This volume examines the tumultuous changes that have occurred and are still occurring in the aftermath of European colonization of the globe since 1492.

Ranging widely over the major themes, regions, theories, and practices of postcolonial study today, the volume presents original essays by the leading proponents of postcolonial study in the Americas, Europe, India, Africa, and East and West Asia. Their contributions provide clear introductions to the major social and political movements underlying colonization and decolonization, accessible histories of the literature and culture in the separate regions affected by European colonization, and introductory essays on the major thinkers and intellectual schools that have informed strategies of national liberation worldwide.

This volume is unique in providing an incisive summary of the long history and theory of modern European colonization in local detail and global scale. It will be a necessary reference tool for years to come.

A Companion to Postcolonial Studies

Blackwell Companions in Cultural Studies

Advisory editor: David Theo Goldberg, Arizona State University

This series aims to provide theoretically ambitious but accessible volumes devoted to the major fields and subfields within Cultural Studies, whether as single disciplines (film studies) inspired and reconfigured by interventionist Cultural Studies approaches, or from broad interdisciplinary and multidisciplinary perspectives (gender studies, race and ethnic studies, postcolonial studies). Each volume sets out to ground and orientate the student through a broad range of specially commissioned articles and also to provide the more experienced scholar and teacher with a convenient and comprehensive overview of the latest trends and critical directions. An over-arching *Companion to Cultural Studies* will map the territory as a whole.

A Companion to Postcolonial Studies

Edited by Henry Schwarz and Sangeeta Ray

BLACKWELL
Publishers

Copyright © Blackwell Publishers Ltd 2000
Editorial apparatus, selection and arrangement copyright © Henry Schwarz and
Sangeeta Ray 2000

First published 2000

2 4 6 8 10 9 7 5 3 1

Blackwell Publishers Inc.
350 Main Street
Malden, Massachusetts 02148
USA

Blackwell Publishers Ltd
108 Cowley Road
Oxford OX4 1JF
UK

Library of Congress Cataloging-in-Publication Data

A companion to postcolonial studies / edited by Henry Schwarz and
Sangeeta Ray.
p.   cm. – (Blackwell companions in cultural studies)
Includes bibliographical references and index.
ISBN 0-631-20662-0 (alk. paper)
1. Postcolonialism.   I. Schwarz, Henry.   II. Ray, Sangeeta.
III. Series.
JV51.C75   2000
325.3 – dc21   99-33933
CIP

British Library Cataloguing in Publication Data

A CIP catalogue record for this book is available from the
British Library.

Typeset in 11 on 13 pt Ehrhardt
by Best-set Typesetter Ltd., Hong Kong
Printed in Great Britain by T. J. International, Padstow, Cornwall

This book is printed on acid-free paper

Contents

Contents

Contributors

Anthony C. Alessandrini is Assistant Professor of English at Kent State University. He is the editor of *Frantz Fanon: Critical Perspectives*, and is currently at work on two books, one on South Asian culture between home and diaspora, the other on the redeployment of humanism in postcolonial writing.

Magda M. Al-Nowaihi is Associate Professor of Arabic Literature at Columbia University. She is the author of *The Poetry of Ibn Khafajah: A Literary Analysis*, and a number of studies on modern Arabic literature. She is currently preparing a manuscript on the Arabic elegy from the pre-Islamic to the Andalusian periods.

Crystal Bartolovich is an Assistant Professor of English and Textual Studies at Syracuse University. She is currently finishing a book entitled *Boundary Disputes*, which considers the counter-national forces at play in the early modern period, and is editing a volume with Neil Lazarus, *Marxism, Postcolonialism and Modernity*, due out in 2000.

Upendra Baxi, former Vice Chancellor, Universities of South Gujarat and Delhi, is currently a Professor of Law, and Director of the Law in Development Program, University of Warwick. His many works include: *The Crisis of the Indian Legal System* (1982); *The Indian Supreme Court and Politics* (1989); *Marx, Law and Justice* (1993); *Inhuman Wrongs and Human Rights* (1994); *Mabrino s Helmet?: Human Rights for a Changing World* (1994); *The Future of Human Rights* (forthcoming.) His current work is focused on globalization of law, and on ways of combating mass impoverishment.

Ali Behdad is an Associate Professor in the English Department at UCLA, and author of *Belated Travellers: Orientalism in the Age of Colonial Dissolution* (1994).

Sandra Buckley teaches Japanese in the English Department at the State University of New York – Albany.

Dipesh Chakrabarty is Professor of History, South Asian Languages and Civilizations, and History of Culture at the University of Chicago. He is a member of the editorial collective of *Subaltern Studies*. His most recent book is *Provincializing Europe: Postcolonial Thought and Historical Difference* (forthcoming 1999).

Rey Chow: beginning in 2000, Dr. Chow is Andrew W. Mellon Professor of the Humanities at Brown University. She is the author of several books, the most recent of which is *Ethics after Idealism: Theory–Culture–Ethnicity–Reading* (1998).

Gaurav Desai teaches in the Department of English at Tulane University and is Co-Director of Tulane's Program in African and African Diaspora Studies.

David Theo Goldberg is Director and Professor of the School of Justice Studies at Arizona State University, Professor in the Graduate Committee on Law and Social Sciences and the Graduate Program in Communications, and Affiliate Professor of Philosophy. He is the author of *Racist Culture: Philosophy and the Politics of Meaning* (1993), *Racial Subjects: Writing on Race in America* (1997) and *Ethical Theory and Social Issues* (1995). Editor of *Anatomy of Racism* (1990) and *Multiculturalism: A Critical Reader* (1995). Co-editor of *Jewish Identity* (1993), and is the founding co-editor of *Social Identities: Journal for the Study of Race, Nation and Culture*.

Anna Johnston is an Associate Lecturer in the English Department at the University of Queensland, Australia. Her research interests include postcolonial literature (particularly in settler-invader cultures), autobiography, postcolonial theory, and the textual interstices of gender, history, and colonialism. In March 1999 she completed a doctoral thesis entitled "Adam's Ribs: Gender, Colonialism, and the Missionaries, 1800–1860," which examined the history and texts of the London Missionary Society's missions in India, Polynesia, and Australia.

Katie King is Associate Professor of Women's Studies at the University of Maryland, College Park. Her last book, *Theory in Its Feminist Travels: Conversations in US Women's Movements*, talked about sites of political struggle in feminist theory, in an examination of histories of feminisms, the forms of writing that produce them, the political alliances that care about them. She is currently preparing *Methodologies Across Fields of Power: Feminisms, Writing Technologies, Global Gay Formations*.

Neil Larsen is professor of Latin American and Comparative Literature at the University of California, Davis, where he directs the Program in Critical Theory. He is the author of *Modernism and Hegemony* (1990) and *Reading North by South* (1995), and is finishing a book on narrative, nationalism and postcolonialism.

Alan Lawson is Deputy Director of the Graduate School and Dean of Post-graduate Students at the University of Queensland where he is also Reader in Postcolonial Literatures. He writes on settler postcolonial theory, cultural institutions, and Australian–Canadian comparative studies. He is co-editor of *Postcolonial Literatures in English: General, Theoretical, and Comparative 1970–1993* (1997), *De-Scribing Empire* (1994), and the *Macmillan Anthology of Australian Literature* (1990).

David Lloyd teaches Irish literature and history in the English Department at Scrips College. His books include *Anomalous States: Irish Writing and the Post-Colonial Moment* (1993).

Walter D. Mignolo is William H. Wannamaker Professor of Literature and Romance Studies, and Professor of Cultural Anthropology at Duke University. Among his most recent publications are *The Darker Side of the Renaissance: Literacy, Territoriality and Colonization* (1995); *Local Histories/Global Designs: Coloniality, Subaltern Knowledges, and Border Thinking* (1999). Co-editor with Elizabeth Hill Boone of *Writing Without Words: Alternative Literacies in Mesoamerica and the Andes* (1994). Founder and co-editor of *Disposition: American Journal of Comparative and Cultural Studies* (1976–) and co-founder and co-editor of *Nepantla: Views from South*. The first issue entitled "Cross-Genealogies and Subaltern Knowledges" will appear in January 2000.

Bart Moore-Gilbert is Reader in English and Postcolonial Studies at Goldsmiths College, University of London. He is the author of *Kipling and "Orientalism"* (1986) and *Postcolonial Theory: Contexts, Practices, Politics* (1997). He is currently completing a monograph on Hanif Kureishi.

Supriya Nair is Associate Professor in the Department of English at Tulane University. She is the author of *Caliban's Curse: George Lamming and the Revisioning of History* (1996).

Tejumola Olaniyan is Associate Professor of English at the University of Virginia, where he teaches African American and postcolonial literatures and theory. He is the author of *Scars of Conquest/Masks of Resistance: The Invention of Cultural Identities in African, African American and Caribbean Drama* (1995).

You-me Park is Assistant Professor of English at the George Washington University in Washington, DC. She is, with Rajeswari Sunder Rajan, the co-editor of *Alternative Austen: Postcolonial Mappings* (2000). She is currently completing a book entitled *States of Emergency: Gender, Postcoloniality, and the Discourse of Expendability*.

Geeta Patel is an Assistant Professor of Women's Studies at Wellesley College. Her book, *Lyrical Movements, Historical Hauntings: On Gender, Colonialism and Desire in Miraji's Urdu Poetry*, is forthcoming in 2000.

Donald E. Pease is the Avalon Foundation Chair of the Humanities at Dartmouth College. The author of *Visionary Compacts: American Renaissance Writing in Cultural Context*, Pease is the editor of nine volumes, including *Cultures of US Imperialism* (with Amy Kaplan), *National Identities and Post-Americanist Narratives* and *Revisionist Interventions into the Canon*. Pease has received Guggenheim and NEH Fellowships and is the General Editor for the book series New Americanists at Duke University Press.

Ato Quayson is a Lecturer in English, Director of the African Studies Centre and Fellow of Pembroke College, University of Cambridge. His publications include *Strategic Transformations in Nigerian Writing* (1997) and *Postcolonialism: Theory, Practice or Process* (1999).

Rajeswari Sunder Rajan is Senior Fellow, Nehru Memorial Museum and Library, New Delhi, and Visiting Professor, English, at George Washington University. Publications include *Real and Imagined Women: Gender, Culture, Post-colonialism* (1993), and two edited volumes: *The Lie of the Land: English Literary Studies in India* (1992), and *Signposts: Gender Issues in Post-Independence India* (1999).

Sangeeta Ray is an associate Professor of English at the University of Maryland, College Park. She has published extensively on postcolonial and gender issues in anthologies and journals such as *Genders*, *Hypatia*, and *Modern Fiction Studies*. Her book *En-Gendering India: Women and Nation in Colonial and Post-colonial India* is in press. She is also currently the Director of the Asian American Studies Project at the University of Maryland, College Park.

Bruce Robbins teaches English and Comparative Literature at Rutgers. He is the author of *Feeling Global: Internationalism in Distress* (1999), *The Servant's Hand: English Fiction from Below* (1986) and *Secular Vocations: Intellectuals, Professionalism, Culture* (1993). He has edited *Intellectuals: Aesthetics, Politics, Academics* (1990) and *The Phantom Public Sphere* (1993), and co-edited *Cosmopolitics: Thinking and Feeling beyond the Nation* (1998). He is also a co-editor of the journal *Social Text*.

Sumit Sarkar teaches history at Delhi University. He is author of many books, including *Modern India: 1885–1947* (1983) and *Writing Cultural History* (1998).

Henry Schwarz teaches in the English Department at Georgetown University, Washington, DC. His publications include *Writing Cultural History in Colonial* *and Postcolonial India* (1997); *Reading the Shape of the World: Toward an International Cultural Studies* (with Richard Dienst) (1996); and *Contributions to Bengal Studies: An Interdisciplinary and International Approach* (with Enayatur Rahim) (1998).

Laurie J. Sears is Associate Professor of History and Adjunct Associate Professor of Women Studies at the University of Washington in Seattle. She teaches colonial and postcolonial histories of Southeast Asia, comparative colonialisms, and theory and historiography. She is author of *Shadows of Empire: Colonial Discourse and Javanese Tales* (1996) and editor of *Fantasizing the Feminine in Indonesia* (1996) and *Autonomous Histories, Particular Truths: Essays in Honor of John R. W. Smail* (1993). She is currently working on *The Prince and the Professor: History, Memoir, Colonial Critique.*

Jenny Sharpe teaches English and Comparative Literature at the University of California at Los Angeles. She is author of *Allegories of Empire: The Figure of Woman in the Colonial Text* (1993) and is currently completing *The Haunting of History: A Literary Archeology of Slave Women's Lives.*

Doris Sommer, Professor of Romance Languages at Harvard University, is author of *Foundational Fiction: The National Romances of Latin America* (1991); and *Proceed with Caution, When Engaged by Minority Writing in the Americas* (1999), which develops a rhetoric of particularism for an ethics of reading difference.

Gayatri Chakravorty Spivak is Avalon Foundation Professor of the Humanities at Columbia University. Her books are *Myself Must I Remake* (1974), *In Other Worlds* (1987), *The Post-Colonial Critic* (1988), *Outside in the Teaching Machine* (1993), and *A Critique of Postcolonial Reason* (1999). She has translated Jacques Derrida's *Of Grammatology* (1978); and Mahasweta Devi's *Imaginary Maps* (1994), *Breast Stories* (1997), and *Old Women* (1999).

Jace Weaver is Associate Professor of American Studies, Religious Studies, and Law at Yale University. He specializes in Native American Studies and is the author of several books, including *That the People Might Live: Native American Literatures and Native American Community.*

Foreword: Upon Reading the
Companion to Postcolonial Studies

Gayatri Chakravorty Spivak

The best of postcolonialism is autocritical. That defining quality is beautifully caught by this *Companion*. Even in so judicious an account as Rajeswari Sunder Rajan and You-me Park's "Postcolonial Feminism/Postcolonialism and Feminism," there is a sense that this peculiar brand of feminism is separated from the vicissitudes of local feminisms. And, indeed, Ipshita Chanda's "Feminist Theory in Perspective" rounds out that sense, diffident for its distance from metropolitan postcolonialism, located as she is in a "real" postcolony. Upendra Baxi reminds us, from the other side of the same position, that much greater attention to gender is paid in actually existing postcolonial constitutions than is allowed by postcolonial theorists (although his argument for the specifically feminist significance of having female heads of state has always left me less than persuaded). We must keep in mind that nothing similar to what the *Companion* establishes as "postcolonialism" came up "spontaneously" in the national and regional languages of the world outside the Euro-US. In a sense, Gaurav Desai's "Rethinking English" exposes the heart of "postcolonial studies."

The worst of postcolonialism, according to some, is its overemphasis upon the South Asian model. This book does not make that mistake. Although the theoretical and historical bits, if grounded, rest in the South Asian model, we do have Africa here – Central, Southern, and Northern – we have the Caribbean, Latin America, Australia, and, straddling two worlds, we have Ireland. The differences in strategy in the treatment of politico–historical spaces is itself instructive. David Theo Goldberg's substitution of heterogeneity for hybridity by way of a consideration of the legacy of slavery is a case in point. Ato Quayson's essay brings in Africa's postmodernity. But it is Tejumola Olaniyan's magisterial "Africa: Varied Colonial Legacies" that sutures slavery and the colonial state, considers the diversity of colonialisms in Africa, takes us through to literary production, attends to women's writing, and moves us into a consideration of neocolonialism in Development, an argument distinct from globalization proper.

The *Companion* includes an essay in Queer Theory – Katie King's "Global Gay Formations" – which relates Queer Theory to postcoloniality in substantive as well as theoretical ways that engage my attention constantly at the moment. If this were an extended essay rather than a brief statement, I would expand on them, for the connections are not always made carefully. Here I can at least record my congratulation to the editors for having thought to include it. Postcoloniality queers the norm.

Two other pieces, not usually a part of postcolonial studies, also deserve our attention: Don Pease's piece on US exceptionalism and Jace Weaver's piece on "Indigenousness and Indigeneity."

The first is important because a great deal of metropolitan multiculturalism – the latter phase of dominant postcolonialism – pre-comprehends US manifest destiny as transformed asylum for the rest of the world. The editors have made it necessary for the reader of this book to come to terms with its forgetting. As Pease suggests, on the basis of much empirical detail: "In restricting the referentiality of the term 'post-colonial' to the political settlements that took place after the decolonization of former european colonies, postcolonial theory has constructed the most recent of the variations on the theme of US exceptionalism."

Rey Chow's "King Kong in Hong Kong" is a fine companion piece to Pease's essay. It connects the strict postcoloniality of Hong Kong with contemporary US political practice. It reminds us that US exceptionalism breeds contempt toward postcoloniality and produces a standing alibi for intervention (which in turn produces the piously justified status of the US-as-asylum): "audiences in the West are obliged to identify with an invisible but adamant moralistic perspective in which the United States is seen as superior." Indeed, the continuity of colonial exceptionalism into postcoloniality is clearly indicated in Chow's essay: "Sovereignty and proprietorship here are not only about the ownership of land or rule but also about ideological self-ownership, that is, about the legitimating terms that allow a people to be." Of course, all miraculating collective identities, not just nationalism, are a covering over of the disymmetry of the singularity of individuals. It is between the negotiating status of the various occlusions that the power games of postcoloniality are played out. Any US triumphalism, however multiculturally destabilized, has a stake in this.

Pease points out that, "[i]nstead of erasing his experiences of exile from memory, [José] Martí transferred his redoubled loss of place into the basis for his refusal to assume a position in the US colonial empire." A tough act to follow, but something to keep in mind as our limit as postcoloniality finds its place in globalization and Asian-American Studies claims postcolonial Asia-s.

It is well-known that "democratization" US-style has something like a relationship with the "civilizing mission" of exceptionalism. More often than not, it becomes a code name for the political restructuring entailed by the transformation of (efficient through inefficient to wild) state capitalisms and their colonies to tributary economies of rationalized global financialization. This is connected by Chow to the British policy of inventing division at departure, particularly well remembered by me as an Indian in her late fifties: "What better way to leave than by implanting the rudimentary structures of democratic elections that would hereafter provide potent grounds for disaffection and dissent against the regime in power?"

If Chow connects "democracy" and globalization in a new way, advancing Pease's argument from manifest destiny, Upendra Baxi's essay takes us further into the new and more general "postcoloniality" of globalization by emphasizing the reduced powers of the state and the greater role of the social movements. Jenny Sharpe brings it home again by commenting that "a 1990 Immigration Reform Act has tripled the question for skilled immigrants, most of whom are from Asia. The priority given to skill over national origins shows that corporate America is willing to tolerate some degree of diversity." From this point on, postcolonialism can investigate what Colleen Lye has called "American Orientalism," the constitution of East Asia and the Asian-American since the end of the nineteenth century.[1]

"Indigenousness and Indigeneity" takes issue with postcolonialism directly. I take the liberty here of quoting two passages that I have recently written:

> The old postcolonial model – very much "India" plus "Fanon" – will not serve now as the master-model for transnational to global cultural studies.[2] We are dealing with heterogeneity on a different scale: "Over the time that the world has known substantial states, . . . empires have been the dominant and largest state form. . . . Only now . . . do we seem to be leaving the age of massive Eurasian empires that began in earnest across a band from the Mediterranean to East Asia almost four thousand years ago. To the extent that we regard such international compacts as the European Union, GATT, and NAFTA as embodying imperial designs, furthermore, even today's requiem may prove premature."[3]

And,

> Jean-Luc Nancy asks: "'Before/after the subject': *who* . . . : not a question of essence, but one of identity . . . The place is *place*." I learn a great deal from the delicacy of Nancy's readings, from his acknowledgment of the risks of the imperative, but I have indeed thought of who will have come after the subject, if we set to work, in the name of who came before, so to speak. Here is the simple answer: the Aboriginal.[4]

Weaver faults Mahasweta Devi for "speaking for" the Indian Aboriginal. Such confusions arise because, as Anna Johnston points out in "Settler Colonies," South Asia model postcolonialists have not come to grips with the fact that India, with its ninety million Aboriginals, is a precapitalist, precolonial, non-European settler colony, where the postcolonial Hindu-majority Indian is, roughly speaking, the first "settler" – and even such a formulation is mired in Aryanist nonsense. At the origin an aporia here, not to be compared to historically tractable situations in Latin America, South Africa, or Australia, each with its own complexity.[5] It is interesting that Ipshita Chanda alone, writing *from* India rather than from a South Asia-centered postcolonial base, quietly compares Kenya and South Bihar as "settler colonizations." Considerations of non-European settler colonies – such as India and Japan – occupy a separate place from current trends in Fourth World Theory. This volume looks at generally capitalist colonialism, whose *longue durée*, as Henry Schwarz points out, begins with that relatively recent event, Columbus's trip. Charting this particular historical formation of the postcolonial, this volume concentrates on the "nation," with here and there a nod at "postnationalism."

I find it difficult to accept the argument that poststructuralism found its origin in the failure of the organized left to support national liberation movements, but it is certainly an argument advanced by some French players. Bruce Robbins lays it out carefully here as one important contribution of Anglo-US postcolonialism. Dipesh Chakrabarty's "A Small History of Subaltern Studies" attempts to counter the "charge that *Subaltern Studies* lost its original way by falling into the bad company of postcolonial theory."

However one treats such apologetics, Chakrabarty's summarizing of that "original way" performs a great service by taking Subaltern Studies out of identitarian "speaking for" debates: "[Ranajit Guha's] gesture [the rejection of Eric Hobsbawm's category 'pre-political'] is radical in that it fundamentally pluralizes the history of power in global modernity and separates it from any universal history of capital." One can restate the Robbins/Chakrabarty argument this way: if French poststructuralism had some connection with the lack of fit between the French Left and the FLN, it is in the work of the pre-US Subaltern Studies that one finds a self-conscious line of connection to the lack of fit between British/South Asian Marxism and national liberation. I remain more committed to the risks of a persistently critiqued humanism which, in my belief, underlies the un-argued space of the ethical entailed by Marx's positing of the "social," before its attempted realization in France, Algeria, or South Asia.

It is refreshing to see Neil Larsen's astute analysis of Lenin heading the volume. Indeed, Larsen's account of the internationalization of aesthetic form as a correlative of the first wave of national liberation movements provides the paradoxical condition of production of the cultural particularisms often associated with current tendencies in "postcolonialism." Crystal Bartolovich situates the current scene within considerations of Western Marxism. Ali Behdad introduces the question of class heterogeneity (within a more general consideration of historical and cultural heterogeneity) into diasporic art and the immigrant everyday. This subtext of the heterogeneous points of contact between Marxism and postcolonialism remains an important component of the *Companion*.

Although the contributors seem generally agreed that postcolonialism arose with Edward W. Said's *Orientalism* and his debt to Gramsci, Fanon, Foucault, there is only one essay on the Arab world in this collection. In "The Middle East;

Or, Arabic Literature and the Postcolonial Predicament," Magda M. Al-Nowaihi mentions the important issue of gender and nationalism, and launches a located critique of mimicry and hybridity. The crucial issue of the suppression of Islam in the construction of Indian nationhood from the nineteenth century down is signaled by default in Laurie Sears' piece "Intellectuals, Theosophy, and Failed Narratives of the Nation in Late Colonial Java." Her discussion of the "displacement of *wayang* mysticism and a rephrasing of it in non-Islamic terms" opens up that other narrative, paradoxically continued in the suppression of grassroots Bengali Sufi by the more orthodox Islamists of Bangladesh.

Some contributors have been kind enough to refer to my work. I take this opportunity to say a few things.

First, facts.

In his "Mission Impossible: Introducing Postcolonial Studies," Henry Schwarz writes that I learned deconstruction and psychoanalysis at Cornell. No. I left Cornell in 1965 to take up an Assistant Professorship at the University of Iowa. De Man met Derrida in 1966, at the Conference on the Structuralist Controversy held at Johns Hopkins. I did not know about this Conference. I ordered *De la grammatologie* from the Minuit catalog because it looked interesting. I did not know who Derrida was. I did not meet him until 1971. Unbeknownst to me, Derrida sat in my audience while I delivered a lecture on allegory. We had had no correspondence prior to that. I got the translation contract by way of a disarmingly reckless query letter to the University of Massachusetts Press written without consultation, in fact because I wanted to write the monograph which became the "Translator's Preface." J. Hillis Miller took the manuscript to Johns Hopkins University Press without my knowledge. I have never attended a class on Derrida. On the contrary, I delivered, with great trepidation, a lecture on varieties of deconstructive practice (thirteen, if I remember right), in de Man's presence in 1982.

As for psychoanalysis, the only Freud I had read at Cornell was an English translation of *Civilization and its Discontents*. I believe it was John Brenkman, who was then my undergraduate student, who brought me a copy of Anthony Wilden's translation of Jacques Lacan's *Discours de Rome* in 1969 and thus began my study of Freud and Lacan.[6] Here, too, absence of instruction has given me a certain autodidactic naiveté. I did certainly point to Freud's "masculine-imperialist ideological formation" in 1982–3, the actual date of composition of "Can the Subaltern Speak?" Again for the record, it should be pointed out that in "Psychoanalysis in Left Field," published in 1994, the criticism is much more sustained and deals with Freud and polytheism; and that, in "Echo" (1996), I try to place Freud within the broader field of ethical instantiation.[7] These two pieces are very much more "postcolonial" than "Can the Subaltern Speak?"

Freud has never been for me an explanatory model. He is, rather, a fellow traveler. As for Lacan, I believe I am just beginning to get a glimpse of his project.

Now for a bit about "Can the Subaltern Speak?" It seems all things to all men. For Neil Larsen, a paean to Derrida, for Dipesh Chakrabarty an essay on a conversation between Foucault and Deleuze. For Moore-Gilbert it reduces itself to essentialism because the subaltern becomes the absolutely other. I don't want to be an essentialist, but the women seem to get the hang of it better. There is Carolyn Boyce Davies:

> In her provocative essay, "Can the Subaltern Speak?," Gayatri Spivak addressed the way the "subaltern" woman as subject is already positioned, represented, spoken for or constructed as absent or silent or not listened to in a variety of discourses. Her speech is already represented as non-speech. Spivak's meanings were forcibly clarified and activated for many by witnessing the way Anita Hill's speech and Lani Guinier's writings (other Black women speakers) were mischaracterized, ignored, distorted, erased.[8]

And Ipshita Chanda, in this collection, not only takes the point, but relates it to the idea of "ethical singularity" from my later work.

Indeed "Can the Subaltern Speak?" is not really about colonialism at all. It is about agency: institutionally validated action. To put it as simply as possible, I will quote a recent piece, written by a woman, in *India Abroad*, a newspaper that has no intellectual pretensions: "Spivak wrote a much-cited article called 'Can the Subaltern Speak?' in which she argued that, unless validated by dominant forms of knowledge and politics, resistance could not be recognized ('heard') as such."[9] What kind of politics can emerge from this, asks Neil Larsen. The politics of demanding and building infrastructure so that when subalterns speak they can be heard. A brief statement is not the place to develop this. Let me simply add that this style of politics has become altogether more important since the World Bank changed Women in Development to Gender and Development without any change in the structural adjustment projects that destroy social redistribution and national infrastructure. I refer the reader to "The New Subaltern."[10]

And no, the subaltern "is" not the absolute other. (Nothing) (is) the absolute other. The "subaltern" describes "the bottom layers of society constituted by specific modes of exclusion from markets, political-legal representation, and the possibility of full membership in dominant social strata."[11] "The absolute other" are words describing a necessary presupposition, as follows:

> Radical alterity – the wholly other – must be thought and must be thought through imaging. To be born human is to be born angled toward an other and others. To account for this the human being presupposes the quite-other. This is the bottom line of being-human as being-in-the-ethical-relation. By definition, we cannot – no self can – reach the quite-other. Thus the ethical situation can only be figured in the ethical experience of the impossible. This is the founding gap in all act or talk, most especially in acts or talk that we understand to be closest to the ethical – the historical and the political.[12]

Finally, in spite of my deep appreciation for his work, Edward W. Said is not my "mentor." He is my friend and ally, my senior colleague. I was already a full Professor for three years before *Orientalism* came out. I certainly meant it when I "described *Orientalism* as 'the source book in our discipline,'" as Moore-Gilbert writes, but I meant it for the sake of the entire discipline.[13] I did not read Gramsci following Said. I read him first at Iowa, in the early seventies Marxist intellectual atmosphere created by Vladimir Padunov. I read him again under the auspices of the Subaltern Studies collective, who had adapted the term, not I, as Moore-Gilbert claims. Also for the record, it should be made clear that the degree to which Said and I "collaborated in the 1980s" with "the Subaltern historians of India" is not comparable. Said graciously agreed to Ranajit Guha's invitation, relayed to him by me, to write a Foreword to the first American edition of *Selected Subaltern Studies* and, at his invitation, Ranajit Guha published his *Dominance Without Hegemony* in Said's series.[14] For better or for worse, I have been closely associated to Subaltern Studies since 1984,[15] published in their collections, participated in their conferences, attended collective meetings in the US and in India, am writing an Introduction for a forthcoming volume, and have been embroiled in the intellectual feuds natural to any volatile and changeful group.

Additionally, I have never sought "to correct" *Orientalism*. My endeavor in "Can the Subaltern Speak?" was to tell the story of Bhubaneswari Bhaduri (and why she could not be heard), not to correct Said. Her name is never mentioned in the discussions of my essay.

I hope postcolonial work, forever autocritical, prospers. I hope metropolitan multiculturalism takes it into account that, in the name of the new "model minorities" (a phrase not encountered in the *Companion*), the obstinate lower reaches of the older minorities are, yes, being "subalternized," if we keep in mind a definition that is upstream from the one I have quoted above: "cut off from the lines of social mobility." If in the larger world, our *Companion* leads us to *After Empire* (see note 3), in the United States it may lead to Rosalyn Deutsche's *Evictions*.[16]

Notes

1 Colleen Lye, "Model Modernity: The Making of Asiatic Racial Form, 1882–1945," Ph.D. dissertation, Columbia University, May 1999.

2 Arif Dirlik, "The Postcolonial Aura: Third World Criticism in the Age of Global Capitalism," *Critical Inquiry*, 20 (winter 1994), pp. 328–56.

3 Charles Tilly, "How Empires End," in Karen Barkey and Mark von Hagen, eds., *After Empire: Multiethnic Societies and Nation-Building; the Soviet Union and the Russian, Ottoman, and Habsburg Empires*. New York: Westview Press, 1997, p. 2.

4   Spivak, *A Critique of Postcolonial Reason: Toward a History of the Vanishing Present*, Chapter 1, note 32. Cambridge: Harvard University Press, 1999; wording slightly altered. The Nancy passage is from Eduardo Cadava *et al.*, eds., *Who Comes After the Subject?* New York: Routledge, 1991, p. 7.

5   Spivak, Interview with Anupama Rao, *Interventions* (forthcoming).

6   Jacques Lacan, *The Language of the Self: The Function of Language in Psychoanalysis*, tr. Anthony Wilden. Baltimore: Johns Hopkins Press, 1968.

7   Spivak, "Psychoanalysis in Left Field; and Fieldworking," in Sonu Shamdasani and Michael Münchow, eds., *Speculations After Freud* (London: Routledge, 1994); "Echo," in Donna Landry and Gerald Maclean, eds., *The Spivak Reader*. New York: Routledge, 1996, pp. 175–202.

8   Carolyn Boyce Davies, "Migratory Subjectivities," in Michael Ryan and Julie Rivkin, eds., *Literary Theory: An Anthology*. Malden: Blackwell, 1998, p. 1009.

9   Ela Dutt, *India Abroad*, May 21, 1999, p. 40.

10 Spivak, "The New Subaltern," forthcoming as Introduction in the next volume of *Subaltern Studies*.

11 Spivak, "Theses on the Subaltern," in Vinayak Chaturvedi, ed., *Mapping Subaltern Studies and the Post-Colonial*. London: Verso, 1999, forthcoming.

12 Spivak, "A Moral Dilemma," forthcoming in an anthology edited by Howard Marchitello.

13 Spivak, "Race Before Racism: The Disappearance of the American," *boundary 2*, 25, no. 2 (summer 1998), p. 35.

14 Ranajit Guha, *Dominance Without Hegemony: History and Power in Colonial India*. Cambridge: Harvard University Press, 1997.

15 The event that Chakrabarty describes without a human subject ("In the same year [1988], an anthology entitled *Selected Subaltern Studies* published from New York launched the global career of the project") was a result of my request to the Collective, placed in 1986 at a discussion held in Calcutta after the Subaltern Studies conference, to make their work more easily available to the nonspecialist audience in the United States. There is more than ample evidence that, for many, "the falling into bad company" dates from this association. Chakrabarty himself has suggested this, with a somewhat disingenuous nonpartisan air, in "Reconstructing Liberalism? Notes Toward a Conversation Between Area Studies and Diasporic Studies," *Public Culture*, vol. 10, no. 3 (spring 1998), pp. 457–81.

16 Deutsche, *Evictions: Art and Spatial Politics*. Cambridge: MIT Press, 1996.

Acknowledgments

This book was born in an office in Washington, DC, and its birth certificate was signed over martinis at the MLA convention there in 1996. It was written literally all over the world, assembled in Philadelphia and College Park, MD, typeset in Hong Kong, and put back together in London. Contributions were handwritten, typed, phoned, faxed, word processed, and email attached. The people who produced this project are true subjects of globalization and understand the meanings and hidden dangers of that now-popular term. They would be reluctant to see its provenance pass into hands less careful than those of Blackwell Publishers.

This book was made possible by the hard work of many people. If it is a baby, its Dr. Spock is Andrew McNeillie, editor extraordinaire at Blackwell. His compatriots Jennifer Lambert and especially Alison Dunnett have shown tremendous resourcefulness in raising it and bringing it to press. Cameron Laux, the Godfather, has seen it through production with fortitude, patience, incredulity, the occasional death threat, and fine, good humor.

The editors have benefitted from discussions with scores of people who listened, criticized, and offered advice. These include presentations and feedback at the conferences of The Marxist Literary Group–Institute on Culture and Society (MLG-ICS); The Commonwealth and Postcolonial Literature Conference at Georgia Southern University; the joint conference of the Peace Studies Association/Consortium on Peace Research, Education and Development (PSA/COPRED); and the Cultural Studies Program at George Mason University, which hosted the wonderful conference on Debunking Intellectuals on April 1, 1999. Our thanks to the audiences who listened and the organizers who invited, especially Gautam Kundu, Don Pease, and Paul Smith. The National Endowment for the Humanities and Georgetown University generously contributed to Henry Schwarz s freedom when he should probably have been doing other things. The University of Pennsylvania Program in Comparative Literature and Literary Theory was an utterly stimulating host while working on this book, and Henry must thank Liliane Weissberg, Gerry Prince, Rita Barnard, and JoAnne

Dubil for their warm hospitality and for distracting him from finishing it sooner. The University of Pennsylvania in general, and the Department of South Asia Regional Studies in particular, must be blamed for all Henry's overdue deadlines. Our colleagues at *Interventions: International Journal of Postcolonial Studies*, Robert Young, Rajeswari Sunder Rajan, and You-me Park in particular, have shown the way to what's next. We are very grateful to Gayatri Spivak, Homi Bhabha, and Fredric Jameson for their kind support in closing.

Henry Schwarz: I would like in particular to thank David Ludden for being the ultimate host in Philadelphia; David Nelson, the finest bibliographer anyone could ask for; Richard Dienst, my best reader; Carmen Lamas for coffee, sugar, and righteous indignation; King Benny the Great and Dr. Spike; Mickey and Timmy; Paul C., Deborah, Max, and Casey Rosier; my brother and sister Michael Brian and Alicia Yvonne, who meticulously oversaw every detail and suggested complexities of which I never would have dreamt; the contributors, whose outstanding work made our lives easy; Agnes Garry, whose life and writing are example enough; Molly, who lived through this book with me.

Sangeeta Ray: I wish to thank David Lloyd, Walter Mignolo, and Ipshita Chanda for their incredible intellectual generosity in allowing me to edit their essays for this anthology. I would also like to thank Bart Moore-Gilbert for his wonderful contribution on very short notice. To Henry who took over when life got in my way. And in the end, yet again, I must say that without Brian Richardson's marvellous wit, intellectual support, and emotional companionship the last year and a half would have been unbearable. And last but not least to Shoham whose presence has helped me re-enter the world of words.

Braithwaite, Kamau. "Metaphors of Underdevelopment." In *The Art of Kamau Braithwaite*. Copyright by Seren. Reprinted by permission of Poetry Wales Press Ltd.

Braithwaite, Kamau. "Islands." In *The Arrivants: A New World Trilogy*. Copyright © 1973 Oxford University Press.

Chow, Rey. "King Kong: Postcolonial China." *Social Text*, 55, (16:2), pp. 93–108. Copyright 1998, Duke University Press. All rights reserved. Reprinted with permission.

Lloyd, David. Introduction, *Ireland after History*, Cork University Press, 1999.

Moore-Gilbert, Bart. *Postcolonial Theory: Contexts, Practices, Politics* (600-word extract). Copyright 1997, Verso. Reproduced with permission.

Patel, Geeta. "Home, Homo, Hybrid: Translating Gender." In *College Literature*, (24:1), pp. 133–150. Copyright 1997, College Literature. Reproduced with permission of West Chester University Press.

Sarkar, Sumit. *Modern India 1885–1947*, pp. 65–86. Copyright 1983, Macmillan. Reproduced with permission of the publisher.

Sears, Laurie J. *Shadows of Empire: Colonial Discourse and Javanese Tales* (excerpt). Copyright 1996, Duke University Press. All rights reserved. Reprinted with permission.

Every effort has been made to contact copyright holders. The publishers apologize for any errors or omissions in the above list and would be grateful to be notified of any corrections that should be incorporated in the next edition or reprint of this book.

Mission Impossible: Introducing Postcolonial Studies in the US Academy

Henry Schwarz

Reading through the thirty essays collected in this book, one is struck by how much more difficult it has become to describe postcolonial studies than it was even five years ago. We see this as a very positive development. Anyone looking for a single, simple definition of this field will be disappointed by what follows. However, those seeking global scale and local commitment brought to the last fifty years of world history will, we feel, be amply rewarded.

Postcolonial studies as a field can be described in several ways. In an historical sense, postcolonial studies describes the movements for national liberation that ended Europe's political domination of the globe, with 1947 an epochal date signaling the emergence of South Asia, "the jewel in the crown" of the British Empire, as an independent region. For the next forty years, one nation after another shook off colonial domination until the United Nations in 1987 numbered some 160 autonomous member-states. The dismantling of the Soviet Union since 1989 has resulted in the emergence of many more, with continuing effects upon the shape of the world, but the question of whether this continues the worldwide movement of decolonization will be taken up in the essay that opens this volume by Neil Larsen.

In either event, this freeing and splintering of political entities has been among the most characteristic and most determining features of the second half of the twentieth century. When postcolonial studies limits itself to these specific events, the political overcoming of colonial/imperial domination, it marks a distinct subfield of certain disciplinary divisions. The so-called Third World that arose as a political entity following the 1955 Bandung Conference on non-alignment has been studied extensively by scholars in disciplines such as Economics, International Relations, Government, History, Sociology, and Literature. In general terms, when we refer to "postcolonial" here we will be using it in this sense, as the historic struggle against European colonialism and the emergence of new political and cultural actors on the world stage during the second half of the twentieth century. These struggles have profoundly reshaped the production of academic knowledge as much as they have reshaped world power.

1

In a larger historical temporality, postcolonial studies also considers the *longue durée* of European expansion, exploration, and conquest during the so-called Renaissance or Early Modern era of European history. In 1492 Christopher Columbus, sailing west from Spain, mistakenly thought he had landed in China. A scant six years later Vasco da Gama, sailing from Portugal and somewhat better informed, found a reliable sea route east to the south Asian port of Calicut. European naval expansion in both directions saw tremendous increases in commodity circulation and resulted in a boom of seafaring navigational technology. Most striking perhaps, considered on a world scale, were the results of contact: the decimation of populations in the Americas and the enforced movement from Africa and Asia of people to the Americas, and from Europe to the settler colonies of the Americas, South Africa, Australia, New Zealand, and other places. Entire continents were cleared of their inhabitants in order to make space for new European settlers, and paradoxically new groups of people, mainly from Africa and Asia, were shipped to the Americas to serve as their slaves. Of course the first people did not entirely disappear, nor were the European reasons given for slaughtering, enslaving, converting, infecting, or neglecting them entirely convincing. Nonetheless, the modern world has been decisively shaped by these events. Many would still argue that the rise of Europe to global dominance from 1500 to 1950, with the holocausts and diasporas thus caused, has been the most significant event structuring world power in the year 2000.

In the Asian hemisphere trade depended on alliances between Europeans and local inhabitants, and conquistadorial practices such as those followed in the Americas were not followed by and large, although very significant displacements and enslavements took place there too and continue to influence the structure of society. The opening of Europe to other worlds through navigation has been deemed a crucial event for the subsequent histories of Asia and the Americas, which soon after their "discoveries" became decisively colonial as European techniques of economic and military organization overwhelmed the early practices of trade. To many contemporary scholars, this description best suits postcolonial studies as the analysis of the historical, technological, socioeconomic, and cultural links between Europe, Asia, and the Americas since 1492, that is, as the emergence of European dominance following the first contact by water.

In the case of the relationship between Europe and Asia, it must be admitted, this date is very arbitrary, as significant trade and cultural links between, say, Italy and China can be traced back to the thirteenth century, and between Greece and India to the fourth century BC. The Iberian peninsula was of course an Islamic enclave from 711 to 1492, and the so-called renaissance in Europe was a direct product of the preservation and transportation of ancient Greek texts by Muslim scholars. Asia has been present in Europe for quite a long time. These historical facts lead us to the necessity of distinguishing a specifically colonial relationship from the long histories of contact and trade between East and West. But the emergence of the Americas and Asia into European consciousness from the fifteenth to eighteenth centuries does seem decisive for any accounting of world history, and the legacy of European civilization in the Americas and Southern Antipodes – the construction of world-historical republics side by side with the genocide of indigenous peoples and the enslavement of Africans and Asians – does seem a persuasive periodizing strategy.

In this perspective, postcolonial studies expands its purview not only historically but disciplinarily. If we are to consider American and Antipodean indigenes as constituent members of the field, not only academic departments of Anthropology but a full range of native practices and knowledges must be included to shape the underlying theory and methodology of the discipline. This inclusion has serious limits, however. On the one hand, why would anyone want to be "included" in a field that obsessively replays his or her destruction? On the other hand, in many formerly colonized countries such attempts to return to pre-colonial traditions of cultural understanding have been charged with "nativism", a naive recovery and celebration of supposedly pure, non-European practices untainted by foreign dominance. What nativists fail to recognize is that colonization in most cases makes any return to the past quite ambiguous, for colonizers are brilliant revisionists who often rewrite ancient traditions to serve their own purposes in the present, thus compromising and transforming the ancient sources of authority themselves. This process renders the ancient traditions fully modern and implicates them in practices of colonial dominance. Several influential books on colonial history in Africa and India, such as Eric Hobsbawm and Terrence Ranger's *The Invention of Tradition*, and Lloyd Rudolph and Susan Rudolph's *The Modernity of Tradition*, make this process painfully clear.

Colonizers also tend to implant modern structures on their territories, such as the exploitive economic system of capitalism, and political structures borrowed from Europe such as territorial boundaries, parliaments, and censuses that *de facto* transform traditional practices into modern ones that can never be repudiated if a new nation is to participate in the international state system once it is liberated. But these so-called modern forms and institutional structures also can function in a profoundly backward fashion. One dramatic example of a colonizer dragging a nation into the backwardness of postcolonial modernity is given in the Portuguese withdrawal from the new nation of Guinea-Bissau in 1975. Upon exiting the newly-liberated country, an autonomy won through an historic struggle that energized the theory and practice of national liberation, the retreatng troops set fire to the National Archives which they in fact had built. Official records of births and deaths, titles to land, government agreements, treaties and diplomatic arrangements, and other business committed to paper during a 400-year occupation were destroyed. Thus Guinea-Bissau became modern and free. Having won back their country, they would now have to begin writing their history.

Long historical temporalities stretching back to the sixteenth century create other demands on scholarship. The range of discrete regional histories, not to mention languages, become research problems of monumental proportion. In this larger configuration of the field, postcolonial studies alerts us that the very forms through which we study the world, the academic disciplines, are implicitly structured by Europe's imperial dominance of the world since 1500. Academic knowledge developed in the modern era in very different ways than those in which it was practiced in medieval European universities, for instance, and the practice of overseas domination had a profound impact on the structure and content of European knowledge. As Edward Said argued so brilliantly in 1978, European knowledge *is* colonialism. The archives of the great Western universities were built from the orientalist acquisition of information about the other. Thus to study this archive is to participate in the politics of dominance. Postcolonial studies works to make this relation of unequal power more visible, with the goal of ending it. Postcolonial studies in this sense is the radical philosophy that interrogates both the past history and ongoing legacies of European colonialism in order to undo them. Thus it is not merely a theory of knowledge but a "theoretical practice," a transformation of knowledge from static disciplinary competence to activist intervention. Postcolonial studies would be pointless as a mere intellectual enterprise, since Western intellectual enterprise itself is fundamentally dependent on Europe's conquest and exploitation of the colonial world. This lesson of Marx's is as relevant today as it was in 1845: "The philosophers have only *interpreted* the world, in various ways; the point is to change it." Postcolonial studies at its best changes the world, providing interpretations that have practical consequences.

Colonial domination has been a fact of life around the world for thousands of years, not just hundreds. If we recognize postcolonial studies in its largest sense as the study of all impositions upon people by other people from foreign territories, we then expand the field to include such phenomena as, for example, the ancient Greek projects of subjugating distant territories to tributary status, the Roman Empire, the Aryan invasion of India (if that in fact occurred at all), the consolidation of the Ch'in Empire in China in third century BC, and the political conquests of outlying groups by the Aztec and Mayan civilizations of Middle America. This Companion is not structured to accommodate this third periodization, although several of its contributors will allude to ancient times and the seemingly universal proclivity of strong civilizations to impose their forms of rule and authority upon weaker ones.

Significantly, however, this third historical horizon influences some contemporary practitioners of the field by isolating a kind of transhistorical cultural imperialism as its essence. Thus the name and practice of postcolonial studies can be invoked at times to describe equally *The Histories* of Herodotus and the *Subaltern Studies* volumes (Chatterjee); the African slave trade and the Greek philosophical appropriation of Egyptian civilization (Bernal); the Mayan conquest of the Yucatan and the Spanish conquest of the Maya (Rabasa); the Roman conquest of Britain and the British conquest of India (Spanos). Although our volume does not treat definitively these long historical scales, many of the sensibilities which inform postcolonial studies in its many permutations stem from such ancient, global conflicts. In this way, postcolonial studies can examine recurring patterns and processes of violence against neighbors and distant peoples over long periods of time. One must be cautious however, as are the exemplary scholars named above, in invoking such seemingly ancient antagonisms lest we fall back into naturalistic excuses such as "human nature" for explaining violence against others. As in all responsible scholarship, one must vigilantly contextualize and historicize the sources of conflict so that world history does not appear as one long succession of colonizing regimes. We feel that the lessons of the last fifty years, derived from the specific struggle against European colonial imperialism, have provided new tools to help us distinguish the specificity of the present from the supposedly ancient antipathies frequently blamed for conflict. In this disciplinary configuration postcolonial studies is allied with Peace Studies, Women's and Gender Studies, World Systems theory, certain strains of Anthropology and Theology, and other diverse projects for the transformation of knowledge into action that attempt to change the present by analyzing the global and local consequences of the European domination of the globe.

Thus it is not sufficient to limit postcolonial studies to strictly historicist explanations. A number of sociological, economic, and philosophical questions have been raised within the field that cannot be contained within historical description. As noted in the third horizon above, postcolonial studies questions the violence that has often accompanied cultural interaction and attempts to frame explanations of it as well as to provide alternate models of accommodation or getting along. It also proposes practical models of ending or channeling conflict, often by rethinking the nature of identity in situations where groups come together and interact. Is it really sufficient, for example, to speak of humans as belonging to particular ethnic or national groupings, and therefore excluded from others? Under what terms? When is one group imposing on another? What is the difference between interaction and imposition? Given that most of the people on this planet have in fact been communicating and traveling for a very long time, postcolonial studies also questions the divisions of humanity into regions ("East is East and West is West, and ne'er the twain shall meet"); the division of knowledges into disciplines; and the seemingly universal tendency to think of fellow humans as "others." For whenever definitions of identity and belonging, inclusion and exclusion, rights and entitlements are posited, they are done for specific, contingent, and situational reasons. Postcolonial studies invites us to examine these reasons in empirical detail and with theoretical precision, recognizing that the world is an integrated ensemble of historical and regional processes, and that particular times and places can rarely be separated out from larger patterns if we are to make interpretations capable of producing change. The reverse is also true: large historical patterns only take on meaning when they can be shown at work in specific contexts.

Despite these various possibilities for periodizing or philosophizing the post-colonial, the fact remains that the term postcolonial itself – as is the case with the other "post"-ed term postmodern – does not have a stable definition and its adoption has been one of situational convenience rather than necessity. And yet a whole body of work has grown up that is identifiable as postcolonial, and academic departments, usually of English literature, seem to have decided that they need people to teach in the field. What is the field? Our first general definition is still the most useful. Postcolonial studies designates the academic study in the West of the cultures and contexts of decolonization. Inevitably, these have been seen to date through the prevailing intellectual paradigms of Western universities. Ato Quayson's essay in Part I discusses the relationship between postcolonialism and postmodernism, one of these intellectual paradigms. Postmodernism has opened the field to serious questionings of identity and belonging, including the possibility that the best way to define the postcolonial may be to recognize from the first that its definition is impossible. Is it not rather preposterous to think that the examination of world cultures, or even the cultures of European colonization arising since the early modern period, is anything new? And yet postcolonial studies is a decidedly new field of scholarship arising in Western universities as the application of postmodern thought to the long history of colonizing practices. There exists a strong suspicion among many scholars, as well as among people implicated in colonial processes, that postcolonialism is merely the bad faith effort of Western scholarship to atone for its sins of knowledge production in the service of imperialism. In another formulation it could be considered the English Department's way of understanding world history as it begins to recognize its crucial role in the domination of the globe.

Yet there are other terminological possibilities worth exploring, as they have at times provided opportunities to think things differently. In a negative characterization, some critics have deplored the recent rise of postcolonial studies, going so far as to caricature it as the opportunism of recent immigrants within the US academy, and to denounce it as a false consciousness that hides the conditions of economic betterment behind the smokescreen of "postcolonialism" (Ahmad, Dirlik). In this turning of the possibilities of the postcolonial perspective into an "ism," such critics fail to recognize the long histories of these forms of scholarship and their connection with real movements of decolonization. This criticism, to our mind, also misses the productive potential of the field in opening new possibilities for understanding ethnicity in the Americas, reducing sophisticated definitions of identity to mere economic enfranchisement. In this book we have tried to show that a materially grounded postcolonial studies is in fact necessary for understanding the complexities of world power, not for avoiding them.

A more positive but difficult lesson is available in the variant "postcoloniality." Critics influenced by poststructuralist and postmodernist thought, especially deconstruction, have moved to shake the foundations of western power/knowledge by invoking the "non-synchronous, multi-spatial events occurring within the folds of a world economy that simultaneously places and displaces, enfranchises and disempowers" (Ray and Schwarz, 1995: 164). Stuart Hall has praised the postcolonial paradigm as offering the opportunity for thinking "at the limit," beyond older oppositions such as colonizer and colonized, colonial and post-colonial, dominated and liberated, First World and Third World. Postcolonial, he argues, describes transformations in the world "that may not be best captured within a paradigm which assumes that all major historical shifts are driven by a necessitarian logic toward a teleological end" (1996: 254). Citing the most influential philosopher of language of our time, Hall continues, "all the key concepts in the 'post-colonial,' as in the general discourse of the 'posts,' are operating, as Derrida would put it, 'under erasure.' They have been subjected to a deep and thorough-going critique, exposing their assumptions as a set of foundational effects. But this deconstruction does not demolish them, in the classic movement of supersession, an *Aufhebung*. It leaves them as the only conceptual instruments and tools with which to think about the present – but only if they are deployed in their deconstructed form" (1996: 255). Homi Bhabha and Gayatri Spivak are the most visible critics to have brought such concepts to our attention. As the essay by Bart Moore-Gilbert in Part III makes clear, "postcoloniality" may well be the rubric of the future in defining postcolonial studies a generation from now. Whatever we call it, this volume is designed as a tool in the contest against the negative effects of European conquest, and to contribute to more equitable projects of knowledge production. This demands the most persistent bringing-to-crisis of those European habits that allowed and condoned world domination. From the psychic constitution of the individual subject to the immensity of the "global economy," all European inventions must be "subjected to a deep and thorough-going critique."

Perhaps the best way to approach the problem is to consider the institutional histories in which postcolonial studies has emerged, contexts which have had varied but decisive effects on how it gets defined and practiced in different times and places.

A Small History of Postcolonial Studies

We are very conscious of describing postcolonial studies in this book as an American phenomenon, or rather of locating ourselves as scholars in the midst of the American manifestations of the field. This necessarily determines certain choices, possibilities, and emphases in what follows. Editing a large collection such as this always carries risks and limitations; some planned essays are never written, and other contributors produce work that changes the original plan. Some readers will be disappointed to find that certain locations are not covered, or are covered in ways they do not agree with. Nonetheless, as scholars located in the US, and drawing from contributors whose experience is largely US-bound, we felt compelled to chart the dimensions of this field within our local institutions. This is by no means to limit postcolonial studies to US-bound frames of reference, but rather to explain our choices and configurations as both enabled

7

and constrained by particular regional and ideological histories. There are obviously very good reasons for studying postcolonial issues differently in different times and places.

A curious and crucial feature of contemporary postcolonial studies in the US emerges in the essays comprising the first Part of this volume. It seems that the disciplinary impulse powering the field has arisen most strongly in the United States, while the most prominent contributors to it have originated elsewhere. This is indeed a strange conjuncture, for as we have argued above, it is the genocidal treatment of the First Nations, the African slave trade to the Americas, and the coming of European settlers that form the most dramatic historical events of modern times on this continent (i.e., since 1492). One would expect residents of the Americas to make the strongest case for inhabiting a properly "post" colonial/imperial region, and so to take the opportunities offered by postcolonial studies to study themselves. But this is not the case. US academia is fractured along multiple disciplinary, regional, and identitarian lines. Some scholars may be skeptical about supporting a field of study which seems at first glance to concentrate on Africa, Asia, or South America while neglecting the internal colonialisms still practiced within the United States. So while postcolonial studies is at present a hot topic in US universities, it has not been seen necessarily as the way to reconfigure American studies. Instead, given the division of knowledges into disciplines and of regions into discrete area studies, postcolonial concerns tend to get added on to departments of national literatures such as English. Given the way that issues of race are generally handled in the US, postcolonial studies often becomes one more mailbox in the department of Ethnic studies, now expanded to include "the rest of the world."

Jenny Sharpe's essay in Part I makes this situation particularly clear. In the US itself, several important disciplinary structures have emerged for the specific study of the various ethnic populations within the country, such as African American, Native American, Asian American, and Latin or Hispanic Studies, with several of these institutional enclaves combined into more generalized programs of Ethnic studies, depending on institutional resources and geographic/demographic location. These are vibrant and viable entities serving dedicated populations of students and faculty which have been crucial in promoting awareness of, and allocating resources for, the academic and activist projects of the vast diversity of peoples in the Americas. Oddly however, the emphasis of much of the visible work done in the US that gets called postcolonial has focused on areas such as South Asia, the Middle East, East Asia, or Africa, seemingly outside the purview of "American" concerns, and has tended to neglect the international experiences of the multiethnic populations of the US including those of its white settlers. This is partially a terminological problem: why would an essay on women in India be published in a journal of postcolonial studies, while an essay on women in the US south would be more suitable for a journal of African American studies? It is also a problem of the politics of knowledge production in this particular context. If postcolonial studies is to take the world as its object, with its long histories of cultural mixing as we suggested above, it must work actively to transcend disciplinary divisions and the compartmentalization of ethnic experience in this country. Our collection of essays on the Americas in Part II goes some way toward addressing these concerns.

One explanation for the contradiction that creates the imaginary divide between postcolonial and other ethnic studies in the US lies in the pervasive academic tradition of "American exceptionalism" that has characterized much scholarly study in this country, and which forms the dominant climate in which American scholars are raised. American exceptionalism claims, in short, that the history of America is fundamentally different from that of Europe, and especially that of England from which most of its early settlers came, in that history began anew with the entry of white settlers into North America. White settlers, on this view, did not reproduce the rigid hierarchies of religion and social class that pertained in England and from which they reportedly fled. Instead, the settlements they created were said to be egalitarian, inclusive structures that benefited from strong interaction with the native populations, thus resulting in utopian communities of tolerance and diversity.

The fundamental beliefs in justice, democracy, and equal opportunity that are said to characterize the American Revolution (1776), the Civil War (1860–5), and today color America's relations with the rest of the world are deeply enshrined in this American mythology and are considered uniquely ("exceptional") American values. Although it is easy to observe the partiality of this view, it is nonetheless ingrained in most school children through the state's educational apparatus and characterizes the professional study of US history and literature to an astonishing degree. To be sure, scholars of American studies are now breaking out of the exceptionalist frame in striking ways, emphasizing the border crossings and ethnic mixings that have long characterized the reality of colonial life in the hemisphere. Yet the older paradigm still conditions the division of academic knowledge in the universities, and postcolonial studies emerged at a time when ethnic exclusivism was still the logic of incorporation within them.

It is important to note the usefulness of American exceptionalism for integrating diverse peoples into a single national project that effectively neutralizes people's differences, positing failure to thrive as the fault of the individual rather than any fundamental inequality of the system itself. Thus the goal of success in America is to "become American," negating one's particular personal history in the drive to approximate what novelist Gish Jen has called "typical American." American exceptionalism reemerged with great force in the post-Second World War period as the US attained superpower status. This was also the era of decolonization, and American ideology reflected the strong cultural nationalisms that accompanied liberation movements, tailoring its promises of "aid" and "development" to the unique identities of recipient nations. In this way individualism and consumerism could be recoded as free choice and national

9

autonomy, and the global spread of American power could appear as a utopian, pluralist accommodation of national and ethnic difference. Both at home and abroad, America styled its image as the one place where diversity could exist. The irony of this image in light of its conquistadorial and slave-holding past required great ideological effort.

American exceptionalism then partially explains the separation of the study of ethnic experience into competing institutions, as people discuss among themselves the strangely unequal terms under which one gains access to "typical American" status. Not yet typical Americans, scholars from the Middle East or South Asia, like those from say Mexico or Canada, were thought to require in America their own house of difference. Yet postcolonial studies in America has by now become a mansion of many rooms representing a wide variety of scholarship about "the rest of the world" that does not fit neatly within the received traditions of the American university or the institutions that had arisen to shelter other kinds of experience. Various configurations of Area Studies arose in the early 1960s to house specialist knowledges about the rest of the world. Yet these institutional locations too have been resistant to the postcolonial phenomenon, at least in part because postcolonial scholars see them as continuing the orientalist tradition of gathering knowledge for the use of state power and as reluctant to engage the radical insights of anticolonial thought. With English as the global language that most postcolonial critics have in common, it is in the English Department that many of their discussions took place. English too in the US was the department most decisively affected by the theoretical currents stirring in Europe as the wars for national liberation raged throughout the fifties and sixties.

By widening the geographical scope of American literary criticism, these scholars challenged the centrality of the US in the English language world-culture that had been emerging since the Second World War. Their research brought other worlds to American consciousness, contesting the dominant story told about exceptional American values and the worldwide spread of Pax Americana. In its place they restored images of marginality and difference to the supposed world order of free markets and bourgeois democracy the US was promoting during the Cold War, and they bore personal witness to the viciousness of the British Empire that dominated the nineteenth century, now succeeded in the twentieth century by that of the US. Since their work did not easily fit the previous definitions of multiethnic Americans, a different terminology developed to stress the "colonial" origins of its practitioners. In the logic of the times the new terminology seemed to herald a new era, just as Star Wars or the New World Order indelibly stamped theirs. There have been many debates about the term postcolonial, as there are in any new field of study. What seems clear is that the perspective is here to stay.

A third sociological explanation for the rise of postcolonial studies and its separation from other forms of American studies involves a shift in immigration laws in the early 1960s to admit larger numbers of educated professionals into the country. According to Sharpe, a new wave of foreign born middle-class professionals began to make their presence felt within academic institutions in the late 1960s and early 1970s due to specific legislation controlling their numbers and qualifications. While the actual numbers of such travelers may have been relatively small, their intellectual impact has been large. The publication of Edward Said's canonical work *Orientalism* in 1978 is widely considered to be the hallmark text of postcolonial studies as a field, and in some ways it can be read as a manifesto of the new influence wielded within the US by this professional class. *Orientalism* can be read as a symptom of the divide between specifically American attitudes toward ethnicity and the general indifference of the American population toward the world at large. *Orientalism* is a profoundly American book in that it views the ideology of American exceptionalism as true; that is to say, it takes America's representation of itself as a given, and then reacts against that representation from the perspective of one excluded from it. It is a brilliant and highly polemical *tour de force* designed to win recognition from the ideological configuration that silences ethnic differences under the guise of pluralist inclusion. It thus places what we could call "foreign ethnicities" on the map of American consciousness, and does so as a general indictment of Western dominance around the world.

While this is not the place for a detailed commentary on *Orientalism* – Anthony Alessandrini's essay in this volume provides that – the figure of Said helps to explain in part the rise of postcolonial studies as an academic pursuit within the particular national context of the US. For one thing, *Orientalism* starkly divided the world into opposing camps – the Orient vs. the Orientalists – that reproduced the rhetoric of the Cold War, now mirrored back onto the colonizing projects of England and France. Americans could identify the stark oppositions of the colonial world in the mutually assured destruction scenarios of their own time. It did this in a dramatically "totalizing" fashion, making the colonial relationship the most determining one in the life of any individual so implicated.

The Orientalists, according to Said, produced the Orient as an object of study and fascination, but mainly one of control. This was reminiscent of the stereotypes hurled back and forth by US and Soviet camps during the period. Moreover, the book was an empassioned plea to listen to the underdog – the Orient – despite a massive, centuries-long effort on the part of Orientalists to speak in the name of the Orient. Indeed, the first epigraph to the book was a famous line taken from Karl Marx, "They cannot represent themselves; they must be represented," which passed sarcastic comment on the Orientalist tendency to silence their objects of study by putting words in their mouths.

Much American postcolonial literary criticism has been produced under these auspices, subscribing to an "us and them" paradigm that pits indomitable enemies against one another. Seminal texts of Third World liberation movements in the 1950s such as Albert Memmi's *The Colonizer and the Colonized* or Octave Mannoni's *Prospero and Caliban* also illustrated these binary oppositions in their

11

titles. Yet Frantz Fanon, the brilliant Martinican psychoanalyst working in Algeria with whom Said has often been compared, originally proposed that the colonial setting created these polarities between white occupiers and black inhabitants in a highly artificial way. These relationships could be compared to Marx's opposition between bourgeoisie and proletariat, but only if they were revised to consider the complex racial and sexual dynamics of vastly different social structures coming into conflict.

Unfortunately, the figure of Fanon was quickly appropriated in the US context of the 1960s as a spokesperson for the "Black revolution that is shaping the world" (blurb to *Wretched of the Earth*), thus reifying his subtle thinking for an utterly different context. In reality Fanon had created a much more flexible and nuanced model of the colonial encounter than he is usually credited with, and certainly one more complex than Said's. For example, as someone sympathetic to the project of building international socialism, but troubled by the exclusion of blacks, women, and Third World peoples generally from many leftist parties in Europe, he quickly qualified his analogy between Third World peoples and the global proletariat by stating, "Marxist analysis should always be slightly stretched every time we have to do with the colonial problem" (Fanon, 1968: 40). Indeed the French Communist Party had difficult debates over the colonial question that could seem off-putting to an observer in French controlled Algeria. Fanon faced the additional burden of "representing" black Africa and the entire Third World within international socialism by virtue of his pigmentation and his scholarly eloquence. His untimely death at the age of 36 cut short this engagement, but his legacy continued to influence discussions around race and class that pervaded leftist organization in the industrialized countries during the wave of decolonizations in the 1960s.

Said on the other hand cleverly mobilized the Marxist slogan ("They cannot represent themselves") within an anti-Marxist rhetoric that was very appropriate for the US context with its history of hysterical anticommunism. In so doing he sidestepped the possible accusation that he was merely another communist apologist for the Third World. We must recall that Russia was the staunchest defender of anticolonial liberation movements throughout the period, from India and China in the 1940s to Vietnam in the 1970s and Africa in the 1980s, while the US tended to oppose liberation movements it could not control directly. Situated thus as an American defense of the Third World within the prevailing Cold War divisions, *Orientalism* proved a marvelous opening salvo to the critical academic study of contemporary non-Western societies, a study which had long been accused of communist sympathies. It brought literary criticism into the world of power and politics, illustrating how innocent purveyors of culture were historically complicit with European imperialism. It showed too that imperialism was an ongoing contemporary process, and that especially in the context of Israel and Palestine, the US was a massively repressive neocolonial force. It also helped to shift the terminology from the earlier Third World slogan to a new phraseology for studying world culture outside the Cold War frame of reference, which reduced other cultures to their strategic and instrumental value in power politics. Said's intervention did however create a context in which postcolonial discussions, at least in the US, tended toward stark oppositions: colonialism as brute domination, resistance as the romanticization of the victims, and a general delinking from leftist politics on a global scale.

Postcolonial studies is practiced as a distinct subfield of literature, philosophy, or history in many places outside the US, and these practices have strongly influenced US scholarship, as discussed by Alan Lawson and Anna Johnston in this volume. Perhaps the strongest exponents of the term have been scholars in the other settler societies of Australia, New Zealand, and Canada (or OZCAN), which have rather different coordinates than those of the EURAM school.

OZCAN postcolonial studies grew in part from the institutions of Commonwealth literature, a distinct subfield of English department activity that tended toward the study of anglophone cultures around the world united by their former or continuing participation in the British Empire. Like the United States, the OZCAN countries undertook strongly nationalist projects in the nineteenth and twentieth centuries to construct for themselves literary and cultural canons distinct from those of Europe. These canons served to undergird a sense of cultural distinction from England, a distinction (or what Pierre Bourdieu has famously called "cultural capital") quite useful and necessary in pressing claims for political and cultural autonomy from the motherland of its white settlers. As in America also, Australian and Canadian institutions of taste tended to write their stories of national distinction as the identity of the settler populations who displaced the preexisting natives. Unlike in the United States, however, Australian and Canadian whites had been more or less peacefully separated from the home country, and their political autonomy had been attained in a somewhat more inclusive fashion.

In 1926, after losing Ireland as the result of a protracted and bloody war, Britain declared that its other "dominions" around the world were in fact "autonomous communities within the British Empire, equal in status," and "united by a common allegiance to the crown." Although they had gained their own political independence in the nineteenth century, Australia and Canada joined this strong international institution, the British Commonwealth of Nations, to enjoy certain preferential terms of trade and migration and to a certain extent to celebrate English culture globally. The claims of English to status as a world language, now spoken practically everywhere for trade and governance, bolstered the claims of English literature to universal greatness. Many anglophone territories, even independent ones, found these claims irresistible in forwarding their own pretensions to national greatness as descended from, but independent of, Britain. Proceeding from the politico–economic model, something called Commonwealth Literature began to be discussed in international conferences and journals as the literary expression of English speakers around the world.

13

With the wave of colonial violence and the massive decolonizations following the Second World War however, the Commonwealth model underwent a shift in meaning. While it did provide members of the former colonies with certain opportunities such as citizenship in Britain and freedom of travel and employment between Commonwealth countries, its ideological connotations became objectionable. If indeed there were commonalities among literatures written in English from the formerly colonized countries, perhaps what was common to them could also be thought of as undesirable. Gandhi himself had claimed in the 1930s that the English language was responsible for enslaving the people of India. By the 1960s, this perception was being articulated with increasing frequency in Africa, the Caribbean, and other regions of Britain's former dominance. The Barbados writer George Lamming's famous reading of Shakespeare's *The Tempest* as the founding text of white oppression in the Americas set the stage for a major revision of the cultural legacy of English internationally.

The 1955 Bandung conference on non-alignment mentioned earlier provided one alternative for discussing the cultural commonalities of newly-independent nations that did not wish to be included either in this false universality nor divided by superpower politics between the First and Second Worlds: Third World. Indeed this slogan was proudly used to generate solidarity among many nations that felt they had suffered at the hands of Europe, even those in Latin America that had achieved independence in the early nineteenth century, or by subcultures internal to superpower states who identified with or otherwise supported the struggles of formerly colonized countries. Although "Third World literature" never really caught on as a coherent rhetoric for studying the cultural expressions of decolonization, it was used informally for thirty years, and is still used today to some extent, to designate both the historical era and a continuing sympathy with its projects.

A decade after the publication of *Orientalism*, an important textbook emerged from Australia which canonized the new term in academic study: *The Empire Writes Back: Theory and Practice in Post-Colonial Literatures* by Bill Ashcroft, Gareth Griffiths, and Helen Tiffin. These authors used the second historical periodization outlined above to define their hyphenated term "post-colonial," the long history of European expansion since 1500. Yet the text tended to focus on the modern period, that is, after decolonization, by elevating contemporary writers as the exponents of the theories which the book endorsed, again mostly derived from contemporary methods in the humanities and social sciences of First World universities. This disjunction between contemporary period versus long continuity, and between Western theories and non-Western authors has continued to characterize postcolonial studies in both EURAM and OZCAN contexts. In another context Gayatri Chakravorty Spivak has termed this paradigm "information retrieval" for First World academic agendas, a painful continuation of the anthropological observation of natives that went hand-in-hand with colonial rule itself. While we would not necessarily single out *The Empire Writes Back* for conviction on this charge, it is worthwhile to note that the "field" of postcolonial studies has blossomed as one that tends to value in the West contemporary literary writers "as if" they represented the long histories of their colonized societies. Thus Salman Rushdie *is* India (or Pakistan), Ngugi wa Thiong'o *is* Africa, Rigoberto Menchu *is* Latin America, and so on. This combination of contemporary celebrity with deep culturalist associations makes the Third World or postcolonial writer vastly overinflated as representative of his or her putative reality. Postcolonial studies only suffers by this reification of the Western craze for otherness.

These difficulties have given us great insights into producing this book. While we too have doubts about the dangers of exceptionalism and celebrity, the continuation of neocolonialism and the postmodern fetishization of otherness, we find it rewarding to call attention to both the efflorescence of work calling itself postcolonial and the institutional rise of postcolonial studies within the US, and to place those events within a global context. To be sure, and despite our criticisms, we feel that postcolonial studies offers one of the most exciting and intellectually responsible paradigms for cultural study in the coming decades. Literary critics and other humanist intellectuals must respond to the world; culture is fundamentally implicated in material processes, especially those of conquest and domination, and no cultural practice is untouched by history. If it has served to draw interested parties into responsible dialogue, we have no qualms with the proliferation of the term. Yet it is obvious that a responsible dialogue is one that will stress complex histories and complicated philosophies informed by great quantities of empirical detail. We reaffirm that the most pressing context for postcolonial studies is the continued attention to decolonization, and the current disposition of world power that has followed in its wake. There is still much to be learned from the histories of contact which made decolonization a world historical event, and still much to be changed before we can definitively put the "post" before colonial.

We hope there will be many intellectual and activist projects for which this book may be useful, but it is designed primarily as an introductory reference for university students interested in studying the many dimensions of the postcolonial. As that is such a vast and unstable term, this section will describe the organization of the book and suggest some ways in which it might function as a textbook for courses in postcolonial culture, world history, commonwealth literature or other fields of study.

The first Part, "Historical and Theoretical Issues," is a thematic summary of the broad outlines of postcolonial studies in the first sense described above, including basic definitions about colonialism, imperialism, and decolonization in the modern world (Larsen). Three symptomatic probes are made into the most visible issues of the field's constitution as an academic discipline in the US and elsewhere: antiracism (Goldberg), feminism (Sunder Rajan and Park), and the contemporary shift in academic discourse towards postmodernism (Quayson). Jenny Sharpe discusses the field's institutional origins in the US. Finally, Crystal

Bartolovich decribes the 1990s vogue for "globalization" and suggests some ways in which postcolonial studies is relevant for our present moment of global capitalism, as well as how the present seems distorted by the claim that the "world economy" is something new. This Part narrates the history of colonialism itself as a term and as a practice; of postcolonial studies in America and Europe; summarizes some major conceptual and political trends in the field as it is practiced in these various places; and extends the interest in this field to other sites in Africa, Latin America, the Middle East, South and Southeast Asia.

The second Part, "The Local and the Global," initiates a discussion, region by region, of the dramatic effects that European colonialism and imperialism have had throughout the world during the modern period, and draws some conclusions about appropriate methods for studying these experiences in a global context while admitting the strong differences in the forms of colonial power and the varied means of overcoming them. Not all of the essays discuss the ways in which postcolonial studies are practiced in their regions; rather, each essay charts the relevance of considering its region through the lens of a postcolonial perspective. Whether this lens is uniquely US-bound becomes a difficult question to ask, as each contributor brings multiple identities into play in the shifting space between the place of the observer and the place of the observed. Although most of our contributors to this section teach within the US, their shifting perspectives reflect the complexity of working through cultural ensembles that are not limited to regions, but rather travel between various locations simultaneously.

The first three essays in this section place the Americas firmly on the map of postcolonial studies. Sommer's provocative title, "A Vindication of Double Consciousness," examines the American exceptionalism described above from the point of view of minority subjects within the US. In her interrogation of the great W. E. B. Du Bois's notion that American blacks are in some sense privileged by their marginality in that they possess a heightened self-consciousness, Sommer extends this insight to the multiethnic populations of the American continents at large. Donald Pease's contribution debunks the American exceptionalist position that the US has not been a colonizing state, and restores the virtually universal perception outside the US that America is in fact a globally dominant oppressor nation whose international relations are pragmatic and self-interested. As we move through the next eight regions covered, we begin to realize that the dominant truth of world history over the last 500 years has been European conquest and control of territory and people everywhere. Jace Weaver's contribution debates the theoretical and practical issues of "who comes first," and thus who has legitimate claim to territory by virtue of prior occupancy. Written from a Native American point of view, this essay discusses the crucial historical and ontological claims to rights made by people variously described as First Nation, Aboriginal, Tribal, or Native who have been displaced by European "discoverers." We find from Weaver's perspective an uncomfortable fit with the academic theories and institutional locations of postcolonial studies, especially in the US where such theories and institutions are often identified with the very settlers who first stole the land.

As the essays spread out to cover the major regions of European colonizing activity – the Caribbean, South Asia, Africa, Middle East, China, Japan, South East Asia, Ireland – we hear recurring themes of displacement, interruption, violence, and exile as the legitimate legacies of European expansion. As Magda Al-Nowaihi's essay reminds us, terms like "Middle East" are uncomfortable reminders of the actual violence that lumped such regions together for strategic purposes, and which continues with every news broadcast. The cumulative purpose of this section is not so much to indict Europe's bloody history – that would be too easy – but to mark the break with tradition which colonial modernity everywhere imposes. David Scott in another context has termed this colonial modernity as "a break beyond which there is no return, and in which what comes after can only be read in, a break beyond which read through, and read against the categories of the modern." (Scott, 1995: 200). Although the phrase seems somewhat awkward out of context, it perhaps deserves rereading to evoke the uncomfortable displacement of "tradition" by modernity which it invokes. The three closing chapters of the Part, on Settler Colonies, Diasporas, and Home respectively, reinforce the notion that Europe really has projected its civilization globally, and that everyone – no matter where they live, how they live, or what they hope to accomplish – must confront European modernity as a fact of life.

The third Part takes account of the richness of theoretical invention which has accompanied the recognition of the postcolonial perspective as the dominant fact of modern world history. Two separate chapters focus on four of the most influential figures in conceptualizing this perspective over the last forty years: Frantz Fanon and Edward Said; Homi Bhabha and Gayatri Spivak. As mentioned earlier, Said's *Orientalism* must be seen as the text which inaugurates the discipline as a field of study in the US. Anthony Alessandrini shows us how the theoretical paradigm first opened by Fanon, writing from within the Algerian movement for national independence in the early 1960s, is transformed for a US context radically different than the one in which Fanon wrote. In a somewhat similar vein, the essay on Bhabha and Spivak illustrates one of Said's central arguments about "travelling theory": both scholars, raised and educated in very different contexts in India, traveled to the West for advanced degrees and encountered extremely rarified theoretical atmospheres. For Spivak, this was deconstruction and psychoanalysis at Cornell; for Bhabha, structuralist Marxism, psychoanalysis, and the advances within British Cultural Studies on race theory at Oxford. When each scholar returned his or her gaze to the colonial context from which s/he came, new identities appeared which had not been evident to colonial history previously. Ambivalence and unraveling replaced collaboration and brute force.

Similarly, Dipesh Chakrabarty's chapter on *Subaltern Studies*, a new school of history writing in South Asia, illustrates how "Western" theories of state and economy such as liberalism and Marxism have been reshaped in their travels East. Subaltern scholars too have discovered identities overlooked by colonial historiography: not the proletarian but the subaltern as the makers of history; not the independent bourgeois state but the colonial comprador state as the achieved form of political autonomy. Ipshita Chanda illustrates the necessary retooling required of Western feminism if it is to prove liberatory for Third World women. In a richly detailed account comparing Indian and African women's movements, Chanda shows us how modern Indian and African women are themselves the products of colonial power relations, and their contemporary disempowerment is in many cases attributable to patriarchal systems invented by colonial rulers to facilitate their power. Who then can recommend that Western feminist theories and tactics are capable of undoing these relations, and what of the precolonial relations these undoings imply? Once again we face a "back to the future" scenario in which authentic traditions of either equitable male-dominated domestic relations, or possibly matriarchal arrangements, are so far lost as to be unrecoverable, and the only way to reestablish women's power is by reforming toward an uncertain future with no proven guides. Thus the global promises of feminist equality confront the practical concerns of specific situations. Since women are not subordinated by all patriarchies in quite the same way, women's paths to freedom must everywhere be different. These facts force to us to consider universal definitions: is freedom the same thing everywhere?

Katie King's essay on "Global Gay Formations and Local Homosexualities" introduces a truly transnational dimension to the volume which, like other processes of planetary scope such as capitalism, demand both global vision and local articulation. Yet King insists that this dialectical vision is still too limited in analyzing the contemporary world dimensions of sexuality: "there are many 'globals,' both kinds and layers of, and many 'locals,' places, particularisms and conceptualizations. Thus it is impossible to ignore that globals and locals are plural, are relative and relational, and that each of these overflowing terms are in fact politicized technologies, in layers of globals and locals, for materially producing people." In a world of such dizzying complexity, "the productive instability of the term Queer" can be read as a code word for truth.

The final Part, "Cultural Studies and the Accommodation of Postcolonialism," addresses some of the dangers and possibilities of postcolonial studies as it attains the professional integrity of an academic discipline but resists the disciplinary and regional fragmentation mentioned earlier. Each contributor in fact challenges the notion of disciplinarity and academic credentialing altogether, and each holds out prospects for the activist nature of intellectual work in a world of rapid information transfers existing side by side with tremendous inequalities. Each would agree that what gets called Cultural Studies in the US (as with postcolonial studies, a hotly contested term that would be discussed very differently in different contexts) is probably the larger organizing rubric for the Humanities, and that postcolonial studies could take its proper place within it; yet for each essayist the question of what to do with postcolonial knowledges and practices outside the academy is more pressing. Thus Gaurav Desai notes the *de facto* spread of English as a world language and questions the very notion of an English department as a place where students fixate on England. Upendra Baxi observes the transformations which newly independent nations such as India have worked on supposedly universal standards of legal rights in writing and amending their national constitutions.

Bruce Robbins despairs of the tired mantra "race, gender, class" in contemporary Cultural Studies – a subject we specifically requested him to write on – and asks what can be added to the Cultural Studies view of the world by including "poco" every time that trio is uttered. His answer is refreshingly productive and humane. The postcolonial perspective, he argues, forces us to confront European defined notions of universality, especially in the field of human rights, and to reimagine the very definitions of being human. If postcolonial theory has offered powerful justifications for colonized states to separate from their oppressors, what can it tell us today of the widespread demands for ethnic and other homelands? How should international organizations such as the UN, not to mention powerful superstates like the US, respond to demands for autonomy such as those in Kosovo, Palestine, or Kashmir? What is the status of the nation today and who decides who gets one, who lives there, and who is to be excluded? How can states which have fought for independence, like India, deny that struggle to smaller groups within their borders, like the Sikhs?

Postcolonial studies alone cannot hope to provide answers or effect solutions to such complex problems, but it can provide more informed histories and theories than those which currently guide public policy. As the tumult of the 1990s becomes the foundation of the new millennium, we hope that scholars, activists, artists, and politicians of all stripes will recognize that postcolonial studies has at least been asking the right questions.

Notes

I would like to thank Richard Dienst, Peter Hulme, You-me Park, and Paul Smith for critical readings of this Introduction.

Suggestions for Further Reading

Ahmad, Aijaz (1992). *In Theory: Nations, Classes, Literatures*. London: Verso.
——. (1987). "Jameson's Rhetoric of Otherness and the 'National Allegory,'" *Social Text*, 17: 3–25.
Ashcroft, Bill, Gareth Griffiths, and Helen Tiffin (1989). *The Empire Writes Back: Theory and Practice in Post-Colonial Literatures*. London: Methuen.

Bernal, Martin (1987). *Black Athena: The Afroasiatic Roots of Classical Civilization*. New Brunswick: Rutgers University Press.

Bhabha, Homi K. (1994). *The Location of Culture*. New York: Routledge.

Breckenridge, Carol A. and Peter van de Veer (1993). *Orientalism and the Postcolonial Predicament*. Philadelphia: University of Pennsylvania Press.

Chatterjee, Partha (1993). *The Nation and Its Fragments: Colonial and Postcolonial Histories*. Princeton: Princeton University Press.

Dirlik, Arif (1994). "The Postcolonial Aura: Third World Criticism in the Age of Global Capitalism," *Critical Inquiry*, 20, no. 2: 328–56.

Fanon, Frantz (1968). *The Wretched of the Earth*, trans. Constance Farrington. New York: Grove Press.

Gates, Henry Louis Jr., ed. (1986). *"Race," Writing and Difference*. Chicago: University of Chicago Press.

Hall, Stuart (1996). "When Was the 'Post-colonial'?: Thinking at the Limit," in *The Post-Colonial Question: Common Skies, Divided Horizons*, eds. Iain Chambers and Lydia Curti. New York: Routledge, 242–60.

Hulme, Peter (1987). *Colonial Encounters: Europe and the Native Caribbean, 1492–1797*. New York: Methuen.

Jameson, Fredric (1986). "Third World Literature in an Age of Multinational Capitalism," *Social Text*, 15: 65–88.

Lamming, George (1960). *The Pleasures of Exile*. London: M. Joseph.

Mangia, Padmia (1996). *Contemporary Postcolonial Theory: A Reader*. New York: Arnold.

Mannoni, Octave (1964). *Prospero and Caliban: The Psychology of Colonization*, trans. Pamela Powesland, 2nd edn. New York: Praeger.

Memmi, Albert (1991). *The Colonizer and the Colonized*, trans. Howard Greenfield, expanded edn. Boston: Beacon.

Mohanty, Chandra Talpade, Ann Russo, and Lourdes Torres, eds. (1991). *Third World Women and the Politics of Feminism*. Indianapolis: Indiana University Press.

Rabasa, José (1993). *Inventing America: Spanish Historiography and the Formation of Eurocentrism*. Norman: University of Oklahoma Press.

Ray, Sangeeta and Henry Schwarz (1995). "Postcolonial Discourse: The Raw and the Cooked," *Ariel: A Review of International English Literature*, 26, no. 1: 147–66.

Said, Edward (1978). *Orientalism*. New York: Pantheon.

——. (1993). *Culture and Imperialism*. New York: Knopf.

Schwarz, Henry and Richard Dienst (1996). *Reading the Shape of the World: Toward an International Cultural Studies*. Boulder: Westview Press.

Scott, David (1995). "Colonial Governmentality," *Social Text*, 43: 191–220.

Spanos, William (1995). *The Errant Art of Moby Dick: The Canon, the Cold War, and the Struggle for American Studies*. Durham: Duke University Press.

Spivak, Gayatri Chakravorty (1987). *In Other Worlds: Essays in Cultural Politics*. New York: Methuen.

——. (1993). *Outside in the Teaching Machine*. New York: Routledge.

PART I

Historical and Theoretical Issues

Chapter 1

Imperialism, Colonialism, Postcolonialism

Neil Larsen

1 Introduction: From Slogans to Jargons

A general introduction to the subject(s) of "imperialism, colonialism and postcolonialism" ought to be a fairly straightforward matter of marshaling the best, or most influential definitions and theoretical illuminations of these terms according to the vaguely historical sequence already implied in this triad. ("Colonialism, imperialism, postcolonialism" would, from this point of view, be the more appropriate sequence.) But this is already a problematic undertaking. However current or fashionable in academic circles, "postcolonialism" is, by anyone's reckoning, a term whose use is also virtually restricted to the metropolitan academy and its satellites. Indeed, its circulation within this academy itself is still far from universal, being further limited mainly to the discourse of literature departments and "cultural studies." (The superficial circumstance of its origins as a term in a 1970s debate between political scientists (Ahmad, 1995) and the fact that historians, sociologists, and even journalists may have now begun to adopt it is largely irrelevant here. The generic use of the term to refer to any formerly colonized political or social entity brings into play none of the polemical and often refractory questions – especially those, as we shall see, regarding the nation – that the term or concept evokes within the humanities, or in volumes such as this one (see Ashcroft *et al.*, 1998: 186).) Yet another "post-al" jargon to its detractors, a challenge to metropolitan, Eurocentrist doxa according to its defenders, the term (in whichever of its variations: postcolonialism, postcoloniality, postcolonial studies, postcolonial theory, etc.) signifies little more than its own (waning) novelty or exoticism *outside* the walls of the academy.

It's possible and sometimes even routine to speak of "colonialism" and "imperialism" *inside* these walls too, but these terms – and the rather more discrete realities they denote – had to force their way in from the outside. I doubt whether the history or social studies textbooks that I read as a 1960s high school student in the midwestern United States made any reference to "colonialism." "Colony" or "colonization," perhaps, as in "the thirteen colonies." "Empire" I do seem to remember (as in "Roman" or "Spanish"); but "imperialism", I am certain, never. "Imperialism" (as in "US") was a term that those of my peers with sufficient temerity had begun to utter after 1967 or so, about a reality entirely outside the textbooks. Its utterance usually meant trouble. With reference to the war in Vietnam, it implied sympathy for the "enemy." "Colonialism" was safer for us, since, so we had been taught, the United States had no "colonies" – only the "commonwealth" or "free associated territory" of Puerto Rico. But one can assume a similarly fraught politics of diction for those speaking of "colonialism" in the Paris of the 1950s, not to mention the Algiers of that same period, or the India or China of decades earlier. These words, whatever else they were, had come to signify injustices, causes, social movements and revolutions, massive historical upheavals and changes. They had their accompanying, opposing slogans: national liberation, revolution, socialism. Perhaps, within its much more modest sphere of common usage, "postcolonialism" has become a slogan as well – powerful enough to secure the publication of an article in a journal, or, on the other hand, troublesome enough to result occasionally in denial of tenure. But no genuinely mass social or political movement I'm aware of paints the word "postcolonialism" on its banners. How, after all, would one know whether to be for it or against it?

"Imperialism, colonialism, postcolonialism," that is, risks conveying an illusion of conceptual parity or symmetry – a species of category mistake – as a result of which a crucial *historical* perspective is eclipsed. To guard against this false, ahistorical symmetry, however, does not require that we drop the last of its terms. (A rather absurd beginning, in any case, for a contribution to a *Companion to Postcolonial Studies*!) That would incur the opposing, anti-intellectual fallacy, according to which academics and intellectuals generally communicate only in esoteric jargons with no bearing on the general form of existence. (Consider whether such could be said of terms such as "relativity," "mode of production," or "the return of the repressed.") "Postcolonialism," despite its intramural genealogy, may in fact point at a concept, or, at least, at a conceptual place-holder, made necessary by the continuation of the same history that turned "imperialism" and "colonialism" into fighting words. For jargons, too, have their histories, and perhaps just enough negativity to point beyond themselves. The gesture of exasperated dismissal on the grounds of "trendiness," unless it can account for the origin of the trend itself, is reduced to the intellectual level of that which it thinks it dismisses.

Think, for instance, of how, before the coinage of "postcolonial," one was accustomed to speak of what the novels of Gabriel García Márquez and Chinua Achebe had in common over and against, say, those of Margaret Drabble and Alain Robbe-Grillet. The reference, unless my memory deceives me, was to the "third world." By way of tarring its utterer as a sixties relic, "third world" conjures up an entire historical conjuncture, and accompanying political culture, in which one naturally went on to utter the above-cited slogans of "national liberation," etc. For reasons that the discussion to follow will, if successful, help to clarify, we who once unself-consciously said "third world" now hesitate, if only for a second, to utter it in the same contexts. This hesitation reflects the decline of the national liberation movements of the "Bandung era" (see below, sections 3 and 4) leaving us with the question of why and with what effect this decline has occurred, but helping to explain in the meantime the currency of "post-colonial" as, if nothing else, a *euphemism* for "third world." Whether the term "postcolonial" or the "theory" and/or the "condition" that are designated this way point us beyond the crisis of third worldism, or merely serve to mystify it yet again, is a matter for genuine debate. But it seems no less certain that a terminology – and thus perhaps a conceptual spectrum – limited to "imperialism" and "colonialism" will incur the risk of historical mystification as well unless it can account for suspicions (often its own) that it has grown somehow anachronistic. There may, in the end, be no particularly good reason for saying "postcolonial" – as distinct from the prior habit of referring to the "neocolonial" – and yet be quite good ones for not saying "third world."

The danger of confusing slogans with jargons, once avoided, still leaves us, however, with certain nagging questions of conceptual protocol. "Postcolonial," within its narrow domain, now routinely qualifies a certain class of "theory" and even of literature and culture. A Gayatri Spivak or Edward Said may now prefer to issue disclaimers, but no one blinks before referring to them (along with the third personage of the celebrated triumvirate, Homi K. Bhabha) as "postcolonial theorists." Salman Rushdie and Derek Walcott are, at least in the world of academic conferences and publications, "postcolonial" authors, and the films of an Ousmane Sembene, a Wang Zhimou and even, perhaps, a Jane Campion may be said to belong to a "postcolonial" cinema. Whether these all, in turn, partake of a common condition or reflect a common ideological standpoint called "postcolonialism" is a more difficult and very likely futile kind of question. (Here already the mechanical utility of the generic gives way to the conceptual counterfeit and nullity of the jargonistic.) But is there, on the other hand, a "colonialist literature," or a "literature of imperialism"? Although it would make obvious sense to designate, say, James Anthony Froude's *The English in the W. Indies, or the Bow of Ulysses* as "colonialist," or the John Wayne movie *The Green Berets* "imperialist," in view of the now transparently apologetic content of such narratives in relation to the ideologies of colonialism and imperialism, what say, of Gertrudis Gómez de Avellaneda's *Sab* or Joseph Conrad's *Heart of Darkness*? Both of these literary works – the former a Cuban abolitionist novel written in the mid nineteenth-century, the latter one of the most celebrated fictional narratives of Britain's late imperial heyday – are also the products of historical periods that gave rise to colonialist and imperialist ideologies, and might even be said to be their cultural products. But the abolitionism of *Sab*, while hardly dreaming of independence from Spain, lends it an incipiently anticolonial flavor nevertheless, and Conrad's novel, however staunch its belief in British (as opposed to Belgian) civilizational probity, is in no *overt* way a defense of imperialism.

Shifting the ideological axis over to the oppostion – the "anti-" – might be the best next move here. Aimé Césaire's *Notebook of a Return to my Native Land* is unambiguoulsy anticolonialist and yet not reducible to a propagandistic core the way Froude's travel narrative is. Bolivian director Jorge Sanjinés' 1960s film *Blood of the Condor* is "anti-imperialist" cinema in an analogous sense. "Postcolonialists" of all stripes ought to find some common ground here in the acknowledgment that conscious opposition to imperialism and colonialism is, while no guarantee of artistic integrity, one of its likelier symptoms.

But *anti*-imperialism/colonialism, in the end, remain no less problematic as indices for literary or cultural research or critique. Most of what furnishes the reader, student, or scholar within the humanistic disciplines with his or her intellectual objects simply stands in too ambiguous, unmediated a relationship to the conceptual domain of imperialism or colonialism. "Postcolonialism" seems better suited to the task, but only insofar as it has been emptied of most ideological referentiality. Although the two are worlds apart ideologically, V. S. Naipaul is as readily classified a "postcolonial" writer as is Ngugi wa Thiong'o. No less ideologically divergent, Hans Magnus Enzenberger and, say, Tom Wolfe are taxonomically if not generically joined in negative correlation with the "postcolonial." There are, no doubt, possible reasons for such pairings, but "postcolonialism" in its currently vernacular usage doesn't get at them.

It is evident, then, that between the intellectual entry-point of a terminology – "Imperialism, Colonialism, Postcolonialism" – and the end-point of these terms' real conceptual purchase for the general-purpose humanist, there are some missing links to be supplied. The most crucial of these, I propose, is the concept that grounds the triad itself, and that, at the same time, mediates between it and the protocols and methodologies of literary or cultural research. This is the concept of *nation*. Imperialism, colonialism, and postcolonialism are, in variant but broadly overlapping ways, things done to, said of, opposed, or embraced by nations. In relation to both imperialism and colonialism, the nation becomes an object or a projected space of emancipation – although, as I shall discuss below, as part of ultimately divergent emancipatory projects. And it is in relation to this nation as a "liberated territory," real or imagined, that the mimetic, narrative, obliquely ideological operations of literature and culture can now be fairly rigorously analyzed and classified. In its outright claim that all third world literature was on some level a "national allegory," Fredric Jameson's celebrated and still controversial essay, "Third World Literature and the Era of Multinational Capitalism," may indeed have overgeneralized this relation to the point of distortion. But its fundamental methodological proposition (not *its* discovery alone, of course) remains a crucial one for postcolonial studies: that "third world" literature (note that when Jameson first published the essay in 1986 the term still needed no apology) is not about imperialism or colonialism as such but about the *nation* as that concrete, lived immediacy that itself, on another historical plane rarely so immediately or concretely experienced, is, or resists being, colonized, etc. (See Part 3 for further discussion of "national allegory.") And only in relation to the question of the nation does postcolonialism shed *its* jargonized and euphemistic properties and begin to assume true, although still perhaps conceptually negative form: albeit here with the difference that the nation has become that lived space in relation to which the liberatory or utopian desire of culture seems, perversely, to have become misplaced.

Keeping the category of the nation in the foreground, what I propose to elaborate in what follows is a general correlation between each of the three terms under discussion, and

A)   a concrete, world-historical conjuncture in relation to which a definite emancipatory politics of the nation (or of nationalism) becomes dominant;

B)   a key theoretical formulation of (A);

C)   an aesthetic or metaliterary idea – in this sense perhaps a "poetics" – of the nation corresponding to (A) and conceptually interlinked with (B).

I should clarify first, however, that the history we are concerned with in what might now be thought of as a material-intellectual genealogy of "imperialism, colonialism, and postcolonialism" begins with the first great global crisis of capitalism in the late nineteenth century (1873–95; cf. Beaud, 1983: 117–44) and is therefore an interval of the *modern*. (Thus the genealogical sequence in which "colonialism" follows on "imperialism" – if not the superficial chronology – is the more accurate one after all.) Neither the imperialisms of the ancient world nor the colonialism of the early modern epoch (1492, etc.) bear on the precise genealogy under scrutiny, except as a source of images and roles in which to play out a modern drama. This is because the national problematic or "question" at the core of postcolonialism presupposes as historically defunct the "classical" national movements of bourgeois Europe, the "great", more or less democratic revolutions and attempted revolutions in England, France, Italy, Germany, etc. However contested or simply nebulous their positions on what the emancipatory powers and spaces of the national are now, postcolonialists are tacitly unanimous in seeking these anywhere but in the metropolitan "West" of today. The nationalisms of a Jean-Marie Le Pen, the Northern Italian "Ligas," or, for that matter, of Michigan or Idaho "militias" are aspects or symptoms of the global conjuncture to which postcolonialism is critically directed, but their neofascist, Eurochauvinist politics place them on the side of a global divide opposite to even the most Eurocentered of postcolonialists. The historical interval that occupies us here dates from that moment, unevenly registered, after which it has become irrevocably clear that the destiny of all modern nations is no longer to become – or to simulate the condition of being – Western . . . if only because the West itself now forbids such an entelechy. Whatever this destiny may be (and perhaps its very thought is already a kind of trap) it cannot avoid the thought of itself as *centered elsewhere.*[1]

2 Imperialism

2.1 *"Oppressed nations"*

Contemporary references to "imperialism," though less and less frequent, it seems, in the discourse of postcolonialism, point to what is fundamentaly still an unlapsed, if much modified historical reality universally heralded in two events: the outbreak of the First World War in 1914, and, in its midst, the Russian Revolution of October 1917. In a more philological sense, such references tend to be conscious or unconscious reinscriptions of a single text, Lenin's *Imperialism, the Highest Stage of Capitalism*, first published in 1916.[2] We shall have more to say in a moment about the general theory of imperialism advanced by Lenin. But it was the events of 1914/1917 themselves that put paid to what had still been, up until then, the widely-held belief that the unity of the European working classes, under the political direction of Social Democracy, would prevail over the predatory interests of monopoly capitalist powers bent on a violent redivision of saturated world markets. As Lenin himself put it in 1915, "the times when the cause of democracy and socialism was associated . . . with Europe alone have gone forever" ("On the Slogan of a United States of Europe," 1970: 664). Only the most reactionary ideologues, shortly to coalesce in European fascism, could any longer affirm that the national destinies of England, France, or Germany were the historical roadsigns pointing to universal emancipation. The European proletariat had defaulted at the decisive moment, and, after the revolutionary shocks brought about by world, "imperialist" war left a beach-head against monopoly capital only in peripheral, semi-colonial, quasi-"Asiatic" Russia, the nation as an "arena of struggle," as a determinate space for a dialectic of emancipation, had suffered a radical transformation. It was now a space in which the centrality and world-historical ascendancy of bourgeois Europe might still be redeemed, but only if the latter looked beyond itself to the margins of its global hegemony for political, not to say spiritual leadership. The multinational, archaeo-imperial territory over which Soviet political organs had assumed a tenuous control was, from a "classical," nineteenth-century European perspective, still a kind of prenational polity, tending towards, but now, it appeared, poised to surpass its bourgeois-revolutionary phase. The nation as emancipatory space had thus seemingly entered into a new historico-philosophical dialectic, unsuspected by Romantic, Hegelian, and even, perhaps, classical-Marxist notions alike: still European in form, if only because Europe still seemed the almost exclusive site of "material civilization," the same nation had become quasi- or even non-European in content. The nation, as one might summarize it here, had become *transeuropeanized*. The highly organized and "cultured" European working class that was to have donned the mantle of eighteenth- and nineteenth-century bourgeois democracy had to look to a fledgling, "underdeveloped" Soviet counterpart for its historical lessons in self-liberation. But this meant in turn looking for such a lesson to an even more "backward" Russian and Central Asian peasantry – only tenuously "Soviet" and just a half-century freed of serfdom – since it was only, in the end, due to the mutinous peasant army of the Czars, in volatile but epoch-making alliance with Soviet power, that the predations of "imperialism" had been dealt a (temporary) historical defeat. The cause of social revolution was, already in the language of the *Communist Manifesto*, pronounced to be international in "substance," but still national in "form" (Marx & Engels, 1998: 49). But 1914/1917 disclosed this form as "national" only if the following corollary were added: there were *oppressor* and *oppressed* nations as well as classes,[3] and the agency of social revolution now appeared to flow from a conjuncture of oppressed class and oppressed nation in relation to which Europe had become "de-centered."

2.2   Lenin

The writings of Lenin on such questions, especially nowadays, are unlikely entries on any academic reading list or bibliography, "postcolonial" or otherwise. And it is important to note that despite what was, for decades, the orthodox left's canonization of Lenin's *Imperialism* as the supreme authority when it came to this subject, Lenin himself had neither coined the term nor cornered the market on theories of imperialism when he wrote his "pamphlet" in Zurich in 1916. His principal empirical source was the work of the English liberal J. A. Hobson and he wrote his own work, as usual for him, in an intensely po-lemical mode, framed by earlier works on the subject by Kautsky, Hilferding, Luxemburg, and Bukharin. In the "postcolonial" mindset that now dominates much radical academic thinking, moreover, references to "imperialism" as the "highest" or "last" stage of capitalism[4] have come to seem painfully anachronis-tic: does not capitalism's ability to survive two world wars, outlast the "really existing" socialism of the USSR and its allies, and, thanks in part to technolo-gies of production and exchange undreamt of by Lenin, to penetrate any and all local, political barriers erected against it, render Lenin's 1916 text finally obsolete?

One might answer here that, electronic capital transfers and the like notwith-standing, to those it most damages, "globalization" (see Part 4) still resembles in most ways what pre-"postcolonial" theory termed "imperialism,"[5] and that "highest" stages can go on much longer than such phrases encourage us to believe. But whether a general, humanistic interest in "imperialism" requires one to read Lenin, or not, the genealogical centrality of his thought in relation to postcolonial studies must be recognized. In *Imperialism* and throughout his writ-ings on the national question, Lenin assumes the social standpoint of those whom modern capitalism as a world system most exploits and oppresses, even when they are not "proletarians" in a conventional sense. As a Marxist, and thus as an inheritor of European "civilization" at what is arguably its intellectual zenith, he nevertheless breaks uncompromisingly with the "oppressor" nations of imperi-alist Europe and North America while still refusing to indulge in the counter-myth of an "inverted Eurocentrism" (Amin, 1989: 124–51). Without discounting in the least the *political* importance of nationalism and national movements in relation to the new imperialist order, Lenin divests the nation of both its Eurocentrist mystique *and* – as we would now say – of its generally "essentialist," fetishized form in oppositional consciousness. Think, for example, of what is implied in the theoretical metaphor most popularly associated with Lenin's theory of imperialism, that of the "weakest link." If the entire globe has now become part of one vast, interlocking system of capitalist production, reproduction, and accumulation – riven, of course, by ever deeper global crises – then the theoretical question of how to rupture or undermine such a system can no longer confine itself to a *national* framework. Given, moreover, the unevenness of this global system in terms of wealth and degrees of exploitation, breaks in the chain are more likely to occur where capitalist development is relatively lacking but where its social impact is, for this reason, most devastating. Czarist Russia, Lenin argued, was such a place, which explained why the relatively small and new Russian proletariat was able to seize and hold power (from a relatively *weak* bourgeoisie, it is true) where its larger, longer-organized European (especially German) counterpart had been unsuccessful in this during the post-war period of crisis. Lenin, indeed, went further and argued that the European labor movement that had failed to stop World War I had been effectively *corrupted* by its higher degree of development. Its leaders, if not its rank and file, had become a "labor aristocracy" with a material interest in keeping the imperialist system – or at least the historical pact with their "own" imperialist bourgeoise – intact (1970: 677). The "weakest link," that is, revealed the existence of a chain that was not only economic but political, and even, in a sense, ideological and cultural in nature. The new reality of imperialism marked the crisis not only of older, nineteenth-century models of national economy but of national culture and civilization as well. It exposed the Western European and North American metropolis as captive to its own global economic and political "reach" – and hence compelled to launch world wars – but also to be a place of moral and spiritual *decadence*. The destiny of the modern, "Western" metropolis was not to become a New Athens but rather a New Babylon.

Historical developments subsequent to 1917 undermine, of course, the erstwhile faith in either the "socialist" citadel of Stalin's USSR or Maoist China's "East Wind" as the new, delinked centers of a post-European, postbourgeois civilization. But the fact that even the most arcane, historically and sociologically oblivious postcolonial theory can regard "Western civilization" as a myth long since shattered rests, genealogically, on the historical and social transformation climaxing in 1914/1917 and on its uncompromising theorization and de-mythification at the hands of Lenin.

"Imperialism," then, understood both as a world-historical conjuncture and as the index of a theoretical and critical discourse denotes an approach to the "national question" that is both "transeuropeanizing" and radically secularizing. By placing the nation in its newly global, economic context, critiques of imperialism such as Lenin's make possible the following step, which is to regard the nation from a consciously historico-political, even strategic perspective. Imperialism's "other" in this sense is not a nationalist "anti-imperialism" but a (proletarian) "internationalism," grasped here, also, as primarily a political and strategic question. The modern nation – the supreme creation of bourgeois Europe – is not something to be reinvented but to be superseded. To do so, however, requires that the nation be confronted theoretically and practically as a form or limit imposed on an internationalist politics.

2.3   An international of form

Can one, then, go on to identify a "poetics" of the nation – or the "inter-nation" – in this sense? As discussed earlier, the links between the literary and imperialism are plentiful but invariably contingent, thematic, or merely propagandistic in nature. But if we reconsider such links in relation to the new, paradoxically "national" experience of the *inter*-nationality brought into being by imperialism – from world wars to mass migrations – we find ourselves in more familiar literary, or, at least, literary-historical territory: is not this "poetics" of internationalism equivalent to that of the twentieth-century avant-garde now (for a "postmodern" culture) canonized in movements such as Cubism, Futurism, and Dada and in figures such as Apollinaire, Grosz, Mayakovsky, etc.? All students of modern "Western" literature and art have learned by heart the art-historical metanarrative that traces the birth of the first, truly cosmopolitan, international aesthetics to the trenches of the First World War. In a four-year interval, as the story goes, the Romantic idols of national culture (European, at any rate) were smashed to pieces. A modern – much less a modern*ist* – aesthetic could no longer be confined within a national tradition, or even experience. Non-Europeans and "postcolonialists" are not long in detecting the Eurocentrist myth that is surreptitiously restored through such a metanarrative. Are Picasso and Breton the redeemers of art after 1914 rather than, say, Diego Rivera and Tagore? To get at the possible degree of truth in the story, I suggest, requires that we both "transeuropeanize" but also deromanticize and amplify it further. For what is generated in the wake of imperialism's first and subsequent global crises is not an international aesthetic culture *per se*; pre-imperialist, not to mention precapitalist societies had all spawned their own. Rather it is an experience of *aesthetic form itself* as "international." Standard conceptions of the avant-garde comprehend this new formal emphasis, but are too parochial in constructing its domain. Imperialism, as the conjunctural, national-theoretical entity posited here, splits off from each other, seemingly forever, the national-cultural paternity of art and its *formal* principle. The latter no longer thinks it needs the former in order to reproduce itself and take on empirical contents. A "revolutionary" world *aesthetic* – as opposed to a tradition, canon or culture – stands forth as the poetics of the new (anti)imperialist internationalism, both proletarian and all-purpose liberal-humanist, and binds together items as apparently antinomial as surrealism and Zhdanovite socialist realism, *Birth of a Nation* and *The Battleship*

Potemkin, Bauhaus and Brechtian epic theater, etc. All conceive of and even (re)produce themselves as instances of a "Weltliteratur" different from the one envisioned by Goethe and even, perhaps, by Marx and Engels. For a "world" that could mobilize, destroy, and reinvent entire nations in the course of months or weeks now no longer paused to seek its universal forms of reflection in particular national histories and experiences. Only aesthetic forms, shorn of culture – montage, *ostranenje*, didactic formulas, style itself – could keep pace. Needless to say, even this "world," trans-European as it was, retained and reproduced, as we shall see in a moment, its extra-universal, distinctly national margins. But after 1914/1917 the new nationalities and nationalisms drawn into its wake would be spared the pre-imperialist illusion of themselves as, on historico-philosophical principles, "peoples without history."

3 Colonialism

3.1 The "Bandung" era

The new imperialist order that obliterates the traditional forms of bourgeois national consciousness in the upheavals of 1914/1917 emerges from the Second World War (1939–45) fundamentally intact. Here again we must guard against the tendency to confuse the rise and fall of terminologies with true epochal transformations. Postcolonialism may, in the end, enjoy more than a trivial degree of historical referentiality, but "postimperialism" – a term that someone somewhere has probably considered coining – still refers (alas) only to a historical possibility.

But the "national question" that had posed itself in radically new ways in the wake of 1914/1917 acquires a still different historical meaning and urgency after the Second World War. For economic and political reasons too complex to be discussed in detail here, the "Allied" colonial empires that had emerged victorious from the First World War (Britain, France, and the USA) as well as those of the "Axis" (Germany, Japan, and Italy) that had sought to (re)establish themselves in direct challenge to Allied supremacy begin a steady decline and disintegration after 1945. This disintegration is not, to be sure, a voluntary affair, as the example of Vietnam in 1945 – liberated from Japan by the Viet Minh only to be handed back to the French by US-backed, armed Japanese POWs – suffices to show. Starting in 1947 with the independence of India and Pakistan, a great period of decolonization begins, ending only in the early 1970s with the liberation of Portugal's remaining colonies in Africa. Following the historical accounts of Samir Amin (1992) and Aijaz Ahmad (1992), I'll refer to this conjuncture in what follows as the "Bandung era," in slightly anachronistic allusion to the conference of newly independent Asian and African nations held in Indonesia ten years after the end of the Second World War. As Ahmad has argued in an especially clarifying essay (cf. "Three Worlds Theory; End of a Debate" in 1992), it is at Bandung that the new national bourgeoisies of what common parlance will henceforth refer to as the "third world" publicly consecrate their emergence as new players in world politics. The most prominent third world statesmen in attendance – Nehru, Nasser, and Sukarno, with Tito as the sole European interloper and Zhou-En-Lai the somewhat anxiously tolerated guest of honor – personify a politics of "oppressed nations" that both guards its left flank against the potentially more radical, revolutionary anti-imperialism of third world peasants and workers but also its right against any attempt by the new imperialist hegemon – the United States – to restrict the third world state's limited national – and capitalist – autonomy.

Not all third world nationalisms conform to the Bandung prototype, of course. The China that, in the course of liberating itself from Japanese imperialism, carries out what is arguably the third great social revolution of the modern era stands in a qualitatively different, effectively exteriorized relation to the neo-imperialist world system. This remains so however much its subsequently counterrevolutionary evolution (not to be confused with any sacrifice of *nationalist* militancy) may now induce us to forget it. China's unique historical development after 1949 has made it, especially in the wake of the collapse of Soviet-modeled socialism and the passing of the Bandung era, one of the great blindspots of postcolonial theory. The Korean, Cuban, Vietnamese, and perhaps also the shorter lived Luso-African revolutions must also be regarded as relatively exceptional in this context.

At the other extreme are the decolonizations that – perhaps because so relatively little was at stake strategically and economically – generate only momentary and superficial nationalist movements and ideologies. One thinks, for example, of certain former British colonies in the West Indies and former French ones in sub-Saharan Africa. But the national-political entity consecrated at Bandung – both actual and ideological – typifies the new historical juncture here under discussion for the following reason: it presupposes the now definitive historical failure of anti-imperialism to take the form of a strategic alliance of metropolitan and third world labor against capital as such, hence the decline, for the then foreseeable future, of "proletarian internationalism." The nationalism of Bandung rests on the *de facto* anti-imperialist alliance, that, in the final analysis, is to take its place: that of third world labor (primarily agrarian at first) and third world capital, under the latter's effective hegemony. An objective assessment of the enormously varied and rich cultural and intellectual output corresponding to this conjuncture – what we might now think of as the canon of third world cultural nationalism – presupposes comprehension of this fundamental historical and political factor, both as constraint and yet also as a deepening of the transeuropeanization signalled by the initial onset of imperialist crisis. By the time the Bandung era comes to its more or less agreed upon close in the 1970s, the ascendancy of the new third world, bourgeois-led states will have come to seem more ambiguous, setting the stage historically for the radical doubts concerning national liberation that are typical of most "postcolonial" theory and criticism. But here too a material genealogy of postcolonialism cannot afford historical embarrassments. The "oppressed nations" of the Bandung era remain, on the most fundamental level, the politico-strategic object of struggle forged out of the first imperialist conjuncture. What is different now is how the new, local political reality of class in ex-colonial nations such as India, Algeria, Vietnam, or Ghana – a reality that either places a fledgling but "really existing" national bourgeoisie in a position of hegemony within the national setting or that makes the creation of such a class the implicit, structural goal of national liberation struggle – reflects itself in what we might term a *re-essentialized*, or even *de-europeanized* national space or imaginary. To emancipate the nation now appears to be something more than to delink it from the chains of imperialist domination, *more* (if not, precisely *other*) than a question of relative class power. It is to attain national *sovereignty*, a *telos* in relation to which categories such as the *popular* and *culture* naturally predominate over those of class, capital, or labor.

3.2   Fanon

Turning now to the question of the theory associated with this new conjunctural reality, we find a broad variation, at first sight confused, of loosely theoretical discourses corresponding to the no less varied reality of anticolonial and national liberation movements stretching across three decades and the better part of the planet. Theory, too, in a sense, reverts to a "national" form, unable to coalesce in a Lenin in the way the theoretical question of imperialism had, out of what now comes to seem an abstract and utopian universalism of class. Mao Zedong, Ho Chi Minh, Gandhi, Nehru, George Padmore, Nkrumah, Nasser, W. E. B. Du Bois, Amilcar Cabral, Che Guevara, Walter Rodney, etc. are the names by which this eclectic theory, in variant degrees of elaboration, is first known. Even so-called "Three Worlds theory", as Ahmad has shown in the above-cited study, breaks down into at least three variants – Bandung or "Non-Aligned," Khrushchevite-Soviet, and Maoist – none of which can claim anything like the critical-analytical rigor of Lenin's *Imperialism*.

Still, certain instances of this more particularistic, nation-bounded "theory" have now shown a capacity to outlive the nationalist movements as part of which they were initially formulated and thus to offer, in more historically and regionally mediated form, a general reflection on the decolonizing/national-liberation process. The theoretical works of Mao Zedong are the first to come to mind here. "Maoism," is, to be sure, a self-conscious continuation of the already universalizing theory of "Marxism-Leninism," and what was, for many years, its enormous authority within not only communist but nationalist circles reflects what we have already noted as the historically exceptional status of China in the Bandung era. The precipitous collapse of this authority after the 1970s with only a few exceptions (e.g., the Shining Path insurgency in 1980s Peru) reflects the no less rapid demotion of Mao to mere national figurehead in the People's

Republic itself. This is no reason at all for not reading the works of Mao Zedong, something no truly serious student of "postcolonial studies" can possibly neglect to do. But in works such as the *Talks at the Ya'nan Conference on Literature and Art* (1980), delivered in the 1940s under Japanese occupation, there is, admittedly, an ironic absence of theoretical concern for the "national question." For Mao, the national self-identity and integrity of China is aleady an axiom; the only question is the strategic, even tactical one of how to liberate it from the Japanese imperialist yoke – something that, let it not be forgotten, the movement led by him went on over a protracted period to do, with shattering results for postwar imperialism.

Far less epoch-making in their own right, but continuously and even increasingly resonant for contemporary intellectual and "postcolonial" sensibilities, are the critical writings of, *inter alia*, a W. E. B. Du Bois, a C. L. R. James, or the Peruvian Marxist and nationalist José Carlos Mariátegui. James' classic history of the Haitian revolution, *The Black Jacobins* (1963), for example, written in the 1930s with a prophetic eye trained on imminent nationalist upheavals in Africa, remains a theoretical reflection of first importance on the national, anticolonial question. But the one name that seems a virtually inevitable reference in the search for theoretical crystallizations of the national-liberation epoch is that of Frantz Fanon. In *Black Skins, White Masks* (1967; first published in 1952), but above all in *The Wretched of the Earth* (1963; first published in 1961), Fanon, a black Martinican who devoted his French training in medicine and psychiatry to the Algerian anticolonial revolution, gives to the Bandung conjuncture (whose final outcome he did not live to see) its most synthesizing, and, at the same time, most self-questioning and prophetic theoretical reflection.

Without ceasing to insist on the struggle for *national* liberation from colonial domination as a precondition for the *social* emancipation of the third world, Fanon presses the plebeian, if not precisely class critique of the third world national bourgeoisie almost to the limits of "third worldist" doctrine. His account of the transformation of pan-Africanist political leadership in the late 1950s from a catalytic into a regressive force that, after independence, "serves to immobilize the people" ("The Pitfalls of National Consciousness," 1963: 171) already anticipates the degeneration of African states into the corrupt, neocolonized instruments of IMF and World Bank diktats many have become today. The fact that *The Wretched of the Earth* still speaks so forcefully to the social experience of contemporary "postcolonial" politics, despite the no less complete political degeneration of the independent Algerian state to which Fanon directed all his energies, is to be explained, I think, by this refusal to credit the third world national bourgeoisie (a class that was, in Fanon's words, "good for nothing" (1963: 176)) with being more than a momentarily strategic ally on the road to a popular sovereignty loosely identified as "socialist." True, Fanon is not a Marxist, a point he clarifies with characteristic directness when he writes, for example, that

> When you examine at close quarters the colonial context, it is evident that what parcels out the world is to begin with the fact of belonging or not belonging to a given race, a given species. In the colonies the economic substructure is also a superstructure. The cause is the consequence; you are rich because you are white, you are white because you are rich. This is why Marxist analysis should always be slightly stretched every time we have to do with the colonial problem. ("Concerning Violence," 1963: 40)

The immediate political realities of the Cold War, including northern ("socialist" and otherwise) labor's *de facto* abandonment of nations such as Algeria to the racist brutalities of French colonialism, appear to Fanon to disprove the universalist claims of Marxism, to unmask it even, as a theory inevitably vulnerable to a West-centered stigmatism. Race has, in the end, prevailed over class in Fanon's third world, a fact that does not, however, lead him to a politics of racial identity but rather to a politics of "national consciousness" as the only rational means of averting the primitive, racially "Manichean" forms of anticolonial awakening. The inevitable violence of decolonization escapes a descent back into pathological forms only if it can be directed outwards at the (neo)colonizer from a *sovereign* subject, fully national (as against ethnic or tribal) in its makeup. The national is the necessary prelude (perhaps a kind of collective Oedipal stage?) to the social, in which form it sheds its adolescent particularisms. As Fanon writes, again in "The Pitfalls of National Consciousness,"

> A bourgeoisie that provides nationalism alone as food for the masses fails in its mission and gets caught up in a whole series of mishaps. But if nationalism is not made explicit, if it is not enriched and deepened by a very rapid transformation into a consciousness of social and political needs, in other words into humanism, it leads up a blind alley. (1963: 204)

It is, of course, difficult to read Fanon today without a good measure of skepticism regarding the very possibility of this "rapid transformation." The broad array of nationalist and third worldist movements that more or less consciously adopted Fanon's call to "national consciousness" often look, from a "postcolonial" standpoint, to have been precisely the "blind alleys" he warned against. Upheld by what he had witnessed in the early years of the Algerian national liberation struggle, Fanon's evident belief that an increasingly popularized national consciousness would burst free of its bourgeois limitations now looks impossibly voluntaristic – a belief, in his own terms, in the capacity of "superstructure" to become "substructure." History in the post-Bandung era has, to say the least, not been kind to this notion. Still, Fanon succeeds here in posing a problem that the Leninist, politico–strategic approach to the national question too easily passes over: if the nation is simply a form or an arena within which the class-based conflict of capital versus labor unfolds (a conflict, recall, pitting "oppressor" against "oppressed" nations) must not this form itself, however demystified or de-"essentialized," have its subjective side? If class must, for its political realization, mediate itself as nation, must not class *consciousness* do likewise? Can the nation become an outpost, a barricade from which to oppose imperialism if those it "interpellates" persist in the colonial psychopathology of seeing themselves as simply inferior versions of a Western (or "Northern") master-subject?

Fanon himself seems to have formulated this question in literally psychiatric terms, whence his consistent emphasis on the violent formation of national consciousness as if virtually a form of collective therapy for the psychoses of colonized subjects. (See the final section of *The Wretched of the Earth*, "Colonial War and Mental Disorders.") But in being recast from a more subjective standpoint, does not the "national question" become in fact the question of national *culture* itself as precisely that sphere within which a "national consciousness" makes the concrete transition from purely objective political theory and strategy to the more subjective level of mass, everyday experience? Once again, *The Wretched of the Earth* reads, here in "On National Culture," like anything but an anachronism. Fanon's familiar dialectical breakdown of the evolution of cultural nationalist intellectuals into the three phases of assimilationism, exoticism, and, finally, authentic nationalism (1963: 222) should placate, up to a point, even the most fervent anti-"essentialist." As the mere "stock of particulars," the "outer garment" of "custom" (224) national culture remains trapped in its reified form, caught in a purely reflexive relationship with the Western, colonizing "civilization" it had once merely aspired to assimilate. National culture only fully realizes its latent possibilities as that "zone of occult instability" (227) that traces in its own movement that of the "people" itself in it self-activity and constant self-creation. The theory of a true "national intellectual" who "addresses his own people" (236) may, like the general idea of a "rapid transformation" of national into social (class) consciousness, arouse suspicion nowadays, but here, it seems to me, Fanon has history a good deal more firmly on his side. For while the third world nationalism of the Bandung era may now be fairly judged, from the perspective of labor, to have been a political failure, its cultural history cannot be so dismissed. Do we not have in literary and artistic figures and movements, from Achebe, Mahfouz, and Neruda to Cuban popular music to contemporary Chinese film, something like the fulfillment of the dialectic that for Fanon culminated in the "national intellectual"? And can any future strategy of "post-colonial" (post)national liberation possibly afford not to steep itself in this tradition?

3.3   "National allegory"

To attempt, now, to define a "poetics" of the nation corresponding to the Bandung conjuncture admittedly carries with it grave risks of overgeneralization. Few critics or literary historians possess the breadth of reading and knowledge required even to begin to determine whether such definition is a valid exercise at all, and I am certainly not one of these few. One thinks inevitably here, again, of the controversy over Fredric Jameson's "Third World Literature in the

Era of Multinational Capitalism" (1986), particularly in the wake of Ahmad's studied and aggressive criticism of this essay for what was reputedly its invention of a grandly mythological abstraction called . . . "third world literature" (Ahmad, 1992). Jameson's claim to have detected a latent "national allegory" in certain writings (e.g., those of China's Lu Hsun) then reread as metonymies for a "third world literature," remains, nevertheless, one of the most prominent definitions of a cultural-nationalist poetics, and is at least a practical point of departure here for what is no more than a speculative exercise. As readers of the essay will recall, the analysis that underlies the "national allegory" theory has to do with the opposition of public and private spheres. Briefly, the social being corresponding to a fully reified capitalist modernity tends to assume purely private forms; that corresponding to the still incompletely, and perhaps never to be fully "modernized" third world national economies and polities does not. This is not to say that third world experience is therefore always *public* in form, but rather that a firm separation between public and private is much more difficult to institute and maintain. The private is always on the point of becoming the public, and thus it is, according to Jameson's reasoning, that the relation of the third world individual to the sphere of national life as a whole forces a break or leap in which the individual or private "destiny" takes on a directly, publicly "national" dimension (69). This subsumption of the particular by the general, and not, as would be the case in the metropolitan bourgeois novel, the reverse, is what Jameson chooses to call "allegory."

The potential for error here, to my thinking, lies in the *a priori* reduction of every individual instance of "third world literature" to such a latent national allegory. But it seems to me correct to regard this allegorizing process as a *structural tendency* in the narrative forms of "peripheral" modernities – a tendency that may, in many instances, never amount to *more* than an abstract possibility. If it can be allowed that the third world nation itself exists, on one plane at least, only as an abstract possibility – as a volatile and unstable form of social self-identity resting on the already volatile and unstable "Bandung" alliance of third world capital and labor – then it follows that attempts to represent this nation, to portray it in a narrative or symbolic medium, will reflect this abstraction within the formal elements of the medium itself.

Not all "third world literature" necessarily undertakes such a form of *national* representation, however; and, indeed, it may be just as typical of the narrative of "developing nations" to *refuse* the "nation" as such an abstract, so to speak, *thematic a priori*. The greatest works of "third world" cinema, from Satyajit Ray's *Apu Trilogy* to Ousmane Sembene's *Xala* to the Brazilian "Cinema Novo" of Pereira dos Santos, Guerra, and Rocha, supersede national-allegorical interpretation – or submit to it only as a noncinematic, dogmatic afterthought. In a Latin American context, I also think here, for example, of the earlier, urban novels of the Peruvian author Mario Vargas Llosa. In *Time of the Hero* (*La ciudad y los perros*, first published in 1962) and *Conversation in the Cathedral* (1969), for instance, there can be noted an almost conscious decision to create *only* characters whose national-allegorical representativity is so complicated and ironized as to be made virtually impossible. "Peru" in these narratives has become an abstract postulate, or "thematic a priori," only in the negative sense of having been *ruled out* as the ultimate, positive meaning of any personal or social emancipation. "¿En qué momento," asks the protagonist of *Conversation in the Cathedral* in its opening pages, "se jodió el Perú?": "When did Peru get fucked up?" True, Vargas Llosa is, already in the 1960s, skeptical of cultural-nationalist formulas, for reasons that at first draw him leftwards towards socialism but that, as his own class and ideological limitations catch up with him, degenerate into rationales for reactionary neoliberalism. Yet *Conversation in the Cathedral* is every bit as "third world" a fiction as the earlier, indigenist, and much more allegorizable fictions of José María Arguedas, Peru's other great literary figure of the fifties and sixties.

The point here is not to launch into the inevitably futile and reductionist attempt to derive ever more authentic canons of third world literature, but rather to note how, for an author such as Vargas Llosa, "national allegory" makes itself felt *structurally* as just that form of representation that must be consciously avoided if certain more socially realistic representations are to become possible. And yet Vargas Llosa's heroes and villains are, in fact, *not* the privatized monads of metropolitan hypermodernity; their destinies unfold precisely on an ever-shifting dividing line between the public and the private that offsets any clean reproduction of national subjectivities. What these novels resist as false is the final, allegorical solution of dissolving this problematic form of individuality into the single, self-identical substance of the "nation." But "Peru" remains no less the "thematic *a priori*" here, if only because it must be consciously and abstractly *negated* as the *positive* content of individual experience if that experience itself is to become fully representable.

The "re-essentialized" third world nation, that is, calls forth a narrative or symbolic process of self-representation that need not be reducible to allegory but that may be obliged to supplement this represenation, even perhaps to interrupt or stop it if it should fail to acknowledge the thematic *a priori*. We can see the result of such a supplementary or ruptural representation not only as outright allegory but also as purely lyrical expression. Think, here, of the Caribbean poetry of negritude and more particularly of the way an Aimé Césaire, René Depestre, Nicolás Guillén, or Luis Palés Matos evoke "Africa" as a poetic presence. In Guillén's "My Last Name" (1972), for example, the poet reconstructs the past scene in which his anonymous Dahoman or Congolese ancestor had his African name blotted out by a Cuban "notary's ink" and a Spanish one ("Guillén") inserted. The history of colonization in its most brutal form is disclosed in the seemingly innocuous fixity and transparency of a few letters on an identity card. But when "My Last Name" comes to invoke the ancestral homeland – the "nation" on its re-essentialized plane – the images Guillén draws upon are of monkeys, spears, rhinoceroses, and baobabs. "Africa" – which is what, after all, motivates and foregrounds the brilliant historical meditation on naming – is a place appearing to lack historical or social specificity, a purely lyrical, even mythical presence. The nation, too, in effect, is only a "name." It is, to cite Césaire's words in the *Discourse on Colonialism*, that place of "profound being" to be found "*beneath* [the] social being" of colonial and neocolonial life (1972: 68; my emphasis). Of course, it is the history of the "middle passage" itself that has placed *objective* limits on the poet's historical imagination in "My Last Name." But the need to gaze back at an effectively unrepresentable ancestral nation – which is simultaneously, for Guillén, the forward gaze into a Cuba freed of its colonialist-racist legacies – cannot wait for history to settle accounts. Here the nation ("Africa," negritude, a black Cuba) must take on a directly representational, symbolic presence, even if it means representation as merely a place of monkeys and baobabs. More, then, than a thematic *a priori*, the nation that colonialism has either suppressed or called forth in defiance (or both) generates a species of *ethno-teleology*, a goal to be reached (or recovered) outside History proper.

Lest it be thought that such "ethno-teleologies" result invariably in aesthetic compromises, however, consider, finally, the work of the famed postrevolutionary Mexican muralists, Diego Rivera, David Siqueiros, and José Clemente Orozco. In addition to virtually recreating the modern iconography of Mexican nationalism with monumental images of pre-Columbian cities, modern workers, and peasant guerrillas, the great murals of the 1920s, 1930s, and 1940s have withstood the crises of that nationalism far better than the state that once subsidized them. In their painterly, but also public-architectural presentation (what Walter Benjamin termed the "tactile") they conserve, somehow, the revolutionary social energies that generated them. Rivera's Zapata looks as defiant of NAFTA as he does of Carranza and erstwhile neocolonial elites. By the 1930s, moreover, the work of the muralists had become an international – even "revolutionary aesthetic" – style in its own right, profoundly influencing the work of depression era North American painters. (In whose hands, admittedly, the painting of national allegories becomes a rather more doubtful affair – think of the work of Thomas Hart Benton or of the young Jackson Pollock.) The mythical, "ethno-teleological" content of the Mexican murals is as transparent as ever. But the mass character, the virtually structural popularity of these "artworks," leaves them permeable to that "zone of occult instability" that for Fanon conserved the formula for a de-europeanized but also *de-bourgeoisified* "national consciousness."

4 Postcolonialism

4.1 "Globalization"

A "material genealogy" of postcolonialism is, to reiterate the point upon which we began, complicated by the disparity between its generative principle – the sweeping history that the term invokes, if often unintentionally – and the narrow, intramural sphere in which postcolonialism is talked about and practiced. To fully reconstruct such a genealogy would require us to go on at considerable length about "Commonwealth Studies," "Colonial Discourse Analysis" symposia, competing postcolonial anthologies, Australian academic clearing-houses, and the like. I take as given here a readerly consensus that there is no time for this – but also that the hypermediated relationship of postcolonialism to secular realities, if carefully abbreviated, will allow us to make some important connections in what follows. In the small world within which volumes like this one are likely to circulate we are now accustomed to speak in the same breath of Bhabha and Fanon, Said and Walter Rodney (i.e., the reader and the read), when a single step outside its walls suffices for these pairings to seem quizzical, and another for them to become incomprehensible. But the fact that relatively few read the reader does not *ipso facto* invalidate the reading nor prevent its genealogical investigation and assessment.

To reiterate further: at some point over the last two decades the same, small but significant class of intellectuals that had learned in the 1960s to say "third world" became more hestitant about saying it. "Postcolonial," a term with far more ambiguous political resonances, fit this hesitation much better and, beginning in the early 1980s, gradually replaced "third world," at least in some contexts. (A similar story could be recounted about "cultural studies" as a euphemistic substitution for "Marxist literary criticism" and even "Critical Theory.") The question for us here is what major historical shift prompted this minor terminological one (among others), and how such a shift effected conceptions, both popular and intellectual, of the entity that is still really at issue here: the nation.

Sticking to the schema employed so far, my answer is to propose a general if highly uneven crisis of "third worldist" or national-liberationist ideology stemming in turn from the progressive collapse of the strategic class and national alliance of third world bourgeoisie and third world labor underwriting this ideology. The more narrowly conjunctural indices of this crisis are many, and it would be difficult to single out any one as more epochal or synthesizing: the overthrow of the Allende regime in Chile in 1973; the fairly rapid economic decline and marketization of "socialist" Vietnam after its final defeat of US and US-backed forces in the mid-1970s; the same nation's border war with "socialist" China a few years later; the increasingly counterrevolutionary direction taken in the People's Republic itself after the triumph of the Deng Xiaoping faction of the Chinese Communist Party; the Islamic Revolution in Iran in 1979; the eventual containment and defeat by the US and its local clients of popular insurgent power in El Salvador and Nicaragua; the collapse of the USSR and its former satellites in the late 1980s and early 1990s, a fact of enormous and disastrous consequences for radical-nationalist regimes from Luso- and North Africa to Cuba; the US invasions of Grenada and Panama; the Persian Gulf War; etc.

It is neither easy nor very safe to speculate about the underlying causes of a crisis that is still very much in process, but these are clearly enough economic as well as political in nature. And the economic theory of choice these days, along an astonishingly broad spectrum from right to left, is that the various attempts of "developing nations" to industrialize without sacrificing national autonomy have succumbed to a new reality of "globalization," a reality in which the sheer scope of market space and activity exceeds the efforts of any but the wealthiest and most powerful nation-states to contain or control it. In most cases the "theory" of globalization functions as a mere apology for US, West European, and Japanese dominance of the world market, belying the fact that the crisis that has all but destroyed nationalized economic regimes in the third (and former "second") world is *itself* global in dimension, and (as recent (1998) developments in East Asia dramatize) dire in its implications for the global hegemons as well.

But apologetics aside, there is little to debate concerning the failure of the economic model more or less vaguely adumbrated by the third world statesmen who had gathered at Bandung in 1955. Perhaps one can point to exceptions here: China, India, South Korea, maybe Brazil and South Africa – although, as this is written, the economic crisis that has shattered the capitalist myth of the "Pacific Tigers" has made the Chinese and even the Japanese "miracles" seem suddenly doubtful. Following the reasoning of political-economists such as Robert Kurz, it seems to me plausible to speak of a general "collapse" of what Kurz terms "recuperative modernization" (*nachholende Modernisierung*) (1991: 189–228) from Mexico to the (post) USSR. In the poorest nations of the third world, where the process of primitive accumulation of capital had yet to be completed, the sheer magnitude of the organic compostion of capital (that is, the ratio of "constant" capital such as plant and infrastructure to "variable" capital, such as wages and labor costs) required within the global process of valorization for such accumulation to occur makes it a practical and increasingly acknowledged impossibility. In the "sub-imperial" economies of China, India, Mexico, Brazil, etc. as well as in the newly "privatized" markets of Russia and Eastern Europe, the rapid selling-off of state-controlled industries – i.e., of the legacy of "Bandung" and "really existing socialism" – is supposed to free up capital for more productive utilization. But "privatization" as often as not is tantamount to a looting spree by financial speculators, signaling in fact the *destruction* of the previously accumulated capital stocks (cf. Kurz, 1993).

The general truth arguably emerging from these particulars of crisis is that the third world national bourgeoisies have, almost without exception, failed as agents of a national modernization that – whether avowedly capitalist, "socialist," or, in that most exotic of Khrushchevite euphemisms, "noncapitalist" – was to bring either a gradual or a revolutionary social emancipation in its wake. To attribute this failure to the inexorability of "globalization" is valid only if we grasp the latter phenomenon in *its* profoundly contradictory reality as a "law" of capitalist development that in fact restricts the very possibility of such development to a constantly narrowing and shrinking base of accumulation. It's not just Nikes and Coke that penetrate all corners of the planet but the negative, often catastrophic effects of "national" and regional capitalist crises themselves. Thus the economic, social failure of bourgeois-led national liberation in the third world (a failure that, we must still recall, has *not* been uniform and that has a flip-side in certain unequivocally progressive changes, especially in areas such as culture) can only be morally condemned if it is first laid at the doorstep of the current beneficiaries and mouthpieces of "globalization" in its guise as the neoliberal panacea now waved in the faces of immiserated third word labor.

But failure is failure. In this context one inevitably comes back to Fanon's astonishingly prophetic insights in *The Wretched of the Earth*, where he warned that the "incapacity of the national middle class to rationalize popular action" – something he clearly understood as a consequence of this class's fundamental incapacity as an agent of development and accumulation – would lead to the "retrogression" in which "the nation is passed over for the race, and the tribe is preferred to the state" (1963: 149). (Fanon's "Bandung," third-worldist outlook is still detectably in force in his simultaneous call for this class to "repudiate its own nature" and "make itself the willing slave of that revolutionary capital which is the people" (150), a demonstration of faith that is the dialectical other of his scathing condemnation of this same class for its weakness and identification with Western bourgeois decadence. But even here the contemporary realities of "globalization" seem almost immanent in his very choice of words, e.g., his dismissal of the third world bourgeoisie for "beginning at the end" of bourgeois civilization in the West. This is, in more strictly political-economic terms, precisely Kurz's argument (1991): that local, neonational attempts to complete the phase of primitive accumulation are doomed by "beginning at the end" of global capitalism's own history of expansionary accumulation.)

Is it not precisely this "retrogression," this failure of "national" to transform itself into "social consciousness," that now unfolds from the Islamic and Hindu demagogies in Western and Southern Asia to the interethnic and, so-to-speak, hypobourgeois wars in Africa and on the immediate southern and eastern flanks of metropolitan Europe? Fanon's insight is in fact needed here to complete the picture of what the "transeuropean" nation as a social, political ideal is now becoming in the course of "globalization": an institutional/ideological entity that, precisely because it has been rendered inoperative as a site for the accumulation and control of capital, seeks to compensate for this in undergoing a radical *reparticularization* verging, in the most extreme cases (e.g., Afghanistan, Serbia) on a *desecularization*. In a strange sense, the earlier, imperialist conjuncture appears to have returned: events such as the rapid collapse of the Soviet bloc, and now the even swifter decimation of East Asian capitalist economies from South Korea to Indonesia, produce a sense of impending global transformation – utopian and catastrophic by turns – for the cognition of which the framework of national consciousness can supply no real vantage point. Where are the strategically "weakest links" to be found now? Seemingly everywhere – has not the hour of the truly "wretched of the earth" come at last? And yet "retrogression" is the near-universal phenomenon. As Asian, African, East European, and Latin American markets threaten to disappear and vast new migrations of unutilizable "human capital" pour out of these regions towards the shrinking bases of accumulating wealth, one begins to speculate that the "weakest" has become, in fact, the strongest, and perhaps soon to be only remaining "link": the neo-imperial metropolis itself.

4.2   Said/Spivak

Suppose now one were to attempt to construct, as a kind of thought experiment, a phenomenology of the nation in its present, conjunctural reality. As just what sort of mental object, or experience, would it present itself to a contemporary critical consciousness, the further objective configuration of which we will leave, for now, unspecified? We might begin with the comparative observation that as an object for a Leninist and a third worldist consciousness, the oppressed nation was endowed with a quality of "historical spatiality": the nation is experienced as a site for a fundamentally unitary, self-contained process of social and historical development. In the "Leninist" instance such spatiality was, in its most general manifestation, already global and not national, but the nation lodged itself discreetly here as a sort of fold within global space, a place one could be inside of without losing sight of the larger enclosure – even, in certain cases, a privileged vantage point from which to experience the spatial connections between all such folds. In short, a "weak link." It is this fold that closes onto itself, becoming coterminous with historical spatiality, in third-worldist or cultural-nationalist consciousness. Or to be still more precise: third worldism (as the enumerative logic of 1,2,3 obviously implies) splits this spatiality into two (or, supposedly, three) opposed spheres. The mechanical, "Manichaean" delusion afflicting such a consciousness – for the transcendental standpoint of phenomenology stipulates that space remain unitary in its essence – is invariably sensed, but only prompts further reflection from an exceptional, dialectical intelligence on the order of Fanon, who simply locates the "universal" historical sphere *within* the particular and seemingly narrower one of "national consciousness," claiming thereby to transform both.

These phenomenological forms of the nation evidently continue to play some experiential role in contemporary consciousness, for which nations in their most immediate, commonsensical self-presentation are, after all, just aggregated, geographical units strung like beads, not linked together in a chain or (except in war) faced off in "Manichean" pairs. But the "globalized"/"reparticularized" nation described above, as a site for the *dis*accumulation of capital and the production of migrancy, as a market increasingly without commodities or consumers, traversed by antimodern, quasi-fascistic fits of religious identity-formation and unraveled along ethnic and tribal lines, seems more and more to be a space emptied of any historical self-relation, not a "people without history" but yet not the place where "people" and "history" meet any longer. "Globalized" nation

space is not the perfectly flattened surface of neo-liberal "Ends of History."
(Even Fukuyama (1989), we recall, acknowledged that there would probably
always be "Albanias" and "Burkina Fasos.") Colonizer and colonized, oppressor
and oppressed, "man" and ethnic (female) "other", rich and poor: these are,
perhaps more than ever, the visible fissures in the "world" that encloses us. But
where does the concrete, historical space of their overcoming, the "historical
spatiality" of *emancipation* begin? A *phenomenology* of the nation seems now
utterly incapable of answering this question. It presents us with the elements of
an emancipatory dialectic, but not with their unifying law of motion, making
them seem, finally (as I have elsewhere described them), "incommensurable"
(Larsen, forthcoming).

But this apparent emptying out of the nation as a *historically* emancipatory
space has not, at least on the *phenomenological* level, enforced a reconciliation of
critical consciousness with "really existing" globalization. For one might concede
the actuality of the latter as a kind of total system and yet still – following in the
philosophical vein of a Nietzsche, for example – posit an opposing principle
outside this, or any, system. Metropolitan critical consciousness, at least of the
academic kind, has for a generation or more been intimate with a modern variation of such antisystemic critique in the form of poststructuralism. Suppose
the globally dominant system could be likened to "discourse" in the Foucaultian sense. This would enable one to account for the seeming absence of the nation
as "historical spatiality," given that the elements of a discursive system bear only
a structural, not spatial or temporal relation to that system. Add to this the idea,
intellectually popularized by theorists such as Foucault and Derrida, that, while
strictly speaking nothing can be outside a discursive system, every such system
has built into it an antisystemic principle, a law of "differance" or a self-
reproducing gap that continuously threatens to undermine it. Suppose further
that the "nation" or its equivalent for contemporary anticolonialism and anti-
imperialism were this sort of antisystemic principle – would not, then, the tables
be turned, or at least turnable, on "globalization"?

The reader may have recognized by now the general theoretical orientation of
Edward Said's *Orientalism* (1978), the work from which virtually all contemporary postcolonial theory derives. The discourse named in its title is one that has,
purportedly since the time of Aeschylus, constructed the Orient not as a "free
subject of thought and action" (3) but as a mere effect, internal to this discourse,
and justifying "in advance" (39) the Western colonization of the East. In an
incorporation of the Foucault of *Discipline and Punish* Said also equates orientalism with a "power/knowledge" for which the Western cognition of a simu-
lacrum called, say, "Egypt" is always already inseparable from the colonization
and domination of the real Egypt. Thus "discourse" (orientalism) and a secular,
historical reality (the Western colonization of the East) are, while not formally
collapsed into each other, nevertheless indistinguishable from the standpoint of
their object. They are two facets of a single, encompassing system that itself
never comes to know or truthfully represent the "other" against which it is

arrayed. Gaining the standpoint of this object would, if possible, be tantamount to subverting the "discourse" that – if we follow strictly the logic of *Orientalism*'s Foucaultian conception – conditions the possibility of the object's colonization.

There is, it is true, a more "worldly," philosophically more "humanist" cast to *Orientalism* as well, for it is a carefully researched work that devotes less time to poststructuralist theorizing than to the focused criticism, loosely historicist in methodology, of a highly specific, empirically "discursive" object: the tradition of eighteenth- and nineteenth-century Western "orientalist" scholarship. Since publishing *Orientalism*, Said has consistently and publicly identified himself with that most historical, extra-discursive movement called Palestinian national liberation, in its decades-long conflict with Zionist nationalism and annexationism. And he would certainly be the last to dissociate himself from the intellectual legacy of "Bandung." Moreover, he concludes his book with a measured advocacy of newer purveyors of orientalist scholarship (e.g., Clifford Geertz) "perfectly capable of freeing themselves from the old ideological straitjackets" (326).

But these aspects of *Orientalism* are not what gradually converted it into the harbinger, if not the paradigm, of postcolonial theory. By invoking a poststructuralist conception of discourse rather than, say, a historical-materialist theory of ideology as the governing category for anticolonialist critique, Said had hit upon a way of salvaging from the post-Bandung crisis of national consciousness (on the level of what we have characterized here as its "phenomenology") a kind of transcendental advantage. As, so to speak, a "globalism" without space and time, "discourse" endows its "other" with, in principle, the same, indeterminate status. The "nation" – the "real," unrepresentable, unknowable "Orient" – acquires automatically subversive potential simply by virtue of its logical exteriority.

As noted, Said himself pulls back from this thought and renders, in the end, a more cautious, but less radical judgment on an orientalism whose "other" may just be a more enlightened, ideologically less "strait-jacketed" orientalist. As a result, *Orientalism* is severely weakened as a theoretically "postcolonial" statement, citing Nietzsche and proclaiming the discursive construction of truth at one moment and denouncing the falsifications of orientalists such as Lane or Gibb in the next, as if unaware of any inconsistency. It has fallen to another, founding text of postcolonial theory – Gayatri Chakravorty Spivak's "Can the Subaltern Speak?" (1988) – to push beyond *Orientalism*'s "humanist" limitations and propose in theoretically less ambiguous terms a "discursive" – more precisely a "textualist" – form of anticolonial/anti-imperialist subversion. In this critical essay – one of the last decade's most widely cited and yet most frequently misconstrued[6] – Spivak executes a Derridean move on Said's Foucaultian reading of colonialism as "discursive practice." The latter now becomes a "social text," an englobing, systemic presence of Western imperialism that obviates *Orientalism*'s vacillation – ideological misrepresentation or "power/knowledge" construct? – on the question of discursive truth content. "Imperialism," as understood by Spivak, does not merely monopolize the power to represent its "other"; *all* such representations have (always) already fallen under the aegis of the Western "Subject." With an implacability that Spivak will mollify in later writings, Foucault himself is rebuked for eliding the "epistemic violence" of the imperialist social text even as he (together with Deleuze) denounces those intellectuals who claim to "represent" the masses: for the self-absenting (Western) intellectual too easily conceals the still more primoridal absence of the third world "subaltern," whose "speech" not even the Nietzschean anarchism of "power/knowledge" can hear.

"In the semioses of the social text, elaborations of insurgency *stand in the place* of the 'utterance.' The 'sender' – 'the peasant' [a.k.a., the subaltern] – is marked only as a pointer to an *irretrievable* consciousness" (287; my emphasis). There can be, from this standpoint, no correcting for "orientalist" misrepresentation, nor even a substitution – "Eastern" for "Western" – of "discursive practices." Such changes would, at best, only make room within the "Subject" for a third world intellectual, or class (or gender) elite, still banishing the "subaltern" to the far side of Spivak's epistemologically constructed "international division of labor." ("Can the Subaltern Speak?" makes no apologies for its post-"Bandung" antibourgeois radicalism – the substance of its otherwise rather puzzling affinity for what was, before Spivak's essay introduced them to a non–Indian public, still the distinctly non-poststructuralist orientation of Ranajit Guha and the Indian "Subaltern Studies" collective (cf. Sarkar, 82–108).) As the social equivalent of "that inaccessible blankness circumscribed by an interpretable text" (Spivak, 1988: 292), the anti-imperialist deconstructor of the "Subject" would, in keeping with the "always already" of its own social/epistemic subjection, *already have performed* its task *before* this Subject could represent/re-subject it, before it could be heard to "speak." From its place outside the global, historical space of representation (but within the "hybrid" space of "textuality") the subaltern *nation* would thus be able to take full, radical advantage of its phenomenological implosion. The sense of not knowing where or when the global system encounters the staging points of its negation becomes evidence, so to speak, for the "textuality" – i.e., the self-negativity but *non-self-transparency* – of this system.

The question hovering over this explication, however, is just what real theoretical validity this sort of thinking has once the phenomenological "brackets" are removed and the postcolonial "thought experiment" is concluded. It will surprise no one by now if I confess to being deeply skeptical on this score. This is not the occasion to pursue my own critical view of "discursive" and "textual" anti-imperialisms, however (cf. Larsen, 1995 and forthcoming). In defense of postcolonial theory in what is, I think, Spivak's paradigmatic formulation, it might be argued that in fact nothing more than a "phenomenology" of the nation, or, in more contemporary parlance, a "reading" of its "text," is being advanced. Moreover, when, in a footnote to "Can the Subaltern Speak?", one reads that "in a certain way . . . the critique of imperialism is deconstruction as such . . ." (311), it is possible to understand Spivak in (at least) two ways: as saying that we must look to Derrida as the true theorist of the "subaltern," or, inversely, that the subaltern, as real, potential agent of deconstruction, makes Derrida superfluous. I will leave this to other readers of "Can the Subaltern Speak?" to decide.

It would, in any case, be erroneous to discard, as some have, the postcolonialist "strategies" now most often denoted by reference to Bhabha's vocabulary of "ambivalence," "hybrids," "migrancy," the "in-between," etc. as being mere confabulations. The retreat from historical standards of thought and critique implicit in such "textualist" strategies responds, defensively or not, to a historical crisis of third worldist nationalism that has left even the most historicizing oppositionalities in a condition of strategical uncertainty. The under- or anti-historicism of postcolonial theory is, ironically, true, up to a point, to its own historical subtext. And while it is wrong to conclude from the phenomenological shrinkage of national-historical space that existing nations themselves are no longer sites of emancipatory possibility (tell that to the Zapatistas, or to striking telephone workers in Puerto Rico), there is also a strong historical case to be made for the progressive reconfiguring of "historical spatiality" along post-national, more transparently global axes. The so-called "third worldization" of the metropolitan centers of global capital resulting from massive labor migrations and the intensifying immiseration of "native" working populations – a trend no one disputes – carries with it profound, if still undertheorized strategical implications.[7] To repeat our earlier, "post"-Leninist metaphor: all "links" increasingly coalesce into one, whose "weakness" grows in direct proportion. Urban rebellions such as the one that erupted in 1992 Los Angeles after the Rodney King verdict was announced are not, in fact, the social manifestations of Spivakian subalternity or Bhabha-ite "hybridity," and postcolonialism could make no claim to function as their virtual theory. But the postcolonial revision of nationalist phenomenologies is clearly attuned to such new political developments, however mystified it may remain about their underlying causes.

4.3 "Narration as nation"

What, finally, might we identify as a "poetics" of the "globalized" nation? Thinking along the lines of the postcolonial theory just discussed, the question itself becomes superfluous: for once it is in terms of "discourse" or the "social text" that we pose the national question, the distinction between politics and poetics is effectively erased. The power to represent the nation is already the power to dominate it, while the power to contest this representation – or to undermine the very logic of representation itself – either preconditions the national-emancipatory act or, depending on one's reading of postcolonial theory, stands in for it. Presupposed in the nationalist poetics of the imperialist and colonialist conjunctures as discussed above, the distinction between the literary or even more generally symbolic form of an object and its practical, secular reality loses force here, at least *qua* the *nation* as secular object. In the vocabulary introduced by Benedict Anderson's *Imagined Communities* (1991) and popularized by post-colonial criticism, the "nation" is predicated in "narration." But what in *Imagined Communities* is still a sociological approach to the symbolic (shared, more or less, in Jameson's theory of third world literature) quickly slides into the anti-symbolism of the textualist insight: why suppose that, in predicating the nation, narration ever stops narrating? What, after all, is the line separating the two, except an authoritarian move towards closure of what is in principle a limitless "chain" of narrative signifiers? Isn't it when the narration stops – or *is* stopped – that the "oppressed" nation becomes, itself, the "oppressor"? So, for example, Bhabha has reasoned in one of his better-known essays, "DissemiNation" (1994).

As we have observed of the postcolonial theory of Spivak and Said, such formulas quickly verge on unreality outside a phenomenological or "semiotic" framing of the colonial relation. Perhaps, after all, a contemporary "poetics" of the nation is what postcolonial theory has been assembling all along, while think-ing of itself as a politics. This is a good place to remind ourselves again that "postcolonialism" is not itself the discourse of national or global movements and formations but of a few odd hundred English departments. Yet if we speculate as to what forms of national experience and imaginary identification would cor-respond to the manifold and "deterritorialized" national spaces of late capitalist globalism, the theory of narrative as a primary constituent of nationality becomes more plausible. To be Nicaraguan in Miami, or Algerian in Marseilles, presum-ably requires a greater investment in symbolic processes than would be neces-sary in the course of daily life in Managua or Algiers. History, of course, is what continues to ground this symbolic compensation – the same history that has generated nations themselves and determined the configurations of the national cultures without which the symbolic process itself would become ephemeral and cease functioning. "Nation" is not ultimately reducible to "narration." But nar-ration, arguably, simulates nation in our globalized, interchangable "locations", now off just about everyone's "cognitive map," and about which stories cannot really be told.

A set of contemporary literatures and cultures (including film, video, music, etc.) already too broad and diverse for canonical abbreviation has now grown up on this new symbolic terrain, so that the "world" increasingly knows something of what it is to "negotiate" South Asian "identities" in London or about how West Indian history also takes place in Brooklyn. To call this manifold corpus, in whole or in part – e.g., the Stephen Frears/Hanif Kureishi film *My Beauti-ful Laundrette* or Paule Marshall's *Brownstones, Brown Girl* – "postcolonial" clearly makes some sense, if only as a matter of terminological expediency. The danger, as critics of postcolonialism such as Ahmad have insisted on reminding us, is that this taxonomy may induce us to forget that, for example, not all nor even most Indian literature is written in English and marketed in *The New York Times Book Review*, or that, conversely, a reading of Morrison's *The Beloved* in

Chicago is not interchangable with its reading in Buenos Aires or, for that matter, in Johannesburg. The third world has long since crowded into the late imperial *fora*, but from there not even the most "hybrid" intelligentsias can see clear across the globe. More than a century of imperialism and colonialism, of national liberations, abdications, and disintegrations, has sedimented out in a global cosmopolis in which literary and intellectual "migrants," once the objects of racial and colonialist exclusion and contempt, now enjoy some legitimacy, and even, in certain cases, immense authority. The old centers of empire, for generations now the objects of a "reverse" colonization by their own peripheries, have tolerated what Said has called "the voyage in" (1993). "Postcolonialism" is among this history's results, and reflects the profound transformation of Eurocentrist intellectual culture that it has made possible. Meanwhile, however, the global inequalities and structures of exploitation and oppression that have led to an ironic "transeuropeanization" of the center imprison unimaginable majorities in catastrophic existences for which even a word like "imperialism" seems too mild. The fortunes of "postcolonialism," along with just about everything else, are inscribed in the history this brute reality portends.

Notes

1   This helps to explain, I think, the uncertain relation of Latin America to post-colonialism. With the historical exceptions of Cuba and Puerto Rico, Latin America's first great national and anticolonial revolutions (1810–25; cf. Halperín Donghi, 1993) consciously model themselves on the bourgeois revolution of Western Europe (especially France) and its political precursor and cognate in the (North) American Revolution of 1776. These are not (conscious) breaks with the hegemony and centrality of the European metropolis, but only with the latter's antidemocratic, antimodern fringe, viz. Spain and Portugal. Beginning with the radical-democratic nationalism of José Martí, born of the new historical conditions affecting the development of the Cuban independence struggle and the global transformations of modern imperialism itself, as heralded, for Latin America, in the events of 1898, this Eurocentrism comes seriously into question for the first time. Thus the radical and revolutionary Latin American nationalisms of the twentieth century, culminating in the Cuban revolution of 1959, are indeed central to the material-intellectual genealogy we wish to trace here. The relative absence of a self-designating "postcolonial studies" among Latin American intellectuals (except in northern universities) has more to do with the history of jargons (e.g., the Anglo-centered, "Commonwealth Studies" ancestry of postcolonialism) than with genuine intellectual differences. To a Latin American political and cultural criticism stretching from Martí to Vasconcelos, Mariátegui, Guevara, Retamar, Schwarz, Quijano, and Sarlo, the question of the nation poses itself just as it has for a Du Bois, a Fanon, or a Said.

2   Up until the outbreak of the First World War in 1914, approving and even utopian evocations of "imperialism" – most famously Cecil Rhodes' observation in 1895 that to avoid civil war "you must become imperialists" – were commonplace. As

Hobsbawm remarks: "In 1914 plenty of politicians were proud to call themselves imperialists, but in the course of our century they have virtually disappeared from sight" (1987: 60).

3   "The bourgeois nationalism of *any* oppressed nation has a general democratic content that is directed *against* oppression, and it is this content we *unconditionally* support." Lenin, "The Right of Nations to Self-Determination" (1970: 611).

4   Hobsbawm (1987: 12) writes, however, that Lenin's original title for his work referred to imperialism as the "latest" not the "highest" stage of capitalism. "Highest" apparently replaced "latest" after his death.

5   Lenin (1970: 737) lists five "basic features" of imperialism: 1) the creation of "monopolies" and their "decisive role in economic life"; 2) the creation of "finance capital" out of a merger of bank and industrial capital; 3) the increased importance of the export of capital relative to the export of commodities; 4) "the formation of international monopoly capitalist associations which share the world among themselves"; 5) the completion of the "territorial division of the whole world among the biggest capitalist powers."

6   A misconstrual already evident in the practice of stressing the last of its terms – "Can the Subaltern *Speak?*" – when the logic of what it is saying would require that the prior term – "Can the *Subaltern* Speak?" – receive the emphasis.

7   Implications chillingly evoked in Kurz's reference to "Welt-Bürgerkrieg" or "world civil war."

References

Ahmad, Aijaz. (1992). *In Theory: Classes, Nations, Literatures*. London: Verso.

——. (1995). "The Politics of Literary Postcoloniality," *Race and Class*, 36, no. 3: 1–20.

Amin, Samir. (1989). *Eurocentrism* (Russell Moore, trans.). New York: Monthly Review Press (original work published in 1988).

——. (1992). *Empire of Chaos* (W. H. Locke Anderson, trans.). New York: Monthly Review Press (originally published in 1992).

Anderson, Benedict. (1991). *Imagined Communities: Reflections on the Origin and Spread of Nationalism*. London: Verso.

Ashcroft, Bill, Griffiths, Gareth, and Tiffin, Helen. (1998). *Key Concepts in Post-colonial Studies*. London: Routledge.

Beaud, Michel. (1983). *A History of Capitalism, 1500–1980* (Tom Dickman and Anny Lefebvre, trans.). New York: Monthly Review Press (originally published in 1981).

Bhabha, Homi K. (1994). *The Location of Culture*. London: Routledge.

Bukharin, Nicolai. (1929). *Imperialism and World Economy*. New York: International Publishers (originally published in 1913).

Césaire, Aimé. (1972). *Discourse on Colonialism* (Joan Pinkham, trans.). New York: Monthly Review Press (originally published in 1955).

Fanon, Frantz. (1963). *The Wretched of the Earth* (Constance Farrington, trans.) New York: Grove Weidenfeld (originally published in 1961).

——. (1967). *Black Skins, White Masks* (Charles Lam Markmann, trans.). New York: Grove Press (originally published in 1952).

Fukuyama, Francis. (1989). "The End of History." *The National Interest*, 16: 3–18.

Guillén, Nicolás. (1972). *Man-making Words: Selected Poems* (Roberto Márquez and David Arthur McMurrray, trans.). Amherst: University of Massachusetts Press (originally published in 1958).

Halperín Donghi, Tulio. (1993). *The Contemporary History of Latin America* (John Charles Chasteen, trans.). Durham: Duke University Press (originally published in 1969).

Hilferding, Rudolf. (1981). *Finance Capital* (Morris Watnick and Sam Gordon, trans.). London: Routledge and Keagan Paul (originally published in 1912).

Hobsbawm, Eric. (1987). *The Age of Empire*. New York: Vintage.

Hobson, J. A. (1938). *Imperialism: A Study*. London: G. Allen & Unwin Ltd (originally published in 1902).

James, C. L. R. (1963). *The Black Jacobins: Toussaint L'Ouverture and the San Domingo Rebellion*. New York: Vintage.

Jameson, Fredric. (1986). "Third World Literature in the Era of Multinational Capitalism." *Social Text*, 15: 65–88.

Kautsky, Karl. (1988). *The Agrarian Question* (Peter Burgess, trans.). London: Zwan Publications (originally published in 1899).

Kurz, Robert. (1991). *Der Kollaps der Modernisierung: von Zusammenburch des Kasernsozialismus zur Krise der Weltökonomie*. Frankfurt am Main: Eichborn Verlag.

——. (1993). *O retorno do Potemkin: capitalismo de fachada e conflito distributivo na Alemanha* (Wolfgang Leo Maar, trans.). São Paulo: Paz e Terra.

Larsen, Neil. (1995). *Reading North by South: on Latin American Literature, Culture and Politics*. Minneapolis: University of Minnesota Press.

——. (forthcoming). "DetermiNation: Postcolonialism, Poststructuralism and the Problem of Ideology." In Kalpana Seshadri-Crooks and Fawzia Afzal-Khan (eds.), *Dimensions of Postcolonial Theory*. Durham: Duke University Press.

Lenin, V. I. (1970). *Selected Works*, vol. I. Moscow: Progress Publishers.

Luxemburg, Rosa. (1976). *The Accumulation of Capital* (Rudolf Wichmann, trans.). New York: Monthly Review Press (originally published in 1913).

Mao Zedong. (1980). *Talks at the Ya'nan Conference on Literature and Art* (Bonnie S. McDougall, trans.). Ann Arbor: Center for Chinese Studies, University of Michigan (originally published in 1942).

Marx, Karl and Engels, Frederick. (1998). *The Manifesto of the Communist Party*. London: Verso.

Said, Edward. (1979). *Orientalism*. New York: Vintage.

——. (1993). *Culture and Imperialism*. New York: Knopf.

Sarkar, Sumit. (1997). *Writing Social History*. Delhi: Oxford University Press/Chennai Mumbai. [See also the extract in this volume.]

Spivak, Gayatri Chakravorty. (1988). "Can the Subaltern Speak?". In Lawrence Grossberg and Cary Nelson (eds.), *Marxism and the Interpretation of Culture*. Urbana-Champagne: University of Illinois Press.

Chapter 2

Postcolonial Feminism/ Postcolonialism and Feminism

Rajeswari Sunder Rajan and You-me Park

Postcolonial feminism cannot be regarded simply as a subset of postcolonial studies, or, alternatively, as another variety of feminism. Rather it is an intervention that is changing the configurations of both postcolonial and feminist studies. Postcolonial feminism is an exploration of and at the intersections of colonialism and neocolonialism with gender, nation, class, race, and sexualities in the different contexts of women's lives, their subjectivities, work, sexuality, and rights. Though such an enterprise is necessarily multidisciplinary in scope, like other postcolonial and feminist studies it primarily inhabits the discursive space of cultural studies, which will provide the focus of this essay. We shall try to identify what we think are, and in some cases what we feel ought to be, the major concerns of postcolonial feminism, within the necessary limits of our scholarship and in the inevitable light of our biases.[1]

"Postcolonial feminism" as a rubric and an aegis under which certain kinds of work are produced (or at least appear) – like postcolonialism itself, the name and the thing – is a product of and circulates mainly within the Anglo-American academy. It is identified with the work of feminists of Third World origin located in the metropolitan university, and it is the agendas set by them that define a recognizable postcolonial feminism. At the same time, however, there are significant women's movements and gender issues in many postcolonial nations which are linked with feminist studies in the academy there, as well as works originating in the First World that relate to women and women's movements in the Third World, which are not often included in postcolonial feminist studies. The reasons for their neglect have to do both with their location as well as their empirical bias (structured as they invariably are by the disciplines of sociology, anthropology, developmental economics, or history). We shall be making a case for the inclusion of this growing body of work within the contours of postcolonial feminism. There are differences (but no contest, either of authenticity or of value, we hasten to add) between the two kinds of work, defined by though not reducible to their locations. The importance of location has to do with the intimate connection between feminist studies and feminist politics, the engagement that is both so necessary and so productive for each. Our understanding therefore has to be highly contextualized, and what follows will be in part an attempt to produce these explanatory frames. But we do not mean to suggest that these are differences without relations; on the contrary broadening the scope of a "postcolonial feminism" should enable us to see the connections among these different sites of engagement, or work at forging them.

II

Postcolonial feminist work in the metropolitan academy, especially as defined by the frame of cultural studies, is, broadly, of two kinds. The first is what we might call "theory," as such; and the other is the newly-motivated study of Third World women's writings in the classroom.

1. The theoretical concerns of metropolitan postcolonial feminism have related mainly to issues of representation and questions of location. Teresa de Lauretis (1988: 138) has suggested that a feminist theory itself became possible only within a "postcolonial mode." The interrogative, interventionary thrust, and the reflexive bias that these enterprises display, have made them vastly influential works for both feminist theory and postcolonial studies.

In their engagement with the issue of representation, postcolonial feminist critics, in common with other US women of color, have attacked both the idea of universal "woman," as well as the reification of the Third World "difference" that produces the "monolithic" Third World woman.[2] They have insisted instead upon the specificities of race, class, nationality, religion, and sexualities that intersect with gender, and the hierarchies, epistemic as well as political, social, and economic that exist among women. First World feminists are called upon to recognize differences, acknowledge the historical specificity of women in other places and times, and abandon their unexamined ethnocentrism and the repro- duction of orientalist categories of thought; nor can these earlier positions be replaced simply by an attitude of easy benevolence towards Third World women- as-victims, "information retrieval" as a way of knowing them, or the celebration of pluralism. Instead First World feminists must enter the hard work of uncov- ering and contesting global power relations, economic, political, military, and cultural-hegemonic.

Questions of location (their own, and those of their subjects) are historicized and politicized as postcolonial feminists enter the terrain of the reflexive that we call theory. The investigators' identities and places of speaking are marked by hybridity, in-betweenness, and hyphenation; pure and authentic "origins" are rendered dubious; their intellectual trajectories are crossed with histories of arrival (in the First World); the autobiographical turn, in anthropology for instance, is seem as specifically feminist. When "Third World Women" speak in the voices of these feminists, it is to repudiate otherness, tokenism, stereotyping, exceptionalism, and the role of "native informant." They seek to resignify the attributes of Third World women – silence, the veil, absence and negativity, for instance.

These reflections are "theoretical" for another obvious reason, their intersection with poststructuralist, specifically Derridean positions. "Theory," as such, however, especially elite continental theory, has also been regarded with great hostility as, precisely, representative of the influential white male epistemologies that trivialize the creative endeavors of black and Third World women writers, as in Barbara Christian's well-known essay "The Race for Theory" (1988). The opposition set up here between White and Black, male and female, theory and literature/literary criticism, may strike us as too schematic, essentialist and starkly oppositional. There are other, more productive forms of engagement with theory, for example the exploration of the uses and limits of First World theoretical insights for reading Third World texts, and also of First World feminist theories in an "international frame," endeavors most systematically undertaken by Gayatri Chakravorty Spivak.[3]

A critique of intellectual endeavor cannot be constructed as a narrative of progress, but nonetheless some kinds of work in a political project appropriately belong to an early stage of its development. Some aspects of postcolonial feminist theory therefore seem to constitute it as primarily a differentiation from mainstream feminism and a ground clearing. The monitory and combative address to First World feminists, the repudiation of the roles and places routinely assigned to women and feminists of/in the Third World, the formation of alliances, the introduction of nuance and complexity into the politics of feminism: these are marks of the pioneering postcolonial feminist work of the eighties and early nineties (though of course they are "discovered" anew and repeated pietistically by subsequent generations of feminists, particularly in more narrowly academic publications). It is not surprising that some of it can sound, like much identity politics, self-indulgent, polemic, and self-righteous. Sara Suleri (1992) offers a sharply critical analysis of some key texts of postcolonial feminist theory, faulting the romanticization of "difference," the claims of "authenticity," the expansive metaphorical uses of postcoloniality, and the narcissism of personal experience, that they are guilty of. Fred Pfeil (1994) opens another important debate when he identifies the "in-difference" to solidarity and political struggle that can become the mark of a politically correct First World feminism that has learnt the lesson of cultural relativism only too well by way of response to postcolonial feminism's talk. Even as we recognize the impact of this kind of postcolonial feminist critique on metropolitan theory – arguably greater than that of any other kind of postcolonialism or feminism – we must circumscribe the limits of its location and its politics.

2.   Another significant development in postcolonial feminism in the metropolitan university is the introduction of Third World women's writings into the curriculum. On the one hand, there are benefits resulting from this expansion of

the canon, benefits not confined to the liberal humanist ideal of expanding the cultural horizons of readers – there are also more explicitly political and tangible goals that teachers of Third World women's writings pursue in the classroom. Not least of these is the opportunity to explore postcolonial issues as they are embedded in the complex and concrete situations of literary or film genres. Though inevitably the texts most accessible to the western academy are written by Anglophone or Francophone writers,[4] there is also a growing body of texts written in other, non-Western languages which are being made available in translation in response to this demand: and the politics and theory of translation are important sites of cross-cultural studies.[5]

On the other hand there exists a certain discomfort on the part of postcolonial feminists concerning the use of Third World women, and their writings, in the First World classroom. The frame and the historical moment of this curricular revolution has, after all, been multiculturalism. While most in the field of postcolonial studies acknowledge the need and desirability of curriculums and academic programs more sensitive to minorities' histories and cultures, they are wary of the liberal humanist tendency in multiculturalism's discourse. Too often Third World women's texts (and by extension Third World women themselves), are objectified and exoticized, or utilized for the convenient and quick edification of Western readers. In the context of global capitalism, where capital flows are seemingly undeterred by national or language barriers, the notion of the equally free and easy flow of cultures is particularly powerful and convincing. Though the texts that are studied finally offer no more than a sampling, they tend to be treated either as representative of whole cultures/national histories, or as exceptional and token documents of a postcolonial intellectual vanguard; and writings from very different places get subsumed into a Third World sameness. Within the limitations of (often, undergraduate) classroom instruction, further, the dangers of an exclusively textualized understanding of the Third World, the suppression of the histories of colonialism and imperialism, and the oscillation between cultural imperialism (complacent enjoyment of Western superiority) and cultural relativism (exemption from any moral discriminations or obligations to act), are real matters of concern.

Not that the ideal of liberal appreciation of other cultures should be too easily discredited in a context of pervasive racism, intolerance, chauvinism, and incomprehension of other cultures. The forging of alliances among women, and the establishment of common ground on which the concepts of justice and freedom as well as respect for differences can be negotiated, are worthy goals of postcolonial feminism which can be promoted within the context defined by multiculturalism. If Third World women's texts are not to become simply objects of consumption in the pluralist intellectual marketplace, the demands of teaching and studying postcolonial literatures must be made rigorous, the concept of (other) cultures needs to be subjected to critical and theoretical examination, and the positionality of the reader in the Western academy, as well as the multiple and complicated relationships between the West and the rest of the world, should be systematically foregrounded. The thinking on these issues by postcolonial feminists involved in teaching in the metropolitan university has resulted in a substantial and significant theoretical intervention.[6]

III

Certain feminist scholars, in both the First World and the Third, are producing a more dialectical and praxis-oriented understanding of postcolonial feminism that links labor sites in the First and Third Worlds and emphasizes the international division of labor as a major concern.[7] They are also actively involved in contesting discriminatory immigration laws in the advanced industrial nations of the First World, and in uncovering the forms of racism and sexism that structure the oppression of women of Third World origin in these countries. These feminists seek to move beyond the discussion of cultural domination, resistance, and subversion with which many postcolonial theorists have so far been largely content.

1.   Feminists from different parts of the world and with different disciplinary backgrounds have jointly produced collections of essays addressing postcolonial and neocolonial concerns from a specifically feminist viewpoint. Inderpal Grewal and Caren Kaplan's *Scattered Hegemonies*, and Chandra Talpade Mohanty and M. Jacqui Alexander's *Feminist Genealogies, Colonial Legacies, and Democratic Futures*, for example, encompass a wide range of topics, sites, and theoretical approaches: such as, investigations into the public policies and legislations that regulate Third World women's lives; explorations of the working conditions of Third World women both in the First World and in postcolonial space; critiques of the hegemonic representations of "other" women; and reports and evaluations of Third World women's movements. Cherrie Moraga and Gloria Anzaldua's *This Bridge Called My Back* (1981) successfully disrupts the prevalent conceptions of Third World women in the United States, and offers various articulations of the multifaceted desires and wishes of minority women from different classes, ethnicities, and sexual orientations (see also Anzaldua, 1990). Resisting the hegemonic readings of Third World women which only either objectify them or render them as hapless victims, feminist writers partaking in these projects seek to forge a sense of urgency and hope at the same time.

This kind of feminism – envisaged as a "transnational feminism" – shares major concerns, subject matter, theoretical interests, and political agendas with what is commonly understood to be postcolonial feminism even though it does not explicitly deal with colonialism; it is, however, centrally engaged with its successor, neocolonialism. Here we argue that the scholarship of these transnational feminists, and other feminists such as Swasti Mitter, Cynthia Enloe, Maria Mies, and Sheila Rowbotham, has particular significance at this historical moment in redefining and reconfiguring the discipline of postcolonial feminism.

Many transnational feminists identify the international division of labor – rather than cultural conflicts or transactions – as the most important defining feature of postcoloniality.[8] The major sites of labor exploitation and resistance are located in the Free Trade Zones in the Third World, in sweatshops in the United States and Europe, and in home-based labor everywhere. By linking these sites, they recognize the spatial interpenetration and integration of the First and Third Worlds; the First World exerts its economic, political, and cultural influence in the Third World, while internal conclaves of a Third World are being constructed within the territorial boundaries of the First World.

In the process of setting up and maintaining labor sites where these women are concentrated, various assumptions concerning Third World women's femininity, their abilities, their sexuality, and their familial obligations all become important factors (see Enloe, 1989; Heyzer, 1986; also Mies, Ong, and Mitter) in the negotiations among transnational capital, indigenous patriarchal structures, and women themselves (see Rowbotham and Mitter, 1994; Sacks, 1984; Ward, 1990).

The issue of dignity is an important one in transnational feminisms because of the kind of work Third World women perform on a global level. As Evelyn Nakano Glenn (1986: intro., ch. 7) points out, third world women's labor and sexuality, as well as their other "desirable" attributes, ranging from their "obedience" to their "nimble fingers," are intricately intertwined in the contemporary global cultural imagination. The issue is not only that they are employed in less than ideal working conditions and that, because of their migrant and often illegal status, they tend to be superexploited, but also that in all instances of sex workers, domestic workers, and factory and sweatshop workers, they are predictably subjected to sexual harassment and assaults. Therefore the degradation of Third World women's labor AND their sexuality needs to be addressed in relation to each other. As Maria Mies and Cynthia Enloe have pointed out, violence is routinely used to keep women in subjection while their sexuality and labor are exploited (see also Peters and Wolper, 1995; Truong, 1990).

Feminists have also mobilized across nations on the issue of sex workers caught in the circuit of global sex tourism. The uneven development of urban and rural areas within the Third World, the degradation and devaluation of women by indigenous patriarchy, and the imperatives of a nationalism that push for rapid economic growth (in rivalry with neighboring countries), all contribute to the entry of women into the sex tourism trade. From the other end, tourism is promoted for specific ends by the workings of global capital. The import and export of domestic workers on a global level also raises a horde of complicated questions. Reports tell us that female domestic workers are subjected to sexual harassment and assaults on a daily basis. The cases of Sara Balabagan and Flor Contemplacion are only the most notorious instances of such a situation. The nature of their employment renders foreign domestic workers isolated and helpless in others' private sphere. Also, as we see in the case of the foreign (mostly

Filipino) domestic workers in Singapore, the concept of feminism itself becomes a highly anxiety-ridden and contradictory term for the state. The supposed "feminism" of the Singaporean state, with its high employment rate and a more egalitarian wage for "their own women," is premised upon the exploitation of foreign domestic workers that they (the state and the women in Singapore) rely upon. The case is even further exacerbated by the outrageous taxation of those domestic workers. The necessity of forging an alliance among women from different classes as well as different nationalities and cultures is highlighted by a situation in which the advancement of the rights of the one group of women depends on the exploitation and violation of another group.[9]

Women workers are generally found in what is termed the "unorganized" sector, which is often home-based labor, in which neither labor's organized resistance in trade unions, nor the protection of labor laws is available.[10] Feminists have sought recognition for women's domestic work, the unpaid agricultural and farm work they often perform in rural areas, and home-based labor, and highlighted the conditions of exploitation under which this work is performed – and they have thereby altered national and global economic profiles. Women workers have organized themselves into collectivities and cooperatives in the struggle for better conditions of work and security. A viable form of transnational feminism is emerging with the formation of groups with widespread networks, like SEWA (Self-Employed Women's Association) in India, which opened its first office abroad, in Durban, South Africa, in 1996. SEWA has also been seeking the protection of international labor laws (via UN organizations like the ILO) rather than those of Indian forums. Postcolonial feminism assumes significance as an effort to grapple with and interpret both the economic-political phenomena of capital and labor, and women's exploitation within and resistance to the system.

2. The presence of Third World populations in Britain and Europe is a direct result of colonialism ("we are here because you were there," as the slogan has it), and is therefore a phenomenon of central importance for postcolonialism. (Immigrants to the United States have a different history, but non-European immigration is also causally connected to US military imperialism.) Discussions of diaspora, exile, borderlands, hybrid identities, and cosmopolitanism have proliferated around this contemporary global demographic reality in mainstream postcolonial theory. But it is feminists who have mobilized around the issues of discriminatory immigration laws and other forms of state racism, and it is the lessons learnt there that have engendered the most radical critiques of both the liberal democratic welfare state and First World feminisms, liberal as well as socialist, that have failed to take race into account.

In Britain feminists have been part of well-established antiracism movements, while also focusing on the specific ways in which immigration laws discriminate against women. Restrictive immigration policies are justified by the state on the grounds that immigrants cause unemployment, overcrowding, and social tensions due to the "differences" of their cultural practices; these arguments justify controls, surveillance, and police brutalities. Kum-Kum Bhavnani and Margaret Coulson (1986: 85) have pointed out some of the sexist aspects of British immigration controls: black women, for instance, were not permitted to bring their fiancés into the UK (until this privilege was abolished for black men as well); only white women are allowed to pass on their citizenship *to children born abroad*. (See also Yuval-Davis, 1997.) Similar restrictions are to be found in US immigration laws. Immigrant women, trapped between patriarchal families and communities on the one hand, and the racist state on the other, are particularly susceptible to family violence. As workers, we saw that they are vulnerable to exploitation, either as undocumented aliens in illegal production sites, or as employees in low-paying jobs and home-based labor.

Radical theoretical insights are made possible by feminist experiences of organizing and activism in the field. Lisa Lowe (1996), and Patricia Williams (1991), for instance, have called into question the very ideal of "universal citizenship" which is contradicted by the systematic categorical exclusions of Third World populations from that discourse and its privileges (see also Ancheta, 1988). Anannya Bhattacharjee (1991) deconstructs the traditional feminist theories of "private" and "public" spaces as they are used to understand violence against women, in light of the different consciousness of "home" that immigrant women bear. "The 'theoretical' component of activism," she insists, "must adhere to a continual process of overturning oppressive definitions" (p. 329). Other feminists have discussed the possibilities and problems of multiculturalist policies that grant rights to groups on the basis of their ethnic identities. While on the one hand these have been a practical way of overcoming racism, Nira Yuval-Davis argues that "women often suffer from the acceptance by the state of the definition of what constitutes 'the cultural needs of the community' in matters of education, marriage and divorce and other provisions such as women's refuges" (1997: 77). There is a stubborn persistence to these questions of gender, posed in relation to race and class in the context of global population flows, that is articulated powerfully in postcolonial feminist theorizing.

IV

Postcolonial feminist studies in, or relating to, the Third World, have a rather different emphasis. The concerns of such work relate predominantly to the following areas: colonialism, and the postcolonial nation–state; religion, especially in the form of religious fundamentalisms, and its connections with nationalism; "development" and its devastating impact upon people of the Third World, and especially upon women in these regions; and engagements, which might be described as themselves "theoretical," with Western feminism and postmodernism.

1. Postcolonial feminist historians' interest in colonialism is reflected in research that involves the recovery and examination of the role of women in freedom struggles;[11] and, further, in understanding the ways women's social roles, the symbolic meanings of femininity and female sexuality (such as "motherhood"), and the relations among women of different castes, classes, and religious communities, were "recast" under colonial modernity, chiefly by way of the colonial state's reformist legislations.[12] The first enterprise led to the realization that the expansion of the sphere of activity and the increase of political influence that participation in anticolonial nationalist struggles had made possible for women, were invariably not sustained into decolonization, except for a small class of elite women who had benefited from access to education and the professions under these conditions. How the demands of nationalism and feminism were reconciled or set at odds with one other, is an important and continuing site of inquiry for postcolonial feminism.

Essays on colonial history like Lata Mani's "Contentious Traditions: the Debate on Sati in Colonial India," and Partha Chatterjee's "The Nationalist Resolution of the Woman Question," in the collection *Recasting Women*, have served as influential paradigms of women under colonialism, despite the specific location of their analysis of early British colonialism and Indian nationalism within a specific class-caste social group in colonial Bengal. Mani's argument that women were merely the "ground" in the debate on *sati* between colonial officials and indigenous reformers on the one hand, and traditionalists on the other, preceding its abolition by law in 1829, is a persuasive one, and has helped to locate the place (really, the entrapment) of women in the conflict between "tradition" and "modernity" in other colonial and postcolonial contexts.[13] Similarly Chatterjee's positing of a resolution of the "women's question" by the indigenous elite, in terms of evolving two spheres of "inner" and "outer," "home" and the "world," "spiritual" and "material," that would correspond to women's and men's spheres, respectively, has highlighted the nationalist "uses" of women and the strategies of containing their freedom.

Outside the South Asian context as well, postcolonial feminists have intervened significantly in colonial historiography, their insistence upon gender as a crucial operative category transforming its contours. One example is their reopening of the issue of comfort women in Asia. While seeking the retrieval of the history of the exploitation of comfort women by the Japanese colonial regime during the Second World War, feminists have also expanded the frame of the debate to include the issue of US military presence in Asia and the comfort women located at these US bases. More than focusing only on the past in pursuing punishment for the former Japanese colonial regime (a necessary and urgent task in itself), Korean feminists insist on the continuities in the history of sexual exploitation and violation of Third World women in the workings of colonial-neocolonial power.[14] Postcolonial feminist studies in colonial history therefore gain political urgency from the relevance of the colonial past for the meanings of the present. In many countries decolonization was simply a transfer of power to national elites who continued colonial structures of rule such as the legal system, the bureaucracy, the military, and other law enforcement bodies, agencies of development, the judiciary. For women's movements as well as other social movements in postcolonial countries, the state is a constitutive site of struggle, both as ally in bringing about desired legal changes and instituting welfare measures, and as adversary on account of its discrimination and coercive measures against women and minorities. Examples of the latter include the state's population-control measures, differential employment opportunities and wages, and custodial rape and other state-supported violence especially against lower-caste and rural women. Above all, women in struggle seek to hold the state to accountability, and to assert their claims as citizens. Women's groups in South Africa such as the Women's National Council and the Rural Women's Movement, for instance, have been active in protecting women's constitutional rights under the new Constitution, and were successful in rejecting the special status sought for tradition and customary law – it was only as a result of this intervention that the priniciple of "nonsexist South Africa" was given superior constitutional authority.

A major, though contested, site of both activism and critical studies is law: its discourses, its reform, its implementation or failures thereof, legislative debates, case law, juridical pronouncements, and legal ethnographies. In a discussion of the landmark Shahbano case in India in 1986, where the judgment that the Muslim husband must pay maintenance to the divorced wife (in this case, Shahbano), led to a long and bitter national controversy over the status of Muslim personal law, Zakia Pathak and I had highlighted the implications for women of the dual structure of law in the Indian constitution, a legacy of British colonialism and a consequence of the exigencies of governance in a multireligious nation-state.[15] Similarly, Jacqui Alexander pointed out in her discussion of the redrafting of the Sexual Offences Bill in Trinidad and Tobago, in 1986, that the state's regulation of sex and (female, nonreproductive) sexuality by constructing norms of morality via legislation, was "not a new dimension of state practice," but was "inextricably bound to colonial rule" (1991). These are only early instances of the kind of critical feminist legal studies, of which there is an increasing number, prompted by postcolonial situations of crisis. Despite the specificity of these studies and their groundedness in discrete historical contexts, clearly it is still possible and valid to use them for careful comparative and cross-cultural study and arrive at some "difficult" generalizations by way of conclusion, so that something called "postcolonial feminism" may be meaningful.[16]

Although the predominance of the state as actor in postcolonial countries constitutes the nation as the most significant scene of activism (not only for women's groups but also for other social movements, organized labor movements, and NGOs), the global as a frame of reference is inescapable, given the massive economic restructuring in progress in most developing nations of the world today, under pressure from international financial institutions and Western governments, the entry of multinational capital, global trade, patent and military agreements, the modernization agendas of development projects, and the cultural impact of global media and telecommunications. Colonialism is mistakenly viewed as a "legacy," if that word is understood only as something left behind with the donor gone; hence the valence of the term neocolonialism, and its resonance with postcolonialism. At the same time, in its interpretations of colonialism, in contemporary struggles with the state, and in understanding religious, ethnic, and cultural nationalisms, postcolonial feminism, like other postcolonialisms, has to contend with the political concepts and practices identified with Western Enlightenment thought as they operate in the different space of postcoloniality (an operation that Gayatri Spivak has described as *catachresis*): secularism, democracy, liberalism, modernity; and not simply by rejection. This is discussed at greater length in what follows.

2. Religious fundamentalism and cultural nationalism have gone hand in hand in many postcolonial countries, especially in South Asia and West Asia. Cultural nationalism – in the form of a valorization of the past, the resurrection of religious symbols, the assertion of pride in indigenous languages, literatures, and the arts, and the resistance to alien knowledges and values – was mobilized in anticolonial struggles in the service of forging a "national" identity. It is women who were invariably called upon to represent this tradition, as symbols and in their persons, often at considerable cost to themselves and to their interests as a group.

Both theocratic and secular (but multireligious) postcolonial nations have continued to rely upon the idiom of nationalism and religious identity to counter Western neo-imperialism, or to prop up the sectarian claims of the majority community. Though the oppression of women under religious laws is a pressing reality, postcolonial feminists have to contend with the equally undeniable reality that it is difficult for women to refuse their communities' demands of loyalty or to relinquish their affiliation to them for the often dubious benefits of their legal rights – nor do they always have this option, where the state's laws are themselves religious. Nor can feminists participate in the simple demonization of Islam and other non-Christian religions that is such a familiar and widespread Western imperialist and Orientalist viewpoint. The phenomena of ethnicity, communalism, and religious fundamentalism have more complex causes than civilizational "backwardness." The attempt to negotiate between the emancipatory goals of feminism and the agendas of nationalism and communalism – all too often posited by its opponents as a conflict – has produced a significant body of postcolonial feminist work. The positions taken range all the way from a rejection of feminism in favor of solidarity with collective "national" or community goals and opposition to colonial modernity (exemplified, for instance, in the work of the Nigerian critic Chikwenye Ogunyemi (1985), who proposes "womanist" as an alternative to "feminist" to designate women committed to the struggle for the "entire people" of Africa and its diaspora), to adherence to clear-cut left-democratic-secular goals (as expressed, for instance, by Kumkum Sangari (1995), in the context of Hindu fundamentalism and communitarian claims in India), with a middle position that attempts to find a way of reconciling these conflicts by revisionary readings of religious texts (for example, the arguments of Riffat Hassan (1993), the Muslim liberation theologist, who believes that the Koran must be understood properly, and those of Madhu Kishwar (1990), editor of an Indian feminist journal, who seeks to highlight the more progressive traditions of Hindu religious thought in the face of reactionary revivalism).

Another complicating reality is that, if women are the most frequent victims of ethnic conflict, riots, pogroms, and civil wars, they are also increasingly visible as participants in and even leaders of revivalist movements, so that the question of female "agency" has had to be radically rethought.[17] Arguably the problem of religion and culture tied to (postcolonial) nationalism is the most pressing and fraught for feminists in these regions to contend with, with the recourse to secularism, democracy, and liberal rights being by no means an uncomplicated alternative, either ideologically or practically.

The debates and negotiations in this area are rehearsed by feminists in the West as well, particularly in Britain and France, where minorities belonging to other races and religions from their former colonies form a significant part of the population. For instance, the tchador affair, as it came to be called, in France, in 1989, was the scene of a controversy in which multiculturalism, as the cultural rights of a community, was pitched against modernity, secularism, a homogeneous nationalism, and women's rights, on the other side. In Britain too, minority rights and the rights and freedom of women in minority communities subjected to oppressive community norms, have to be fought for and reconciled in the context of white racism. Feminist activists and activist-academics in these situations produce a contingent, complex and radical rethinking of gender issues.

3. Feminist critiques of developmental ideology and practice in the "developing" world (the euphemistic description of the poor nations of the world that, not coincidentally, were at one time Europe's colonies), have arguably carried the most weight in effecting change in the condition of women, particularly poor and rural women, in the Third World. Following independence from colonial rule, these countries set out on the path of a "development" targeted primarily at economic growth, and committed to a modernization consisting of technological advancement, industrialization, and urbanization. Postcolonial governments received both "aid" and directions from the advanced countries of the West, from international agencies, the United Nations and its organizations, other international donors, and international funding agencies. These programs, however, made no appreciable impact upon poverty alleviation, reducing women in particular to even further levels of destitution as mechanization displaced them from their traditional occupations, the devastation of natural resources made their subsistence labor more difficult, male migration to urban centers in

search of employment left them to cope with family responsibilities and struggles with land, and few governmental welfare measures, land reforms, or health, literacy, and employment programs touched them.

It was this realization that brought forth the earliest of feminist demands for considering the question of "women's role in economic development," initiated by Ester Boserup's landmark work of that name in 1970. The implications, both the gains and the limitations, of this and subsequent modifications, corrections, and critiques of gendered analysis of development, have been conveniently reviewed in Naila Kabeer's recent book, *Reversed Realities* (1994).[18] The influence of feminist academics, those employed in development organizations (international, government, and nongovernmental), and, crucially, of rural women themselves as they came together in collectivities of different kinds, is reflected in the sensitization of institutions to the central place of gender in addressing these issues. A series of measures, beginning with the UN Decade for Women (1975–85), and culminating in the recent UN Human Development Index, reflect the international dimension and impact of this problematic.

Making women beneficiaries of development programs began as a matter of "social welfare" (with all the problems attendant upon that concept), quickly moved to a recognition of their "merit" (women's proven hard work, thrift, sacrifice to family interests, cooperation, pragmatism), and have only recently shifted to considerations of empowerment, equality, justice, and "capabilities."[19] Policy, praxis, and theory in different fields are therefore crucially intertwined in development matters.

Though admittedly gender talk has been co-opted by funding agencies (on this, see John, 1997), and women's development projects have been a series of trials and errors, the gains of learning and the actual empowerment and improvement of the status of women locally and globally have resulted from feminist thought and experience in development, and constitute a significant component of postcolonial feminist studies.

4.   Postcolonial feminists have necessarily to negotiate the relationship of their feminism not only with Western feminism, but also, as we have seen, with other contending ideologies such as nationalism, socialist-feminism, and liberalism, an endeavor that is both politically fraught and theoretically complex. Feminism itself is closely identified with, indeed understood as a Western movement – as historically it unquestionably is – and is criticized on this basis from an influential antiwestern standpoint. In various international forums – such as the United Nations Conference for Women in Nairobi (1985), the UN International Conference on Population and Development (1994), and the Fourth UN World Conference on Women in Beijing (1995) – the differences and conflicts between the agendas of women's groups in developing and in advanced Western countries, were only too evident. Within academic circles the hostility of Third World feminists to the ethnocentrism, ignorance, and condescension of feminists from the First World has often been undisguised.[20]

But the emphasis on individualism, equality, rights struggles, and identity politics in the Western women's movement had in any case already begun to seem insufficient in the light of women's more complicated positioning as citizens and subjects in both Western and non-Western contexts. As a result, some post-structuralist feminist critiques have provided feminists in the Third World a point of entry into reading postcolonial subaltern subjectivities and the "social text," for example in the essay on "Shahbano" referred to earlier. Other examples of theoretical critique (I use the word in preference to "application," to suggest a critical engagement) in Indian feminist work include: Susie Tharu and K. Lalitha's introduction to the two-volume anthology edited by them, *Women Writing in India*, in which they reflect upon their indebtedness to and differences from Anglo–American "gynocriticism"; Nivedita Menon's discussion of the limits of "justice" and rights claims in the context of specific gender issues in India; and Susie Tharu and Tejaswini Niranjana's criticism of the liberal humanist assumptions underlying the conception of the secular citizen subject that has currency in Indian political thinking. Elsewhere (as in the psychoanalytical insights in the work of Assia Djebar, or Nawal el-Saadwi), we see other deployments of "elite, Western" theories by postcolonial feminists in Third World contexts. Overall, postcolonial feminisms have established a discursive space where constructive critiques and dialogue are being made possible. Rather than blindly embrace or reject Western theories, postcolonial feminists in their best moments have successfully anchored these theories in historically and geographically specific social realities. In postcolonial space, where political and economic contradictions are more plainly visible and less skillfully disguised than in the First World, postcolonial feminists have had opportunities to "try out" the theories for fit – and in some cases they have significantly and even fundamentally revised the theories themselves.

V

The most urgent significance of postcolonial feminism does not merely lie in its ability to protest the oppression of Third World women or correct unjust situations. The nature of postcolonial feminism, which insists on local readings of "ordinary women" in the necessarily global context, does not allow postcolonial feminists to collect data without considering theoretical and more far-reaching causes and consequences for the "facts," or to indulge in a bird's-eye view of the situation without paying attention to the most minute detail of everyday lives. In that sense, postcolonial feminism inevitably requires a rigorously historical and dialectical approach to its objects of study, and in its understanding of itself. As a theoretical paradigm, then, a postcolonial feminism that addresses the issues concerning the most "backward" parts of the world may claim the most advanced understanding of the contemporary "reality."

This is not to deny that postcolonial feminism, at this historical moment, is not so much a stable entity or an institutionalized academic discipline as an aggregate of political and cultural movements sharing the goal of approximating a more egalitarian and dignified reality. Nevertheless, we believe that "postcolonical feminism" distinguishes itself from other cultural and theoretical endeavors (which, as in the case of postcolonial feminism, also attempt to approach a more integrated and complex understanding of cultural, economic, historical, and political aspects of contemporary reality) in its insistence on understanding colonialism (and its legacy) and neocolonialism as one of the most important obstacles for the attainment of the more egalitarian and just world, and in its emphasis on women as the group who will not only benefit most from the changed world but also lead this particular historical transformation of humanity in the future.

Notes

1   We have scanted, for instance, an entire body of significant work produced in Latin America, and made only intermittent references to feminism in Africa and the Caribbean; these gaps have to be made good by more exhaustive researches than appear here.

2   The phrase appears in Mohanty (1991: 51), Spivak (1988b: 296–304). Some of the relevant works here would be: Martin and Mohanty (1986); Trinh T. Minh-ha (1986) and (1989); Visweswaran (1996); John (1996); Mani (1989).

3   In "A Literary Representation of the Subaltern: A Woman's Text from the Third World," and "French Feminism in an International Frame," both in Spivak (1988a). It is also Spivak who links the histories of western feminist individualism with those of the colonial woman's abjection in her landmark essay, "Three Women's Texts and a Critique of Imperialism" (1985).

4   In university classrooms and in the discipline of postcolonial studies itself, heavy emphases have been given to texts by African and South Asian writers who command English and French fluently (Bessie Head, Ama Ata Aidoo, Mariama Ba, Buchi Emecheta, and Shashi Deshpande). By comparison, Asian writers' works, even though they directly address the issues of colonial legacy and postcolonial conditions, rarely receive recognition. Ngugi wa Thiong'o from Kenya drew attention to the politics of language in the context of postcoloniality, when he decided to write novels only in Kikuyu rather than in English so that his works would not be turned into cultural commodities for quick and easy consumption by the West.

5   On postcolonial translation theory and politics, see Niranjana (1992); Spivak, "The Politics of Translation," in *Outside in the Teaching Machine* (1993); Dingwaney and Maier (1996).

6   These include Spivak (1996) and (1990), and Needham (1990).

7   See Mies (1986), Mitter (1986), Nash and Fernandez-Kelly (1983), and Ong (1987).

67

8   Teresa L. Ebert defines postcoloniality as "the articulation of the international division of labor" (1996: 285).

9   See Heng, "'A Great Way to Fly': Nationalism, the State, and the Varieties of Third-World feminism" in Mohanty *et al.* (1991). For a discussion of the case of Flor Contemplacion, a Filipina domestic helper convicted and executed for the murder of her employer in Singapore, see Rafael (1997).

10   A number of accounts may be found in Rowbotham and Mitter, 1994.

11   The most comprehensive of these accounts is Jayawardena (1986).

12   See, for example, the essays in Sangari and Vaid, eds. (1989). Also in the collection edited by Uberoi (1996).

13   In the Indian context, the colonial debates around *sati* have been the focus of much attention from feminists, especially in the wake of a contemporary resurgence of *sati* events in India.

14   See *Positions: East Asia Cultures Critique*, fall 1997, special issue on comfort women; and Kim and Choi (1998).

15   Pathak and Rajan (1989). Also reprinted in Judith Butler and Joan Scott, eds., *Feminists Theorize the Political* (London and New York: Routledge, 1992).

16   On the legitimacy and the need for "difficult generalizations," see Robbins (1992).

17   On the question of agency, see Sangari (1993). Also, several essays in Sarkar and Butalia (1996).

18   Feminist publications on women's work, development, ecology, and the new social movements, in India, include Mies (1982), Shiva (1993), Omvedt (1993), Agarwal (1994).

19   The concept of "capabilities" is developed by Amartya Sen in a number of works – see, especially, "Equality of What?" in (1982); and (1985); and Dreze and Sen (1998). A number of contributors, including Sen, use it in the context of gender and development in the volume edited by Glover and Nussbaum (1996).

20   See, for instance, Amadiume (1987), esp. the preface, 1–9.

References

Agarwal, Bina. (1994). *A Field of One's Own: Gender and Land Rights in South Asia.* Cambridge: Cambridge University Press.

Alexander, M. Jacqui. (1991). "Redrafting Morality: The Postcolonial State and the Sexual Offences Bill of Trinidad and Tobago," in Mohanty *et al.*, eds., *Third World Women and the Politics of Feminism*. Bloomington: Indiana University Press, 133–52.

Amadiume, Ifa. (1987). *Male Daughters, Female Husbands: Gender and Sex in an African Society.* Londona nd New Jersey: Zed.

Ancheta, Angelo N. (1988). *Race, Rights, and the Asian American Experience.* New Brunswick: Rutgers University Press.

Anzaldua, Gloria, ed. (1990). *Making Face, Making Soul*/Haciendo Caras: *Creative and Critical Perspectives by Women of Color*. San Francisco: Aunt Lute.

Bhattacharjee, Anannya. (1991). "The Public/Private Mirage: Mapping Homes and Undomesticating Violence Work in the South Asian Immigrant Community," in

Mohanty *et al.*, eds., *Third World Women and the Politics of Feminism*. Bloomington: Indiana University Press, 308–29.

Bhavnani, Kum-Kum and Margaret Coulson. (1986). "Transforming Socialist-Feminism: The Challenge of Racism," *Feminist Review*, 23 (June): 81–92.

Boserup, Ester. (1970). *Women's Role in Economic Development*. New York: St. Martin's Press.

Christian, Barbara. (1988). "The Race for Theory," *Feminist Studies*, 14, no. 1 (spring): 67–79.

de Lauretis, Teresa. (1988). "Displacing Hegemonic Discourses: Reflections on Feminist Theory in the 1980s," *Inscriptions*, 3/4 (special issue on Feminism and the Critique of Colonial Discourse): 127–44.

Dreze, Jean and Amartya Sen. (1998). *India: Economic Development and Social Opportunity*. New Delhi: Oxford University Press.

Ebert, Teresa L. (1996). *Ludic Feminism and After*. Ann Arbor: Michigan University Press.

el-Saadawi, Nawal. (1980). *The Hidden Face of Eve: Women in the Arab World*. London: Zed.

Enloe, Cynthia. (1989). *Bananas, Beaches, and Bases: Making Feminist Sense of International Politics*. Berkeley: University of California Press.

Glenn, Evelyn Nakano. (1986). *Issei, Nisei, Warbride: Three Generations of Japanese American Women in Domestic Service*. Philadelphia: Temple University Press.

Glover, Jonathan and Martha Nussbaum. (1996). *Women, Culture, and Development*. Oxford: Clarendon Press.

Hassan, Riffat. (1993). "The Issue of Women's and Men's Equality in the Islamic Tradition," in L. Grob *et al.*, eds., *Women's and Men's Liberation: Testimonies of Spirit*. New York: Greenwood.

Heng, Geraldine. (1991). "'A Great Way to Fly': Nationalism, the State, and the Varieties of Third-World Feminism," in Mohanty *et al.*, eds., *Third World Women and the Politics of Feminism*. Bloomington: Indiana University Press.

Heyzer, Noeleen. (1986). *Working Women in South-East Asia*. Philadelphia: Open University Press.

Jayawardena, Kumari. (1986). *Feminism and Nationalism in the Third World*. London: Zed.

John, Mary E. (1996). *Discrepant Dislocation: Feminism, Theory and Postcolonial Histories*. Berkeley: University of California Press.

———. (1997). "Gender and Development: Problems for a History of the Present," *Thamyris*, 4, no. 1 (spring): 137–54.

Kabeer, Naila. (1994). *Reversed Realities*. London: Verso.

Kishwar, Madhu. (1990). "In Defence of our Dharma," *Manushi*, 60 (Sept./Oct.): 2–15.

Lowe, Lisa. (1996). *Immigrant Acts: On Asian American Cultural Politics*. Durham: Duke University Press.

Kim, Elaine and Chungmoo Choi, eds. (1998). *Dangerous Women: Gender and Korean Nationalism*. New York: Routledge.

Mani, Lata. (1989). "Multiple Mediations: Feminist Scholarship in the Age of Multinational Reception," *Inscriptions*, 5: 1–23.

Martin, Biddy and Chandra Mohanty. (1986). "Feminist Politics: What's Home Got to Do with It?" in Teresa de Lauretis, ed., *Feminist Studies, Critical Studies*. Bloomington: Indiana University Press, 191–212.

Mies, Maria. (1982). *The Lace-Makers of Narsapur: Indian Housewives Produce for the World Market*. London: Zed.

——. (1986). *Patriarchy and Accumulation on a World Scale: Women in the International Division of Labor*. London: Zed.

Minh-ha, Trinh T. (1986). "Difference: 'A Special Third World Women Issue,'" *Discourse: Journal for Theoretical Studies in Media and Culture*, 8 (fall/winter): 11–36. (A special issue, edited by Trinh T. Minh-ha, titled "She, The Inappropriate/d Other.")

——. (1989). *Woman, Native, Other*. Bloomington: Indiana University Press.

Mitter, Swasti. (1986). *Common Fate, Common Bond: Women in the Global Economy*. London: Pluto.

Mohanty, Chandra. (1991). "Under Western Eyes: Feminist Scholarship and Colonial Discourses," in Mohanty *et al.*, eds., *Third World Women and the Politics of Feminism*. Bloomington: Indiana University Press, 51–80.

Moraga, Cherrie and Gloria Anzaldua, eds. (1981). *This Bridge Called My Back: Writings by Radical Women of Color*. Watertown: Persephone Press.

Nash, June and Maria Patricia Fernandez-Kelly, eds. (1983). *Women, Men, and the International Division of Labor*. Albany: State University of New York Press.

Needham, Anuradha Dingwaney. (1990). "At the Receiving End: 'Third' World Texts in 'First' World Contexts," *Women's Studies Quarterly*, 18, no. 3/4: 91–9.

Niranjana, Tejaswini. (1992). *Siting Translation: History, Post-structuralism, and the Colonial Context*. Berkeley: University of California Press.

Ogunyemi, Chickwenye Okonjo. (1985). "The Dynamics of the Contemporary Black Female Novel in English," *Signs*, 11, no. 1 (autumn): 63–80.

Omvedt, Gail. (1993). *Reinventing Revolution: New Social Movements and the Socialist Tradition in India*. New York and London: M. E. Sharpe.

Ong, Aihwa. (1987). *Spirits of Resistance and Capitalist Discipline: Factory Women in Malaysia*. Albany: State University of New York Press.

Pathak, Zakia and Rajeswari Sunder Rajan. (1989). "Shahbano," *Signs*, 14, no. 3 (spring): 558–82.

Peters, Julie and Andrea Wolper, eds. (1995). *Women's Rights, Human Rights: International Feminist Perspectives*. New York: Routledge.

Pfeil, Fred. (1994). "No Basta Teorizar: In-difference to Solidarity in Contemporary Fiction, Theory and Practice," in Inderpal Grewal and Caren Kaplan, eds., *Scattered Hegemonies: Postmodernity and Transnational Feminist Practices*. Minneapolis: University of Minnesota Press, 197–231.

Positions: East Asia Cultures Critique. (fall, 1997). Special issue on comfort women.

Rafael, Vincente. (1997). "'Your Grief is Our Gossip': Overseas Filipinos and Other Spectral Presences," *Public Culture*, 9, no. 2 (winter).

Robbins, Bruce. (1992). "Comparative Cosmopolitanism," *Social Text*, 31/32: 169–86.

Rowbotham, Sheila and Swasti Mitter. (1994). *Dignity and Daily Bread: New Forms of Economic Organizing Among Poor Women in the Third World and the First*. New York: Routledge.

Sacks, Karen Brodkin. (1984). *My Troubles Are Going to Have Trouble with Me: Everyday Trials and Triumphs of Women Workers*. New Brunswick: Rutgers University Press.

Sangari, Kumkum. (1993). "Consent, Agency and the Rhetorics of Incitement," *Economic and Political Weekly*, 1 May: 867–82.

——. (1995). "Politics of Diversity: Religious Communities and Multiple Patriarchies," *Economic and Political Weekly*, 23 Dec.: 3287–311.

—— and Sudesh Vaid, eds. (1989). *Recasting Women: Essays in Colonial History*. New Delhi: Kali for Women.

Sarkar, Tanika and Urvashi Butalia, eds. (1996). *Women and the Hindu Right*. New Delhi: Kali for Women.

Sen, Amartya. (1982). "Equality of What?" in *Choice, Welfare and Measurement*. Oxford: Blackwell.

——. (1985). *Commodities and Capabilities*. Amsterdam: North Holland.

Shiva, Vandana. (1993). *Ecofeminism*. London: Zed.

Spivak, Gayatri Chakravorty. (1985). "Three Women's Texts and a Critique of Imperialism," *Critical Inquiry*, 12, no. 1 (autumn): 243–61.

——. (1988a). *In Other Worlds: Essays in Cultural Politics*. London and New York: Routledge.

——. (1988b). "Can the Subaltern Speak?" in Cary Nelson and Lawrence Grosberg, eds., *Marxism and the Interpretation of Culture*. Urbana: University of Illinois Press, 271–313.

——. (1990). "The Making of Americans, the Teaching of English, and the Future of Culture Studies," *New Literary History*, 21, no. 4 (autumn): 781–98.

——. (1993). *Outside in the Teaching Machine*. London and New York: Routledge.

——. (1996). "How to Teach a Culturally Different Book," in Donna Landry and Gerald Maclean, eds., *The Spivak Reader*. London and New York: Routledge.

Suleri, Sara. (1992). "Woman Skin Deep: Feminism and the Postcolonial Condition," *Critical Inquiry*, 18, no. 4 (summer): 756–69.

Tharu, Susie and K. Lalitha, eds. (1991; 1993). *Women Writing in India*. 2 vols. New Delhi: Oxford University Press.

Truong, Thanh-Dam. (1990). *Sex, Money, and Morality: Prostitution and Tourism in Southeast Asia*. London: Zed.

Uberoi, Patricia, ed. (1996). *Social Reform, Sexuality and the State*. New Delhi: Sage.

Visweswaran, Kamala. (1996). *Fictions of Feminist Ethnography*. Minneapolis: University of Minnesota Press.

Ward, Kathryn, ed. (1990). *Women Workers and Global Restructuring*. Ithaca: Cornell University Press.

Williams, Patricia. (1991). *The Alchemy of Race and Rights: Diary of a Law Professor*. Cambridge: Harvard University Press.

Yuval-Davis, Nira. (1997). *Gender and Nation*. London: Sage.

Chapter 3

Heterogeneity and Hybridity: Colonial Legacy, Postcolonial Heresy

David Theo Goldberg

"All the best signs . . . are not so different from all the worst."

Richard Ford, *The Sportswriter*, 265

Hybridity has become invested with impossible conceptual promise, hope bound to be dashed, faith destined to turn bad, in the desperate drive away from race as it at once predicates itself on racial distinction, in the rush to theorize the betwixt and between of cultural expression, group formation, and social conditions. Hybridity itself is taken as conceptually catching the in-between, as the product if not the very expression of mixture, of the antipure, of Becoming in the face of Being's stasis. Hybridity is "a scandal," as Anne McClintock puts it provocatively (1995: 299ff), precisely because in the face of claims to the virtues of racial purity, of racial apartness and the imperative of racialized divides, it is deemed inherently, automatically transgressive. Perhaps once culturally and politically to be shunned, it is now in some circles fashionably (Colker, 1996), avant-gardedly (Bhabha, 1993) embraced.

Now no concept perhaps can bear such epistemological, let alone political, burden. Not least in this case because the concept of hybridity, as Robert Young chronicles for those who haven't read the primary texts, has a history (Young, 1995). Its history precisely is racial, and it long precedes its celebrated moment of late. The longer fate of the hybrid's conceptual legacy testifies to the danger of essentializing definitional commitments, no matter the purity of heart, the benevolence of intentions, the radical nature of theoretical intervention.

To see this history, not just in its conceptual form but in its material manifestation, to engage its implications, it would help to understand hybridity conceived against the background of heterogeneity, its conceptual and material expression and delimitation. For the concept of "the hybrid" waxes and wanes and waxes again in light of perceived threats and interventionary challenges of growing demographic heterogeneity in the nineteenth and twentieth centuries.

In a different though related context, Ali Rattansi criticizes as instantiating a "binary opposition" the distinction I draw here between heterogeneity and homogeneity (Rattansi, 1998). Elsewhere (Goldberg, 1994) I argue that those committed to monoculturalism in social formations predicate their arguments on an underlying assumption of cultural – ethnoracial – homogeneity. Because, as I note there, historical tendencies to migration have largely meant heterogenous social spaces, increasingly so throughout modernity, monocultural commitment is necessarily bought at the expense of cultural and political repression. If there is "a binary" at work here – and Rattansi nowhere says what is wrong with this particular distinction – it is introduced by the repressive forces insisting upon instituting homogeneity (oftentimes under the cover of assuming its naturalness). "Heterogeneity" is simply the general characterization for diverse social arrangements that in fact have been historically fashioned. It really doesn't help in this respect to say, as Rattansi does, that we should have "both/and." What exactly would a multiculturalism predicated on homogeneity look like, the very point being that homogeneity, conceptually as much as politically, is denial of the possibilities of the multicultural? Nor is it productive to suggest that homogeneity *historically* has come about through repression, because a cultural homogeneity that would not be exclusive and exclusionary is precisely equivalent to the undoing of homogeneity, to opening homogeneity to transformation at the hands of critical forces. And this precisely is to say that the social formation is no longer homogenous. So much for clichéd criticism.

One dominant view concerned with periodizing the history of growing demographic and cultural heterogeneity in the West and among northern countries has reduced the dramatic nature of this heterogeneity to the second half of the twentieth century. Thus growth in racial heterogeneity among populations and in culture is considered a function of growing global integration following the Second World War and dying colonialism following the 1950s, those "winds of change" that swept not just through Africa but the entire colonized and colonizing worlds. These changes produced massive dislocations, prompted large-scale migrations, opened up borders and boundaries, transnationally and culturally, challenged prevailing hegemonies as they at once stormed the bastions of haute culture. A compelling picture, one obviously resonating with the drama of twentieth-century events, economic, political, cultural, intellectual.

But this picture, prevailing as it might be, is parochial in the sense that it occludes the heterogeneity of past ages, the perhaps slower yet steady intermixing of peoples and interfacing of cultures migrations have always produced. Its framing has hidden from view the longstanding differences and distinctions flowing through the hearts of colonizing darkness, the capitals of colonial powers at the very height of their imperial spread. And so too it has made less than visible the significance of the notion of "hybridity" at different historical moments. This restriction in the recognition of heterogeneity, political and theoretical, is tied up with the thick ways in which modern state formation has been racialized, with the ways in which modern states have predicated themselves on racial differentiation and racist exclusion and exploitation. Thus modern states fashioned themselves not as heterogenous spaces but homogenous ones, falsely as fact and repressively as value, and so have acted variously to guarantee, to (rein)force, materially what they have claimed (to be committed to) conceptually and axiologically.

The transformation of medieval city-states into modern states brought increasing urban heterogeneity, even in racial terms. So colonizing cities like Amsterdam and London began to see diversity in their populations as early as the seventeenth century that at the same time has been virtually ignored in mainstream historical studies. Well-regarded histories of these cities, for instance, usually presume that their racial diversity is only a post-Second World War phenomenon. There is no doubt that these trends accelerated dramatically from the mid-twentieth century on, but to cast it thus is already to acknowledge that there were trends, relatively longstanding trends, already at play, however minimal by comparison. Notions of hybridity took hold, in part, in relation to responses to the nineteenth-century tensions such heterogeneity supposedly effected, played out intellectually (in science, philosophy, anthropology) and politically (in law and policy). Racial hybridity accordingly constituted then, as it continues to constitute now, an object of fear and celebration, paranoia and persistence, repression and resistance, a point to which I will return in conclusion.

With the onset of modernity, the advent of vigorous transnational commerce, and the rising dominance of Dutch among European imperial and colonial powers, class structure in the Netherlands, and in Amsterdam particularly, assumed plurality and fluidity. This fluidity became especially manifest as the Netherlands consolidated as a nation in the seventeenth and eighteenth centuries. The Dutch were "a people," if it makes sense to refer in the singular to the people of any nation state in modernity, whose very constitution was a product of immigration, not least within Europe: Flemish and Huguenots fleeing religious intolerance, Sephardic Jews fleeing Catholic terror in Spain and Portugal, Ashkenazi Jews from Eastern Europe. Two-thirds of Amsterdam's 7,500 Jews at the close of the seventeenth century were Ashkenazi. German domestic workers arrived in droves in the nineteenth century, many staying to marry Dutch men. Starting in 1610, colonies were acquired throughout the seventeenth century. But the first inkling of the racial diversification that would challenge the sense of singularity in Dutch society, as elsewhere, in the aftermath of colonialism centuries later landed in Zeeland in 1596. A Dutch privateer that had captured 130 slaves off a Portuguese slave ship delivered its hopeless bounty to port. To their credit the Dutch at the time outlawed slavery (overturned less than a decade later once the profits and "benefits" of slave trading became evident), and the slaves were freed. Within a century the Dutch had become major players in the slave trade, shipping their "wares" from the west coast of Africa to the Caribbean and Brazil.

As the mark of revolutionary transformation began to sweep across Europe late in the eighteenth century, Amsterdam exhibited a sort of local heterogeneity, in classical terms more ethnic than racial in its constitution. By the eighteenth century fully 20 percent of those arrested in Amsterdam were of German background, though there was no indication that they were criminologically discriminated against (Schama, 1997: 582), Amsterdam after all being the center of political and cultural tolerance. Where there were slaves they would have been house slaves, the occasional symbols of status and curiosity, "like a souvenir collected on long travels, which you show to family, friends and others interested," like impressing business colleagues, as Philomena Essed has put it to me in conversation. I think here of Rembrandt's haunting painting of *Two Negroes* (1661), Rubens' four drawings of a "negro figure", or Van Dyck's early seventeenth-century inclusion of a black woman servant (*The Discovery of Moses*) or of a satyr (*Bacchanalia*). Some slaves there were locally, though most got shipped on, and too few people who could be said to be nonwhite or non-European to be more than objects of curious (in)difference and sometime derision. It is remarkable thus that Simon Schama could write his masterful history of Dutch culture in "the golden age" without mentioning slavery or blacks; indeed, without any extended discussion of the importance of colonies to or influence of colonial culture on Dutch wealth and forms of desire, points made impressively by Ann Stoler (Stoler, 1995).

If racial heterogeneity came slowly to Dutch modernity, it touched London life early on even as it was also downplayed or largely absent from the prevailing histories of that city. The earliest black people appeared in "modern" London (at least on one account) in 1555 (Gerzina, 1995), when five West Africans arrived to acquire the English language as a way to promote commerce – slave commerce, it seems. There is evidence though of the employment of black musicians in the English and Scottish courts nearly a century earlier, the appearance of North African pirates as far north as Scotland by the end of the fifteenth century, and two African friars in Edinburgh early in the sixteenth (Gundara and Duffield, 1992: 15–18; Fryer, 1984: 2).[1] The dramatic modern shift in disposition towards black people is signaled by the fact that at the close of that century Queen Elizabeth had passed an edict requiring all black people to leave England (Gerzina, 1995: 3). The population of greater London, totalling just 200,000 in 1600, doubled in half a century, and spiraled to 575,000 by century's end. A century later yet, the metropolis was just short of one million (900,000 by the census of 1801), bolstered by the flow predominantly from country to town, and later by Irish migration and Ashkenazi Jews "going and resting" (Josipovici, 1993) to flee persecution in Eastern and Central Europe who concentrated themselves in the East End, and less so by Germans, Dutch, and Portuguese. Census counts topped 4.5 million in 1881 and had risen staggeringly to seven million just 30 years later (Porter, 1995: 205). By the latter part of the eighteenth century the number of black people in London, largely from the West Indies, and Indian seamen working for the English East Indies Company, counted at least as much as 10,000 and quite possibly half more than that, about one percent of the population (Rude, 1971: 6–8). Indeed, as early as April 1721 one London daily was warning that "there is a great number of Blacks come daily into this city, so that 'tis thought in a short time, if they be not suppressed, the city will swarm with them" (quoted in Dabydeen, 1992: 31).

Slaves were not uncommon in London also, largely brought back from the West Indies by British planters and mixing with black sailors, students, and musicians. As early as 1696 there appeared heartbreakingly cruel advertisements in the local press for the return of runaway slaves or the sale of black boys as young as eleven or twelve (Gerzina, 1995: 5–8). By the end of the eighteenth century, as the abolitionist movement gained ground, these advertisements for the sale of slaves had largely disappeared, the emergent English culture of civility ordering commercial sensibilities regarding blacks (Lorimer, 1992: 70). And by the mid to later Enlightenment there was evidence also of wealthy black men parading undisturbed with white women on Oxford Street, accompanied neverthless by bemoaning observations of mixed race progeny, the first inklings possibly of more vociferous concerns to emerge regarding hybridity in the nineteenth century: "in every town, nay in almost every village, are to be seen a little race of mulattoes, mischievous as monkeys, and infinitely more dangerous."[2] Black women were much scarcer, usually brought to London by West Indian slavers bearing in tow their concubines veiled as servants. In larger measure though, David Dabydeen points out in *Hogarth's Blacks* that even more than the demographic presence of black people, London was "visually black," signboards and business cards imprinting the emblem of a black man as the mark of commerce, the icon of blackness curiously serving as a measure of commercial success (Dabydeen, 1987: 18). And by the middle of the nineteenth century, Topsy wallpaper and dolls were the rage through fashionable London (Gerzina, 1995: 25).

It is remarkable then that Gareth Steadman Jones (1971) and Roy Porter (1995) each can write justly influential histories of London – Victorian class relations in that city in the former case, a more broadly social history in the latter – without so much as a single mention of blacks or of the influence upon the life of that capital of finance, colonial commerce, and administration of slave trading colonies or colonialism. Similarly Steadman Jones co-edits a book with David Feldman (Feldman and Steadman Jones, 1989) on the history of metropolitan London. The book is concerned with a wide range of London's demographic and cultural diversity, detailing the importance to London life and "identities" (the title of a section in the book) of Irish and Jews, women and the working classes, but which has no word whatsoever about black people either narrowly construed as people of African descent or more broadly including Asians. This is more remarkable in light of the fact not only that by the 1770s London-owned slave ships were transporting close to 10,000 slaves a year in the triangular trade – not nearly as large as Liverpool or Bristol admittedly, but significant nevertheless (Fryer, 1984: 36). The silence is more deeply troubling, the influence of Africans on London public performance and musical culture notwithstanding, given the centrality of London in financing the slave trade (by mid-eighteenth century London was handling three-quarters of all sugar imported into Britain), the importance of the trade not only to London's economy but to its political life. Many influential politicians were caught up in one way or another in the benefits of slave trading, and West Indian absentee plantation proprietors were able quite easily to buy seats in the House of Commons, a practice that became, well, common. So strong, highly organized, and well-heeled was the West Indies lobby that the abolitionist movement found itself facing significant resistance at the end of the "enlightened century" (Fryer, 1984: 44–50).

Two points are worth emphasizing here. First, the obvious lesson of this tale of two cities is that the heterogenous mix of populations making up the capitals of colonial empires has largely been downplayed, and indeed until quite recently all but ignored. Second, relatedly but more deeply, the occlusion of blacks from the representational historical record of this urban diversity indicates by extension that blacks for the most part were rendered invisible in the daily political life of those cities. This can be seen in sharp contrast to the persistent, one might say insistent, concern with colonized black people deemed administratively problematic by the colonizers (consider, for instance, the exchange in 1849 between Thomas Carlyle and John Stuart Mill concerning the "Nigger/Negro problem" (August, 1971; Goldberg, 1998)). It is significant then, both as a mark of urban life and of historical scholarship, that accounts of blacks in Britain and the Netherlands (Gundara and Duffield, 1992; Gerzina, 1995; Fryer, 1984; Fryer, 1988; Scobie, 1972; Blakely, 1993; West, 1996; and Arthur Japin's historical novel, Japin, 1997) are exceptional, are (regarded as) outside of – not properly belonging to – standard historical accounts of those societies, and take this exclusion as their almost exclusive motivating or inspirational focus. This exceptionalism, it should be clear, is not a product principally of self-determining "minority" separation, an infantilizing celebration of ethnic self-identification. Rather, it is a product primarily of that initial ignoring, the rendering invisible, of peoples designated black so that representational exceptionalism, an emphatic foregrounding focus, becomes the only possibility for writing Strangers and Outsiders, black people in particular, back into the historical record.

A prevailing problematic of the nineteenth century, representative at least in that strand of modernism articulated through the positivity of science, concerned control of both natural and social conditions. But beneath this, perhaps as a Hobbesian-like motivation, lay anxiety – about the unknown, about that which could not be controled, concerning natural forces beyond control. Heterogeneity may be read as challenge or threat, opportunity or potential problem. In the nineteenth century, especially in its racial interpretation, heterogeneity was interpreted very much in the latter vein, taken to inject into the safety and stability of the known, predictable, and controllable worlds elements of the unknown, the unpredictable, the uncontrollable. The concept of "hybridism" appears then to inject control (or at least to claim it), to furnish comprehension (and perhaps comprehensibility) where it otherwise is clearly absent, or to reestablish determination in the face of threatened indeterminacy.

In the wake of abolition of slave trading throughout the British Empire in 1807, and of slavery altogether in 1834, black people seemed freer to come and go from Britain than they had been, although their movement was not always unrestricted. This trend was more obvious in Britain than in Holland, owing to the greater global spread of Britain's empire in the nineteenth century, its heavier engagement in the slave trade, the public prominence there of the abolitionist movement in comparison to conditions in the Netherlands, as well as the fact that slavery continued under the Dutch until the middle of 1863. It is in light of this expedited movement that black presence in Britain especially became more obvious, that mixed race populations began to become more apparent (as they did too in wake of the Civil War in the United States), and to be focused upon more readily as anomalous. The remarkable increase in flows – of populations to and from colonies, of commodities and raw materials, indeed of miscegenation and its offspring – prompted heightened population heterogeneity and cultural bricolage. Coupled with fears and anxieties, challenges to established orders, and manifest changes in prevailing socioscientific interpretation of human differentiation, there emerged concerns, theoretical and political, articulated in terms of the concept of hybridity.

Theoretically, the concern with "hybridism" – the static substantivizing of the term indicative of the worry – was a product of the nineteenth-century theoretical shift from mono- to polygenism. If races are separate species, as polygenists claimed definitionally, mating of their members should not produce offspring at all (Nott, 1843). "Mixed race" or "hybrid" offspring, the product of miscegenation nominated "mulatto" in the second half of the nineteenth century, increased as a result of greater cross-racial contact, not least following abolition of slavery, migrations in the wake of colonial commerce, and the promise of reconstructed societies – in Britain, on the Continent, in the United States. Mixed race presence offered an obvious challenge to polygenic presumption. If races are species, and species are defined by capacity to reproduce only among species members, the existence of mixed race (or cross-species) offspring suggests failure to meet a crucial condition of the theory. Nevertheless, existence of hybrid offspring prompted revisions in polygenic theory rather than its initial abandonment. The first revision was to insist that hybrids themselves would be infertile; later that more "distant" groups are much more likely to be infertile than more "proximate" ones (Broca, 1860; cf. Young, 1995). When counterevidence quickly emerged, predictions were revised to the longer-term view that hybrid offspring eventually – over a number of (unspecified) generations – would degenerate and ultimately die out (Knox, 1862; cf. Broca, 1860). The failure of this prediction to materialize coincided more or less with the demise of polygenic theory in the face of Darwinian evolution, on one hand, and Darwinist-prompted eugenics, on the other.

Scientific hybridity thus failed theoretically (that is, on scientific criteria). In the wake of Darwin there began a shift – long, slow, and incomplete – away from strictly scientific technologies of race and racism. Where science continued to contribute to racial thinking it was now less direct, less focused straightforwardly on advancing racial science for its own sake. From the close of the nineteenth century scientific thinking about race became more applied. The invocation of scientific technologies developed with more general purpose in mind – for their own sake or with other object(ive)s at issue – and were adopted or adapted to address questions of race, as in the application of IQ testing. In that sense the prevalence of eugenics in the first few decades of the twentieth century may be considered the tail end of "pure" racial science, scientific racism's more or less last spree. Those who considered the nineteenth century, and scientific racism in particular, the apex of racist expression have thought this a shift away also from racist expression as such, a revealing of racism's intellectual vacuity, its essential irrationality, in the wake of racism's failure to exhibit scientific legitimacy. But this would be a mistake. For as the longer-term legacy of Darwin may have signaled a shift from the viability of a scientifically sustained sense of race and racist expression, culturalist and class centered expressions of racist exclusion began to dominate. And along with this shift away from physicalist-based notions, the concept of hybridity began in turn increasingly to assume reified culturalist expression (cf. Young, 1995: 6). Thus at century's turn Kipling ironically has a Russian speaking in French to a Frenchman refer to "the monstrous hybridism of East and West" in characterizing the effects of British imperialism upon India, the degenerating pollution of cultural mixing, as earlier sexual mixing was considered to result in physical degeneracy (Kipling, 1913/1901: 382).

So in the nineteenth century the concept of hybridity represented dominant concerns that white or European-based purity, power, and privilege would be polluted, and in being polluted diluted. If whites were supposedly superior intellectually and culturally to those not white, then on amalgamationist assumptions the mixing of those nonwhite with white generative capacity *ex hypothesi* would imperil the power of the latter, would result in their degeneration. Hybridity thus assumed the conceptual expression of anxiety, of white people's paranoia, signaling the ultimate powerlessness of the powerful. Powerlessness precisely in that hybridity poses a challenge to the guardians of purity, power, and privilege, a challenge channeled through desire: the libidinal pull of sexual desire, the lure of forbidden fruit, in the one instance; the exciting, energizing magnet of cultural renewal, and so an implicit judgment concerning the static predisposition of "the pure", in the other. Nowhere is this more evident than in the case of South Africa in the first half of the twentieth century, that colonially produced hybrid of Africa, Asia (Indians, Malaysians, Chinese), and Europe (British and Dutch principally, but East European Jews, Italians, Greeks, and Portuguese also, all combined not quite indistinguishably into the invention of whiteness). Thus Afrikaner politicians readily invoked eugenics-inflected phrases concerning "virile" and "vigorous" blacks "flooding" city space, "swamping" whites who were in the minority, and threatening the safety of vulnerable white women. More than one election was won on the tailcoats of such rhetoric. In 1927 the Immorality Act (*sic*) was passed, prohibiting miscegenation between whites and Africans. Attempts were later made to extend the legislation to prohibit all inter-racial sexual intercourse, including government commissions of inquiry regarding such legislation in the late 1930s, but the fuller restriction manifested only eventually in 1949 with the passing of the Mixed Marriages Act as a cornerstone in the systematic institutionalization of the apartheid state. Similarly, the state began moving in the mid-1950s against the perceived threat of cultural pollution, stamping out hip hybrid urban neighborhoods in Johannesburg, Durban, and Cape Town that just might prove enticing to white youth (cf. Dubow, 1995: 180ff). Growing up close to and interactive with one such neighborhood, I could be said to be a beneficiary, the product in part, of its cultural contribution, and an indirect victim of its partial destruction, as in a more or less extended sense one might say all South Africans were, like it or not.

As negative critique, then, the concept of hybridity becomes an outward expression of the repressed, and in such expression assumes the power of the repressive itself. As the product of two differentiated elements, the hybrid is supposed to fuse them together, assuming features of each into a transformed "third" element. Historically, such elements have stood to each other in hierarchical relations of power. As a critical concept, the hybrid thus is supposed to blunt power's point, to shift power's oppressive expression, but it does so only by assuming some of the hierarchical aspects of power. Homi Bhabha's "hybrid third space" in this respect is altogether romanticized. On the other side, the denial of hybridity, physiologically or culturally conceived, accordingly becomes the refusal of possibility to the mixed, the repression of conditions of possibility for hybridity to materialize. Consider, for instance, the "assault" on European languages maintained to manifest in creolization, and the authoritarian restriction of their use by colonial (and postcolonial) administrations (cf. Stoler, 1995: 43). Hence the multitude of laws against racially defined immigration, miscegenation, cross-racial intercourse (sexual or cultural), institutionalization of segregation, racial conceived cultural expressions and practices identified with otherness (like Ebonics as a teaching medium), and so on.

There lies here an apparent paradox: Precisely at the moment we find greater likelihood of heterogeneity among and between population groups, however conceived or defined, the greater the denial through racial fixity and reification. Where a degree of racial homogeneity could be more or less safely assumed, as in early modern Britain and Holland, the less race seemed necessary as an explicit self-reference. Here race referred to the outside, the strange and exotic at a distance. The more heterogenous such societies grew, the more racial definition came to mark self-characterization. The question then becomes, in the face and wake of the colonial condition which helped to produce demographic heterogeneity, why race is invoked in a variety of denials to face such heterogeneity off. The genealogy of hybridity I have offered suggests something of a response, if not to resolving the paradox, then to why it should arise. On one hand, hybridity has been invoked to rationalize (away) the fears and anxieties, not least concerning "species corruption" (White, 1972: 14–15) and the threat of impurity, that mobilized one side of the paradoxical equation, and in rationalizing thus to legitimate them. On the other, hybridity has been pushed more recently as a celebration of the possibilities to which heterogeneity gives rise, yet exacerbating again the very fears, now in culturalist terms and precisely in those (formerly) colonizing societies once considering themselves more or less homogenous, that hybridity was initially invoked to quell.

We may see this played out in societies like the United States and Britain, the Netherlands and France, concerning language and dress, census categories and mixed race recognition, and perhaps most extremely in immigration policy and opportunity. But one can find versions of this in the academy also, expressed in terms of disciplinarity and indeed epistemologically. I have suggested elsewhere that disciplines are to the academy, to intellectual pursuit, as borders are more broadly to nation-states (Goldberg, 1994). The transgressive threats possible in multi- and transdisciplinarity seem as unsettling to some locally as migration and transnationalism seem to the relatively privileged more globally, and for related sorts of reasons. Settled ideas, practices, and institutions are challenged as a result, sometimes at considerable existential cost. The threat is not just that some or other discipline might transform, but that it might turn out to be redundant and disappear completely, that the power and privilege it has secured may be lost. Hence the investment in a conserving resistance. Relatedly, epistemological hybridity suggests new forms of thinking, new categories of knowing rather than resting (in)secure in settled ways of seeing and comprehending the world. As Bakhtin (1981: 344) suggests, authoritarian language – epistemologically, disciplinarily, politically – is necessarily antihybrid as it depends upon the singularity and static fixity of meaning, the insistence of the given and ordered, the silencing of voice(s) at odds with the authorial power.

It bears pointing out here the inherently homogenizing logic of institutions. In their dominant logical form, institutions are predicated principally on instituting, operating, and (re)producing homogeneity. If the state minimally is a collection of institutions, manifesting and (re)ordering itself necessarily in and through the logic of such institutional arrangement, then one could say that the state inherently is the institutionalization of homogeneity. Liberal states like Britain, the Netherlands, and the US that claim to furnish the structures for heterogeneity to flourish in this sense actually promote contradictory aims, purposes that pull in competing directions. Hence the anachronistic language one hears of "managing diversity," of "ordering difference," of "unifying in difference." The homogenizing imperative is revealed on both sides of these "hybrid" nomenclatures, for curiously the active expression is born in the restricting pursuit (managing, ordering, unifying), the passive in the reified substantivization – the rendering passive – of what one would have thought to be creative and energizing (diversity, difference). This homogenizing logic is internal to administration and governmentality. To run counter to it, even in an administrative capacity, is to run counter to administrative or governmental logic. The state – and nation-state especially, where nation here becomes the cultural reproduction of hegemonic consensus to state administrative mandates – is in that sense all about institutionally reproductive homogenization.[3] On the other side, though, hybridity is conceived as about Becoming, about transformation and so the reiterative undoing of form ("the permanent revolution of forms," as Young characterizes Homi Bhabha's view), about flow and flux, a term that apparently "captures" the logic of history itself (cf. Young, 1995: 25). As such, the substantivization of hybridity in the form of reifying resistance – in a movement, as a (more or less) self-consciously cohering intervention – at once homogenizes the heterogenous, fixes the flux and flow, orders the dis-orderly, renders more or less safe by "capturing" the transgressive expression of the hybrid. Here, at best, the critical conception of hybridity is reduced to the fusional or amalgamational; at worst, any possibility of hybridity is obliterated altogether.

So, like race, indeed, as a sometime proxy for it, hybridity in its ethnoracial connotation assumes a variety of forms. Initially biological in relation to demography, it may connote aesthetically, morally, obviously always politically in any of these senses, as well as in the less obvious epistemological one. Bakhtin reveals, in Young's helpful terms, the "hybridity of hybridity" itself. As I hint at in the preceding paragraph, there are at least two ways in which hybridity may manifest: as combinatory of otherwise clashing categories, on one hand, fusing their antithetical senses into new expression and form, the new here possibly assuming renewed homogeneity; and as self-consciously critical, on the other, as social unmasking, a studied commitment to undoing the necessary singularity of the authoritative voice, wherever and whenever expressed (a point turned to some effect by Bhabha in his critique of colonial power, though in romancing the resistive he overlooks the conservationist element inherent equally in any conception of the hybrid and the resistant) (Bakhtin, 1981: 344ff; Bhabha, 1993; Young, 1995: 20–8).

Colonialism, John Comaroff has made abundantly clear in a scintillating rethinking of the colonial state (Comaroff, 1998), was about managing heterogeneity, dealing with difference through imposition and restriction, regulation and repression. Seemingly by contrast but in fact relatedly, colonizing states like Britain and the Netherlands proceeded on an assumption of population homogeneity, of ethnoracial sameness and of externalizing difference, purporting at least nominally to keep the different out and at bay lest they undo by infecting the rationality of brotherhood, thus toppling reason's rule. Implicit here is a distinction between two forms of regulation and imposition, the restrictive or exclusionary disciplining of difference and (one might say in the name of) the rule of sameness. The combining of racial hybridism with colonialism in the nineteenth century was a "social-scientific" way of managing these related concerns:

keeping the Other from polluting and diluting the Same by keeping the former at arm's length; but at once benefiting from the material and libidinal pleasures exploitation of colonized Others made possible. Under the aegis of restricting hybridity physiologically and culturally, otherness, difference, and heterogeneity were reduced to racial management. In the late twentieth century, by contrast, the regulative force of colonialism has broken down and the unsettling capacity of hybridity can no longer be kept (colonially) marginal by modern forms of control. Indeed, the heterogenous and hybrid have come to occupy and challenge modernity's centers. Under these altered conditions, hybridity's unsettling capacity has been celebrated and embraced, but also fiercely resisted. Indeed, it has become a contested domain – epistemologically, disciplinarily, aesthetically, culturally, politically.

What I have been suggesting, nevertheless, is that in *both* expressions of racially imposed and racially conceived hybridity – the repressive and the resistive – there are always at least delimiting hints of the other. Thus it is not just that heterogeneity is or has been a challenge *or* threat, opportunity *or* potential problem. In the context of racial history, and the history of racial theorizing, it has always been both. Perhaps a concept at once neutering and neutralizing the sexually provocative conditions that are a necessary underpinning of hybridity's very conception cannot help but suffer the anxiety of its ambiguity in this way. It is the value invested in the concept in relation to the material historical contexts in which it is embedded accordingly that will determine hybridity's critical capacity in specific space-time conditions, whether to be shunned or embraced, critically discarded or exploited. So Anne McClintock's general warning regarding historical agency and colonialism, in quiet criticism of Homi Bhabha, might serve also to warn against uncritical invocations of hybridity. "Taking the question of historical agency seriously ('How . . . is authority displaced?')," she writes,

> entails interrogating more than the ambivalences of form; it also entails interrogating the messy imprecisions of history, the embattled negotations and strategies of the disempowered, the militarization of masculinity, the elision of women from political and economic power, the decisive foreclosures of ethnic violence and so on. Ambivalence may well be a critical aspect of subversion, but it is not a sufficient agent of colonial failure. (McClintock, 1995: 66–7)

So though hybridity continues to be scandalous,[4] it is perhaps equally outrageous for an anti-essentialist intellectual politics that it has failed to take seriously the doubleness of hybrid consciousness, not just its in-betweenness but its "caught-betweenness," and accordingly not just the ambivalence it produces but its almost inevitable duplicity. Thus it is never just its transgression that marks racially imposed and racially conceived hybridity as attractive but the type of scandal it stands for, time and place specifically. And this, as McClintock rightfully insists, is tied up with the specificities of material exclusions, repressions, and subjugations. In short, with the microdetails of racial power and privilege and their articulation with other forms through which its domination is worked.[5]

Notes

1 Fryer (1984: 1, 4) notes the presence of a "division of Moors" assigned by the Roman imperial army to defend Hadrian's wall in the third century AD. He also offers evidence of a black trumpeter in the English court in London as early as 1507.
2 Philip Thicknesse writing in 1778, quoted in Gerzina, 1995: 22.
3 Not one to use the substantivizing form lightly – it is used much too readily – I think in this case (homogenization) the use is exactly what is called for.
4 McClintock (1995: 299–328, esp. 300–2) never says why hybridity is scandalous, only why some presumably hybridly produced and constituted text in the specific historical contexts of postapartheid South Africa is.
5 This paper benefited from considerable conversation with Philomena Essed, who directed me to especially helpful sources on Dutch history. I am grateful also for the patience exhibited by the volume's editors through very trying times. There were moments when they no doubt wondered whether my initial commitment was merely idle.

References

August, E., ed. (1971). *Carlyle, The Nigger Question and Mill, The Negro Question*. New York, Appleton Century Crofts.
Bakhtin, Mikhail. (1981). *The Dialogic Imagination: Four Essays*. Austin: University of Texas Press.
Bhabha, Homi. (1993). *The Location of Culture*. London: Routledge.
Blakely, Allison. (1993). *Blacks in the Dutch World: The Evolution of Racial Imagery in a Modern Society*. Bloomington: Indiana University Press.
Broca, Paul. (1860). "On the Phenomena of Hybridity in the Genus Homo," in Count ed. 1950, 68–74.
Colker, Ruth. (1996). *Hybrid: Bisexuals, Multiracials, and Other Misfits under American Law*. New York: New York University Press.
Comaroff, John. (1998). "Reflections on the Colonial State, in South Africa and Elsewhere: Factions, Fragments, Facts and Fictions," *Social Identities* 4, no. 3 (fall): 317–58.
Count, Earl, ed. (1950). *This is Race: An Anthology Selected from the International Literature on the Races of Man*. New York: Henry Schuman.
Dabydeen, David. (1992). "The Role of Black People in William Hogarth's Criticism of Eighteenth Century English Culture and Society," in Gundara and Duffield, eds., 1992.

Dabydeen, David. (1987). *Hogarth s Blacks*. Manchester: Manchester University Press.

Darwin, Charles. (1859). *The Origin of Species by Means of Natural Selection, or the Preservation of the Favored Races in the Struggle for Life*. London.

Dubow, Saul. (1995). *Illicit Union: Scientific Racism in Modern South Africa*. Johannesburg: Witwatersrand University Press.

Feldman, David and Gareth Stedman Jones, eds. (1989). *Metropolis. London: Histories and Representations Since 1800*. London: Routledge.

Ford, Richard. (1986). *The Sportswriter*. New York: Vintage Books.

Fryer, Peter. (1984). *Staying Power: The History of Black People in Britain*. London: Pluto.

——. (1988). *Black People in the British Empire: An Introduction*. London: Pluto.

Gerzina, Gretchen. (1995). *Black London: Life Before Emancipation*. New Brunswick: Rutgers University Press.

Goldberg, David Theo. (1994). *Multiculturalism: A Critical Reader*. Oxford: Blackwell.

——. (1998). "Liberalism s Limits: Carlyle and Mill on The Negro Question. " *Nineteenth Century Contexts*.

Gundara, Jagdish and Ian Duffield, eds. (1992). *Essays on the History of Blacks in Britain*. Aldershot: Avebury.

Japin, Arthur. (1997). *De Zwarte met het Witte Hart: Roman*. Amsterdam: Uitgeverij De Arbeidspers.

Josipovici, Gabriel. (1993). "Going and Resting," in David Theo Goldberg and Michael Krausz, eds., *Jewish Identity*. Philadelphia: Temple University Press.

Kipling, Rudyard. (1913). *Kim* (1901). New York: Doubleday.

Knox, Robert. (1862). *The Races of Men: A Philosophical Enquiry into the Influence of Race over the Destinies of Nations*, 2nd ed. London: Renshaw.

Lorimer, Douglas. (1992). "Black Resistance to Slavery and Racism in Eighteenth-Century England," in Gundara and Duffield, eds., 1992.

McClintock, Anne. (1995). *Imperial Leather: Race, Gender and Sexuality in the Colonial Contest*. New York: Routledge.

Nott, Josiah. (1843). "The Mulatto a Hybrid – Probable Extermination of the Two Races if the Whites and Blacks are Allowed to Intermarry," *American Journal of the Medical Sciences*, 6: 252–6.

Porter, Roy. (1995). *London: A Social History*. Cambridge: Harvard University Press.

Rattansi, Ali. (1998). "Racism, Postmodernism and Reflexive Multiculturalism," in *Critical Multiculturalism: Rethinking Multicultural and Antiracist Education*, ed. Stephen May. London: Falmer Press.

Steadman Jones, Gareth. (1971). *Outcast London: A Study in the Relationship Between Classes in Victorian Society*. Oxford: Oxford University Press.

Rude, George. (1971). *Hanoverian London: 1714–1808*. Berkeley: University of California Press.

Schama, Simon. (1997). *The Embarrassment of Riches: An Interpretation of Dutch Culture in the Golden Age*. New York: Vintage.

Scobie, Edward. (1972). *Black Britannia: A History of Blacks in Britain*. Chicago: Johnson Publishing.

Stoler, Ann Laura. (1995). *Race and the Education of Desire: Foucault s History of Sexuality and the Colonial Order of Things*. Durham: Duke University Press.

West, Shearer, ed. (1996). *The Victorians and Race*. Aldershot: Scolar Press.

White, Hayden. (1972). "The Forms of Wildness: Archaeology of an Idea," *in The Wild Man Within: An Image in Western Thought from the Renaissance to Romanticism*, eds. E. Dudley and A. Novak. Pittsburgh: University of Pittsburgh Press.

Young, Robert. (1995). *Colonial Desire: Hybridity in Theory, Culture and Race*. London: Routledge.

Chapter 4

Postcolonialism and Postmodernism

Ato Quayson

The terms postcolonialism and postmodernism are both extremely elusive to classify, and the attempt to bring them together might be thought only to further compound the difficulties. For some critics, any attempt to fuse the two in a common theoretical inquiry is bound to occlude serious problems of the degree to which the unfinished business of late capitalism differently affects postmodern and postcolonial conditions. More crucially, it is also argued that the postmodern is part of an ensemble of the hierarchizing impulse of Western discourses, and that even though it hints at pluralism and seems to favor an attack on hegemonic discourses, it is ultimately apolitical and does not feed into larger projects of emancipation. To collocate the two, then, is somehow to disempower the postcolonial, which is conceived to be more concerned with pressing economic, political, and cultural inequalities (Sangari, 1987 and Tiffin, 1988). In fact, for some commentators such as Nigerian Denis Ekpo, postmodernism is nothing but another stage in the West's crisis of consciousness:

> The crisis of the subject and its radical and violent deflation – the focal point of postmodern critique – are logical consequences of the absurd self-inflation that the European subjectivity had undergone in its modernist ambition to be the salt of the earth, the measure and master of all things.
>
> For cultures (such as ours) that neither absolutized, i.e. deified, human reason in the past nor saw the necessity for it in the present, the postmodern project of de-deification, de-absolutization of reason, of man, of history, etc., on the one hand, and of a return to, or a rehabilitation of, obscurity, the unknown, the non-transparent, the paralogical on the other hand, cannot at all be felt like the cultural and epistemological earthquake that it appears to be for the European man. In fact, it cannot even be seen as a problem at all. . . . [W]hen such a being settles for the indeterminate, the paradoxical, the strange and absurd, it is probably because he bears no more resemblance to the man as we know him, especially here in Africa; he is a post-man whose society, having overfed him and spoilt him, has delivered him over to irremediable boredom. Nothing therefore, stops the African from viewing the celebrated postmodern condition a little

sarcastically as nothing but the hypocritical self-flattering cry of the bored and spoilt children of hypercapitalism. (Ekpo, 1995)

For Ekpo postmodernism has to be seen as the hubristic consequence of a desire to dominate the world, one that, linked to the universalizing rationality of science and anthropology, has to face its own unraveling when confronted by the loss of empire. For critics such as Linda Hutcheon (1989) and Steven Connor (1997: 263–8), however, there is a productive way of seeing the two as mutually reinforcing. The two may be brought together in common thematic, rhetorical, and strategic concerns, especially as these are brought to bear on questions of marginality. The conjuncture is sometimes thought to be best expressed in the literary genre of magical realism. In magical realism a happy conjuncture is settled upon: magical realism is the literary genre that simultaneously shows a suspicion towards metanarratives, whatever their provenance might be in the Enlightenment, in nationalist historiography, and in literary realism. As Stephen Slemon notes about the genre, it is one in which a sustained opposition between realism and its opposite "forestalls the possibility of interpretive closure through any act of naturalizing the text to an established system of representation" (Slemon, 1995: 410). And so an affinity of concerns and strategies has been deemed applicable on behalf of both terms, at least in the area of literary studies.

In the general usage of both terms, there is an uneasy oscillation between social referencing and the analysis of representations, with this oscillation frequently being resolved by subsuming the analysis of social referents under the analysis of regimes of representation. This creates a number of serious problems which we shall comment on later. Thus, postmodernism is related to a literary and philosophical tradition of representation which could be said to have its own peculiar historical and social trajectory in Western thought. Some postmodernist critics maintain that no reality can be thought of outside the way in which it is represented and that any attempt to do so is to ignore the implicatedness of any perspective within the very object that is being described and vice versa (see, for instance, Natoli, 1997: 5–8, 21–5). Because the desire of what passes under the rubric of postcolonial theory is also frequently concerned with representational discourses, postcolonialism also regularly takes representations as the primary target of analysis, with material conditions being accessed only insofar as they can be related in varying ways to representational regimes. A simple way of viewing this similarity would be to see both theoretical terms as being the descendants of what has been called the "linguistic turn" in the social sciences and humanities, but this approach is not always helpful as it does not take account of the different emphases the two areas place on the relation between representation and a possible praxis, something to which we shall attend more fully in the third part of this chapter.[1]

There are other areas of perceived overlap between them. The prefix "post" in postcolonialism and postmodernism aligns them both to similar problematics of temporal sequence and transcendence in relation to their second terms, colonialism and modernism. The relation of temporal or other supercession raises problems of continuity and rupture for both terms, something which has been pointed out in different directions by critics alert to the easy triumphalism inherent in such "posts." Alex Callinicos (1989) shows how much the definitions of postmodernism actually reproduce definitions that had been applied to high modernism, while Anne McClintock (1992) provides a stimulating critique of postcolonialism and shows how much, in its implicit temporal trajectory, it ends up reproducing elements of Enlightenment notions of progress which it seems inclined to challenge. On the other hand, the "ism" in both indicates their shared mutuality as second-order meditations, which, even though not coalescing into clear-cut ideologies, nonetheless seek to distinguish themselves from central positions in their various fields of inquiry. Both are thought to be second-order meditations upon real (and imagined) conditions in the contemporary world and are to be taken seriously as contributing to an understanding of the world in which we live.

2   The Concerns of Postmodernism

A fruitful way to proceed in defining the potential conjunctures and distinctions between the two terms is to attend to their different theoretical inspirations and ultimate social referents. As a means of mapping out the theoretical terrain of postmodernism, it is perhaps best to typify it according to a number of regular concerns. These concerns get different treatment in the hands of different critics, and there are bound to be disagreements on what things are most representative of the postmodernist paradigm.

A key area of dispute is how postmodernism is to be related to modernism. Ihab Hassan, one of the earliest commentators on postmodernism, addresses the question by discussing schematically the differences between modernism and postmodernism. Part of his table is as follows:

Modernism	Postmodernism
romanticism/Symbolism	paraphysics/Dadaism
form (conjunctive, closed)	antiform (disjunctive/open)
purpose	play
design	chance
hierarchy	anarchy
mastery/logos	exhaustion/silence
art object/finished work	process/performance/happening
distance	participation
creation/totalization/synthesis	decreation/deconstruction/antithesis
presence	absence
centering	dispersal
genre/boundary	text/intertext

root/depth	rhizome/surface
interpretation/reading	against interpretation/misreading
narrative/*grande histoire*	antinarrative/*petite histoire*
master code	idiolect
paranoia	schizophrenia
origin/cause	difference–*différance*/trace
determinacy	indeterminacy
God the Father	The Holy Ghost
transcendence	immanence

(Hassan, 1985: 123–4)

These are mainly stylistic oppositions and it runs the danger, as others have pointed out, of reducing complex relations to simple polarizations. The significant thing, as Harvey (1989: 42–65) shows in his discussion of this table in the context of the wider questions of definition more generally, is that Hassan draws on a variety of fields as diverse as linguistics, anthropology, philosophy, rhetoric, political science, and theology in setting up the distinctions. Thus, Hassan's table attempts to encompass all aspects of contemporary society and culture and how elements within them distinguish them from modernism and mark them out as postmodernist. These schematic polarizations, though useful as a starting point, are by no means beyond dispute. In the area of architecture, for instance, there have been disputes about the ways in which contemporary buildings are either modernist or postmodernist. One such disagreement has been on the status of John Portman's Bonaventure Hotel, between Charles Jencks and Fredric Jameson, with the first seeing the hotel as late modernist and the second interpreting it as postmodernist. (See Jencks, 1980: 15, 70 and Jameson, 1991: 38–45.)

As can be seen from the debates on terminology, the discussion of what constitutes postmodernism often highlights borrowings from linguistic metaphors and their application to social and cultural discourses. Indeed, easily traceable to the theoretical genealogy of postmodernism has to be the poststructuralism(s) that proliferated in the 1960s. In fact, for some, postmodernism is the operationalization of concepts developed initially within poststructuralism. At a rather basic level, it is the split in language between the sign and its referent, the understanding that language does not actually name an objective reality, that has acted as the main import from poststructuralism into postmodernism. This split between sign and referent is then taken also to be homologous with a series of other splits, such as those between history and its narrative representation, and between the author's intention and the meaning(s) of the text.

At one level, then, postmodernism can be typified as a vigorously antisystemic mode of understanding, with pluralism, borders, and multiple perspectives being highlighted as a means of disrupting the centralizing impulse of any system. This in itself has a fascinating history in Western philosophy and has been discussed by Robert C. Holub (1995) in terms of the ways in which, from the period of German Romanticism, the maxim, the apothegm, the aphorism, the anecdote, and the essay were used as a discursive means of expressing the irreducibility of human subjectivity to totalized frameworks. Holub analyses this in relation to three historical moments in Western philosophy: the elevation of the fragment into a legitimate literary and philosophical genre in the early writings of Friedrich Schlegel and Novalis; the scrupulous plurality in the thought of Friedrich Nietzsche and his attempts to take apart the fundamental categories of Western thought through various attacks on conceptions of the subject, value, representation, causality, truth value, and system; and, finally, the critique of totality expressed in poststructuralist thought. Holub comes to two important conclusions in his account. The first is that the three phases have different understandings of totality. For the Romantics he discusses, the fragment, though seeming to stand in contrast to any totalized whole, was thought to actually be capable of capturing the essence of totality. Thus the fragment was ultimately itself totalized and wound up being a "religiously recuperated totality" (1995: 89). In Nietszche's work, on the other hand, it is evident that his robust attacks on totality are themselves undergirded by an implicit impulse towards totalization. This is best seen in the oppositions in the antagonistic value scales he frequently sets up in the course of his philosophizing, which he labels variously the Dionysian and the Apollonian or Socratic, the Greek and the Judeo-Christian, or describes by the oppositions good versus bad and good versus evil. Holub notes that on all such scales two common features are evident: the first term is always valorized over the second and the second and nonfavored designation or category is viewed as an "outgrowth of sickness, deceit, deception, or an illicit attempt to gain and secure power" (p. 94). In poststructuralist thought, exemplified for Holub by the work of Lyotard, the same entanglement with a totalizing impulse is evident, particularly in his implicit claim to oversee all historical development while tracing the factors that have led to the postmodernist loss of belief in metanarratives (p. 98). The important thing for us here is not so much whether Holub's own account fully explicates the central antisystemic impulses behind postmodernism or not, but that historically, the antisystemic focus on fragments and other forms of apodictic discourses has been related to specific historical and aesthetic configurations.

Jean-François Lyotard, in his book *The Postmodern Condition*, provides another dimension to the antisystemic disposition in postmodernism. Among other things, Lyotard argues that both scientific knowledge and ordinary anthropological knowledge are governed by narrative. However, there is a historical break from about the eighteenth century, when science suppresses forms of knowledge that depend upon narrative. The crucial distinction comes when the mode of assigning truth value in scientific knowledge is set apart from the ways in which such assignings are achieved through narrative in ordinary knowledge. For Lyotard, the central feature of the postmodern condition is an incredulity towards metanarratives produced by science, Marxism, and Enlightenment theories of progress, and one of the ways in which the postmodern is set to counter the institutions and discourses that seek to validate such metanarratives is by way of "the atomization of the social into flexible networks of language games" (1984: 17ff). Lyotard's position might be fruitfully aligned to that of the Frankfurt School's contention that scientific universalism comes at the price of the peripheralization if not distortion of specificities. For Adorno, Horkheimer, and others in the Frankfurt School tradition, there was always an excess of social and historical reality over and above the appropriative grasp of conceptualization that Enlightenment thinkers produced in generating a basis for scientific rationality (see Horkheimer and Adorno, *Dialectic of Enlightenment*). For postmodernism, it is precisely this problematic excess that is widened and rendered into the dominant epistemological truth of existence under late capitalism, and a number of strategies are produced to support this key informing premise. These include a focus on indeterminacy, ambiguity, and deferral; on the deliberate fragmentation and misarticulation of the text, whether this is conceived of as social or literary; on the proliferation of aporias where meaning is deliberately made unretrievable; and a carefully parodic style that appropriates everything from tradition, history, and other genres and respects nothing. There is a focus on surfaces, on play, on the dissolution of boundaries, and on narrative and other jumpstarts that do not necessarily lead anywhere. The key theoretical terms in postmodernism are dissemination, dispersal, indeterminacy, hyperreality, normless pastiche, bricolage, *différance*, aporia, play, and such like.

The third major concern of postmodernism to be highlighted in our account has to do with the way in which the contemporary condition of globalized economics and culture are interpreted. Again following on from the implications of the linguistic turn already mentioned, postmodernist thinkers have attacked economistic models of the interpretation of social reality in favor of more attention to representation. Marxism was the prime candidate for critique, and the nature of the postmodernist rereading of Marx is best seen in the work of Jean Baudrillard. Classical Marxism has a three-tier interpretation of the growth of the market and its central feature, exchange-value. For Marx, the phase of industrial production is that in which things are produced primarily for exchange; use-value becomes secondary to exchange-value, unlike the case that might be thought to have pertained under feudalism, where only a small proportion of what was produced as handicrafts, agricultural products, etc. was available for exchange. The third phase discussed by Marx is when abstract values such as love, virtue, knowledge, previously thought to be immune from market forces, themselves enter into the realm of exchange-value. For Baudrillard in works like *The Mirror of Production* (1975) and "The Orders of Simulacra" (1983), it is no longer possible or desirable to separate the second from the third stages, since in the "postindustrial world" (Bell, 1973) all abstract human qualities, images, and representations have become part of the economic world. Thus, Baudrillard argues that a "political economy of the sign" has come to predominate contemporary life, to the degree that all reality, including the economic, is ultimately understandable in relation to signs. Television, the media, and popular culture then become significant areas of analysis for postmodernists because it is in these areas that the economy of the sign is best seen in its varying operation.

Furthermore, this postindustrial scenario is thought to proliferate a number of important social and cultural features. As David Harvey puts it in *The Condition of Postmodernity*:

> Postmodernism also ought to be looked at as mimetic of social, economic, and political practices in society. But since it is mimetic of different facets of those practices it appears in very different guises. The superimposition of different worlds in many a postmodern novel, worlds between which an uncommunicative "otherness" prevails in the space of coexistence, bears an uncanny relationship to the increasing ghettoization, disempowerment, and isolation of poverty and minority populations in the inner cities of both Britain and the United States. (Harvey, 1989: 113–14)

Harvey contextualizes this within a larger discussion of shifts in economic patterns. Like Baudrillard, he believes that postmodernity is due to the vast assimilation of more and more areas of life to the logic of the marketplace in place of the clear division of economic interest between labor and capital along with clear patterns of social antagonism and identification. There is now a "space-time" compression brought on by accelerations in travel and communications. Under these conditions, production is now organized on a global scale, with the manufacturing process being spread out across many countries and plants with each being responsible for a minor part of the finished product. This contrasts sharply with the model he describes as exemplified in the carmaker Ford, where cars of the same make were made in the same plant and distributed to thousands of consumers all over the world. Such a form of production was centralized, dedicated to the mass production of minimally varied items, and was driven by economies of scale demanding and providing stable and continuous patterns of employment. In the post-Fordist era, economies of scale are replaced by economies of scope, where shifts in demands of taste and fashion are met by increased differentiation in the product (Harvey, 1989: 125ff). Within such contexts, and given the "uncommunicative otherness" that reflects the ghettoization of minority populations, one then sees how multiculturalism becomes the "praxis" by which a sense of identity is negotiated within a seemingly incomprehensible postmodern social realm.[2]

2.1 Genealogies of postcolonialism

Like postmodernism and poststructuralism, postcolonialism designates critical practice that is highly eclectic and difficult to define. A possible working definition for postcolonialism is that it involves a studied engagement with the experience of colonialism and its past and present effects, both at the local level of ex-colonial societies, as well as at the level of more general global developments thought to be the after-effects of empire. Postcolonialism often involves the discussion of experiences of various kinds such as those of slavery, migration, suppression, and resistance, difference, race, gender, place, and the responses to the discourses of imperial Europe such as history, philosophy, anthropology, and linguistics. The term is as much about conditions under imperialism and colonialism proper as about conditions coming after the historical end of colonialism. A growing concern among postcolonial critics has also been with racial minorities in the West, embracing native and African Americans in the US, British Asians and African Caribbeans in the UK, and Aborigines in Australia among others. Because of these features, postcolonialism allows for a wide range of applications, designating a constant interplay and slippage between the sense of a historical transition, a sociocultural location, and an epochal configuration (Slemon, 1994). However the term is construed, a central underlying assumption is that there is as much focus on the discourse and ideology of colonialism as on the material effects of subjugation under colonialism and after.

Some of the overlap between the antisystemic concerns of postmodernism and those of postcolonialism can be gleaned from a definition of postcolonialism advanced by Homi Bhabha, one of the key theorists of the field:

> Postcolonial criticism bears witness to the unequal and uneven forces of cultural representation involved in the contest for political and social authority within the modern world order. Postcolonial perspectives emerge from the colonial testimony of Third World countries and the discourses of "minorities" within the geopolitical divisions of east and west, north and south. They intervene in those ideological discourses of modernity that attempt to give a hegemonic "normality" to the uneven development and the differential, often disadvantaged, histories of nations, races, communities, peoples. They formulate their critical revisions around issues of cultural difference, social authority, and political discrimination in order to reveal the antagonistic and ambivalent moments within the "rationalizations" of modernity. To bend Jürgen Habermas to our purposes, we could also argue that the postcolonial project, at the most general theoretical level, seeks to explore those social pathologies – "loss of meaning, conditions of anomie" – that no longer simply cluster around class antagonism, [but] break up into widely scattered historical contingencies. (Bhabha, 1992)

Lyotard's understanding of the incredulity towards metanarratives that he argues defines postmodernism is evident in Bhabha's formulation here, with the difference that Bhabha's formulation seeks to highlight the fight against perceived inequalities as being central to postcolonialism.

It is generally agreed that the single most influential work to define the purview of the term was Edward W. Said's *Orientalism*, published in 1978. Drawing on the work of Michel Foucault, Said's main thesis was that the Western academic discipline of Orientalism was strictly speaking a means by which the Orient was produced as a figment of the Western imagination for consumption in the West and also as a means of subserving the ultimate project of imperial domination. Said's main ideas have been both criticized and extrapolated across various disciplines, and it is mainly thanks to his book that what is known as colonial discourse analysis gained coherence. Among studies inspired by his work have been those by Gauri Viswanathan (1990), looking at the introduction of the paradigm of English studies in India and the degree to which it attempted to shape local attitudes to empire; Patrick Brantlinger (1988), which looks at the forms of imperial ideology as perceivable in the literary writings of the period 1830–1914; Martin Bernal (1987; 1991), which through a careful analysis of the sources of Greek civilization sought not only to show that this was heavily indebted to the influence of a black Egyptian civilization but, also, the degree to which the discipline of classical studies in the eighteenth century sought to obscure this contribution in the dominant disciplinary paradigms that were in use; and Valentin Mudimbe (1988), which showed that the notion of African systems of knowledge had always been governed by Western forms of knowledge.

Even though Edward Said's work provides a useful starting point for defining the field of postcolonial studies, it is important also to take account of the composite genealogy of its formation. This can be fruitfully linked to what Benita Parry has noted, in an echo of Bhabha, as the "wide-ranging retrospect taken in the 1980s on the exclusionary forms of reason and universality composed by a Western modernity complicit with imperial expansion and colonialist rule" (Parry, 1997: 4). Directly significant for postcolonialism was the gradual and increasingly important research done in the areas of feminist, multicultural, minority, and gay and lesbian studies. The impulse they shared in common with postcolonial studies was the desire to contest the centrality and authority of distinctive systems of domination, jointly contributing to deciphering systems of representation thought to have been either designed or apropriated to validate institutional subordination and silence the voice of competitors. This major critical and retrospective glance was itself filiated to the broader criticisms of Western philosophy which, though having a long history, gained a special coherence in the hands of poststructuralists such as Jacques Derrida, Jacques Lacan, Michel Foucault, Deleuze and Guattari, and others from the late 1960s and early 1970s. Quite often, work of a thorough interdisciplinary nature was pursued, such as that by Gayatri Spivak in her linking of Marxism, feminism, and an eclectic cultural criticism, or that of Homi Bhabha himself, which combines Lacanian psychoanalysis with discourse theory.

Even though postcolonial theory and criticism has been heavily influenced by developments in Western philosophy, it is also the case that this has been joined to an impulse to formulate non-Western modes of discourse as significant ways of challenging the West. Though this idea is first forcefully spelt out in Ashcroft *et al.*'s *The Empire Writes Back* (1989), it is perhaps Bart Moore-Gilbert who provides a more interesting genealogy of this tendency, particularly as he is able to show how some of the key concepts in postcolonial theory were worked out in the writing and criticism of authors such as Chinua Achebe, Kamau

Braithwaite, Wilson Harris, Wole Soyinka, and others (Moore-Gilbert, 1997: 152–84). Postcolonialism is seen by some of its practitioners as the paradigmatic antihegemonic theorietical orientation, with colonialism taken to be the archetypal and most brutal expression of hegemony; any theoretical tendency that sees itself as antihegemonic is then easily taken to be affiliated to postcolonialism. For others, however, it is its productive circularity that calls the postcolonial object of study into being while allowing unreflexive notions of nationhood, race, and identity and even of colonialism itself to be deployed without attention to the specificities of each discipline, or, indeed of particular local conditions (see Ahmad, 1992 and Thomas, 1994: 33–65).

Another inspiration behind postcolonial theory is the theories and processes of decolonization of the 1950s and 1960s. The centrality of thinkers like Frantz Fanon, Aimé Césaire, Albert Memmi, and C. L. R. James ensures that this link is kept alive, even though there is as yet no steady coherence in how these thinkers have been appropriated. There have been increasingly strong calls for a firmer acknowledgment of this dimension of postcolonialism's genealogy, especially because the work of decolonization is thought not to be completely over (see, for instance, Williams and Chrisman, 1993, Ato Sekyi-Otu, 1996, and Benita Parry, 1997).

The differences between postmodernism and postcolonialism become starker when their different social referents are disentangled from their representational domains and brought out into the open. Postmodernism references a particular sociocultural configuration in the West and theorizes globalization from an essentially Western standpoint, generalizing about global economics and culture as it is seen from the vantage point of the Western metropolis. As has been noted earlier, postmodernity is the era of surfaces, of the flattening out of affect, of multiple and shifting subjectivities, and of the total subordination of the real under the irreality of the images generated by visual culture. For postcolonialism, however, even though all of these might be granted as pertaining to postcolonial existence, the central problem is really the double vision that a peripheral existence in the world engenders. This doubleness can be theorized in many ways. Du Bois provides something of a significant lead in the area of African American subjectivity when he writes in *The Souls of Black Folk* that the African American is a product of double consciousness: "It is a peculiar sensation, this double-consciousness, this sense of always looking at one's self through the eyes of others, of measuring one's soul by the tape of a world that looks on in amused contempt and pity. One feels his twoness, – an American, a Negro; two souls, two thoughts, two unreconciled strivings; two warring ideals in one dark body, whose dogged strength alone keeps it from being torn asunder" (1997: 615). Coming from different theoretical and personal inspirations others such as Frantz Fanon in *Black Skin, White Masks* (1967) and Ngugi wa Thiong'o in *Decolonizing the Mind* (1986) and others have also theorized the same idea in postcolonialism both in the domain of subjectiviy and in that of language more generally.

3 Reading across the "Posts": Towards a Methodological Agenda

Without attempting to read the two fields in their fullest comparative possibilities (something which would be self-defeatist if not utterly hubristic) I want at this stage to focus on two areas as a means of pointing out possible directions that such a comparative approach might take. The two areas I want to focus on are 1) that of the problematic nature of identity formation in the light of aestheticized images of privilege, and 2) the "political unconscious" of popular filmic and televisual images of otherness and the implications these have for the *reception* of otherness in the metropolitan West. I do this by drawing examples from postcolonial and postmodern texts, as well as with reference to the popular television series *The X-Files*, among others.

3.1   *The social life of images*

Something of the potential for a fruitful cross-reading of concepts between postmodernism and postcolonialism can be extrapolated from Arjun Appadurai's introductory essay to *The Social Life of Things* (1986). In this superb essay, Appadurai boldly joins Baudrillard with Simmel, Mauss, and others to define how exchange value is created for commodities through what he carefully elaborates as their "social life." This, he shows, is not a secondary offshoot of exchange relations but is part and parcel of economic exchange and the creation of value in all societies. His comments are much too complicated and rich to be properly summarized here, but for my purposes I want to focus on the comments he makes about the work of Sombart (1967). Sombart argues that the principal cause of the expansion of trade, industry, and finance capital in the West was the demand for luxury goods, principally on the part of the newly rich, the courts, and the aristocracy. He locates the source of this increased demand, in turn, in the new understanding of "free" love, sensual refinement, and the political economy of courtship during this period. To Sombart fashion becomes a driving force for the upper classes, who are satiated only by ever-increasing quantities and ever-differentiated qualities of articles of consumption (Appadurai, 1986: 36–7). Appadurai makes a direct link between Sombart and certain postmodernist theorists before adding his own interpretive gloss to Sombart's ideas:

> In his emphasis on demand, in his key observations about the politics of fashion, in his placement of economic drives in the context of transformations of sexuality, and in his dialectical view of the relationship between luxury and necessity, Sombart anticipates recent semiotic approaches to economic behaviour, such as those of Baudrillard, Bourdieu, Kristeva, and others.
>
> . . . For our purposes, the importance of Sombart's model of the relationship between luxury goods and early capitalism lies less in the temporal and spatial specifics of his argument (which is a matter for historians of early modern Europe),

than in the generalizability of the *logic* of his argument regarding the cultural basis of demand for at least some kinds of commodities, those that he calls luxury goods.

I propose that we regard luxury goods not so much in contrast to necessities (a contrast filled with problems), but as goods whose principal use is *rhetorical* and *social*, goods that are simply *incarnated signs*. (Appadurai, 1986: 37, 38)

Following Appadurai, we can see how a focus on commodities as incarnated signs allows us to discern more clearly the economic basis for the dual consciousness that I spoke of at the end of the last section. Two literary examples will help bring this point home. In 1915, a play was produced by the Ghanaian national-ist Kobina Sekyi called *The Blinkards*. This play seemed on the surface to be merely a dramatic satirization of the up-and-coming newly rich who (mis)appro-poriate what they think are forms of Western bourgeois civility and luxury items as a means of giving themselves a distinctive standing among the local popula-tion. There is much that is pathetic and hilarious in Sekyi's dramatization of the concerns of this class of people. Among other things, Mrs. Brofusem, who has returned to Ghana with her husband after a brief spell in England, insists on speaking English to her husband and her servants. What is more intriguing, however, is that she also insists that her husband smoke his cigars and drop the ashes on the carpet in the living room. The English, she insists, do this to give the carpets a special look. But she is not the only one afflicted by this misappre-hension of bourgeois domestic social practices; as the action unfolds a local farmer, Mr. Tsiba, brings his daughter to live with Mrs. Brofusem, so she can be brought up in the proper ways of civilization as only the redoubtable Mrs. Brofusem is thought to be able to instill. But Mr. Tsiba is inspired by an odd sense of doubleness, part of which is due to the fact that he keeps a small book with him of English sayings and proverbs which he tries to translate directly into his understanding of life. The results are unsettling:

MR TSI: Mrs Brofusem, some book I have reading say "All modest young ladies blush at certain times." I look in the dickhendry, and I see "blush" means to redden in the face," also I look "modest," and I see "chaste." I know "chaste": the minister explain this to me. But I think "blush" is some English powder for face. I have never seen it here. Order some for my daughter I have many cocoa . . .

MRS BROFUSEM: (*Laughing*) Ah! Blush: Your daughter can't be able to blush.

MR TSI: (*Offended*) You mean my daughter too raw? I say I give her to you free, gratis. Make her blush. I will pay.

MRS BROFUSEM: I mean her skin don't allow it to be clear when she will blush.

MR TSI: But she has fine black skin, – velvet black. My great-grandmother he say, in old times, the blackest ladies are most beautifullest. I think my daugh-ter's skin is alright.

MRS BROFUSEM: You don't understand –

MR TSI: Ma'm I went to standard sever. I understand –

MRS BROFUSEM: I don't men to say you don't understand English. How can you talk what you don't understand? You understand English but you don't know that white peoples' skin is transparent; so you can see the blood running into their faces when they are having some emotional state.

MR TSI: Ah! What fine big words you use. "Transparent – Transparent." Wait (*Takes out a pocket Dictionary, and looks in*) Ah! here it is: "Transparent – that may be seen through, clear." (*To himself*) Well, my daughter's skin is clear, my skin is clear, my wife's skin is clear, my wife's skin is clear. We get no sickness. (*Reflects a moment*) Oh, "see through": I see! I see! Very funny. "Transparent" is like glass: no colour; so it is the blood make him red. You call that "blush." All right! Teach Barbara all the things . . . (Sekyi, 1974: 32–3)

It is interesting to note how the hapless Mr. Tsiba has to trace the liminal meanings of English words through the dictionary. In piecing such meanings together, of course, it is evident that he is never able to come to a full understanding of their meaning. This is of course a function of his semiliteracy; but more important is the fact that the dictionary essentially atomizes the meanings of words and treats them largely in isolation from their full cultural context. The inklings of a postmodernist problematic are in evidence here. But this has to be seen alongside the larger colonial and postcolonial problematic of double consciousness. Mr. Tsiba is bringing his daughter to be trained so that her "market value" in the marriage world can be augmented; in choosing this option he simultaneously enters the realm of imagined Western fashion and thus allows the further consolidation of a Western idea of selfhood which, as Sombart argues, comes from the sexual economy that ultimately undergirded the industrial expansion of the eighteenth century in the first place. But Mr. Tsiba has to square these new ideas of feminine desirability which he wants for his daughter with indigenous ideas of beauty. As he recalls it, his great-grandmother always said that the darker the skin, the more beautiful. Because the play is essentially a comedy, it resolves the contradictions happily, allowing us to laugh at these people on stage while remembering the more tragic ways in which this doubleness was played out in the social life of the newly educated classes of the period.[3]

Another good example of the incarnated significatory valence of commodities, this time taken from African American literature, is provided in Toni Morrison's *The Bluest Eye*. This jump to African American literature is strategic.[4] *The Bluest Eye* is at a primary level about the crisis of identity faced by the teenage Pecola Breedlove, who, because of the dysfunctional nature of her family and her own lack of beauty and grace, craves for blue eyes in the forlorn hope of gaining herself acceptability. But the "blue eyes" have entered a commodified domain; they are no longer just part of the white man's anatomy. Aided by marketing, the proliferation of images of blue eyes on dolls, cups, films, and even sweets, blue eyes become a disembodied object of aesthetic intensity. Though this is by no means the place to pursue a full study of this phenomenon, it would be interesting for example to trace how this objective fact – blue eyes – is detached from its objective domain and then transferred into the domain of commodification, accruing an exchange value through its social life, and becoming a desirable commodity to "own" as a means of identity affirmation. One might, in such a study, cast a passing glance at the eyes of Dr. T. J. Eckelburg in F. Scott Fitzgerald's *The Great Gatsby*, which, implanted on an oculist's fast-fading billboard, nonetheless create the social conception of the eyes of God in the novel. One might also want to study the Black Consciousness Movement of the 1960s and 1970s and the popular culture that they spawned, the ways in which the "I am black and proud" of the likes of James Brown was a reaction to this commodification of blue eyes and white ideas of beauty. How do such objects shift epistemologically from a human domain through a quasi-theological one and into an area of aesthetic commodification? What are the moments of intensity in this process and what social formations disguise AND support their transformations?

The important thing for us at this point, however, is the effect that the desire for blue eyes has on Pecola. Partly at the mercy of an image culture, and partly because of the domestic crises of lovelessness she is constantly exposed to, she gets a split consciousness. For it is patently clear to her that she cannot get blue eyes, and yet she insistently desires them. When she does finally get the blue eyes, through the agency of the religious charlatan Soapherd Church, she is completely split within her psyche and becomes mad. She can only attain the aestheticized object of a commodified image culture by tragically doubling herself, being her own ontological interlocutor with an immediacy only allowed the insane.

Are these examples postcolonial or postmodern? They appear amenable to both perspectives. In both cases things, both abstract and concrete, are interpreted as efficacious signs of identification and become invested with desire. They are first and foremost incarnated signs, and mark, as Appadurai points out, a "register of consumption." But they are signs that are not entirely free of power; there is a certain discursivity in both cases that places the desired objects within cycles that define a nebulous but regulative capitalist or Western or white area of power. Mrs. Brofusem and Mr. Tsiba in Sekyi's text define themselves in relation to a Western bourgeois civility, one that cannot be fully attained precisely because the incarnated signs of luxury they activate and aspire to conceal behind them is a complicated hinterland of Western cultural significance. For Pecola, the problem is obviously more pressingly ontological. Having blue eyes is not in itself enough; for the blue eyes to be efficacious in giving her a sense of worth, she would also have to be part of the middle-class ethos defined by the family captured in the words of the primer with which Morrison opens her text. Without reducing the two theoretical perspectives to simple polarities, we might say that the key dimension that postcolonialism forces us to consider is that of agency, whilst the postmodernist angle would make us settle on the economy of the image and the potetnial for the proliferation of subject positions. For postcolonial theory, the question of agency is crucial because merely identifying the purview or ambit of the regulative parameters set up by images is not enough.

The next step has to be how such images ought to be subverted or how, if at all, their effects are to be challenged with a view to setting up a better order of effects. As the Igbos of Nigeria succinctly put it: "When we ask where the rain is hitting us, it is to prevent us from getting wet in the future," or, in another useful formulation, "The anthill survives so that the new grass will have memory of the fire that devastated the savannah in the previous season."

3.2   Films, TV, and freedom

Following this thread on agency, it is important to note the difference between postmodernism's interest in image culture and the multiplication of realities, and postcolonialism's focus on the politics of representation. For some postmodernists, the proliferation of images is a reflection of a problematically empowering subjectivity, one that allows people greater leeway in continually reimagining themselves. This is how Douglas Kellner puts it in *Media Culture*:

> My analysis suggests that in a postmodern image culture, the images, scenes, stories, and cultural texts of media culture offer a wealth of subject positions which in turn help structure individual identity. These images project role and gender models, appropriate and inappropriate forms of behavior, style, and fashion, and subtle enticements to emulate and identify with certain identities while avoiding others. Rather than identity disappearing in a postmodern society, it is merely subject to new determinations and new forces while offering as well new possibilities, styles, models, and forms. Yet the overwhelming variety of possibilities for identity in an affluent image culture no doubt creates highly unstable identities while constantly providing new openings to restructure one's identity. (Kellner, 1995: 257)

Even though this notion of freedom cannot by any means be taken as a generalizable opinion, it is interesting that it is asserted at all as a form of the possibility for the individual's appropriation of the postmodern moment. In postcolonial theory, the emphasis is placed elsewhere. Whereas representations, especially residual colonialist ones, proliferate everywhere, it is by no means the case that the mere recognition of their proliferation gives access to freedom; such proliferations must be understood in their social content and historic projects before they can be aligned potentially to questions of freedom.

Something of the difference in the implications of the two positions for the issue of freedom may be glimpsed from the implications that televisual and filmic images of otherness have for postcolonial diasporas, and beyond them for multicultural agendas in general. It is significant to note, along with Robert Stam and Ella Shohat (1995), that the beginnings of Western cinema coincided with the intensification of empire in the late nineteenth century. This had a correlation with the content of films, especially as the medium was used for documentary and propaganda purposes in the heyday of empire. And Stam and Shohat additionally make the point that the popular images of the cinema helped to secure an image of otherness whose efficacy it is difficult to deny. From Tarzan to Disney's Aladdin, the popular televisual and filmic media have succeeded in creating images of otherness that, even though a part of the proliferation of images that postmodernists speak of, nonetheless attempt to stabilize subliminal images of otherness whose contestation can never be completely successful until their import in a hierarchical world is fully grasped.

This contention is given even greater relevance if seen in the light of the changing demographics of cities in the West and the historical implications these have had for imagining individual subjectivity. The Western city, as an idea and peculiar place for the meeting and mingling of strangers, was an important organizing paradigm behind modernism. Many well-known characters of the modernist novel struggled for an identity within the hustle and bustle of the city, and this struggle for identity provided the rationale for their interiorization and the focus on the mediation of the external bustle through the psychology of the individual. While modernism relentlessly defined the individual against an engulfing urban background, it also succeeded in producing an important opposition between interiority and exteriority, the masses and the individual. But, crucially, it also subsumed under this typology a dialectic of otherness, in which the individual sensibility was shown to have to shore up a sense of (in)coherence in the face of the burgeoning and spreading city. These typologies by no means die with the waning of modernism, and postmodern culture has repeatedly returned to a number of these typologies in the face of the changing demographic configuration of the city. There is, for instance, a more subtle logic to be seen at play in the noir films of the 1950s, where filmic techniques sought to inscribe the typology of otherness on the landscape of the city itself. In the various metropolitan cities in which noir was set, such as Los Angeles, New York, Detroit, etc., it was clear that a postwar movement of nonwhite populations was moving into the major cities and, thereby, producing anxiety about urban space. The noir films of the fifties confronted this phenomenon, but not directly. They grappled with otherness by inscribing the polarities of race and of good and evil within the dynamics of filmic technique itself. This was realized in the foregrounding of the affectivity given to the perambulations of the civic hero in the dark, mean, and lonely streets of the city. Julian Murphet puts the point succinctly in his nuanced analysis of the "racial unconscious" of film noir: "These run–down, dark, mean and empty streets resound with the fear and hatred of a race/class faction that has lost its hold over them. The anger and bewilderment of the protagonists as they run along these avenues, casting nervous glances into every niche and side–alley, is as much an expression of bereaved loss as it is of haunted terror." (Murphet, 1998: 29)

If noir is taken to be a "modernist" filmic genre, supremely subtle in conceptualizing the shaping forces of otherness in the city, it is no less true to say that this concern retains its force in current popular TV series such as *The X-Files*. *The X-Files* is a curious hybrid. On the one hand it is clearly a police-detective drama, with a subliminal sexual synergy between the two cops, Scully and Mulder. (It is perhaps not idle to note that Scully always keeps her lips partially apart, even when she is not speaking, in a barely concealed sexualized gesture much reminiscent of advertisements in women's magazines.) More important, though, is that the series is specifically about the esoteric crimes that consistently baffle the established protocols of investigation and which the police protagonists of the series are always brought in to tackle. "The truth," as the opening words in the title score says, "is out there."

The series is predominantly set in the city, and in many respects extends one of the concerns of the noir genre, namely the ontological inscription of otherness onto the geography of the city itself. In one particular episode called "Teliko: The Case of the Missing Pigment," this concern with an ontological otherness manifests itself at both the explicit level of the story as well as at the level of the cityscape. The episode opens with a flight from an African country which we later learn is Burkina Faso in West Africa. One of the passengers gets up to visit the toilet, and, while washing his hands, looks up and sees something off-camera that obviously frightens him. The scene is cut back to the passengers in the plane and we see a flight attendant asking people to prepare for landing. Asking about the whereabouts of the missing passenger, she goes to the toilet and, on seeing the body of the man, now dead, screams. He is chalk white and no longer black. The action begins.

We are next taken to the police department where we follow Scully and Mulder on their early attempts to make sense of a spate of strange deaths of black men from inner city areas. The cadavers, all African American, are distinguished by their uncanny chalk whiteness. Things resolve themselves into a clearer pattern when a new character is quickly introduced who happens to have traveled on the flight from Burkina Faso (and of whom we caught a brief glimpse coming from another toilet in the plane). He is Samuel Aboah, and seeks emigrant status that would allow him to remain and work in the United States. As the program unfolds we are gradually given more information about Samuel Aboah. He is visited by a black social worker who promises to help him get his papers; captures another victim in whom he induces a kind of trancelike state by shooting him with poisoned darts from a small reed-like object; is momentarily interrupted by the police inserting the reedlike object into the nose of his victim; and is later captured and sent to hospital but makes a dramatic escape. There is a final showdown in which the black social worker and Mulder are almost made victims of Samuel Aboah before he is shot in the stomach by Scully.

This truncated account by no means conveys the tension and mystery/thriller-like impact of the episode as the two detectives attempt to unravel the mystery of the missing pigment. But the "truth" is pieced together methodically. It turns out that Samuel Aboah is a member of a tribe in Burkina Faso who have been rumored to regularly kill other tribesmen, and, magically, to leave them chalky white. For the Burkinabe victims of this strange plague, this can only be the sign of a feared magic. But Scully unearths a more rational explanation. Aboah's tribespeople are, according to her, in an earlier stage of evolution, when their bodies lack the capacity for producing the life-sustaining melanin that is the cause of the black pigment. But without it they cannot live. Their solution to this is to kill others and to somehow drain them of their pigmentation to supplement their own deficient supplies. This is what leaves their black victims chalk white.

A number of things need to be noted if this remarkable episode is to be fully understood in relation to the typology of othering that we noted earlier. The first thing is the subtle integration of the esoteric, in this case located in Samuel Aboah's mysterious vampire powers of draining melanin, with the discourse of illegal immigration. At a point during the film, Scully asks Mulder why this melanin deficient African tribesman should want to come to America in the first place. His answer is revealing. He has come, M. says, for the same reasons that all people come to America, to enjoy freedom, a place to live, and work. However, this universal desire for American life is in this episode criminalized, firstly by the fact that Samuel Aboah is nothing other than a melanin-extracting vampire, and secondly by the fact that he seems so desperate to get residence that he is prepared to use any means, fair or foul. Thus, the esoteric in this particular episode is no other than the illegal immigrant.

Samuel Aboah is an "illegal" in another respect also. He is an illegal immigrant into a more advanced stage of human evolution. It is perhaps not entirely accidental that his surname is the Akan name for animal. In his case he is underdeveloped even in respect to other African tribespeople. When he comes to the United States, his entrapment in an earlier stage of evolution reveals itself also in the curious tools by which he captures and works on his victims. Opposed to the guns of the detectives, his mouth-blown weapon is a throw back to superseded stages of civilization. Curiously enough, however, this evolutionarily retarded species is linked in the program to a more modern African in the person of the Burkina Faso ambassador to the United States. It is from him that Mulder learns of this strange tribe in a story the ambassador tells from his childhood about the death of a cousin of his. The ambassador, it turns out, has the body of the man killed in the plane secretly sent back to Burkina Faso for a postmortem in the hope that some light might be shed on his own cousin's uncanny death. But the tale the ambassador tells is clearly supposed to be opposed to Scully's more elaborate and scientific explanation. Aboah is to civilization what the Burkina Faso ambassador is to Scully: evolutionarily and scientifically retarded species, respectively.

If this play with otherness manifests itself in such a blatant way, it is folded back into the informing logic of *The X-Files* by being staged in the recognizable geographical background of the inner city that gets incessantly revisited in the series. The inner city is a chronotope. As Bakhtin defines it, the chronotope is a time-space organization that calls up a specific affective response and allows us to relate an image to specific spatiotemporal and historical coordinates. Many of *The X-Files* episodes end in chases through dark streets and alleys. Even though these dark streets are by no means racially coded, it is also the case that inner cities, especially in the United States, have a specific demographic character. The chronotope of the alleyways and dark streets, then, serves to signal a concern with the otherness of the cityscape even as a variegated racial (and class) demography is written onto it.

A critical question remains to be answered. In what ways can a TV series such as *The X-Files* be submitted to a postmodernist reading? It is a curious hybrid form, embodying a belief in the supernatural as a principle of relativizing scientific rationality. This is captured most critically in the fact that the other people in the police department regularly scoff at Scully and Mulder's often bizarre explanations for events. However, and this is a regular movement in the series, the esoteric is always submitted to veridical police procedures and, ultimately, shown to be explicable in scientific terms. But the scientific terms of explanation no longer remain the same. The contact with the supernatural leads to various kinds of short-circuiting of the rational procedures to be applied. In the pigment episode we have described, for instance, this short-circuiting is shown in the fact that no rational explanation is offered for how the draining of the melanin out of Samuel Aboah's victims in supposed to have been done. Also, no explanation is given for how, even granted that he is able to drain his victims of melanin, he is able to inject or take it into himself to give him his life-sustaining blackness.

Police departments in all big cities face increasingly strident criticisms about their competence in combating crime. Crime, the "other" of the civic and of law and order, is frequently seen to be uncontainable. But it is uncontainable for specific social causes. The genius of *The X-Files* is to transfer these causes onto the esoteric, while simultaneously placing emphasis on the supremacy of a newly-sensitized mode of police work. All the esoteric characters in *The X-Files* are strangers, visitants from elsewhere, not fully integratable into the spheres of civil order. Most of them reside on the social peripheries of the city (naturally, one might add), but this periphery often coincides with destitution, and the more run-down areas of the city, where the lower classes and racial minorities are traditionally known to reside. The esoteric is coded along a specific chronotope of the city, which, like the genre of film noir, hides a particular racial unconscious. The discourse of scientific, veridical police procedures are always shown to be found wanting; however, this apparent questioning of the efficacy of police procedures is not meant to completely replace it with a postrealist or esoteric procedure. On the contrary. The postrealist or esoteric is shown to subtend the rationalistic discourse of science. Ultimately, just as the esoteric other is contained by the handcuffs of scientific police procedures, so the social other, whether racial minority or lower-class fraction, is contained by the apparatuses of power.

How, we might ask, does all this fit into a postcolonial understanding of the world? What sustains *The X-Files'* imagining of otherness is not merely the strangeness of the esoteric, but its coding as opposed to the Law and to civic order. Mapped onto the chronotopes of the dark alleyways of the inner city, this other of the civic order is then easily imagined as that other which resists the

Law or, more usually, fails to be fully integrated into the civil order. In the Teliko example I have noted from *The X-Files*, this other is of course the illegal immigrant who lives among the ethnic minorities of his own color and preys upon them. Thus, the image of otherness in *The X-Files* is conjoined to a major concern of political systems in the West: how are illegal immigrants to be surveilled, checked, and policed, considering that they are so "different," so given to "uncivilized" behaviour, and so utterly and irredeemably other? It is not only police departments that are interested in surveilling otherness. The police represent one of the instituional apparatuses that most strongly articulate this interest. But the interest in surveilling otherness is dispersed everywhere, sometimes making itself manifest in the constantly asked "where do you really come from" question put to newly arrived immigrants, to second and third generation children of immigrants, and, most irritatingly, to those of mixed descent in the various postcolonial diasporas of the West. For, the question "Where are you from?" is never an innocent one; it is a question of origin that, posed to particular subjects and in particular contexts also involves a question of return (see Visweswaran, 1994: 114–40). Thus the city chronotopes of *The X-Files* and other series like them have to be seen in a general popular anxiety about the very constitution of Western identity in general. This cannot be taken solely as a postmodernist question of the dissolution of the centrality of the West; it is a postcolonial one as well because the demographic changes in the West today cannot be thought of outside the various histories of empire (and slavery, in the case of the United States) which stretch back into previous centuries. And the mass media are critical in the dissemination of specific understandings of the West's history and its relationship to the rest of the world. A postcolonial perspective allows us to see how these media relate to continuing problems of racial anxiety in the world today, and how we might think of a way of transcending such anxiety.

4 Conclusion: Postmodernism as Postcolonialism

I would like to conclude polemically by suggesting that postmodernism can never fully explain the state of the contemporary world without first becoming postcolonial and vice versa. The cross-reading of the two domains that we have attempted provides some pointers to possible directions. The first thing to note is the need to simultaneously factor images, tropes, and texts into specific sociocultural domains while at the same time attempting to alienate them from themselves by reading them against other images, tropes, and texts that do not seem to share historical similarities. The purpose of this would in my view be not only to "read awry," as Slavoj Žižek (1991) puts it, but to force the phenomenon under analysis into a mode of alienation or estrangement from itself by means of which it would be made to deliver a truth-value that ramifies far beyond its own domain of circulation. This does not preclude the filling in of context. On the contrary, the specification of historical context is one of the first principles to be observed. But this has to be aligned to a more pressing requirement. Following the insights about the proliferation of perspectives that postmodernism offers, it is useful to try and fill out as many dimensions of context as possible, even when these might seem to contradict each other at various points. In our transfer of Appadurai to a reading of Sekyi and Morrison, for instance, we applied his ideas to two texts from very different contexts, one being that of late nineteenth-century cultural nationalism in West Africa and the other being that of early seventies African America. The point of it was to estrange the two texts from their normal grids of interpretation and to show how a similarity of effects could be said to have impinged upon the formation of subjectivity in both contexts. In this comparative approach, it would be critical to attend to certain inherent dangers in comparative analysis. Marilyn Strathern makes interesting observations about precisely these problems in respect of anthropology. Observing in *Partial Connections* that "complexity is intrinsic both to the ethnographic and comparative enterprise," she points out how, in the attempt to demonstrate the social and cultural entailments of phenomena, simplification is necessary for complexity to be made visible (1991: xiii). She adds further:

> The perception of increasable complication – that there are always potentially "more" things to take into account – contributes to a muted skepticism about the utility of comparison at all. However, anthropologists do not produce this sense of complexity unaided. *Their discipline has developed in a cultural milieu committed to ideas of pluralism and enumeration and with an internal faculty for the perpetual multiplication of things to know.* (Strathern, 1991: xiii, xiv, emphasis added)

Her remark about the cultural milieu, in the West, of pluralism *and* enumeration is particularly relevant for any cross-reading, comparative or otherwise. For the impulse towards pluralism and enumeration conjoins the objectivist impulses of scientific rationality with its implicit negation in the detailing and proliferation of phenomena that constantly threaten to outstrip the capacity for description. But these impulses have to be relocated within grids that allow for challenges to be posed to any overweening systemic or hegemonic rationalization: not, it has to be noted, as a means of merely negating the systemic or the hegemonic, but to bring these into dialectical confrontation with their denied logics. This would be to engraft provisionality into any systemic analysis even while finding ways of making ethically grounded proclamations about the projects we pursue.

The next plank of reading postcolonialism and postmodernism together is of course to try and grasp the social life of ideas, whether these inhere in images of fashion, as was the case in the Sekyi and Morrison texts, or in popular cultural images of otherness, as was observed in the example from *The X-Files*. The point here is to unearth incipient or fully-formed social values both in their formation (in terms of process) and historicity (in terms of completeness from the perspective of the moment of analysis). In doing this we would arguably be going a

107

step further than Appadurai by moving the discussion of commodification from the domain of things to embrace that of images as well, while sidestepping the more extreme forms of postmodernist and postcolonial interpretations that hyperinflate images and take them as unmediated stand-ins for society and culture. Thus the images of otherness in *The X-Files* were related in our account to general problems of the surveilling of immigrants and racial others in the West. The key thing would be not to dubiously hyperinflate, but to read such images alongside other socially relevant configurations. Finally, however, any cross-reading has to have a commitment to integrate the analysis into a larger affirmative project. This is by no means easy when both theorietical domains (but more especially postmodernism) run shy of making definitive ethical and evaluative statements about the phenomena they engage with. The fear of being thought prescriptive and hegemonic is one that most people no longer think worth risking in a world of pluralism. I happen to think otherwise. Recognizing that there is much destitution, poverty, and sheer despair in the world, it seems to me increasingly imperative that the risk of appearing prescriptive is one worth taking if one is not to surrender completely to a debilitating anomie brought on by the comprehension of persistent social tragedies. Those who lose their limbs to landmines, are displaced due to refugee crises, or merely subsist in the intermittent but regularly frustrated hope that the world can become a better place, cannot wait for complete moral certitude before they take action to improve their existence. It is partly in the implicit (and often real) alliance with those who, to appropriate a phrase from Julian Murphet, "keep running all the time simply to keep pace with events," that we ought to take courage to make ethical judgments even in the full knowledge that we may be proved wrong. To this larger picture, and in the service of this larger affirmation we ought to commit our critical enterprises. Both postmodernism *and* postcolonialism have a part to play in this.

Notes

1   The "linguistic turn" has now been noted to have influenced developments in various disciplines. See for example, Sherry B. Ortner (1984), Bryan D. Palmer (1990); and, from a more social theory perspective, Quentin Skinner (1985).

2   This is not the place to discuss how multiculturalism becomes the preferred praxis of postmodernism, but for critical accounts, see Slavoj Žižek, "Multiculturalism, Or, the Cultural Logic of Multinational Capitalism" (1997); Kobena Mercer, "'1968': Periodizing Postmodern Politics and Identity" (1992); Peter McLaren, "White Terror and Oppositional Agency: Towards a Critical Multiculturalism" (1994).

3   The notion of the double consciousness of the period given full treatment across the West African region in the various essays in *Self-Assertion and Brokerage: Early Cultural Nationalism in West Africa*, eds. P. F. de Moraes Farias and Karin Barber (1990).

4 Even though there are significant differences between any putative postcolonial condition and that of African America, its is arguably the case that the history of slavery and the peripheralization of blacks in that culture makes them amenable to a postcolonial analysis. For a recent discussion of this point, especially in relation to new multicultural pedagogies, see the special issue of *Wasafiri*, no. 27 (1998) devoted to African American literature, especially the interview by bell hooks and the essay by Julian Murphet on Anna Deveare Smith and the question of the staging of racial identification.

References

Ahmad, Aijaz. (1992). *In Theory: Classes, Nations, Literatures*. London: Verso.

Appadurai, Arjun. (1986). "Commodities and the Politics of Value," in *The Social Life of Things*. Cambridge: Cambridge University Press, 3–63.

Ashcroft, Bill, Gareth Griffiths, and Helen Tiffin. (1989). *The Empire Writes Back: Theory and Practice in Post-Colonial Literatures*. London: Routledge.

——, ——, and ——. (1994). *The Post-Colonial Studies Reader*. London: Routledge.

Baudrillard, Jean. (1975). *The Mirror of Production*, trans. Mark Poster. St. Louis: Telos Press.

——. (1983). "The Orders of Simulacra," trans. Paul Foss, Paul Patton, and Philip Bleitchman, in *Simulations*. New York: Semiotext(e).

Bell, Daniel. (1973). *The Coming of Post-Industrial Society*. Harmondsworth: Penguin.

Bernal, Martin. (1987). *Black Athena*, vol. 1. London: Free Association Press.

——. (1991). *Black Athena*, vol. 2. London: Free Association Press.

Bhabha, Homi. (1992). "Postcolonial Criticism," in *Redrawing the Boundaries: The Transformation of English and American Literary Studies*, eds. Stephen Greenblatt and Giles Dunn. New York: Modern Language Association of America, 1992.

Brantlinger, Patrick. (1988). *Rule of Darkness: British Literature and Imperialism, 1830–1914*. Ithaca: Cornell University Press.

Callinicos, Alex. (1989). *Against Postmodernism: A Marxist Critique*. Cambridge: Polity.

Connor, Steven. (1997). *Postmodernist Culture: An Introduction to Theories of the Contemporary*, 2nd ed. Oxford: Blackwell; first published 1989.

de Moraes Farias, P. F. and Karin Barber, eds. (1990). *Self-Assertion and Brokerage: Early Cultural Nationalism in West Africa*. Birmingham: Centre for West African Studies.

Du Bois, W. E. B. (1997). *The Souls of Black Folk*, in *The Norton Anthology of African American Literature*, eds. Henry Louis Gates, Jr. and Nellie Y. McKay. New York: W. W. Norton and Co., 613–740; first published 1903.

Eagleton, Terry. (1997). *The Illusions of Posmodernism*. Oxford: Blackwell.

Ekpo, Denis. (1995). "Towards a Post-Africanism: Contemporary African Thought and Postmodernism," *Textual Practice*, 9, no. 1: 121–35.

Fanon, Frantz. (1967). *Black Skin, White Masks*, trans Charles Lam Markham. New York: Grove Press; first published 1952.

Harvey, David. (1989). *The Condition of Postmodernity*. Oxford: Blackwell.

Hassan, Ihab. (1985). "The Culture of Postmodernism," *Theory, Culture and Society*, 2, no. 3: 119–32.

Holub, Robert C. (1995). "Fragmentary Totalities and Totalized Fragments: On the Politics of Anti-Systemic Thought," in *Postmodern Pluralism and Concepts of Totality*, ed. Jost Hermand. New York: Peter Lang, 83–104.

Hutcheon, Linda. (1989). "Circling the Downpost of Empire," *Ariel*, 20, no. 4: 149–75; rpt. in Ashcroft *et al.*, 1995.

Jameson, Fredric. (1991). *Postmodernism, Or, The Cultural Logic of Late Capitalism*. London: Verso.

Jencks, Charles. (1980). *Late Modern Architecture*. London: Academy Editions.

Kellner, Douglas. (1995). *Media Culture: Cultural Studies, Identity and Politics Between the Modern and the Postmodern*. London: Routledge.

Lyotard, Jean-François. (1984). *The Postmodern Condition: A Report on Knowledge*. Manchester: Manchester University Press, 1984.

McClintock, Anne. (1992). "The Angel of Progress: Pitfalls of the Term "Post-colonialism,'" in *Colonial Discourse and Post-Colonial Theory*, eds. Patrick Williams and Laura Chrisman. New York: Harvester Wheatsheaf, 291–304.

McLaren, Peter. (1994). "White Terror and Oppositional Agency: Towards a Critical Multiculturalism," in *Multiculturalism: A Critical Reader*, ed. David Theo Goldberg, Oxford: Blackwell, 45–74.

Mercer, Kobena. (1992). "'1968': Periodizing Postmodern Politics and Identity," in *Cutural Studies*, eds. Lawrence Grossberg, Cary Nelson, and Paul Treichler. London: Routledge, 424–37.

Moore-Gilbert, Bart. (1997). *Postcolonial Theory: Contexts, Practices, Politics*. London: Verso.

Mudimbe, Valentin Y. (1988). *The Invention of Africa: Gnosis, Philosophy and the Order of Knowledge*. Bloomington and London: Indiana University Press and James Currey.

Murphet, Julian. (1998). "Noir and the Racial Unconscious," *Screen*, 39, no. 1: 22–35.

Natoli, Joseph. (1997). *A Primer to Postmodernity*. Oxford: Blackwell.

Ortner, Sherry B. (1984). "Theory in Anthropology since the Sixties," *Comparative Studies in Society and History*, 26, no. 1: 126–66.

Palmer, Bryan D. (1990). *Descent into Discourse: The Reification of Language and the Writing of Social History*. Philadelphia: Temple University Press.

Parry, Benita. (1997). "The Postcolonial: Conceptual Category or Chimera?" In *The Yearbook of English Studies*, 27: 3–21.

Said, Edward. (1978). *Orientalism*. London: Chatto and Windus.

Sangari, Kumkum. (1987). "The Politics of the Possible," *Cultural Critique*, 7: 157–186; rpt. in Ashcroft *et al.*, 1995.

Sekyi, Kobina. (1974). *The Blinkards*. London: Heinemann.

Sekyi-Otu, Ato. (1996). *Fanon's Dialectic of Experience*. Cambridge: Harvard University Press.

Skinner, Quentin. (1985). Introduction to *The Return of Grand Theory in the Human Sciences*. Cambridge: Cambridge University Press.

Slemon, Stephen. (1994) "The Scramble for Post-Colonialism," Ashcroft *et al.*, 1994.

——. (1995). "Magic Realism as Postcolonial Discourse," in *Magic Realism: Theory, History, Community*, eds. Lois Parkinson Zamora and Wendy B. Faris. Durham: Duke University Press.

Sombart, Werner. (1967). *Luxury and Capitalism*, trans. W. R. Dittmar. Ann Arbor: University of Michigan Press.

Stam, Robert and Ella Shohat. (1995). Unthinking Eurocentrism, Multiculturalism and the Media. New York and London: Routledge.

Strathern, Marilyn. (1991). *Partial Connections*. Savage, Md.: Rowman and Littlefield.

Thomas, Nicholas. (1994). *Colonialism's Culture: Anthropology, Travel and Government*. Cambridge: Polity Press.

Tiffin, Helen. (1988). "Post-Colonialism, Post-Modernism and the Rehabilitation of Post-Colonial History," *Journal of Commonwealth Literature*, 23, no. 1: 169–81.

Viswanathan, Gauri. (1990). *Masks of Conquest: Literary Studies and British Rule in India*. London: Faber.

Visweswaran, Kamala. (1994) *Fictions of Feminist Ethnography*. Minneapolis: University of Minnesota Press.

wa Thiong'o, Ngugi. (1986). *Decolonizing the Mind*. London: James Currey.

Williams, Patrick and Laura Chrisman. (1993). Introduction to *Colonial Discourse and Post-Colonial Theory*. New York: Harvester Wheatsheaf.

Žižek, Slavoj. (1991). *Looking Awry: An Introduction to Jacques Lacan Through Popular Culture*. Cambridge: MIT Press.

——. (1997). "Multiculturalism, Or, the Cultural Logic of Multinational Capitalism," *New Left Review*, 225: 29–51.

Chapter 5

Postcolonial Studies in the House of US Multiculturalism

Jenny Sharpe

This essay gives an overview of the institutional history of postcolonial studies in order to provide a map for future developments in the field. More specifically, it locates postcolonial studies within the larger project of US multicultural educational reform. The beginnings of this reform can be traced to the mid-sixties, when the instituting of black and ethnic studies was seen as a way of redressing the historical under-representation of racial minorities in traditionally white colleges. Multiculturalism was expanded during the eighties through a main-streaming of US minority and non–Western cultures into core curriculum. This stage of multicultural educational reform was as much a response to the increased presence of people from Third World countries in the United States as to the historical under-representation of racial minorities in universities. Since many practioners of postcolonial studies belonged to these new immigrant groups, it is not accidental that they began to see an intersection between their field and ethnic studies. The intersection became all the more apparent once critics began using "postcolonial" as a descriptive term for the United States. The nineties, however, introduced a new challenge for multicultural education, that of prepar-ing students for a global economy in which cultural diversity is defined more strongly in international terms. Here we find postcolonial studies at a crossroad. What role will it play in a global multiculturalism? This is the question my essay intends to address.

Since postcolonial studies is not housed in a single discipline or program, it is difficult to pinpoint its exact emergence as an academic field. A single "event" that can be identified as initiating the field is the 1978 publication of Edward W. Said's *Orientalism*. Said described Oriental studies (known today as Middle East or Near Eastern studies) as a Western style of thought and institution of power for exercising control over Arabs and Islam. What was different about this book from previous intellectual histories was that it implicated academic learning in colonialism. By extending Michel Foucault's critique of disciplinary knowledge to Orientalism, Said established connections between images and institutions, the production of knowledge and the securing of power. His highly influential work cleared the space for a new field of study known as "colonial discourse analysis," which later evolved into postcolonial studies. Said's Foucauldian methodology coupled with the poststructuralist training of subsequent critics gave the field its strong theoretical foundation.

If one expands this picture to see what was happening in other parts of the globe, it becomes clear that colonial discourse analysis was part of a larger anticolonial critique. The late seventies was an era in which recently decolonized nations were struggling to find their own identities, and in order to do so they had to break the authority Western culture had over indigenous languages, forms of knowledge, and literary production. In 1977, just one year before Said's study, Kenyan writer Ngugi wa Thiong'o published *Petals of Blood*, his last creative writing in the English language. He announced that he would write all subsequent novels, plays, and children's stories in his native Gĩkũyũ, while continuing to write nonfictional essays in English. His essays, which describe the debilitating effects of colonialism on African culture, appeared as *Decolonising the Mind* (1986), his final nonfictional publication in English. On the other side of the hemisphere, at Carifesta 76 in Jamaica, poet-historian Edward Kamau Brathwaite described how nation language, the creolized speech of the people, was becoming the authoritative language of Caribbean poetic expression.

Unlike criticism from the ex-colonies, which engaged in the two-pronged project of decentering imperial culture while forging emergent national identities from local traditions, Said's study centered on the Western consumption of an imaginary Orient. It took critics like Gayatri Chakravorty Spivak and Homi Bhabha to shift the center of colonial discourse analysis from Europe to its colonies. Spivak, who like Said is trained in Comparative Literature, charted the difficulty of recovering colonized women's subjectivities in the wake of what she called the "epistemic violence" of imperialism. She also introduced into the US academy the writings of the Subaltern Studies group, a collective of intellectuals in Britain, India, and Australia who began working on peasant resistance as an intervention into the seventies nation-state crisis in India. Bhabha, a critic of Commonwealth literary studies in Britain, turned to the writings of Antillean psychoanalyst and guerrilla-activist, Frantz Fanon, for reworking Said's paradigm. In contrast to Said's characterization of "the Orient [as] the stage on which the whole East is confined" (1978: 63), Fanon described how the drama of decolonization disturbed exotic images fixed within the Western imagination. "The Western 'model' is being attacked in its essence and in its finality," he announced in the FLN (Algerian National Liberation Front) newspaper, *El Moudjahid*, in 1958. "The Orientals, the Arabs, and the Negroes, today, want to present their plans, want to affirm their values, want to define their relations with the world" (1970: 125). Combining a Fanonian model of resistance with Lacanian psychoanalytic theory, Bhabha identified in colonial discourse an inherent "ambivalence" that allowed for slippages and native appropriations.

113

The literature of decolonization to which Fanon's writing belongs is often identified as the intellectual antecedent to postcolonial studies. While the process of decolonization has played a central role in shaping the political objectives of the field, it is also important to remember that the writings of Frantz Fanon, C. L. R. James, Aimé Césaire, Amilcar Cabral, Ngũgĩ wa Thiong'o, and Albert Memmi (among others) were geographically and historically removed from the institutional development of postcolonial studies. Unlike the literature of decolonization, which was bound up with the Third World national liberation movements of the sixties and seventies, postcolonial studies is primarily a First World academic discourse of the eighties and nineties. In calling attention to the temporal and geographical distance between anticolonial and academic writing, I do not mean to say that postcolonial studies should be narrowly defined in terms of what is produced in the university. Nor am I arguing that academic discourse has no political efficacy. What I am saying is that the term "postcolonial" has greater currency in imperial centers like Britain and the United States, as well as former settler colonies like Australia, New Zealand, and Canada, than in Third World nations. As such, it is bound up with multicultural education, which is a concern of racially diversified First World nations alone.

US Multiculturalism first made its appearance on college campuses during the late sixties and early seventies through the establishing of Afro-American, American Indian, Chicano, and Asian American Studies programs and centers. Inasmuch as racial minorities and their cultures were excluded from the curriculum of traditionally white colleges, the campuses were a microcosm of segregated America. Student activists drew on the anticolonial writings of Third World liberation movements to suggest that the disenfranchisement of racial minorities was a form of colonization. Rejecting the preexisting national paradigm of immigration and assimilation, they declared the ghettos, barrios, internment camps, and reservations to be the "internal colonies" of the United States. Initiated at San Francisco State College, the coalition of students known as the Third World Movement soon spread to other campuses (Liu, 1976).

Sociologists, together with political activists outside the university, further developed the idea of US racial minorities as internal colonized "nations." They argued that these groups experienced the underdevelopment and dependency of Third World economies. As sociologist Robert Blauner declared in *Racial Oppression in America* (1972: 52): "The third world perspective returns us to the origins of the American experience, reminding us that this nation owes its very existence to colonialism, and that along with settlers and immigrants there have always been conquered Indians and black slaves, and later defeated Mexicans – that is, colonial subjects – on national soil." The *internal colonization model* drew a sharp line between those people who came over to the New World as immigrants and those who were conquered or brought over against their will. In doing so, it drew attention to the racial homogeneity of white colleges as the end-product of a long history of discrimination and unequal opportunities for racial minorities. Multicultural education, in its earliest configuration, was thus seen as a means of redressing the disadvantages racial groups had suffered in the past.

A contending multicultural paradigm emerged in the early seventies. Proponents of cultural pluralism challenged the melting pot hypothesis by claiming that, instead of melding into an undifferentiated nation, social groups maintained distinct ethnic identities to form a nation of nations. The idea of the US nation as a "mosaic" or "quilt" (rather than a melting pot) was paradoxically indebted to the race pride movements but primarily interested in articulating the identities of white ethnics.[1] As a consequence, it blurred the distinction between a *racial identity* formed in opposition to the idea of the United States as a nation of immigrants, and an *ethnic identity* formed around the idea of the United States as a nation of *unmeltable immigrants*. The primacy of ethnic over racial identities expanded the category of historically under-represented groups to include unassimilated immigrants who maintained their unique cultural identities. In this manner, the nation of nations paradigm conflated the divergent histories of native and immigrant populations and homogenized the specific histories of different racial and ethnic groups. The appearance of an ancestry question for the first time in the 1980 Census is but one indication of how this new way of imagining the nation had become the norm.[2]

The legacy of the nation of nations paradigm was a *liberal multiculturalism* that informed the eighties project of introducing minority cultures across the curriculum. Constituted around diversity and difference rather than racism and the unequal distribution of power, liberal multiculturalism weakened the original goals of multicultural education, which were to redress the debilitating effects of racial (and sexual) discrimination. In short, it disassociated multicultural education from questions of affirmative action. Or, conversely, it allowed for the argument that "affirmative action . . . must not be restricted to African-, Asian-, Mexican-, and Native-American writers; it must be extended to include the writers from European ethnic groups that have historically been ignored or marginalized by the Anglo–American literary-academic establishment" (Oliver, 1991: 806).

In many instances, the canon wars that dominated the eighties were not only fought over whether marginalized cultures should be mainstreamed into Western and American civilization courses, which is how the debates are generally described. They were also fought over whether a radical or liberal paradigm should predominate. There were those who argued in favor of multiculturalism being determined according to questions of race and gender hierarchies. Others defined diversity as the representation of different ethnic minority cultures rather than a corrective to a history of racial and sexual exclusion. The liberal paradigm won and, during the eighties, multicultural education became rearticulated as a means of enabling students to cope in an increasingly diversified workplace.

As a field that emerged during the eighties, postcolonial studies entered the fray of the canon wars. Critics took up the challenge of "moving the center" of

Western civilization (to use Ngugi's phrase) by demonstrating the existence of multiple centers that could not be reduced to a Universal Subject. They showed how this Subject had been historically constituted through a colonial civilizing mission that sought to remake the rest of the world in the image of the West. On being confronted with the limitations of simply identifying colonial structures of power and knowledge, critics turned to non-Western literature and systems of thought as alternative frames of reference.[3] What began as colonial discourse analysis, the study of Western power and domination, was subsequently reshaped as postcolonial studies, which addressed minority discourses, nationalisms, and cultural identities following the end of Empire. But, even as I describe the shift from colonial discourse analysis to postcolonial studies as being initiated by intellectuals, I also want to stress that it is not so easy to disentangle their critical interventions from the institutional demands placed on them.

Most scholars who consider themselves postcolonial literary critics were hired by English departments to teach the Anglophone writings of Britain's ex-colonies. (Although I am restricting my discussion to my own discipline, a similar pattern of hiring exists in other institutional sites of postcolonial studies, which are comparative literature, history, anthropology, and some area studies.) A glance at any English department's course offerings will reveal that Third World literatures are now essential to the curriculum. Their inclusion represents an effort to reshape British literature in the same way that the canon of American literature was transformed by the introduction of racial minority literatures. In this regard, postcolonial literature belongs to the larger multicultural project of introducing cultural diversity across the curriculum. At the same time, the tendency of universities to identify diasporic Third World intellectuals with the literatures they teach extends to postcolonial studies the identity politics of US minority programs, even though there are no affirmative-action policies behind such hirings. This practice has led to some confusion as to the exact relationship of postcolonial studies to black and ethnic studies.

Despite the formal resemblances between postcolonial and black/ethnic studies, it is important to remember that they do not share the same institutional history. Postcolonial studies did not emerge in response to student demands or a political activism that spilled over onto college campuses. Rather, it constitutes an institutional reform "from within." In order to develop a multicultural curriculum that included the Anglophone writings of the ex-colonies, English departments (whose decision-makers often did not include the practioners of postcolonial studies) turned to the preexisting field of Commonwealth Studies. Initiated at the Leeds conference of 1964, Commonwealth Studies was formed around the English-language literature of Africa, Australia, Canada, South Asia, New Zealand, and the West Indies. For intellectuals in Britain's ex-colonies laboring under the hegemony of "Englishness," Commonwealth Studies brought recognition to the vast body of national literatures in English that had previously been ignored. Institutionally, however, Commonwealth Literature was more often than not treated as marginal (and, by implication, inferior) to English literature. Hence, when postcolonial studies began to emerge in the United States, Commonwealth literary critics saw an opportunity to bring greater legitimacy to their field.

Bill Ashcroft, Gareth Griffiths, and Helen Tiffin, who teach at universities in Australia and New Zealand, co-authored the first primer on postcolonial studies, *The Empire Writes Back* (1989). They explain that the term "postcolonial," which emphasizes an "after" to colonialism, is preferable to "Commonwealth," which subordinates the ex-colonies to the old imperial center. They also extend the category of "the postcolonial" to include the United States because "its relationship with the metropolitan centre as it evolved over the last two centuries has been paradigmatic for post-colonial literature everywhere" (1989: 2). Ashcroft *et al.* do not explain exactly how the United States serves as a paradigm for ex-colonies *everywhere*, and their statement appears to be more relevant to former settler colonies like Australia and New Zealand than territorial colonies in Asia, Africa, and the Caribbean. When used to describe *all* cultures that have come through the colonial experience, "postcolonial" elides the unequal distribution of power between European immigrants and the indigenous populations of the lands they settled, and conflates different forms of colonization.

There exists a similar homogenization of colonial cultures in Commonwealth literary critics' use of the term to describe Third World peoples inhabiting the imperial centers. Their designation of Western Europe as "postcolonial" signals how decolonization initiated an unprecedented migration of peoples from the ex-colonies to metropolitan centers. For example, in *The Location of Culture*, Bhabha characterizes Britain as a postcolonial nation in order to draw attention to a repressed colonial past that is responsible for problems appearing to have originated with the arrival of "immigrants," a term reserved for nonpatrial (i.e. non-white) immigrants alone. Yet, he also employs the condition of the Third World migrant as a theoretical model for explaining *all* colonized cultures, past and present. When Bhabha offers Toni Morrison's *Beloved* as an instance of the "transnational histories of migrants, the colonized, or political refugees" (1994: 12), he brings the diasporic experience of African slaves into a narrative of postwar urban migration. The editors of Columbia University Press's *Colonial Discourse and Post-Colonial Theory: A Reader* similarly collapse the history of US racism into that of Europe's overseas empires when they feature writings by African American critics under the rubric of "postcolonial" as a category that "includes diasporic communities, 'ethnic minority' communities within the overdeveloped world as well as formerly colonized national cultures" (Williams and Chrisman, 1994: 373). Routledge's *Post-Colonial Studies Reader*, edited by Ashcroft *et al.*, also includes African American critical writings. While Blacks in Britain, who are immigrants from its former colonies, might properly be called "postcolonial," the term does not accurately describe Black America.

It is easy for those of us working within postcolonial studies to forget that the internal colonization model was developed in response to immigration as a national paradigm. Since people from Third World countries now inhabit the

United States, the migrant can all too easily become the figure of racial exclusion. In this manner, a prior history is written over (or worse yet, appropriated). Ruth Frankenberg and Lata Mani argue against using "postcolonial" as a descriptive term for the United States because it does not fully capture the history of a white settler colony that appropriated land from Native Americans, incorporated parts of Mexico, imported slaves and indentured labor from Africa and Asia, and whose foreign policy in East Asia, the Philippines, Central and Latin America, and the Caribbean accounts, in part, for its new immigrants. They suggest *post-Civil Rights* as a parallel to the anti-colonial struggles that define the "after" to colonialism, although they admit that the term is inadequate for explaining the experience of recent immigrants and refugees (1993: 293). If *postcolonial* is to have any descriptive force at all, we need to account for uneven historical formations and dispersed geographical locales rather than think in terms of a simple center/margins opposition.

Many of the epistemological problems with an academic use of "postcolonial" have been imported from Commonwealth Studies. By uniting the cultures of such diverse regions as Kenya, Nigeria, India, Australia, Canada, and Jamaica, it ignores historical differences between the nations that emerged from decolonization. Since there is nothing that holds these cultures together other than their past relationship to England, it re-centers their cultures around Europe. For this reason, Salman Rushdie calls the category of Commonwealth Literature a chimera, "a monster . . . composed of elements which could not possibly be joined together in the real world" (1991: 63). Does postcolonial studies risk becoming an imaginary beast of this sort? Critics from within the field seem to think so.

In her pointed critique of an academic use of "postcolonial," Anne McClintock shows how the colonial/postcolonial division defines global relations according to a binary axis of time rather than power. As an organizing principle, postcolonialism not only provides an imaginative geography that recenters Europe, it also elides the uneven development of colonialism, particularly the emergence of the United States as an imperial power and its replacement of Britain as a center. In this regard, a field that developed as a critique of colonialism renders invisible the neocolonial relations into which the ex-colonies entered. In their haste to name a postcolonial-*ism*, critics reintroduced the colonial systems of knowledge they were seeking to escape.

Spivak indicates that the teaching of postcolonial literatures, in its current form, has failed to dislodge a colonial value system. Indicating how a canon of Third World Literature in translation serves as a "new orientalism," she advises that the study of colonial and postcolonial discourse not be undertaken within the discipline of English. Instead, she suggests revising Comparative Literature into an interdisciplinary program – a *transnational cultural studies* – that couples English with, say, History or African Studies and which requires the study of at least one "colonized vernacular" language (1993: 277). Arjun Appadurai also recommends that postcolonial studies be reconfigured as a transnational cultural studies. Speaking from within the discipline of Anthropology, where the study of vernacular languages is required, he is more concerned about the presumed equation of postcoloniality with the ex-colonies. Since he sees this equation as a form of containing the Third World as exotic cultures existing "out there," he suggests a *postnational approach* that draws attention to the Third World within the United States.

Appadurai's caveat is that theoretical models derived from the study of nations and empires cannot account for a postindustrial culture of *transnationalisms* and *diasporas*. Transnationalism denotes the permeability of national borders in the electronic transmission of capital, labor, technology, and media images. Diaspora designates the political and economic refugees, Third World immigrant and exile communities that inhabit advanced industrial and newly-industrializing nations and city-states. Since travel and telecommunications permit immigrants to maintain close ties with their countries of origin, they exist as transnational diasporas that do not assimilate into the nation. Appadurai concludes that postcolonial critics should enter debates on US racism, affirmative action, and multiculturalism in order to show that the idea of the United States as an autonomous and self-contained nation is no longer tenable. His argument is a response to the nativism and xenophobia of the nineties, a decade characterized by a withholding of social services to noncitizens and increased patrolling of the Mexican-American border. Yet, one also has to contend with what this anti-immigrant sentiment means if one considers that a 1990 Immigration Reform Act has tripled the quotas for skilled immigrants, most of whom are from Asia. The priority given to skill over national origins shows that corporate America is willing to tolerate some degree of diversity.

Arif Dirlik and Masao Miyoshi are less convinced that the diasporic diversity of immigrant communities goes against the grain of the cultural dominant. Dirlik reminds us that the earliest advocates of multiculturalism were business administrators and managers of transnational corporations (TNCs), because in today's global market diversity (defined in international rather than national terms) makes good economic sense (1994: 354–5). Miyoshi observes that transnational identities are not necessarily the answer to the democratic failures of the nation-state when TNCs "are at least officially and superficially trained to be color-blind and multicultural" (1993: 741). Diasporic communities may threaten the integrity of the US nation, but this does not mean that they disrupt the interlinked economies of North America, Europe, and Japan (with Taiwan, Hong Kong, and Singapore as their junior partners). TNCs rely on a transnational class of professionals who can move freely between First and Third World cultures. Miyoshi concludes that postcolonial studies should be demonstrating how, instead of liberating ex-colonials from the nation, globalization has intensified colonialism.

There is some value to Appadurai's contention that postcolonial critics should be concerned with US racism, multiculturalism, and affirmative action.

Unassimilated immigrants from Third World countries represent a demographic shift that figured into the eighties reform if not the actual debates on multi-cultural education. Take, for example, the SUNY-Buffalo report on its 1991 decision to introduce an American Pluralism course requirement. It justifies the course with statistics from demographers who predict that by the year 2000, 85 percent of the workforce will consist of women, minorities, and immigrants. Citing one demographer's reaction to the 1990 Census, the report states that "cultural diversity probably accelerated more in the 1980s than in any other decade." What made the United States more of a multicultural society in the eighties – a transformation that universities felt compelled to address – was the existence of large communities of immigrants from Third World countries. The eighties, the economic boom years during which the US demand for immigrant labor reached its peak, are now called "the decade of immigration" (Usdansky). The SUNY-Buffalo report is telling inasmuch as it demonstrates that multicultural education was not simply a response to the historical under-representation of racial minorities but also the presence of new immigrant groups. The sudden emergence of these new ethnicities was the result of immigration laws introduced since the mid-sixties.

Following fast on the passage of the 1964 Civil Rights Act, the 1965 Immigration and Nationality Act, which became effective on July 1, 1968, reversed earlier legislation that restricted the immigration of non-Europeans. Prior to 1965, race was a determining factor for laws that prevented the unification of non-European families. The new law eliminated prior restrictions by assigning a uniform quota for all countries in the Eastern and Western hemispheres and giving special preferences to immigrants who were technically skilled or had capital to invest, regardless of race. It also included provisions for political refugees. Policy-makers at the time did not anticipate any dramatic change in the racial make-up of immigrants. Instead, they saw the reform as social redress for Catholics and Jews from southern and eastern Europe who were also affected by the 1924 Immigration Act, which established quotas for northern European nations alone (Glazer, 1985: 7). They were unprepared for the demographic shift that would take place.

Asians, Central Americans, Mexicans, and Caribbeans now comprise 80 percent of all immigrants to the United States. Because of preferences given to business and professional classes there is also, for the first time, a sizable population of educated urban middle-class immigrants, particularly from Asia. This class has a social and financial interest in maintaining close ties with their countries of origin, thereby forming satellite communities that resist an assimilation into dominant American culture. Women also constitute a larger percentage of the immigrants than ever before, a factor that has contributed to diasporic communities being able to maintain their cultural autonomy. Since post-1965, immigrants experience a racism having less to do with the slaveholding or colonial past of the United States than its possession of overseas colonies, its policies in the Third World, and anti-immigrant sentiments during times of economic hardship. The failure of the radical multicultural paradigm can, in part, be attributed to its inability to account for these new social groups.

The weakness of the internal colonization model is that, by equating immigration with assimilation and colonization with racial exclusion, it draws too sharp a distinction between voluntary and involuntary movements of populations. Asian Americans, for whom immigration was voluntary but who nonetheless experienced racism, have always had an ambivalent relationship to the model. Unable to explain their condition as simply colonized, Blauner is forced to call the ghettos in which Chinese-owned businesses exploited other Chinese, "neocolonial enclaves" (1972: 88). Since the analogy between American racism and European colonialism was a politically strategic move designed to harness the language of decolonization, his argument is now judged to be "politically not analytically grounded" (Omi and Winant, 1994: 50).

Asian American studies is in the process of rethinking the internal colonization model on which it was founded. Twenty-five years ago most Asian Americans were descendants of unskilled Chinese and Japanese workers who came over prior to 1924; today, the majority are foreign-born. Asian Americans have gone from being an under-represented to becoming an over-represented minority in American universities, particularly in California, where the majority of post-1965 Asian immigrants reside. Hence, it is not accidental that this particular racial group has served as a "model minority" in the effort to end affirmative action. The anti-affirmative action lobby holds up the success of Asian Americans as a model for other minorities to overcome the racial discrimination (coded as economic disadvantages) they face. What this argument fails to recognize is that many of the successful Asian Americans belong to the class of immigrants who have benefited from the preferences given to professionals and entrepreneurs. Moreover, as critics of the model minority hypothesis point out, the grouping together of people from diverse historical and economic backgrounds permits the media to present successful sectors of the Asian population as representative of the larger community as such. The visibility of successful groups renders invisible (and without access to social services) those members who are economically impoverished.

The term *Asian American* no longer holds together a diverse group that includes, not only American-born Chinese and Japanese, but also skilled Chinese immigrants and undocumented sweatshop workers, Filipino and Korean small business owners, as well as Vietnamese, Hmong, and Mien refugees. Asian emigration to the United States also cannot be understood in the absence of US imperialism in Hawaii, Vietnam, and the Philippines and its economic relations with Taiwan, South Korea, and, more recently, the People's Republic of China. For intellectuals working in Asian American studies, the global frame of race politics and ethnic identities is impossible to ignore.[4]

Postcolonial critics, particularly those of South Asian descent, are also interested in bridging the gap between postcolonial and ethnic studies. For example, Inderpal Grewal addresses the status of Bharati Mukherjee's novel *Jasmine*, whose protagonist emigrates from India to the United States, as a standard text for ethnic literatures and Asian American courses. She makes a case for situating the ethnic American novel within the global relations of the modern Indian nation-state so that its antiracist perspective on American culture can be read alongside its conservative class, caste, and regional position on Indian culture. The fact that *Jasmine* is included in Asian American literature courses speaks to the visible presence of Indian Americans as a new ethnicity since 1965. Alluding to the communities of South Asian immigrants, R. Radhakrishnan agrees with Appadurai that postcolonial studies should be concerned with "the third world within" the United States. However, he sees the free-floating status of diasporic subjectivities as working against forming political constituencies and, for this reason, makes a case for the positive value of ethnic identities (1996: 155–84). Radhakrishnan concludes that the "postcolonial–diasporic–ethnic conjuncture" can open up new utopian spaces by forcing the United States to remember its own settler colonial and slaveholding past that has engendered the current conditions of oppression (xxvi).

Given its history of imported slave and contract labor, continental expansion, and overseas imperialism, an implication of the United States in postcolonial studies is perhaps long overdue. As Amy Kaplan points out in her introduction to *Cultures of United States Imperialism*, American culture is equally absent from the postcolonial study of empires as a discussion of imperialism is missing from the study of American culture. Yet, even as postcolonial studies has expanded its scope to include the United States, it has not addressed its status as an imperial power, past or present. Rather, the post-1965 immigrant has become the privileged object of critical attention.

It is possible to describe the shift in center of postcolonial studies, from decolonized space to "the third world within" the United States, as an outcome of the contradictory demands of multicultural education. The institutional requirement that diasporic Third World intellectuals represent the cultures of their countries of origin unwittingly introduced the identity politics of black and ethnic studies to the field. Since most postcolonial critics are first or second generation immigrants, they rearticulated this institutional demand in terms of an identity politics based on their own diasporic or immigrant experience. This is perhaps why Dirlik observes that the term "postcolonial" designates less the emergence of a field than the arrival of Third World intellectuals in First World universities. He is critical of a conflation of the field with its practitioners and argues for distinguishing the use of "postcolonial" as a description of intellectuals from "postcolonial" as a description of global relations (1994: 330–1).

Spivak is equally critical of a naming that permits diasporic intellectuals in American universities to represent the margins. In particular, she is concerned with how the paradigmatic status of the race, class, and gender oppression of the Third World migrant obscures the contingency of neocolonialism upon the cooperation of indigenous elites in the Third World proper (1993: 55–7). Dirlik and Spivak observe that once the term "postcolonial" becomes detached from decolonized space, the global is generalized from the local, which allows the latter to act in its place. Although the objective of a postnational approach was to bring the Third World into the imperial center, its effect has been to further marginalize the ex-colonies.

Where does this leave postcolonial studies today? In its current configuration, the field is pulled between questions of ethnicity and those of globalization, although they may well be two sides to the same coin. If, as postcolonial critics, we are going to claim ethnic identities, then we need to be all the more attentive to the specific histories of such identities, or else we risk playing into a liberal multiculturalism that obfuscates the category of race. Although liberal multiculturalism was initiated in the white ethnicity movement, it is being reconfigured to accommodate globalism. With the erosion of affirmative action, diversity on college campuses is being redefined in international rather than national terms. In his study of how the logic of global markets has influenced the running of universities. Bill Readings predicts that, as the nation-state becomes less important, the humanities will no longer be charged with the mission of producing citizen-subjects for the nation but rather, multicultural subjects for transnational corporations. What part will postcolonial studies play in a global multiculturalism? I have mapped the emergence of the field onto that of US multiculturalism in order to demonstrate that a discourse on postcolonialism, transnationalism, and globalization are First World concerns. In so-called developing parts of the world, the problems of nation and neocolonialism have not gone away. To begin with that simple acknowledgment is to ensure that postcolonial studies not become a new universalism of the sort it was established to critique.

Notes

1 My discussion of the white ethnicity movement is from an unpublished paper by Jeffrey Louis Decker, "Blood Lines: The 1970s Movement for White Ethnicity."
2 Although the impulse behind the ancestry question was to bring race under the hegemony of an ethnic identity, its instructions reveal the limits to the immigrant paradigm on which the idea of ethnic identities is based. A history of colonial conquest, which accounts for the misnaming of the indigenous peoples, is visible in the demand for specificity: "If ancestry is 'Indian,' specify whether American Indian, Asian Indian, or West Indian." The examples for different ancestries provided – "Afro-Amer., English, French, German, Honduran, Hungarian, Irish, Italian, Jamaican, Korean, Lebanese, Mexican, Nigerian, Polish, Ukrainian, Venezuelan, etc." – denote the absence a country of origins for Afro-Americans but not Afro-Caribbeans. While the descendants of slaves on the mainland cannot be made to conform to an immigrant paradigm, those who have emigrated from the islands split the racial identity of Black America.

3   The problem should be familiar to anyone who has attempted to teach Conrad's *Heart of Darkness* without the accompanying reversal of perspective offered by Chinua Achebe's *Things Fall Apart*. African culture and history, indeed its humanity, have been so successfully effaced that students have no conceptual framework with which to understand the colonial encounter other than the highly circumscribed one of Conrad's novel.

4   See Sau-Ling Wong's excellent evaluation of the shift in Asian American studies from a cultural nationalist to a diasporic perspective.

References

Appadurai, A. (1993). "The Heart of Whiteness," *Callaloo*, 16: 796–807.

Ashcroft, B., G. Griffiths, and H. Tiffin. (1989). *The Empire Writes Back: Theory and Practice in Post-Colonial Literatures*. New York: Routledge.

——, ——, and ——. (1995). *The Post-Colonial Studies Reader*. New York: Routledge.

Bhabha, H. K. (1994). *The Location of Culture*. New York: Routledge.

Blauner, R. (1972). *Racial Oppression in America*. New York: Harper.

Brathwaite, E. K. (1984). *History of the Voice: The Development of Nation Language in Anglophone Caribbean Poetry*. London: New Beacon.

Dirlik, A. (1994). "The Postcolonial Aura: Third World Criticism in the Age of Global Capitalism," *Critical Inquiry*, 20: 328–56.

Fanon, F. (1970). *Toward the African Revolution*. (H. Chevalier, Trans.). Harmondsworth: Penguin (Original work published 1964).

Frankenberg, R. and L. Mani. (1993). "Crosscurrents, Crosstalk: Race, 'Postcoloniality' and the Politics of Location," *Cultural Studies*, 7: 292–310.

Glazer, N., ed. (1985). *Clamor at the Gates: The New American Immigration*. San Francisco: Institute for Contemporary Studies.

Kaplan, A. and D. Pease, eds. (1993). *Cultures of United States Imperialism*. Durham: Duke University Press.

Liu, J. (1976). "Towards an Understanding of the Internal Colonial Model," in *Counterpoint: Perspectives on Asian America*, ed. Emma Gee. Los Angeles: Asian American Studies Center, UCLA, 160–8.

McClintock, A. (1992). "The Angel of Progress: Pitfalls of the Term 'Post-Colonialism,'" *Social Text*, 31/32: 84–98.

Miyoshi, M. (1993). "A Borderless World? From Colonialism to Transnationalism and the Decline of the Nation-State," *Critical Inquiry*, 19: 726–51.

Ngũgĩ wa Thiong'o. (1977). *Petals of Blood*. London: Heinemann.

——. (1986). *Decolonising the Mind: The Politics of Language in African Literature*. London: James Currey.

Oliver, L. J. (1991). "Deconstruction or Affirmative Action: The Literary-Political Debate over the 'Ethnic Question,'" *American Literary History*, 3: 792–808.

Omi, M. and H. Winant. (1994). *Racial Formation in the United States: From the 1960s to the 1990s*. New York: Routledge.

Radhakrishnan, R. (1996). *Diasporic Mediations: Between Home and Location*. Minneapolis: University of Minnesota Press.

Readings, B. (1996). *The University in Ruins*. Cambridge: Harvard University Press.

Rushdie, S. (1991). "'Commonwealth Literature' Does Not Exist," in *Imaginary Homelands: Essays and Criticism 1981–1991*. London: Granta, 61–70.

Said, E. W. (1978). *Orientalism*. New York: Vintage.

Spivak, G. C. (1993). *Outside in the Teaching Machine*. New York: Routledge.

Usdansky, M. (1992). "'Diverse' Fits Nation Better than 'Normal,'" *USA Today*, 29–30 May: 1A; 6A–7A.

Williams, P. and L. Chrisman, eds. (1994). *Colonial Discourse and Post-Colonial Theory: A Reader*. New York: Columbia University Press.

Wong, S. C. (1995). "Denationalization Reconsidered: Asian American Cultural Criticism at a Theoretical Crossroads," *Amerasia Journal*, 21, nos. 1 & 2: 1–27.

Chapter 6

Global Capital and Transnationalism

Crystal Bartolovich

"Every boundary line is a myth."[1]

Wilson Harris

"The need for a constantly expanding market for its products chases the bourgeoisie over the whole surface of the globe. It must nestle everywhere, settle everywhere, establish connections everywhere."

Karl Marx and Friedrich Engels

The cover of a recent issue of the mass market London entertainment weekly *Time Out* featured a refashioned tube (subway) symbol (a red circle with a blue horizontal bar bisecting it), in which the red from the circle had been evacuated and replaced by a representation of the perimeter of a globe; "The World" was printed across the bar, where station stops are usually designated. Below this transformed symbol a caption suggested: "Travel the globe without leaving London." Inside the magazine this theme is further developed and we learn that "what's really making the capitol's pulse race is not the Britishness of it, but the unfamiliar and the exotic." Then we are offered an "insider's guide to the . . . most exotic restaurants, bars, shops and sites," organized according to ethnicities. The magazine also includes a "round the world" (without leaving London) tour with Michael Palin (of BBC travel show fame), which offers "stops" in the "West Indies" (Brixton), " Armenia" (Kensington), "Iran" (Olympia), "Japan" (Colindale), "India" (Neasden), "Poland" (South Kensington), "Africa" (Covent Garden), and "South America" (Shaftesbury Avenue). In this fantasy, London is not simply the center of the world, it *is* the world.

I begin with this description of a (very ordinary) issue of *Time Out* to foreground for readers what they probably already know: it is difficult to pick up a magazine or newspaper – not to mention a corporate annual report – these days without being confronted with the discourse of "globalization," a term which – in mainstream and academic venues alike – typically refers to a process Roland Robertson (1992) has described as "the compression of the world into a single place (6).[2] If London can contain "Africa" and "South America" within itself, continental drift surely has taken on a whole new meaning. And the discourse of "globalization" implies that this process is ubiquitous (if uneven – which I will come to in a bit) – that is to say that "London" is in "South America" as well as vice versa. As popular forms of this discourse have proliferated since its emergence in the 1970s, so, too, have theoretical explanations in the universities.[3] Conjuring up an image of a decentered, multiply-determined world, postcolonial theorist Arjun Appadurai (1996) has proposed that "we begin to think of the configuration of cultural forms . . . as fundamentally fractal, that is, as possessing no Euclidean boundaries, structures, or regularities" (46). Boundaries persist – such as those of nation-states – but these boundaries are insufficient to contain or explain *culture* as flows of people, images, technologies, ideologies, and capital spill over traditional political boundaries and create novel "uncertain landscapes" through their complex interaction (43).[4]

Alternatively, from a specifically Marxist perspective, Fredric Jameson (1988) attributes the boundary-troubling of globalization to the expansive dynamic of capitalism alone, which in his view has – through (neo)colonialism – interconnected the world in such a way that: "the truth of [subjective] experience no longer coincides with the place in which it takes place. The truth of that limited daily experience of London [for example] lies, rather, in India or Jamaica or Hong Kong" (349). The expansive and intensive thrust of capital not only fractures subjective experience as it penetrates into more and more areas of everyday life, but it undermines the quintessential spatial forms of modernity in the process, transforming the city and the nation-state into "ruined archaic remnants of earlier stages in the development of capital" (350). "Strong" globalization theorists (of whom Jameson and Appadurai are only two of many), varied as they are in their political and theoretical commitments, tend to see the nation-state as imperiled or outmoded at the current conjuncture due to the collective impact of *transnational* forces such as the global, computer-aided circulation of credit, capital, currency, and information, the movements of diaspora populations, the intermixing of commodified fragments of distant cultures, the beaming of media images simultaneously into vastly separated households, the escalation in awareness of environmental threats which refuse to respect state borders, the availability (and increased use) of swift means of transportation and communication, the stocking of store shelves with commodities whose routes of production read like the itineraries of a world tour, as well as the putative decline of resistance to the global reach of "free market" (or "neoliberal") capitalism with the implosion of Soviet communism – forces which have produced a world that a recent UN report described as ("for the first time in human history") a " single, unified global system" (74).[5]

However, in spite (or perhaps because) of the pervasiveness of globalization discourses, and the fervor of the strongest claims, "globalization" – including its progress, timeline, and effects – is a hotly disputed concept. For example, while Appadurai and Jameson share a view of the nation-state as a less significant space today than in the past, they disagree about whether a single force (capitalism) or multiple autonomous forces (diaspora, communications, etc.) have produced this effect.[6] Other unsettled questions among theorists of "globalization" include even the most fundamental ones: Does it really exist in so dramatic a form as claimed? If so, what are its main aspects? If not, why is something called "globalization" on everyone's lips? Is it really new?[7] And, most importantly, is the nation–state really at risk in our supposedly "globalizing" world? This latter question will most concern me here, as it gets to the heart of the question begged by the title of this chapter: is "global" capital "*trans*national"? This is to say, has capitalism in its most recent form somehow transcended the strictures of the nation–state which had been so important to its development – as commentators as diverse as Robert Reich (1992), Kinichi Ohmae (1990), Arjun Appadurai, and Fredric Jameson suggest? A focus on the "nation" is also a compelling way to examine "globalization" for the purposes of this volume, since it is the site of one of the most intensive (and revealing) disagreements between current trends in Marxist and postcolonial theorizations. While there are proponents of "strong globalization" almost everywhere, including within Marxism (as Jameson's remarks cited above indicate), there has been a strong return to interest among Marxists recently in the *power* of the nation–state, as indicated by studies which examine the efforts of some states to maintain privileged positions in the New World Order as well as those which foreground the potential resistance to "global" forces which states can provide. On the other hand, much postcolonial theory remains committed to interrogating the nation–state as a unit of analysis and a political form, claiming that it gives rise to dangerous myths of "pure culture" and remains within a "binary logic." These views are not *necessarily* mutually exclusive, but they *do* correspond to very different theoretical commitments and levels of analysis, and the reasons for these different emphases are important and need to be noted, especially since the history of nationalist struggles for decolonization and a history of internationalism in Marxism, might have encouraged one to predict exactly the opposite developments in the two groups.

As is no doubt now evident to students of "postcolonial" studies, the debates around "globalization" intersect at numerous points with the field's concerns to the extent that it has focused on global inequalities and how they are effected and maintained. In the inaugural issue of the journal *Interventions*, for example, Robert Young (1998/9) explicitly describes postcolonial studies as: "a certain kind of interdisciplinary political, theoretical and historical academic work that sets out to serve as a transnational forum for studies grounded in the historical context of colonialism, as well as in the political context of contemporary problems of globalization" (4). These themes are plainly visible even in the field's "founding" texts. *Orientalism*, for example, tracks what Edward Said (1979) calls the "worldwide hegemony of imperialism," and insists on the importance of taking a "worldwide" perspective to understand historical conditions even in a "local" site, a view which, in a variety of forms, has persisted in postcolonial criticism and theory (328). The other widely recognized senior figures in the field, Gayatri Spivak and Homi Bhabha, too, have touched upon the themes of "globalization." Spivak has done so explicitly, especially in her concerns with the "international division of labor" and the place of subaltern women in it.[8] Bhabha's influence, alternatively, has been to encourage a tendency to examine problems of "globalization" by way of issues of identity, hybridity, and diaspora in postcolonial studies. This perspective has prevailed – in a variety of forms – over the binarism of Said's early work, which has given way to an interest in cultural intermixing, syncretism, and creolization throughout much of the field.[9] Indeed, some of the most influential recent interventions in the study of "globalization" have been contributed by theorists associated with postcolonial studies *and* a critique of binary thinking, including not only Arjun Appadurai, but also Stuart Hall, Paul Gilroy, and Kobena Mercer. All of this work shows the mark of the various "post" theories which have emerged in the years following the Second World War (postcolonial, postmarxist, poststructuralist, and postmodernist).

It also follows in the wake of the radical social and political disruptions of mid-century, the various reactionary countermovements (Thatcherism, Reaganism) which succeeded them, as well as the hyperproduction of "globalization" discourse in popular and scholarly venues in the 1980s.[10] The "postwar" period saw a continuation of war on many different fronts. Anticolonial struggles were the most prominent of these, but turmoil unsettled the "most developed" nations, too, as the so-called "New Social Movements" against racism, sexism, homophobia, nuclear annihilation, and environmental degradation, among other injustices and problems, emerged. Old verities, especially the revolutionary vanguard role of the Western working class, were called into question, not only by the proliferation of struggles and the seeming cooptation of the Western working class by the pleasures of consumerism, but also by the apparent assumption of the revolutionary task by "Third World" peoples. Out of the decolonization movements came the stirring insurgent voices of Frantz Fanon, Aimé Césaire, Amilcar Cabral, Ngugi wa Thiong'o, and numerous other revolutionary intellectuals attempting to come to terms with the legacy of colonialism and the continuing efforts to forge new nations once the Europeans were thrust out of official meddling in affairs of state if not the economy.

"Language," "culture," and "nation" were their battlegrounds as well as the economy and state, as colonized peoples worked to extricate themselves from a colonial *system* of oppression which had infiltrated their everyday lives: labor relations and language, state and psyche. As Cabral (1994) put it: "national liberation is necessarily an act of culture" since "to dominate a people is, above all, to take up arms to destroy, or at least to neutralize, to paralyze, its cultural life." In the Western nations, at this same time a rather different conquest by culture was underway as capitalism intensified its encroachment into more and more aspects of everyday life via consumer appeals and the power of the media, until even "identity" politics were tapped as "lifestyles."[11] These two "cultural" crises – "North" and "South" – converged as diaspora flows from the former colonies altered the social landscape of the imperial nations (and media images of capital – if not capital itself – trickled into the former colonies). Margaret Thatcher, among other leaders, were able to manipulate the anxieties provoked under such conditions, turning "culture" into a major political issue; "culture wars" erupted around the globe in various forms as groups (re)defined themselves along religious, ethnic, racial, and "moral" lines. I am *not* suggesting either that "cultural" issues (in some narrow sense) were exclusive or paramount in decolonization or even for the New Social Movements, nor am I suggesting that "culture" means the same thing in both instances. I am simply pointing out that "culture" was the idiom in which many economic, political, and social struggles were waged, both in and out of the industrialized world, in the postwar period. Poststructuralist and postmodernist theorists surveyed at least the Euro–US parts of this terrain, especially the ferment and disappointments of 1968, and turned their attention increasingly to cultural matters, since that appeared to be where the action was. For advocates of this shift (e.g. Ernesto Laclau), poststructuralism opened up politics to new possibilities for democratic coalition and freed subjects from reified roles and practices.[12] For critics (e.g. Perry Anderson), however, poststructuralism seemed to announce the death of the political as such.[13]

The impact of the cultural and textual turn on postcolonial studies can hardly be overestimated. I have outlined (in very broad strokes) above two distinct, but interconnected processes: decolonization and the rise of the New Social Movements as well as the "cultural" concerns of each, because both underwrite the emergence of postcolonial studies, to which this volume is devoted. Without decolonization and diaspora, there would be no postcolonial studies as we know it in the Western academy; ditto for identity politics and poststructuralism. Edward Said's *Orientalism* spawned a large number of colonial *discourse* analyses, drawing to greater or lesser degree on Foucault, while the prominence of Homi Bhabha's and Gayatri Spivak's work assured that at least some attention was given to Lacan and Derrida as well – or at least to problems of subjectivity, language, and textuality. The problematizing of the "colonizer/colonized" binary – and the nation – follows from these developments and parallels debates about "ideology" within Marxism, especially as it relates to "consumption" and "reception." Whereas older models of ideology within Marxism had emphasized the "duping" of the "oppressed" by the "oppressors," more recent models in the area of cultural studies, including the sites in which it overlaps with postcolonial studies, have instead emphasized the flexible and interactive nature of ideology – drawing on Althusser's Marxism and Gramsci's theory of hegemony.[14] Just as "ideology" began to be depicted as (at least) a two-way street, so too did the culture of colonialism – and not only in the sense that the preexisting conditions, responses, resistances, and independent initiatives of the colonized shaped their society as much as the activities and directives of the colonizer, but also in the sense that the colonial encounter had effects on the colonizer's "home" society as well. Hence, in studies of both colonial culture and globalization, the emphasis in postcolonial studies has been on undermining the notion that "culture" is an effect of a unilateral imposition. To the contrary, culture is depicted as a site of active intermixing and transcoding of novel elements in "local" terms. Growing up out of a soil fertilized with poststructuralist critiques of subjectivity and anthropological critiques of "authenticity," this strand of postcolonial theory insists on the "hybridity" of all cultures, the irreducible dividedness of subjectivity and constructedness, and the contingency of "identity."

At the moment that postcolonial theory was increasingly turning its attention to the "micropolitics" of subjectivity, however, the specific crisis which ushers in the moment of emergence of globalization discourses in the mid-1970s, was decidedly macro and politico-economic: a shift in the postwar global balance of power dominated by the US.[15] Most significantly, currency markets were deregulated, which gave individual nations, even the US, far less control over their own currencies, at the same time as it opened up additional options for speculators. Furthermore, while the US was unquestionably the preeminent capitalist industrial power during the period in which Europe and Japan (as well as the Soviet Union) were struggling to rebuild their war-ravaged countries, by the 1970s, infrastructures had been rebuilt, home markets saturated, and capacity (and motivation) for economic competition with the US (at least on the part of Europe and Japan) strong. A glance at the shift in Foreign Direct Investment figures tells this story quite dramatically; whereas there was virtually no "external" capital invested in the US before the mid-1970s, by 1985 its "ratio of outward to inward investment [was] . . . almost in balance" (Dicken, 1992: 55). The practices of corporate capital have also changed along with these changes in finance and investment. Most importantly, while dispersed *trade* relations are very old – far older than capitalism as a mode of production – dispersed *production* on a large scale is a relatively recent phenomenon, in the view of many recent authors on the subject of globalization.[16]

Supported by lower costs in transport, and the coordination of vastly separated facilities made possible by advances in communications, as well as encouraged by the lure of vast pools of highly exploitable (non-unionized) labor outside the "First World," corporations exported capital into new areas, some of which became the Newly Industrialized Countries (NICs – e.g. Singapore, Brazil), who experienced rapid – though fragile – economic growth. Taking the itinerary of a blouse on the racks of any suburban US shopping mall as an example of these new networks: the cotton may be grown and harvested, the polyester manufactured, the cloth woven and dyed, the pattern cut and sewn, the final product "prewashed," packed, stored, and, finally, sold, all in different countries, typically (in the garment industry, at least) involving a movement from South to North.[17] Automobiles and electronics might have even longer and more intricate production chains, although large chunks of the globe (Africa in particular) remained largely unconnected by them, though still linked to the global market through cash crops and natural resources. Along with a (relative) dispersion of productive facilities have come other novelties, which in the view of David

131

Harvey (1990), among others, attempt to make capital more "flexible": speeding up delivery time, for example, and fragmenting markets to target very specific consumption habits or "lifestyles." Such practices have been described as "post-fordist," a term which is used not only to mark new production practices and organizational forms of corporations, but also changes in the aggregate global economy and the international division of labor which have accompanied them, including the increased feminization of the proletariat.[18]

Under such conditions, the most emphatic and ubiquitously mentioned effect of globalization is the ostensible demise, or at least relative decline, of the coherence and integrity of nation-states, brought about by the increasing power of "transnational" corporations. The following passage from *Global Dreams – Imperial Corporations and the New World Order* is typical in this respect:

> The emerging global order is spearheaded by a few hundred corporate giants, many of them bigger than most sovereign nations. Ford's economy is larger than Saudi Arabia's and Norway's. Philip Morris's annual sales exceed New Zealand's gross domestic product. The multinational corporation of twenty years ago carried on separate operations in many different countries and tailored its operations to local conditions. In the 1990s large business enterprises, even some smaller ones, have the technological means and strategic vision to burst old limits – of time, space, national boundaries, language, custom and ideology. (Barnet and Cavanagh, 1994: 14)

Such claims seem appropriate at a time in which not only are the "economies" of major global corporations larger than those of many nation-states, as Barnet and Cavanagh note, but also private capital flows from transnational corporations into "Third World" nations far exceed the "foreign aid" programs of even the largest nation-states, mercenary armies such as Executive Outcomes can be hired to protect these corporate interests, and the largest corporations see themselves, as one CEO put it, as devoted in the first instance to the making of money which "has no heart, soul, conscience, [or] homeland."[19] A Coca Cola ad campaign, which features portraits of Napoleon and Lenin next to a bottle of the soft drink, asserts just such a triumphal ascendancy of corporations over polities: "only one launched a campaign that conquered the world," it suggests.[20]

In the face of such material manifestations and claims of "globalization," virtually everyone writing on the topic concedes some changes in global inter-relations have occurred in the past twenty years – in degree if not in kind – but, nevertheless, the more dramatic assertions of "burst[ing] old limits . . . of national boundaries" have not been without their critics, who have raised hard questions not only about the extent and scope of "globalization," but also its effects, and how to deal with them. Empirically driven accounts and critical essays, including the work of Frances Fox Piven (1995), Chris Harman (1996), Paul Hirst and Greg Thompson (1996), among others, have observed that (1) national economies are not necessarily more open now than at various points in the past; (2) few multinationals move around rapidly, or very far; and (3) foreign direct investment is largely concentrated among the wealthiest nations, not draining capital from the so-called First World to the Third as has often been claimed, or at least implied. The main purpose of such work has been to remind readers that the so-called "one world" we inhabit is a starkly *uneven* one, in which some people and geographical areas benefit from the whole system more than others, as is immediately evident through examination of UN publications, such as the annual *Human Development Report.*[21] Even leaving aside questions of justice, however, the "progress" of globalization is by no means a settled question. Kinichi Ohmae (1990), one of the most fervent business cheerleaders of globalization, admits freely that truly global companies must "denationalize their operations and create a system of values shared by company managers around the globe to replace the glue a nation-based orientation once provided," and that "few if any companies have learned how to operate entirely in such a fashion" (91). Rumors of the death of the nation-state, it appears, have been much exaggerated.

After all, in a world in which civil wars and other nationalist struggles abound, it seems impossible to deny the continued power of the *idea* of the nation-state at the very least, and for many theorists – Marxists in particular – its material effects continue to be pertinent as well.[22] The question becomes, then, is the persistence of the "nation" a progressive or regressive force in the contemporary world? Much recent work on the subject (on both the right and the left, but especially among Marxists) notes that "globalization" (like capitalism in general) seems to entail a host of simultaneous and *contradictory* processes – for example, national boundaries may have become more "porous" for flows of capital, while for labor they may be far less so – and, thus, that globalization cannot be seen as simply a drive to burst all barriers and render all areas of the world exactly alike; to the contrary, globalization is characterized by Andrew McGrew (1996) as giving rise to a set of opposing trends: "universalization versus particularization"; "homogenization versus differentiation"; "integration versus fragmentation"; "centralization versus decentralization"; "juxtaposition versus syncretization" (478–9). Nationalisms, in such a contradictory world, some argue, can be either progressive or reactionary, liberating or oppressive: it depends upon specific geopolitical relations in which the nationalism plays itself out (I shall return to this point below). In any case, despite widespread capitalist rhetoric about a desire for "global markets" – seemingly without borders – not only do the contradictions of globalization indicate that the actual practice of capitalism does not correspond fully to the less temperate claims of its rhetoric, but also that full globalization – in the sense of a "borderless world" – "could not be completed as a global system in its proper capitalist form" since (from a Marxist perspective, at least) these contradictions are irreducible within the capitalist mode of production as it attempts to resolve the crises generated by its own expansionary thrust through reliance on the state, or other "non-economic" institutions (Meszaros, 1998: 30). This desire to have the state and exceed it too is one of capital's fatal flaws, John Rees (1994) explains:

"capital can only exist as many competing capitals, [so] it still needs a state that can try to stand above the fray and attempt to regulate the competition. The move to international capital does not dispense with this requirement, but raises it to the level of conflicts between states and trading blocs" (104). In this contradictory world, if "globalization" discourse that proclaims successful destruction, or at least demotion, of the nation-state isn't merely descriptive, what is it?

Paul Smith (1997) has emphasized that "globalization" as it is used in much popular discourse, as well as in much of the business literature, is primarily *ideological*: it acts as if a "borderless world" has already been accomplished for capitalism, realizing in fantasy what has not yet been (and cannot – within capitalism – be) materially achieved.[23] Not only does such a fantasy naturalize and render seemingly inevitable a process that can only be (partially) effected with considerable struggle, but it downplays the very significant roles still played by nation-states in the "North" to secure their ascendancy over the states of the "South." This attempt to present capital's globalization as inevitable has garnered much criticism on the left, including Tim Brennan's (1997) critique of the "gullibility" of those on the left who (he claims) have bought this line uncritically; along these lines, much recent Marxist work on globalization has been directed to asserting both the continued power of the nation-state and thus the dangerous effects of dismissing it as an analytic category too soon – not the least of which is the denial of one of the main ideological and practical forms of political organizing for subaltern states and peoples who have not yet achieved desired nationhood in the here and now, as well as discounting – and helping to render invisible – the heroic tradition of socialist insurgent struggles against both colonialism and capitalism.[24] For Smith the reality of massive global inequalities calls for an unapologetic return to the "binaristic" definitions of the situation rejected by poststructuralists, since they are "an indication of the binary demarcation which are still being made all across the space of the fundamentalist capitalist dream" (1997: 16).[25] Such Marxist critiques are – at minimum – a powerful, and a much-needed *tactical* corrective to both the celebratory discourse of corporate globalization, and a tendency for vague assertion rather than careful theoretical and empirical work in some of the earlier studies on the left.

However, since this Marxist insistence on the power of nation-states arranged in a global hierarchy of "center" over "periphery," "colonizer" over "colonized," or "North" over "South," has been rejected as not only "binaristic," but also "Eurocentric" by many postcolonial theorists, we must examine it further. In the *Black Atlantic*, Paul Gilroy (1993) argues that the nation-state is not an appropriate unit of analysis for the study of black diaspora populations (historically or currently), and that it leads to a counterproductive, even destructive "ethnic absolutism" rather than a truly liberatory politics (5). Alternatively, he proposes "the Black Atlantic" (which links the black peoples of the Caribbean, Britain, and the US to Africa – though not discussed in his book) as an alternative area for study of the "compound culture" of blacks. Instead of relying on "national culture" (or even an insurgent "national popular" culture) as securing identity, Gilroy places more emphasis on identity formation through "routes" (the circulation of peoples and cultural forms and forces) than "roots" (a distinct and "authentic" culture embedded in a particular place): "dealing equally with the significance of roots and routes . . . should undermine the purified appeal of either Africentrism or the Eurocentrisms it struggles to answer. This book has been more concerned with the flows, exchanges and in-between elements that call the very desire to center into question" (190). His argument's implications are that all "cultures" would show the same intermixing and transculturation, although this is ordinarily disavowed and suppressed in the interest of various nationalisms.

One effect of this disavowal, he claims, is an inability to see the contributions made by nondominant peoples, since the very notion of "culture" is (often) predicated on a distinctive, autonomous, and exclusive development. Gilroy counters the ("white") culture of modernity with the assertion that Black people, though often omitted from accounts of the making of the modern world, have been crucial to its emergence as such: "the concentrated intensity of the slave experience is something that marked out blacks as the first truly modern people" (221). He is not here simply reversing the usual paradigm (whites produce modernity and are, therefore, always a bit ahead), but rather insisting that the usual paradigm simply obliterates the irreducible and crucial place of blacks in the production of modernity. In a move typical of early Derridian deconstruction, not only does the putatively marginal turn out to be central – but this reversal displaces the debate, opening up a space to see the world differently. Gilroy bases his claim on the ravages of the experience of slavery, which he sees as wrenching black peoples into the modern crises of identity (what Du Bois called "double consciousness") which would confront non-enslaved subjects only later. Thus, Gilroy's strategy for attacking the unquestionable inequalities of global relations relies on *dismantling from within* the pretensions of "pure culture" through which, historically, such inequalities have been explained and/or justified, and asserting the transnational against the exclusionary force of the national.

For Gilroy and similar theorists not only is "globalization" not new, but the elements which characterize it are not either – as long as you look in the right places. What is (seemingly) new to (privileged subjects in) the "First World" is not new to the oppressed. What had changed in the 1970s, then, is not so much the *process* of globalization, but the distribution pattern of the deleterious experience of it. When George Bush admits in a 1992 speech that the US is beset with "economic problems," he asserts specifically that these problems derive from recalcitrance on the part of Democrats to his programs at a time of heightened "global economic competition." Thus he urges: "in order to keep succeeding in . . . global economic competition we've got to change America" (1992: 420). However, while seemingly appearing as novel to leaders in the US and Europe, the "global" pressures to which Bush refers look all too familiar to

135

peoples in the former colonies, for whom the destruction and restructuring of local economies and cultures in the interests of "external" capitalist forces is old news, as is what we might call the convergence (and contestation) of cultures – "syncretism" being the subjective conditions of existence in the former colonies and the post-independence nation-states, where people have long lived, as Chinua Achebe (1973) evocatively put it, at the "crossroads" of global forces.[26] When "globalization" is examined in a truly "global" context, then, we can readily see that it implies a politics of history as well as geography: its "newness" depends to a large extent not only on how it is conceptualized, but where you look for it.

Indeed, in a world in which everything – all history, all progress – was supposed to emanate from "the West," a revisionist global perspective would mean not only a reexamination of the processes of spatial division and interaction, but a more nuanced – and, as Samir Amin (1989: 146) would put it, "truly universalist" – understanding of contributions to history. C. L. R. James (1980a) made this point in a wonderfully subversive way long ago when he compiled the following list of contributors to "Western Civilization": "Touissant L'Overture, Alexander Hamilton, Alexander Dumas (the father), Leconte Delisle, Jose Maria de Heredia, Marcus Garvey, Rene Maran, Saint-John Perse, Aimé Césaire, George Padmore, Frantz Fanon . . . Alejo Carpentier. . . . [and] Garfield Sobers" (190). One might quibble with the particular figures chosen (on gender grounds, among others) but I am more interested here in the work this list performs in deconstructing "the West" in ways that seem absolutely essential to any "postcolonial" materialism. Revolutionary leaders from the Caribbean, North America, Europe, and Africa rub shoulders with an equally varied assortment of cultural heroes – indeed, sometimes both roles are combined in a single figure; in addition, all of the figures and their work "travel" in Edward Said's (1983), if not in Jim Clifford's (1997) sense: their books, their political activism, or both, have had an impact on sites far distant from the land of their births.[27] Working against the binary logic of so-called "Western Civilization," which imagined a progressive European "self" imparting wisdom on the benighted colonial "other," and defined itself through disavowal, devaluation, "assimilation," or containment of all that is contributed from "outside" itself, James refuses to nurture the illusion that "Western" states have independently created cultural, political, economic, and social forms "internally," and, then, because these were "superior" to other such forms, diffused them out to a more or less grateful world.

For James (1980b), to the contrary, peoples engaged in anticapitalist struggles, or cultural production, wherever geographically situated, were linked to each other because of the "worldwide experience" of capitalism (direct or indirect): "whenever a revolutionary class moves, it establishes a stage for the international movement." Ultimately, emphasizing this connection over local differences, James goes on: "when Marxists talk about class, they have in mind the history of civilization" (117). Recent postcolonial theory engages in a similar deconstruction, but without the link to Marxism for the most part. Indeed, in spite of the engagement with Marxism of anticolonial theorists of the period of decolonization, such as James and Amilcar Cabral, much recent postcolonial theory is suspicious of, or simply indifferent to, Marxism, associating it with "European" modes of thought, especially Enlightenment "totalizing" tendencies, and even a complicity with colonialism, which renders it either superfluous – or downright antagonistic – to postcolonial analysis.[28] A typical critique is David Washbrook's, which suggests that World Systems theories perpetuate the view that the motor of all progress is "the West," by deploying the "center" and "periphery" vocabulary (and logic), a view which Gilroy, Hall, Chakrabarty, and similar theorists, vehemently reject. Said's (1979) damning judgment in *Orientalism* of Marx's writings on India ("Marx's economic analyses are perfectly fitted . . . to a standard Orientalist undertaking, even though Marx's humanity, his sympathy for the misery of people, are clearly engaged") set the stage for later dismissals of Marxism in the work of other postcolonial critics, including even more severe critiques, such as Robert Young's (1990) rejection of all dialectics on the grounds that (he suggests) it is the theoretical form of the Master/Slave narrative actually enacted by Europe in the colonial world. Even those postcolonial critics with the greatest investment in attempting to "open the texts of Marx beyond his European provenance" (Spivak, 1988: 211) are forced to point out the massive ignorance of the non-European world on which Marx's writings, and "Western Marxisms" which follow from it, were sometimes predicated.[29] Thus, the trend within dominant postcolonial criticism has been to focus on the instances of disruption of fluidity, transgression, and excess which disrupt " the metaphorical and mythical binariness presented by empire" (Gikandi, 1997: 17), without reference to Marxist ways of telling the story.[30]

Numerous alternative formulations to center/periphery have thus been adopted, including a wide variety of "global/local" dynamics (e.g. "glocalization"); a Deleuzian problematic (deterritorialization/reterritorialization); and "disembedding" (Giddens) – all of which evade defining a "center."[31] The interest in "the local" in such studies arises from a desire to indicate the resistance and transformative energies collected in specific sites, such that elements entering from "outside" a local cultural matrix do not simply obliterate and displace elements they encounter *in situ*, but are reworked by their entrance into the new milieu. Thinking through the relation of "local" and "global," postcolonial theory has emphasized that interculturation is not only a process at work in the so-called Third World, but in the First as well. Anthony King (1990) has argued, for example, that London is as much a "Caribbean" city as a "British" one, and that diaspora movements tie it materially to multiple "nations." King has also proposed that the colonial city is actually the paradigm case of what is now called the "postmodern" predicament of multiple inscription and creolization, crosshatched as it necessarily was with "outside" forces (also see Benitez-Rojo, 1992). Similarly, analyses of "world cities" and "global cities" (London is ubiquitously named as one) have emphasized the ties linking this grid of urban spaces to each other rather than their ties to any individual "nation." In this way, spaces such as the "global city" undermine a tidy map of nation-states – theorists such as Saskia Sassen (1991) have suggested – and urge an alternative spatial analysis in order to understand properly how they work in the contemporary world. The proliferation of analyses of "the city" in various contexts fits in with a broad range of inquiries in postcolonial theory about "alternative" spaces to the nation-state, and the raising of questions about what "local" means in a "globalizing" world.

Along these lines, for recent postcolonial theorists, colonial culture is often viewed as permeating the "local" of both colonizer and colonized as mutually constituting. As Stuart Hall (1996: 246) has put it:

> it ["post-colonial"] refers to a general process of decolonization which, like colonization itself, has marked the colonizing societies as powerfully as it has the colonized (of course in different ways). Hence the subverting of the old coloniz-ing/colonized binary in the new conjuncture. Indeed, one of the principal values of the term "post colonial" has been to direct our attention to the many ways in which colonization was never simply external to the societies of the imperial metropolis. It was always inscribed deeply within them – as it become indelibly inscribed in the cultures of the colonized.

This gesture has been foregrounded in postcolonial studies because while no one disputes that the colonization process left its mark on the colonies, the reverse had been less often marked. For the Said (1993) of *Culture and Imperialism* this absence of address to the "dependence" of the "West" on the "non-West" to form "itself" is symptomatic, and demands that we "regard imperial concerns as constitutively significant to the culture of the modern West," and at the same time pay attention to resistance to these colonial pressures in the colonies them-selves, a reading practice he calls "contrapuntal," a metaphor from music which refers to different melodic lines confronting each other in a compositional whole (66). An extension of this process for Stuart Hall (1996), among others, is a rethinking of the nation-state itself at the current conjuncture, in order to reread "colonization as part of an essentially transnational and transcultural global process [which] produces a decentered, diasporic or 'global' rewriting of earlier, nation-centered imperial grand narratives" (247). Along similar lines, Inderpal Grewal and Caren Kaplan (1994) have claimed that: "the terms generally used by the left (such as dominant/dominated, colonizer/colonized) to mark the interplay of power in the era of imperialism often overlook complex, multiply constituted identities that cannot be accounted for by binary oppositions" (10). Anthony Appiah (1992), too, insists that "talk of the production of marginality by the culture of the center is wholly inadequate by itself. For it ignores the reciprocal nature of power relations" (72). He argues instead for attention to "the mutual interdependencies history has thrust upon us." This emphasis on "interdependency" – and the shift to a focus on *culture* (as opposed to "political economy" in the Marxist sense) on which it is usually predicated (both because of the impact of the "cultural turn" in theory in general, and because intermixing is often easily and satisfyingly tracked in cultural forms) – characterizes the vast bulk of postcolonial work today informed by poststructuralism. From this perspective, the much vaunted (and disputed) claims of current globalization discourse about the "porousness" of the nation–state can be seen as an unveiling of an enabling fiction of the nation–state, rather than an observation about a novel development.

To many Marxists, however, even those who also take up questions of culture, such views can sound utterly preposterous; they might point out, for example, that Appiah resorts to the passive voice when he discusses "interdependencies history *has thrust* upon us," and suggest that such constructions are part of the problem in a world in which "history" doesn't do anything all by itself: people make it, even if not under conditions of their own choosing. *Armies* attack and pillage, *politicians* sign charters and laws, European *colonists* and officials settled on confiscated local land in the colonies, and the *colonized* resist. And such polarities do not end with decolonization: more recently, World Bank debt, transnational corporations, and US weaponry produce and manage the global imbalances that the colonial chartered companies and state apparatuses used to oversee directly. As a result, nation-states struggle among themselves for power in the global system, and some of them are in a position to dominate and exploit while others must struggle to eke out a fragile existence, the effect of which has been a globe in which a handful of nations (20 percent of the world's population) control 80 percent of global wealth. With these historical conditions in mind, a vexed Marxist colleague of mine once responded in exasperation to a poststructuralist interlocutor: "How can't you see it? The colonizers are the ones with the *guns!*" – suggesting something of the incomprehension and mutual antagonism that has been inspired by these differences between Marxism and poststructurally-inflected postcolonialism.

On the one side, Paul Gilroy's (1993) lyrical and provocative *Black Atlantic* claims (confirming the worst fears of some Marxists as he pushes the consequences of a poststructural perspective to its limit): "the reflexive cultures and consciousness of the European settlers and those of the Africans they enslaved, the 'Indians' they slaughtered, and the Asians they indentured were not, even in situations of the most extreme brutality, sealed off hermetically from each other" (2). On the other side, Tim Brennan's (1997) lucid and nuanced Marxist study of the effects of such observations in actual historical struggles, suggests that these groups might not be sealed off "hermetically" from each other, but they certainly *are* sealed off politically – and this is what matters most: a "scrupulously inclusive 'we' – as in the phrases 'we live in-between,' or 'we are all cosmopolitans' – is complete as identity and incomplete as situation." In other words, such formulations as Gilroy's, in his (neo-Fanonist) view, while strictly speaking "true," are disabling in the context of "anticolonial war," where a unified front against a distinct oppressive power is needed, and a distinct

139

insurgent "culture" is born out of that struggle (18). Whereas the Marxist approach tends to emphasize material unevenness – and resistance to exploitation – the postcolonial approach has emphasized instead the intermixing of cultures which make it impossible to, say, definitively separate the *cultures* of "exploiter" and "exploited."

The unwillingness to engage in this sort of sorting exercise which might expose definite "sides" to a struggle, has evoked charges of "complicity" on the part of critics of postcolonial discourse.[32] While, as I have noted above, Marxists are often charged with remaining within a "colonial" binary logic, Postcolonial theorists have been charged with engaging in a theoretical exercise which encourages an exploitative status quo. Masao Miyoshi (1996), for example, has argued that when we fail to consider "political and economic inequalities" – and the causes for them – and engage in discourses of "postcoloniality" (which for him implies – falsely – the end of colonialism in a neocolonial world) "we are fully collaborating with the hegemonic ideology, which looks, as usual, as if it were no ideology at all" (98). Similarly, Arif Dirlik (1994b: 356) suggests that

> Postcolonial critics . . . in their repudiation of structure and affirmation of the local in problems of oppression and liberation, . . . have mystified the ways in which totalizing structures persist in the midst of apparent disintegration and fluidity. They have rendered into problems of subjectivity and epistemology concrete and material problems of the everyday world. While capital in its motions continues to structure the world, refusing it foundational status renders impossible the cognitive mapping that must be the point of departure for any practice of resistance and leaves such mapping as there is in the domain of those who manage the capitalist world economy.

For Dirlik, this state of affairs means that "postcoloniality is the condition of the intelligentsia of global capitalism," whose ends they further however unwittingly.

Nowhere, perhaps, is the impasse between "Marxism" and "Poststructuralism" more evident than in Aijaz Ahmad's (1992) stern and magisterial defense of Marxism as political praxis: *In Theory*. His charges against the metropolitan left (he is most concerned with the US) on this score are many. To his mind, even in the heyday of the 1960s metropolitan radicals were more invested in what he calls "Third-Worldist nationalism" (bad – because it homogenizes the "Third World" and evades a class analysis) than with insurgent socialism, when they took up international issues at all, and, in any case, they soon abandoned even a limited nationalist perspective after poststructuralism offered its distracting charms. The effect of this latter move, according to Ahmad, has been the replacement of a left "activist culture" in the universities with a "textual culture" (1), which has forgone any meaningful engagement with the working class for a "conversation" (2) among academics in which "reading" becomes "the appropriate from of politics" (3). According to Ahmad, in these "readings," Marxism – as a living politics – is either ignored, denounced, or transformed into a mere "analytic of textual elucidation among other such analytics" (4). Insofar as this "conversation" has been concerned with "empire, colony, nation, migrancy, post-coloniality, and so on" it has moved from an earlier uncritical advocacy of "Third-Worldist nationalism" to an even worse position: "against the categories of nation and nationalism" *tout court* (3). These trends in "theory," he suggests, have coincided – not accidentally – with decolonization – and the globalization of capital – "which brought all zones . . . into a single integrated market, entirely dominated by this extreme imperialist power [of the US]" (21). The important point of Ahmad's historical tale – all its extraordinary elisions and oversimplifications notwithstanding – is to insist that insurgent socialism has never got the support that it has deserved from the metropolitan left, to the detriment of anticapitalist struggles.[33] From Ahmad's perspective, poststructuralism in particular stands in the way of such struggles by – among other things – calling into question the nation as a potentially (though, of course, not universally) liberatory and progressive organizing site for anticapitalist movements.

At an earlier moment, the place within Marxism where many of these issues had been battled out in the postwar period include "dependency," "underdevelopment," and "world systems" theories, which argue in various forms that the development of the wealthier and more powerful regions of the world is underwritten not only by exploitation of poorer regions, but also that the poorer regions are actively "underdeveloped" – prevented from developing – by the dominant states to keep them subaltern. Though these theories have been much criticized, they nevertheless have intervened in important ways in theoretical debates within Marxism and without, by insisting on studying the globe as a whole when analyzing economies in any part, and paying attention, in particular, to the role of geography in exploitation, as well as class relations. Hence, Neil Lazarus (1999) takes Gilroy to task for neglecting this Marxist tradition which seems so pertinent to his own concerns ("there is not a single reference . . . [in his work] to world-system theory or to the work of such writers as Immanuel Wallerstein, Samir Amin, or Andre Gundar Frank"). For Lazarus, this neglect is particularly unfortunate since:

> Marxism can credibly claim to have been (for over a hundred years now) the source and inspiration of the most coherent and principled theories both of the advent of capitalist modernity and of the universalizing propensities and global reach (the systematicity) of capitalism as an historical formation. Central to these theories from the outset has been a critique of nationalism, an insistence that the determinants of social life are secured globally and not at the level of the nation-state, and that, therefore, the only form of politics capable of presenting a decisive challenge to the globalism of actually existing capitalism is an internationalist socialism.

While it is difficult to disagree with Lazarus's contention that Gilroy's failure to address Marxist political economy[34] impoverishes his analysis, the claims that the

"Marxist" theories he names have been "central" to its debates in the West, or that the "national question" has been settled as he suggests within Marxism are debatable. To the contrary, as Mike Sprinker (1993) notes in his thoughtful review of Aijaz Ahmad's *In Theory*, the typical Marxist understanding of resistance to capital has been that it must be conducted "through the nation-state" if not for the nation-state (4). Indeed, the vehement return to the nation-state as the appropriate unit through which to analyze (and resist) globalization in so much recent Marxist work certainly affirms this still to be the case.

To be sure, some strands of underdevelopment and dependency theory, as well as many anticolonial critics within Marxism, *have* argued that unequal global trade, slavery, and colonies have underwritten not only continuing global inequality, but also the development of capitalism in the core, and thus they *might* be read as "deconstructive" of any easy divide between "center" and "periphery," or the enclosure of "national economies."[35] Fanon (1963), after all, argued that "Europe is literally the creation of the Third World," pointing to the wealth in money, labor, and resources which moved from the South to the benefit of the North from the slave trade, colonial exploitation, and outright theft, an argument typical of various critiques of (neo)colonialism. Eric Williams's (1944) *Capitalism in Slavery*, for example, adamantly argues that the capital for the industrial revolution in England was extracted directly from the slave trade and slave-based colonial production, replicating in an economic argument a position seemingly congenial to Gilroy's own cultural one: that the supposedly marginal contributors to modernity have been central. Also potentially congenial to Gilroy's argument are the claims of "world systems" theorists, such as Immanuel Wallerstein and Giovanni Arrighi, who have long emphasized that nations did not spring fully formed (or, even incrementally) out of the English common law or the French Revolution. They have emerged rather in an interaction of *global* forces underwritten by *capitalism* – including colonization, trade, wars – relations from which the development of "individual" states are inextricable. The emphasis in the analysis of world systems theorists is *always* on relations and exchanges among *capitalists*, since from its perspective there is *no* autonomous capitalist development "internal" to a given state which can be meaningfully detached from the larger system in which states function. Wallerstein argues, for example, that "the [global] balance of power [was not] merely a relationship between state-machineries, because the internal actors within any given state regularly acted beyond their own boundaries either directly or via alliances with actors elsewhere. Therefore, in assessing the politics of a given state, the internal/external distinction is quite formal and it is not too helpful to an understanding of how the political struggles actually occurred" (1983: 60). From this perspective it makes more sense to say that capitalism gave birth to a certain Great Britain than the other way around, as is typical in the European historiography on the part of both the left and right. It also reminds us that the "dependency" in dependency theory means not only that of the "periphery" on the "center" but also vice versa. As A. G. Frank (1969) put it: "development and underdevelop-

142

ment each cause and are caused by the other in the total development of capitalism" (240). At first glance, in any case, these theories within Marxism seem as if they might be especially useful to the postcolonial critiques mistrustful of the nation-state.

However, there are two main reasons why they are not entirely welcoming sites for Gilroy's – or other forms of postcolonial/poststructuralist – analysis to be articulated with Marxism. The first has to do with the ways in which dependency theory remains caught up in the very binary oppositions that postcolonial theorists wish to undo, since the vocabulary of center/periphery, originating in Frank's work on "underdevelopment," for example, persist in the work of others who study the empirically unquestionable economic disparities between some nations and others within the global system. As noted above, this vocabulary conflicts with the preference for intermixing and unstable borders in postcolonial discourse. A second reason is more complex, deriving from the now long-standing ambivalence within Marxism itself to "dependency" oriented analyses in *any* form. J. M. Blaut (1993), for example, has noted that there has been a precipitous dropping away of interest in assessing the "Third World's" role in *global* development since the 1960s, even among Marxists, who, after a period of infatuation dropped virtually all affiliation with "dependency" theories and the like, to the point where "Eurocentric Marxists who dismissed the role of the Third World both historically and in the present now became virtually the only Marxists within the academic world to pronounce upon issues related to the Third World" (137–8). He has in mind in particular the legacy of the critiques of dependency theory by Bill Warren (1980) and Robert Brenner (1977), as well as the vast output in England on the "transition" to capitalism, which, following Brenner's early essays, often emphasize Europe's endogenous development, and the "diffusion" of capitalism from Europe.[36] Blaut's point is not that there is nothing in dependency theory, etc., to critique, but rather that (Western) Marxism has not fully divested of Eurocentric concepts and habits, which sometimes leads to unsatisfactory critiques. My interest in this chapter lies in the possibility that revisiting this Marxist tradition might indicate a way to bring Marxism and postcolonial theory together in a way that acknowledges limits to actually-existing Marxism as well as postcolonial studies – especially now that theorists such as Amin and Wallerstein have turned to questions of culture so conspicuously absent from their earlier work.[37]

At the very least the return to questions of global political economy posed by "dependency" theories, grafted to the concerns of postcolonial studies with culture, might make it less easy for actually-existing Marxists to claims such things as "only in England did capitalism emerge, in the early modern period, as an indigenous national economy" (Wood, 1991: 1). From the perspective of *both* dependency theory and postcolonial studies, to assume "England" to be a tidy enclosure in which capitalism was incubated and readied for export making use of only "indigenous" elements, is problematic. First of all, there are the problems of "internal colonialism" (Hechter) and incipient extra-European colonialism to contend with, but also such matters as the slave trade, import/re-export joint stock companies, and the transnational circulation of craftsmen, techniques, raw materials, and knowledge to consider. Given these conditions, defining the "England" that capitalism could be born in is no simple matter, and yet the myths of enclosure and even possessive nationalism persist. Even so influential and venerable a figure as E. P. Thompson (1966) – whose practical politics were emphatically internationalist, and who was as outspoken a critic of imperialism as any other Englishman of his period – managed to write over 800 pages on the "making of the English working class" without any consideration of colonialism to speak of – not even the destruction of the indigenous cotton industry in India, which clearly had an impact on the fate of mill workers in England, as Marx himself emphasizes in his notorious short comments on India for the *New York Daily Tribune*.[38] Apparently, to Thompson's brilliant and politically-astute mind, the "social life" of the English working class was not "secured globally" to any appreciable extent. This curious divided consciousness – avowedly (or at least nominally) "internationalist" in political commitment, but utterly "national," if not nationalist, in the production of academic work – is pervasive in Marxism.

Hence, Leslie Sklair (1991) has observed that "classical Marxists refuse to accept, either empirically or theoretically, that the state is the most important actor in the global system. . . . In practice, however, most contemporary Marxism is state-centered to a greater or lesser extent" (4). The very critique that Lazarus (properly) directs at Gilroy – that he fails to acknowledge the tradition within Marxism that asserts that the "determinants of social life are secured globally" – could, then, apparently, be directed to Marxism itself in many of its currently extant forms. I emphasize this *not* to discount or discredit Marxism, but because a selective reading of Marxist history might make postcolonial theory's neglect or rejection of Marxism seem either entirely inexplicable, or the result of a facile and craven infatuation with "poststructuralism" alone, as if, *in context*, the rise of postcolonialism had *nothing* to do with problems with Marxist positions in practice, and thus that postcolonial theory has nothing to offer Marxist analysis of the globalization today because as an intellectual enterprise it has been fundamentally self-serving, elitist, and complicit with metropolitan interests (as Ahmad, among others, suggests). In some cases this is no doubt an accurate assessment (there is a good deal of unthinkingly repetitive – and even bad – work in any field), but I am interested in a different issue: what did the poststructuralist critique of "identity" – especially in relation to the "nation" – provide to postcolonial theory which Marxism seemed less able (or eager) to provide, at least in its seemingly most widely disseminated and accepted positions in the academy? Answering this question requires a historical excursus.

Much work in the second generation of Cultural Studies in Britain – which is now intertwined with postcolonial critique (see Morley and Chen, 1996) – focused on the very questions of "race" and "Britishness" side-stepped in many popular press accounts of globalization, such as the one offered in the issue of

Time Out I described at the beginning of this chapter.[39] It is only in the context of this history, it seems to me, that the current difference between "postcolonial" and "Marxist" approaches to the "nation" under "globalization" make any sense. Postcolonial theory and criticism is suspicious of the nation not only because of theoretical investments, but because it was born at a moment when diaspora populations flowed into the homelands of the former colonizers and discovered "nation" deployed against them.[40] Assumptions of a pure and coherent nation-state are, of course, far easier for any state to manage when, ideologically, militarily, and fiscally, its status as a world power is secure. Although the trace of Empire is evident virtually everywhere in prewar British society, from the booty on display in museums and the tea and sugar in cupboards, to the returns on investments piled in the bank vaults, these inflows were all managed and assimilated, however ambivalently, as part of "British" culture. However, as loss of empire and competition with the US eroded Britain's global position in the post-Second World War period, relations with its "others" became a more fraught proposition. In addition, large, vocal diaspora populations in, say, London, are more challenging to local norms than the traces of their presence in commodities and capital that had flowed in already for centuries. Yet (de)colonization is simply overlooked for the most part by the earliest work in cultural studies, while the influx of "American" mass culture is everywhere deplored and feared, marking a perceived change in cultural ascendancy, among other things. However, by the 1980s, not only mainstream racism, but certain Eurocentric strains within [Western] Marxism and Feminism came under attack from a specifically *postcolonial* position. In *Black British Cultural Studies* Hazel Carby (1996: 64) observes, for example, that:

> too often concepts of historical progress are invoked by the left and feminists alike, to create a single sliding scale of "civilized liberties." When barbarous sexual practices are to be described the "Third World" is placed on display and compared to the "First World" which is seen as more "enlightened" or "progressive." The metropolitan centers of the West define the question to be asked of other social systems and, at the same time, provide the measure against which all "foreign" practices are gauged. In a particular combination of Marxism and feminism, capitalism becomes the vehicle of reforms, which allows for progress toward the emancipation of women.

Postcolonial critiques emerged at a moment when metropolitan Marxisms (and Feminisms) were perceived to be inadequate – at least as practiced.

It was in *this* context that one of the most influential British Cultural Studies texts of this period, Paul Gilroy's (1991) *Ain't No Black in the Union Jack*, foregrounded the oppressiveness of nation-state imaginaries themselves, which function by disavowal and exclusion, differentiation and phantasmatic purification, themes which he would later develop in the *Black Atlantic*. Cultural Studies critiques of (extant) Marxisms, in spite of Ahmad's quite different argument, were,

145

it seems to me, responding to real limitations in the Marxisms of the period, and exerted – to my mind at least – healthy pressures, which have not been entirely worked through even now. This moment has been decisive, it seems to me, in giving rise to the very different ways in which "Marxist" critiques and "Postcolonial" critiques of globalization have unfolded. While the currently ascendant strain of the former has emphasized the continued power and force of the nation-state in a world ostensibly undermining it, specifically postcolonial critiques have tended to interrogate the nation-state and emphasize its inadequacy as a unit of analysis from its emergence, focused as they are on diaspora and the very real dilemmas it poses for nations as "imagined communities" faced with disruptive "global" flows.

Historically, for Marxism, "the national question" has been complicated. The recent return to insistence on the importance of the nation-state as a unit of analysis (e.g. Smith, Callinicos), and, also, in certain instances, as a site of resistance (Brennan, Blaut, Ahmad, Beinefeld), follows in the wake of a long history of debates about what the nation might mean for an "internationalist" movement. As Blaut (1987) has argued, though the prewar Marxisms tend to emphasize "internationalism" (on the assumption that capitalism was breaking down national differences, and would continue to do so), both Marx's and Engels' comments on Ireland (and the Irish in England), indicate that they saw progressive possibilities in a quest for nationhood as well, which only find their full development later, in the work of Lenin, and Cabral, who provided Marxism with a fuller theorization of "the right to national self-determination" and of insurgent nationalism, as opposed to a rejection of nationalism *tout court* as bourgeois in Luxemburg and Trotsky.[41] The recent return to the importance of the nation-state draws on both traditions within Marxism, making a distinction between "insurgent" and "bourgeois" nationalisms, arguing for their continued pertinence as part of the struggle against "global" capital, which divides the world into oppressor and oppressed nations.

As I have emphasized throughout this chapter, much recent work in postcolonial theory has taken a different tack, and mistrusts the assertion of the nation – even the insurgent nation – as a primary site of struggle or analysis. There are real limits to this trend – limits which have been amply noted by the small but vocal contingent of Marxists who "cross over" into the issues discussed by postcolonial theorists. In their view, postcolonialism, having abandoned "materialist" imperatives for "culturalist" ones, can no longer properly analyze exploitation and domination – indeed sometimes does not even seem to be able to *see* it. Some of the blindness stems, in the view of Marxist critics, from an elitist metropolitan culturalist point of view (if not physical location) which renders material unevenness less visible, leading Terry Eagleton (1998/9) to fault postcolonial theory for "failing to make a rather significant distinction between Mussolini and Mozambique" in their assessment of nationalism (25). From the vantage-point of many Marxists, the poststructuralist postcolonial theorists have muddled crucial concepts with their insistence on imbrication and intermixing. As Brennan cautions, "if hybridity can be said to characterize ["native cultures"] then it is a hybridity reclaimed and reinvented as indigenous, defiantly posed against an increasingly insistent metropolitan norm" (310). Often focusing on the metropolitan nationalisms, and the oppressive pressures they continue to exert, postcolonial critics see the nation as a very different sort of construct than the Marxists looking to insurgent socialisms.

Unquestionably, Marxism has dealt in more impressive detail with the economic aspects of globalization, and also with the "cultural" aspects of a still operating "(neo)colonial" relation between "North" and "South," a point conceded by at least some of the more prominent poststructuralist postcolonialists.[42] There are nonetheless important insights to be gleaned for Marxism from the postcolonial approach to the "contestation of cultures" thesis I have identified with such figures as Gilroy and Hall – just as there would be much to be gained by an attention to specifically Marxist concerns and concepts in postcolonial theory. For one thing, the intactness of what looks like a persistent "North"/"South" divide should not distract us from recognizing the ways in which this binary is insufficient to characterize current global relations.[43] As Armand Mattelart *et al.*, (1984) have argued, such divides sometimes lead to the unfortunate claims that anything (even a "Third World" transnational corporation that operates to enforce local inequalities) is "good" if it resists the incursion of the "North." To the contrary, they suggest that "whether viewed in terms of the formation of multimedia groups or in terms of communications hardware production, 'Third World' appears today as an increasingly meaningless term. A whole series of interchangeable terms (the South, developing countries, peripheral countries, etc.) no longer grasp the realities they supposedly refer to" (432). What must be resisted, rather, is capitalism, wherever it arises – a proposition with which a Marxist could hardly disagree.[44] At the current conjuncture it may well be that such an analysis, as it calls upon us to attend to the historical specificity of any given geopolitical situation, may push us toward an analysis of spaces not yet fully examined by classical Marxism (London as a Caribbean city, for example). Of course this analysis would not *preclude* examination of the interplay of nation-states, nor would it necessarily insist that no "national struggle" can be progressive.

According to the Marxist geographer David Harvey (1995), it is when we take up such questions that neither "globalization" nor "neocolonialism" adequately serves to assess current global relations, and he proposes "uneven spatio-temporal development" as an alternative. He rejects "globalization" on the grounds that many other Marxist writers on the subject do: it presupposes a full triumph of a capitalism still engaged in struggle with resistant forces (and its own contradictions), and therefore not as omnipotent or ubiquitous as it would like us to believe. His quarrel with "neocolonialism," however, brings him into contention with many other Marxists, for whom the subterfuge of "globalization" is to be best countered by returning it to the discourse of imperialism, which at least calls attention to power relations. Harvey, however, declares "imperialism" inadequate on grounds similar to Mattelart's: it is, he claims, "too crude to express the geopolitical complexities within which class struggles must now unfold" (1995: 14). All national space, Harvey insists, "when scrutinized more closely, turns out to be a space within an international space of flows of capital, labor, information and so on, in turn comprised of immediate smaller spaces, each with its own characteristics" (4). This situation demands more specific units of analysis and organization than classical Marxism offers, he argues.

In the *Manifesto*, Marx and Engels, too, concerned themselves with the selection of appropriate analytic and organizational units, understanding well the problems posed by them: "though not in substance," they observed, "yet in *form*, the struggle of the proletariat with the bourgeoisie is at first a national struggle" (1848: 14, emphasis added). Not "national" in "substance," of course, because the proletarian struggle was always-already "international," since capital was. Yet, the struggle was still "national" in "form" – this they argued consistently. Is this still the case? Has capitalism perhaps changed so much that a change in "form" of resistance is needed as well? The "return" to the "nation" in so much recent Marxist writing on globalization marks an important grappling with this problem of form, and it answers the questions I pose in the previous sentences in the negative. And yet the postcolonial critiques of the "nation" continue to haunt me. Does an *articulation* of struggles (antiracist, antipatriarchal, proletarian . . .) require a different "form" than the "proletarian struggle"? What about diaspora? When "national" populations are dispersed, what "form" does struggle take? Can there be "transnational" sites of resistance? What would they took like? What "form" furthers most effectively "globalization from below" – the formation of transnational alliances among unions and other groups resisting corporate globalization?[45] Such questions suggest, it seems to me, that a continued – critical, careful, thoughtful – quest for a convergence of postcolonial and Marxist critiques is still worthwhile as we continue to try to understand – and resist – "global capital."

Notes

1   Although this line from Harris's *Palace of the Peacock* emanates from the mouth of the loathsome colonizer Donne as he attempts to establish himself as universal ("I'm everything. Midwife, yes, doctor, yes, gaoler, judge, hangman, every blasted thing to the labouring people," 22), it is thematically related to the novel as a whole, which calls into question numerous conventional boundaries of space (e.g. is Mariella a woman, a town, or both?) and time (C. L. R. James describes the novel's method as "Heideggerian" in this respect) in order to explore the politics of memory

and property, which Harris, who worked for some years as a land surveyor, well appreciated. See also Harris's *The Womb of Space: the Cross Cultural Imagination*; Ashcroft, Griffiths, and Tiffin, "Wilson Harris and the Synchretic vision" (149–54 in *The Empire Writes Back*); and James's "On Wilson Harris," in *Spheres of Existence*.

2 Some version of this "small world" thesis can be found in virtually all recent accounts of globalization (if only to refute it). Although it does not itself use the term "globalization," David Harvey's 1990 book *The Condition of Postmodernity* has greatly influenced discussion of it, especially in its description of "time-space compression" – "processes that so revolutionize the objective qualities of space and time that we are forced to alter, sometimes in quite radical ways, how we represent the world to ourselves. I use the word 'compression' because a strong case can be made that the history of capitalism has been characterized by speed-up in the pace of life, while so overcoming spatial barriers that the world sometimes seems to collapse inwards upon us" (240). See in particular Part III, "The Experience of Space and Time" (201–323).

3 For a discussion of the emergence of the term, see Robertson (1992).

4 For Appadurai, each of these transnational flows produces a corresponding distinct, disjunct, and ever-changing "space" or "scape": ethnoscape, mediascape, technoscape, ideoscape, and financescape.

5 "Strong globalization" is a term I borrow from Neil Lazarus's (1999) excellent survey and discussion of globalization discourse, which I find congenial in general, though we differ on some of the details, as will be evident below. He uses the term to distinguish those theorists of globalization who see the changes wrought by space-time compression and capital's production/use of it to be "epochal" – that is to say, so significant as to propel us into a distinct regime of capital accumulation. He includes not only "postmodernists" in this group, such as Arjun Appadurai and Stuart Hall, but also Marxists, such as Eric Hobsbawn, David Harvey, and Anthony McGrew, and includes an excellent bibliography of pertinent work. See note no. 7 below also. The (strong globalization!) "UN report" to which I refer is the 1992 *Human Development Report*, which, at the same time as it declares the world a "*single*" space, also emphasizes that it is *not* a homogenous one, marked as it is by spectacularly high levels of inequality, as the most recent (1998) report also overwhelmingly confirms.

6 Like Appadurai, Barrie Axford (1995) attributes globalization to multiple causes: "a fluid and contingent state which is the expression of interactions within and between societal and intersocietal systems" (8). He faults theorists such as Wallerstein who persist in seeing the "world system" as determined by the "single implacable logic" of capitalism, a view which characterizes the (self-proclaimed) Marxist accounts for the most part, though not exclusively (see Dirlik's *After the Revolution* for an exception). This distinction – which provides the grist for one of the major ongoing debates on globalization – can be seen as separating the work of (for example) Giddens, Hall, Robertson, Dirlik, and Axford from that of Jameson, Sklair, Lazarus, Sivanandan, and Wallerstein.

7 Relying on a stagist model borrowed from Ernest Mandel, Jameson argues that globalization is characteristic of "postmodernism" and a new stage of capitalism, which has the effect of massive social disorientation as subjects attempt to negotiate its

complex – and historically novel – terrain. A. Sivanandan and the *Race and Class* collective, too, theorize "globalization" as ruptural, and thus as requiring new forms of resistance (as well as modes of theorization) than those adopted by earlier critics of capitalism (see his debate with Ellen Wood in *Monthly Review* 48, no. 9). This is a view he shares with critics with whom he is otherwise at odds, such as the *New Times* group in London, who have proposed that Marxism itself must be changed in order to meet the needs of current conditions so radically different from those faced by earlier Marxists (see the 1990 anthology edited by Hall and Jacques on this topic). Assorted conservative and liberal commentators as well have touted the novelty of globalization, and heralded the dawning of a new age, whether they see this age as needing to be celebrated or feared (as Ohmae and Reich, respectively). A significant contingent of recent theorists – especially Marxists – have, however, disputed this "rupture" model, emphasizing continuity with previous strategies of capital expansion rather than a break. For example, an influential 1993 article (reprinted 1996) by Masao Miyoshi situates the emergence of globalization discourse in the shift from a "colonial" system predicated on the explicitly territorial conquest by nation-states to a more indirect conquest by transnational corporations, and he emphasizes the continuity between the two forms of exploitation. "World System" theorists, too, such as Giovanni Arrighi (1994), have long stressed a continuity (even cycling) in historical processes, suggesting, for example, that "the financial expansion of the 1970s and 1980s does indeed appear to be the predominant tendency of processes of capital accumulation on a world scale. But it does not appear to be a "revolutionary" tendency at all. Financial expansions of this kind have recurred since the fourteenth century as the characteristic reaction of capital to the intensification of competitive pressures" (300). The debate over the timeline of globalization is one of the major current disputes among its theorists, and it has significant implications for how we think about space-time under current conditions, especially as they impact upon strategies of resistance to capitalism.

8   Of the three "first generation" postcolonial theorists, Spivak's is the most concerned with Marxist problematics, and has been crucial in teasing out the (non)place of the subaltern woman under conditions of global capital. See, for example, "Woman in Difference" in *Outside in the Teaching Machine* and "Scattered Speculation on the Question of Value" in *In Other Worlds*.

9   These lines from Homi Bhabha are typical: "all forms of culture are continually in a process of hybridity. But for me the importance of hybridity is not to be able to trace two original moments from which the third emerges, rather hybridity to me is the 'third space' which enables other positions to emerge" (211). See "The Third Space. Interview with Homi Bhabha" (1990). Variations on this general theme are widely dispersed in Postcolonial Studies, such that Timothy Brennan (1997) observes: "most under attack has been the dichotomy between colonizer and colonized, though without denying inequality as such. We have for some time now been witnessing a shift from a binary otherness to a single, internally rich and disparate plurality: a varity of levels within and sites between, rather than the lonely outposts on either side of belief's wall" (2).

10   For a wide-ranging introductory overview of postwar social, economic, cultural, and political history, see Hobsbawm (1994).

11   See Clarke (1991).

12   See Laclau (1990).

13   See Anderson (1984), especially "Structure and Subject."

14   See Hall (1988).

15   For the US, a (mid-century) movement toward, and then away from, a more equitable distribution of wealth as the struggle for hegemony among US, Japanese, and German capitalist interests heated up, has been chronicled by Robert Brenner in *New Left Review* 229 (1998).

16   For discussion of such "production chains," see Dicken (1992), especially pages 189–227. It should be noted here, however, that there has been much dispute about whether or not such "chains" are new. Wallerstein has persistently argued that they are not. Much of the dispute has to do with whether or not "circulation" should be considered part of "production," as well as how far back the process of "transnational production" goes (see Wallerstein, 1991: 31). One of the harshist "Marxist" criticisms of "dependency," "underdevelopment," and "world systems" theories (which attempted to account in various ways for the globally uneven development of capitalism) was that they emphasized "trade" over "production." See, in particular, Brenner (1977). Alternatively, theorists such as Giovanni Arrighi (1994) have taken the position that (even aside from the clearcut cases of early transnational commodity production chains) circulation (whether across town, or across the ocean) adds value, and thus is part of the production process itself: "the reshuffling of goods in space and time, which is what trade is all about, can involve as much human effort and can add as much use-value ('utility') to the goods so reshuffled as does extracting them from nature and changing their form and substance, which is what we understand by production in a narrow sense" (177); see also Blaut (1987), esp. p. 274. See notes 35 and 36 below.

17   See Enloe (1989), esp. ch. 7.

18   Although it obviously does not address the current scene, Nash and Fernandez-Kelly (1983) contains helpful essays for understanding the earlier trends, as does Enloe (1989). More recent overviews include Mitter (1994) and Mohanty *et al.* (1997). In addition, Zed Books publishes numerous specialized volumes on women and development, environment and so on.

19   *The Nation* (Nov. 10, 1997) reported "the replacement of industrial nations' foreign aid programs with reliance on transnational investment and charitable giving. In 1996 private capital flows to developing countries totaled $234 billion – four times the size of the industrial world's foreign aid programs combined" (3). See "St. George and the Kremlin." The comment from the CEO is borrowed from Doug Henwood's enormously informative *Wall Street*.

20   A reproduction of this advertisement is included with the illustrations to Eric Hobsbawm's, *The Age of Extremes* (1996).

21   For an analysis of globalization which draws extensively upon these reports, see Robinson (1996).

22   For a detailed discussion of the material significance of "the national question" in times of "globalization," see Blaut (1987). For an account of "the nation" that more closely corresponds to the dominant understanding in postcolonial studies, see Chatterjee (1986).

23 For a useful distinction between "globalization" (to describe a historical process) and "globalism" (to describe the *discourse* which Smith draws our attention to here), see Sivanandan (1998/9).

24 This is a particular incentive for Brennan's critique of an elitist and uncritical "cosmopolitanism": "the new cosmopolitanism drifts into view as an act of avoidance if not hostitity and disarticulation toward states in formation" (2), and for this reason, among others, he thinks it is important to preserve a sense of "dichotomy between colonizer and colonized" in full realization with all the problems entailed in such a formulation (2). Other Marxist defenses of the colonial/colonized binary abound. See, for example, Smith (who couches the binary in North/South terms) and also the essays collected in *Marxism and the New Imperialism*. In that collection, Alex Callinicos, for example, describes as a "left . . . orthodoxy" the position that "decolonization represented a purely superficial change in the relationships between rich and poor countries. The ties of economic dependence on the advanced countries have, on this account, kept the ex-colonies in effectively the same position as they were before independence. Constitutionally these 'neo-colonies' or 'semi-colonies' may be sovereign, but the real relations of global power mean that they are still finally subordinated to the Western imperialist countries" (46). Callinicos goes on to critique the crudest versions of this view, but emphasizes in his discussion of globalization just the same that: An "imbalance in economic power is reflected in the politico–military hierarchy which exists among the world's states, and in particular the dominant role of the Western imperialist powers," thus indicating a need for retaining the older vocabulary (51).

25 Smith actually makes this point by way of a surprisingly culturalist gesture, an anecdote about a group of Czechoslovakian students hailing Vaclav Havel "Godot has arrived," several days after Beckett's death, an incident which he reads, allegorically, as illustrating Eastern Europe's temporal alterity (still "Modernist") in relation to ("postmodern") Europe. Elsewhere in the text, however, he grounds this alterity in the vast material inequalities that are his main concern.

26 Chinua Achebe (1973) writes: under colonization "we lived at the crossroads of cultures. We still do today." This "crossroads" condition had been variously theorized as "hybridity" (Bhabha); "creolization" (Hannerz); and "postmodern" (Benitiz-Rojo; King). Perhaps the most sophisticated elucidation of the resulting contest in the colonial situation is Ranajit Guha's "Dominance Without Hegemony," which describes the multiple ways in which "external" forces were integrated, resisted, and transformed under colonial conditions, with a particular focus on the aspects of the colonial situation in which an interactive "hegemony" did not pertain, and colonial power exerted a brute force resulting in what can only be called domination.

27 For the various uses of "travel" in contemporary theory, see Kaplan (1996).

28 There have also, however, been a number of theorists committed to bringing a specifically Marxist perspective to/against Postcolonial Studies, including Aijaz Ahmad, Tim Brennan, Laura Chrisman, Arif Dirlik, Neil Larsen, Neil Lazarus, Masao Miyoshi, Benita Parry, E. San Juan, Sangeeta Ray and Henry Schwarz, and Gayatri Chakravorty Spivak. See the References for selected relevant work.

29 See Chakrabarty; Prakash. Aijaz Ahmad's chapter on Marx's writings on India in *In Theory* is particularly interesting on this score since it is, on the one hand, deeply

critical of postcolonial theory for a too-easy rejection of Marxism (among other things), but, on the other hand, does also note that Marx did seem to rely on a overly-scanty knowledge base when he discussed Asia in the journalism: "the fact that Marx did not have the more modern research at his disposal explains the origin of his errors, but the fact that he accepted the available evidence as conclusive enough to base certain categorical assertions on it was undoubtedly an error of judgment as well" (244).

30 For a (brief) Marxist critique see Parry (1998).

31 The essays collected in two recent anthologies illustrate this full range of approaches; see Wilson and Dissanayake (1996) *Global/Local* and Featherstone, Lash, and Robertson (1995), *Global Modernities*.

32 For bibliography and discussion, see Hall (1996); also Ahmad, Brennan. Even in the midst of a virulent critique of most of its acutally existing forms, however, Arif Dirlik observes that "postcoloniality represents a response to a genuine need, the need to overcome a crisis of understanding produced by the inability of old categories to account for the world" (353). It is in this sense, that I use postcolonial here – with the proviso that most Marxist categories (if not the practice of some users of them) *are* adequate to the current conjuncture, though some do need reinscription or abandonment in response to new conditions or in light of new knowledge (for example, "the Oriental Mode of Production" – for a critique of which, see Ahmad).

33 On some of the "elisions and oversimplifications" as discussed by generally appreciative readers, see: Brennan (1994), Lazarus (1993), Sprinker (1993).

34 Actually, Gilroy does cite the "Marxist tradition" in the likes of Benjamin, Adorno, and others of the more "cultural" and speculative practitioners, but it is certainly the case that he has nothing to say about the specifically political-economic studies Lazarus cites, nor does he draw attention to the "Marxist" aspects of the work of the Frankfurt School theorists when he makes use of them.

35 A word is in order here about "dependency," "underdevelopment," and "world systems" theories, which differ from each other in important details (discussed in Larrain (sympathetically), Brewer (unsympathetically), and Axford), though they are all concerned with exposing and explaining inequalities among nations in the world economy. Andre Gunder Frank's work on Latin America initiated not only a school of "dependency theory," but has also influenced government policy in that region. Working against the hegemony of "modernization" theory (e.g. Rostow), which insisted that the marvels of capitalist development were available to "Third World" countries if they would only follow the lead of the First World, Frank argued that capitalist intervention in Latin America had failed to be progressive not because of local "backwardness," but rather because capitalism worked by subordinating "peripheral" economies to dominant "central" ones, which actively (if not consciously) hindered growth in the peripheral states by forcing their economies only down those avenues most favorable to the center. "Underdevelopment" theories – such as those of Walter Rodney – brought a similar set of analyses to the African context, arguing that colonialism and neocolonialism "underdeveloped" Africa, in its own interest. "World System" theories (e.g. Wallerstein, Arrighi), influenced by both dependency theory and Annales school historians, argued that the world could only be understood as an interacting totality, and that states could

be sorted into "core," "periphery," and "semi-periphery" according to the relative subordination of economies to other states. Also influential has been Samir Amin, who distinguishes himself from these other schools, though his work overlaps with them in important respects. He, too, insists that some national economies become subordinated to others, and favors a policy of economic "delinking" in order to sever these ties (NOT an isolationism, but a conscious policy of making economic decisions in favor of the subordinated state rather than dominating economies). See notes 16, 36.

36 Supporting Blaut's assessment, even now Brenner's early essays – and critiques of dependency, world systems, and underdevelopment theory predicated on it – are ubiquitously (favorably) echoed in the standard reference works in Marxism such as the *Dictionary of Marxist Thought*, which in each of the relevant entries (on "underdevelopment" and "dependency" for example) cite Brenner as having decisively undermined would systems and related theories, *and* cite favorably Bill Warren, who fired one of the first salvos against what he saw as over-eager Third-Worldism, in a book-length defense of the (one-sided, West-initiated) "progressiveness" of colonialism. Robert Brewer's widely circulated *Marxist Theories of Imperialism* – reprinted 5 times since 1980 and appearing in a second edition in 1990 – also mentions Warren favorably, dismisses emphatically *all* the figures cited by Lazarus as central to a "global" perspective, and emphatically asserts that "dependency theory" (which Brewer associates with Amin in particular) is "alien to the mainstream of Marxist thought" – an assessment pervasive enough for Amin to assume a defensive position in recent work, such as *Eurocentrism* (1989: 198). From another direction, Blaut (1987), while sympathetic to Amin, is suspicious of "world systems" theory, which he critiques on the ground that it provides for no autonomy of nation-states (43–4). It should be noted, however, that Brenner's own most recent work calls into question his earlier thesis rather dramatically, though he does not seem able or willing to register this himself. See Callinicos's review of *Merchants and Revolution* for *NLR*. It should also be noted that much of the critique of these theories is thoughtful and has led to important development and revisions. See notes 16, 35 above.

37 Much of Wallerstein's more recent work moves in this direction, including *Historical Capitalism, Geopolitics and Geoculture*, as well as his collaborative volume with Balibar. See also Amin (1997).

38 C. L. R. James implicitly critiques this insularity in alluding to Thompson's title, while employing a quite different methodology, in his "Making of the Caribbean People," just as he critiques Raymond Williams's insularity in "Marxism and Intellectuals." Both essays are collected in *Spheres of Existence*.

39 See Alan Sinfield's *Literature, Politics and Culture in Postwar Britain*, Lin Chun's *The British New Left*, and Dennis Dworkin's *Cultural Marxism in Postwar Britain* for some context.

40 Another factor, of course, was the disappointing decline of many nationalist movements in the postcolonial period, thwarted in some instances by corrupt and dictatorial regimes, or in the breakdown of fragile anticolonial coalitions into mutually-contending factions, or in the recognition that nationalism in itself did nothing to end patriarchy, class divisions, or, for that matter, neocolonial pressures of the global economy.

41 Luxemburg's comments on "the national question" have been collected into a volume, *The National Question*. Lenin's "Critical Remarks on the National Question" and "The Right of Nations to Self Determination" are in Volume 20 of *Works*. Trotsky's "The Program of International Revolution or a Program of Socialism in One Country" is collected in *The Third International After Lenin*. Cabral's "National Liberation and Culture" is collected in *Return to the Source*, and *Colonial Discourse and Postcolonial Theory: A Reader*.

42 Stuart Hall (1996) concedes that "two halves of the current debate about 'late modernity' – the postcolonial and the analysis of the new developments in global capitalism – have indeed largely proceeded in relative isolation from one another, and to their mutual cost" (258).

43 Even within the "industrialized" nations, inequalities are manifest, and signal a problem of thinking simply in "national" terms when attempting to understand the workings of the contemporary world system. Factors of race, gender, ethnicity, and the labor diaspora in the most highly developed nations, as well as dramatic inequalities within the underdeveloped nations themselves, complicate any absolute separation of "North" from "South" in purely geographical terms at the current conjuncture. Though the standard of living for US whites is highest in the world, blacks and Hispanics seem to live in a different country, according to all the standard UN measures, which rank US blacks 27th and US Hispanics 32nd (1995, 22). For whites, as well, even those with a college education, all is not what it once was. Unemployment is lower in the US than in Europe, and the economy is growing, but, as the *NY Times* special report explained, "the sting is in the nature of the . . . work. Whereas 25 years ago the vast majority of the people who were laid off found jobs that paid as well as their old ones, Labor Department numbers show that now only about 35% of laid-off, full-time workers end up in equally remunerative or better-paid jobs. Compounding this frustration are stagnant wages and an increasingly unequal distribution of wealth" (1996: 6). In the US, 97% of the 10% rise in household income between 1979 and 1994 went to the wealthiest 20% of the population. And these figures are even more chilling in the context of the world as a whole. The UN has speculated that if income disparity within countries worldwide were taken into account, the already huge gap between peoples, understood in terms of per capita income, would skyrocket: perhaps rising as high as 150 to 1 (1992: 34). In corporate celebratory discourse about globalization, much of these inequalities seem to fall away, shielded from sight by the networks of computer links, phone lines, and satellite feed which link the corporations and elites to each other, whatever conditions may pertain for the rest of the world's peoples. I am not, of course, suggesting that we only need to look at the troubles of the so-called "First World" because all the world's problems can be found there (and, presumably, solved there as well). To the contrary, I am suggesting that the specific conditions in particular sites need to be examined, wherever they may be. I question the claim that the nation is, or should be, the priviledged site of such analysis, although I am equally suspicious of any analysis that would reject it *tout court*. It is of the greatest consequence that we assess this inequality properly, and there are many reasons to suspect that the nation–state may not provide the most useful – certainly not the exclusive – unit of analysis.

44 A related point: By judging nations only in terms of per capita income, for example, the statistics upon which the divide between North and South is usually based (and undeniable), one remains locked within Western (capitalist) assumptions of progress, as Amartya Sen's work has indicated. The UN's *Human Development Report* (1992) actually deploys a different optic so that it takes into account other factors besides income in recognition that quality of life is not solely predicated on it.

45 "Globalization from below" is a term used by Brecher and Costello (1994) to describe "a democratic or people's internationalism" based on transnational alliances among various groups resisting the adverse effects of globalizing capital, from environmental to labor (78).

References and Further Reading

Achebe, Chinua. (1973). "Named for Victoria, Queen of England," *New Letters* 40, no. 3.

Ahmad, Aijaz. (1992). *In Theory*. London and New York: Verso.

Amin, Samir. (1989). *Eurocentrism*, trans. Russell Moore. New York: Monthly Review.

——. (1997). *Capitalism in the Age of Globalization*. London: Zed.

Anderson, Perry. (1984). *In the Tracks of Historical Materialism*. Chicago: University of Chicago Press.

Appadurai, Arjun. (1996). *Modernity at Large*. Minneapolis and London: University of Minnesota Press.

Appiah, Kwame Anthony. (1992). *In My Father's House*. New York and Oxford: Oxford University Press.

Arrighi, Giovanni. (1994). *The Long Twentieth Century*. London and New York: Verso.

Ashcroft, Bill, Gareth Griffiths, and Helen Tiffin. (1989). *The Empire Writes Back*. London and New York: Routledge.

Axford, Barrie. (1995). *The Global System: Economics, Politics and Culture*. New York: St. Martins Press.

Balibar, Etienne and Immanuel Wallerstein. (1991). *Race, Nation, Class: Ambiguous Identities*, trans. Chris Turner. London and New York: Verso.

Barnet, Richard and John Cavanagh. (1994). *Global Dreams: Imperial Corporations and the New World Order*. New York: Touchstone.

Benitez-Rojo, Antonio. (1992). *The Repeating Island: The Carribbean and the Postmodern Perspective*. Durham: Duke University Press.

Bienefeld, Manfred. (1994). "Capitalism and the Nation-State in the Dog Days of the Twentieth Century," in *Between Globalism and Nationalism*, eds. Ralph Milliband and Leo Panitch. London: Merlin.

Bhabha, Homi. (1990). "The Third Space. Interview with Homi Bhabha," in *Identity, Community, Culture, Difference*, ed. J. Rutherford. London: Lawrence and Wishart.

——. (1990). "DissemiNation: Time, Narrative, and the Margins of the Modern Nation," in *Nation and Narration*, ed. Homi Bhabha. London and New York: Routledge.

Blaut, J. M. (1993). *The Colonizer's Model of the World*. New York: Guilford.

——. (1987). *The National Question: Decolonizing the Theory of Nationalism*. London and New Jersey: Zed.

Brecher, Jeremy and Tim Costello. (1994). *Global Village or Global Pillage*. Boston: South End.

Brennan, Timothy. (1997). *At Home in the World*. Cambridge, Mass. and London: Harvard University Press.

——. (1994). "Aijaz Ahmad, In Theory," *Textual Practice*, 8, no. 2: 327–35.

Brenner, Robert. (1977). "The Origins of Capitalist Development: A Critique of Neo-Smithian Marxism," *New Left Review*, 104: 25–92.

——. (1993). *Merchants and Revolution*. Princeton: Princeton University Press.

Brewer, Robert. (1990). *Marxist Theories of Imperialism: A Critical Survey*, 2nd ed. London and New York: Routledge.

Bush, George. (1992). "Economic Growth," *Vital Speeches of the Day*, 58, no. 14: 418–21.

Cabral, Amilcar. (1994). "National Liberation and Culture," in *Colonial Discourse and Post-Colonial Theory: A Reader*, eds. Patrick Williams and Laura Chrisman. New York: Columbia University Press, 53–65. First published 1973 in *Return to the Source*.

Callinicos, Alex. (1994). "Imperialism Today," in *Marxism and the New Imperialism*. London: Bookmarks, 11–66.

Césaire, Aimé. (1972). *Discourse on Colonialism*. New York: Monthly Review Press.

Carby, Hazel. (1996). "White Woman Listen! Black Feminism and the Boundaries of Sisterhood," in *Black British Cultural Studies: A Reader*, eds. Houston A. Baker, Jr., Manthia Diawara, and Ruth H. Lindeborg. Chicago and London: University of Chicago Press, 61–86.

Castells, Manuel. (1985). "High Technology, Economic Restructuring and the Urban-Regional Process in the Unites States," in *High Technology, Space and Society*, ed. Manuel Castells. Beverly Hills and London: Sage.

Chatterjee, Partha. (1986). *Nationalist Thought in the Colonial World: A Derivative Discourse*. London: Zed.

Chun, Lin. (1993). *The British New Left*. Edinburgh: Edinburgh University Press.

Chrisman, Laura. (1997). "Journeying to Death: Gilroy's Black Atlantic," *Race and Class*, 39, no. 2: 51–64.

Clarke, John. (1991). *New Times and Old Enemies*. London: HarperCollins Academic.

Clifford, James. (1997). *Routes*. Cambridge, Mass. and London: Harvard University Press.

Dicken, Peter. (1992). *Global Shift: The Internationalization of Economic Activity*, 2nd ed. New York: Guilford.

Dirlik, Arif. (1994a). *After the Revolution*. Hanover and London: Weselyan University Press.

——. (1994b). "The Postcolonial Aura: Third World Criticism in the Age of Global Capitalism," *Critical Inquiry*, 20: 328–56.

Dworkin, Dennis. (1997). *Cultural Marxism in Postwar Britain*. Durham: Duke University Press.

Eagleton, Terry. (1998/9). "Postcolonialism and 'Postcolonialism,'" *Interventions*, no. 1: 24–6.

Enloe, Cynthia. (1989). *Bananas, Beaches and Bases: Making Feminist Sense of International Politics*. Berkeley and Los Angeles: University of California Press.

157

Fanon, Frantz. (1963). *The Wretched of the Earth*, trans. Constance Farrington. New York: Grove Press.

Featherstone, Mike, Scott Lash, and Roland Robertson, eds. (1995). *Global Modernities*. London: Sage.

Frank, A. G. (1969). *Capitalism and Underdevelopment in Latin America*. New York Monthly Review Press.

Giddens, Anthony. (1990). *Consequences of Modernity*. Stanford: Stanford University Press.

Gikandi, Simon. (1997). *Maps of Englishness*. New York: Columbia University Press.

Gilroy, Paul. (1993). *The Black Atlantic*. Cambridge: Harvard University Press.

——. (1991). *There Ain't No Black in the Union Jack*. Chicago: University of Chicago Press.

Grewal, Inderpal and Caren Kaplan, eds. (1994). *Scattered Hegemonies*. London and Minneapolis: University of Minnesota Press.

Guha, Ranajit. (1989). "Dominance Without Hegemony and its Historiography," *Subaltern Studies* VI. Delhi: Oxford University Press, 210–309.

Hall, Stuart. (1997). "The Local and the Global: Globalization and Ethnicity," in *Culture, Globalization and the World-System*, ed. Anthony King. Minneapolis: University of Minnesota Press, 19–39. First published 1991.

——. (1996). "When was the Postcolonial?" in *The Postcolonial Question*, eds. Iain Chambers and Lidia Curti. London and New York: Routledge, 242–60.

——. (1988). "A Toad in the Garden: Thatcherism among the Theorists," in *Marxism and the Interpretation of Culture*, eds. Cary Nelson and Lawrence Grossberg. Urbana and Chicago: University of Illinois Press.

——, *et al.* (1978). *Policing the Crisis*. London: Macmillan.

—— and Martin Jacques, eds. (1990). *New Times: The Changing Face of Politics in the 1990s*. London: Lawrence and Wishart.

Hannerz, Ulf. (1989). "Notes on the Global Ecumene," *Public Culture*, no. 2: 66–75.

——. (1987). "The World in Creolisation," *Africa*, 57, no. 4: 546–59.

Harman, Chris. (1996). "Globalization: A Critique of the New Orthodoxy," *International Socialism*, 73: 3–33.

Harris, Wilson. (1998). *Palace of the Peacock*. London: Faber and Faber. First published 1960.

——. (1983). *The Womb of Space: The Cross-Cultural Imagination*. Westport, Conn.: Greenwood.

Harvey, David. (1990). *The Condition of Postmodernity*. Oxford: Blackwell.

——. (1995). "Globalization in Question," *Rethinking Marxism*, 8, no. 4: 1–17.

Hechter, Michael. (1975). *Internal Colonialism: The Celtic Fringe in British National Development*. Berkeley: University of California Press.

Henwood, Douglas. (1997). *Wall Street*. London: Verso.

Hirst, Paul and Greg Thompson. (1996). *Globalization in Question*. Oxford: Polity.

Hobsbawm, Eric. (1996). *The Age of Extremes*. New York: Vintage. First Published 1994.

——. (1995). *The Age of Capital*. New York: Scribner's.

James, C. L. R. (1980a). "The Making of the Caribbean People," in *Spheres of Existence*. Westport, Conn.: Lawrence hill & Co., 173–190. First published 1966.

——. (1980b). "Marxism and the Intellectuals," in *Spheres of Existence*, 113–30. First published 1962.

Jameson, Fredric. (1988). "Cognitive Mapping," in *Marxism and the Interpretation of Culture*, eds. Cary Nelson and Lawrence Grossberg. Urbana and Chicago: University of Illinois Press, 347–60.

Kaplan, Caren. (1996). *Questions of Travel*. Durham: Duke University Press.

King, Anthony. (1997). "The Global, the Urban and the World," in *Culture, Globalization and the World System*, ed. Anthony King. Minneapolis: University of Minnesota Press.

——. (1990). *Urbanism, Colonialism and the World-Economy*. London: Routledge.

Laclau, Ernesto. (1990). *New Reflections on the Revolution of Our Time*. London: Verso.

Larrain, Jorge. (1989). *Theories of Development: Capitalism, Colonialism and Dependency*. Cambridge: Polity.

Lazarus, Neil. (1999). *Nationalism and Cultural Practice in the Postcolonial World*. Cambridge: Cambridge University Press.

——. (1993). "Postcolonialism and the Dilemma of Nationalism: Aijaz Ahmad's Critique of Third-Worldism," *Diaspora*, 9, no. 3: 373–400.

Lenin, V. I. (various dates). *Collected Works*. Moscow: Progress.

Luxemburg, Rosa. (1976). *The National Question: Selected Writings of Rosa Luxemburg*, ed. Horace B. Davis. New York and London: Monthly Review Press.

Mandel, Ernest. (1993). *Late Capitalism*. London and New York: Verso.

Marx, Karl and Friedrich Engels. (1992). *The Communist Manifesto*, ed. David McLellan. Oxford and New York: Oxford University Press. First published 1848.

Massey, Doreen. (1992). "A Place Called Home?" *New Formations*, 17: 3–15.

Mattelart, Armand, *et al.* (1984). *International Image Markets*, trans. David Buxton. London: Comedia.

McGrew, Andrew. (1996). "A Global Society?" in *Modernity: An Introduction to Modern Societies*, eds. Stuart Hall, *et al.* Cambridge, Mass. and Oxford: Blackwell.

Mercer, Kobena. (1994). *Welcome to the Jungle: New Positions in Black Cultural Studies*. London: Routledge.

Meszaros, Istvan. (1998). "The Uncontrollability of Globalizing Capital," *Monthly Review*, 49, no. 9: 27–37.

Mitter, Swasti. (1994). "On Organizing Women in Casualised Work," in *Dignity and Daily Bread: New Forms of Economic Organizing Among Poor Women in the Third World and the First*, eds. Sheila Rowbotham and Swasti Mitter. New York: Routledge.

Miyoshi, Masao. (1996). "A Borderless World? From Colonialism to Transnationalism and the Decline of the Nation-State," in *Global/Local*, eds. Rob Wilson and Wial Dissanayake. Durham: Duke University Press.

Mohanty, C. T., *et al.*, eds. (1997). *Feminist Genealogies, Colonial Legacies, Democratic Futures*. New York and London: Routledge.

Morley, David and Kuan-Hsing Chen. (1996). *Stuart Hall: Critical Dialogues in Cultural Studies*. London and New York: Routledge.

Nash, June and Maria Fernandez-Kelly, eds. (1983). *Women, Men and the International Division of Labor*. Albany: State University of New York Press.

New York Times. (1996). *The Downsizing of America*. New York: Random House.

Ngugi wa Thiong'o. (1986). *Decolonizing the Mind*. Portsmouth: Heinemann.

Ohmae, Kinichi. (1990). *The Borderless World: Power and Strategy in an Interlinked Economy*. London: HarperCollins.

159

Parry, Benita. (1998). "Post-Colonial Ambiguity," *New Formations*, 33: 149–53.

Piven, Frances Fox. (1995). "Is it Global Economics or Neo-Laissez-Faire?" *New Left Review*, 213: 107-14.

Prakash, Gyan. (1990). "Writing Post-Orientalist Histories of the Third World: Perspectives from Indian Historiography," *Comparative Studies in Society and History*, 32, no. 2: 383–408.

Ray, Sangeeta and Henry Schwarz. (1995). "Postcolonial Discourse: The Raw and the Cooked," *Ariel*, 26, no. 1: 147–66.

Rees, John. (1994). "The New Imperialism," in *Marxism and the New Imperialism*. London: Bookmarks, 67–121.

Reich, Robert. (1992). *The Work of Nations*. New York: Vintage.

Robertson, Roland. (1992). *Globalization: Social Theory and Global Culture*. London: Sage.

Robinson, William. (1996). "Globalisation: Nine Theses on Our Epoch," *Race and Class*, 38, no. 2: 13–31.

Rodney, Walter. (1972). *How Europe Underdeveloped Africa*. Harare: Zimbabwe Publishing.

Rostow, W. W. (1985). *The Stages of Economic Growth: A Non-Communist Manifesto*. Cambridge: Cambridge University Press.

Said, Edward. (1993). *Culture and Imperialism*. New York: Knopf.

——. (1979). *Orientalism*. New York: Vintage.

——. (1983). "Traveling Theory," in *The World, the Text and the Critic*. Cambridge: Harvard University Press, 226–47.

San Juan, E. (1995). "On the Limits of 'Postcolonial' Theory," *Ariel*, 26, no. 3.

Sassen, Saskia. (1991). *The Global City: New York, London, Tokyo*. Princeton: Princeton University Press.

Sivanandan, A. (1998/9). "Globalism and the Left," *Race and Class*, 40, nos. 2–3: 5–19.

—— and Ellen Meiksins Wood. (1997). "Capitalism, Globalization and Epochal Shifts: An Exchange," *Monthly Review*, 48, no. 9: 19–32.

Sklair, Leslie. (1991). *Sociology of the Global System*. Baltimore: Johns Hopkins University Press.

Smith, Paul. (1997). *Millennial Dreams*. London and New York: Verso.

Spivak, Gayatri Chakravorty. (1993). *Outside in the Teaching Machine*. New York and London: Routledge.

——. (1988). *In Other Worlds: Essays in Cultural Politics*. New York and London: Routledge.

Sprinker, Michael. (1993). "The National Question: Said, Ahmad, Jameson," *Public Culture*, 6: 3–29.

"St. George and the Kremlin." (1997). *The Nation*, 265, no. 15: 3–4.

Thompson, E. P. (1966). *The Making of the English Working Class*. New York: Vintage. First published 1963.

Trotsky, Leon. (1996). *The Third International after Lenin*. New York: Pathfinder.

United Nations. (1992). *Human Development Report*. New York and Oxford: Oxford University Press.

Wallerstein, Immanuel. (1991). *Geopolitics and Geoculture*. Cambridge: Cambridge University Press.

——. (1983). *Historical Capitalism*. London: Verso.

Warren, Bill. (1980). *Imperialism: Pioneer of Capitalism.* London: Verso.

Washbrook, David. (1990). "South Asia, the World System, and World Capitalism," *Journal of Asian Studies*, 49, no. 3: 479–508.

Williams, Eric. (1944). *Capitalism and Slavery.* Chapel Hill: University of North Carolina Press.

Wilson, Rob and Wimal Dissanayake, eds. (1996). *Global/Local: Cultural Production and the Transnational Imaginary.* Durham: Duke University Press.

Wood, Ellen. (1991). *The Pristine Culture of Capitalism.* London: Verso.

Young, Robert. (1998/9). "Ideologies of the Postcolonial," *Interventions*, 1, no. 1: 4–8.

——. (1990). *White Mythologies: Writing History and the West.* London: Routledge.

PART II

The Local and the Global

Chapter 7

A Vindication of Double Consciousness

Doris Sommer

"How does it feel to be a problem?" This is what whitepeople are always asking Blacks, says W. E. B. Du Bois at the beginning of *Souls of Black Folk* (1903), even when they are being compassionate or feeling vicariously outraged at things "that make your blood boil." Du Bois reduces his own boiling point to a simmer, as he puts it, in order to ventriloquize for whites who don't dare ask about the "problem" outright. Delicacy doesn't cover up the question; it obstructs any possible answer. So Du Bois asks boldly, and responds: Feeling yourself to be a problem, he says, "is a peculiar sensation, this double-consciousness, this sense of always looking at one's self through the eyes of others, of measuring one's soul by the tape of a world that looks on in amused contempt and pity. One ever feels this twoness, – an American, a Negro; two souls, two thoughts, two unreconciled strivings" (1903: 215).

Double consciousness is a double bind for Du Bois. This wasn't the case for Ralph Waldo Emerson, who coined the term to describe a productive dynamism.[1] Nor will it necessarily bind up postmodern citizens in self-destructive contradictions. On the contrary, and this is the point of my essay. Double consciousness may be our best cultural safeguard for democratic practice, because doubleness won't allow the meanness of one thought, one striving, one measure of value. Democracy prizes non-normative procedure over political substance. In the seam between particular cultures that fit badly together democracy can work procedurally, to define universal rights and obligations. Good fits leave little room for serious play. But differences that are admitted and continue to strain against one another show the gap where debate and procedure can work. Du Bois himself opens leads in this direction when he refuses to "bleach his Negro soul" in order to fit into white America, as we will see. But mostly, *Souls of Black Folk* complains that seeing double means losing focus. Emerson's coinage of double consciousness amounted to social bankruptcy for Blacks, who were pulled in opposite directions and getting nowhere.

1 Collusion and Collision

For Emerson, double consciousness had meant the dynamics of American progress, the principle of coordination between opposing forces. It was the productive relationship between nature and freedom, between racial inheritance and universal purpose. He formulated this mixture of optimism and resignation in "Fate," written during the troubled decade before the Civil War. The first draft was a lecture in 1851 (just after the war that annexed half of Mexico to the United States) and the published essay appeared in 1860.

> One key, one solution to the mysteries of human condition, one solution to the old knots of fate, freedom, and foreknowledge, exists, the propounding, namely, of the double consciousness. A man must ride alternately on the horses of his private and his public nature, as the equestrians in the circus throw themselves nimbly from horse to horse, or plant one foot on the back of one, and the other foot on the back of the other.[2]

Thanks to Americans' emotional agility to move from public to private passions, and thanks also to their coming late into history with long views that show suffering as part of the grand scheme of human progress, doubleness is resolved into "one solution." The horse on the left and the horse on the right both move forward, as the skillful rider stays on top. Emerson wrote this, as I said, after the triumph against Mexico and just before the war to end slavery. If a disastrous struggle at home was foreseeable, so too was the welcome release from an unbearable contradiction for the young democracy. The future carnage of so prolonged a civil war was unforeseeable and could not have cramped Emerson's optimism, nor could the unimagined frustrations that followed have yet crippled his faith. So the condition of double consciousness doesn't need a cure for Emerson. Man's maturity brings an acknowledgment that one's particular possibilities and limitations are part of a universal design. While inheritance (temperament, race) drags him down, purpose in the divine scheme lifts the spirit. Why tinker with the asymmetry between a narrow (racial) consciousness and a broad consciousness of participating in the Universe? Divine Law takes care of that, straightening out the divided self and generally overriding apparent oppositions. Instead of cures, Emerson commissioned monuments to the grand solution:

> Let us build altars to the Blessed Unity which holds nature and souls in perfect solution, and compels every atom to serve an universal end . . . Let us build altars to the Beautiful Necessity, which secures that all is made of one piece; that plaintiff and defendant, friend and enemy, animal and planet, food and eater, are of one kind . . . Why should we fear to be crushed by savage elements, we who are made up of the same elements? (1860: 816)

This is not a rhetorical question for everyone. Those who are crushed ask it differently from those who benefit by the crushing. Emerson's abstract universalist language (loosely Buddhist, even more loosely Hegelian, or Schopenhaurean turned perversely optimistic) builds towards this final coordination of universal "Fate" with particular destiny. But the movement has been so effortless, the fit between his particular triumphalist racial consciousness with the consciousness of divine Law has been so seamless, that the concluding exhortation to praise the design seems callow if not downright cruel. "We like the nervous and victorious habit of our own branch of the family," he had proudly said early in the essay: "Cold and sea will train an imperial Saxon race, which nature cannot bear to lose, and, after cooping it up for a thousand years in yonder England, gives a hundred Englands, a hundred Mexicos. All the bloods it shall absorb and domineer: and more than Mexicos, – the secrets of water and steam, the spasms of electricity, the ductility of metals, the chariot of the air, the ruddered balloon are awaiting you" (1860: 808). Meanwhile, other races deteriorate when you dislodge them, and literally become fertilizer for the heartier race: "The German and Irish millions, like the Negro, have a great deal of guano in their destiny. They are ferried over the Atlantic, and carted over America, to ditch and to drudge, to make corn cheap, and then to lie down prematurely to make a spot of green grass on the prairie" (1860: 801). All this makes the closing injunction suspiciously self-serving. Blameless, in the big picture, the Anglo-Saxon race smiles exultant, effortlessly aligned with the Universe, while other races can share the design by embracing humility, resigning themselves to an appointed role, and wisely grateful to have performed services for their betters.

No wonder Emerson welcomed Whitman, the poet who dared to speak for the master and for the slave, for the hunter and the hunted, husband and the wife. No wonder both live on in Jorge Luis Borges' version of Schopenhauerean fate, "La nadería de la personalidad" which expounds the emptiness of personal identities. They are mere masks that cover the "nothingness" of roles such as victim or murderer. Borges, like most of Whitman's fans, also loved his jumbled catalogues that joined unlikely neighbors and flattened dramatic differences into more of the same familiar rhythm during the drone of long lists. (Emerson's "Fate" shows some of the same love of lists, the lushness of more than enough examples that train us in familiar expectations as much as they convince readers through argument.) The down-to-earth equality of Whitman's *Leaves* is also worth mentioning, with Emerson's bias toward material history in mind. Not even Nietzsche promised as much relief from dualism as did Whitman, say Deleuze and Guattari, because he respatialized our political imagination from thinking in terms of circles, or poles, or dialectical spirals, to thinking in terms of the rhizome (1983: 9, 43, 48). The figure is "an underground stem" that proliferates laterally without any center or goal, so that each growth is equal to and connects with all others. This radically American image allegedly sets the model for the "successive lateral shoots" that can loosen Europe's fixation on deep roots. (They might also have gone back to Jefferson's ideally repeatable Cartesian plots of land,[3] and to Emerson's repeatable self-reliant citizen.) The problem with proliferation is that it assumes a model that is endlessly repeated. Who establishes that representative man, seemingly humble, commonest, and cheapest? And how can its endless repetition accommodate the different styles, interests, desires that Deleuze and Guattari had defended in *Anti-Oedipus*? Emerson's candid version of this philosophical vanishing point is to identify Americans as Anglo-Saxons, to celebrate their proliferation in the spaces fertilized by disappearing races.

An open-ended reading of Emerson's "New Yet Unapproachable America" might seem to mitigate the racialized triumphalism of "Fate." America, says Stanley Cavell (1989) on this reading, is best understood as a project rather than a product. It is a purposefully unfulfilled desire for fulfillment, for spiritual coherence. And the desire moves Emersonian thought onward, asymptotically, towards the unreachable shore. Desire for an evenly aligned society doesn't falter if the existing country falls short of perfection. Instead, yearning renews itself in Emerson's dialectic of romantic becoming. His steadfastness is hardly generous to all concerned. It daunts anyone who isn't moving along. Americans who embrace Emerson's goal of coordination, but who cannot make their double consciousness budge, are frustrated by the desire. And others may be offended by the very program to brace the doubleness in a movement towards coherence. They may intuit that double consciousness is no problem at all, but rather Americans' most promising feature. I'll return more than once to the suggestion that doubled identities safeguard democracy because they show a gap between cultures, an empty space where culture has no answers, and politics can work in the nonnormative procedures that democracy depends on. Without the experience of cultural contradictions, one might mistake the empty space of politics for a place occupied by one particular culture, the way Emerson did. Anti-Emersonians will refuse to count themselves either among conquistadorial Anglo-Saxons, or among the vanquished who fuel progress with their own expendable existence.

Du Bois has seemed to readers more frustrated than offended, though we will see him complicated enough to occupy both positions. It is true that *Souls of Black Folk* begins at the end of Emersonian optimism, without lifting the now hopeless burden of coordination. "The history of the American Negro is the history of this strife, – this longing to attain self-conscious manhood, to merge his double self into a better and truer self" (1965: 215). The first pages eulogize the slaves' limitless faith in freedom, then follows a long and bitter review of the anticlimax to that faith when Reconstruction broke one promise after another. Du Bois lingers on the rash of local sabotage that undid the federal government's ambitious program of reparations for Blacks and their initiation into a market economy; the lynchings; and the experiences of ex-slaves themselves, unable to adapt to these unpromising circumstances. Fifty years after Emerson's rhapsody on Fate, freedom began to feel like another form of bondage for Blacks, and a frustrated Du Bois protested that no amount of equestrian skill could save the Black rider of Emerson's contending horses. Blacks are crushed between the furious hoofs as race consciousness collides with racist national consciousness; or they are torn apart as the strains of a divided consciousness pull in contrary directions. Agility and stamina only prolong the torment for divided souls. For Emerson, Fate was the classical name for something close to Providence. But the (familiar Christian) paradox of suffering that brings salvation looses its charm for Du Bois; it flattens into an ugly contradiction for American Blacks who neither choose to suffer nor benefit by it. Instead of progress borne by conflicting forces, Du Bois describes an insoluble conflict for the Black intellectual, as one force wastes the other.

> The innate love of harmony and beauty that set the ruder souls of his people a-dancing and a-singing raised but confusion and doubt in the soul of the black artist; for the beauty revealed to him was the soul-beauty of a race which his larger audience despised, and he could not articulate the message of another people. This waste of double aims, this seeking to satisfy two unreconciled ideals, has wrought sad havoc with the courage and faith and deeds of ten thousand thousand people, has sent them often wooing false gods and invoking false means of salvation, and at times has even seemed about to make them ashamed of themselves. (1965: 216)

Ever since then, double consciousness has been the bane of American minorities, an obstacle to acculturation.[4] It has been the unproductive tension between contradictory identities, one particular the other universal. This is an unhappy consciousness by definition, in its structural duplicity. In fact, double consciousness makes a mockery of the word "identity," which literally means some single thing, by splitting it into contending signs held apart by hyphens (African-American; Jewish-American; Hispanic-American; Irish-American . . .). Or the signs are braced together by that hyphen in an unstable, transitional cluster, as the citizen develops towards a more perfect alignment with a universal spirit. Braces are a nice figure, I think, for the voluntary growing pains of becoming American; they are a necessary nuisance that is scheduled to disappear once citizens achieve an unencumbered and attractive maturity. The young country was absorbing citizens from many different backgrounds. And their lingering ties to a culture based elsewhere interrupted a sense of belonging here. The unhappy, but understandable and transitory, result was a fissured "double consciousness" that could be straightened out through training and through time. The orthopedic image would have seemed unnecessary meddling to Emerson, since the Anglo-Saxon race would naturally align itself to history. Double consciousness was a kind of juvenile inability to adjust fate to freedom. Adults would normally make the adjustment (as cultivators of the soil or as guano for it). If they could not adjust they would, evidently, become problems for the country.

"How does it feel to be a problem?" is a question that makes a self-fulfilling assumption. Perhaps Du Bois is also asking if the question is off the mark. It is probably making trouble instead of probing it. The question assumes that Blacks "feel" themselves to be a problem. This is a reflexive move; it imposes the double-consciousness that burdens Du Bois: one self identifies the problem, and the other self embodies it. To unburden himself, with that slow burn he recommends to evaporate pretense and reserve the thick words that should flow, Du Bois delivers an answer that shifts the focus from Black to White, from contemporary misfits ("an outcast and stranger in mine own house" – 1965: 214) to a sketch of slavery, heroic resistance, insufficient efforts at Reconstruction, all of which engrave the indelible racial line that fissures Black consciousness into African and American selves locked in struggle with each other. Double consciousness is indeed a problem for Du Bois, and it's doubly unfair. First Blacks are short-changed by America, and then they fall short of their own American ideals.

To feel oneself as a problem breeds the kind of self-hatred that members of any minority group are likely to experience, to the degree that they also belong to the majority group that hates them. To the extent that Blacks have a national (racist) consciousness which they share with inquiring Whites, Blacks also share the assumptions that Whites make in their discreet but nagging question. Sander Gilman's *Jewish Self-Hatred* (1986) repeats the structure that Du Bois called "two warring ideals in one dark body," while looking at another body. Gilman's prologue explains that his particular focus on Jews is circumstantial, autobiographical. He could have written about almost any minority group: Blacks, Irish, homosexuals, women, Moslems, etc. Paradoxically enough, the predicament of self-hating particularist identities is rather universal.

2   Choose and Lose

Doubleness has not always been a predicament, though. A long history of some premodern societies is instructive. Nor does doubleness necessarily mean trouble for a postmodern society, where the overload of cultural differences demands, as I said, an empty, public space for coordination. Consider medieval England, where Normans were wise enough to know that they ruled a nation of foreigners. Jews, Germans, Danes, and others could not "speak the same language" in any literal way, but they were enjoined to deal fairly with one another. Prudent listening for the "differend" was a medieval practice, long before it became Lyotard's postmodern hope. A medieval mixed jury, which combined local subjects and foreigners as members of the same tribunal, would hear cases between culturally different litigants who could not be subject to one existing rule. The mixed jury predates the contradiction between nation and republic that Lyotard locates at the inconsistent core of modern polities (1993: 139). Perhaps American law would do well to retrieve and adapt medieval respect for cultural specificity as a vehicle and safeguard for justice (see Constable, 1994). Now that our postmodern nations are adjusting to culturally mixed populations, unstoppable waves of immigration, the continuing sounds of different languages in public places, we might take a lead from the Normans, and from the Moors in Spain, to cite one more example. They used to tax thriving infidels rather than to eliminate them as so much guano for conquest. More rational than Christian tradition has portrayed them, Moslem empires have traditionally been hosts to the cultural differences that Christendom does not abide. Spanish modernity came with cultural and political coherence: the consolidation of reluctant and even embattled kingdoms, the expulsion of miscreants, and the continued surveillance of private devotions by public authority. Modernity drove England to overcome internal differences too: a uniform Common Law replaced the *ad hoc* mixed jury, and Jews were expelled (as elsewhere) because they preferred double consciousness over the coherence of one intolerant culture.

Today, universal rights is an idea that parts company with what Europeans had assumed to be a universal culture. Ernesto Laclau argues provocatively along with some critical legal scholars, that universalism is promising today because it depends on difference.[5] It has survived classical philosophy's dismissal of particularity as deviation, and it has outlived a European Enlightenment that conflated the universal (subject, class, culture) with particular (French) incarnations. Today's universalism is a paradox for the past, because it is grounded in particularist demands. They unmoor universalism from any fixed cultural content and keep it open to an "always receding horizon."[6] Precisely because citizens cannot presume to feel, or to think, or to perform alike, their ear for otherness makes justice possible.[7] That is why political philosophy and ethics, from Benjamin and Arendt to Bakhtin and Levinas, caution against empathy, which plays treacherously in a subject-centered key that overwhelms unfamiliar voices to repeat solitary sounds of the self.[8]

This is not the time to lead the horses of double consciousness in one direction, with Emerson's agile Anglo-Saxons who drive others aground; not the time to revive his easy and airless fit between Americans and America. Nor is this the time to follow Du Bois in vicious circles as race and nation dig each other into a ground that requires acculturation but does not permit it. Today we might notice that double consciousness is a normal and ever more universal condition of contemporary subjects. It is also, I have been saying, a structure of democratic feeling. Du Bois called it a curse, we know, but he hinted that double consciousness could also be a double blessing, for Blacks in particular and for America in general. Anything less impoverishes both:

> In the merging he wants neither of the older selves to be lost. He would not Africanize America, for America has too much to teach the world and Africa. He would not bleach his Negro soul in a flood of white Americans, for he knows that Negro blood has a message for the world. He simply wishes to make it possible for a man to be both a Negro and an American, without being cursed and spit upon by his fellows, without having the doors of Opportunity closed roughly in his face.

> This, then, is the end of his striving; to be a co-worker in the kingdom of culture, to escape both death and isolation, to husband and use his best powers and his latent genius. (1965: 215)

The difference between acculturation and this syncretic program may be lost on some American readers, since we have been trained to value assimilation as the process of becoming American. For many immigrants, the process begins with cutting loose, leaving a home culture to join the New World. Mary Antin's example is telling, for its popularity as much as for its power. Consider the opening lines of her autobiography, *The Promised Land* (1997: 1): "I was born, I have lived, and I have been made over. Is it not time to write my life's story? I am just as much out of the way as if I were dead, for I am absolutely other than the person whose story I have to tell." Not everyone, though, was so categorical or sanguine about letting go. Jews who were more attached to tradition than was Antin, Blacks who immigrated involuntarily including some of Du Bois's forebears, Chicanos who never crossed the border but were crossed by it, might well read her enthusiasm for America as intolerance for variety, the dream of purification rather than the drive of dialectics. For them, the Promised Land has meant a place where they prosper, not where they become extinct. Yet the standard meaning of acculturation demands taking sides, nurturing our common new culture and letting the others wither, as if their extinction were a positive goal. Antin herself recoiled from the consequences, after the Great War aroused unfriendly passions in her German-American husband. We hardly know how to name Du Bois's reluctance to cut and to choose when different cultures claim him. What does one call the cultural process of amalgamation that embraces difference, but apparently absorbs it in a new homogeneous mix?

3   Lost in the Mix [*Juntos y Revueltos*]

Latin Americans know several names for it. *Mestizaje* is probably the most familiar. In English, the counterpart would be miscegenation, and the clumsy translation is a sign of the bad fit between the codes (see Sollors, 1997). Miscegenation has been pronounced with mistrust or revulsion, while Latin American racial mixing has often been an official slogan in Spanish and Portuguese. *Mestizaje* endorses the particularity of New World peoples through a rhetoric of national brotherhood that is meant to ease racial tensions, not necessarily to address material equity. Latin Americans would immediately recognize Du Bois's manifesto for merging as a conventional banner of cultural pride. It was, for example, the standard of the Independence movement throughout the continent, when Simón Bolívar proclaimed that Spanish Americans have many fathers, but only one mother, that they are neither Spanish, nor Indian, nor Black, but all of these. A century later, to mention just one more of many examples, *mestizaje* reaffirmed Mexico as a modern country with a mission to the world. For a hundred years, the republic had been torn between indigenist liberals like President Benito Juárez, and Europeanizing monarchists who replaced him with Maximillian. Both sides would contribute, said the minister of education during the Mexican Revolution, to making the new man. Whites and Indians would be joined by Blacks and Asians in the unprecedented culmination of one "cosmic race." This would happen in Mexico, José Vasconcelos wrote in 1925, because no other country was as free from the racial prejudice that obstructs human progress. Anglo-Saxons (like Emerson and Whitman) seemed to prosper by divine will, but, Vasconcelos underlined, "*they committed the sin of destroying those races, while we assimilated them, and this gives us new rights and hopes for admission without precedent in History*" (1979: 15).

In 1940, Fernando Ortiz proposed a new word for merging, in *Cuban Counterpoint of Tobacco and Sugar*. "Transculturation" would emphasize cultural process over racial inheritance, the way syncretism and hybridity already did for contemporary anthropology. Ortiz's innovation was to take account of the pain and the costs (mostly to Blacks) of amalgamation, even though the end product was an admirable and fascinating Cuban culture. Existing words like syncretism and hybridity described the results but ignored the tortuous process. And, as we saw in the case of assimilationists in the United States, a word like acculturation missed the novelty altogether by reducing New World clashes of culture into a one-way

> process of transition from one culture to another, and its manifold social repercussions. But *transculturation* is a more fitting term . . . Men, economies, cultures, ambitions were all foreigners here, provisional, changing, "birds of passage" over the country, at its cost, against its wishes, and without its approval. All those above and those below, living together in the same atmosphere of terror and oppression, the oppressed in terror of punishment, the oppressor in terror of reprisals, all beside justice, beside adjustment, beside themselves. And all in the painful process of transculturation. (Ortiz, 1995: 98–102).

Ortiz was a cultural anthropologist (he began as an ethnomusicologist fascinated by African forms that flourished in Cuba), not an ideologue. Unlike institution-builder Vasconcelos, who promoted *The Cosmic Race* (subtitled *The Mission of the Ibero American Race*), Ortiz was describing an already existing cosmic culture. Cubans were not all equally flattered by the black and white boldness of the picture, to be sure. An autochthonous culture that owed as much to Africa as to Europe could not have appealed to the white elitism that official Cuba had cultivated since the Conquest. To the extent that *Cuban Counterpoint* affirms a more complicated culture, the book is political. It requires acknowledgment of the difference within, the admission for example, that the cult of Orishas plays in counterpoint to the cult of Catholic saints. To this same extent, however, any politics of change is superfluous and distracting. The only sensible response is to celebrate a complex (rather than simply coherent) New World self. Understandably, transculturation (along with *mestizaje* and the cosmic race) has lately come under criticism as an ideology of social affirmation that amounts to control.[9] If difference is already part of the self, neutralized and melted down to merge with its agonist, how can transculturation promote political vitality? How can it focus on the unequal histories of participants?

4   A Republic of Hyphens

I wonder if this kind of stabilized merging is what Du Bois yearned for. It is possible, of course; even probable. He was troubled by the incommensurability of a Black and an American consciousness. But he was also offended at the requirement to acculturate one to the other, to "bleach his Negro soul." Bilateral exchanges seemed to promise more. If Africa and America would produce a new consciousness together, the way Ortiz said they had in Cuba and the way Malinowski had theorized in general about parent cultures producing a new culture that takes from both and yet is different from either one (Ortiz, 1995: 103), then Black and White America could be equally proud of their future offspring. Until very late in his life, Du Bois kept yearning for this bilateral creativity. Everything seemed to hang on the mutuality of acknowledgment, on winning the partnership of whites by cultivating the most gifted Blacks. The elitism (and the patient efforts to arouse indifferent whites) keeps some of his best students at a respectful distance (see West, 1996).

I want to risk a less likely but still possible reading of Du Bois. It hesitates at the point before differences would merge, and lingers on the tension between ill-fitting partners. In part, this slightly willful reading follows from Ortiz's historically inflected improvement on effortlessly friendly words like syncretism and hybridity. But it also departs from Ortiz, along the very faultline that he described between cultural partners trapped in a forced marriage. Transculturation is creativity derived from antagonism. I prefer to focus on Du Bois's scorn for the requirement to bleach one's soul and to ignore racial antagonism, and to downplay his goal of a coherent consciousness. That scorn is an expression of pride in one's difference, and the energy that keeps one cultural particularity in productive tension with others. Thanks to this tension, to incommensurability itself when one thinks of history, taste, preferences, the empty space opens up for a truly universal, non-normative, public sphere of rights and obligations. This is postmodernity's response to the dialectics of modernization: to appreciate the emphasis on procedure in modern politics, and also to value cultural variety (that demands tolerance and flexibility) over modernity's taste for normalization. Does the Du Bois who would modernize through merging convince postmodern readers? Do we still believe in an incrementally truer and more coherent consciousness, along with the eugenic arguments for *mestizaje* and a single cosmic race?

174

If you allow me to pose the question in perhaps impertinently personal terms, I might ask if you would cure your double consciousness if you could. Or would you prefer to continue under its burden? Suppose that you could wake up tomorrow, no longer a Jewish-American, lesbian-American, Latino-, African-, Asian-, gay-, Moslem-American, or any other particular variation but simply American, would you do it? If you could suppress the hyphen of your oxymoronic, more than single, "identity," would you want to? Well, . . . would you? Almost everyone else I have asked has answered *no*, even when they show surprise at their own response. What would predict the resistance, when so much of our civic and cultural training in the United States demonizes the doubleness? Even Du Bois showed reluctance to cure the problem at the cost of racial pride. Perhaps we sense, sometimes without saying it, that the cure is far worse than the complaint.

Some contemporary theorists do say it, urgently and boldly. I mentioned Ernesto Laclau, an Argentine in Europe (in the contradictions between universal rights and a presumptively universal culture) who defends an empty, nonnormative universality cleared away by the bad fit of cultural particularities. I should mention Mari Matsuda too, a Japanese-Hawaiian legal scholar who also defends the play of cultural differences. This is America's best safeguard for democracy, she argues, because the promise of fairness has been mired in a practice of monocultural intolerance for difference.[10] This is certainly not an argument for a Tower of Babel that will quake and crumble with the frustrations of incomprehension. Instead, I want to defend code-switching as one of democracy's most effective speech-acts, along with translation and speaking English through heavy accents, because they all slow down communication and labor through the difficulties of understanding and reaching agreement.

To these theorists and others, one could add a variety of authors who live happily on the hyphen, cultivating the space for personal self-fashioning and for political flexibility. Pérez Firmat (delighted with the paradox) easily becomes American *because* he already is Cuban. Cuba, after all, coined the word *transculturation*, the self-conscious process of admitting difference into the self. But Pérez Firmat's (1994) postmodern *biculturation* refuses the merger that Ortiz had described and that Du Bois had probably desired. "The Cuban-American Way" doesn't fuse the contending cultures but braces them together, on either side of a spacing device that leaves room for creativity. Coco Fusco continues the game in *English is Broken Here* (1995), a manifesto for keeping the country fractured, linguistically, and open to the play of difference. Even Richard Rodriguez, infamous among Chicano rights advocates for arguing against bilingual education and for seamless assimilation in *Hunger of Memory* (1981), keeps his distance. In afterthoughts to Anglos about his tenacious home culture, Rodriguez writes, "I might surprise, even offend, you by how inconveniently Mexican I can be." And like Pérez Firmat, Rodriguez credits his home culture, not the United States, for promoting assimilation. "As someone whose blood springs from Mexico, I am created by an assimilationist culture. Mexico, not the United States, is the true assimilationist example. Most Mexicans do not belong to a single race" (1997: 9–10). In the US, though, Rodriguez remains inconveniently different, bicultural and incoherent. Is this an unhappy consciousness that double identifies define, as they did for Du Bois? Or is it more defiant to monoculturalism than disappointed at not fitting in?

Double consciousness may indeed be a challenge today for the United States, and for other countries reluctant to let go of the dialectical dream of coherence. But it is no longer a rush of contrary forces that human progress should gradually coordinate, as it was for Emerson. Instead, double consciousness is the challenge to develop stamina for the incoherence. Matsuda and others will not be satisfied by mere tolerance for different accents in the courtroom, different flavors of food on streetcorner stands, and complicated personal webs of belonging and sympathies. America needs to value these differences, to celebrate them as the fissures that keep the country from congealing into the meanness of one standard style. Now that Mexican and Central American immigration is virtually uncontainable, that African Americans are taking stock of what is to be gained through assimilation, now that class struggle throughout the hemisphere takes on ethnic inflections, it is time to admit that the dream of cultural coherence is a greater danger to democracy than any obstacle it could hope to overcome.

Is double consciousness in fact bad for democracy, as Du Bois evidently worried it was? Does it block responsible conversation in a vertigo of particular self-hatred and universal contempt for misfits? There is good reason to believe the opposite: that double consciousness enables conversation between parties who respect the differences that separate them, because they acknowledge stubborn differences that fissure their own identities. Perhaps double consciousness ensures democracy by embracing the particularities of citizens who must be tolerated in their difference from others. Otherwise, what would tolerance mean? Anyone who imagines that it means defining difference away, as more of the same "universal" human character, is surely more afflicted by an unhappy consciousness than those of us who learn to live happily on the hyphen and to deal fairly with other fissured subjects.

Notes

1 I thank Werner Sollors for pointing out helpful recent explorations of the philosophical origins of the term double consciousness and of its meanings in contemporary America. See Zamir (1995), Early (1993), and Gooding-Williams (1994).

2 I thank Sacvan Bercovitch for general conversations about this subject, for leading me back to Emerson on the question of double consciousness and locating this quote. See Emerson (1860: 1–42).

3 See Fisher's section on "Jefferson's Map" (1988: 72–7).

4   I am grateful to Werner Sollors for pointing me to the book edited by Gerald Early (1993). See also Sollors (1997).

5   See Gotanda (1991: 53) Citing Robert Paul Wolff, in *A Critique of Pure Tolerance* (Robert Paul Wolff, Barrington Moore, Jr., and Herbert Marcuse, eds., 1965), pp. 4, 17, Gotanda defends racial-cultural diversity as a positive good in the polity, rather than something to be merely tolerated and benignly overlooked. Gotanda also quotes Justice Brennan, whose decision in *Metro Broadcasting* v. *FCC* draws from *Regents of University of California* v. *Bakke*: "Just as a 'diverse student body' contributing to a 'robust exchange of ideas' is a 'constitutionally permissible goal' on which a race-conscious university admissions program may be predicated, the diversity of views and information on the airwaves serves important First Amendment values. The benefits of such diversity are not limited to the members of minority groups . . . ; rather, the benefits redound to all members of the viewing and listening audience" (57). Thanks to Susan Keller for directing me to this article.

6   Laclau (1995: 107). Judith Butler cautiously agrees that universality can be a site of translation. See Benhabib *et al.* (1995: 130): "the universal is always culturally articulated, and . . . the complex process of learning how to read that claim is not something any of us can do outside of the difficult process of cultural translation. [but definition is in the process of defining, *el camino se hace al caminar*] . . . the terms made to stand for one another are transformed in the process, and where the movement of that unanticipated transformation establishes the universal as that which is yet to be achieved and which, in order to resist domestication, may never be fully or finally achievable."

    See also Butler (1997), where she argues for the efficacy of "performative contradictions" in the contestatory translations of "universal." "Performative contradiction" is a term Habermas (1987: xv) had used to discredit Foucault's critique of reason via reason. I'm not sure, however, how different in practice is Butler's project of open-ended translation from Habermas's pursuit of the universal as an ideal. (See Habermas, 1987: 198.) Who could ever reach an ideal? And yet, in the heuristic spirit of Seyla's Benhabib's work, how can one have a political engagement without imagining ideals?

    Homi K. Bhabha also makes translation the cite of the movable nature of modernity in general. See (1994: esp. 32, 242). Translation is the favored strategy for keeping the promise of modernity usably alive.

7   This is a commonplace of political philosophy, one that Mari Matsuda (1991) develops for the practice of law. See Rawls (1985: 248): "[L]iberalism as a political doctrine supposes that there are many conflicting and incommensurable conceptions of the good, each compatible with the full rationality of human persons"; Dahl (1982); Fisk (1993: 1): "There has to be at least a conflict based on an actual lack of homogeneity for what is distinctive about justice to become relevant." See also Benhabib, *Situating the Self.*

8   Benjamin, (1969). In thesis VII of "Theses on the Philosophy of History" (256) he disdains historicism for cultivating empathy, that lazy attachment to the past that has survived in documents, necessarily of the oppressive winners.

    Arendt (1963), see the long section in chapter 2, "The Social Question." Because compassion abolishes the distance where politics can happen, it is irrelevant for worldly affairs (81), and worse, speaking for (weak) others may be a pretext for lust for power (84).

Bakhtin (1990: 64, 81, 88); and Emmanuel Levinas throughout *Totality and Infinity* and *Otherwise Than Being*.

For a proceduralist critique of grounding politics in positive feeling, see, for example, Dahl (1982), esp. ch. 7, "Changing Civic Orientations," 147: "To love a member of one's family or a friend is not at all like 'loving' abstract 'others' whom one does not know, never expects to know, and may not even want to know."

9 I am referring primarily to debates among authors of the New Cultural History of Latin America, being prepared under the leadership of Mario Valdés and Linda Hutcheon.

10 See Matsuda (1991). She celebrates cultural difference beyond the tolerance that liberals like Rorty defend. I am grateful to Professor Susan Keller for this reference.

References

Antin, Mary. (1997). *The Promised Land*, intro. and notes by Werner Sollors. New York: Penguin.

Arendt, Hannah. (1963). *On Revolution*. New York: Viking.

Bakhtin, M. M. (1990). *Art and Answerability: Early Philosophical Essays*, eds. Michael Holquist and Vadim Liapunov. Austin: University of Texas Press.

Benhabib, Seyla. (1992). *Situating the Self: Gender, Community, and Postmodernism in Contemporary Ethics*. Cambridge: Polity.

——, Judith Butler, Drucilla Cornell, and Nancy Fraser. (1995). *Feminist Contentions: A Philosophical Exchange*. New York and London: Routledge. Introduction by Linda Nicholson.

Benjamin, Walter. (1969). *Illuminations*, ed. with an intro. by Hannah Arendt, trans. Harry Zohn. New York: Schocken.

Bhabha, Homi K. (1994). *The Location of Culture*. New York: Routledge.

Butler, Judith. (1997). "Sovereign Performatives in the Contemporary Scene of Utterance," *Critical Inquiry*, 23, no. 2.

Cavell, Stanley. (1989). *This New Yet Unapproachable America: Lecture after Emerson after Wittgenstein*. Albuquerque: Living Batch Press.

Constable, Marianne. (1994). *The Law of the Other: The Mixed Jury and Changing Conceptions of Citizenship*, Law, and Knowledge. Chicago: University of Chicago Press.

Dahl, Robert. (1982). *Dilemmas of Pluralist Democracy: Autonomy Versus Control*. New Haven: Yale University Press.

Deleuze, Gilles and Félix Guattari. (1983). *On the Line*, trans. John Johnston, Semiotext(e), Inc. New York: Columbia University Press.

Du Bois, W. E. B. (1965). *The Souls of Black Folk*, in *Three Negro Classics*. New York: Avon Books, 213–390. First published 1903.

Early, Gerald, ed. (1993). *Lure and Loathing: Essays on Race, Identity, and the Ambivalence of Assimilation*. New York: Allen Lane, Penguin Press.

Emerson, Ralph Waldo. (1860). "Fate," in *The Conduct of Life*. Boston: Ticknor and Fields.

Fisher, Philip. (1988). "Democratic Social Space: Whitman, Melville and the Promise of American Transparency," *Representations*, 24 (Fall): 60–101.

Fisk, Milton. (1993). "Introduction: The Problem of Justice," in *Key Concepts in Critical Theory: Justice*. Atlantic Highlands, NJ: Humanities Press, 1–8.

Fusco, Coco. (1995). *English is Broken Here: Notes on Cultural Fusion in the Americas*. New York: The New Press.

Gilman, Sander. (1986). *Jewish Self-Hatred*. Baltimore: Johns Hopkins University Press.

Gooding-Williams, Robert, ed. (1994). *W. E. B. Du Bois: Of Cultural and Racial Identity*, special issue of *The Massachusetts Review*, 35, no. 2 (summer).

Gotanda, Neil. (1991). "A Critique of 'Our Constitution is Color-Blind,'" *Stanford Law Review*, 44, no. 1 (Nov.): 1–68.

Habermas, Jürgen. (1987). *The Philosophical Discourse of Modernity*, trans. Frederick Lawrence. Cambridge: MIT Press. Introduction by Thomas McCarthy.

Laclau, Ernesto. (1995). "Universalism, Particularism and the Question of Identity," in *The Identity In Question*, ed. John Rajchman. New York: Routledge, 93–108.

Lyotard, Jean-François. (1993). "The Ohter's Rights," in *On Human Rights: The Oxford Amnesty Lectures 1993*, eds. Stephen Shute and Susan Hurley. New York: Harper-Collins, 136–47.

Matsuda, Mari J. (1991). "Voices of America: Accent, Antidiscrimination Law, and a Jurisprudence for the Last Reconstruction," *Yale Law Journal*, 100, no. 5 (March): 1329–1407.

Ortiz, Fernando. (1995). *Cuban Counterpoint of Tobacco and Sugar*, intro by B. Malinowski. First published 1940.

Pérez Firmat, Gustavo. (1994). *Life on the Hyphen: The Cuban-American Way*. Austin: University of Texas Press.

Rawls, John. (1985). "Justice as Fairness: Political Not Metaphysical," in *Philosophy and Public Affairs*, 14: 223–51.

Rodriguez, Richard. (1997). "An American Writer," in Sollors (1997).

Sollors, Werner, ed. (1997). *Neither Black nor White, but Both: Thematic Explorations of Interracial Literature*. New York: Oxford University Press.

Vasconcelos, José. (1979). *The Cosmic Race (The Mission of the Ibero American Race)*, trans. Didier T. Jaén. Los Angeles: California State University Press.

West, Cornell. (1996). "Black Strivings in a Twilight Civilization," in *The Future of Race*, eds. Henry L. Gates, Jr. and C. West. New York: Alfred A. Knopf.

Zamir, Shamoon. (1995). *Dark Voices: W. E. B. Du Bois and American Thought, 1888–1903*. Chicago and London: University of Chicago Press.

Chapter 8

Human Understanding and (Latin) American Interests – The Politics and Sensibilities of Geohistorical Locations

Walter D. Mignolo

1 Transculturation and Loci of Enunciation: Writing at and Writing from Groundless Grounds

What follows is an essay on theorizing postcolonial cultural histories. While I am aware of the difficulties involved in the uses and abuses of the term "postcolonial" (Prakash 1990; Shohat 1992), I am more interested at this point in its advantages. It allows me to think of modernity and postmodernity from a postcolonial perspective, that is, to view "modernity" and understand it from the fringes of colonial histories from the sixteenth to the twentieth century.

The distinctiveness and complementarity of the postmodern and the post-colonial in Latin American intellectual production is clearly, if indirectly, indicated by the authors of two articles in a recent special issue of *boundary 2* on "The Postmodernism Debate in Latin America." While José Joaquín Brunner's article conceptualizes modernity and postmodernity in Latin America, Enrique Dussel's contribution is akin to what I am here calling "postcolonial theories and cultural histories." This program is clearly outlined in Dussel's opening paragraph:

> Modernity is, for many (for Jürgen Habermas or Charles Taylor, for example), an essentially or exclusively European phenomenon, but one constituted in a dialectical relation with a non-European alterity that is its ultimate content. Modernity appears when Europe affirms itself as the "center" of a *World* History that it inaugurates; the "periphery" that surrounds this center is consequently part of its self-definition. The occlusion of this periphery (and of the role of Spain and Portugal in the formation of the modern world system from the late fifteenth to the mid-seventeenth centuries) lead the major contemporary thinkers of the "center" into a Eurocentric fallacy in their understanding of modernity. If their understanding of the genealogy of modernity is thus partial and provincial, their attempts at a critique or defense of it are likewise unilateral and, in part, false.[1] (Dussel 1993: 65)

The identification of the self-same rather than the representation of the other is what flows through literary and philosophical practices in (Latin) America. Geohistorical identification is a complex issue: it is a struggle between colonial allocation and oppositional (neocolonial or postcolonial) relocations on a number of fronts. It strives for the (auto)identification (relocation) of people in a cultural place allocated by successive imperialisms, namely, the New World, the Indies, America during the period of Spanish and Portuguese imperial dominion, and Latin America, as invented by nineteenth-century French imperialism, where the goal was to relocate, in Europe, those cultures whose languages had Latin roots and to defend their own imperial domains against a newly emerging imperial force expanding across the Atlantic: the United States. A second geohistorical identification was largely an intellectual exercise affecting a segment of the population but not the society at large.[2] The extent to which social movements and popular cultures throughout the history of (Latin) America from the sixteenth to the twentieth century assumed or enacted any geohistorical politics of identification, as conceived by the intellectual elite, is an issue that has yet to be explored. Furthermore, precisely how and to what extent such identifications have been reshaped, in practice (by emerging communities and social movements) or in theory (by transforming the human sciences, where understanding and sensibilities have eroded the stability of the persistent Western legacy of viewing knowledge as equivalent to *techné*), during a period of increasing globalization and regional reshaping remains to be seen.

The complexity of this issue stems predominantly from the increasing relevance of borders, boundaries, and borderlines in dislocating national ontologies of geohistorical location and reinscribing, in a transnational world, the spaces-in-between (*nepantla* was coined by Nahuatl-speaking people to refer to the space-in-between the Spanish and the Mexican) engendered by colonial expansion since the end of the fifteenth century.[3] "Mestizaje" and, more recently, "transculturation" are two enduring concepts of discursive formation referring to the Latin American cultural history of defining the self-same as a place of dwelling and of speaking. There have been significant transformations, however, in the ways that these terms were employed until recently and in the meanings that they have acquired. For a long time, "mestizaje" and "transculturation" were used in the context of national configurations. More recently, they have begun to play a role in redefining the transnational locations of cultures (see Kaplan 1992), that is, the movable borders of nations and the fuzzy domains of continental and subcontinental configurations. One such transformation was marked by the significant differences in travel writing between Americans traveling to Europe (e.g., Sarmiento or Emerson) and Europeans traveling to America (e.g., Chauteaubriand or Humboldt).[4] The complicitous identification of the self-same with national territories emerged as a postcolonial concern in both North and South America, while otherness was the focus of European travelers to the New World and to such peripheral areas of the Old World as Africa and Asia.

During the colonial period, administrators in the Americas were not concerned with their own geohistorical and territorial locations, for *where they were* was a place to which they *did not belong*. The situation today is radically different, since the contemporary transnational migrations, borderlands, and other displacements have spawned a territorially detached politics of location. A new configuration of places (rather than any non-place or non-location) is engendering a new geohistorical politics of location in *place* of national- or territorial-identity politics. The transnational does not, of course, erase the national, in the sense of the place where one is born and educated (even if that place is a borderland), but it does imply such erasure. Nor is the transnational necessarily the postnational. It is, rather, the coexistence of regional languages, smells, tastes, objects, pictures, and so forth, with international communications, interactions, and the activities of daily life. The politics of geohistorical location does not imply, then, a defense of the national, but rather the recognition that one is always *from* and *at* (Gilroy 1993), whether or not those locations happen to be the same place (see Shammas 1994).

I have no problem saying that I am Argentinian and Latin American, although I live in the United States and am a naturalized American. As Anton Shammas's dictum goes, "Home is the only thing you do not leave home without" (ibid.). I do, however, balk at saying that I am American when the implication is "from the United States," even though I have developed a sensibility for "its" objects, situations, memories, and places.

Discussions about *loci of enunciation* and *imaginary constructions* of/in the Americas arose several years ago from the combined feeling of *being* "American," properly speaking, that is, coming *from* Argentina and living *in* the United States, *feeling* (Latin) American at the intersection of *coming from* and *being at*. I do not know what being (Latin) American is, but I do know how it feels to be *here*. There are certain imprints left on the body of the place where one grew up (a place that could also be no-place, the no-place of constant migration or continuous exile). I cannot feel European instead, born in Italy and living in London, for instance. Or African, born in Cairo and living in Tangier. This is perhaps what "being at" and "being from" ultimately signify in a transnational world.

In Latin America and the Caribbean there is a long discursive tradition of searching for specifically American geohistorical identities (see Stabb 1967; La Page 1985; Chanady 1993). Nowadays, we might regard this pursuit as an attempt to legitimize *loci of enunciation*; a decolonizing impulse first prompted such quests, although nineteenth-century decolonization now seems to us (if not to its participants then) more like a recolonization, in the sense that while the creole elite emancipated themselves from Spain, Portugal established new connections and dependencies with France and England, and later with the United States. The politics of geohistorical identity created a double bind for the (Latin) American, since an identification constructed by European intellectuals as a *description of an object* inevitably clashed with (Latin) American constructions of the same identification as a *description of the self and of the speaking subject.*

Thus it is the *process of constructing identification* rather than the *description (or definition) of identity* that should be our concern. This change of cognitive terrain has had serious epistemological consequences, as it suggests a shift from the analysis of *representations* to the analysis of the *interactions* that engender representations. This is not to say that those who in the past sought a hidden representational identity were wrong or that they should have conceived of what they were doing as performance rather than representation. I am suggesting, rather, that the performance of representation be read as part of its conceptual structure. In this context, epistemology operates not as "the mirror of nature," but as a site for the regulation of human interactions at both the local and the global level.

As a result of this epistemological shift, the geohistorical question "Who are we?" (Chilean, Argentinian, Caribbean, Andean, Latin American, etc.) can be broken down into two, more penetrating questions: (1) Who is constructing what image? and (2) How does one construct a self-image in the face of one's definition or identification by others (whether by other people or by institutions)? As the question shifts, so does the orientation of theoretical and philosophical concerns. The mimetic game and the desire of intellectuals living in (i.e., *being at*) the colonies or the neocolonial nations (at the periphery or, if you wish, in the colonial or neocolonial centers) or become players in the games played elsewhere prevents them (more often than not) from striving for a theoretical construct grounded in the local needs that are in constant tension with global forces. Such tensions nourish particular kinds of sensibilities, which in turn engender geohistorical identifications at the intersection of imaginary constructions and loci of enunciation.

While I am aware that the center/periphery distinction is suspect in this era of mass globalization, I would like to maintain it, if only because globalization has neither erased nor supplanted this distinction, which has been maintained through 500 years of Western religious, economic, and cultural expansion, a distinction now maintained by an electronic network of power. In my view, both the modern distinction and its postmodern and postcolonial interrogations coexist, even in that electronic intellectual arena where geographical displacement allows people from different corners of the world to move freely, interactively, from periphery to center, and vice versa. There are several respects in which the center/periphery distinction could be said to still hold, such as the food one grows up eating or the music one grows up hearing. Obviously, growing up in Argentina to the beats of Elvis Presley, the tango, and northern Argentinian country music will not be the same as growing up on Elvis Presley in Los Angeles, New York, or Owosso, Michigan.

There is one aspect of the center/periphery distinction that is especially important in relation to the question of loci of enunciation: that is, language and its identification with nations and empires. When the British Empire began to replace those of Spain and Portugal, intellectual colonization went hand in hand with economic expansion (Baumgart 1982; Smith 1981). Spanish and Portuguese

183

lost their allure and were replaced by the major imperial languages (French, German, and English), which have dominated intellectual production from the eighteenth century to the present. In the process by which these "major" languages were canonized (i.e., in the complicity of language with intellectual production), lesser languages (Spanish and Portuguese) were marginalized and those languages that had already been marginalized during the course of Spanish and Portuguese expansion (native languages in America, Africa, and Asia) were suppressed. What "center" and "periphery" mean in a linguistic context and from a global perspective, then, is the difference between writing in Spanish to publish in Mexico City, Bogotá, or Buenos Aires and writing in English to publish in London or New York (see Mignolo 1994).

A tradition of looking for geohistorical specificities was invented in Latin America, as I mentioned earlier, a tradition too long and complex to summarize here. It would be no less complex to debate the logical impossibility, as opposed to the empirical difficulty, of defining or describing geohistorical identities. Therefore, I will focus instead on some of the issues entailed by the search for geohistorical specificities and identities that impinge on loci of enunciation and imaginary constructions. The concept of a *locus of enunciation* invites a change of orientation and enables us to think in terms of *identification* rather than identity, of location as a process related to a place of speaking rather than a description intended to capture a correspondence between what one is and what one ought to be according to some preexisting cultural reality.

While the quest for a Latin American identification is a nineteenth-century phenomenon, the Americas and the Caribbean are historical configurations shaped by conflictive encounters between pre-Columbian European nations and pre-Columbian regional territories, such as Tawantinsuyu (the Andean region today shared by Peru, Bolivia, and Ecuador), Mesoamerica (extending from what is now northern Mexico to Central America), and the islands which were soon to become – in Columbus's imagination – a semantic configuration between cannibals and the Caribbean (see Hulme 1987). The Inkas[5] conceived of the world as a whole divided into four parts, a world they called "Tawantinsuyu." The Aztecs (or Mexica, as they preferred to call themselves) named their own territory in the Gulf of Mexico "Anáhuac" (place surrounded by water) and conceived of the entire world as "Cemanáhuac," thus siting their own region between the two oceans known today as the Pacific and the Atlantic. The Aztecs believed that both oceans were part of a larger body of water surrounding the land mass on which they lived. The emigration of Europeans (from Spain and Portugal to South America during the sixteenth and seventeenth centuries, and from France and England to North America and the Caribbean during the eighteenth and nineteenth centuries) and their transactions with the inhabitants of the lands to which they emigrated, created a "New World" out of the discontinuities of reinscribing both European and Amerindian traditions. Given these discontinuities, reflections on New World identities require a pluritopical hermeneutic capable of articulating both traditions – European and Amerindian

– as these were transformed in their colonial reinscriptions. A pluritopical hermeneutic is required in order to understand new cultures emerging not only from the ruins of disrupted Amerindian civilizations, but also from the fragments of a civilization trying to constitute itself at once as "European" and as the center of a civilizing campaign exported to the New World.

2 Transculturation, Pluritopical Hermeneutics, Colonial and Neocolonial Semiosis

Before I go on with my argument, I should explain what I mean by "pluritopical hermeneutics," beginning with Hindu historian of religion Raimundo Pannikar's definition of "diatopical hermeneutics" as

> the required method of interpretation when the distance to overcome, needed for any understanding, is not just a distance within one single culture (morphological hermeneutics), or a temporal one (diachronic hermeneutics), but rather the distance between two (or more) cultures, *which have independently developed in different spaces* (topoi) their own methods of philosophizing [or of telling stories, creating rhythmic verbal patterns and recording in nonalphabetic writing systems] and *ways of reading* intelligibility along with their proper categories. (Pannikar 1988: 129; my emphases and bracketed addendum)

The paradigmatic example of Pannikar's hermeneutics would be a comparative analysis of two independent and divergent cultures. For instance, while we could compare pre-Columbian European Christianity with pre-Columbian Andean articulations of the relations between human beings and the cosmos, we would not be comparing the "religions" of these cultures since the concept of "religion" would apply to only one of them; its application to the other one would constitute a blatantly monotopical move in comparative studies. The experience of the "Americas" foregrounds a different example: the conflictive encounters and subsequent negotiations between people of unrelated, invented geohistorical traditions. That is, the elements to be compared must be traced to the emergence of cultural patterns and performances. (By "culture" I mean what guides actions or patterns of behavior, not the accumulated achievements or accomplishments by which "cultures" are often measured and ranked; by "performances" I mean the enactment of such behavioral patterns in survival, pleasure, love, hate, etc.) These negotiations between different cultural traditions (in shifting imperial and national contexts) become major forces in the articulation of emergent geohistorical complexes. "Mestizaje," for example, has become a widely used term for describing racial or ethnic hybridity, while "transculturation," a more recently coined term, is used to describe mixed cultural patterns and ways of life (see Arguedas 1975). Both terms may lead to the mistaken assumption that a happy mingling of different bloodlines and ways of life underlies America's unique identity, instead of understanding mestizaje and transculturation as conditions under which such a discourse of identification has been produced and reproduced. In order to avoid such idealistic images, let's foreground "mestizaje" and "transculturation" in the context of colonial legacies and postcolonial theories – a move that will lead us through the back door to the issue of (Latin) American identifications.

The history of the Americas and the Caribbean from 1492 on is not only the history of Western European linguistic, economic, and religious expansion, but also the history of the ways of life adopted by those who were there before this expansion occurred. That history is one of resistance to the imposition of new lifestyles, of accommodation to new situations, and of survival under new social structures of domination. These "new situations" were imposed – in Mesoamerica and the Andes – both on the dominated and on those in dominating positions. But this history is also the story of those who (mainly in the nineteenth century) created a neo- or post-colonial state in South America by gaining independence from Spain and then falling into the net of the new imperial forces, the British economy and French education. And it is finally the history of those "in between": the natives or immigrants who had to deal with colonial situations and the postcolonial intellectuals who had to negotiate a cognitive space between the fragments of the European legacy and the forces of Amerindian ruins. Thus "mestizaje" and "transculturation" cannot be detached from the structure of domination underpinning both colonial situations and postcolonial negotiations, lest they contribute to the idealized construct of a happily multiracial and multicultural society emerging from "cultures in contact" (Malinowski 1943).

"Mestizaje" and "transculturation" could be understood as two different types of discursive configurations, the first accounting for cultural complexities based on bloodlines (and, as such, having strong racial connotations), the other accounting for cultural complexities based on social and semiotic interactions. This understanding would be justified, given that "mestizaje" was first coined by nineteenth-century nation builders (i.e., "first generation") when South American nations were beginning to emerge and the notion of "Latin America" was being promulgated by French intellectuals to counter US (Anglo–American) expansion in Mexico. "Transculturation," on the other hand, was coined by postcolonial intellectuals (i.e., "second generation"), who witnessed the advent of socialism and communism and the crises of the Western world in two successive world wars. Thus while "mestizaje" implied a convivial hybridization of contact zones in the liberal imagination, "transculturation" has implied mutual transformation through continual interaction and negotiation among people of different cultural backgrounds. "Transculturation," with its connotations of social and cultural transformation, is more amenable to a conceptualization of processes of identification (allocation and relocation) than to one of fixed identity states.

As is well-known among Latinoamericanists, the concept of "transcultura-tion" was introduced by the Cuban anthropologist Fernando Ortíz (1881–1969) in an attempt to account for the complex mix of people in Cuba's cultural history and to offer an alternative or counter-construct to Bronislaw Malinowski's notion of "acculturation," a concept meant to account for particular phenomena in areas (or zones) of "cultural contact" (Malinowski 1943). Ortíz explained his concept of "transculturation" as follows:

I understand that *transculturation* better captures the different stages of the tran-sition from one culture to another because such a process is not simply the acqui-sition of a culture different from one's own (which is what *acculturation* suggests); it also implies the loss of or uprooting from a previous culture. In other words, the process implies a partial *disacculturation* and, at the same time, the creation of new phenomena, which could be called *neoculturation*. Briefly, and as Malinowski's school has made clear, every cultural contact [*abrazos de cultura*] is like a genetic coupling between individuals: the newborn shares the features of his or her parents while being different from both. Thus the process is one of *transculturation*, and this notion embraces all the different facets of the analogy.

Questions of sociological lexicons are very important to a better understanding of social phenomena, particularly in Cuba, whose history, unlike that of any other place in America, is one of intense, complex, and endless *transculturation* of numer-ous human masses, all of them in constant transitional process. (Ortíz 1978 [1943]: 96–7; my translation)

One can surmise that the experiences which led Ortíz to articulate the notion of transculturation were very similar to those that led Brazilian writer and critic Silviano Santiago (b. 1936) to formulate his notion of "discourse in between." While Ortíz drew on the anthropological discourse of his day, Santiago was responding in the late sixties and early seventies to poststructuralism and Derridean deconstruction. Furthermore, Santiago, like Ortíz, was sensitive to the marginality of his "Westernness" and to the particularities of loci of enun-ciation under transcultural, bilingual, and "in-between" conditions. For Santiago (1978), "transculturation" became the "entre-lugar do discurso latino-americano" (in-between of Latin American discourse). He stressed the "hybrid" (Santiago's word) character of any colonial process and, in particular, the colo-nization of the New World by means of which the expansion of Western culture became a process of continual reinscription of the New World from the Old. The New World/Old World distinction was the first and the foundational gesture of that process, since it was from the European geohistorical politics of location that Tawantinsuyu or Anáhuac became part and parcel of the imaginary construction of a "New World," with all the properties of the young and the immature attrib-uted to it by that same mentality. The foundational moment of the dialectic between the New and the Old coincided with the foundational moment of the "entre-lugar" as the articulation of a new locus of enunciation (or as a new

187

politics of geohistorical location), challenging such concepts as *unity* and *purity*. "Latin America," according to Santiago, "claims its place on the map of Western civilization due to a constant detour from the norm, a movement which is at the same time active and destructive, which constantly transforms the elements (already made and unchangeable) that Europeans exported to the New World" (ibid.: 18). The Latin American intellectual, in Santiago's view, always acted and wrote *against the same*, so to speak, attempting to detach himself from colonial legacy. Thus "the place in-between" is a place without roots, a place for negotiating the fragments of European civilization in the New World and – in the case of Brazil – the linguistic ruins of Amerindian civilizations (e.g., the *tupiguarani*), as well as the uprooted cultures resulting from African slavery.

There is, no doubt, a radical difference between postcolonial intellectuals of the first and second generations in Latin America. While the first generation promoted mimicry of and alignment with European civilization (mainly the Europe conceptualized by Hegel), postcolonial intellectuals of the second generation – who experienced the socialist revolution as well as the growing influence of the United States in Latin America – replaced the first-generation imaginary construction with a transcultural or hybrid one in and by which Latin America's topography became multilingual and pluricultural, a place where the conflictive politics of cultural differences were articulated in and by distinctive loci of enunciation, as so aptly illustrated by Ortíz and Santiago.

3   Rethinking Europe and How the West Was Born

Before I go any further, I should clarify the context in which I refer to "Europe" and the "West." My use of both notions follows Hegel, who stated in his lectures on the philosophy of history that "the history of the World travels from East to West, for Europe is absolutely the end of History" (Hegel 1956: 103). However, Europe was not a homogeneous entity in Hegel's mind; he perceived it as divided into three parts: "The first part is Southern Europe – looking towards the Mediterranean. Greece also belongs to this part of Europe. Greece and Italy long presented the theater of the World's History; and while the middle and north of Europe were uncultivated, the World's Spirit found its home here" (ibid.: 102). But of particular relevance to my argument is the paragraph in which Hegel described the second part of Europe as "its heart":

> The second portion is *the heart* of Europe, which Caesar opened when conquering Gaul. *This achievement was one of manhood* on the part of the Roman general, and more productive than that youthful one of Alexander, who undertook to exalt the East to a participation in Greek life; and whose work, though in its purport the noblest and fairest for the imagination, soon vanished, as a mere Ideal, in the sequel. *In this center of Europe, France, Germany and England are the principal countries.* (ibid., my emphases)

Briefly stated, "the heart of Europe" included the three colonizing countries which, since the eighteenth century, have replaced Spain and Portugal as the ruling powers over most non-European areas of the world. Finally, the third part of Europe was mentioned by Hegel simply to be dismissed, relegated to the "beginning" of History: "The third part consists of the northeastern states of Europe – Poland, Russia, and the Slavonic Kingdoms. They come only late into the series of historical States, and form and perpetuate the connection with Asia" (ibid.). Thus, by the beginning of the nineteenth century, Spain and Portugal, the great empires of only a few centuries before, had fallen off the European map. This observation is not, I hasten to add, a patriotic or nationalistic complaint; what I have in mind is the overwhelming tendency in current scholarship to set the clock of modernity at the hour of the eighteenth century instead of turning it back to those forgotten days of the thirteenth century when Roger Bacon, looking with admiration toward China and Islam, wished to uplift a lesser community which was in the process of constructing the place where they lived as Europe rather than Christendom.

The "modern period" thus has a double face: a monotopical face, on which universal history is portrayed as a succession of European epochs (Middle Ages, Renaissance, Enlightenment), and a pluritopical face, on which history is expressed as a succession of colonial empires and situations and as the coexistence of complex histories linking the "heart of Europe" (or its empires) with centers constituted in their own rights (i.e., borders, spaces-in-between, or places of transculturation), not as its peripheral colonial dominions. China and Tawantinsuyu were centers in themselves, but were constituted as peripheral from the perspective of the colonizing institutions and the production of knowledge.[6] They were peripheral only from a colonial and European point of view. The concurrent coexistence of centers and the succession of ages might be better understood from within a pluritopical hermeneutics. In colonial situations, loci of enunciation are constructed in two different directions: the celebratory imitation of the colonial power, and the creative counter-discourse of transculturation and the space-in-between. Their consequences for the politics and ethics of intellectual inquiry are quite simple: they invite us to move away from both the *temporal* conceptualization of world history central to modernity (and to postmodern thinking) and monotopical hermeneutics toward the *spatial* conceptualization of world histories and relations central to postcolonial theories and pluritopical hermeneutics. Let's take a closer look at these two perspectives.

4 Colonies Recentered: The Displacement of Imperial Languages and the Emergence of New Loci of Enunciation

The so-called modern period thus had different faces in different centers (Seville, Tawantinsuyu, Peru, Lisbon, Paris, London, Argentina, the Caribbean, Canada, or the border between Mexico and the United States) and in different periods (the sixteenth, nineteenth, or twentieth centuries). In other words, "modernity" is a manifold geohistorical category which was interpreted chronologically within the reduced space of the heart of Europe. In Canada, for instance, toward the end of the nineteenth century, George Robert Parkin was proud to locate his country at the center of the British Empire. Parkin (1895) believed that the amazing spread of the "human race" was the main fact of modern history and would surely have the greatest impact on the future of mankind.

Parkin's discourse exemplifies hundreds of others that could be labeled "colonial discourses from the margins of the West" (taking "colonial discourse" to mean the discourse of the colonizer), by which the intelligentsia of the colonized countries expressed their pride in belonging to or enrolling themselves in the Western tradition. Such discourse reflects the darker side of the more familiar image of the "modern period." Through it, the idea of Europe as a civilizing mission has been kept alive from the sixteenth century to our own by the ideologues of colonial expansion.

While Parkin's work illustrates the discourse of assimilation produced in the Americas of the nineteenth century (as does Domingo Faustino Sarmiento's Argentinian discourse), Frantz Fanon's illustrates the paradigmatic construction of mid-twentieth-century oppositional loci of enunciation. For Fanon's (1952, 1961) critique of colonialism is not only important in its own right, but also for what it reveals about how the transfiguration of the imaginary construction of the Americas went hand in hand with the construction of new centers of enunciation. Fanon's critique thus complemented what Ortíz was doing earlier in Cuba, what Antônio Cândido (1959) was doing in Brazil concurrently with Fanon's efforts, and what Santiago and Roberto Schwartz would do, also in Brazil, some twenty years later.

One of Fanon's major contributions to the critique of colonial discourse was his displacement of the language of the empire, the tool of colonial discourse. While the language of the empire was generally accepted or only weakly challenged by first-generation postcolonial intellectuals, such as Andrés Bello (1781–1865) or Sarmiento, and second-generation intellectuals like Ortíz, it came under heavy fire in Fanon's work. Fanon (1952) established a clear distinction between two levels on which the French language operated, its official use in France and her colonies, and its appropriation by non-French native speakers in the French colonies. He used the figurative terms "white mask" and "black skin" to designate these two levels of French, respectively. Thus were new loci of enunciation constructed out of the fragments of imperial languages that had been transculturated in the ruins of native Caribbean cultures and along with the transplanted languages of uprooted African peoples. Fanon's displacement of the imperial language in the French Antilles was followed up by, among others, Michelle Cliff in Jamaica.

Cliff foregrounded differences (of use and usage) in the English language of the West Indies and, by implication, alternative loci of enunciation in a colonial space. The differences highlighted by Cliff were not those of accent or lexicon, but rather pertained to the language's political dimension. Born into a wealthy family, Cliff pursued her graduate studies at the Warburg Institute in London. Her dissertation on game playing in the Italian Renaissance took her to Siena, Florence, and Urbino, a journey which led her to become active in the feminist movement and to rediscover an identity she had been taught to despise. I will let Cliff speak for herself, quoting extensively from her preface to *The Land of Look-Behind*.

> I originated in the Caribbean, specifically on the island of Jamaica, and although I have lived in the United States and England, I travel as a Jamaican. It is Jamaica that forms my writing for the most part, and which has formed for the most part, myself. Even though I often feel what Derek Walcott expresses in his poem "The Schooner Flight": "I had no nation now but the imagination." It is a complicated business. Jamaica is a place halfway between Africa and England, to put it simply, although historically one culture (guess which one) has been esteemed and the other denigrated (both are understatements) – at least among those who control the culture and politics of the Island – the Afro-Saxons. As a child among these people, indeed of these people, as one of them, I received the message of anglocentrism, of white supremacy, and I internalized it. As a writer, as a human being, I have had to accept that reality and deal with its effect on me, as well as finding what has been lost to me from the darker side, and what may be hidden, to be dredged from memory and dream. And it is there to be dredged. As my writing delved longer and deeper into this part of myself, I began to dream and imagine. . . .
>
> One of the effects of assimilation, indoctrination, passing into the anglocentrism of the British West Indian culture is that you believe absolutely in the hegemony of the King's English and in the form in which it is meant to be expressed. Or else your writing is not literature; it is folklore, and folklore can never be art. Read some poetry by West Indian writers – some, not all – and you will see what I mean. You have to dissect stanza after extraordinarily Anglican stanza for Afro-Caribbean truth; you may never find the latter. But this has been our education. The Anglican ideal – Milton, Wordsworth, Keats – was held before us with an assurance that we were unable, and would never be enabled, to compose a work of similar correctness. No reggae spoken here. (Cliff 1985: 12–13)

Imaginary constructions and loci of enunciation permeate these paragraphs, from the Walcott quotation to the sustained dialectic between the island's English and the King's English, especially the King's English on the island. The same language, the same syntactic rules, but the language game, played under different conditions, yields different kinds of enunciations (literature or folklore) from different loci of enunciation.

Fanon's displacement of imperial French and Cliff's of the King's English are complemented by Gloria Anzaldúa's displacement of Spanish. To read her *Borderland/La frontera* is to read three languages and three literatures at the same time, in the same book – a book that is not only trilingual (Spanish, English,

Nahuatl), but also, of course, tricultural. While Cliff and Fanon likewise molded their respective loci of enunciation from colonial spaces-in-between, Anzaldúa's "in-between" is the pressured space squeezed from between the layers of successive colonizations: first the Spanish colonization of Nahuatl, and later the American English colonization of Spanish. Chapter 6 of Anzaldúa's book is entitled "*Tlilli, Tlapalli*: The Path of the Red and Black Ink," which she explains as follows:

> For the ancient Aztecs, *tlilli, tlapalli, la tinta negra y roja de sus códices* (the black and red ink painted on codices) were the colors symbolizing *escritura y sabiduría* (writing and wisdom) . . . An image is a bridge between evoked emotion and conscious knowledge; words are cables that hold up the bridge. Images are more direct, more immediate than words, and closer to the unconscious. Picture language precedes thinking in words, the metaphorical mind precedes analytical consciousness. . . .
>
> I write the myths in me, the myths I am, the myths I want to become. The word, the image and the feeling have a palatable energy, a kind of power. *Con imágenes domo mi miedo, cruzo los abismos que tengo por dentro. Con palabras me hago piedra, pájaro, puente de serpientes arrastrando a ras del suelo todo lo que osy, todo lo que algún día seré.*
>
> Los que están mirando (leyendo),
> los que cuentan (o refieren lo que leen).
> Los que vuelven ruidosamente las hojas de los códices
> los que tienen en su poder
> la tinta negra y roja (la sabiduría)
> y lo pintado,
> ellos nos llevan, nos guían
> nos dicen el camino. (Anzaldúa 1985: 71)

Anzaldúa's juxtaposition of Spanish and English also juxtaposes prose and poetry, as in her quotation, cast in verse and transcribed in Spanish, of the *Coloquios y doctrina cristiana* (León-Portilla 1986), a dialogue between Mexicans and the first twelve Franciscan friars arriving in Mexico in 1524, after the fall of Mexico-Tenochtitlán. Originally recorded in Nahuatl, then collected and translated into Spanish by Bernardino de Sahagún around 1565, Anzaldúa's excerpt quotes the answers of Mexican noblemen to the Franciscans' questions and their expressed wish that the Mexicans embrace Christian doctrine. Here, the noblemen refer to the *tlamatinime* ("wise men," i.e., those who can read the black and red ink, or the writing in the codices). Anzaldúa not only mixes three languages (two of which – Spanish and English – have strong "literary" traditions, while the third, Nahuatl, was and still is predominantly oral), but she also invokes two kinds of writing: the alphabetic writing imported by the colonizer and the pictographic writing of the Mexican (and Mesoamerican) civilizations. By bringing together three languages, two writing systems, and both the oral and the written tradition, Anzaldúa invites the reader to go beyond the narrow boundaries of the *letter* (*littera*, as in *littera-ture*), the complicities between national languages and nation-states, and the linguistic legacies of colonization.

Imaginary constructions go hand in hand with *enunciations*, and loci of enunciation are unthinkable without a language, in the most general sense of the term. In the more restricted domains of speech and writing, modernity's loci of enunciation have been bound up with the colonial languages of modern Europe (as conceived of by Hegel and Habermas). Fanon's and Cliff's observations on the cultural, ideological, and literary dimensions of French and English directly address an issue which has often been voiced by West Indian writers (e.g., Lamming and Braithwaite) as well as by those of the French Caribbean (e.g., Césaire, Glissant). Anzaldúa offers a more revealing example of the point I am trying to make. Insofar as loci of enunciation are *territorial*, in the conditions of both their possibilities and their performances, Fanon, Cliff, and Anzaldúa all enact a displacement of the understanding subject, who is relocated at the limits (both as margin and as discontinuity) of the Western tradition and colonial expansion.

5   Caliban and Cornel West

There is an intriguing paragraph in Gayatri Spivak's (1993) reflections on post-structuralism and marginality, "Marginality in the Teaching Machine." Spivak quotes the following sentence from a grant proposal by a "brilliant young Marxist academic": "Taking the 'magic realism' of García Márquez as a paradigmatic case of Third World literary production, I will argue that science fiction . . . may be considered, so to speak, the Third World fiction of the industrial nations." Emphasizing the model ("magic realism") rather than the project ("science fiction"), Spivak comments as follows:

> Why is "magic realism" paradigmatic of Third World literary production? . . . In a bit, and in the hands of the less gifted teacher, only that literary style will begin to count as ethnically authentic. There is, after all, a reason why Latin America qualifies as the norm of "the Third World" for the United States, even as India used to be the authentic margin for the British. It is interesting that "magic realism," a style of Latin American provenance, has been used to great effect by some expatriate or diasporic subcontinentals writing in English. Yet, as the Ariel–Caliban debates dramatize, Latin America has *not* participated in decolonization. Certainly this formal conduct of magic realism can be said to allegorize, in the strictest possible sense, a social and a political configuration where "decolonization" cannot be narrativized. What are the complications of pedagogic gestures that monumentalize *this* style as the right Third World style? In the greater part of the Third World, the problem is that the declared rupture of "decolonization" boringly repeats the rhythms of colonization with the consolidation of recognizable styles. (ibid.: 57–8)

193

What is interesting about both the sentence Spivak quotes and her comments on it are the connections made among magic realism, the third world (particularly Latin America), and decolonization (also particularly in Latin America, which, according to Spivak, has not participated in decolonization). There are questions of sensibility and knowledge here that I would like to disentangle.

Fernández Retamar, writing in Cuba after the Cuban Revolution, proposed Caliban as the paradigmatic figure of Latin America. Many years before, during the late fifties, George Lamming had read *The Tempest* with his eyes trained on Caliban. In a chapter of *The Pleasures of Exile* entitled "Caliban Order History," Lamming capitalized on the Caliban allegory to place François Toussaint L'Ouverture, the leader of the slave rebellion on the island of San Domingo, on a par with Napoleon, endowing Toussaint with an awareness of the hierarchies established by the official histories of France, England, and Europe as a whole. Lamming also called attention to a neglected classic of Caribbean cultural history, C. L. R. James's *Black Jacobins*, in which the story of Toussaint L'Ouverture and the San Domingo slave revolt were also told:

> In August 1791, after two years of the French Revolution and its repercussions in San Domingo, the slaves revolted. The struggle lasted for twelve years. The slaves defeated in turn the local whites and the soldiers of the French monarchy, a Spanish invasion, a British expedition of some 60,000 men, and a French expedition of similar size under Bonaparte's brother-in-law. The defeat of Bonaparte's expedition in 1803 resulted in the establishment of the Negro state of Haiti which has lasted to this day. (James 1989 [1938]: ix)

The interplay between Toussaint's revolution and James's account of it, as well as that between Lamming's reading of James and James's reading of Caribbean history, suggests a different angle on the relationship between imaginary constructions and loci of enunciation, between Caliban's ordering history and authorizing a discursive site. In his preface to the 1963 edition of *The Black Jacobins*, James addressed this issue with exemplary force and clarity:

> I have retained the concluding pages which envisage and were intended to stimulate the coming emancipation of Africa. They are a part of the history of our time. In 1938 only the writer and a handful of close associates thought, wrote and spoke as if the African events of the last quarter of a century were imminent.
>
> The Appendix, "From Toussaint L'Ouverture to Fidel Castro," attempts for the future of the West Indies, all of them, what was done for Africa in 1938. Writers on the West Indies always relate them to their approximation to Britain, France, Spain and America, that is to say, to Western civilization, never in relation to their own history. This is here attempted for the first time. (ibid.)

The force of James's writing lies precisely in its constant movement between self-reflection and the construction of loci of enunciation and representation of the slave revolts as small victories achieved throughout the colonial and postcolonial world. Moreover, its force comes from its dislocation of hegemonic models of thinking. In his *Notes on Dialectics*, James (1980) emphasized that philosophical cognition had nothing to do with Hegel or Kant or any particular philosopher; rather, Western philosophers became paradigmatic examples of the increasing influence of the notion of thinking and of its practice. James went beyond articulating mere oppositions to get at the content of colonial discourse, which undercut philosophy's very foundations, questioning not just what may be concluded from Western philosophical premises, but the privileging of those premises and conclusions as the uncontested grounds of human cognition and understanding. James insisted that human cognition and understanding are, first, independent of Western philosophy and its conceptualization of cognition, and second, grounded on the capabilities of the brains and nervous systems of living organisms who have been historically conceived in the West as "human beings." Human cognition and understanding were part and parcel of human life, entwined with the materiality of the body and actualized according to personal sensibilities, gender, class, and geopolitical forces. One of the goals of decolonizing discourse is not simply to construct semantic oppositions, but precisely to dismantle the presuppositions on which Western colonial discourse has been constructed. Whether dislodging colonial discourse from its epistemic and hermeneutic foundations is a similar operation to deconstructing Western metaphysics is a different question and one that I cannot take up here.

My university years in Argentina coincided with the rise of "magic realism." When I went to France at the end of the sixties, "magic realism" was becoming "le dernier gadget d'outre-mer." There was a conflict, then, between how I experienced "magic realism" in Argentina, reading Spanish, and how I experienced it in Paris, reading French translations and discussing it in French with "les copains." Sometimes I was not sure that we were talking about the same thing. Several years later, confronted with Carl Pletsche's (1981) article on the epistemological distribution of the "three worlds," I began to understand my mixed feelings in Paris about the French consumption of magic realism. Pletsche pointed out that the socioeconomic division of the three worlds was paralleled by an epistemological one, according to which the first world produced knowledge, the second world ideology, and the third world "culture." (By "culture" here, Pletsche meant what anthropology has claimed as its field of study.) In this context, then, a partial answer to Spivak's question about how magic realism came to be seen as the "right Third World style" is that magic realism mixes first-world knowledge with the third-world "culture" of passion, emotion, irrationality, and the uncharted domains of folklore. And that is what magic realism explored in art and proposed as an ontology: Latin America *is* magic-realistic.

From "within" however, magic realism is only one of several, not *the* representative style of Latin America, as if Latin America could be identified with any one representative style. Thus has Latin America been allocated once more, this time, however, not by colonial administrators and historians but by oppositional intellectuals. While magic realism (or "marvelous realism") in the hands of Latin American writers (e.g., Carpentier and Asturias) became a means of relocating imaginary constructions and loci of enunciation, it was also reconverted into a new allocation; as such, the agencies producing magic or marvelous realism in Latin America were appropriated and replaced by new agencies that theorized the cultural production of Latin America.

But why, after all, did Spivak assert that there is no intellectual "decolonization" occurring in Latin America? Perhaps, as I believe, she assumes that Latin America is the continental parcel which was once under Spanish rule. The French and the British Caribbean have been constructed by successive colonial discourses as other peripheral entities, although northern Brazil, Venezuela, Colombia, and Mexico are all part of the Caribbean as well. Alejo Carpentier and García Márquez are considered Latin American writers, although they are (belle à bien) Caribbean. José Martí was a postcolonial Caribbean intellectual, in today's sense of "postcolonial." To "decolonize" at the beginning of the nineteenth century, when being free of the Spanish or the Portuguese monarch meant falling into the hands of the British or the French Empire, was a different experience from the decolonizing movements which took place after the Second World War.

Finally, I would like to bring Cornel West's reading of American philosophy into the picture in order to compare geohistorical politics and the sensibilities of location with personal and community interests. In his genealogy of pragmaticism, West (1989) perceives a common thread running through the intellectual history of Anglo-America, namely, the evasion of philosophy, from Ralph Waldo Emerson through Charles Sanders Peirce to Richard Rorty. There has always been a concern in Western philosophy, argues West, with being inside or outside the boundaries of disciplines, as inherited from the Western tradition and as practiced in Western Europe. One might recall in this context Ortega y Gasset's reference to "a philosopher in partibus infidelum," which expressed his own feelings as a philosopher in Spain in the early twentieth century, after returning from studying philosophy in Germany with Husserl and Heidegger to a country whose national language was considered ill-suited to philosophical discourse (see Ortega y Gasset 1984). Of course, several similarities as well as some enormous differences are encountered in other areas when the United States is compared to Spain.

During the modern era Spain remained pretty much on "the margins of the Occident" (to borrow Leopoldo Zea's (1958, 1988) phrase), as the social and historical conditions that made the preservation and expansion of a philosophical tradition possible in Europe were not present in Spain, Argentina, or the United States. Thus, if the locus of enunciation is not given, but is always constructed as a politics of location (whether in geohistorical terms or in those of gender, race, class, etc.), its construction is determined by the situations, possibilities, and sensibilities of sociohistorical conditions, on the one hand, and the way in which these impinge upon disciplinary practices, on the other. Returning to West's analysis, one might suggest that in a country in which Western "civilization" has entailed colonizing the "wilderness" and where cities (with a few exceptions) do not have the contours or the spirit of European urban spaces four or five times as old, a philosophical practice which corresponds to the history of such cities would be difficult to achieve. Charles Sanders Peirce, the most "logical" and "philosophical" of American philosophers and the founder of Anglo-American semiotics, could not restrain himself from devoting time and energy to thinking about ethical issues, including Christianity and the configuration of human communities. On the other hand, his logic and his semiotics "suffered" (from the point of view of a disciplinary concept of philosophy) from the unachieved, the repetitious, and the splendid insights of an open thinking process.

How is the "American evasion of philosophy" finally linked to a geohistorical politics of location? Here is what Cornel West has to tell us:

> It is no accident that American pragmatics once again rises to the surface of North Atlantic intellectual life at the present moment. For its major themes of evading epistemology-centered philosophy, accenting human powers, and transforming antiquated modes of social hierarchies in light of religious and/or ethical ideals make it relevant and attractive. The distinctive appeal of American pragmatism in our postmodern moment is its unashamedly moral emphasis and its unequivocally ameliorative impulse. In this world-weary period of pervasive cynicisms, nihilisms, terrorisms, and possible extermination, there is a longing for norms and values that can make a difference, a yearning for principled resistance and struggle that can change our desperate plight.
>
> The irony of the contemporary intellectual scene in North America is that after an obsession with European theories and philosophies, *we are discovering some of what is needed in the American heritage. This intellectual turn to our heritage ought to be neither a simplistic pro-Americanism in the life of the mind nor a naive parochialism that shuns international outlooks. But this turn is a symptom of just how blinded we often are to certain riches in the American intellectual and political past.* . . . I understand American Pragmatism as a specific historical and cultural product of American civilization, a particular set of social practices that articulate certain American desires, values, and responses and that are elaborated in institutional apparatuses principally controlled by a significant slice of the American middle class. (West 1989: 4)

Briefly stated, West is looking for a location from which to speak, a location that engenders not only ways of saying and seeing, but also ways of feeling and desiring.

And so is José Saldívar, as he rearticulates traditions and constructs a borderland locus of enunciation which allows him to erase previous borders traced by the imaginary constructions of colonial discourse. Colonial distinctions based on colonial languages, on the gap between the English and Spanish languages and literatures, are addressed by Saldívar in a way that reminds us of James's translinguistic concept of the Caribbean:

> What lies behind this essay, then, is a growing awareness on my part of the extremely narrow confines and conservative practices of literary study as it is now performed in the academy, and with that, a growing conviction about the social and political implications of this exclusionary practice. As a literary theoretician outside the mainstream and educated in a segregated farm society in south Texas, I have been particularly sensitive to the absence of writers from . . . "our America." . . . In my view, the greatest shortcoming of the work being done on the American canon is not its lack of theoretical rigor but rather its parochial vision. Literary historians (even the newer ones) and critics working on the reconstruction of American literary history characteristically know little in depth about the history, cultures, and discourses of the Americas as a totality. One of the values of a comparative focus is that it permits us to escape from . . . the provincial, limiting set of tacit assumptions that tend to result from perpetual immersion in the study of a single American culture or literature.[7] (Saldívar 1990: 63)

Saldívar transforms the earlier Ariel-Caliban version of decolonization into the dialectics of "Our America" and thereby relocates José Martí and Roberto Fernández Retamar at the forefront of postcolonial intellectuals. Like Leopoldo Zea and other (Latin) American and Caribbean writers, Fernández Retamar has contributed to the effort of relocating America in the discourse of the West. By taking up this relocation where he has left off, Saldívar addresses the question of loci of enunciation and theoretical production: "A radical decentering of postcolonial theory is currently under way in the hybrid works of such writers as Kumkum Sangari, Barbara Harlow, and Norma Alarcón" (Saldívar 1990: 149).

By liberating "theory," a decentering of discursive production and loci of enunciation could begin. If we limit our speculations to (Latin) America, we can see that what has been a long tradition of allocating (Latin) American cultures is beginning to be reconstructed as a relocation: a new, transnational geopolitics that emphasizes borders, languages across nations, and plurilingualism within nations – briefly, a reconfiguration of linguistic maps that can lead to the imagining of new cultural geographies and new loci of enunciation. In this process, new agencies will claim their places and voices in the dialogue, as social movements transform cultural spaces such that imaginary constructions and loci of enunciation are no longer the sole province of writers and intellectuals.[8] In other words, loci of enunciation are also the spaces in which social movements are already transforming imaginary constructions (see Evers 1985; Findji 1992; Westwood and Radcliffe 1993; Alvarez and Escobar 1992). If, as Arturo Escobar (1992) and Orin Stern (1992) maintain, collective social actors construct their identities and produce fresh political visions through a creative process of engagement with the conditions of everyday life, and if, as Tilman

Evers (1985) claims, social movements transform not just the political but the cultural social space, then the geohistorical politics of location and the conflictive politics of difference can no longer be defined by academic intellectuals alone, but should emerge from a dialogue between them and the newly emerging intellectuals who are leading social movements. In the early 1970s, Paul Ricoeur could imagine social actions as texts. By now, we are accustomed to imagining texts as social actions. We still need to work on understanding that such relations are not a matter of "high" and "low" cultures, of "thought" versus "action," but rather of different ways of striving for social and cultural transformations.

Notes

I am indebted to José Rabasa and the students in his seminar on "Subaltern Studies in the Americas" at the University of Maryland for a long and lasting discussion of this paper.

1   Dussel (1992) articulates the same idea in more detail. For a similar argument, see Homi Bhabha (1994a, 1994b), Paul Gilroy (1993), and Walter Mignolo (1993, forthcoming (a), and forthcoming (b)).
2   See, for instance, Tilman Evers (1985) and S. Westwood and S. A. Radcliffe (1993) on the question of identification and social movements.
3   This particular notion of "hybridity" or "space-in-between" has been exploited by such Chicana/o writers as Gloria Anzaldúa (1987) and Pat Mora (1993).
    For similar theoretical constructions in the context of different colonial legacies, see Fernando Ortíz (1978 [1943]) on the Spanish Caribbean (on Ortíz, see Coronil 1995; James 1980, 1989 [1938], 1993 [1963]); M. N. Philip (1992) on the British Caribbean (on James, see Winter 1992; Henry and Buhle 1992); on the French Caribbean, see Maryse Condé (1978) and Edouard Glissant (1981). (On Condé, see Clark 1991; on Glissant, see Case 1989.)
4   On such travel writing, see Beatriz Urraca (1993), Ottmar Ette and Andrea Pagni (1992), and Mary Louise Pratt (1992).
5   Here I am following the spelling used by J. C. Mariátegui in *Siete ensayos de interpretación de la realidad peruana* (1928).
6   See Marshall Hodgson (1993) for a similar argument using the examples of Islam and Christianity.
7   See also Saldívar (1990: 4). For the relevance of this paragraph in a larger context, see Mignolo (1991, 1992a).
8   During the discussion of this paper in José Rabasa's seminar on subaltern studies, Ms Urquilla, one of the participants, suggested that I should also think in terms of "loci of enactment" and not only of "enunciation." Ms Urquilla argued that the phrase "loci of enunciation" maintains the privileging of speech and writing over other kinds of social action. I take her critique seriously and believe that "social movements" are clearly examples of "loci of enactment." I therefore think of loci of enunciation as enactment and of loci of enactment as enunciation.

199

References

Alvarez, Sonia E., and Arturo Escobar, eds. (1992). *The Making of Social Movements in Latin America: Identily, Strategy and Democracy* (Boulder: Westview Press).

Anzaldúa, Gloria. (1987). *Borderland/La frontera* (San Francisco: Aunt Lutte).

Arguedas, José María. (1975). *Formación de una cultura nacional indoamericana* (Mexico City: F.C.E.).

Baumgart, Winfried. (1982). *Imperialism: The Idea and Reality of British and French Colonial Expansion, 1880–1924* (New York: Oxford University Press).

Bhabha, Homi K. (1994a). "Introduction: Locations of Culture," *The Location of Culture*, 1–18 (New York: Routledge).

——. (1994b). "The Postcolonial and the Postmodern: The Question of Agency," *The Location of Culture*, 171–97 (New York: Routledge).

Brunner, José Joaquín. (1993). "Notes on Modernity and Postmodernity in Latin America," in *The Postmodernism Debate in Latin America*, eds. J. Beverley, J. Oviedo, and M. Aronna (Durham: Duke University Press).

Cândido, Antônio. (1959). *Formacao da Literatura Brasileira* (São Paulo: Martins).

Case, Frederick Ivor. (1989). "Edouard Glissant and the Poetics of Cultural Marginalisation," *World Literature Today*, 63 (4): 593–98.

Chanady, Amaryll, ed. (1993). Latin American Identity and Constructions of Difference. *Hispanic Issues*, 10.

Clark VéVé, A. (1991). "I Have Made Peace with My Island: An Interview with Maryse Condé," *Callaloo*, 142: 381–88.

Cliff, Michelle. (1985). *The Land of Look-Behind* (Ithaca: Firebrand Books).

Condé, Maryse. (1978). *La Parole des femmes: Essais sur des romancières des Antilles de langues française* (Paris: L'Harmattan).

Coronil, Fernando. (1995). "Transculturation and the Politics of Theory: Countering the Center, Cuban Counterpoint." Introduction to F. Ortíz, *Cuban Counterpoint: Tobacco and Sugar*, trans. Harriet de Onís (Durham: Duke University Press).

Dussel, Enrique. (1992). *1492. El encubrimiento del otro: Hacia el origen del mito de la modernidad* (Madrid: Nueva Utopía).

——. (1993). "Eurocentrism and Modernity (Introduction to the Frankfurt Lectures)," *boundary 2*, 20 (3): 65–76.

Escobar, Arturo. (1992). "Culture, Economics, and Politics in Latin American Social Movements: Theory and Research," in Alvarez and Escobar 1992: 62–87.

Ette, Ottmar, and Andrea Pagni. (1992). Crossing the Atlantic: Travel Literature and the Reception of the Other. Special issue of *Dispositio: Revista Americana de Estudios Comparados y Culturales/American Journal of Comparative and Cultural Studies*, 18 (42/43).

Evers, Tilman. (1985). "Identity: The Hidden Side of New Social Movements in Latin America," in *New Social Movements and the State in Latin America*, ed. David Slater, 43–72 (Amsterdam: CEDLA).

Fabian, Johannes. (1982). *Time and the Other: How Anthropology Makes Its Object* (New York: Columbia University Press).

Fanon, Frantz. (1952). *Peau noire, masques blanc* (Paris: Seuil).

——. (1961). *Les Damnés de la terre* (Paris: Maspero).

Findji, Maria Teresa. (1992). "From Resistance to Social Movement: The Indigenous Authorities Movement in Colombia," in Alvarez and Escobar 1992.

Gilroy, Paul. (1993). *The Black Atlantic: Modernity and Double Consciousness* (Cambridge, Mass.: Harvard University Press).

Glissant, Edouard. (1981). *Le Discours antillais* (Paris: Seuil).

Hegel, G. W. F. (1956). *Philosophy of History*, trans. J. Sibree (New York: Dover).

Henry, P. and P. Buhle. (1992). "Caliban as Deconstructionist: C. L. R. James and Post-colonial Discourse," in *C. L. R. James's Caribbean*, eds. P. Henry and P. Buhle, 111–44 (Durham: Duke University Press).

Hodgson, Marshall G. S. (1993 [1956]). "In the Center of the Map: Nations See Themselves as the Hub of History," in *Rethinking World History: Essays on Europe, Islam and World History*, ed. Edmund Burke III (New York: Cambridge University Press).

Hulme, Peter. (1987). *Colonial Encounters: Europe and the Native Caribbean, 1492–1797* (New York: Methuen).

James, C. L. R. (1980). *Notes on Dialectics* (London: Allison and Busby).

——. (1989 [1938]). *The Black Jacobins: Toussaint L'Ouverture and the San Domingo Revolution* (New York: Vintage Books).

——. (1993 [1963]). *Beyond a Boundary* (Durham: Duke University Press).

Kaplan, Caren. (1992). "Resisting Autobiography: Out-Law Genres and Transnational Feminist Subjects," in *De/Colonizing the Subject*, eds. S. Smith and J. Watson, 115–38 (Minneapolis: University of Minnesota Press).

La Page, R. G. (1985). *Acts of Identity: Creole-Based Approaches to Language and Ethnicity* (New York: Cambridge University Press).

León-Portilla, Miguel, ed. (1986). *Coloquios y doctrina cristiana* [1565]. Collected by Fray Bernardino de Sahagún (Mexico City: Universidad Nacional Autónoma de México).

Malinowski, Bronislaw. (1943). "The Pan-African Problem of Culture in Contact," *American Journal of Sociology*, 48: 6.

Mignolo, Walter D. (1991). "Canon and Corpus: Nuevas Perspectivas en los Estudios Literarios Latinoamericanos." Lecture delivered at Freiburg University, Germany, Nov. 1991.

——. (1992a). "Canon and Corpus: Alternative Views of Comparative Literature in Colonial Situations," *Dedalus: Revista Portuguesa de Literatura Comparada*, 1: 219–44.

——. (1992b). "Canons A(nd)Cross-Cultural Boundaries (Or, Whose Canon Are We Talking About?)," *Poetics Today*, 12 (1): 1–28.

——. (1993). "Colonial and Postcolonial Discourse: Cultural Critique or Academic Colonialism?" *Latin American Research Review*, 28 (3): 120–34.

——. (1994). "Linguistic Maps and Literary Geographies: Nations, Languages and Migrations." Lecture delivered at "II Encuentro Internacional sobre teorías y prácticas críticas: La responsabilidad del intelectual en el final del milenio," Mendoza, Argentina, Aug. 1994.

——. (1995) "Occidentalización, imperialismo, globalización: Colonización y razón post-colonial," *Revista Iberoamericana*, 170/171: 27–40.

——. Forthcoming (b). "The Postcolonial Reason: Colonial Legacies and Postcolonial Theories," in *Dimensions of Postcolonial Studies*, eds. Fawzia Afzal-Khan and Kalpana Seshadri-Crooks.

Mora, Pat. (1993). *Nepantla: Essays from the Land in the Middle* (Albuquerque: University of New Mexico Press).

Ortega y Gasset, José. (1984). *Meditaciones del Quijote* (Madrid: Cátedra).

Ortíz, Fernando. (1978 [1943]). *Contrapunteo cubano del tabaco y del azúcar* (Caracas: Biblioteca Ayacucho).

201

Pannikar, Raimundo. (1988). "What Is Comparative Philosophy Comparing?" In *Interpreting across Boundaries*, eds. G. Larson and D. Eliot, 116–36 (Princeton: Princeton University Press).

Parkin, George Robert. (1895). *The Great Dominion: Studies of Canada* (London and New York: Macmillan).

Philip, Marlene Nourbese. (1992). *Frontiers: Essays and Writings on Racism and Culture* (Ontario: Mercury Press).

Pletsche, Carl. (1981). "The Three Worlds, or the Division of Social Scientific Labor, circa 1950–1975," *Comparative Studies in Society and History*, 23 (4): 565–90.

Prakash, Gyan. (1990). "Writing Post-Orientalist Histories of the Third World: Perspectives from Indian Historiography," *Comparative Studies in Society and History*, 32: 383–408.

Pratt, Mary Louise. (1992). *Imperial Eyes: Travel Writing and Transculturation* (New York: Routledge).

Saldívar, José. (1990). "The Dialectics of Our America," in *Do the Americas Have a Common Literature?*, ed. Gustavo Pérez-Firmat, 62–84 (Durham: Duke University Press).

Santiago, Silvano. (1978). "O entre-lugar do discurso latino-americano," *Uma literatura nos tropicos: Ensaios sobre dependencia cultural* (São Paulo: Editora Perspectiva).

Shammas, Anton. (1994). "Going Home: The Case of Palestine, Michigan," Lecture delivered at the 1994 Littauer Foundation Lecture Series, Duke University, Feb. 23.

Shohat, Ella. (1992). "Notes on the 'Post-Colonial,'" *Social Text*, 31/32: 99–113.

Smith, Tony. (1981). *The Pattern of Imperialism: The United States, Great Britain, and the Late Industrializing World Since 1815* (New York: Cambridge University Press).

Spivak, Gayatri C. (1993). "Marginality in the Teaching Machine," *Outside the Teaching Machine* (New York and London: Routledge).

Stabb, Martin S. (1967). *In Quest of Identity: Patterns in the Spanish American Essay of Ideas, 1890–1960* (Chapel Hill: University of North Carolina Press).

Stern, Orin. (1992). "'I Dreamed of Foxes and Hawks': Reflections on Peasant Protest, New Social Movements, and the *Rondas Campesinas* of Northern Peru," in Alvarez and Escobar 1992: 89–111.

Urraca, Beatriz. (1993). "The Literary Construction of National Identities: Argentina and the US, 1845–1898." University of Michigan Dissertation Microfilms.

West, Cornel. (1989). *The American Evasion of Philosophy: A Genealogical Pragmaticism* (Madison: University Books).

Westwood, S. and S. A. Radcliffe. (1993). "Gender, Racism and the Politics of Identities in Latin America," *VIVA: Women and Popular Protest in Latin America* (Boulder: Westwood Press).

Winter, Sylvia. (1992). "Beyond the Categories of the Master Conception: The Counterdoctrine of the Jamesian Poiesis," in *C. L. R. James's Caribbean*, eds. P. Henry and P. Buhle, 63–91 (Durham: Duke University Press).

Zea, Leopoldo. (1958) *América en la historia* (Mexico City: Universidad Nacional Autónoma de México).

———. (1988). *Discurso desde la marginación y la barbarie* (Barcelona: Anthropos).

Chapter 9

US Imperialism: Global Dominance without Colonies

Donald E. Pease

The incompatible phrases in the title of this essay rehearse the contradictory stances that US policy-makers have adopted regarding the nation's colonial history. When linked with "US Imperialism," the phrase "without colonies" reveals disavowal and selective amnesia as conjoined strategies through which the state has accomplished the denial of US colonialism. Historians have adapted these strategies to a terminology that would recognize the existence of US imperialism only when qualified as "informal," "accidental," "involuntary," or otherwise differentiated from the european kind. But from the time of its founding, the state administered colonial institutions that included "indian removal" policies, slave plantations, and settlements for defeated populations. While it confined itself to the exercise of internal colonialism during most of the nineteenth century, at the turn of the twentieth the US acquired a colonial empire overseas. After The Second World War, the cold war state engaged in neocolonial policies with newly decolonized countries.

Indeed throughout most of its history, the US participated in the imperial world system. But its official representatives have proposed that US imperialism be conceptualized as an adventure that the state accomplished without US imperialists who would claim knowledge of or responsibility for this fact. The disparity between the United States' imperial policies and the refusal to acknowledge them bears powerful witness to the power of the doctrine of US exceptionalism which authorized the refusal.

US exceptionalism is a political doctrine as well as a regulatory ideal assigned responsibility for defining, supporting, and transmitting the US national identity. The power of that doctrine to solicit belief is discernible in the clause set in apposition to "US imperialism." "Global dominance without colonies" occupies two utterly different spaces in the US political order. When elaborated into the proposition that the nation achieved worldly power without acquiring colonies, the phrase confirms the core tenet of the doctrine of US exceptionalism. But when invoked by the state in the administration of its colonies, the clause has also empowered the state to produce legal exceptions to this tenet.

Despite the incompatibilty in the state's usages of this clause, however, the doctrine of exceptionalism has not construed the state's exceptions as refutations of its core beliefs.

The authority of the doctrine is discernible in its power actively to ignore the state's exceptions. It supplied its adherents with the absences they required to maintain their foundational beliefs. The doctrine was a composite construction that involved an alliance among cultural workers, the economic sector, and the state in refusing to acknowledge the realities of political domination. The strategies whereby the doctrine acquired critical mass in the culture at large were shaped in a network of discourses correlating US foreign and domestic policies with the work of official historians, literary critics, economists, museum directors, ethnographers, journalists, sociologists, canonical writers, theologians, pragmatists, and postcolonial theorists. In this broad-ranging network of discourses, the doctrine has served as at once an object of study and an instrument of rule.

The doctrine also shaped the contours of the academic field of American Studies out of the prolonged debate conducted therein over whether the nation was a variation upon or a deviation from European models. Whether and how it differed released a range of problems that delimited the scope of the field's inquiry. In restricting its understanding of US culture to these standpoints, American Studies has in turn provided the discourse an operational context determining how US culture gets taught, administered and pronounced upon. When historians have linked the doctrine of exceptionalism to their narratives, it has regulated how US citizens represented themselves and their history. The state has linked this web of representations to its domestic and foreign policies.

What the doctrine of exceptionalism declared exceptional in the US political economy referred to european institutions – like feudalism, monarchical rule, and colonial territories – that were reputedly absent from its history. But while the state was constituted in explicit opposition to monarchical rule and was resolute in its rejection of feudalism, its relation to colonialism was decidedly more complicated.

The complications did not arise from the historical fact that such colonies existed. They arose instead from the state's representation of their political status as exceptions and from the role exceptionalism played in sustaining that condition. The doctrine of exceptionalism regulated how citizens responded to the historical existence of US colonies by characterizing them as exceptions to its norms. The relations between exceptionalism and the state's exceptions to its beliefs are best described in psychological terms as structures of denial. The psychological processes of disavowal and forgetting that exceptionalism facilitated might as a consequence be understood as efforts to produce the absences in which the doctrine is grounded. These and related forms of denial reconstituted US citizens' adherence to the nation's exceptionality by excluding historical facts that might disconfirm that belief.

While the doctrine installed US exceptionalism as a transhistorical model, specifications of the doctrine's content have changed with historical circumstances. Exponents of exceptionality have placed in nomination various descriptions of the nation's world historical role. Candidates have included the "redeemer nation," "nation of nations," "leader of the free world," "conqueror of the world's markets." But each of these variations on the nation's exceptional place in the world order is derivable from the conviction that colonialism was absent from US history.

But if the doctrine of exceptionalism produced this belief to which the state regularly took exception, the state thereafter required the doctrine to solicit its citizenry's assent. The doctrine of exceptionalism enjoined belief in the proposition that in lacking a colonial empire, the US occupied a position significantly different from that of other powerful nation-states. But that belief, as has already been observed, coincided with the state's acquisition of internal colonies. In its disavowal of this historical fact, exceptionalism supplied US citizens with an imaginary relation to actual state colonialism.

Exceptionalism and the state's exceptions to it at once require one another's operations, yet they are also set in opposition. The power of the state's exceptions becomes evident in what the discourse of exceptionalism is compelled to disavow. By way of its exceptions the state includes instances of what the doctrine of exceptionalism has described as missing from the national history. The state can thereafter exercise the sovereign power to produce the absence that exceptionalism has described as foundational. US exceptionalism, on the other hand, can describe persons that the state has declared exceptions to its rules as representing political ideologies – like communism or colonialism – that lacked a foundation in the history of the republic.

In the case of colonialism the state has exercised both options. It has referred to the doctrinal belief in the historical absence of colonialism, for example, as pretext for the immigration policies banishing certain colonial refugees. But in its Jim Crow legislation and civil rights policies, the state has also declared itself exempt from exceptionalism's ruling norms. In adding to the polity the colonial condition that its governing rules had described the nation as constitutively lacking, the state has positioned itself as an exception to the norms through which it governed. Persons that the state had constructed as exceptions to its exceptionalist norms – slaves, migrant laborers, involuntary immigrants – were likewise situated in the space of the exception. They were inside the state but treated as if outside its conditions of belonging.

The disavowal that was crucial to the production of these exceptions discloses the willfulness through which the US misrepresented its history as well as its place in the world. Official historians have fashioned their accounts of US domestic policies out of the conviction that the nation was different from european imperial states in that it repudiated the acquisition of colonies. Disowning knowledge of the historical realities of imported slave labor, of overseas colonialism, of the economic exploitation of refugees has entailed historians' differentiating the US government's domestic policies from the *realpolitik* of the international arena. But in their distribution of ethnic and "racialist" differences into hierarchical social rankings, US immigration laws in particular have depended upon stereotypes developed out of a residual colonial discourse. Moreover, throughout much of the nation's history, US foreign policy has worked in more or less open violation of democratic ideals. The historical struggles of asian, hispanic and amerindian groups for recognition of their equal rights reveal linkages between domestic and foreign policies that US exceptionalism effaced.

State historians have grounded the narrative through which they have ignored the contradiction between the nation's democratic ideals and subsequent imperialist practices in the discourse of exceptionalism. The narrative linked the United States' place in world history into a quasi-messianic national ideology. This ideology was believed to have originated in the Puritans' conviction that providential design had assigned them the unique world historical task of dispossessing amerindians of their lands as the precondition for the redemption of their souls.

Early New England settlers successfully tallied the incorporation of vast expanses of the natives' geography with this belief. But following the settlers' separation from the "mother country," the religious aspects of the doctrine of exceptionalism underwent transformation into a state credo. But historical events never in fact coincided with the credo's idealized image of the US as a democracy founded in defiance of imperial norms. In accomplishing a position of dominance in the hierarchy of nations, the US practiced the imperialism that it disavowed in principle.

William Appleman Williams has succinctly described the dissociative reasoning through which historians have recounted the exceptionalist narrative:

> One of the central themes of American historiography is that there is no American Empire. Most historians will admit, if pressed, that the United States once had an empire. They then promptly insist that it was given away. But they also speak persistently of America as a world power. (1980: 380)

In between US historians' admission of a US colonial empire and their insistence "that it was given away," an entire imperial history comes into visibility as what cannot become straightforwardly referential in the exceptionalist metanarrative.

Throughout his historical project, Williams has demonstrated how the stratagems through which US imperial history has been misremembered also permit the construction of counterhistories. But the "remembering" of imperial events at the site of official historians' amnesia has required strategic and far-reaching historical revisionisms. Effective revisionist histories have often been composed by representatives of the communities whose pasts were displaced from within official historical narratives. In bearing collective witness against historical forgetting, writers like Frederick Douglass, José Martí, Louise Erdrich, and Joy Kogawa have struggled to come to adequate terms with collective historical traumas like the institutional slavery and internal colonialism of the nineteenth century and border patrols, Japanese internment camps, not to mention HUAC in the twentieth. In refusing the cultural stereotypes and conventions through which the official historical narrative had represented them, their alternative narrations have materialized the experiences – of imperial aggression and neocolonialist exploitation – that US exceptionalism had denied referentiality.

But the doctrine of US exceptionalism has also undergone significant revisions designed to assimilate these counterhistories to its encompassing narration of them. Whenever the state's imperialist foreign policies openly violated democratic norms, the narrative has proposed significant reinterpretations of the doctrine. In accommodating its beliefs to these revisions, the doctrine of US exceptionalism has hollowed out an exception to the nation's foundational norms. The exception has described the state as at times obliged to enact policies in open violation of its declared opposition to the imperialism of european nations. The doctrine has also restricted the state's power to invoke these exceptional powers to the event of a national emergency or for the purpose of demonstrating US moral superiority.

The second of these restrictions has proven elastic enough to permit a moral interpretation of practically any state policy. The "Mexican-American War" is exemplary for its having stretched the moral imagination of US exceptionalists to invent an auxiliary belief as its rationale. Throughout this war, the state's military strategists had coordinated the annexation of vast territories in the Southwest and the displacement of entire populations. Since the greed and brutality in evidence throughout the expansionist campaign constituted behavior more typically associated with ambitious imperial states, the war proved vexing for the state intellectuals assigned the task of explaining its moral purpose. The nation would not be relieved of this ethical dilemma until its moral arbiters added manifest destiny as a new tenet in the civil religion. Manifest destiny solicited belief in the fiction that US soldiers and Mexican peoples were acting out a moral allegory that divine providence assigned them as the way to realize the fate of both nations.

Approximately every fifty years since the Mexican War, the US has invoked a logic of the exception to justify policies significantly different from its anti-imperial norms. Throughout the "Spanish-American War" the US rationalized its imperialist foreign policies by recasting them as the state's exercise of emergency powers required to defend the nation's commercial interests abroad. In 1949, Harry Truman inaugurated the fifty-year reign of the cold war's state of emergency when he invoked National Security Position Paper 68 as its rationale. That document explained that the national security state had emerged out of the necessity to defend the nation against Russian imperialism. It further described that state's emergency powers as exempt from the democracy's normal procedures of checks and balances.

In restricting the referentiality of the term "postcolonial" to the political settlements that took place after the decolonization of former european colonies, postcolonial theory has constructed the most recent of the variations on the theme of US exceptionalism. With notable exceptions, postcolonial theorists have argued against interpreting US policies toward racial minorities and immigrants as evidence of what Robert Blauner (1972) has called "internal colonialism." Observing that postcolonialism does not happen now because colonialism did not happen in the nation's past, they have concluded that colonialism had little or nothing to do with the formation of the US national identity and that the study of US culture will not affect their understanding of postcoloniality.

In support of this conclusion, postcolonial exceptionalists have proposed that the US be understood as different from other imperial nations in that it did not require colonies to advance in status from nationhood to world domination. With this proposition as warrant, postcolonial critics have recently argued that racial minorities and third world immigrants did not undergo a history of colonial relations with the US, and have recommended that their struggles against state oppression be interpreted exclusively in the aftermath of the 1960s civil–rights movements.

While the advocates of a post–civil rights perspective would repudiate belief in US exceptionalism, their viewpoint nevertheless accepts the state's official account of colonialism as an exception. Like the state policies it criticizes, this account tends to efface the history of state oppression that subordinated certain persons and groups to the status of internal colonials as well as the role played by the logic of the exception in the history of US colonialism.

By way of its status as an exception to the anticolonial norms by which it has governed, the state established a paradoxical relation to its colonial possessions. Through the acquisition of colonies, the state demonstrated its power to exempt itself from the norms it regulated. The state acquired its colonies as a negative reference for the political formation that it also solicited its citizens to disavow. US domestic policies have as a consequence of this disavowal divided the national peoples into two nonsymmetrical populations: individuals who found their relation to the nation represented by the discourse of exceptionalism and groups who were bound to the state as exceptions. The oppositional practices of US populations subject to the state as exceptions have brought into visibility the history of colonial relations that the exceptionalists would disown.

Alluding to this revisionist history, Sangeeta Ray and Henry Schwarz have provided an account of the differences between the US and other ex–settler states that has challenged the exceptionalists' doctrine. The US was alone of all the postcolonies around the world, Ray and Schwarz have observed, in "turning the colonial relation on its head." Having redescribed the difference between US and other postcolonies in terms of its succesfully mutating into an oppressor state, Ray and Schwarz also suggest why state historians have preferred the doctrine of US exceptionalism as an alternative description.

Prior to the US declaration of independence, Great Britain included the United States among the settler colonies in the anglo-american empire. While its white settlers would later picture themselves as anticolonialist with regard to British rule, they nevertheless collaborated in the British Empire's colonial domination of indigenous populations. After formally separating from Britain, the members of the US postcolony continued British colonial practices in their relations with native populations of neighboring territories and with migrants from other european colonies.

Policy-makers have described these colonial practices as an aspect of a more inclusive process of decolonization that was implemented to defend the territorial US against europe's imperial states. But the state's anticolonial colonialism remained indebted to the imperial model for the construction of its rule of law. In designating for exclusion from membership in the imagined national community a non-indigenous population that had been transported to the colony as slaves, the US constitution revealed the lingering effects of British imperial law.

Even after their acquiring the formal status of US citizenship, African-Americans have been demarcated as a racially distinct group and deprived of their civil and political rights throughout the majority of US history. Traces of US imperial history are likewise discernible in events – the dispossession of Native Americans' lands, the importation of slave labor from Asia, the acquisition of territorial and informal colonies in Central and Latin America, East Asia, the Philippines, and the Caribbean – that the narrative of US exceptionalism has selectively forgotten.

Having now arrived at these examples of its doctrinal limits, we might recall the relationships between US imperialism and the doctrine of exceptionalism proposed in the discussion thus far. The doctrine has functioned as a regulatory ideal invoked by institutions assigned responsibility for defining, supporting, transmitting, administering, and reproducing the US national identity. In performing these functions the doctrine has operated on at least three different discursive registers: as a normative presupposition, as an historical paradigm, and as a national narrative through which the paradigm linked imperial events to the norms that had already interpreted them as exceptions. Overall US exceptionalism supplied the discourse through which US citizens could plausibly disavow knowledge of US colonialism.

The discussion has also proposed the logic of the exception as the basis for the absence of US imperialism from accounts of postcolonialism. With this proposition as warrant, it has described revisionist historians as empowering the recollection of US colonialism's disavowed histories by bringing to a crisis the exceptionalist norms through which they had been forgotten. Whereas disavowal supplied an historically effective psychological structure linking a national community to US exceptionalism, remembering their disavowed histories has mobilized the diverse peoples that the US fashioned as exceptions.

In what follows I do not intend a continuation of this historical overview of the macropolitics of US exceptionalism. Instead I want to shift the focus of this discussion to a specific moment in the 1890s when US imperial policies flagrantly violated exceptionalist norms and threatened their regulatory powers. This change of focus will permit a micropolitical analysis of exceptionalism as a discursive formation. In an effort to accomplish that analysis I will consider specific discursive strategies that the state intellectual William Wilson deployed in his efforts to consolidate and that the (post)colonial activist José Martí mobilized in his struggle to disrupt the hegemony of the phrase "US imperialism: global dominance without colonies."

This discussion will conclude with a brief review of the itinerary of that phrase through three distinct historical periods: the 1890s, when William Wilson helped to establish its hegemony; to the period after the Second World War, when the cold war proposed that it be construed as the reason of state; and into the present, where the phrase has been used to describe processes of globalization that have continued US global dominance by other means.

Presupposing Exceptionalism – Disavowing Colonialism

In 1893 the botanist William Wilson opened the doors of his Commercial Museum in Philadelphia to a fierce debate that transpired throughout the United States over the question of imperialism. The debate was conducted within and across the cultural, political, and economic spheres and set those who favored the imperialist foreign policy that the US had recently adopted against those who believed US imperialism incompatible with the nation's principles.

When William Wilson founded his museum, he did so in order to recover exceptionalism's power to anchor the competing sides in this debate. In refusing to acknowledge the distinction between US and European imperialism, as Wilson observed, both antagonists had ignored the doctrine that provided the nation with its identity. Because Wilson had committed himself to the work of recovering the hegemony of US exceptionalism, he considered the resolution of the argument over the nature of US imperialism the museum's primary task. But Wilson's solution did not entail proposing still another standpoint on the question of US imperialism. The purpose of the museum tour involved replacing his visitors' antagonistic standpoints on the question of US imperialism with a belief about US uniqueness that would no longer be subject to debate.

In accomplishing this purpose, Wilson did not take the side of the anti-imperialists nor did he endorse the policy of territorial expansion. Wilson's efforts at reorienting the debate instead required that he appear aloof from it.

The appearance his aloofness assumed was that of the founder of Philadelphia's Commercial Museum, dedicated to the proposition that the US could achieve global dominance by conquering the world's markets.

Wilson's primary identification as a botanist supplied his project with scientific authority. Museum exhibits borrowed from botany an evolutionary discourse interconnecting military concerns overseas with domestic business and political interests. In fashioning the knowledge produced in his commercial museum after models developed within the discipline of botany, Wilson associated his academic expertise with the worldly power to construct, naturalize, and manage representations of US imperialism.

The displays that William Wilson arranged for the Commercial Museum represented the rise and fall of empires as if these historical events were more or less interchangable with the growth and decay of plant life. By staging such interconnections, Wilson constructed a relay of relations linking imperial norms to the public's idealization of the partnership of science and commerce. After he adapted it to the academic discipline of botany, Wilson's quasi-scientific discourse also designated imperialism as the groundwork for an evolutionary process that unfolded into commerce's advance over territorial aggression. What commerce had made possible for the United States in particular Wilson extrapolated as the purpose of world civilization in general. By way of the itinerary of the connections it established between commerce and empire, Wilson's museum advocated for an understanding of commercial enterprise as a "civilized" advance over territorial imperialism.

This association of questions of foreign policy and commerce with the scientific discipline underwriting his museum's exhibits, depended on Wilson's awareness of the role that discourse played in fashioning the public's knowledge of US imperialism. As it circulated through the ensemble of museum displays, the discourse of exceptionalism produced an isomorphism across their otherwise unrelated discourses. Its network of relations encompassed disparate elements from the political, cultural, and economic spheres. Functioning as a regulative ideal internal to the ensemble through which it passed, exceptionalism became a practicable knowledge. It solicited the public's consent to imperialism as a US foreign policy but also to the domestic arrangements that policy valorized.

Wilson's adaptation of this discourse exhibited the process of empire as taking place across the otherwise unrelated terrains of business interests and ethnographic exhibits. The relays he put into place between the museum's ethnographic and commercial exhibits effected an illusion of agreement among their contradictory elements. The inclusive discursive formation that he fashioned out of the tenets of US exceptionalism integrated these displays within the extensive network of linguistic and extralinguistic practices that naturalized imperial norms.

Oddly, Wilson's museum discourse did not conceal the fact that economic exploitation had been inextricably connected with territorial colonization. But the exhibits redescribed the latter process as an unevolved manifestation of commercial development. In subordinating imperial adventure to the more enlightened interests of commercial enterpreneurs, this history downplayed the violent jingoism of imperial adventurers like Roosevelt along with significant portions of the national history connected with that violence. The museum narrative recast slavery, territorial conquest, and involuntary immigration as the raw materials out of which commerce had evolved.

After his visitors learned how to distinguish commercial from territorial imperialism, the distinction underwent a change in logical status from a debatable proposition to a presupposition that regulated the conditions of debate. In order to stay in place as a presupposition, the distinction actively excluded questions about the terms comprising it. Operating as a normative presupposition this essentialized antithesis organized the conceptual frame through which museum visitors gauged their attitude toward US imperialism. After it became embedded within the interpretive framework informing the museum public's discussion of US imperialism, the distinction supplanted debate over the United States' proper role in the arena of world power.

While Wilson readily acknowledged the fact that commercial interests were allied with US imperial ambitions, he also believed that the US public did not want to acknowledge this fact. Wilson was also convinced that the relationship the public wanted to disavow had to be materially in place before they could successfully perform its derecognition. As a consequence of this conviction Wilson built contradictions to his museum's primary beliefs into its structure. The logic of Wilson's conviction can be replicated as the relationship between antecedent and consequent clauses: before museum visitors could overcome the contradictions that were fully in place before they walked through the museum's doors, the museum had to reproduce them within its precincts.

Because he wanted museum visitors thoroughly to ignore the relays linking business interests to US imperial policy, Wilson produced flat-footed evidence of that partnership for the public to negate. The museum's dual classification system placed the contradiction between business and empire into its basis for its taxonomy. This system arranged the museum's exhibits into geographic displays – including examples of a country's representative cultural artifacts – and monographic exhibits – with data concerning the comparative cost of labor and the availability of raw materials. Whereas the museum's geographic displays represented places in the colonial world system, the monographic exhibits distributed information crucial to the system's mode of production. Their tables of comparison typically correlated the artifacts in the geographical display with knowledge about the costs of doing business in the various regions from which those artifacts had originated. The vital importance of this information to the nation's commercial interests led to its affiliation with the United States Bureau of Information.

This dual classification operated incompatible logics in relation to the knowledge it produced. In its function as a purveyor of scientific knowledge, the museum accumulated cultural artifacts in the interests of their preservation, but in its commercial function the museum associated its epistemic aspect with an unacknowledged imperial project. The artifacts that the museum had acquired through its participation in the imperial world order were in fact indistinguishable from Europe's colonial acquisitions. As an Information Bureau facilitating their distribution, Wilson's museum at once directly participated in a colonial enterprise, yet simultaneously disowned knowledge of its place in the imperialist world system.

The museum's structure also provided its visitors with a way to take up their places within that system by disowning the knowledge of their participation within it. As these exhibits demonstrated to consumers and manufacturers alike the knowledges used to construct a US empire, they also installed the museum's visitors as subjects within a discursive formation enabling their misrecognition. In producing a model with which to explain the difference between the museum's colonial and commercial acquistions, the museum's official epistemology disclaimed knowledge of its role as an extension of colonial relations. It permitted museum visitors to enjoy the fruits of colonialism without knowing that it was colonialism they were enjoying.

Through this process of negative reference to imperialism, Wilson's museum supported its visitors' (dis)belief. The museum's contradictory relation to its displays operated a structural denegation whereby US imperialism was at once effaced yet evoked. The commercialism through which the visitors knew imperialism never coincided with imperialism in its material aspects, and the imperialism that the visitors practiced could not be known.

In its role as an ideology, Wilson's museum tour solicited US visitors' voluntary consent to their participating in the imperial world system. If this consent initially assumed the restricted form of a museum tour, that event also initiated US tourists into everyday practices of euro–american imperialism. The United States, the Philadelphia Commercial Museum might be represented as having explained, was that branch of the euro–american imperial system that disavowed its involvement with the European system.

The (Post)Colonial Exception

Wilson understood how US imperial policies in Cuba and the Philippines had violated the norms of exceptionalism and rendered vulnerable its hegemony. He designed his museum to transform the citizenry's imperial anxieties into a renewal of their belief in the nation's exceptionality. A tour of Wilson's museum promoted the understanding that the US was singular among world powers in that it did not possess a colonial empire. The most powerful challenge to this belief would be posed by José Martí, a Cuban in exile who, so far as I know, never took Wilson's museum tour. Unlike the museum's visitors, Martí represented the spaces within the US to which he was exiled as part of the world's colonial system.

213

From 1881 until his death on a battlefield in Cuba on May 19, 1895, José Martí was exiled in New York City as a political refugee. His period of exile coincided with the historical moment in which the annexation of Cuba was under discussion in the US Congress. As a political exile, Martí was alienated from both United States civil society as well as the Cuban political authorities responsible for his deportation. But the purpose of his prolonged stay in the US was not assimilation, and immigration did not constitute for Martí an adequate model for political reform.

Instead of erasing his experiences of exile from memory, Martí transferred his redoubled loss of place into the basis for his refusal to assume a position in the US colonial empire. Martí advocated independence from Spain while opposing annexation to the United States. In campaigning against imperial nationalism, Martí did not attempt to replace them with a single imagined community or to return to his native land. *Our America*, a political manifesto that Martí published in 1891, convoked a transnational coalition throughout the Americas whose members associated its democratizing force with the shared condition of exile.

Martí harnessed his political aptitude to the project of dismantling the various nationalisms that would impede the emergence of this irrecuperably transnational movement. In travelling back and forth between New York's hispanic ghettoes and the territories the US contemplates annexing in Latin and South America, Martí delineated the contours of a vast internal colony. Because Martí's decolonization efforts took place within a political formation that interrelated multiple international as well as transnational locales, it might be described as anticolonial and postcolonial at once.

The phrase "Our America" named the colonial conditions from which Martí wanted to be dispossessed and the movement through which he stuggled to gratify this desire. He configured "our America" at sites where political refugees, migrant populations, nomads, expellees and the dispossessed intersected with the international trade and immigration policies constructed to regulate their movements. It was this movement rather than Cuba or the US that Martí identified a his homeland.

The coalition that Martí organized was positioned in a space that Foucault has called a "heterotopia." In remaining outside of the imperial norms of other cultural spaces, "our America" permitted of their analysis, contestation, and reversal. The counterhegemonic strategies Martí devised here required that he confront US citizens with the hard facts concerning their colonial history. But promoting such knowledge required that Martí upset the relay of cultural relations that supported its denial. Two of the nodal points in this network of relations linked the ethnographic exhibits in places like Wilson's museum to the categories informing the deliberations of bureaucrats in the Department of Immigration and Naturalization over who was and who was not culturally assimilable.

An explanation of the strategies Martí deployed to disjoin these relays requires an understanding of the circular causality conjoining them. Such a circle originated when US citizens practiced the exceptionality they had learned in Wilson's museum by sorting persons from other cultures according to their distinguishable differences from the US. When resituated within the semiotic field brought into coherence by the INS, the taxonomies of cultural types that the public had learned from museum ethnographical exhibits were made to signify a ranked hierarchical order.

The INS in turn conscripted citizens' visual perceptions to reproduce and thereby authorize its categorizations. In visualizing "foreigners" according to INS categories, US citizens linked them to formulations that also evaluated them. Members of other cultures thereafter became servants of INS categories that they could not escape and that seemingly legislated their existence.

When they recognized immigrants as functions of distinguishable traits, US citizens practiced what might be called visual imperialism. Visually sorting immigrants according to the INS's taxonomy involved citizens in the imperial practices whereby the US colonized other lifeworlds. But if US imperialism constituted the optical unconscious for its citizens' visualization of cultural otherness, the assimilationist model through which they comprehended these processes rendered them unable to become conscious of this fact. Assimilation was the form exceptionalism assumed when it "naturalized" its citizens' cultural stereotyping. Assimilation actively disavowed the cultural imperialism that immigration policies and visualization practices reproduced.

A difference in the allocation of looking privileges distinguished naturalized immigants from resident aliens. In conferring upon newly americanized immigrants the power visually to colonize other cultures, the cultural imperium compensated ethnic nationals for having submitted themselves to the cultural stereotyping whereby they had become naturalized as American citizens. The procedures of visualization subordinating immigrants to these general types underwent reversal thereafter into the visual capital required to enframe their former native lands within a US world picture.

Immigrant narratives that represented the US as a haven from colonial and political oppression closed this circle by authorizing indirectly immigration policies of exclusion and denaturalization. Each story that represented the US as a safe haven from colonial oppression abroad eclipsed the history of US colonial relations. The myth of the US as a promised land erased the middle passage narrative of slaves who were brought to the US against their will, and the stories of migrant laborers the state had newly colonized, and of immigrants who felt their conditions had worsened.

Martí thoroughly understood how the negative reference to colonialism regulated the citizenry's political unconscious. He dedicated himself to work of representing to US citizens examples of the colonialism that the discourse could not include without breaking down. But before he could break down exceptionalism's hegemony Martí was obliged to dismantle the structures supporting the disavowal through which it ruled. Martí contested this hegemony most vigorously at border crossings and ports of entry. The political work Martí performed there revealed an isomorphism between the assimilation of immigrants and the annexation of colonies.

In each of his negotiations with the discursive formation that exceptionalism regulated, Martí exposed the colonial conditions that its relay of circular relations could not accommodate. To reveal the complicity between citizens' negative stereotypes and cultural imperialism, Martí interrupted the imperial gaze right after it disclosed its imperializing intent yet just before an immigrant assumed a negative stereotype.

Following his representation of the assimilationist model as a form of neo-colonialism, Martí erected a distinction between his political condition as a Cuban exile and the processes of naturalization. The construal of Cuban-Americans as second-class citizens on the domestic sphere, Martí explained, was a direct consequence of United States foreign policy. Dependency in the one sphere authorized subordination in the other.

In *Our America*, Martí constructed a counternarrative to the promised land by recounting the stories of the economic and political refugees who inhabited the barrios, ghettoes, and indian reservations comprising a colonial empire internal to the US. Upon remembering the colonial history that the discourse of exceptionalism had suppressed, Martí deployed this countermemory as a weapon in combating its hegemony. By organizing his anticolonialist activities from within this space, Martí disclosed the role the US played in the imperial world order. Martí described the state's acquisition of colonies as an assertion of its exemption from the anticolonialist norms it regulated. But in place of acknowledging the state's power to construct such exceptions, Martí asserted the democracy's right to oppose them. Martí thereafter diagnosed the state's exceptions as indicative of a form of colonial state oppression that was internal to the territorial US.

Martí successfully exposed to sight the presence of the colonial empire that Wilson founded his museum to disavow. Instead of countering Martí's tactics, however, William Wilson never explicitly acknowledged them. Nor did his museum ever take notice of the Spanish-American-Cuban War on one of whose battlefields Martí lost his life. But shortly after Spain officially signed over to the United States the rights of territorial possession to Hawaii, Guam, Puerto Rico, and the Philippines in December of 1898, the US acquired colonial territories that Wilson could no longer ignore.

In 1904, William Howard Taft, who was then Governor of the Philippines, asked Wilson to take a leave of absence from the museum to mount the Philippines display in the St. Louis World's Fair. Acclaimed as the most significant since Chicago's Columbian Exposition of 1893, the St. Louis fair commemorated the Louisiana Purchase as the inaugural event in a century of US expansionism. In response to Taft's request, William Wilson assembled a group of natives he had exported from the Philippines. The exhibit's copy described this *mise-en-scène* as an accurate ethnographical representation of a vanishing Filipino culture.

In mounting this ethnographical spectacle before the eyes of spectators whose government had recently acquired territorial rights over the natives' land, Wilson also provided them with a perspective from which they might take visual possession of the state's newly acquired colony. The timing and placement of this exhibit are as noteworthy as the fact that Wilson exported living Filipinos to represesent it.

As the founder of a museum grounded in the conviction that the US government was different from european imperial states in repudiating the acquisition of colonies, Wilson had dedicated himself to the work of instructing the public in how to presuppose this distinction in their assessments of the nation's foreign policy. But in transporting this portion of a territorial colony onto national grounds, Wilson would appear to have re-performed an imperial practice. That neither Wilson nor the visitors to his Filipino exhibit considered it a contradiction to their convictions bears powerful witness to the procedures through which Wilson's *mise-en-scène* governed their perceptions.

This exhibit provided vivid evidence of the US territorial colonialism that Wilson pledged to disavow. It re-presented the vanishing of a Filipino culture as an historical event taking place before the eyes of onlookers gathered to observe it. But after the exhibit's discourse recoded this event as an example of US exceptionality, it underwent a dramatic change of registers. In staging an unabashedly colonial spectacle, Wilson involved the visitors in a visual practice that complemented the strategies of denegation they had learned in their other transactions at the St. Louis Fair.

Proposing that the live exhibit be understood as an unforgettable lesson in ethnography, Wilson erased all signs of imperial aggression from its landscape and cast the Filipinos as willing collaborators in this colonial enterprise. Although they were alive and in the flesh, after they assumed their places in this scenario, these living Filipinos at once became lifelike actors whose rehearsal of bygone customs explained the disappearance of their way of life.

In thus eliminating any discernible distinction between commercial imperialism as trade between cultures and as the expropriation of an entire culture, Wilson's exhibit might also be understood as having overcome the time lag between the presence and representation of this event. The exhibit simultaneously detached a "historyless" Filipino culture from the flow of world historical events and represented it as participating in an inexorable evoutionary process. As they observed the disappearance of this territorial colony from within their visual field, the bedazzled spectators' bore witness as well to the materialization of their belief that the US had achieved its global dominance without colonies. That belief had quite literally taken place not merely before but *through* their own eyes.

Seeing Like a State

Wilson never explicitly articulated the belief that the US had become a dominant global power without colonies. But his authorization of this belief, which has since become the core tenet within the credo of US exceptionalism, may have constituted Wilson's greatest contribution to the recovery of that doctrine's hegemony. In the century since Wilson opened the doors to his museum this tenet has become the governing rule for very different geopolitical formations.

Neil Smith has described the state's official adoption of this self-representation as the outcome of a meeting between President Franklin Delano Roosevelt and the British diplomatic corps that was held at the White House on St. Patrick's day 1944. "In day-to-day operations, the *Pax Americana* was to be an economic before a political or military empire," Smith summarizes the minutes of this meeting. "It was imperialism without colonies" (Godlewska and Smith, 1994: 273). Smith also indicates that some policy-makers perceived this distinction as a cosmetic device intended to keep up the appearances of US exceptionalism. A member of Roosevelt's Council of Foreign Relations who observed that "the British empire as it was created in the past will never reap-pear and the United States may have to take its place" was perhaps more blunt in his assessment of the purpose for this postwar settlement (1994: 273).

Throughout the cold war, US citizens' belief in US exceptionalism sometimes coincided and occasionally collided with the interests of the national security state. Because the cold war state advanced the claim that the nation was in a per-manent state of emergency, it required its citizenry to construe US neocolonial-ism as a necessary means of combating soviet imperialism. In seeing the world from the perspective of the state's imperial anti-imperialism, citizens need not recognize any disitinction between exceptionalism and the state's exceptions. The state historian Arthur Schlesinger has supplied this misrecognition with an irreproachable rationale. The US empire, according to Schlesinger, "was pro-duced not by the economic system demanding expansion but in order to survive; not by the quest for material prosperity but by the quest for physical security in order to feel safe; not by businessmen and farmers seeking private profit but by politicians and military men seeking national power; not by a *Weltanschauung* peculiar to American capitalism but by *raisons d'état* common to all nations" (1986: 141). Because the security state acts in the interests of the preservation of the nation-state, Schlesinger explains, it is free to protect those interests by any means necessary and without the posibility of challenge.

Schlesinger articulated this rationale in the last years of the cold war but before the US officially acknowledged the era of globalization. While imperial-ism, nationalism, and colonialism may no longer provide adequate units of analy-sis for an understanding of a global economy, the state remains necessary to regulate global traffic.

The phrase "global dominance without colonies" has empowered the emergence of a discourse of multiculturalism within the US domestic political economy and diasporism globally. But whether globalism has superseded US global dominance or describes the effects of US imperialism by way of another name depends upon the semantics described by new economic dispensation of the phrase "without colonies." If that phrase in interpreted to mean that there are no longer populations that the global economy exploits as biopower or places whose resource it depletes, globalization may have replaced exceptionalism in providing still another way to disavow US colonization.

References and Further Reading

Balibar, Etienne and Immanuel Wallerstein. (1991). *Race, Nation and Class: Ambiguous Identities*. London: Verso.

Bhabha, Homi. (1994). *The Location of Culture*. New York: Routledge.

Blauner, Robert. (1972). "Internal Colonization and Ghetto Revolt," in *Racial Oppression in America*, 82–110. New York: Harper and Row.

Collins, Jane and Catherine Lutz. (1993). *Reading National Geographic*. Chicago: University of Chicago Press.

Conn, Stephen. (1998). "An Epistemology for Empire: The Philadelphia Commercial Museum, 1893–1926," *Diplomatic History*, 22: 533–63.

Drinnon, Richard. (1980). *Facing West: The Metaphysics of Indian-Hating and Empire-Building*. New York: NAL.

Enloe, Cynthia. (1990). *Bananas, Beaches, and Bases: Making Feminist Sense of International Politics*. Berkeley: University of California Press.

Foucault, Michel. (1998)."Different Spaces," in *Aesthetics, Method and Epistemology*, ed. James B. Faubion. New York: The New Press.

Godlewska, Anne and Neil Smith. (1994). *Geography and Empire*. Oxford: Blackwell.

Frankenberg, Ruth and Lata Mani. (1993). "Crosscurrents, Crosstalk: Race, 'Post-coloniality', and the Politics of Location," *Cultural Studies*, 7: 292–310.

Hinsley, Curtis. (1981). *Savages and Scientists: The Smithsonian Museum and the Development of American Anthropology, 1846–1910*. Washington, DC: Smithsonian Institution Press.

Kaplan, Amy. (1990). "Romancing the Empire," *American Literary History*, 2 (Winter): 659–90.

Kaplan, Amy and Donald E. Pease, eds. (1993). *Cultures of United States Imperialism*. Durham: Duke University Press.

LaFeber, Walter. (1989). *The American Age: United States Foreign Policy at Home and Abroad since 1750*. New York,: Norton.

Martí, José. (1891). *Nuestra America*, in *El Partido Liberal, Obras Completas* (Havana: Editorial Nacional de Cuba, 1963–5).

Mills, Sara. (1991). *Discourses of Difference: An Analysis of Women's Travel Writing and Colonialism*. London: Routledge.

Miyoshi, Masao. (1993). "A Borderless World? From Colonialism to Transnationalism and the Decline of the Nation-State," *Critical Inquiry*, 19: 726–51.

Pease, Donald E. (1997). "Regulating Multi-Adhoccerisits: Fish's Rules," *Critical Inquiry*, 23: 396–418.

——. (1997). "National Narratives, Postnational Narration," *Modern Fiction Studies*, 43: 1–26.

——. (1998). "Imperial Dicourse," *Diplomatic History*, 22: 605–15.

Pratt, Mary Louise. (1992). *Imperial Eyes: Writing and Tranculturation*. London: Routledge.

Ray, Sangeeta and Henry Schwarz. (1995). "Postcolonial Discourse: The Raw and the Cooked," *Ariel*, 26: 147–66.

Robertson, Roland. (1992). *Globalization, Social Theory and Global Culture*. London: Sage.

Rony, Fatimah Tobing. (1996). *The Third Eye: Race, Cinema and Ethnographic Spectacle*. Durham: Duke University Press.

Rydell, Robert. (1984). *All the World's a Fair: Visions of Empire in American International Expositions 1876–1916*. Chicago: University of Chicago Press.

Said, Edward. (1993). *Culture and Imperialism*. New York: Oxford, 1993.

Salman, Michael. (1991) "In our Orientalist Imagination: Historiography and the Culture of Colonialism in the US," *Radical History Review*, 50: 221–32.

Schlesinger, Arhur M. (1986). *The Cycles of American History*. Boston: Houghton-Mifflin.

Spurr, David Spurr. (1993). *The Rhetoric of Empire: Colonial Discourse in Journalism, Travel Writing and Imperial Administration*. Durham: Duke University Press.

Williams, William Appleman. (1955). "The Frontier Thesis and American Foreign Policy," *Pacific Historical Review*, 24: 379–95.

——. (1980 [1959]). *The Tragedy of American Diplomacy*. New York: Random House.

——. (1980). *Empire as a Way of Life*. New York: Dell.

Wilson, William. (1899). "The Philadelphia Commercial Museum," *Forum*, Sept. 28, 1899: 114–29.

Zinn, Howard. (1980). *A People's History of the United States*. New York: Harper.

Chapter 10

Indigenousness and Indigeneity

Jace Weaver

1   Introduction

Indigeneity is one of the most contentiously debated concepts in postcolonial studies. According to Bill Ashcroft, Gareth Griffiths, and Helen Tiffin, the way in which it "intersects with notions of race, marginality, imperialism, and identity, leads to a constantly shifting theoretical ground, a ground continually contested. . . . At its simplest the argument boils down to a dispute over whether . . . the indigenous people of an invaded colony are the only 'truly colonised' group" (1995: 213). When one considers that it is also woven together in an intricate web of ideas such as hybridity, essentialism, authenticity, diaspora, Third World, and Fourth World, and the way those ideas are developed and "owned," that shifting theoretical ground seems even more like quicksand. Even the term itself is disputed, as some Native American scholars prefer to think in terms of "indigenousness" as more descriptive of the place of indigenous groups in the Americas – thus deliberately divorcing themselves from what has emerged as the mainstream of postcolonial theory. Before one can adequately analyze "indigeneity," postcoloniality itself must be considered.

2   The Postcolonial Problem

The idea of the *postcolonial*, referring to "a general process of decolonisation which, like colonisation itself, has marked the colonising societies as powerfully as it has the colonised (of course, in different ways)," has gained a great deal of currency in academic circles and exerted an important influence on the developing discipline of cultural studies (Hall, 1996: 246). It has been articulated most fully by literary critics. To a certain extent this is natural because "literature offers one of the most important ways in which these new perceptions are expressed and it is in their writing, and through other arts such as painting, sculpture, music and dance that the day-to-day realities experienced by colonized peoples have been powerfully encoded and so profoundly influential" (Ashcroft *et al.*, 1989: 1). Yet this has also posed a limitation for postcolonial analysis because these same literary scholars "have been reluctant to make the break across disciplinary (even post-disciplinary) boundaries required to advance the argument" (Hall, 1996: 58) or, indeed, truly to test its utility as a way of apprehending the lived reality of persons and peoples.

On its face, the concept has much to recommend it to scholars in discussing the situation of indigenous peoples around the globe. Religious studies scholar William Baldridge, a Cherokee, writes, "For Native Americans, perhaps the most pervasive result of colonialism is that we cannot even begin a conversation without referencing our words to definitions imposed or rooted in 1492. The arrival of Columbus marks the beginning of colonial hubris in America, a pride so severe that it must answer the charge of blasphemy" (1993: 24). As this statement demonstrates, native cultures (not only in the Americas but throughout the world) were decisively different after the ruptures of invasion and colonization. It is self-evident that they were different from how they would have developed if left in isolation. New and extreme pressures, erratic and oppressive government policies, and, in some countries, the reduction of indigenes to small percentages of the population have led to new constellations of identity.

Stuart Hall, a leading force in cultural studies, observes:

> The argument is not that, thereafter, everything has remained the same – colonisation repeating itself in perpetuity to the end of time. It is, rather, that colonisation so refigured the terrain that, ever since, the very idea of a world of separate identities, of isolated or separable and self-sufficient cultures and economies, has been obliged to yield to a variety of paradigms designed to capture these different but related forms of relationship, interconnection and discontinuity. (1996: 252–3)

While I do not want to be accused of the charge of "banal reductionism," which Hall hurls at critic Arif Dirlik, a number of indigenous scholars, myself among them, do believe that there are potentially troubling aspects of postcolonial discourse that must be debated seriously before it can be determined whether it is useful to hop aboard the postcolonial bandwagon.

If Ella Shohat (1992) is correct about the ahistorical, universalizing, depoliticizing effects of the post-colonial, there is nothing in that analysis for indigenous peoples. If Ruth Frankenberg and Lata Mani (1992) are right in their assertion that too often the sole function of postcolonial analysis seems to serve is a critique of dominant, Western philosophical discourse – "merely a detour to return to the position of the Other as a resource for rethinking the Western self" – then indigenous peoples will want little part of it. Unquestionably, as Dirlik states, "post-coloniality represents a response to a genuine need, the need to overcome a crisis of understanding produced by the inability of old categories to account for the world" (1992: 353). The "old categories" of Western discourse, however, never accounted for native worldviews, and since the time of first contact with Europeans, the reality of the world's indigenous populations has been all too much monotonously the same, controled by those who conquered them.

A basic question concerning postcoloniality is that raised by Hall in the title of his essay "When Was the 'Post-Colonial'? Thinking at the Limit." Shohat has pointed out the "problematic temporality" of the term. Ashcroft, Griffiths, and Tiffin contend that the postcolonial is that period which commences at the moment of colonization and continues to the present day. Hall, for his part, maintains that one thing the postcolonial is not is a periodization based on epochal stages "when everything is reversed at the same moment, all the old relations disappear for ever [*sic*] and entirely new ones replace them." For him, the term is not merely descriptive of *there* versus *here* or *then* versus *now*. Nevertheless, in Hall's thinking, as for many postcolonial critics, the term has a temporal scope much more limited than that given to it by Ashcroft, Griffiths, and Tiffin. *Postcolonial* truly represents a time *after* colonialism and temporally means that time of postindependence of the former colonial world, even if the struggle for decolonization is not yet complete (Aschcroft *et al.*, 1989: 2, 6; Hall, 1996: 247).

The problem is that for much of that two-thirds of the world colonialism is not dead. It is not merely living as "after-effects," as Hall implies. Indigenous peoples around the world remain colonized peoples, victims of internal colonialism. *Internal colonialism* differs from classic colonialism (sometimes called blue water colonialism) in that in colonialism's classic form a small group of colonists occupy a land far from the colonial metropolis (*métropole*[1]) and remain a minority, exercising control over a large indigenous population. By contrast, in internal colonialism, the native population is swamped by a large mass of colonial settlers who, after generations, no longer have a *métropole* to which to return. *Métropole* and colony thus become geographically coextensive. In post-colonial theory, this distinction is usually called the difference between "invaded" colonies (classic colonies, primarily those in Africa and Asia) and "settler" colonies (i.e., instances of internal colonialism, such as Australia, Palestine, New Zealand, Canada, and the United States). Native American writer and critic Gerald Vizenor (1994) terms settler colonies, *paracolonialism*. Confronting this temporal anomaly squarely, Elizabeth Cook-Lynn, also Native American and one of those who eschews the concept of indigeneity in favor of indigenousness, writes:

Postcolonial theories became the pronouncements of the day. Postcolonial study has always been defined by Euro-American scholars [in the case of the United States] as the discourse that *begins from the moment of what is called "colonial contact*," not from the moment that imperial nations rejected colonizing as an *illegal* activity, because that time has never come. In the past twenty or thirty years, postcolonial theories have been propounded by modern scholars as though Native populations in the United States were no longer trapped in the vise of twentieth-century colonialism but were freed of government hegemony and ready to become whatever they wanted, which, of course, they were not. Today, colonizing, unlike slavery, is not a crime anywhere in the world. Even the use of the word *contact* in the definition of "postcolonial" studies disguises a history of invasion and genocide. (1997: 13)

Cook-Lynn's remarks could be amplified to take in indigenous peoples anywhere.

Beyond its temporal definition, another fundamental issue concerning postcolonial discourse for indigenous peoples is its geographic scope. With a few notable exceptions, the concept of postcoloniality has been advanced almost exclusively in the Anglocolonial world (Australia, New Zealand, Canada, the United States, and India). To a certain extent, as with its articulation in literary theory, this too is natural: the indigenous peoples in those nations share what Maori lawyer Moana Jackson has termed a "culture of dispossession" given an aura of legitimacy by doctrines of discovery and conquest, treaties, and the "gift" of "civilization" ([Roberts], 1996: 28–9). They each suffered (and continue to suffer) paternalistic, colonial systems predicated "both on a pragmatic concern to ensure that native peoples did not become obstacles or a nuisance to settlement and on an official perception of indigenous peoples as 'primitives' who would be quickly eradicated by European settlers if they were not protected by authorities" (Dyck, 1985: 9).

Its primary proponents, however, often have been racial/ethnic minority scholars (such as Stuart Hall or Gayatri Chakravorty Spivak) who reside and work in the *métropole* and scholars of European descent or origin who are similarly situated. Even when what may be called postcolonial analysis is produced by a critic living in his or her native country, it is most often produced in the non-autochthonous language of the colonizer – English. Thus, in a stirring inconsistency of thought, Indian thinker Ashis Nandy can criticize revolutionary writer Frantz Fanon for attacking the West in French "in the elegant style of Jean-Paul Sartre," even though Nandy himself produced *The Intimate Enemy: Loss and Recovery of Self under Colonialism* in English, for which he has "developed a taste" despite the fact that he forms his thoughts "in my native Begali and then translate when I have to put them down on paper" (1983: xii, xix). Often postcolonial writing seems oddly detached when discussing indigenous peoples and their lives. It often displays – as in the work of Mahasweta Devi (1995: ix–xxii) about and on behalf of the tribal peoples of India – the same sense of patronizing care reflected by those in the dominant, Western culture.[2] With its geographic and linguistic limitations, postcolonial discourse says little about indigenous liberation struggles in Africa, Palestine, Central America, Scandinavia, or Japan – to select only a few examples. Nor does it truly say much about movements among Native Americans in the United States, Aborigines in Australia, or Maoris in New Zealand.

In sum, postcolonial theories deal with the Third World but say nothing to or about the Fourth World. "Third World," as a collective term for developing, non-European countries, is today well known. It was first employed by Alfred Sauvy in an article in France in 1952. The appellation "Fourth World" was coined in Canada in the 1970s to distinguish indigenous peoples around the planet from the Third World, in whose countries they may nonetheless reside. Hence the argument within postcolonial discourse, set forth at the outset of this paper, as to whether or not indigenous populations – that is to say, the Fourth World – are the only truly colonized peoples – whether they are in invaded or settler colonies.

A further ironic aspect of postcolonial critique for indigenous peoples is its relationship to postmodernism. Poststructuralist discourse provides its "philosophic and theoretical grounding," and like poststructuralism, it is "anti-foundational" (Hall, 1996: 255–6). To fully understand the irony of this predicament, one must turn back to the previous century. In the late nineteenth century, two great rationalizing sciences rose to prominence, sociology and anthropology. The former purported to study that which is normative in the dominant culture. The latter, which Claude Lévi-Strauss labels "the handmaiden of colonialism," studied the Other and advised colonial masters in the manners and mores of native peoples that they might be more effectively controled (Said, 1993: 152). In like manner, in the late twentieth century two systems of critical thought have arisen to explain the world. It is no coincidence that just as the people of the Two-Thirds World (i.e., non-First World) begin to find their voices and assert their own agency and subjectivity, postmodernism proclaims the end of subjectivity. By finding its theoretical roots in European intellectual discourse, postcolonialism continues, by inadvertence, the philosophical hegemony of the West.

Like postmodernism, postcolonialism is obsessed with the issues of identity and subjectivity. Hall writes that

> questions of hybridity, syncretism, of cultural undecidability and the complexities of disaporic identification . . . interrupt any "return" to ethnically closed and "centred" original histories. Understood in its global and transcultural context, colonisation has made ethnic absolutism an increasingly untenable cultural strategy. It made "colonies" themselves, and even more, large tracts of the "postcolonial" world, always-already "diasporic" in relation to what might be thought of as their cultures of origin. (1996: 250)

Similarly, Trinh T. Minh-Ha writes, "This is not to say that the historical 'I' can be obscured or ignored, and that differentiation cannot be made; but that 'I' is not unitary, culture has never been monolithic, and more or less is always more or less in relation to a judging subject. Differences do not only exist between outsider and insider – two entities –, they are also at work within the outsider or the insider – a single entity" (1991). Trinh is correct in pointing up that indigenous cultures and experience are not monoliths, no matter how much they are portrayed as such by the dominant cultures. Yet, putting aside for the moment the diasporic nature of much of modern indigenous existence, one must nevertheless admit that there is something real, concrete, and centered in that existence and identity. Joseph Conrad can become a major figure of English letters despite being born in Poland, and Léopold Sédar Senghor, an African, can become a member of the French Academy, but one is either Native American – or Maori, or Aborigine – or one is not. And certain genuine consequences flow from those accidents of birth and culture. It is part of the distinction drawn by Palestinian critic Edward Said between filiation and affiliation (1983: 19–20).

The problem is that, at base, postcolonial discourse *is* depoliticized. As Shohat notes, in its legitimate and sincere effort to escape essentialism, "post-colonial discourse sometimes seems to define *any* attempt to recover or inscribe a communal past as a form of idealization, despite its significance as a site of resistance and collective identity" (cited in Hall, 1996: 251). Its error, like that of postmodernism, is that it mistakes having deconstructed something theoretically for having displaced it politically (Hall, 1996: 249). Jacqueline Rose, in her book *States of Fantasy*, observes that the postmodern in its "vision of free-wheeling identity . . . seems bereft of history and passion" (1996). Said responds, "Just so, particularly at a moment when, all over the globe, identities, civilizations, religions, cultures seem more bloodily at odds than ever before. Postmodernism can do nothing to try to understand this" (1996: 7). The same case could be made against postcolonialism.

Like postmodernism, postcolonial theory opposes *essentialism*, the contention that there is a "real" *essence* in a given racial/ethnic category or identity. In the place of essentialism, it promotes hybridity, synchreticity, and cosmopolitanism; "it favors voluntary affiliations as opposed to inherent identities" (Velie, forthcoming). In his book *Postethnic America: Beyond Multiculturalism*, David Hollinger avers, "Cosmopolitanism promotes multiple identities"; it "emphasizes the dynamic and changing character of many groups, and is responsive to the potential for creating new cultural combinations." He contrasts cosmopolitanism with *pluralism*, which he sees as highly essentializing because it "respects inherited boundaries and locates individuals within one or another of a series of ethno–racial groups to be protected and preserved" (1995: 3).

Yet a growing number of theorists, some of them writing from a postcolonial position themselves, question the value, and even the accuracy, of a rigid opposition to essentialism, as demonstrated by Shohat's critique quoted above. Cook-Lynn notes that indigenous scholars have suggested that essentialism is, in fact, a "defensible notion," as indigenous groups use it to "fight off domination by outsiders in order to make themselves heard within their own experiences." Charges of essentialism have been used, according to her, to defuse and disempower the indigenous voice (1997: 20). In stressing the hybridity of modern indigenous existence, charges of essentialism as indigenous peoples assert their identities are themselves essentializing, positing in contemporary existence a descent from a racially/ethnically pure past. G. C. Spivak notes, "Identity is a very different word from essence. We 'write' a running biography with life-language rather than only word-language in order to 'be.' Call this identity! Deconstruction, whatever it may be, is not most valuably an exposure of error, certainly not other people's error, other people's essentialism. The most serious critique in deconstruction is the critique of things that are extremely useful, things without which we cannot live on, take chances; like our running self-iden-tikit. That should be the approach of how we are essentialists." Thus we must run "the risk of essence," the "*strategic* use of a positivist essentialism in a scrupulously visible political interest" (Spivak, 1993: 3–7). Such strategic essen-tialism is increasingly employed by indigenous groups as they assert their iden-tity, sovereignty, even their primacy in a given location.

On another level, however, a discussion of an indigenous people's identity, beliefs, or culture is not to engage in essentialism in a critical theory sense. To view it as such is to misunderstand the fundamental differences between native and Western cultures. Central to a Native's sense of self is the individ-ual's sense of how he or she fits into the native community. Anthropologist Clif-ford Geertz states that "the Western conception of the person as a bounded, unique, more or less integrated motivational and cognitive universe, a dynamic center of awareness, emotion, judgement, and action organized into a distinctive whole and set contrastively both against other such wholes and against its social and natural background, is . . . a rather peculiar idea within the context of the world's cultures." Indigenous societies are *synedochic* (part-to-whole) rather than the more Western conception that is *metonymic* (part-to-part). As Native American historian Donald Fixico notes, Natives tend to see themselves in terms of "self in society" rather than "self and society." It is an "enlarged sense of self" (Weaver, 1997: 39). It is, in a profound sense, a mentality that declares, "I am We." One is thus able to speak more broadly about commonly shared atti-tudes and beliefs within a given grouping than is possible in discussing Western cultures.

3 Indigeneity and the Semiotic Field

As already noted, it is self-evident that indigenous cultures are different by virtue of the contact with European cultures and colonialism that they have experi-enced. They are, in fact, living cultures. Colonialism and international move-ments of peoples have created new identities, such as pan-Indianism in the United States or "indigenism" or Fourth World identification worldwide. Indige-nous cultures have always been dynamic rather than static, which is a European construct. As Aboriginal novelist Mudrooroo Nyoongah (Colin Johnson) states, "They, like every other culture on the globe, are subject to change and are chang-ing constantly. I want to emphasise that such a thing as a stone-age culture (static and unchanging), is a myth created by those who should have known better and still put forth by those who should know better" (1995: 228). The only cultures that do not change are dead cultures, and colonialism has always posited indigenous societies as dying or dead. An extinct people do not change. Their story is complete. Once they are removed – literally or figuratively – from the landscape, the colonial conquest of territory that was once theirs can be completed unimpeded with only a nod of sentimental regret expressed at their passing. Thus one hears in Canada a great deal about the no longer extant Beothuk people of Newfoundland but less about the First Nations (as indigenous groups are known there) that still struggle for their rights. In similar fashion, colonial authorities declared the indigenous peoples of Tasmania extinct, despite the fact that there were, and are, still many mixed-blood Tasmanians.

The declaration of indigenous cultures as vanishing or extinct becomes a means in settler colonies of establishing an uneasy illusion of indigeneity (indigenousness) on the part of the colonizers. For the North American context, Native lawyer, teacher, and activist, Vine Deloria, Jr., put the matter succinctly, "Underneath all the conflicting images of the Indian, one fundamental truth emerges: the white man knows that he is alien and he knows that North America is Indian – and he will never let go of the Indian image because he thinks by some clever manipulation he can achieve an authenticity which can never be his" (1980: xvi; see also Weaver, 1994: 27–39). This quest for indigeneity shows itself most clearly in literature. It has been a constant in settler colonies from their inception: from Hector St. John de Crèvecoeur, boasting (1981: 60–70, 120–4) of the "new man" being born as colonists tilled the fields of North America, to New Zealand poet Allen Curnow, marveling at how "something different, something nobody counted on" (Ashcroft *et al.*, 1989: 136) resulted from living in the new environment, to Reinhold Niebuhr, observing that in America "all the races of Europe were formed into a new amalgam of races, not quite Anglo–Saxon, but prevailingly European" (1964: 11). It can be seen in attempts to bring native literatures into the national canons to establish the indigeneity of settler literatures as part of national literatures rooted in the soil of the new place. It validates attempts such as those of Jerome Rothenberg and the ethnopoetics movement in the United States or the Jindyworobak movement in Australia in the 1930s and 1940s, both of which sought to incorporate or utilize indigenous forms and aesthetics as part of "an enriching cultural appropriation" (see Ashcroft *et al.*, 1989: 143). Begged, of course, is the question of precisely who is "enriched" and who diminished in the process.

This contest between the falsely asserted indigeneity of colonizers and that of Natives is waged on a semiotic (battle)field whose fluid boundaries include not only literature but history, science, language, and sovereignty.

Albert Memmi, Frantz Fanon, and Edward Said all point out that it is not enough for the colonizer to control the present and future of the colonized but, in the effort to prove his own indigeneity, he must rewrite the past as well. According to Fanon, "Colonialism is not satisfied merely with holding a people in its grip and emptying the native's brain of all form and content. By a kind of perverted logic, it turns to the past of the people, and distorts, disfigures, and destroys it. This work of devaluing pre-colonial history takes on a dialectical significance today" (1961: 210; see also Memmi, 1967; Said, 1993). Author Howard Adams, one of the Métis people of Canada, elaborates on Fanon's observation for American indigenes:

> The native people in a colony are not allowed a valid interpretation of their history, because the conquered do not write their own history. They must endure a history that shames them, destroys their confidence, and causes them to reject their heritage. Those in power command the present and shape the future by controlling the past, particularly for natives. A fact of imperialism is that it systematically denies native people a dignified history. Whites claim that Métis and Indians have no history or national identity, or, if they do, then it is a disgraceful and pathetic one. When natives renounce their nationalism and deny their Indianness, it is a sure sign that colonizing schemes of inferiorization have been successful. (1989: 43)

Across the globe, indigenous peoples became objects of study. In the United States, not only their material culture and sacred objects, but their physical remains as well, were shipped to museums for scientific scrutiny. Anthropologists, motivated by the belief that indigenous cultures were about to vanish undocumented, swarmed into the field wherever such cultures could be found – from Africa to Samoa. Speaking of this invasion, Native Canadian scholar Georges Sioui (1992: 101) writes, "Far from bringing benefits to the peoples whose 'cultural conduct is being studied,' these scientific games have the unhappy effect of overshadowing their socio-economic condition and of dashing their efforts to restore their historic dignity," too often drowning out their attempts at assertion of their own subjectivity in a sea of "scientificity." Johannes Fabian, in his *Time and the Other: How Anthropology Makes Its Object*, agrees, noting the primitivism the discipline imposes on indigenous cultures: "Anthropology contributed above all to the intellectual justification of the colonial enterprise. It gave politics and economics – both concerned with human Time – a firm belief in 'natural,' i.e., evolutionary Time. It promoted a scheme in terms of which not only past cultures, but all living societies were placed on a temporal slope, a stream of Time – some upstream, others downstream" (1983: 17). Further, anthropology has contributed to essentialism in its contention that the cultural adaptations of indigenous cultures represent that "descent from a racially pure past" and thus helped to justify the colonial endeavor. As Noel Dyck observes, "[T]he anthropological assumption that aboriginal peoples until recently possessed neatly bounded and self-perpetuating cultures or 'designs for living' amounts to a tacit erasure of hundreds of years of colonial history. In effect, the mythology of the 'only-recently-departed pristine primitive' ignores relationships and involvements that have been instrumental in shaping the lives of minority indigenous peoples within settler societies" (1985: 237).

The issue of language has been of especial importance in indigenous communities as they struggle both for its preservation and to make their ways through

229

contemporary life in the foreign tongues of their colonizers. Ashcroft, Griffiths, and Tiffin observe that a distinctive characteristic of settler colonies is the maintenance of a nonautochthonous language following political independence from the *métropole*. They write, "Having no ancestral contact with the land, they [colonizers] dealt with their sense of displacement by unquestioningly clinging to a belief in the adequacy of the imported language – where mistranslation could not be overlooked it was the land or the season which was 'wrong.' Yet in all these areas [of the politically independent, decolonized world] writers have come, in different ways, to question the appropriateness of imported language to place" (1989: 25). Some postcolonial theorists, following Fanon and Memmi, argue that colonization can only be put behind by achieving "full independence" of culture, language, and political organization. Thus, for example, Sukarno, realizing that Indonesia could not sever its colonial ties without ridding itself of Dutch, banned its teaching in all schools. Others, like Guyanese Denis Williams, argue "that not only is this impossible but that cultural syncreticity is a valuable as well as an inescapable and characteristic feature of all post-colonial societies and indeed is the source of their peculiar strength" (Ashcroft *et al.*, 1989: 30). Homi K. Bhabha agrees, claiming that the "interstitial passage between fixed identifications opens up the possibility of a cultural hybridity that entertains difference without an assumed or imposed hierarchy" (1994: 4).

The final, and most important, boundary of the semiotic field upon which indigenous peoples vie with their colonizers is that of sovereignty. Immediately this touches upon both history and science. For instance, in Australia, Aborigines, citing privacy grounds, "are demanding full control over who inspects archival records concerning their people." Non-Aboriginal historian Ann McGrath responds:

> This is an understandable position as it follows decades of the State exerting control over their private lives. Many things have also been insensitively published by anthropologists and other academics, including photographs or names of the recently deceased or sacred materials. Aborigines have every right to distrust white promises. Yet to "lock up" this information from non-family members threatens to deny access to vital knowledge relevant to understanding colonial power relations. (1997: 380)

Similar charges have been made against Native Americans who seek the return of human remains pursuant to the provisions of the Native American Graves Protection and Repatriation Act.[3] Though McGrath couches her plea in terms of understanding "colonial power relations," most arguments are made in the name of academic freedom or the unfettered pursuit of knowledge. In so doing, they fail to understand the fact/value dichotomy – that no knowledge is value-neutral and that, when it comes to scholarship on indigenous cultures, there is no such thing ultimately as "knowledge for knowledge's sake."

Indigenous peoples all over the world increasingly have been involved in demands for sovereignty. Though, as will be seen, this concept, like so many involved in indigeneity, is a contested one, at base it involves two different, but related, things: control over lands and self-determination for indigenous peoples themselves. Thus the Maya in Guatemala, after hundreds of years of oppression and a brutal 30-year civil war, have secured recognition of their existence and are experiencing a tentative, but growing, renaissance. In Canada, First Nations have engaged in sophisticated political maneuvering to protect their rights in the struggle over patriation of the Canadian constitution. The Saami Action Group in Norway undertook a hunger strike to dramatize their demands for fair treatment by the dominant culture. Maoris in New Zealand have held a series of convocations (or *hui*) to state their claim to *tino rangatiratanga* (or total control or authority) over Aotearoa (New Zealand) as part of negotiations over the "Crown Proposals for the Settlement of Treaty of Waitangi Claims" (commonly referred to as the "fiscal envelope"). These are but a few examples of indigenous assertion of sovereignty. Many others could be cited. Although the situation in each locale is unique, "much of Fourth World politics is about turning physical powerlessness into moral power and then putting that to good political account" (Paine, 1985: 190).

A baseline problem with such assertions is the very nature of the modern nation-state. There is a "fundamental asymmetry" in the power of the parties involved – a people versus a state. As Dyck observes, "Although indigenous peoples are culturally and often geographically and socioeconomically distinct from the rest of the nation, government leaders . . . take great pains to minimize the perceived social and political differences between indigenous and non-indigenous sectors of the population" (1985: 7–8). Likewise postcolonial critics and scholars seek to minimize differences in their valorization of cosmopolitanism over essentialism. While not denying the history of colonialism, they view past actions as lamentable "but largely irrelevant to the contemporary situation," ignoring ongoing exercises of that same colonialism (Dyck, 1985: 11).

Nation-states are capable of recognizing only a "single category of citizenship." In contrast, indigenous peoples are asserting their refusal to be considered simply an "ethnic minority" within the nation-state. While not all may be political separatists, they will "no longer accept being recognized as anything less than distinctive members with special rights" (Dyck, 1985: 11, 22). This is what might be termed "pluralist separatism." This "special rather than stigmatized status for autochthones" is stated in diverse terms in different countries (see Sanson, 1985). In the United States it is the declaration of Native peoples as "nations within a nation," guaranteed by treaty and by the US Constitution. In Canada it is called "citizenship-plus" status. Among Maoris in New Zealand it is a focus on *tino rangatiratanga*. In each case, it is rooted in the unique history of relations between the colonizer and colonized. And in each instance, its goal is "the protection and preservation of specific social systems, languages, land, and resources" (Cook-Lynn, 1997: 27).

There is no unanimity among indigenous peoples (or even within given groups) as to how to achieve sovereignty or even as to the precise meaning of sovereignty itself. "Sovereignty" has perhaps become a retronym, a word that has lost its original meaning through different usages so that it can no longer be employed without an adjectival modifier. It may now be necessary to refer to "multiple sovereignties" and to distinguish among them – political, cultural, territorial, economic, intellectual, etc.

It is one of the ironies of the colonial history that even as colonizers seek an illusory indigeneity and are drawn to the image of the indigenes within their claimed territory, they simultaneously fear that same indigeneity. The great fear of the colonial enterprise is that members of the colonialist class will "go native," a fear manifested in the person of Kurz in Conrad's *Heart of Darkness*, in the English aristocrat in *A Man Called Horse*, or in the naive Lieutenant Dunbar of *Dances with Wolves*. Terry Goldie has captured this twinning of desire and trepidation in his book *Fear and Temptation: The Image of the Indigene in Canadian, Australian, and New Zealand Literatures* (1989). It illustrates the truth of Deloria's claim that the colonizer will "never let go" of the indigenous image and the reasons why.

4   Conclusion

Elizabeth Cook-Lynn and other native critics explicitly link, in Cook-Lynn's term, indigenousness and sovereignty. It is in this linking that postcolonial theory fails indigenous peoples. According to Cook-Lynn:

> For American Indians . . . and for the indigenes everywhere in the world, post-colonial studies has little to do with independence, nor does it have much to do with the actual deconstruction of oppressive colonial systems. It is not like the end of slavery in 1865, for example, when owning other human beings for economic reasons became illegal and a new status for African Americans as free citizens could become the focus of the discourse. Postcolonial thought in indigenous history, as a result of the prevailing definition, has emerged as a subversion rather than a revolution. This fact has been a huge disappointment to those scholars whose interest has been in Native-nation status and independence. (1997: 14)

Gayatri Spivak notes that Europe constructed the "Other" to consolidate its own subject status (1988: 271–313). Similarly, indigenous critics remain suspicious that postcolonial theory was developed as a "subversive tactic" to create "a new kind of imperial domination" as the old forms of more overt colonial power failed (Cook-Lynn, 1997: 21).

After more than 500 years of ongoing colonialism, indigenous peoples everywhere wrestle with two divergent pulls of identity, one settled and the other diasporic (Said, 1996: 7). The settled is that of traditional lands and territories that were once wholly theirs. The diasporic is that of new homes to which they were exiled by their conquerors, of urban existence far removed from even those places, of a grim realization that their colonizers are here to stay and that they are, in most cases, seemingly "fated always to be minority populations in their own lands" (Dyck, 1985: 1). Only the most winsome dreamer and the most prophetic visionary believe that the colonizers are going anywhere – short of the success of the Ghost Dance in North America or cataclysmic destruction brought upon themselves. Postcolonial critique provides a useful tool for analyzing Native literatures, which reflect these different pulls on identity, and for deconstructing the ironic and destructive images imposed upon indigenes. As long, however, as Western nation-states remain kleptocracies based on the taking of native lands, as long as autochthones are denied sovereignty and are pushed toward assimilation into the dominant culture, the postcolonial moment for indigenous peoples will not have arrived.

Notes

1   Both metropolis and *métropole* come from the Greek *metropolis*, meaning the mother city or state of a colony. In postcolonial discourse, metropolis is the term most commonly used for the colonial center. In English, however, this word more commonly designates a large or important city. I prefer the use of the French term, which will, I hope, allow the reader more distantiation and allow her or him to recognize the colonial implications of the term.
2   Devi writes about and works for the tribal peoples of India, though not from any of those groups herself. She does write in Bengali and not in English, but neither does she write in the languages of those whom she represents in print. *Imaginary Maps* is dedicated to "all indigenous peoples of the world."
3   I have previously discussed this in my essay "Indian Presence with No Indians Present: NAGPRA and Its Discontents," Weaver (1998).

References

Adams, Howard. (1989). *Prison of Grass: Canada from a Native Point of View*, rev. ed. Saskatoon: Fifth House.

Ashcroft, Bill, Gareth Griffiths, and Helen Tiffin, eds. (1989). *The Empire Writes Back: Theory and Practice in Post-Colonial Literatures*. London: Routledge.

——, ——, and ——, eds. (1995). *The Post-Colonial Studies Reader*. London Routledge.

Baldridge, William. (1993). "Reclaiming Our Histories," in *New Visions for the Americas: Religious Engagement and Social Transformation*, ed. David Batstone. Minneapolis: Fortress Press.

Bhabha, Homi K. (1994). *The Location of Culture*. New York: Routledge.

Cook-Lyn, Elizabeth. (1997). "Who Stole Native American Studies," *Wicazo Sa Review* (spring).

Crèvecoeur, Hector St. John de. (1981). *Letters from an American Farmer*. Rpt. New York: Penguin.

Deloria, Vine, Jr. (1980). "Foreword: American Fantasy," in *The Pretend Indians: Images of Native Americans in the Movies*, eds. Gretchen Bataille and Charles Silet. Ames: Iowa State University Press.

Devi, Mahasweta. (1995). *Imaginary Maps*. New York: Routledge.

Dirlik, Arif. (1992). "The Postcolonial Aura: Third World Criticism in the Age of Global Capitalism," *Critical Inquiry* (winter).

Dyck, Noel, ed. (1985). *Indigenous Peoples and the Nation-State: Fourth World Politics in Canada, Australia and Norway*, Social and Economic Papers No. 14. St. John's: Institute of Social and Economic Research, Memorial University of Newfoundland.

Fabian, Johannes. (1983). *Time and the Other: How Anthropology Makes Its Object*. New York: Columbia University Press.

Fanon, Frantz. (1961). *The Wretched of the Earth*. New York: Grove. Rpt. 1968.

Frankenberg, Ruth and Lata Mani. (1992). "Crosscurrents, Crosstalk: Race, 'Postcoloniality,' and the Politics of Location," *Cultural Studies*, 7, no. 2.

Goldie, Terry. (1989). *Fear and Temptation: The Image of the Indigene in Canadian, Australian, and New Zealand Literatures*. Kingston, Ont.: McGill-Queen's University Press.

Hall, Stuart. (1996). "*When was the 'Post-Colonial'? Thinking at the Limit*," in *The Post-Colonial Question: Common Skies, Divided Horizons*, eds. Iain Chambers and Lidia Curti. London: Routledge.

Hollinger, David. (1995). *Postethnic America: Beyond Multiculturalism*. New York: Basic Books.

McGrath, Ann. (1997). "Contested Ground: What is 'Aboriginal History'?" in *Contested Ground: Australian Aborigines under the British Crown*. Sydney: Allen & Unwin.

Memmi, Albert. (1967). *The Colonizer and the Colonized*. Expanded ed. Boston: Beacon Press.

Mudrooroo Nyoongah. (1995). "White Forms, Aboriginal Content," in Ashcroft *et al.*, eds., 1995.

Nandy, Ashis. (1983). *The Intimate Enemy: Loss and Recovery of Self under Colonialism*. Delhi: Oxford University Press.

Niebuhr, Reinhold and Alan Heimert. (1964). *A Nation So Conceived*. London: Faber & Faber.

Paine, Robert. (1985). "Ethnodrama and the 'Fourth World': The Saami Action Group in Norway, 1979–1981," in Dyck, ed., 1985.

[Roberts, John.] (1996). *Alternative Vision/He moemoea ano*. Wellington: Joint Public Questions Committee of the Methodist Church of New Zealand and Presbyterian Church of Aotearoa New Zealand.

Rose, Jacqueline. (1996). *States of Fantasy*. New York: Oxford University Press.

Said, Edward. (1983). *The World, the Text, and the Critic*. Cambridge: Harvard University Press.

——. (1993). *Culture and Imperialism*. New York: Alfred A. Knopf.

——. (1996). "Fantasy's Role in the Making of Nations," *Times Literary Supplement*, Aug. 9, p. 7.

Sanson, Basil. (1985). "Aborigines, Anthropologists and Leviathan," in Dyck, ed., 1985.

Shohat, Ella. (1992). "Notes on the Postcolonial," *Social Text*, 31/32.

Sioui, Georges. (1992). *For an Amerindian Autohistory*. Montreal: McGill-Queen's University Press.

Spivak, Gayatri Chakravorty. (1988). "Can the Subaltern Speak?" in *Marxism and the Interpretation of Culture*, eds. Cary Nelson and Lawrence Grossberg. London: Macmillan.

——. (1993). *Outside in the Teaching Machine*. New York: Routledge.

Trinh T. Minh-Ha. (1991). *When the Moon Waxes Red: Representation, Gender and Cultural Politics*. New York: Routledge.

Velie, Alan. (forthcoming). "Ethnicity, Indian Identity, and Indian Literature," *American Indian Culture and Research Journal*.

Vizenor, Gerald. (1994). *Manifest Manners: Postindian Warriors of Survivance*. Hanover: Wesleyan University Press/University Press of New England.

Weaver, Jace. (1994). "Ethnic Cleansing, Homestyle," *Wicazo Sa Review*, 10, no. 1 (spring): 27–39.

——. (1997). *That the People Might Live: Native American Literatures and Native American Community*. New York: Oxford University Press.

——. (1998). "Indian Presence with No Indians Present: NAGPRA and Its Discontents," in *Native American Religious Freedom: Unforgotten Gods*, ed. Jace Weaver. Maryknoll, NY: Orbis Books.

Chapter 11

Creolization, Orality, and Nation Language in the Caribbean

Supriya Nair

it is not
it is not
it is not enough
it is not enough to be free
of the whips, principalities and powers
where is your kingdom of the Word?

Kamau Brathwaite, "Islands," The Arrivants

but then, you see, colonial caliban is not supposed to get it right.
Kamau Brathwaite, "Metaphors of Underdevelopment: A Proem for Hernan Cortez"

What might seem a rather intransigent refusal "to get it right," to preside, instead, over a kingdom of "Calibanisms" or neologisms is really an attempt both to describe and to create a very specific Caribbean predicament. Edward Kamau Brathwaite, the historian, poet, literary and cultural critic from Barbados, provides an appropriate point of entry into the embroiled debates on creolization, orality, and nation language since his work demonstrates a sustained preoccupation with all three issues. While notions of the creole and creolization extend far beyond the Caribbean, they have a particular resonance in the archipelago that Brathwaite astutely grasps as the embodiment of error. If one recollects that at least in some minds the repopulation and transformation of the Caribbean colonies in their explosive modern configurations began with the navigational error of Christopher Columbus in 1492, Brathwaite s insistence on not getting it right as the prerogative of a colonial subject gains significance. Speaking, for instance, of the powerful if often irrelevant influence of English culture on the anglophone West Indian native s education, he refers to an essay by a schoolgirl who writes of snow falling on the cane fields. Unable to quite make the transcendence to the snow falling on the fields of Shropshire, she switches registers to her local reality, presenting an implausible if imaginative meteorological phenomenon. "The child had not yet reached the obvious statement that it wasn t snow at all, but rain that was probably falling on the cane fields. She was trying to have both cultures at the same time. But that is creolization," concludes Brathwaite (1993: 264). This little anecdote sums up his own thesis about the muddled, contradictory yet creative possibilities of creolized cultures.

1 Creolization

Although Brathwaite and other proponents of creolization are ultimately concerned with articulating a distinctively Caribbean contribution to the New World, the history of the term "Creole" indicates a complex heritage that reflects its varying contexts both within the geographical Caribbean and in the rest of the Americas. Brathwaite, citing various experts in his definitions, attributes the term itself to "two Spanish words '_criar_' (to create, to imagine, to establish, to found, to settle) and '_colon_' (a colonist, a founder, a settler)" which, combined into "_criollo_," refers generally to a settler in the New World of the Americas (1974: 10). He is, however, aware of the differences in definition depending on the specific context. In the case of Peru, the term was used to refer to those born of Spanish parents in the New World whereas in Jamaica it was used simply to refer to anyone born in the New World without racial, class, or labor distinction (which is the usage he prefers). In Brazil the term was applied to black slaves born there and in Sierra Leone it referred to the descendants of relocated slaves who were returned to Africa and who often considered themselves superior to the locals. In Trinidad, adds Brathwaite, creoles were principally black descendants of slaves as distinguished from the East Indian (and Chinese) descendants of "coolies." There are other markers that complicate the term. Racial, as in white or black Creole, with both sides claiming precedence as in the case of Louisiana; national, as in French creole or Spanish creole; linguistic, as in the (French) Creoles spoken in Haiti or Martinique; mixed race, as in mulatto creole or mestizo creole. In these already slippery categories are other slippages of class, color, bloodline, continental ancestry, and native lineage. And further muddying the waters of this formidable contextualization are the various cultural nuances to the process of creolization, depending again on specific historical and political contingencies.

Considering that Brathwaite is aware of the enormous range compressed in the use of the above terms, the attention he gives to the dualistic categories of white and black and Europe and Africa might at first seem baffling and even shortsighted. In fact, Brathwaite's controversial stance on the marginal contribution of "white Creoles" such as Jean Rhys, and of Asian, particularly Indian and Chinese populations, to the creolizing process in the Caribbean have led to accusations of Afrocentricity and anti-West Indian racial prejudice. Historically, discussions of the Caribbean have been informed by the predominantly dualistic tensions between white and black, master and slave, Europe and Africa that characterize the colonial history of the region. But more recent analyses have urged for a broader reading that takes into account the presence of varied national and racial mixtures. Such a recognition is pragmatic, even banal, for an area stretching across a myriad of island and continental nations, inhabited by migrant communities from various parts of Europe and the West coast of Africa, by East Indians, Chinese, Jews, Malays, Syrians, and Lebanese, all of whom brought their diverse customs and languages with them. In fact, in the Caribbean, "indigenous" and "native" were terms that could strictly be applied only to a small and decimated population of Amerindians whose besieged cultures struggled to survive the ravages of virtual genocide.

The expansion of the term to include other groups in a global syncretic exchange and transfer shifted the emphasis from a binary relationship in which one of the two categories was privileged over the other. In preferring the term "transculturation" as used by the Cuban scholar Fernando Ortiz in the forties, Nancy Morejón signals the shift toward the process of creolization as a "constant interaction, transmutation between two or more cultural components whose unconscious end is the creation of a third cultural whole – that is, culture – new and independent, although its bases, its roots, rest on preceding elements" (Morejón, 1993: 229). The movement to reciprocity and newness, unlike the passive assimilation implied in terms like "assimilation" or "acculturation," in which the stronger subsumes the subordinate, by no means ignores the asymmetrical power structures of colonial relationships. Nor does the reference to a third culture suggest singularity and wholeness. Spain itself, Ortiz is quick to say, was a creation of miscegenized peoples. The point is to acknowledge the cultural motley but to move, in the teleological scheme mapped by Ortiz, from hostility (against the black), to compromise (by the slyly subversive slave), to adaptation (on the part of imitative mulattos), to vindication (of the blacks and mulattos), and finally to integration. Not surprisingly, Ortiz defers this synthesis to a utopian future, where the "tertium quid, a third identity and culture" of racial integration and harmony will flourish (Ortiz, 1993: 33).

Ortiz's own politics matched his progressive mapping of race relations in Cuba, since his study of Africanisms was motivated by an initial discomfort with his subject before he proceeded to align himself with black struggles (Moore, 1997: 34). In fact, as in Ortiz's own work, attitudes toward Afro-Cubans and the Afro-hispanic heritage continue to be marked by ambivalence. Even noted figures of the Afrocubanismo movement in the late twenties, which inspired the later rhetoric of the Communist party, often provided only qualified approval and middle-class benevolence toward the so-called color and vitality of black cultures. As in the case of the larger Caribbean, folk arts and performance were deeply embedded in the twinned modalities of race and class in which black subjects usually occupied the lower end of the class spectrum.

Given the continuity of these tensions, those who summarily dismiss Brathwaite's emphasis on Africa overlook a crucial political impetus behind the creolization thesis in the Caribbean. Especially in the case of Barbados, Brathwaite's native island, Europe's overwhelming cultural presence in a colony that was one of the first to achieve a self-sustaining and majority black population from

African slaves cannot be underestimated. The tag of Little England was appropriate given the ideology that made Barbados a cultural derivative of the colonial metropolis not just for the white planters, who, in one reading of creole, believed themselves to be still British, just born in the Caribbean. England was "mother country" to the Afro-Caribbean peoples as well, some of whom took their cultural allegiance to England so seriously that it led to the creation of the "Afro-Saxon" subject. Absurd as it might seem, such cultural identification was what led to the incongruity of conceptualizing snow on canefields, the consequence of a massive ideological aggrandizement of English culture and the colonial masters, with a simultaneous dismissal of Africa and of the slaves and their descendants. In the above example, the "whitening" of Caribbean reality testifies that the creolization process is not necessarily a relationship between equals. As Brathwaite and Édouard Glissant, another major theorist of creolization from Martinique, argue, the very association of creolization with the plantation systems of the New World presupposed the tensions of dominance and subordination between the two principle constituting factors. Brathwaite does mention "lateral creolization," the interaction between the various subordinate groups such as "poor whites and coloureds; between Syrians, Chinese and Jews; between these and blacks; between blacks and East Indians," and so on, but he makes the focus of his study what he considers primary to the creation of the modern Caribbean: the Europe–Africa connection (1974: 63).

Interestingly, the appropriation of creolization by the emerging nationalist movements in the Caribbean as early as the twenties was multifaceted and some might say paradoxical. Nationalist rhetoric argued that the diverse mixtures on the islands did not preclude a common identity but could allow for the possibility of unification through a blended culture, the tertium quid. The politics of creolization was simultaneously engaged to articulate nationalism, pan-Caribbeanism, and pan-Africanism as black cultures became the new domain of struggle. The marginal majority, the disenfranchised black people, became the central referents in the national culture of the "common man," as the global processes of democratization and decolonization coincided with the emergence of black consciousness and working-class struggles. Even later, creole language politics in Martinique in the 1970s was aligned with a demand for autonomy from French metropolitan control, pride in black indigeneity, and a call for legitimating the language of the masses.

Admittedly, creolization, with its stress on cultural exchange and synthesis, could accommodate the demands of global flows in an increasingly capitalist ethos, and at the same time satisfy the needs of an anti-imperial Caribbean nationalism that sought an indigenous common cultural intermixture as its new substructure. But these broad, materialistic, and all-inclusive goals were secondary, in the case of intellectuals like Brathwaite, to reviving the "diluted," "submerged," "cultural wreck" of Africa suppressed, as the above metaphors indicate, in the upheaval of the Middle Passage (1993: 200). While Brathwaite would be the first to argue that the cultures of the slaves survived the depredations of the brutal transportation and the disruptions of plantation life and labor, he also emphasizes the struggle involved in that survival, often at great cost to resisting slaves. Regardless of the complexities of class and ethnicity, gender and nation, race and class, the reading of creole in some of these islands as denoting a Caucasian, European lineage underlines the dominant, even triumphalist, category in the history of the Caribbean. Appropriating creole and creolization to include the cultures of the African slaves, however fragmentary and invented, was a political act of reclamation in a history of silence and contempt. When Brathwaite hails Africa as the "submerged mother of the creole system," it is a reaction, however problematic, to centuries of the institutional lack of recognition given to African influences in the Caribbean region (1974: 6).

Ironically, "creole" as the marker of a superior heritage of whiteness was not a stable one, and its exclusionary appropriation by the slave-owning plantocracy revealed a historical anxiety about and antagonism toward the colonial metropolis. The Englishman Edward Rochester's pungent epithet, "bad, mad, and embruted," describing Bertha Mason in Charlotte Brontë's *Jane Eyre*, is stereotypically emblematic of the degenerate white Creole woman of the Caribbean (Brontë, 1847: 295), whose colored sister was the tragic and overly sexualized mulatta. But despite the fact that each metropolis itself had a turbulent relationship with its overseas colonial representatives in the tropics, or perhaps because of it, the white European colonialists generally insisted on their cultural superiority to the indigenized African populations. Their systematic efforts at suppressing the cultural characteristics of the latter led to a skewed emphasis on only one side of the colonial equation, and to a false impression, as Brathwaite and others were to argue, that blacks simply imitated whites and borrowed their culture. While such "mimic men" were an undeniable consequence of the colonial encounter, some of the revisionist advocates of creolization mentioned below, in fighting to balance the equation, may have caused the pendulum to swing to the other extreme. Still, given that African cultures were virtually ignored in the educational curriculum of the islands for centuries, Brathwaite may have a point in deriding anxieties about an overemphasis on Africa (1993: 199). He attacks the tendency in literary criticism and social sciences to question a significant link between the Caribbean and Africa (1993: 121; 1974: 42–3). The debasement of Africa should call not for a dismissal of its influence, he believes, but for a more committed inquiry into what has been so deformed that it is considered to be nonexistent or at best minimal.

Restoring African influences to the cultural mechanisms of creolization was not restricted to the anglophone islands alone. In their manifesto, *Éloge de la créolité*, published in 1989, and later translated into English as "In Praise of Creoleness," Jean Bernabé, Patrick Chamoiseau, and Raphaël Confiant momentarily laud the Martinican poet Aimé Césaire for giving "Creole society its African dimension" through Negritude, although they ultimately stand opposed to Césaire's assimilative politics and to the Afrocentric essentialism of Negritude. They go on to embrace the other national or continental cultures that form the Caribbean and reject the "exteriority" of both Europe and Africa to call for a specifically Caribbean "interior" vision (1990: 888). Their manifesto on "Créolité," heavily influenced by the concept of "antillanité" derived from Édouard Glissant (whom they quote extensively), seeks to combine the use of French Creole with an all-inclusive celebration of the various continents that contributed to the rich cultural diversity of the Caribbean. Ironically, Glissant distances himself from "Créolité" because of its French-language centered politics in a region that speaks as many, if not more, languages than the European colonies that ruled it (1989: 263). The general tags anglophone, francophone, Dutch-speaking, and so on signify more than the linguistic control of the islands. They inscribe their derivative cultural character as well. The French overseas departments in the Caribbean, with their ideology of assimilation, were arguably more in need of such revisions. Like Negritude, Haitian indigenism both reflected and rejected the obsession with Europe, specifically with France. Jean Price-Mars's *Ainsi Parla l'Oncle* (1928) critiqued the dominance of the French language in a country where the majority of the population spoke Haitian Creole, considered a debased form of French because of the changes wrought by the African and, in a few cases, indigenous languages that creolized it.

The editorial subheading "Rescuing Africa from Oblivion," in a section translated from Walterio Carbonell's *Como surgió la cultura nacional* (1961), stresses the Afro-Latin links that also need to be rediscovered (1993: 195). Here, too, the possibilities for Cuban national culture, anti-imperialism, pan-Caribbeanism, and a larger culture of the Americas are articulated in conjunction with the obscured significance of black African presence. The poetry of Nicolas Guillen, himself a mulatto, while acknowledging the multivalenced "social hydrography" of Cuba, nevertheless gives priority to the overlooked African "capillary" (Prologue to *Sóngoro cosongo*, cited in Morejón, 1993: 235). In an account that shares Brathwaite's perception of "contradictory omens," the two editors of *AfroCuba* justify the title and their focus thus: "We both share the conviction that the creolization process has affected all groupings to such a degree that it is difficult to talk of any form of racial purity. . . . Nonetheless, we also feel that the 'melting pot' approach begs the question of strong racial differences, which must be recognized and respected as such, if 'assimilation to white' assumptions are to be challenged" (see Carbonell, 1993: 13–14, for the main reference.). So although the Hispanic Caribbean is creolized to the point where race ceases to be a biologically viable category, the politics of creolization demand its strategic appropriation to challenge the cultural supremacy of white culture, although white is equally fluid in the creole world.

Pointing out the class rivalries that flourished among planters, for example, Gordon Lewis (1983) argues that race sentiments took a back seat to property affiliations. Rich planters found their impoverished inferiors particularly despicable. When Tia in *Wide Sargasso Sea*, Rhys's imaginative supplement to *Jane Eyre*, shrewdly declares that "black nigger better than white nigger" (1996: 21) she inexorably maintains not only her historical racial separation from

241

Antoinette, who would like to claim affinity, but also the rigid class distinctions that often undermined racial solidarity. In addition to internal schisms, there were external rifts in the creole planter class. "The new social class of colonial settlers, planters, and entrepreneurs was at once, in the English settlements, Anglo-Saxon and anti-English, in the Spanish settlements pro-Hispanic and anti-Spanish, in the French settlements Gallic and anti-French," says Lewis, using the designation of class rather than race perhaps deliberately (1983: 75). Clearly, in the ambivalent affiliations of the colonies, not only the liberated slaves and servants but also the wealthy land-owning elites desired independence from the mother country, to which they on occasion paid loyal obeisance.

However, Brathwaite ultimately valorizes the African and black element in "authentic" creolization, leading to his theory that white involvement was structural, materialistic, and limited (1974: 32), and Asian participation more in the realm of style rather than substance because of the rigid insularity of these groups (1974: 53). He asserts, on the one hand, that Africa is an important if overlooked element in the creolizing process of black slaves but, on the other hand, that the borrowed "great tradition" of the Indian subcontinent was an impediment in the creolizing process, since the migrant Indian laborers ignored their "authentic" folk traditions, like the black slaves once did. There are other contradictions that are not resolved, perhaps inevitably, and even self-consciously. Although Brathwaite seems to view creolization as producing a certain core or common culture that the different cultural components can share, he also notes that the inevitably incomplete reconciliation and the lack of homogeneity between different elements is precisely what makes creolized cultures innovative, inventive, and unique.

While the charge that Brathwaite tends to homogenize diverse African cultures and languages is fair, critiques leveled against his socially static view of creolization are not. Occasionally he does envisage creolization creating a homogeneous "third" culture, but he is not completely oblivious either to class conflicts or to the internally "contentious" nature of creolization, as Nigel Bolland argues (1992: 73). Using the historical experience of the rape of black women by white men, Bolland critiques Brathwaite for obscuring the brutal power structures underlying the new demographics of colored people on plantations. While Bolland is sympathetic to the need to recuperate Caribbean links with African structures, his dialectical theory insists on the social specificity of various cultural practices in both contexts. Underlining the conflicted and dynamic nature of creolization, he draws attention not to its supposed end result of cultural homogeneity, but to the heterogeneous and uneven struggle between its different cultural factors. Nevertheless, even if the "folk" or Africa are sometimes presented as easily containable, reified categories, Brathwaite, like Glissant (who eschews the more static term "creoleness"), insists on the process implied in creolization, ultimately denying a fixed or monolithic character to any of its components.

2   Orality

The call for a revival of lost Africanisms might seem at odds with the nationalist and pan-Caribbean agendas that fueled the drive toward creolization. But like the latter, the diasporic quest for an anterior cultural foundation had similar investments in extending historical agency from the conquerors and owners to the slaves and laborers. Using history in the sense of quotidian practices rather than grand narratives allowed ordinary "folk," the "common people," to also be active agents and not just passive recipients of culture. However, this shift was usually based on an assumption that folk culture was largely the domain of the slaves and their descendants, which then made the turn to Africa the consequence of the search for primary influences. Indeed, for Brathwaite, the African aspect of the creole heritage was the "authentic" source of folk culture which was taking center stage with the independence of colonies. And this African element most clearly reveals itself, he believes, in the rich oral traditions of the Caribbean. In his words, "the African presence in Caribbean literature cannot be fully or easily perceived until we redefine the term "literature" to include the nonscribal material of the folk/oral tradition, which, on examination, turns out to have a much longer history than our scribal tradition, to have been relevant to the majority of our people, and to have had unquestionably wider provenance" (1993: 204–5).

Africa, for him, is not just the fundamental constituent of Caribbean folk culture, it emerges everywhere in the language, in everyday practices, and in the communal and spiritual values of his society. However, Brathwaite later goes on to say that the reading voice of T. S. Eliot was a major influence on Caribbean poetry and it helped the poets conceive of a conversational tone in written language (1993: 286). He also mentions the "Lawrence–Faulkner–Hemingway tradition of folk-talk and rhythmic prose," more disparagingly, as one of the literary models of Caribbean writers in English (1993: 52). Yet he uses "folk" and "oral" interchangably in a substitution that is now fairly common in the bourgeois academy. Brathwaite does not entirely ignore the appropriation of "folk-talk" by largely middle-class writers, with the additional problem, in the case of the Caribbean, of writers of his generation generally in exile in the metropolis. This sense of double distance and historical alienation must attend any discussion of orality and nation language as cautionary notes on the engagement in print of folk sources and the language of the people. As Bernabé points out in a recent interview, the French Creole used in fiction is itself a new language, creatively imagined by the author and not necessarily an authentic reflection of actual speech anymore than the fiction itself is a mirror image of reality (Taylor, 1998: 146).

In a largely migrant culture underwritten by a severely dependent national economy and haunted by a rootless past, the need to stake a claim in some sort

of hopeful foundation must be urgent. It is, of course, quite likely that exile actually contributes to a deeper and perhaps more committed sense of home and
nation. Brathwaite, for instance, has made it clear that his sojourns in England
and Ghana have only reinforced his sense of belonging to the Caribbean.
However, not every acknowledgment of rootlessness is accompanied by a concomitant desire for a firm and singular base: some prefer the thickly spreading
diffusion of rhizomes. As Michael Dash says of one of the most serious advocates of the latter, "it is the composite reality of the bastard that obsesses
Glissant, not the longing for a remote paternity" (in Glissant, 1989: xli). While
Édouard Glissant is equally emphatic about the importance of orality, he also
alerts us to the possibility of an unreflected return to the oral sources of folklore
and to a romanticized notion of the folk as an authentic source of literary expression or political activism. But he praises Brathwaite for graphically reconnecting
the written word with the oral (1989: 109), and insists that the binary split
between them in modern literary tradition misrepresents the intimacy between
the oral and the scribal.

Brathwaite's discussion of orality reorients the modern reader used to the
silent visual experience of print to the aural experience of sound. Using what he
claims is the African-derived concept of "nommo," he pays tribute to the explosive power of the word, "the atomic core of language" (1993: 236). Referring not
just to the material but also to the psychic effects of the vibrations of sound,
Brathwaite insists that sound affects meaning and communication in ways
that the printed word cannot hope to imitate. When he tries to illustrate his
concept of nation language, for instance, he brings a tape recorder to the lecture
to make his point to the audience. It is worth noting that in his attempt to give
orality the respectability it lacks in the modern print world, Brathwaite goes
beyond folk conventions in deploying the wonders of technology. Apart from the
tape recorder, the typewriter and the word-processor allow him to work with
printed type in order to re-present the more fluid structures of sound. The
playfulness that the computer encourages in formulating words, emphasizing
their sound qualities through visual graphs, and breaking up linear structures of
print, proves that the industrialized world is not entirely devoid of imaginative
possibilities.

His experimental *Dreamstories*, for instance, defies the generic and structural
distinctions between poetry and prose primarily through the use of the computer. As Gordon Rohlehr states in his excellent introduction to the collection,
the "video" style that the poet chooses exploits fonts, line (dis)placement, type-
face, typographic symbols, wordplay and page margins to render in graphic form
the "nuances of language" (Brathwaite, 1994: viii). As the words disintegrate,
reformulate, blur, bounce, leap off the page, the constant adjustments that the
eyes have to make challenge the traditionally linear visual response to static print.
The ocular representations are not simply a demonstration of the power of the
computer, but are directly connected to the poet's psychological and cerebral
acrobatics in the dream visions. Brathwaite nevertheless ascribes more power to

the oral artists since their words rely on human breath and not on "technology outside themselves" (1993: 273). One can argue that the microphone is now an integral aspect of the sound experience, but Brathwaite's point about the performative aspect of the spoken word is a salient one, particularly for audiences whose primary world was and continues to be the oral rather than the written one. The title of his lecture, "The History of the Voice" (included in his 1993 collection), which he gave in 1976, is a poignant statement on the historic struggle for cultural expression on the part of the slaves who were largely excluded from print culture but who refused to remain voiceless.

Reading is usually an individual, private, and silent experience whereas the oral tradition is more often rooted in the communal, listening audience. Listening to English spoken by various speech communities in the colonies is sometimes a more acute reminder of the recontextualization or transformation of the dominant colonial language. In other words, even if one were to read aloud a passage written in standard English that mimicked its Great Tradition, the accent and inflection would strike the ear with their particular notes, often revealing the speech community of the speaker. But Brathwaite's use for the oral is more ambitious since he is dealing with writing that speaks to us, as Glissant points out. Take, for instance, the following verses in "Islands":

wid we hat in hand
no speak when we spoken to;
for too

long now we was 'fraid to speak
for too long frighten an' weak.
But the time is come

when you got to speak
when you got to face fac's
when you got to ax

for an answer. . . .   ("Islands", *The Arrivants*: 227)

One hears these words not just because they are presented in the form of poetry, a form more suited to a listening audience, but also because they portray language as it would be used in a conversation, even if it is visually broken up. The gaps, or conversely, the repetition in the poetic form, often enable an antiphonic response, as in the case of a "dub" verse to which an audience can add their words, once again highlighting the communal participation. The refraction of the oral through the written word achieves the necessary distortion (and I use this word in the positive sense) of regulated standard usage into the Caribbean "kingdom(s) of the Word," creating a new realm of expression that Brathwaite defines as "nation language."

3 Nation Language

We might begin with what nation language is not. According to Brathwaite, it is not the imperial language of the colonizer (English, French, Spanish, Dutch, etc.), nor is it the creoles that emerged as each of the above languages came into contact with those spoken by the colonized populations. It is also not the specific languages of the Indian and Chinese communities nor the surviving Amerindian or African languages. And although Brathwaite says that nation language is "the kind of English spoken by the . . . slaves and labourers, the servants who were brought in by the conquistadors," in other references nation language does not seem to be tied to the specific borders of a nation nor to a particular class (1993: 260). However, Brathwaite's African focus returns to the fore in his conceptualization of the term which was influenced, he says, by the different "nations" through which Africans in the New World identified themselves. In "The African Presence in Caribbean Literature," nation language is linked to Afro-creolized languages. The African speech patterns, the rhythms, the ideas and images, the tonality, and even the lexical and grammatical structures of languages such as Yoruba, Housa, Ibo, and Twi underlying the use of English, for instance, transform it into an "intransigent un-English," the master's language, but often in a form unrecognizable to the master, who consequently demeans its "improper" use (1993: 219).

However, in addition to the African influences, Brathwaite places emphasis on a more local cultural context. Earlier poetic renditions in the anglophone Caribbean were understandably influenced by the rhyme and metrical structures of English poetry. It was not uncommon to find odes and sonnets as poetic models in this stage. The dominance of English literary models was only one manifestation of the lived experience of alienation in which English culture and history seemed more real, more accessible than the local versions. As Brathwaite protests, "we haven't got the syllables, the syllabic intelligence, to describe the hurricane, which is our own experience; whereas we can describe the imported alien experience of the snowfall" (1993: 263). But, he goes on to argue in a now famous line, "the hurricane does not roar in pentameter" (1993: 265). The attempt to find a rhythm, a meter, a language that approximates more precisely and passionately the experience of the Caribbean is the creolizing impetus behind nation language. The risks of using terms like "dominant" and "subordinate" are brought to the fore with a concept that defiantly appropriates the mass collectivity implied in nation. What one tends to forget is that the masses in these islands do indeed speak different versions of the colonial languages as a consequence of the creolizing influences which produce them. So while standard English, for example, may be the prestige language, the so-called dominant version, it is spoken only by a minority. Even the middle classes who strive for the prestige language, switch to the creolized form when it suits them. The particular register that is selected is about more than linguistic communication because it reveals an entire social dynamics at work. Standard English can function more appropriately, for instance, as the formal language of business, whereas the creolized form may be used in more intimate, personal situations. In a more cynical example, middle-class nationalists often use the local patois to claim oneness with lower-class communities. In any case, what needs emphasis is the paradox that the supposedly subordinate language is the language of the masses. This may explain Brathwaite's choice of the term "nation language."

Subordination, however, has less to do with numerical minority than with the political fact that power is restricted to the hands of a few. Literary standards are not exempt from such political imbalances. Louise Bennett, the Jamaican poet who adapted oral cultural forms and "nonstandard" Jamaican English into her performance poetry, went unrecognized for years by the literary establishments although she was very popular with the discerning public in Jamaica. She herself wryly acknowledges in an interview that the social stigma associated with using the language of the "common man" excluded her from serious consideration as a poet (1989: 49).

But it is to her poetry that Brathwaite turns to demonstrate a successful and original formulation of nation language. In Bennett's case, she uses a Jamaican creole that bears only a faint resemblance to English lexical and grammatical structures, as in a verse from "Jamaica Oman":

Jamaica oman cunny, sah!
Is how dem jinnal so?
Look how long dem liberated
An de man dem never know!   (1989: 53)

In the fused oral and scribal traditions at work in this poem, explains Carolyn Cooper, the folk hero, the trickster spider Anancy, takes on a female avatar as a "cunny Jamaica(n) woman" (1995: 59). As she argues, "oracy is not merely the absence of literacy; it is a way of seeing, a knowledge system" (1995: 81). The master's language is encoded in the canny locution of Bennett's folk, so camouflaged that the masters themselves "never know" what to make of it. This is not to suggest that creole languages deliberately evolved through the medium of trickery and subversion, but to ascribe to them a certain level of independent will and abstraction that were denied when they were simply seen as bad or inferior usage. Cooper's attempts to gain respectability for Jamaican creole led to dismissals similar to the kind faced by Bennett herself. Like Bennett, Cooper refused to back down and actually includes a literary analysis of Sistren Theater Collective's *Lionhearted Gal* in the orthographic system developed by linguist Frederic Cassidy, who believed that English orthography was inadequate in presenting the difference between standard English and Jamaican creole. This is how she begins: "A so Ava se Sistrin staat aaf: a tel wananada stuori. So yu tel, mi tel, so tel di huol a wi fain out se a di wan stuori wi a tel: Uman stuori. Di siem ting uova an uova" (Cooper, 1995: 91). Readers unfamiliar with this script may be forgiven for wondering if this is a foreign language because they may now be more receptive to Brathwaite's emphasis on nation languages that reflect the *differences* of Caribbean speech from the standardized prestige versions.

Together with orality, nation language traces its sources back to the folk culture of slaves, peasants, and laborers. However, technology and print culture have a role to play here as well. Nation language poetry, or "dub poetry," in the coinage of Linton Kwesi Johnson, deploys electronic media to combine poetry with music. Dub poets like Johnson, Michael (Mikey) Smith, and Mutabaruka utilized Jamaican disk jockey traditions in which the dub side (with the vocals removed from the music) made a "live" on-site space available for performative intervention and commentary. In Smith's "Me Cyaan Believe It," the initial poetic insistence on the incredibility of the various social ills he observes, turns to a question to the audience, "Yuh believe it?" and concludes, "Lawwwwwwwwd / me know yuh believe it" (1989: 286). The tautly interactive, explosive, and dialogic verse is a direct reflection of the immediate social conditions from which such poetry emerges. Smith's own brutal murder, cutting him down in the midst of his success, is itself a grim comment on the legacy of violence that continues to haunt the Caribbean.

To some writers, the social context for such violence in/to language goes even further back. As Marlene Nourbese Philip notes:

> The formal standard language was subverted, turned upside down, inside out and sometimes even erased. Nouns became strangers to verbs and vice versa; tonal accentuation took the place of several words at times; rhythms held sway. This used to be and sometimes still is referred to as bad English, broken English, patois, dialect or ideolect, but it is also the living legacy of an experience, the living legacy of a people trying and succeeding in giving voice to their experience in the best and sometimes the only way possible. We may even suggest that the havoc that was wreaked upon the English language metaphorically expresses the experience of the African being brought to the New World and all the havoc that that entailed for them. (*sic*) (Philip, 1990: 275)

Brathwaite would not stop with the idea of an almost revengeful violence alone, although he would certainly approve of Philip's recasting of nation languages from failed attempts at linguistic accommodation to a successful rebellion against learning the correct version.

Shakespeare's Caliban learning Prospero's language only to curse fluently in it is now a familiar trope in the New World, particularly in the Caribbean. But in an interview, Brathwaite suggests that too much has perhaps been made of invective as Caliban's sole recourse, considering that this character has the "most beautiful lines in the play." Rather than limit Caliban's scope to one of mere reaction to Prospero, Brathwaite prefers seeing the former "hack his way back to the language of the forgotten, submerged mother, Sycorax" (Mackey, 1995: 16).

248

Édouard Glissant also attributes the violence of creoles to this "hacking" back (though with less emphasis on the African roots), and he believes that the forced poetics of the imposed languages is cracked open by the barely concealed fault-lines of the creole languages. Like Brathwaite, in a defiant appropriation of contemptuous colonial terminology, Glissant describes such languages as "din," "noise," "verbal delirium," the "natural" outcome of communities that have long been silenced (1989: "Poetics"). In his later *Poetics of Relation*, dedicated to Michael Smith, Glissant emphasizes diverse languages as a necesssary feature of the "multiply dispersed zone" of the Caribbean, and indeed the world (1997: 109). Arguing against the propagation of any one language as the norm, as in his own educational experience where Martinican French Creole was suppressed in favor of standard French, Glissant finds the "unicity" of any language a conceptual impossibility, since every active, living language already exists in many versions. Contrary to Bernabé, Chamoiseau, and Confiant, Glissant is not particularly invested in retrieving Martinican French Creole as a "first language" out of the "compost" heap of Caribbean languages ("Praise," 1989: 899). In a somewhat different approach to the exhilaration of not getting it right, Glissant refuses even to consider that there is any one right way of getting it: "even correctness is variable" (1997: 101). He encourages the building of the "tower" so that one may enjoy the "vertigo" of different languages that the world's multitudes have to offer, to view Babel/babble not as the biblical curse of discord that punished humanity for arrogance in Genesis but as the "liberation of the imagination" (1997: 109).

This is a view shared by Bernabé and the others who see Babel rise as "cultures melt" and the world itself becomes creolized ("Praise," 1989: 902). However, while they acknowledge that creolization is a global process, the vast continent of Africa itself providing examples of creolized cultures, they insist rather controversially that creolization in the Caribbean is distinct in its sudden violence and forced contact of different cultures as compared to the gradual, even organic cultural transformations elsewhere. When the defining characteristic is "chaos," they argue, "there never comes a time of general synthesis, with everyone beatifically at one with one another" (in Taylor, 1998: 136). Answering charges against the movement as an elitist and exoticized cultural indulgence that caters to Parisian literary cravings of the moment, they respond that creolization instead provides a useful corrective to the homogenization of globalization, usually a disguise for North American capitalism. Conversely, while once the bastard lineage of creole cultures was a cause for shame, now the Caribbean sets a vanguardist example for an attractive and globalized impurity of origins.

Brathwaite's version of the tower is slightly different from the French intellectuals discussed above, particularly with the eulogistic abstractions of "In Praise," in which Creoleness runs the risk of being everything and nothing. More concerned with articulating a specific Caribbean topology and less so with a global poetics of transformation, he says on a more somber note, "we start with the ruins and our responsibility is to rebuild those fragments into a whole society" (Mackey, 1995: 23). Although sources and origins contribute to an imaginative foundation for this new cultural architecture, Brathwaite is clearly aware of its invented nature, its antipodal yet conciliatory ability to "see the fragments/whole" (1974: 7). "Destitution" and "re-storation" form an unceasing dialectic in the Caribbean region, and for Brathwaite, active, (re)constructive intervention in all the varied facets of cultural work is the essential task of Caribbean artists and intellectuals.

References and Further Reading

Bennett, Louise. (1989). "Jamaica Oman," in E. A. Markham (ed.), *Hinterland: Caribbean Poetry from the West Indies and Britain*. Newcastle upon Tyne: Bloodaxe Books.

Bernabé, Jean, Patrick Chamoiseau, and Raphaël Confiant. (1990). "In Praise of Creoleness," trans. Mohamed B. Taleb Khyar, *Callaloo*, 13: 886–909. Original work published in 1989.

Bolland, Nigel O. (1992). "Creolization and Creole Societies: A Cultural Nationalist View of Caribbean Social History," in Alistair Hennessy (ed.), *Intellectuals in the Twentieth-Century Caribbean, Volume 1: Spectre of the New Class: The Commonwealth Caribbean*. London: Macmillan Caribbean.

Braithwaite, Edward Kamau. (1971). *The Development of Creole Society in Jamaica, 1770–1820*. Oxford: Clarendon Press.

——. (1973). *The Arrivants: A New World Trilogy*. Oxford: Oxford University Press.

——. (1974). *Contradictory Omens: Cultural Diversity and Integration in the Caribbean*. Mona, Jamaica: Savacou.

——. (1985). "Metaphors of Underdevelopment: A Proem for Hernan Cortez," *New England Review*, 7, no. 4: 453–76.

——. (1993). *Roots*. Ann Arbor: University of Michigan Press.

——. (1994). *Dreamstories*. Essex, England: Longman.

Brontë, Charlotte. (1975). *Jane Eyre*. Oxford: Oxford University Press. Originally published in 1847.

Burton, Richard. (1992). "Between the Particular and the Universal: Dilemmas of the Martinican Intellectual," in Alistair Hennessy (ed.), *Intellectuals in the Twentieth-Century Caribbean, Volume 2: Unity in Variety: The Hispanic and Francophone Caribbean*. London: Macmillan Caribbean.

Carbonell, Walterio. (1993). "Birth of a National Culture," in Pedro Perez Sarduy and Jean Stubbs (eds. and trans.), *AfroCuba: An Anthology of Cuban Writing on Race, Politics and Culture*. New York: Latin America Bureau. Original work published 1961.

Charles, Jeannette. (1990). "Leh We Talk See," in Selwyn R. Cudjoe (ed.), *Caribbean Women Writers: Essays from the First International Conference*. Wellesley, Mass.: Calaloux Publications.

Cooper, Carolyn. (1995). *Noises in the Blood: Orality, Gender and the "Vulgar" Body of Jamaican Popular Culture*. Durham: Duke University Press.

Craton, Michael. (1991). "Reluctant Creoles: The Planters' World in the British West Indies," in Bernard Bailyn and Philip D. Morgan (eds.), *Strangers Within the Realm:*

Cultural Margins of the First British Empire. Chapel Hill: The University of North Carolina Press.

Dalphinis, Morgan. (1985). *Caribbean and African Languages: Social History, Language, Literature and Education*. London: Karia Press.

Glissant, Édouard. (1989). *Caribbean Discourse: Selected Essays*, trans. J. Michael Dash. Charlottesville: University Press of Virginia. Original work published in 1981.

——. (1997). *Poetics of Relation*, trans. Betsy Wing. Ann Arbor: University of Michigan Press. Original work published in 1990.

Green, William. (1996). "The Creolization of Caribbean History: The Emancipation Era and a Critique of Dialectical Analysis," in Hilary Beckles and Verene Shepherd (eds.), *Caribbean Freedom: Economy and Society from Emancipation to the Present, A Student Reader*. Princeton: Markus Weiner.

Lewis, Gordon K. (1983). *Main Currents in Caribbean Thought: The Historical Evolution of Caribbean Society in its Ideological Aspects, 1492–1900*. Baltimore: The Johns Hopkins University Press.

Mackey, Nathaniel. (1995). "An Interview with Kamau Brathwaite," in Stewart Brown (ed.), *The Art of Kamau Brathwaite*. Mid Glamorgan, Wales: Seren.

Mesh, Cynthia J. (1997). "Empowering the Mother Tongue: The Creole Movement in Guadeloupe," in Consuelo Lopez Springfield (ed.), *Daughters of Caliban: Caribbean Women in the Twentieth Century*. Bloomington: Indiana University Press.

Moore, Robin. (1997). *Nationalizing Blackness: Afrocubanismo and Artistic Revolution in Havana, 1920–1940*. Pittsburgh: University of Pittsburgh Press.

Morejón, Nancy. (1993). "Race and Nation," in Pedro Perez Sarduy and Jean Stubbs (eds. and trans.), *AfroCuba: An Anthology of Cuban Writing on Race, Politics and Culture*. New York: Latin America Bureau. Original work published in 1982.

Ortiz, Fernando. (1993). "For a Cuban Integration of Whites and Blacks," in Pedro Perez Sarduy and Jean Stubbs (eds. and trans.), *AfroCuba: An Anthology of Cuban Writing on Race, Politics and Culture*. New York: Latin America Bureau. Original work published in 1960.

Philip, Marlene Nourbese. (1990). "The Absence of Writing or How I Almost Became a Spy," in Carole Boyce Davies and Elaine Savory Fido (eds.), *Out of the Kumbla: Caribbean Women and Literature*. Trenton, NJ: Africa World Press.

Price-Mars, Jean. (1928). *Ainsi Parla L'Oncle: Essais d'Ethnographie*. Port-au-Prince, Haiti: Imprimerie de Compiegne.

Raiskin, Judith. (1996). *Snow on the Cane Fields: Women's Writing and Creole Subjectivity*. Minneapolis: University of Minnesota Press.

Rhys, Jean. (1966). *Wide Sargasso Sea*. Middlesex, England: Penguin.

Smith, Michael. (1989). "Me Cyaan Believe It," in E. A. Markham (ed.), *Hinterland: Caribbean Poetry from the West Indies and Britain*. Newcastle upon Tyne: Bloodaxe Books.

Taylor, Lucien. (1998). "Creolite Bites: A Conversation with Patrick Chamoiseau, Raphaël Confiant, and Jean Bernabé," *Transition*, 74: 124–60.

Thomas, John Jacob. (1969). *The Theory and Practice of Creole Grammar*. London: New Beacon Books. Original work published 1869.

Chapter 12

"Middle-class" Consciousness and Patriotic Literature in South Asia

Sumit Sarkar

1   Social Roots of the Intelligentsia

By the 1880s, the total number of English-educated Indians was approaching the 50,000 mark, if the number of matriculates may be taken as a rough indicator (only 5,000 as yet had BA degrees). The number of those studying English went up fairly rapidly from 298,000 in 1887 to 505,000 in 1907, while the circulation of English-language newspapers climbed from 90,000 in 1885 to 276,000 in 1905. (J. R. McLane, *Indian Nationalism and the Early Congress*, p. 4) A "microscopic minority," as the British never tired of pointing out (the literacy figures even in 1911 were only 1 percent for English and 6 percent for the vernaculars), this emerging social group enjoyed an importance far in excess of its size. English education gave its beneficiaries a unique capacity to establish contacts on a countrywide scale. English-educated government employees, lawyers, teachers, journalists, or doctors worked fairly often outside their home regions. Already in the 1870s, for instance, the existence of colonies of educated Bengalis in many north Indian towns enabled Surendranath Banerji to make several successful political tours and the Indian Association to set up a large number of branches outside Bengal. Above all, Western education did bring with it an awareness of world currents and ideologies, without which it would have been difficult to formulate conscious theories of nationalism. At the same time, the alienating and divisive effects of education through a foreign medium were evident enough from the beginning, and have persisted right up to the present day. In 1883–4, only 9 percent of college students in Bengal came from families with annual incomes of less than Rs 200 – which was but to be expected, as the tuition fees in the Calcutta Hindu College had already been Rs 5 per month in the 1820s. Sharp regional disparities posed another problem, causing provincial tensions as English education increasingly became the sole path to good jobs. The Public Service Commission report of 1886–7 found 18,390 "educated natives" in Madras, 16,639 in Bengal, 7,196 in Bombay – but only 3,200 in the United Provinces, 1,944 in Punjab, 608 in the Central Provinces, and 274 in Assam.

The early research of Anil Seal and John Broomfield made it very fashionable for a time to consider the English-educated as "elite-groups" defined basically by their upper-caste status. It is certainly true that the traditional "literary" castes tended to take more easily to the new education. Thus 84.7 percent of Hindu College students in Bengal came from the three *bhadralok* castes of Brahman, Kayastha, or Vaidya in 1883–4. Brahman students predominated in Madras, Bombay, or Poona, Kayasthas were prominent in UP. But the value of this whole approach has come under serious questioning today. As Seal admitted in 1973 in a moment of self-criticism, the "truisms of the Raj" had "become the dogmas of historians" – official categories had been accepted a little too uncritically. Not all Bengali Brahmans were accepted as *bhadralok* by any means (e.g., the Brahman cooks, or even sometimes the *purohit*, custodian of family ritual), while in Bombay city in 1864 the allegedly "dominant elite" of Chitpavan and Saraswat Brahmans included 10,000 beggars and 1,880 domestic servants. The very use of the term "elite" is dubious in this context, as the one genuine and truly exclusive elite in colonial India consisted of the whites. The ideology of the English-educated was seldom one of conscious defence or restriction of its privileges, whether educational or caste – which is what one would have expected of a true elite, and what one sees with the Englishmen in India. Rather, some of them made considerable personal sacrifices in social reform movements often aimed directly or indirectly against upper-caste privileges, and many more did their best to extend education through starting private schools and colleges in their home towns or villages. With the cutting-down of government aid to higher education following the recommendations of the Hunter Commission (1882), this was in fact the principal way in which education spread in India. The number of private unaided colleges went up from 11 to 53 between 1881–2 and 1901–2. It should also be remembered that the first bill to make primary education compulsory (and free for families earning less than Rs 10 a month) was moved in the Imperial Council by G. K. Gokhale in 1911, and was rejected by the official majority. The Bombay Governor in a private letter to the Viceroy stated the real reason: nationalist "power to stir up discontent would be immensely increased if every cultivator could read" (B. R. Nanda, *Gokhale*, p. 392).

A more fruitful way of studying the intelligentsia is through a simultaneous analysis of its ideas and its socio-economic roots. This immediately reveals a significant contrast between broadly bourgeois ideals derived from a growing awareness of contemporary developments in the West, and a predominantly non-bourgeois social base. The contrast was perhaps clearest in Bengal. Here the nineteenth-century intelligentsia diligently cultivated the self-image of a "middle class" (*madhyabitta-sreni*), below the *zamindars* but above the toilers. It searched for its model in the European "middle class," which, as it learned through Western education, had brought about the great transformation from medieval to modern times through movements like the Renaissance, the Reformation, the Enlightenment, and democratic revolution or reform. Yet its own social roots lay not in industry or trade, increasingly controlled by British managing agency firms and their Marwari subordinates, but in government service or the professions of law, education, journalism, or medicine – with which was very often combined some connection with land in the shape of the intermediate tenures which were rapidly proliferating in Permanent Settlement Bengal. The *Amrita Bazar Patrika* of December 9, 1869 vividly expressed this dualism: "Middle-class ('madhyabitta') people are always considered the most useful group in any society. Our country's welfare depends to a large extent on this class. If there is ever to be a social or any other revolution in this country, it will be by the middle class. All the beneficial institutions or activities that we see in our country today have been started by this class . . . The livelihood of middle-class people comes from landed property and the services . . . Middle-class people are often, 'gantidars.'" (A form of intermediate tenure common in the Jessore-Nadia region, from which the *Amrita Bazar Patrika* was then being published.)

It must be added that the Bengali intelligentsia's aloofness from business did not really come from any *bhadralok* aversion to trade, for "middle-class" journals throughout the nineteenth century never tired of urging their readers to take to independent industry or trade. The link with a semifeudal land system did not prevent bourgeois aspirations, but it did inhibit, as we shall have to repeatedly note, radical thought and action on agrarian issues – a limitation of ultimately momentous consequence for Bengal, with its large Muslim peasant population.

A broadly similar pattern can be seen in other provinces, though with some interesting regional variations. Thus in Madras Suntharalingam talks of an early prominence of a "commercial elite," with merchants like Lakshmanarasu Chetti, important in the Madras Native Association of the 1850s, giving place to "administrative" and "professional elites" for reasons which he unfortunately fails to analyze. The Western-educated groups were once again often connected with petty landholding, though Washbrook has recently emphasized the behind the scenes role in the activities of the Madras Mahajana Sabha of the 1880s and the Congress run by it, of financial patrons coming from prosperous business groups like the Chettis of Madras town or the Komati merchants of the Andhra delta, as well as some big *zamindars*.

In Maharashtra the Poona intelligentsia, based on a town with virtually no industrial or commercial importance, could have little connection with business except through *swadeshi* aspiration. Tilak's journal *Mahratta*, however, noted an interesting and important paradox here in its issue of September 6, 1891, while commenting on the initiative taken by Poona in starting an annual Industrial Conference. "Poona is, we freely admit, not a manufacturing or commercial centre. It is rich . . . in political traditions. . . . Bombay is richer than Poona, but the attention as well as the time of our Bombay commercial men, is entirely taken up by their pursuits, and in consequence the work of formulating a scheme of commercial revival must be done by other hands." A link with land was once again often present in the form of petty rent-collecting *khoti* rights, particularly in a district like Ratnagiri which supplied a disproportionately large number of Maharashtrian intellectuals (both Tilak and Gokhale came from families with *khoti* rights in Ratnagiri). As in Bengal, the social basis did not mechanically determine the ideology, but it did fix some limits. A Bombay Government move to restrain transfer of peasant lands to moneylenders in 1901 was bitterly opposed by Tilak as well as Gokhale, and the father of Extremism once even made the following revealing comments: "Just as the government has no right to rob the sowcar (moneylender) and distribute his wealth among the poor, in the same way the government has no right to deprive the *khot* of his rightful income and distribute the money to the peasant. This is a question of rights and not of humanity" (quoted in Bhagwat and Pradhan, *Lokamanya Tilak*, p. 134).

Bourgeois connections were naturally somewhat more prominent in Bombay city. Though relations between *shetia* merchant-princes and "Young Bombay" intellectuals had been rather uncertain and at times quite hostile, more stable links were forged between the new Bombay intelligentsia leadership of the 1880s and 1890s (headed by the lawyer-triumvirate of Pherozeshah Mehta, K. T. Telang, and Badruddin Tyabji) and the mill-owners through agitation over issues like abolition of import duties on Lancashire cottons and imposition of the countervailing excise. The connection was symbolized by the career of Dinshaw Wacha – principal contact of Naoroji in Bombay, secretary of the Bombay Presidency Association (1885–1915), general secretary of the Congress (1896–1913), member of 38 years of the Bombay Millowners' Association executive committee, and managing agent of several textile mills. And yet Wacha's letters to Naoroji are full of complaints about the parsimony of Bombay businessmen – it was quite a job to obtain the paltry sum of Rs 500 from J. N. Tata for the Congress, for instance, in 1889. Indian capitalists were to unloosen their purse-strings for the nationalists only a generation later, after the First World War and with the rise of Gandhi.

In northern India, Bayly's microstudy of Allahabad brings out once again the connections between professional groups and small landlordism. He emphasizes more, however, the link between politicians like Madan Mohan Malaviya and Khattri and Agarwal banking and trading families (themselves, it should be noted, often also landlords – 12 of the 24 major Allahabad commercial families listed by Bayly owned *zamindaris*) – a link mediated primarily through Arya Samajist and Hindu-revivalist cultural and religious activities.

Two general statements are commonly made about the pattern of thought and activity of the intelligentsia in the last quarter of the nineteenth century. Social and religious reform movements, so prominent down to the 1870s, were being swamped, we are told, by a rising tide of revivalism, and the latter again was intimately bound up with the emergence of more extreme varieties of nationalism. Like many generalizations, both these statements require some qualifications.

2 Hindu Reform and Revival

That reform movements were past their peak in Bengal was obvious enough after the 1870s, with the Brahmos torn by internal quarrels and losing influence, and Iswarchandra Vidyasagar retiring into tragic isolation. The pattern was by no means so unambiguous in western India, where M. G. Ranade remained a commanding influence in the intellectual world till his death in 1901. Along with his friend K. T. Telang (Prarthana Samajist and reformer as well as one of the pillars of the early Congress), Ranade followed a cautious policy of pursuing social reform "along the lines of least resistance" – a caution which by the late 1890s was being attacked by men like R. G. Bhandarkar and N. C. Chandavarkar. A reform group had also emerged in the south, where Virasalingam of the Telegu-speaking country founded the Rajahmundri Social Reform Association in 1878 with promotion of widow remarriage as its principal objective, and K. N. Natarajan started the influential *Indian Social Reformer* in 1890. A Hindu Social Reform Association was also started in Madras in 1892 by the "young Madras party" associated with that journal. For the first time, too, something like an all-India social reform movement had been launched with Ranade from 1887 organizing an annual National Social Conference which met in the Congress *pandal* till Tilak drove it out at Poona in 1895. Behramji Malabari's *Notes* on infant marriage and enforced widowhood in 1884 started a countrywide debate among intellectuals, and his sustained campaign (directed, it is true, as much if not more towards public opinion in England and British officials as to winning over Indians) did pressurize the government to pass the first major social reform legislation since the legalization of widow remarriage in 1856 – the Age of Consent Act of 1891.

The short-lived but intense storm aroused over the Age of Consent issue, however, revealed how much the climate of educated opinion had changed since 1860, when sexual intercourse with a girl below the age of ten had been declared to be rape without much protest from anyone. The relatively minor reform raising this age from ten to twelve, which was all that the government eventually accepted of Malabari's far more wide-ranging proposals directed against child-marriage, now provoked massive opposition, particularly in Bengal and Maharashtra. Frankly conservative and obscurantist sentiments mingled here with the nationalist argument, put forward most notably by Tilak, that foreign rulers had no right to interfere with religious and social customs. The latter argument, it must be added, was slightly specious, since Hindu orthodox groups in the same period seldom hesitated to plead for legislation against cow-slaughter. Such legislation would surely also have been an interference with the religious and social customs of a big part of Indian society – the Muslims. The Bengal movement spearheaded by the newspaper *Bangabasi* (which attained a circulation of 20,000 as against 4,000 of the pro-reform Brahmo journal *Sanjibani*, and against which a sedition case was launched) briefly anticipated some *swadeshi* moods and methods, with huge meetings at the Calcutta Maidan, a great *puja* at Kalighat, and even calls for boycott and a few efforts at organizing indigenous enterprises.

In Bengal, the intellectual mood had been changing under a variety of influences from the 1870s. Defence of Hindu traditions became more respectable as scholars like Max Müller rediscovered the glories of ancient Aryans, and as a romantic cult of the exotic Orient developed in the West, bearing strange and more than a little dubious fruit in the Theosophical movement of Olcott and Blavatsky. A small but influential group headed in the 1880s and 1890s by Jogendrochandra Ghosh used Comte's Positivism to formulate a *via media* for intellectuals who had lost their traditional faith but still wanted social conformity. Sophisticated and intellectualized revivalism was best represented by the Bankimchandra of the 1880s, reinterpreting Krishna as ideal man, culture-hero, and nation builder. At a more obscurantist level revivalism was represented by Sasadhar Tarkachudamani and Krishnaprasanna Sen, who claimed *shastric* precedents for all the discoveries of modern western science. But revivalism was most effective when it sought to appeal to emotions rather than to the intellect: through the neo-Vaishnavism of the *Amrita Bazar Patrika*, seeking inspiration in Chaitanya rather than the Krishna of the epics whom Bankim had sought to idealize, and above all through Ramakrishna Paramhansa, the saintly Dakshineswar priest who cast a spell over Calcutta's sophisticated intellectuals precisely through his eclecticism and rustic simplicity. In the 1890s, his disciple Vivekananda leapt to fame after a memorable appearance at the Chicago Congress of Religions. Vivekananda was very far from being an obscurantist or revivalist in any crude sense. One major effect of his work still was to weaken social reform further by condemning it (no doubt with considerable justice) as elitist and inspired by alien models and replacing it by the ideal of social service, and the Ramakrishna Mission founded by him in 1897 has proved an efficient philanthropic organization with no claims to social radicalism. Yet Vivekananda himself had combined passionate evocation of the glories of the Aryan tradition and Hinduism (particularly before Western audiences) with bitter attacks on present-day degeneration: "Our religion is in the kitchen. Our God is the cooking pot." "As if religion consisted in making a girl a mother at the age of twelve or thirteen," was his private comment on the Age of Consent furore, and Vivekananda's remark about the cult of the cow – "like mother, like son," deserves to be recalled. He preached a this-worldly type of religion, emphasizing self-help and the building-up of manly strength: "What our country now wants are muscles of iron and nerves of steel." Equally remarkable was Vivekananda's concern for the plight of the "Daridra-narayana," the Shudra and the untouchable, his occasional vague predictions about their gaining "supremacy in every society . . . Socialism, Anarchism, Nihilism, and other like sects are the vanguard of the social revolution that is to follow" – as well as his famous appeal to "forget not that the lower classes, the ignorant, the poor, the illiterate, the cobbler, the sweeper, are thy flesh and blood, thy brothers." Such rhetoric, however, was combined with a near-total lack of clarity about concrete socio-economic programs, methods of mass contact, or even political objectives. Yet in eclecticism precisely lay the strength of Vivekananda's appeal, and his mixture of patriotism with the cult of manly virtues, vague populism, and evocation of Hindu glory was to prove heady wine indeed for young men in the coming *Swadeshi* periods.

In Maharashtra, revivalism had its centre at Poona, and took on a more narrowly Brahmanical character than in Bengal. Connected initially with the declining position of the traditional literati of *shastris* who saw their *dakshinas* or stipends gradually drying up under British rule, the evocation of lost Hindu, Brahman, and Maratha glory began finding increasing support from the English-educated, through the influence of Vishnu Krishna Chiplunkar's *Nibandhmala* essays (1874–81). Tilak's alliance with the Poona revivalists in the 1890s, forged through opposition to the Age of Consent bill, the starting of the Ganapati Utsava, and the refusal to permit Ranade to hold his National Social Conference at the Congress *pandal* in 1895, may be best regarded perhaps as political utilization of an already existing reality – for personally he was hardly an obscurantist. He had even sponsored with Ranade, as late as 1890, a circular letter advocating women's education and raising of the age of marriage. In south India, where indigenous movements of reform or revival were relatively weak, the Theosophical Society founded at Adyar in 1882 acquired considerable influence among the English-educated, particularly after the arrival in 1893 of Annie Besant. In the 1890s, Mrs. Besant repeatedly attacked social reformers and extolled the virtues of traditional Hinduism, though her views on this as well as on many other subjects were to change dramatically later on.

The one "reform" movement, however, that was making spectacular advances in the 1880s and 1890s was the Arya Samaj, founded by the wandering *sanyasi* from Kathiawar, Dayanand Saraswati (1824–83) but acquiring its principal base in northern India (Punjab and parts of western UP). The message of Dayanand attained success perhaps through its very ambiguity, for it combined sharp criticism of many existing Hindu practices (idolatry and polytheism, child marriage, the taboos on widow remarriage and foreign travel, Brahman predominance and the multiplicity of castes based on birth alone) with an extremely aggressive assertion of the superiority over all other faiths, Christianity, Islam, or Sikhism, of purified Hinduism based on Vedic infallibility. The specific goals of the social reformers were thus absorbed into a dominant pan-Hindu revivalist framework. The Arya Samaj soon overshadowed the Brahmos in the contest for the loyalties of reform-minded educated young men of northern India, offering as it did a doctrine at once safer, less alienating, and unconnected with an increasingly unpopular Bengali immigrant community, which had initially occupied an undue portion of administrative and professional jobs due to its early lead in English education. The Arya Samajists also struck deep roots among the trading castes. The principal early Punjab leaders, Guru Dutt, Lala Hans Raj, Lala Lajpat Rai, and Lala Munshi Ram (Swami Shraddhanand), all came from Khatri, Arora, or

Aggarwal families. Kenneth Jones relates the four principal bases of the Samaj in the Punjab (Peshawar-Rawalpindi, Multan, Rohtak-Hissar, and the Jullundur Doab) partly to local business support. From 1900 onwards, they also went in for largescale *shuddhi* or mass purification and conversion of lower castes – Rahtias, Odhs, Meghs, and Jats. With them as with trading groups, the Arya Samaj had thus become something like a channel for "Sanskritizing" processes. Membership consequently rose in a spectacular manner: 40,000 in 1891, 92,000 in 1901, half a million by 1921 (the Brahmos in sharp contrast never numbered more than a few thousands in the census figures).

In 1893, the Arya Samaj split on the two issues of meat-eating versus vegetarianism and Anglicized versus Sanskrit-based education. The moderate "College" faction led by Hans Raj and Lajpat Rai henceforward concentrated on building up a chain of "Dayanand Anglo-Vedic" colleges, and also developed a somewhat sporadic interest in Congress politics as well as a more sustained involvement in *swadeshi* enterprise. The more openly revivalist and militant "Gurukul" faction founded by Lekh Ram and Munshi Ram started the Hardwar Gurukul in 1902 (unaffiliated to the official educational system, unlike the DAV, and based on principles of *brahmacharya* and Vedic training). They emphasized proselytization through paid preachers and *shuddhi*. Within both groups, however, the general trend was towards a shift "from Arya Dharm to Hindu consciousness" (Kenneth Jones) – and a consciousness quite often openly communal and anti–Muslim. Lekh Ram's bitter polemics with the Ahmediya Muslim sect led to his assassination in 1897, while in February 1909 Lajpat's associate Lala Lal Chand clearly anticipated much of later Hindu Mahasabha and RSS ideology in his *Panjabee* article, "Self-Abnegation in Politics." Lal Chand bitterly attacked the Congress for ignoring the specific problems and demands of the Hindus. "The consciousness must arise in the mind of each Hindu that he is a Hindu, and not merely an Indian" – and hence there was need for "the substitution of Hindu Sabhas for Congress Committees, of a Hindu Press for the Congress Press, organization of a Hindu Defence Fund with regular office and machinery for collecting information and seeking redress by self-help . . ." Thus despite much initial hostility (which had even included some plots against Dayanand's life), the Arya Samaj in practice was coming fairly close to the postures of orthodox Hinduism – an orthodoxy which was also trying to organize itself by the late nineteenth century through Hari Sabhas and Sanatan Dharma Sabhas, conferences at Kumbha Melas, and a big conference at Delhi in 1900 which started a Bharat Dharma Mahamandal – organizational efforts which have not drawn sufficient interest yet from historians.

"Revivalism" thus obviously contributed to the assertion of an aggressive Hindu identity. But one has to add that the difference here with the "reform" movements was of degree rather than kind. Not only had "modernistic" trends like the Brahmo or Prarthana Samajas or the more secular movements of Young Bengal or Vidyasagar been entirely Hindu in composition; with few exceptions, they too had operated with a conception of "Muslim tyranny" or a "medieval" dark age (an assumption we meet with in Rammohun and among Derozians almost as much as in Bankimchandra) from which British rule with its accompanying alleged "renaissance" or "awakening" had been a deliverance. This was not a theory which could ever hope to appeal to Muslim intellectuals, while the attempts to purge Hindu religion and society of "medieval" crudities and superstitions in the name of ancient standards and an emerging code of middle-class respectability also at times involved attacks on syncretist popular customs, like the worship in common of Hindu and Muslim holy men or shrines. As similar movements were developing at about the same time within Indian Islam too (e.g., the attack on Sufi eclecticism from the standpoint of a return to the purity and rigor of early Islam), the two communities tended to drift apart both at the level of the elite (where the unifying bond of a common Urdu-based culture was under severe strain in northern India) and of the peasant masses. District Gazetteers and biographical literature written in Bengal at about the turn of the century, for instance, frequently recall common participation in festivals like Durga Puja or Muharram and a variety of syncretist popular cults as important but diminishing phenomena.

3   Trends in Indian Islam

A pattern of clear-cut reformist-revivalist conflict, with the first tending to be loyalist and the second anti-British, seems at first to be evident in late-nineteenth-century Indian Islam, the two poles being represented by Sir Sayyid Ahmed Khan's Aligarh movement and the Deoband Dar-ul-Ulum or seminary founded in 1867 by two Mutiny veterans, Muhammad Qasim Nanawtawi and Rashid Ahmed Gangohi. Sayyid Ahmed tried to convert upper-class Muslims of western UP to the virtues and benefits of English education through a Scientific Society (1864), a modernistic Urdu journal *Tahzib al-akhlaq* (1870), and the Aligarh Anglo-Muhammadan Oriental College (1875). His interpretation of Islam emphasized the validity of free enquiry (*ijtihad*) and the alleged similarities between Koranic revelation and the laws of nature discovered by modern science. Yet the theology classes in Aligarh were directed by orthodox *mullahs*, and the modernistic elements in the Aligarh movement came to be considerably toned down over time, particularly under Muhsin al-Mulk. What is more important, Sayyid Ahmed had always stressed the need to import Western education to upper-class Muslims as Muslims, and to thus foster in them a sense of corporate unity. His program dovetailed neatly with the aims of the new British policy as formulated by Hunter's *Indian Mussalmans*, commissioned by Mayo in 1871: the British should help to "develop a rising generation of Muhammedans ... tinctured with the sober and genial knowledge of the West. At the same time they would have a sufficient acquaintance with their religious code to command the respect of their own community ..." Aligarh consequently got a quite unusual amount of British patronage, including a personal donation of Rs 10,000 from the Viceroy, Lord Northbrooke. As Francis Robinson has pointed out, it was through British support, above all, that "a man whose religious views were so unorthodox that the majority of his co-religionists branded him an infidel was raised up as the advocate of his community" (*Separatism among Indian Muslims*, p. 131).

The social basis for Sayyid Ahmed was provided by UP Muslim landlords (numerous in the Aligarh-Bulandshahr region and comprising 76 out of the 272 *taluqdar* families of Avadh) and traditional service families – a privileged but slowly declining group, which held 63.9 percent of subordinate judicial and executive posts in the province in 1857, 45.1 percent in 1886–7, and 34.7 percent in 1913 (the percentage of Muslims to the total population in NW Provinces and Avadh was only 13.4 in 1886–7). Thus, contrary to Hunter's generalization on the basis of the rather special Bengal case (where urban upper- or middle-class Muslims were relatively few in number), a generalization which was taken over by many British officials and Muslim leaders, separatism developed initially not for reasons of "backwardness," but because a traditional elite felt increasingly threatened by Hindu trader, moneylender, and professional groups buying up land, capturing municipalities, and obtaining jobs at its expense. A similar case – in reverse – is to be seen in the Punjab, where Kenneth Jones links the growing appeal of Arya Samajist revivalism in part to a Muslim challenge to earlier Khatri, Arora, and Badia predominance in business and the professions.

The initial British support for Aligarh was due not so much to the need for a counterpoise against Congress-type nationalism (which was not yet much of a threat), but to official fears concerning certain other trends within Indian Islam – the so-called "fanaticism" and antiforeign mentality preached by some religious leaders, which often seemed to find a ready response among what Peter Hardy has described as the "pre-industrial lower middle class of petty land-holders, country-town mullahs, teachers, booksellers, small shopkeepers, minor officials and skilled artisans . . . men literate in the vernacular . . . quick to be seized by religious passion" (*Muslims of British India*, p. 58). Broadly similar groups among Hindus were being attracted to revivalism and Extremist nationalism by the late nineteenth century. In this case, memories of 1857 which exaggerated somewhat the specific role of the Muslims merged with the panic caused by the "Wahhabi" frontier wars and conspiracies of the 1860s. By the net decade, however, the political, anti-British aspects of the Wahhabi (more correctly, *Tariqah-i-Muhammediyah*) movement had been suppressed; what survived was a sustained campaign of Islamization active particularly in rural Bengal, directed against syncretist cults, *shirk* and *bid'ah* (polytheism and sinful innovation). Such puritanical movements were thus curiously double-edged – heroically anti-British at times, they could also contribute to internal conflicts. An almost exact parallel here would be the Kuka sect among the Sikhs. Having faced British guns in 1872, they have been hailed occasionally as freedom-fighters, and yet their activities principally concerned bitter attacks on Islam on the cow-slaughter issue, culminating in the murder of some Muslim butchers at Amritsar and Ludhiana in 1871.

A more muted kind of anti-British temper survived in the religious seminary started at Deoband in 1867. Rigidly orthodox, unlike the Wahhabis, and hostile to Sayyid Ahmed for his theological innovations and political loyalism alike, Deoband attracted relatively poor students who could not afford Western education, remained influential through the *madrasah* teachers it produced and in the twentieth century provided fairly consistent support to Congress nationalism. What alarmed the British in our period much more, however, was the occasional evidence of pan-Islamic sentiments aroused by the distant figure of the Ottoman Sultan-Khalifa, particularly during the Balkan war of 1876–8 and the Graeco-Turkish war of 1896–7. The founder of modern pan-Islamism, Jamal al-Din al-Afghani, was himself in India between 1879 and 1882, writing and giving lectures in Hyderabad and Calcutta. Though Jamal al-Din made a violent attack on Sayyid Ahmed in a *Refutation of the Materialists* (1882), modern research has established that his real quarrel was against the latter's subserviency towards the British. Al-Afghani's own theological ideas were at least as heterodox, and he passionately pleaded for Hindu–Muslim unity in lectures to Calcutta students, one at the Albert Hall in College Street, now the Coffee House. The immediate impact seems to have been small, but a new trend was emerging, once again profoundly ambiguous. By the late 1890s, there is some evidence that even Calcutta Muslim jute workers were being taught to look upon the Sultan as a distant but mighty protector. Pan-Islamism contributed to the Calcutta riots of 1897; twenty years later it was to become for some time a powerful anti-imperialist force through the Khilafat movement.

As would be evident from the above survey, very many of the conflicts in late-nineteenth-century Indian society were intracommunal disputes among various trends within Hinduism or Islam, rather than confrontations between the two big religious communities. But "communalism" proper was also acquiring, for the first time in the 1880s and 1890s, something like an all-India dimension. The two principal issues were the Urdu–Devanagri controversy and cow-protection. The demand for the use of the Devanagri script, first made by some Benares Hindus in 1868 and granted by Lt.-Governor Macdonnell in 1900, was clearly connected with the tension between old and new elites in the UP. It is interesting that Sayyid Ahmed started talking in terms of Muslims as a separate entity for the first time in 1869, and explicitly in the context of the script controversy – his Scientific Society had actually had more Hindu members than Muslim. Ultimately more significant, however, was the cow-protection issue, for it served as a link between elite and popular communalism, as McLane has shown in a recently-published study. Hindu defenders of the cow hoped and agitated for legislation on the subject, and in many UP municipalities passed bylaws restricting slaughter-houses, and *kabab*-shops on allegedly "hygienic" grounds. Muslim politicians feared that the Hindu majorities which would result from the introduction of elections would further curb what many felt was an essential part of their religion. Dayanand had published a pamphlet on the subject, *Gaukarunanidhi*, in 1881, and local *gaurakshini sabhas* began springing up in many parts of northern India from the late 1880s, encouraged by the patronage of some lawyers and *zamindars*, as well as by the activities of some wandering *sadhus*. The cow was not only an age-old religious symbol, but also the most vital economic asset for the peasant, apart from his land – while educated Hindus were attracted by the argument that cow-protection would improve the health and prosperity of all Indians. *Gaurakshini sabhas* were becoming more militant after 1892–3, perhaps reflecting to some extent orthodox resentment at the passing of the Age of Consent Act the previous year. There were reports of forcible inter-ference with the sale or slaughter of cows and even of setting up of *sabha* courts which punished sale to butchers by fine or social boycott. As Islamic revivalist trends were simultaneously insisting on the necessity of the Bakr-Id sacrifice, the ground was prepared for the large-scale riots of June–July 1893. These started at Mau in Azamgarh, where a big Muslim population was attacked by crowds coming in from Ghazipur and Ballia districts. Riots were most organized in Ballia, where a Rajput *zamindar* was extremely active; most widespread (22 in all) in Saran, Gaya, and Patna, the locale of many large cattle fairs; and most violent in Bombay city, where 80 were killed, and the disturbances were sparked off by the issue of whether Hindu processions could play music before mosques. The two other places affected were Junagadh and far-off Rangoon. This was rioting on a quite unprecedented, almost countrywide, scale – a poor augury, indeed, for the modern national movement which was only just getting into its stride.

The connection often assumed between revivalism and extremer varieties of nationalism appears a bit dubious insofar as the former led up to riots which Sec-retary of State Kimberley welcomed as cutting "at the roots of the Congress agi-tation for the formation of a united Indian people" (Kimberley to Lansdowne, August 25, 1893). Even otherwise, it must be remembered that the biggest single contribution made to nationalism in the pre-1905 period – the formulation of a systematic critique of the economic aspects of British rule through the drain of wealth theory – was the work of men like Dadabhai Naoroji, Ranade, G. V. Joshi, and R. C. Dutt, all broadly associated with modernistic reformers. Nor were social reform enthusiasts always necessarily milk and water moderates in poli-tics. In 1876, the Brahmo leader Sivanath Sastri inspired a group of young men (including Bepinchandra Pal) to take a remarkable pledge abjuring government service and declaring that "self-government is the only form of political gov-ernment ordained by God." G. G. Agarkar, who started the Deccan Education Society and the journals *Kesari* and *Mahratta* along with Tilak but later quar-relled with him, had the reputation of being a radical in both social and politi-cal matters. Patwardhan, who succeeded Agarkar as editor of the reformist *Sudharak* after the latter's untimely death in 1895, was suspended as a teacher and threatened with sedition charges during the plague disturbances in Poona in 1897. Conversely, not all advocates of orthodoxy or revivalism were political fire-brands. An orthodox rally of 10,000 at Benares in 1892 ended with three cheers for the Sanatan Dharma and Queen Victoria. Annie Besant became politically active only after her conversion to social reform, and the more orthodox Gurukul section of the Aryas kept away from nationalist politics, unlike Lajpat's College faction. As late as 1913, the Gurukul was parading its loyalism through an osten-tatious welcome to Lt.-Governor Meston.

What was happening from roughly the 1870s was a gradual, incomplete, often inconsistent, but still extremely important shift within the whole universe of dis-course and action of the intelligentsia towards various forms of nationalism, a shift which affected many (though by no means all) reformers and revivalists alike. The attempt to explain this phenomenon in terms of growing educated unemployment is not entirely satisfactory. It is true that Indian newspapers (as well as many official reports) repeatedly complained of diminishing prospects for graduates (itself a product of colonialism, one must add: the very slow growth of industry and the humanistic bias given to English education right from its beginnings under Macaulay made overcrowding of the liberal professions and government services inevitable). Yet it has to be remembered that competition for jobs by itself could lead as easily to sectional consciousness along regional or communal lines. We have already seen examples of this happening, in the Hindu–Muslim elite conflict in UP and the growing unpopularity of Bengalis in much of northern India. The leaders and most of the participants in the early Congress were not unemployed youths, but successful and fairly prosperous pro-fessional men. Much more important factors were racism, of which the Ilbert Bill furore was only one major manifestation, and the growing awareness of the link between British policies and the stark poverty of the country (made more obvious by the repeated famines of the 1870s and 1890s). If explanations are still to be sought at the microlevel, one could point to the fact that the successful lawyer leaders of the early Congress often had to overcome considerable white obstructions in their early careers. Pherozeshah Mehta, for instance, decided to concentrate on *mofussil* practice after complaining about unfair British competi-tion in Bombay in 1873. W. C. Bonnerji was passed over for appointment to standing counsel in 1881, and Indian *vakils* in Madras and Calcutta won the right to appear without barristers in High Court original suits only after refusing to serve as junior counsels to whites. Patriotism of a necessarily more muted kind was bred also at times by discrimination within the Civil Service – in men like Brojendranath De, for example, who was repeatedly passed over in promotions after he had intervened on behalf of Indians ill-treated by white mine-owners at Ranigunj, and had then added to his sins by defending the Ilbert Bill against the wishes of his superior John Beames. Another, much more obscure Bengal offi-cial, a district *munsiff* named Gyanchandra Banerji, has left an unpublished diary marked throughout by remarkably intense anti-British feelings, sparked off by the twin issues of racial discrimination and mass poverty.

264

4 Patriotism in Literature

The initial and natural form of expression of the patriotism of the intelligentsia was through literature in the regional languages. Modern literature in the various Indian languages (and particularly prose, which was largely undeveloped prior to the nineteenth century) everywhere emerged in close association with reform movements (one might recall, for instance, the role of Rammohun and particularly Vidyasagar in the development of Bengali prose). It was then taken over by the new patriotic mood. Bengal in the 1860s and 1870s produced a large number of patriotic poems and songs bemoaning the plight of the country and at times even directly referring to the decline of handicrafts. Many of these were written for the Hindu Mela organized for some years from 1867 by Nabagopal Mitra with the backing of the Tagore family. The newly-established theater was even more directly anti-British, from Dinabandhu Mitra's exposure of indigo-planters in *Nil-Darpan* (1860) down to certain plays in the 1870s which led directly to Lytton's Dramatic Performances Act in 1876. The greatest single influence was Bankimchandra, with his historical novels climaxed by *Anandmath* (1882) with its *Bande Mataram* hymn. Through essays as well as novels, Bankimchandra sought to evoke a new interest in the history of the country, striking a note typical of nationalism the world over. It is interesting, however, that the 1880s and 1890s which saw Hindu revivalism at its height in Bengal seem to have been marked by a certain decline of political interest. The theater was now dominated by Girishchandra Ghosh's sentimental domestic dramas or plays on Puranic themes with little direct political content. In 1903 Bepinchandra Pal stated that since the Ilbert Bill days, "Politics have been neglected in the interest of abstract religion. And in consequence religious songs have supplanted the old national songs" (*New India*, March 19, 1903).

A broadly similar pattern of connection between nationalism and the development of regional literature can be seen in other parts of the country, along a varied timescale which again corresponded roughly to the emergence of patriotic activity in particular areas. M. G. Ranade's *Note on the Growth of Marathi Literature* (1898) cataloged the rapid increase in the number of Marathi publications (only 3 in the years 1818–27, 102 in 1847–57, 1,530 in 1865–74, 3,824 in 1885–96), and emphasized the move to publish new editions of the medieval Marathi *bhakti* poets from the 1840s onwards. This was followed by publications of old Marathi chronicles (*bakhars*), and Ranade's own historical works and articles in a sense began the cult of Shivaji which Tilak took up from 1895. Ranade, however, tried to portray the seventeenth-century revival as a kind of protestant movement inspired by *bhakti* saints who sought to transcend caste differences. He felt that the orthodoxy of the later Peshwas was partly responsible for the Maratha decline. A quite different view of Shivaji, emphasizing the role of his *guru* Ramdas as an apostle of Hindu militancy, was put forward from the 1890s by Tilak, Kelkar, and Rajwade; it is obvious that contemporary differences were

265

being projected back into the past on both sides. There was also a third view, projecting Shivaji as a Shudra king, as Jotiba Phule tried to do in a ballad composed in 1869. More directly political themes were developed, again from contrasting points of view, by "Lokahitavadi" Gopal Hari Deshmukh in his *Satapatra* series (1848–50) which called for social reforms, advocated indigenous enterprise, but broadly welcomed British rule, and a generation later by Vishnukrishna Chiplunkar's journal *Nibandhamala* (1874–81) with its strong revivalist and anti-British note.

As the examples of Bengali and Marathi make clear, however, the development of patriotic literature in the languages of the various Indian peoples contained certain ambiguities. It tended to foster, more or less at the same time, national, regional, and communal consciousness. Thus Bankimchandra was concerned essentially with the history of Bengal, repeatedly asserted that Bengal had lost her independence with Bakhtiyar Khilji and not with Plassey, emphasized the harmful effects of Mughal centralization on regional life, and liberally distributed abuse of Muslims in his later historical novels (particularly *Anandamath*, *Debi Chaudhurani*, and *Sitaram*). Tod's romantic mythmaking about Rajput chivalry and valor directed against Muslim invaders was taken up on a large scale in Bengali poetry, drama, novels, and even books for children. Attempts were made also to import the cult of Shivaji, though the principal historical link of Bengal with the Maratha power had been through the extremely destructive *bargi* raids of the 1740s. Thus developed what Bipan Chandra has appropriately called "vicarious nationalism," which has been justified at times by the argument that it would have been dangerous (for Bankim as a government official, for instance) to write openly against British rule. But the use of Muslims as convenient whipping-boys for the British could not but have extremely harmful consequences. Bankimchandra was idolized by *swadeshi* Hindu youth particularly from 1905, but even Muslim journals like the *Mussalman*, broadly sympathetic to nationalism, repeatedly attacked him for the abuse of *Yavanas* contained in many of his works. Muslim intellectuals were soon developing their own variety of vicarious nationalism, glorifying precisely the periods and figures (like Aurangzeb) abused by the Hindus and evoking nostalgic feelings for the lost glories of Islam on a world scale. This was the note struck by late-nineteenth-century Urdu poets like Altaf Husain Hali and Shibli Nomani. In Bengal, this trend was expressed by the Muslim poet Kaikobad.

Things were even more complicated in two major regions – Tamilnadu, and what is today described as the "Hindi" belt. The evocation of Tamil history and classical Tamil literature, encouraged by British scholars like Robert Caldwell and J. H. Nelson, was acquiring by the early twentieth century a strongly anti-Brahmanical note which could easily become anti-north Indian Aryan also – a development occasionally encouraged by British officials like Governor Grant-Duff in 1886. Literary Hindi, again, was very much of an artificial creation closely associated with Hindu revivalist movements. "Bharatendu" Harishchandra (1850–85), often regarded as the "father" of modern Hindi due to his plays, poems, and journalism, combined pleas for use of *swadeshi* articles with demands for replacement of Urdu by Hindi in courts, and a ban on cow-slaughter. He remained also fundamentally a loyalist in politics. In the eighteenth and much of the nineteenth century, Urdu had been the language of polite culture over a big part of north India, for Hindus quite as much as Muslims. As late as the decade 1881–90, 4,380 Urdu books had been published in UP, as compared to 2,793 in Hindi, while the corresponding circulation figures for newspapers were 16,256 for Urdu and 8,002 for Hindi. Even Premchand wrote mainly in Urdu down to 1915, till he found publishers difficult to obtain. The campaign for Hindi in the Devangari script launched by Arya Samajists and orthodox Hindus did have a certain populist appeal, for Persianized Urdu had been the language of an elite. But the highly Sanskritized Hindi which was increasingly propagated, and later sought by some enthusiasts to be given the stature of the "national" language, was really quite far removed from the various popular vernaculars of the region (Punjabi, Haryanvi, Pahari, Rajasthani, Avadhi, Bhojpuri, Maithili, Magadhi, etc.). What was much more ominous was the way in which differences of script and language came to be progressively identified with differences in religion, embedding communalism at a very deep level in the popular consciousness. Thus in north India as well as in the south, problems were emerging that have remained to trouble independent India right up to the present day.

References and Further Reading

Western histories of the fifteen official Indian languages are available in the series published by Otto Harrassowitz, Weisbaden; and edited by Jan Gonda.

The National Literature Academy of India (Sahitya Akademi) has issued it own set of regional literary histories.

Banerjee, Sumanta. (1989). *The Parlour and the Streets: Elite and Popular Culture in Nineteenth Century Calcutta*. Calcutta: Seagull Books.

Bayly, C. A. (1996). *Empire and Information: Intelligence Gathering and Social Communication in India, 1780–1870*. Cambridge: Cambridge University Press.

Chandra, Sudir. (1992). *The Oppressive Present: Literature and Social Consciousness in Colonial India*. New Delhi: Oxford University Press.

Dimock, Edward C., Jr., *et al.* (1974). *The Literatures of India: An Introduction*. Chicago and London: University of Chicago Press.

Hasan, Muhammad. (1990). *Thought Patterns of Nineteenth Century Literature of North India*. Karachi: Royal Book Co.

Joshi, Svati, ed. (1991). *Rethinking English: Essays in Literature, Language, History*. New Delhi: Trianka.

Ramaswamy, Sumathi. (1997). *Passions of the Tongue: Language Devotion in Tamil India*. Berkeley: University of California Press.

Sarkar, Sumit. (1997). *Writing Social History*. New Delhi: Oxford University Press.

Sarkar, Tanika. (1985). "Bengali Middle-Class Nationalism and Literature: A Study of Saratchandra's 'Pather Dabi' and Rabindranath's 'Char Adhyay,'" in D. N. Panigrahi, ed., *Economy, Society and Politics in Modern India*. New Delhi: Vikas, 449–462.

———. (1987). "Nationalist Iconography: Image of Women in 19th Century Bengali Literature," *Economic and Political Weekly*, WS (Nov.): 2011–15.

———. (1992). "The Hindu Wife and the Hindu Nation: Domesticity and Nationalism in Nineteenth Century Bengal," *Studies in History*, 8, no. 2, n.s. (1992): 213–35.

Schwarz, Henry. (1996). "Sexing the Pundits: Gender, Romance and Realism in the Cultural Politics of Colonial Bengal," in Henry Schwarz and Richard Dienst, eds., *Reading the Shape of the World: Toward an International Cultural Studies*. Boulder, Colo.: Westview Press, 224–60.

Sunder Rajan, Rajeswari, ed. (1992). *The Lie of the Land: English Literary Studies in India*. New Delhi: Oxford University Press.

Vishwanathan, Gauri. (1989). *Masks of Conquest: Literary Study and British Rule in India*. New York: Columbia University Press.

Chapter 13

Africa: Varied Colonial Legacies

Tejumola Olaniyan

To understand the varied legacies of colonialism in Africa with any measure of depth, we must specify the particular nature of colonialism experienced by the continent. The current ubiquitous usage of "colonialism" as a catch-all to describe the disparate experiences of many societies under imperial rule is not useless; it only needs specific details in particular instances for productive illumination. One of the earliest and most famous of such specifications of the nature of African colonial experience is offered by Aimé Césaire when he writes in his classic work, *Discourse on Colonialism*, that:

> the great historical tragedy of Africa has been not so much that it was too late in making contact with the rest of the world, as the manner in which that contact was brought about; that Europe began to "propagate" at a time when it had fallen into the hands of the most unscrupulous financiers and captains of industry; that it was our misfortune to encounter that particular Europe on our path, and that Europe is responsible before the human community for the highest heap of corpses in human history. (1972: 23)

It is an implicit tribute to the cogency of Césaire's specification that very few historians today contest "the Scramble for Africa," a descriptive phrase that Césaire could very well have used, as the most appropriate characterization of that "historical tragedy."

But even Césaire's delineation needs more precise clarification, and that is provided by Mahmood Mamdani in his *Citizen and Subject: Contemporary Africa and the Legacy of Late Colonialism*. The distinct trajectory of European imperial rule that most shaped contemporary Africa, he says, is "late colonialism." Africa was Europe's last colonial possession, therefore Europe came to it with a wealth of experience. The fields of India – especially after the 1852 Mutiny – and Indochina had given its initial ideological mask of "civilizing mission" a severe and irreparable dent and made the pretense outdated. Africa was never the "jewel in the crown," with all the colonial psychological investment that that naming entails. By the time of the Scramble, that hypocritical "civilizing mission" had given way to a wholly avaricious "incorporation mission" and an obssession with "law and order" in the colonies by any means (Mamdani, 1996: 49–50, 109). The effect of this late colonialism on Africa has been enormous.

What defines the enormity is an all-embracing marginality of Africa, produced by the tripartite elements of the "colonizing structure" (Mudimbe, 1988: 2): the domination of physical space, the reformation of *natives*' minds, and the integration of local economic histories into the Western perspective. This structure of *complementary* acts "completely embraces the physical, human, and spiritual aspects of the colonizing experience" (Mudimbe, 1988: 2). I have found it quite productive to organize my considerations of the legacies of colonialism in Africa around this "colonizing structure." Although Mudimbe suggests that the structure has the tendency, if not the goal, to arrange and transform non-European areas into "fundamentally European constructs" (1988: 1), I will insist that what actually happened was not any such transformation – because Africa could only, in the circumstances, be incorporated *unequally* into the orbit of the West – but a general arrest and devastation of the colonized societies' capacities for self-directed evolution. Because this is a structured marginality, changes occasioned by political independence such as the deracialization of politics and civil society, have proved to be of little effect in reversing the marginality. I take this marginality to be the content of what is called "postcoloniality": an ambivalent temporality situated between the end of formal empire and an inability to tame or transcend imperial institutional structures. In our more hopeful moments, we can describe the temporality as an "interregnum," bound to end one day, though full of a "great variety of morbid symptoms" (Gramsci, 1987: 276) now. It is the central *composite* legacy of colonialism in Africa.

1   The Domination of Physical Space

Since the wave of decolonization in Africa in the 1960s, colonialism has often been invoked more in the context of considerations of the continued *economic* exploitation and underdevelopment of erstwhile colonized regions. That was how "neocolonialism" came into currency as a description of politically independent countries that are still deeply tied to the economic apron-strings of Europe and America. This overly strong emphasis on the economic is not unjustified, but I will insist that the economic pales into secondariness when we consider the legacies of colonial territorial domination on much of the African continent.

The geopolitical boundaries of contemporary African nations were determined solely by the exigencies of colonial conquest. They had very little to do with the demands or logics of indigenous ethnic, linguistic, or cultural communities, and everything to do with which colonizing country got where first or with treaties of whatever kind signed among them. This has led to countless cross-boundary clashes, exacerbated by the fact of the principle of sovereignty of modern nation-states which dictates a far more puritanical conception – and therefore, uncompromising policing – of geopolitical borders and boundaries than ever before. Perhaps such remorseless marking may have been less problematic where the lines follow entrenched cultural communities, but colonialism created African countries as *states first, then nations if ever possible*. This unusual backward mode of formation implies force, coercion, and arbitrariness as norm. Part of the contemporary crisis of the African state is its inability to forge a nation from its awkwardly thrown together constituent parts, parts that were routinely manipulated into fierce competition and set off against one another by the colonizers during colonial rule. In Nigeria, for instance, the then Northern Region, composed mainly of Hausa–Fulani, had the coziest relationship with the British and even rejected proposals for independence when brought up by the South, inhabited by the Yoruba and the Igbo. Part of the distrust preceded colonial rule, but colonialism, in binding the diverse regions artificially together in an unprecedentedly tight manner, greatly exacerbated and more substantively formalized it. Since the postcolonial period, the antagonism, basically originating from the problematics of resource exploration and allocation within the nation, has led to the enthronement of an atavistic ethnic consciousness, a major civil war, and an epidemic of *coup d'états*. Similar scenarios abound in many other African countries.

But there is a legacy more fundamental than awkward boundaries, ethnic chauvinism, or absence of national cohesion. That legacy is the perpetual crisis and instability of the African state. It is the consequence of Africa's *loss of power* in the shaping and direction of its affairs after the imposition of colonial rule. The notable historian, Walter Rodney, best describes the ramifications of that loss:

> The decisiveness of the short period of colonialism and its negative consequences for Africa spring mainly from the fact that Africa lost power. Power is the ultimate determinant in human society, being basic to the relations within any group and between groups. It implies the ability to defend one's interests and if necessary to impose one's will by any means available. In relations between peoples, the question of power determines maneuverability in bargaining, the extent to which a people survive as a physical and cultural entity. When one society finds itself forced to relinquish power entirely to another society, that in itself is a form of underdevelopment. (Rodney, 1972: 224)

In other words, the seven or so decades of colonial rule remain the most destructive, even more than the centuries of trans-Atlantic slavery, in African history; they are the source of contemporary African underdevelopment. All this because it was a period when, to the *unequal trade relations* characteristic of the preceding epoch of slavery, was added *outright territorial and political domination*.

271

Basil Davidson, the distinguished historian, affirms Rodney's argument by describing the decades of colonial rule as "wasted" in terms of crucial "political and structural development" of the continent" (1992: 72). "[I]n every crucial field of life," writes Davidson, "the British had frozen the indigenous institutions while at the same time robbing colonized peoples of every scope and freedom for self-development" (1992: 72). European territorial domination broke up and reorganized in its own interest settled African political communities (Chabal, 1994: 38) with recognized rules and institutions for the exercise of power and modalities for the management of crises. In the imposed new dispensation, power either flowed from entirely alien and alienating sources, or from the old sources as reshaped by the colonizers and not by the processes of autonomous indigenous evolution. Colonial political community was constituted by a hierarchy of European officials who dispensed absolute power through a myriad of local chiefs, "traditional" or created, who themselves ruled the "natives" with closed fists. The nationalists who opposed both on behalf of the African masses were themselves the creation of colonial society. Their claim to legitimacy was based more on a mastery of colonial language and civilization than on their representativeness within the indigenous society. They wanted freedom and independence, but very few questioned the strange geopolitical boundaries or the despotic political communities and associated institutions erected everywhere by colonial rule. The nationalists' vision rarely went beyond the capture or, more expressively, the deracialization of the colonial state and its apparatuses. But deracialization is not democratization. The colonial state was neither democratized, nor was or has much serious thought been given, by politicians or social scientists, to how African sociopolitical institutions that have worked well before colonial rule could be figured into the continent's perennial search for enduring democratic rule.

With the colonial dissolution of precolonial African political communities also followed the dissolution of established indigenous African political accountability. This is especially important given the epidemic of tyrannical rules that have bedeviled the African continent since the end of colonial rule. Patrick Chabal defines political accountability as

> the institutional, traditional and symbolic mechanisms by which, on the one hand, the governed called their governors to account for their deeds and, on the other, the governors discharge the responsibilities of political obligation. It is, nore broadly, the ensemble of formal and informal factors which impinge on the way in which rulers and the ruled relate to each other in a political community. (Chabal, 1994: 54)

Political accountability is not static but historical and dynamic. It is not change as such that destroys it but change that is not catalyzed by the indigenous evolution of the people, such as the type occasioned by colonialism. The irrefutable evidence is that the postcolonial crisis of the African state, so lamented globally, is without precedent in the entire precolonial history of Africa.

The postcolonial African state was determined mainly by the colonial state. But the colonial state was in description and practice an imposed, dictatorial state. It was a conquest state and not a product of the changing autonomous history of the people, as with most European states. As a conquest state, it was accountable only to the colonial office in the metropole, never to the people it governed in the colonies. Colonial accountability was, in essence, dictatorial. As a result, the colonial state had no structures of representation, ruled more by force than by consent, had absolute control of economic resources, created a bureaucracy with an extraverted mentality, and established a rural–urban divide that has been the nemesis of even well-meaning development programs. These features still define postcolonial African states today, military or civilian.

2 Reformation of Natives' Minds

From the "crude and inchoate prejudices" of the era of slavery, colonialism fashioned an elaborate "skein of racist ideology" (Davidson, 1992: 41) based on the supposed natural inferiority of the African. This is the self-serving fount of much of the zeal of the missionaries, the arrogance of colonial bureaucrats, the soggy subjectivism of early anthropologists, and the smugness of a whole array of peripheral colonial operatives, travelers, adventurers, and writers. The project of the reformation of natives' minds, by assigning the mark of the negative to everything African and the positive to everything European, was designed to socialize Africans to despise their history and culture and, therefore, themselves. It was to impart in them, to make them freely accept, an inferiority complex that perpetually yearns for Europeanness. This transformation of subjection (colonial racism) into subjectivity has been famously explored by Fanon in *Black Skin, White Masks*. The Christian missions and the colonial school, backed by the coercive force of the colonial state, were the primary agents of the transformation.

Space and place are the objects of colonial territorial control, but the soul is the object of its reformation of minds. It is in the realm of the reformation of minds – the realm of culture – that history is processed into nature, and contingency into inevitability; where the subjective *I* is simultaneously real and illusory, and acting is also and at the same time the illusion of acting. It is *simultaneously* the *process* and *space* of securing discursive reproduction and stability. It is thus the realm of the formation of subjectivity and the subject, the latter both as self-knowledge and as subjection to the dictates of "someone else." It is also, therefore, the realm of the contest and refusal of subjectivity and subjection. What underscores the importance of this site *and* stake of social struggles is that it is "where the identity of individuals and groups is at stake, and where order in its broadest meaning is taking form. This is the realm in which culture and power are most closely intertwined" (Rabinow, 1986: 260).

The project of reforming minds was marked by an ambiguity from the start. Its ostensible goal was to "civilize," that is, Europeanize, the natives. However, to civilize the native is paradoxically to confound the basis of the racist hierarchical scheme of civilized/barbaric. But paradox does not necessarily disable power – it is, in fact, very often its handmaiden – and so it was that "civilized," meaning Christianized and Western-educated, Africans were usually the targets of the worst forms of colonial racism precisely because they lived and demanded the recognition that their "civilized" status conferred on them. The "holy" frock or strings of academic degrees from Cambridge or the Sorbonne proved to be brittle shields against the arrows of prejudice. This frustration is structural to the colonial project of reformation of minds, and it soon led to movements for counterreformation and reorientation of consciousness. This is the origin of that first major Afrocentric discursive formation, Negritude (Abiola, 1981) and other cultural nationalist movements such as African Personality, African Aesthetic, as well as subsequent political nationalisms that led to independence.

Just as its origins, the legacy of the colonial reformation of minds remains equivocal. Postcolonial deracialization of colonial culture has been met with phenomenal successes on a variety of fronts. The content and themes of Western education were Africanized and procedures tailored to fit the goals of the "new nations." Even the most mainstream or conservative of Christian denominations incorporated African materials and practices, while new denominations based on African religious practices expanded exponentially. Indigenous artistic traditions, long maligned and suppressed by colonialism, became the source-pool of inspiration for many writers, artists, and performers, and many have created exquisite and truly uplifting works from a hybrid of both indigenous African and European traditions. This cultural-artistic decolonization, this fashioning of creative originality from both indigenous and borrowed materials, techniques, and media of transmission, is phenomenal in its success and is worthy of more attention.

African cinema, in quality as well as quantity of full-length feature productions, is becoming an increasingly distinct artistic presence both in and outside the continent, and only severe capital constraints, not availability of requisite skills, impede its faster expansion. A variety of styles of innovative African music are flourishing; and with the technology of mass reproduction, not a few African musicians – Mariam Makeba, Fela Anikulapo-Kuti, Alpha Blondy, Youssou N'Dour, Manu Dibango, Sunny Ade, and more – have achieved global fame. But the creative art that most decisively registered postcolonial African subjectivity, because the most visible worldwide, is literature, written in the languages of the former colonizing powers. There are three major phases in the development of this literature.

The first phase covers the earliest African written creative expressions in European languages to the 1950s. This phase is characterized, thematically, by a fundamental ambiguity about European imperialism in Africa: the writers, though all are assimilated into European culture as far as that process could go, are not absolutely in support of colonial domination but at the same time are very much enamored of the West and the products of its modernity – organized religious and secular education and their rituals, discourse of political liberalism though not applied to the colonies, and advanced technology. The protest against empire or colonialism is thus generally of the mild type, very often Christian-inspired. The lessons are sometimes heavy-handed and the artistry affected, the latter a result of uncritical immersion in European forms. The literature of this phase is generally optimistic about the ultimate resolution of the colonial problem and the future greatness of Africa – within the framework of a synthesis of the best from Africa and Europe. Some of these pioneers and their works include Olaudah Equiano, *The Interesting Narrative of the Life of Olaudah Equiano* (1789), Joseph Casely-Hayford, *Ethiopia Unbound* (1911); Kobina Sekyi, *The Blinkards* (1915); H. I. E. Dhlomo, *Girl Who killed to Save* (1935); R. E. Obeng, *Eighteenpence* (1943); R. E. G. Armattoe, *Between the Forest and the Sea* (1950); Dennis Osadebey, *Africa Sings* (1952), Amos Tutuola, *The Palmwine Drinkard* (1952). Also belonging to this phase is Negritude, the literary movement founded in Paris in the 1930s by French-speaking intellectuals from Africa and the Caribbean. Negritude, meaning an affirmation of the black African world against European racist prejudices, had as its main themes the psychological redemption of the colonized black, a valorization of African cultural traditions, a critique of the colonial and quest for independence. Stylistically, Negritude borrowed from European – mainly avant-garde or nonmainstream – literary traditions, tempered with imagery drawn from African sources. Negritude is ideologically uneven, as the more cultural-nationalist writers such as Léopold Sédar Senghor (who subsequently became the first president of independent Senegal) and Birago Diop, to name two examples, are to be distinguished from the more radical and left-leaning writers such as David Diop and Mongo Beti. Although the emphasis of the literature of the first phase is overwhelmingly African in content and in a few instances in form too, the implied audience is European.

The second phase, the late 1950s to the 1970s, stretches across two main historical developments. The late fifties through the decade of the sixties was marked by intense anticolonial nationalist activity and political decolonization throughout much of the continent. By the late 1970s, however, the heights of hope – of building stable, prosperous, and egalitarian nations – occasioned by political independence, had given way to depths of despair – at the endemic dictatorship, mass pauperization, and civil unrest – in one country after another. Most of the household names in African literature today achieved their fame by articulating the complexities of this unique history: Wole Soyinka, winner of the 1996 Nobel Prize in Literature, Chinua Achebe, Camara Laye, Ngugi wa Thiong'O, Flora Nwapa, Peter Abrahams, Ayi Kwei Armah, Sembene Ousmane, Ama Ata Aidoo, Ahmadou Kourouma, Yambo Ouloguem, Cheikh Hamidou

Kane, Okot p'Bitek. Their literature is characterized, stylistically, by a surer grasp of artistry evident in the simultaneous refashioning of borrowed European, and the critical appropriation of indigenous African, forms. Thematically, the literature evinced a bolder nationalism; a more realistic revisiting of African history to counter years of racist stereotyping; critical interrogations of indigenous traditions; a savage, unrelenting critique of African political leadership and the African state, and of African neocolonial relations with the West that subtend the failure of African political independence. Because opposition is the foundational principle upon which the literature of this phase found its voice – opposition to both the colonizers and the new postcolonial leaders as well as the exploited and gullible masses – satire and irony are its predominant artistic modes. Unlike in the previous phase, the implied audience is most assuredly African.

The literature of the post-1970s, the third phase, shares the features of the second phase. Additionally, there has been a phenomenal self-consciousness about style (experimentation with various forms, serious interrogation of the medium and elements of communication) as well as about themes and social relations (for instances, gender and interethnic issues came to be foregrounded as never before). In addition to the older African writers who are also changing with the times, some of the writers uniquely of the third phase include Femi Osofisan, Niyi Osundare, Buchi Emecheta, Nawal El Saadawi, Dambudzo Marechera, Ben Okri, Bessie Head, Kofi Anyidoho, Mariama Ba, Tsitsi Dangarembga, Karen King-Aribisala. From being a borrowed alien tool, African literature in European languages has become an *authentic* and indispensable part of postcolonial African intellectual life; its language notwithstanding, it has all over it the imprints of the gargantuan agency of Africa.

However, the counterreformation of minds was in many instances only half-heartedly pursued and thus has proven to be shallower than is apparent.

The colonial languages still remain the languages of government and commerce in most countries, a situation that alienates the state and its formal sectors from the majority of the population who are not literate in such languages. The contents and themes of Western education may have been decolonized, but as Olufemi Taiwo argued in a seminal essay, neither in material structure nor in accompanying social relations has the Western "mode of knowledge production" taken any solid and really productive root (1993), nor an applicable local mode fashioned and firmly in place. The result has been a crippling intellectual dependence on, or, in Mudimbe's more charitable description, an "epistemological filiation" to, the West (Mudimbe, 1988: 185). African literature now may be considered as African as the harmattan, but the debate begun in the 1960s as to the appropriateness of "African" literature in European languages, has by no means ended. The old anxiety that the relationship between the colonial languages and the indigenous African languages is a murderous, culturally deracinating zero-sum in favor of the former, has barely been allayed or proven wrong; and neither have all the palliative arguments about globalism and hybridity – arguments with a peculiar ability to turn historical accident into destiny – been able to sell the fact of African literature in European languages as anything but a constant reminder of African dependence. It is questions such as these that led Ngugi wa Thiong'O, after a distinguished record of several major novels and plays in English, to begin writing in his Gikuyu language in 1980. The success of Ngugi's efforts has been followed by translations into African languages of some of the works of notable writers such Wole Soyinka and Femi Osofisan, works originally published in English. This is still far from being a trend, though it ought to be so.

And very obviously, the widespread indigenization of Christianity has not deceived abandoned African deities: African prayers – for visionary leadership, good health, and economic prosperity – continue unanswered as the continent self-destructively bows to this and that alien god. Outside of bland pronouncements of freedom of worship, there is no African country where the kind of official regard accorded Christianity or Islam is extended to any indigenous religion.

Overall, "black skin, white masks," while no longer the grave generic social problem it was in Fanon's time, is still so prevalent a disease as to be a regular subject of caricature in the press by cartoonists and journalists: the Minister of Culture who addresses a press conference to denounce local radicals and marxists who are "corrupting our culture with alien ideas." He speaks in English or French or Portuguese. His three-piece suit is imported from West End London, his shoes from Italy, his wristwatch from Switzerland, and he drives away from the conference venue in a custom-built Mercedes Benz! Such is the vapidity of postcolonial cultural nationalism. Because it conceives culture and cultural identity as static rather than dynamic, it is easy for it to create such oppositions as "material culture," and "nonmaterial culture" or values, then sanction the acceptance of the former (for instance, European technology, under the guise that "our culture must modernize itself"), while insisting that "local" values must remain unchanged – as if "material culture" is neutral and value-free. This is the logic behind such historically famous statements as "[a] society or a culture can stay itself while undergoing economic development, provided it takes the necessary steps," enshrined in the Organization of African Unity's Pan-African Cultural Manifesto (1969: 794), released at the end of the First All African Cultural Festival held in Algiers, Algeria from July 21 to August 1, 1969.

3   Economic Underdevelopment and Dependence

This is often the realm of elaborate figures and statistics, and perhaps they are not entirely avoidable, for comparative purposes, in considerations of contemporary African economic underdevelopment. But figures and statistics do have a clinically antiseptic side to them that can deaden our responses to the human dimensions of Africa's economic crisis. Who hasn't seen those harrowing recuring pictures of famine and malnutrition, of epidemics of a variety of diseases and of rudimentary or nonexistent health care, of collapsed infrastructures, of rural areas bled dry to feed the cities and then completely neglected, of vast, sprawling slums called "cities" where seas of African humanity live? And what of the phenomena of the "vanishing middle class" and "brain drain"? These problems were far less severe in the late 1970s when a panel of international leaders and statesmen, under Willy Brandt of Germany, formed the famous "North–South Commission" to report on global inequality. The report noted that while the "North including Eastern Europe has a quarter of the world's population and four-fifths of its income; the South including China has three billion people – three-quarters of the world's population but living on one-fifth of the world's income" (Brandt *et al.*, 1980: 32). This fact caused extremely divergent life expectancies, standards of living, infant mortality rates, and so on between the two regions. More revealing, however, is what the report noted as "the fundamental inequality of economic strength" that propped up the differences:

> It is not just that the North is so much richer than the South. Over 90% of the world's manufacturing industry is in the North. Most patents and new technology are the property of multinational corporations of the North, which conduct a large share of world investment and world trade in raw materials and manufactures. Because of this economic power northern countries dominate the international economic system – its rules and regulations, and its international institutions of trade, money and finance. (Brandt *et al.*, 1980: 32)

The report stopped short of historicizing the disparity in economic strength, though it noted that many countries of the south are bound together by many things, including "their colonial experience" (1980: 32). This unexplained "colonial experience," however, is key to understanding the economic underdevelopment of many formerly colonized countries, especially in Africa.

In a way, it is redundant to argue that European colonization of Africa resulted in African economic underdevelopment and subsequent postcolonial dependence on the West. Colonialism, as handmaiden of capitalist imperialism, is supposed to do little else. It incorporated Africa unequally into the international capitalist economy as a source of raw materials and cheap labor to feed its industries, and as a market for processed goods. Its goal and practical effect were to pauperize the colonies as economic value is extracted and shipped out to European capitals. This is an essential part of how Europe, in Rodney's expression, "underdeveloped" Africa:

> Colonialism was not merely a system of exploitation, but one whose essential purpose was to repatriate the profits to the so-called mother country. From an African viewpoint, that amounted to consistent expatriation of surplus produced

by African labor out of African resources. It meant the development of Europe as part of the same dialectical process in which Africa was underdeveloped. (1972: 149)

We are in effect dealing with a "double jeopardy" for Africa: not only was its labor exploited but the continent was denied the benefits that would have accrued from a reinvestment of the extracted surplus value, the multiplier effect that that would have had on several sectors of its economy.

European trading companies such as the French Compagnie Française d'Afrique Occidentale (CFAO) and Société Commercial Ouest Africaine (SCOA), the British United Africa Company (UAC), and Unilever, operated as virtual monopolies transporting produce within colonies and between colonies and Europe. They discriminated in hiring and paying African workers and grossly underpaid the peasants from whom they obtained their wares. Their exploitative practices led in part to major peasant uprisings such as the Maji Maji in Tanzania and the Agbekoya in Nigeria. After detailing the unbridled exploitation of Africans by the companies, Walter Rodney concludes with laconic plainness: "In a way, the companies were simply receiving tribute from a conquered people . . ." (1972: 158).

The "trading" companies were in part responsible for the perversion of indigenous agricultural patterns as their activities steered the efforts of many farmers away from self-sufficient subsistence into cash crop farming to feed European industries. A few farmers benefitted and became rich, but many were impoverished or went bankrupt as they became totally dependent on cash crop prices set solely by the Europeans. And because the production of such crops was not in response to demands of the local economy which therefore could not absorb it, there was nothing the farmers could do but sell. To them, a thousand bags of cocoa were only as good as what the trading companies were willing to pay for them. Cocoa or palm oil, as "primary produce," had first to be transported to European factories and then return as exorbitantly-priced consumables such as chocolate, margarine, or soap. Unequal terms of trade were the norm, and the loop of exploitation of Africa seemed endless.

Carefully managing African exploitation by virtue of its monopoly of coercion, lawmaking, and taxation was the colonial state. It was not just an economic exploiter in its own right, but it was also the main economic actor. It created and managed currency, directed markets, formulated policies on labor and land use and population movements, and controled import and export trades. Its aim was the creation of optimum conditions for the exploitation of the colonies. The private enterprises and economic initiatives that were actively promoted and supported were the European trading companies, and in most times, the colonial state and the companies worked hand in hand to institutionalize conditions for the maximum exploitation of the colonies.

In the fourth decade *after* colonial rule, the foregoing structural features – systemic inequality in the global economy dominated by the West, domination of local economies by multinational companies, uncontroled capital outflow (through repatriation of profits, mindless expenditure on imports, and transfers of embezzled public funds to banks abroad), decline of indigenous agriculture and industry, overemphasis on shallow and rudimentary industries such as assembly plants in which all the parts are manufactured and imported from overseas, underdevelopment of infrastructure, and the concentration of economic power in the hands of the state, leading to corruption, overly politicized economic policies, and the underdevelopment of an accountable, business-minded business class – still constitute the source of much of postcolonial economic underdevelopment and of the harrowing mass media pictures of poverty that have come to stand for Africa in the last two and half decades.

4   Conclusion: Reading the Colonial Legacy

It would be a grave mistake to assume that colonialism is wholly and immediately responsible for every contemporary African problem. If this were so, the gargantuan efforts of a host of African scholars, politicians, and activists in exposing and attacking the tyranny and endemic corruption of the postcolonial African state, the widespread misallocation of resources, the sacrifice of quality and efficiency on the altar of nepotism and ethnic chauvinism, would have been in vain. No, African agency cannot be subtracted from the equation. To do that would be as vulgar and unproductive as subscribing to the opposite view which holds that colonialism had nothing to do with the postcolonial African crisis, that colonialism in fact ended too soon and that Africa should be recolonized to save it from itself (Johnson, 1993: 22). I have implicitly suggested a different and useful approach in the foregoing pages, which is, to consider contemporary African agency within the structure of constraints and possibilities that produces it. That structure, I argue, was determined and shaped largely by European colonization of Africa. Although that colonization is formally over, the basic inequality which subtended it – and which sponsored everything from economic exploitation to racism, destruction of indigenous African institutions, and epistemological dependency – is still firmly in place.

References

Abiola. (1981). "Negritude and Nationalism", in *The African Experience in Literature and Ideology*. London: Heinemann, 67–124.

Brandt, Willy, *et al.* (1980). *North–South: A Program for Survival*. Cambridge: MIT Press.

Césaire, A. (1972). *Discourse on Colonialism*. New York: Monthly Review Press.

Chabal, Patrick. (1994). *Power in Africa: An Essay in Political Interpretation*. New York: St. Martin's Press.

Davidson, Basil. (1992). *The Black Man's Burden: Africa and the Curse of the Nation State*. New York: Random House.

Escobar, Arturo. (1995). *Encountering Development: The Making and Unmaking of the Third World*. New Jersey: Princeton University Press.

Fanon, Frantz. (1967). *Black Skin, White Masks*, trans. C. L. Markmann. New York: Grove Press. Original work published 1952.

Gramsci, Antonio. (1987). *Selections from the Prison Notebooks*, eds. and trans. Quintin Hoare and Geoffrey N. Smith. New York: International Publishers.

Johnson, Paul. (1993). "Colonialism's Back – and Not a Moment Too Soon: Let's Face It: Some Countries are Just Not Fit to Govern Themselves," *New York Times Magazine*, April 18, pp. 22, 43–4.

Mamdani, M. (1996). *Citizen and Subject: Contemporary Africa and the Legacy of Late Colonialism*. Princeton: Princeton University Press.

Mowoe, J. I. and R. Bjornson, eds. (1986). *Africa and the West: Legacies of Empire*. New York: Greenwood Press.

Mudimbe, V. Y. (1988). *The Invention of Africa: Gnosis, Philosophy, and the Order of Knowledge*. Bloomington: Indiana University Press.

Ngugi wa Thiong'O. (1986). *Decolonising the Mind: The Politics of Language in African Literature*. London: James Currey.

Organization of African Unity. (1969). "Cultural Manifesto", in J. Ayo Langley, ed., *Ideologies of Liberation in Black Africa 1856–1970: Documents on Modern African Political Thought from Colonial Times to the Present*. London: Rex Collings, 1979.

Rabinow, Paul. (1986). "Representations Are Social Facts: Modernity and Postmodernity in Anthropology", in *Writing Culture: The Poetics and Politics of Ethnography*, eds. J. Clifford and G. E. Marcus. Berkeley: University of California Press, 234–61.

Rodney, Walter. (1972). *How Europe Underdeveloped Africa*. Washington, DC: Howard University Press.

Taiwo, Olufemi. (1993). "Colonialism and Its Aftermath: The Crisis of Knowledge Production," *Callaloo*, 16, no. 3: 891–908.

Chapter 14

The "Middle East"? Or . . . / Arabic Literature and the Postcolonial Predicament

Magda M. Al-Nowaihi

1   The "Middle East"? Or . . .

When I was initially invited to participate in this volume, the request was to submit a paper of 7,500–8,000 words on "The Middle East." This I felt I could not do, and after some negotiations with the editors, we agreed that I would focus on Arabic literature, after briefly explaining my reasons for rejecting the initial category "Middle East."

"The Middle East" stands for over a dozen countries situated in two continents (Africa and Asia), with at least four official languages (Arabic, Hebrew, Persian, and Turkish) as well as a handful of unofficial ones (Armenian and Kurdish, for example). Those countries mainly were colonized by two European powers, England and France (and Italy if we include North Africa) in a variety of arrangements and under differing conditions. Resistance to colonization also took on many different forms. If we look back to before the nineteenth century, recorded history offers us examples of indigenous groups in the area imposing their will and power over others, under the pretext of religion or even racial superiority, to forge dynasties or empires (the Abbassid dynasty and the Ottoman empire, to mention just two examples), and there were what may perhaps be termed anticolonial movements dating back to over a thousand years (the *shu'u-biyya*, for example). Attempting to cover all this in an essay of 7,500–8,000 words risks homogenizing the differences and glossing over the specific histories and multiple contextual nuances of the peoples and cultures of this geographical area both in their relations with one another as well as with the phenomenon of colonialism *per se*. Ironically, this homogenization of the "other" is itself one of the basic strategies of colonialism, as has been demonstrated repeatedly by different scholars over the last two decades. This classification, "Middle East," could easily push us into a discussion of "us" versus "them," a discussion which is of lesser value the wider and more amorphous the categories of "us" and "them" are.

Nor would this be the only way in which sticking to the category "Middle East" replicates colonial premises and tactics. In this context I would like to quote

Rey Chow critiquing the continued and persistent use of national categories as a basis for classification in literary studies:

> Of all the prominent features of Eurocentrism, the one that stands out in the context of the university is the conception of culture as based on the modern European notion of the nation-state. In this light, comparative literature has been rightly criticized for having concentrated on the literatures of a few strong nation-states in modern Europe. But the problem does not go away if we simply substitute India, China, and Japan for England, France, and Germany. To this day we still witness publications that bear titles such as "comparative approaches to masterpieces of Asian literature" which adopt precisely this Eurocentric, nation-oriented model of literature *in the name of the other* . . . The critique of Eurocentrism, if it is to be thorough and fundamental, cannot take place at the level of replacing one set of texts with another set of texts – not even if the former are European and the latter are Asian, African, or Latin American. (Chow, 1995: 109)

But why does the term "Middle East" not serve as a rallying call for an empowering unity that transcends national and linguistic boundaries? Why has it never functioned as a basis for enabling agendas of resistance? The reason lies in the origins of the concept, which is not a consequence of a grassroots awareness or indigenous movements. The very appellation is a creation of colonialism, for this region is "Middle" simply because the point of reference, in more than one way, is Europe. People who live in these countries understand themselves to be "Middle Easterners" only in relation to the West, and use the term primarily within the context of discussion of geopolitical considerations and configurations of world powers. Their own self-designated parameters of identity would not include this category. No one would say: "As a Middle Easterner, I . . .", while people do say, "as an Arab," "an Egyptian," "a Muslim," in addition to "as a woman," "a physician," "a Marxist," etc. If people of the region want to use a more encompassing designation that transcends national, linguistic, or religious classifications, they tend to use the term "peoples of the third world."[1]

The field of "Middle Eastern Studies" suffers from similar problems. Departments of Middle Eastern Studies are usually composed of scholars working on different "regions" within the area, each within one language, and these scholars are more often than not interested in and capable of talking to colleagues in other departments, such as English literature, rather than with one another. The colonial barriers which divide the different peoples in the physical "Middle East" are reenacted within the space of the western academy, and these departments amount to a number of individual scholars who have been forcibly lumped together as a matter of convenience for powers that need to look at the countries they focus on as one region. The ghettoization of these departments within the western academy parallels the disenfranchisement of the cultures they represent in the power games on the world arena, and their lack of inner cohesion and solidarity is reminiscent of the sad divisions between the different nation-states of the Middle East. The historical roots behind this state of affairs were aptly analyzed over twenty years ago by Edward Said in *Orientalism*.

But I do not want to imply that the peoples and cultures of that geographical area have nothing in common, for they do and have done for many centuries now. And of course artificial barriers should be crossed in the virtual "Middle East," and fences, to borrow Mary Louise Pratt's metaphor, ought to be jumped over within the academy. The troubled state of affairs in the Middle East lies well beyond my expertise. I might instead say a few words about the study of that area. Like many third-world peoples, we in the Middle East, and in the field of Middle Eastern Studies, have mostly lost the ability to talk to one another in any language other than English (and occasionally French), and in reference to any terms outside those set by western discourses. It is rare indeed that we encounter one another and experience each other's cultural productions without the mediation of the West. I know no Hebrew, Turkish, or Armenian, but my English, French, and even German are quite good, and the only reason I learned some Persian, to be quite honest, is because it was required by my department at that august American academic institution, Harvard University, where I conducted my graduate studies. In that I am quite representative of the field, I think. But the fact that I am forced to rely on English translations to experience a Turkish novel troubles me, not because I hold on to the belief that only cultural insiders who read the material in the original language are authorized to represent it. Rather, my anxiety stems from my knowledge, through my own first-hand experience in dealing with translations from Arabic, that the works that make it into English, and the English forms they take, offer more insights into the politics of reception in the host culture than the cultural dynamics of the target one. At best, what makes it into English replicates an elitist and hegemonic canon in the original culture, at worst it creates an alternative English canon that privileges works easily consumed by western audiences because they reinforce preexisting stereotypes and misconceptions.[2]

While many of our limitations as scholars in Middle Eastern Studies are results of the very processes of colonialism which we are now attempting to struggle against, we have not been entirely blameless, and have participated in the mechanisms that keep us apart, or at least we have not been as committed to fighting them as we ought to be. Our department of Middle Eastern and Asian Studies at Columbia University is attempting to initiate and sustain conversations through team-teaching, devising courses that are not limited to one national context, and perhaps most importantly, encouraging our students to do comparative literature *within* our own department and between our cultures rather than with the more customary English or French. Only last year we voted, not without internal opposition I should add, that the two research languages required of doctoral candidates do not have to be French and German, which is the case in almost all departments of the Middle East in this country, but can include Arabic,

Hebrew, Persian, etc. We are hopeful that this new group of scholars will be able to transcend artificial barriers and forge empowering alliances. Meanwhile, while understanding that "Arabic Literature" as a category of analysis does not eliminate all the difficulties I have with the alternative one of the "Middle East," at least it is one within which I feel more comfortable with my abilities to overcome externally imposed, and internalized, limitations.

2   Arabic Literature and the Postcolonial Predicament

In Nabil Naoum Gorgy's surrealistic short story "The Slave's Dream", a young man is captured and enslaved by a group of lepers who force him to witness their horrifying acts of rape, torture, and murder – yet there are moments when he can escape these horrors through dreaming. As his slavery continues, however, his dreams of escape and freedom make way for fantasies in which he participates in the lepers' sadistic activities, and as the story concludes, we are told that "night after night I dream of the coming of the new slave" (1993: 63–8).

Writing an essay on Arabic literature for a volume on "postcolonial studies," I am well aware of the dangers of participating in what Aijaz Ahmad has described thus: "efforts are now underway also to designate the contemporary literatures of Asia and Africa as 'postcolonial' and thus to make them available for being read according to the protocols that metropolitan criticism has developed for reading what it calls 'minority literatures'" (1996: 282). There is no doubt that the organizing principal and terms of reference for this essay will privilege concepts, issues, and strategies closely affiliated with the field of "postcolonial studies," and will exclude other equally valid prisms through which to look at Arabic literature. But I am also convinced that in spite of the well-warranted criticisms, this field has touched on and brought about discussions of some of the most serious and persistent preoccupations of Arab authors and intellectuals who predate and/or know nothing about "postcolonial studies," and therefore cannot be said to be mindlessly mimicking it in their own work. Arab literary works have continued to exhibit and illustrate a sophisticated awareness of the structures of power and manipulation between nations, as well as between different segments of society whose competing interests result in different allegiances to such notions as modernity, democracy, nationalism, etc.[3]

Arabic literature has a long, rich, and varied history that includes both prose and poetry and encompasses a variety of genres, with records dating back to the sixth century AD. Yet most literary histories consider the period from roughly the sixteenth through the eighteenth centuries to be one of cultural and literary decadence, and connect the renaissance (*nahda*) in the nineteenth century to Napoleon Bonaparte's invasion of Egypt in 1798. The story goes that although this French campaign lasted only three years, it shocked the Egyptians so, showing them the amazing technological and military advantage the Europeans had over them, and stimulating the impulse towards modernization initiated by Muhammad Ali, who ruled Egypt 1805–48. Ali sent missions of students to Europe, especially France, and commissioned the translation of various French texts to Arabic, whose spread was facilitated by the Arabic printing press that was set up in Bulaq in 1822. This process of education and translation quickly widened its scope to include literary, historical, philosophical texts, etc. But because Arabic culture has an established written history, as compared to some other colonized societies with primarily oral cultural histories, soon reprinted works from the *turath* (heritage) circulated widely and took their place next to the translated works to push forth the *nahda* or renaissance.[4] It is between these two general impulses that modern Arabic literature is said to have developed, and at least in its early stages, the *nahda* had an important component of looking backwards to the past as well as looking westwards to Europe.[5] Much of the early works were deemed "neoclassical," with the "neo" somehow being seen as the outcome of the European influence, and the "classical" of the Arab one. In fact, histories of Arabic literature have been quite obsessed with the issue of origins, with one camp, for example, arguing that the novel emerged from indigenous narrative forms, while another insists that it is absolutely and undoubtedly a borrowed European form – arguments that unfortunately seem to go on forever and lead nowhere.

More recently, a number of younger scholars have suggested that this account of the birth of modern Arabic literature shows a historiographical bias in privileging the violent confrontation between east and west as the moment of inception; that the sixteenth to the eighteenth centuries were decadent only if we have a rather narrow and limited definition of what "good culture" is, and that the *nahda* actually had begun earlier than is generally acknowledged, due to internal as well as external reasons. And yet Bonaparte's invasion of Egypt was an important moment in the development of modern Arabic literature, to say the least, when Europe became an integral part of the worldview of the Arabs; a central component of the landscape that was impossible to shut out. From then on, the Arab world could not just let Europe be because Europe, and later the United States, did not let the Arab world be: militarily, economically, or culturally.[6]

The earliest groups of fiction writers around the turn of the twentieth century were mostly, though not exclusively, middle or upper class and western educated, and their story is not an uncommon one. Through their education and training, they developed a taste for European music, art, and literature, and their class affiliations made a certain liberal humanism attractive to them, at the same time creating a painful ambivalence in their relationship to the "masses" who came to represent indigenous culture. On the one hand, ideals of equality and social justice under the model of the nation state were central to the evolving hopes for the future and necessitated including these "masses" into the emerging body politic. But at the same time these elite intellectuals also bought into the perception of these "masses" as ignorant, dirty, backward, undemocratic, unfair to women – in short: uncivilized, and requiring their intervention as intermediaries in the civilizing mission.

But the admiration for European civilization was tempered, if not sometimes actually reversed, by the way actual Europeans behaved in the Arab countries, with arrogance and ruthlessness that were in such stark opposition, or so it seemed, with the ideals of liberal humanism which symbolized European culture.[7] This "superior," infuriatingly aggressive and oppressive west, with its master narratives of nationalism, democracy, individualism, and modernity, its schools of thought and intellectual giants, and its material power over the Arab world, in the various guises that this material power takes, is at least one of the crucial parameters within which, and *against* which, a sense of identity: individual, collective, and national, is negotiated. I would like to trace some of the most significant moments in this negotiation process as represented in, and through, narrative texts, starting with the deep resentment against colonial powers, made even more painful by the enthrallment with European modernity in the earlier part of the century, on to the emerging subaltern voices talking back around the middle of the century, and concluding with the most recent narratives exposing globalism, cultural hybridity, and the new world order as the new masks of empire that are more difficult to resist precisely because they are "postcolonial." Within this schema I will discuss how different Arab writers have dealt with such issues as sexual morality, gendered oppressions, class conflicts, the tensions between individuality and collectivism, and nationalism. On the surface, my organization may look like a neat history of linear development, so I want to emphasize that there have always been multiple intellectual and political crosscurrents at any given historical moment, sometimes even within the works of one and the same writer.

Arabic narratives are generally considered to have reached their full artistic maturity in the twenties of this century in Egypt, by a group of writers who, though not all of Egyptian origin by any means, were actively involved in launching an "authentic national Egyptian Literature" (*adab Misri qawmi*) as a necessary part of envisioning the Egyptian nation.[8] One such important group of writers was *Jama'at al-Madrasa al-Haditha* (the New School), whose nucleus was formed in 1917, and who published the weekly journal *Al-Fajr* (Dawn) starting in 1925. The group was interested in establishing a national narrative literature which did not simply contain Egyptian local color or address the concerns of their readers, but also applied Max Weber's notion of "ideal types" to "real Egyptians" (Hafez, 1993: 217). The short stories of Mahmud Tahir Lashin, one of the most important members of the group, are an excellent illustration of the ambivalent feelings towards the West and "real Egyptians" that were typical of intellectual life at the time.[9] The European characters who appear in his stories seem to bring doom and destruction in their wake, and an important theme is the growing power of the British in Egypt. Whether it is a soldier in the army of 'Urabi, who fought and was defeated by the British in the battle of Tal al-Kabir, after which the British occupied Egypt in 1882, or a brilliant university student who participated in the 1919 revolution, or even a lawyer who marries a French woman, Egyptians who cross paths with Europeans suffer rather unhappy fates. Sabry Hafez is absolutely right that "it is not mere coincidence that Lashin chose a soldier to portray the deep suffering and humiliation of Egypt's defeat by the occupying British forces and a clever student to portray the far-reaching effect of the crushing of the country's hopes for independence [from the British]" (Hafez, 1993: 21).[10]

But the resistance against British military, political, and economic presence in Egypt should not lead us to underestimate the degree to which European ideas on secularism, rationality, and democracy were infiltrating Lashin's and his colleagues' minds. A brief analysis of Lashin's arguably most successful short story, and the only one that takes place outside the city, is a good illustration. In "Village Small Talk," the narrator accompanies a friend, a son of the aristocratic landowning classes presumably, for a day's visit to "his village," nameless to symbolize rural Egypt in its entirety (Lashin, 1929: 262–8).[11] While impressed with the natural beauty of the countryside, he is horrified by the peasants, who are described by him in terms that hardly distinguish them from the animals they live with. His friend, on the other hand, believes this lifestyle to be quite suitable for these peasants whose "primitive exteriors" hide "the treachery of wolves and the cunning of foxes." A meeting with the peasants quickly disintegrates into strained silence, during which the narrator and his friend actually exchange a few words in English. Finally, the peasants invite the village sheik, or religious leader, to converse with the two gentlemen. His speech is replete with lies and superstitions according to the narrator, who tries to counter what he sees as the sheik's negative influence by lecturing the peasants on free will and how they could better their lives. They respond by "staring open-mouthed in dumb amazement," then abruptly change the subject and ask the sheik to retell the story of a certain 'Abd el Sami', a peasant who was lured to the city with promises of a better life by a city dweller whose real purpose, it transpires, is to carry out an affair with the pretty wife of 'Abd el Sami'. Upon discovering the affair, 'Abd el Sami' kills both of them and ends up in prison. The message is not a subtle one, and the narrator dejectedly realizes that he has not and cannot reach the peasants.

What is lacking, however, is any awareness of how the narrator, on his part, has "othered" these peasants, and transformed them into alien entities, to the extent that he asks with astonishing naiveté what they could possibly talk to their wives about, and whether they ever noticed how impoverished their lives were. His attempt to sell them an Egyptian version of the American dream – a better life achieved through belief in free will and ambition, quite deserves their "open-mouthed amazement." But this othering of the peasants does not stop with the narrator and his friend, for the author draws the two gentlemen from the city as distinct personalities with different attitudes and views, whereas the peasants remain a mass of undifferentiated bodies, a bunch of subalterns who, if they can speak at all, do so in chorus fashion, incapable of thinking for themselves and merely echoing the sheik's views. The sheik's depiction is negatively one-sided, the story concluding with him going to meet with the mayor and notables, implying his collaboration with a corrupt political system, but there is no similar attempt to explore the narrator's own complicity in these structures of power. The peasants are "happy to follow their teacher into the darkness," and again there is no attempt to delve into the complexities of their relationship with the sheik. Rather, the ending indicates their unchanging, undemocratic nature, so that we may ask to what extent the narrator, and Lashin, are different from the friend who believes that these peasants are actually quite satisfied with and deserving of their poverty and oppression. The figure of the woman is interesting as well, for 'Abd el Sami's wife is not sacrificed at the altar of honor by her husband and the peasants alone, but also, in an arrangement where discourse mirrors reality, by the narrator and the author. The tragic hero, for the characters within the story as well as the readers of the story, is not the murdered wife, who is nothing more than a shadowy background figure, but rather either the unfortunate duped husband or the anguished narrator.[12] For Lashin and his westernized, fairly affluent middle- and upper-class colleagues, resisting the British and being well aware of their exploitativeness and cruelty did not preclude believing that reason, secularism, and democracy must do battle with the religious and traditional powers of darkness in order to move ahead on the path to progress and develop a strong, civilized nation, and for this lofty cause poor ignorant peasants had to be educated in the virtues of modernity.

"The masses" do talk back in subsequent narratives, written from the forties to the sixties by writers with different class and political affiliations, and a strong sympathy to Marxist and socialist ideologies. The interest in socialism was concurrent with the beginnings of success in the struggles for independence from colonial powers, and the emerging empowering concepts of pan-Arabism and pan-Africanism, strongly advocated by the immensely popular Egyptian president Gamal 'Abd al-Nasser (1952–70). Writers like Naguib Mahfouz, Yusuf Idris, and 'Abd al-Hakim Qasim came from more modest backgrounds than the older generation of writers generally did, and were capable of more nuanced depictions of the lives and characters of the lower and lower-middle classes. Representations of "the masses" now balanced depictions of poverty, ignorance, etc., with strong expositions of the forces, both internal and external, that contribute to these conditions. While the harsh realities of lower-class life were not glossed over, there was also an understanding of some of the more joyful aspects of that life, and, in some cases, of the capacity of the underprivileged to resist and bring about change.[13] And although alleviating the suffering of the masses was still seen very much as best realized within the rubric of a strong modern nation, and the solidarity of that nation with other "third world" nations undergoing similar struggles, ambivalence towards a number of values linked to a western-style modernity began to creep into the narratives. 'Abd al-Hakim Qasim's *The Seven Days of Man* (1969) is one such novel in which the complex tensions between tradition and modernity are richly explored. In seven chapters, the novel skillfully links seven stages in a village's pilgrimage to a saint's annual festival in a nearby city to the changing worldview of the protagonist, 'Abd al-'Aziz, as he moves from childhood to late adolescence and is exposed to city life. 'Abd al-'Aziz's increasing alienation from the village is never free from a deep sense of loss, for if religious faith, for example, makes the villagers seem like an unquestioning herd, he also understands that it creates a sense of communal solidarity, of warmth and loyalty that he sorely misses as he moves towards autonomy and independence. Moreover, his initial infatuation with the city gives way to an understanding of the manipulative and coercive relation it has with the village. As he painfully witnesses the derisive tone of the small businessmen as they cheat the villagers, or the outright cruelty of the policemen as they control them, and the humiliated acquiescence of the villagers who cannot answer back, he understands that their dumb silence is a condition of their sense of displacement in the hostile city, for within the village and with each other they can certainly speak intelligently, argue passionately, laugh robustly, and sing movingly. 'Abd al-'Aziz's irresolvable inbetweenness allows us to hear the subalterns' voices as well as witness their silencing, and to admire the very qualities which we recognize as causes for their exploitation by the forces of modernity. Mahmud Diyab's *A City's Sorrows: A Child in the Arab Quarter* (1971) links the growing sense of alienation and loss of the protagonist/narrator, who here belongs to the urban lower middle class, with western intervention in Egyptian affairs. The events take place in the thirties and forties, on one street in the coastal city of Ismailiyyah in which eight families form a closely-knit community, making decisions collectively, and celebrating happy and sad occasions as a group. As a result, the children grow up in a caring, protective atmosphere that also offers rich and varied interpersonal relationships and experiences. As the protagonist moves towards adolescence, his difficult individuation is made more painful because it parallels the displacement of that warm communal life with a new lifestyle that is more affluent, but that is characterized by materialism, rampant consumerism, and personal greed. This new lifestyle is linked to the general changes brought about by the European powers involved in the Second World War, who used Egypt as one of the playing fields for their conflicts and created havoc in the country's economy and social fabric.[14]

If for the generation of Lashin a favored motif was that of the individual, often an elite modern intellectual, facing the uncomprehending, intractable masses, and for Qasim and Diyab's generation it was that of a young man torn between the desire to melt into the collective on the one hand and to live out the modern paradigm of individual autonomy on the other, some of the works of the exiled Saudi writer 'Abd al-Rahman Munif[15] offer a different model. Here the conflict is no longer between the individual and the group, but rather between competing interests and forces in which individuals are mere playthings. Many of Munif's works take place in unnamed gulf countries closely resembling Saudi Arabia. In *Endings* (1978), he focuses on the imaginary village of al-Tiba during one of its draught seasons. Technology does not come to al-Tiba in the form of the water dam which the villagers had been pleading with city officials to build for years, but in the shape of sophisticated machine guns and Jeeps which city dwellers, in search of adventure and attempting to recapture some notion they have of the past, use for hunting the animals and birds which the villagers survive on. The resulting deaths of these creatures are very different from those caused by the traditional way of hunting, when man was forced to come close to his prey, and thus achieve an understanding and respect for the various creatures surrounding him, and learn to distinguish, for example, between a male and a pregnant or nursing female. Death through the old hunting style was an integral part of a natural cycle of regeneration, whereas the new type of hunting only brings abrupt, meaningless endings. As Munif mourns a dying world, he does so in a narrative style reminiscent of that world. Instead of a biography of various characters we have detailed descriptions of the geography and weather patterns of the village. There is no exploration of inner thoughts and feelings in the psychoanalytic language of modern narrative, but rather an external witnessing of people's actions and the various interpretations the community gives to these actions. The relationship between a man and his dog, or between a litter of puppies and a flock of birds, is given considerably more narrative space than the typical romance storyline. Animal stories written by the medieval author al-Jahiz are blended in with stories issuing from the collective memory of the village, told and retold by unnamed narrators at funerals and similar occasions to bring the community together and help them determine future plans and strategies, which are thus made inseparable from their past and their specific conditions. Munif's rejection of an exploitative form of modernity thus extends from the content to the form of his narration, which is innovative precisely because it is traditional.[16] Munif continues his campaign in his five-volume masterpiece *Cities of Salt* (1984–9), which traces the destructive effects of the discovery of oil in a poor oasis community in a desert kingdom during the thirties, and the descent upon the area of large numbers of American oil company employees who, in collaboration with short-sighted, uncaring, and corrupt authorities, do not hesitate to trample on the people and culture in their pursuit of profit.

When the European powers officially "left" the region, one of their other major legacies was the creation of the state of Israel in 1948, resulting in the forced dispersal and living under occupation of millions of Palestinians.[17] Palestinian literature has not been arrested in a reactive mode because it has not moved to a "postcolonial" state and still lives within the parameters of colonialism.[18] It presents us with a rich and varied body of narratives that struggle with courageous honesty with various facets of the relationship between individual and national identity, including the ethics of resistance, the bitter travails, and sometimes unexpected pleasures, of a diasporic existence, and the multiple costs of living under occupation. Much of this corpus of works goes well beyond easy finger pointing, and looks deep into the regional and global forces that have resulted in this disaster. Ghassan Kanafani's masterpiece *Men in the Sun* (1963), for example, depicts the attempts of three Palestinian refugees to cross the borders into Kuwait to fulfill their dreams of a better life, focusing on the complicity of Arab bureaucracy in their tragedy.[19] Imil Habibi's darkly humorous *The Pessoptimist* (1974) traces the failed attempts of its protagonist, Said, to be accepted or even spared the constant humiliations of being an Arab citizen of the state of Israel. Although the Israeli state comes out as no angel, Said himself is also a target of the biting humor, and his fumbling endeavors to show the Israelis what a good loyal citizen of the state he is lead him from one disaster to the next. Sahar Khalifah's *Wild Thorns* concentrates on Palestinians in the occupied territories, whose competing personal and national obligations are played out in their struggles with the decision of whether or not to work within the state of Israel. These jobs are usually building houses for new Jewish immigrants, often enough on the rubble of torn down Palestinian homes, while at the same time the Israeli authorities are demolishing the construction workers' own homes on the West Bank for any suspected "illegal activities." Khalifah (1976) does not hesitate to reveal the differences within the Palestinian community along generational and class lines. For example, while there is no doubt that the dismal employment situation in the occupied territories is primarily due to the enforcement of unjust Israeli economic policies, she also shows the weak ties some of the hired help or temporary workers have to the land as a result of their disenfranchisement well before the Israeli occupation. Khalifah brings in an important gendered dimension to issues of resistance and national affiliation in her later *Saha Gate* (1990), in which women from different backgrounds passionately debate whether the cost of constantly doing battle against the Israelis is worth it, particularly in view of the fact that their own concerns as women have often been given short shrift in the liberation agenda.[20]

Gender as a prism through which to analyze the problematics of nationhood and nationalist feelings is not of course limited to the Palestinians. Some of the most powerful novels critiquing the Lebanese civil war that culminated with the Israeli invasion of Lebanon in 1982, for example, have been by women. Hanan Al-Shaykh's *The Story of Zahra* (1986) attempts to understand the attraction of war through telling the story of a lower middle-class, not very attractive, not particularly well-educated or self-aware, and in fact somewhat mad woman. The men who desire Zahra, her own love affair with a sniper, and the see-sawing political affiliations of her brother allow for a masterful excavation of the normalizing effects of war on frustrated individuals who were already misfits in a society that did not successfully include any but its most powerful members in the body politic. Hoda Barakat's *The Stone of Laughter* (1990) takes a gay male as its protagonist: Khalil's "femininity" results in his exclusion from society, and he himself tries to keep his life separate from the madness of the war. Eventually, however, the temptations of the war, indeed the basic need to survive it, lead him to surrender and assume a more acceptable "masculine" identity. As Fadia Faqir notes in her introduction to the translation (Barakat, 1990: vi–vii): "One of the main characters of this novel is the beleaguered city of Beirut . . . all parties of different persuasions are mocked and ridiculed. From the sidelines,

Barakat blasts her city with words, trying to 'betray' it in order to reconstruct it." Ahlam Mosteghanemi's *The Body's Memory* (1993), remarkably the first Algerian novel written by a woman in Arabic,[21] uses a failed love affair between a painter and a novelist to dissect the artistic and intellectual Algerian community living in France. Disillusioned by the failure of their revolutionary aspirations to materialize after independence from France; disappointed by their former comrades in the resistance movement who have now turned into self-satisfied businessmen with no national vision or collective dreams; and equally dissatisfied with life in France, these exiles wallow in guilt and despair that make their alienation impotent rather than oppositional.

Even Egypt, arguably the Arab country with the oldest and most solid sense of nationhood, has witnessed a recent onslaught of critiques of the state. Comparing two novels by Latifa al-Zayyat illustrates some of the changes in attitudes towards different agendas of liberation and the possibilities of linking them together. In al-Zayyat's first novel *Open Door* (1960), whose events take place in the forties, the protagonist Layla is oppressed as a young person in a society where authority is mostly in the hands of the elders; as a woman in a bourgeois family whose values tie a woman's worth to superficial qualities of attractiveness; and as an Egyptian in an Egypt ruled by the iron fist of England. After a number of misguided attempts at rebellion, Layla recognizes that her self-realization and liberation as a woman and an Egyptian are one and the same and she enters into an equal relationship with a young man who, like her, is fighting the British and the Egyptian monarchy. As the novel concludes, we realize with Layla that although the road ahead is not easy, the door, at least, is open. Compare that to the claustrophobic atmosphere that pervades *The Owner of the House* (1994), in which Samia is running away from the Egyptian political police with her husband and their comrade Rafiq, and hides in a house which is gradually transformed in her mind from a safe haven to a prison, and its owner from a guardian angel to a jailer. Samia comes to realize the degree to which she is infantalized by the men and consistently excluded from full membership in their brotherhood. She finally understands that the liberation agenda will not include her unless she is willing to assert herself, through violent confrontation with the owner of the house if need be. This is a remarkable novel considering the fact that al-Zayyat, up until the end of her life, rejected the application of the term "feminist" to herself, and insisted that the only category or general label she would be willing to accept would be that of communist. (See, for example, al-Zayyat, 1994a.) It is clear, though, that the al-Zayyat of the eighties and nineties recognizes that it is not enough for the British to leave Egypt, or even for the communists to come to power, for a state of harmony and social justice to prevail and equally include all citizens, and that multiple oppressions related to class, gender, sexual orientation etc. need to be fought simultaneously on different, even competing, fronts. Also, it is not unreasonable to see shades of president Gamal 'Abd al-Nasser in the figure of the owner of the house, or rather perhaps in the dependent relationship that develops between a powerful and charismatic figure like 'Abd al-Nasser and a people desperate for a leader to protect and empower them, with their hero-worship ultimately stifling their own inner strength and independence.

In her autobiography *The Search* (1992), al-Zayyat explicitly voices some of her ambivalent feelings towards 'Abd al-Nasser – an ambivalence shared by many other intellectuals throughout the Arab world.[22] The Nasserist era, at least in its earlier phases, marked an end to foreign domination and outmoded corrupt monarchies, a strong sense of solidarity with other struggling countries finding expression in the movements of pan-Arabism, pan-Africanism, and treaties with non-aligned countries, and the spread of socialist ideals and laws guaranteeing, among other rights, a free education and affordable healthcare to all. On the other hand, 'Abd al-Nasser soon showed very low tolerance for internal dissent, whether from the right (the Muslim brotherhood) or the left (the communist party), and exercised repressive measures against writers and thinkers which included state censorship, and sometimes imprisonment and torture. The low point of his presidency and leadership was the defeat of the Arab forces by Israel in six days in 1967, which was a shocking and humiliating end to an era of dreams and hopes. But in spite of the disappointments of the Nasserist era, which at least represented a genuine if failed attempt at liberation and social justice,[23] it often appears as a shining period compared to the following Sadatist period (1970–81). President Sadat knew how the winds of the new world order were blowing, and decided to be swayed by them rather than take any oppositional stance. His Camp David agreement with Israel, brokered by the United States in 1978, effectively put an end to the dream of a united Arab nation, at least for a while, and signaled his abandonment of the Palestinian cause and the ideals of "third world" solidarity.[24] His "Open Door" policy privatized large sections of the economy and changed laws to encourage foreign investment in Egypt, at the same time cutting down on welfare-like programs and promoting the philosophy that those who were unsuccessful had brought this fate upon themselves through their laziness, lack of motivation, and conversely, envy. In response, the eighties and nineties have presented us with a rich assortment of innovative narratives mourning the failed dreams of freedom and independence and critiquing the new Arab world that has emerged within the neocolonial world order.

Baha Taher's *Love in Exile* (1995) bitterly indicts the new yet strikingly familiar forms of injustice while showing how no one parameter is sufficient for explaining these emerging structures that somehow succeed in continuing the older patterns of manipulation and exploitation. The protagonist is a middle-aged Nasserist journalist banished by his Cairene newspaper to an unnamed European city where he ostensibly serves as foreign correspondent. He comes into close contact with a group of journalists, healthcare professionals, and lawyers of different nationalities and ethnic backgrounds trying to publicize and fight against human rights abuses in different parts of the world. He is not alone in failing to get stories that matter printed by his paper, so that, with the exception of a few leftist newspapers with minuscule circulations, horrifying facts about torture in Chili, for example, are not disclosed to the public. New forms of censorship, determined primarily by material factors, are in place, and are no less intractable because they are executed with a smile rather than a whip. The glimmer of hope offered by the promises of a wealthy Arab prince to establish a new progressive Arabic newspaper in Europe collapses when it transpires that the "progressive prince" is a close ally of a wealthy Jewish businessman involved in gentrifying poor neighborhoods and supplying the Israeli army with plentiful aid. Nor is this the only unholy alliance that crosses national lines, for the brutal massacres of poor Palestinians in the refugee camps of Sabra and Shatila which are a central event in the novel are seen to be a result of the collaboration of Israelis with Lebanese militia forces, and made possible by the silence and implicit acceptance of most Arab regimes. And while the lone figures who fight the brutality are of various nationalities (two of the most powerful testimonies about the massacres are by a Norwegian nurse and an American Jewish journalist who exist in real life, as Taher tells us at the end of the novel), their efforts are relentlessly crushed on every level. Thus while it is true that there are many individuals who can transcend racial, religious, or national boundaries, it is also clear that structural racism is as pervasive as ever, and the narrator is convinced that left-wing and right-wing parties are ultimately indistinguishable when it comes to the treatment of poor non-European countries. But while structures of oppression, whose victims are most often nonwhites and the poor, persist and gain in strength, agendas of resistance, whether class or nationalist based, have failed dismally. The narrator, in one of the many heated arguments he has with his communist friend Ibrahim, screams in anguish: "If you ask me where are the Arabs I will ask you where are the workers of the world who have united." Finally, even private love, grasped at by those in exile as one of the last possible refuges, also collapses under pressures from the outside world. For example, the love between a European woman and her African husband cannot survive the pervading racist hostility, culminating in a rape attempt against her by a group of white youths who cause her to miscarry her baby, while her husband is being held down, taunted, and humiliated with racial epithets.[25] Taher's bleak vision does not underrate the power of personal salvation, but will not allow us the comforting myths of individual escape so long as structures of oppression continue to flourish.

The bleak visions of quite a few novels of the period are couched in a bitterly irreverent humor that has the capacity to shock readers out of their apathy and self-pity; to produce an angry laughter that is hopefully more productive than despair; to disorient in order to reorient. Salwa Bakr's *The Golden Chariot Does Not Ascend to Heaven* (1991), which takes place in a women's prison where all the inmates are slightly mad, juxtaposes thematic and stylistic spaces to create a disorienting humor that leaves no myth intact: whether it is love, marriage and family life, state apparatuses like the judiciary, the army, and the police, the languages of the media, political ideologies of all colors, and the novelistic medium itself. The result is a fiercely original narrative which creates a pathos that is both hysterically funny and devastatingly tragic, and which overcomes many of the limitations of the middle-class novel when it seeks to represent the underprivileged. Salwa Bakr's mad criminal women neither speak for themselves in the self-aware language of modern narrative, nor are they spoken for by the narrator, who seems just as befuddled as they. The meaning of the novel emerges from the irreconcilable gaps between their realities and their dreams, between their lives and the various discourses that attempt to represent them, and between their madness and what society has decreed as sanity.[26]

The last two works of Son'allah Ibrahim have concentrated on the fate of Egypt as one of those poor non-European countries whose citizens have fallen under the spell of globalization and cultural hybridity. The front cover of *Dhat* (1992) is at once an instance and indictment of "cultural hybridity." A woman with the Islamic headdress and a face empty of features except for lips painted with a glaring red lipstick is standing in front of, or just under, a construction which is a kitchen shelf that resembles a crown (or heavy weight) on her head, covered with foreign consumer goods such as 7UP, Tang, and Nescafe. The novel alternates chapters on the life of its female protagonist Dhat (meaning self or identity), with actual clippings from newspapers and magazines, and soon a link is established between the life and character of Dhat and the material conditions which make it impossible for her to be anything other than what she has become. Dhat's story, also told with a great deal of humor, is an all-too-typical one of a middle-class young woman who gets married in the sixties, and whose aspirations become progressively limited to the acquisition of more consumer goods than all her neighbors – the more foreign and unnecessary the goods the better – this at the same time that the most basic needs of the majority of the population: for education, healthcare, housing etc., are unsatisfied. The chapters with the newspaper clippings direct the responsibility clearly towards the deals transacted between Egyptian politicians, government officials, and public religious figures on the one hand, and western and multinational corporations as well as political figures on the other – all of whose appetites for ever-increasing profits make any notion of integrity or ethics quite quaint. We learn from the clippings, for example, that while the King of Saudi Arabia has declared himself "the servant of the two holiest places [of Islam]," the amount of money deposited in European and American banks by oil-rich Gulf countries is enough, according to United Nations figures, to create job opportunities for millions of individuals in the industrialized world, at the same time that unemployment reaches unprecedented levels in the Muslim Arab countries. We find out that the well-known officially-sanctioned Muslim sheik who guides Dhat and many like her towards a "virtuous life" has announced that women should cover themselves up, that listening to Beethoven at bedtime is a sin, and also that good Muslims should not covet or envy the rich their wealth. Meanwhile, the sheik has accepted a gift of a fabulous mansion from some of these very same rich, who have acquired their money from making deals with foreign companies, pushing forth laws that give these companies amazing tax breaks, effectively killing off their local competition. The imported products are not just foot massage machines and the latest shades of lipstick, but also expired foods and medicines, and pesticides that cannot be used in the producing countries because of their proven links to cancer. What is extremely impressive is the amount of research that Ibrahim has put into *Dhat*, and his courage in naming names and meticulously building up his cases so that they cannot be dismissed as the rantings of an angry ideologue.[27]

If Dhat has a momentary tweak of consciousness every now and then (after all, she did grow up during the idealistic Nasserist era), in *Sharaf* (1997) we are confronted with a protagonist who is totally vacuous and unaware, whose only concerns are to wear Calvin Klein jeans, Ray Ban sunglasses, a Polo shirt, etc. Young Sharaf, whose name means honor, grew up in the Sadatist "postcolonial" era, when imperialism, colonialism, etc. were thought of as things of the past, over and done with, and as a result Sharaf seems like a trapped animal – fearful and wanting but uncomprehending of the real dangers surrounding him. Sharaf's sexuality becomes a metaphor for his exploitation. A European tourist attempts to seduce him with some imported goods, but Sharaf holds on to his "honor," which he equates with not allowing another man to penetrate his bodily orifices, and he therefore kills the attempted rapist and ends up in jail. Prison is a microcosm of the outside world, and the privatization efforts sweeping the country extend to it, so that the richest prisoners end up with quite a comfortable incarceration experience, while those less fortunate, like Sharaf, clean their toilets, wash their clothes, etc. By the end of the novel, Sharaf has already hidden illicit drugs up his anus, and is shaving his bodily hair in preparation for becoming the lover-boy of one of those powerful and wealthy prisoners, in a relationship very unlike an earlier one of mutual affection, respect, and budding passion which had begun to develop between him and another equally powerless inmate, and which came to an abrupt end when the other inmate was moved to another prison. In acquiescing to hiding the drugs and shaving his legs, Sharaf has finally understood the degree to which he has already been penetrated.

Intellectuals like Ibrahim may have come a long way from Lashin and his contemporaries, both in their more nuanced understanding of the versions of modernity and "progress" made available to the third world by the West, and in their respectfully critical rather than nobly condescending representation of the masses. And yet young men like Sharaf, decked in the latest European and American fashions and dancing to rap music, are no less disenfranchised than the "dirty, ignorant" peasants who populated Lashin's village, and may be even more so. While those who experienced European colonialism were, for the most part, well aware of what they were dealing with, Sharaf, the product of a "postcolonial" era, is a mimic whose mimickry is neither a real understanding of western culture nor a form of resistance against western hegemony, but rather a half-conscious attempt to belong to a "civilized" world which promotes and feeds on this misguided desire for its own profit. Compared to his naiveté, Lashin's peasants, with their wily suspiciousness of city dwellers, speakers of English, and those who promise them better lives if only they believed in free will and were ambitious, seem extremely sophisticated. Unfortunately, Sharaf's only act of awareness may precisely be his final decision that the only way left for him to hold on to a shred of dignity and honor is to learn to be the compliant slave and bide his time, until a new slave is ushered in.

Notes

1 In a discussion of this issue I had with the Israeli literary critic Hannan Hever, he pointed out that the term "Middle Eastern" is sometimes used by Israelis in much the same way that, according to his analysis, the term Mediterranean is used, as part of "the Zionist narrative and the mode in which this narrative makes use of the Mediterranean as a tool to strengthen and fortify the national narrative." "Such a reading will expose the Zionist national appropriation of the Mediterranean as an apparatus of repression and erasure of the violence with which territorial representations are saturated, as they always include traces of the conflict that occurred in space, traces of the violence accompanying occupation, as the people living in this territory disrupt the smooth progression of the narrative of integration in space." Hever also points out that whereas the term "Middle East" erases the territorial violence of occupation, the term Mediterranean "erases the Palestinian and the Mizrahi, the Arab Jew [Jews from Arab countries] as others, and the Mediterranean becomes the new otherness: not so much Morocco and Tunis, but the shores which are perceived as non-Arabic – Italy, France, Greece, and Spain. They now appear as the culture to relate to as a mirroring one, as the one to adopt as its origin and proximity." Hannan Hever, "Zionist Albatross: Symbolism and Nationalism in Modern Hebrew Poetry" (unpublished paper).

2 Excellent work is being done on this issue for the field of Arabic by a number of younger scholars, including Amal Amiereh, Nancy Coffin, Jenine Dallal, and Therese Saliba.

3 Due to the limitations in space, this essay is extremely selective, and while I have made an effort to choose material that gives an honest picture of the field, it is of necessity a limited one. I have excluded works not originally written in Arabic despite their importance, as these involve a somewhat different constellation of issues. I have also decided to focus on narratives in order to give the discussion some cohesion. An extremely important and rather complicated topic which I did not feel I could adequately cover in this limited format is the relationship of literary theory, criticism, and history of the Arab world to western literary studies. I would just like to briefly mention that the term "postcoloniality" has only recently made its appearance in literary journals in the Arab world. The literary journal *Fusul* is currently preparing an issue on the subject, and a recent issue of the magazine *Al-Qahira* (Cairo, Nov. 97) had a "file" devoted to *ma-ba'd al-kuluniyaliyya* (the "coloniality" part of the term is not translated). This file is composed of either translated material, or analysis of non-Arab works, with Edward Said the only Arab writer discussed. What is encouraging, though, is that some of the authors whose work is analyzed are not westerners, breaking the general pattern of talking back to a West

that rarely listens, and hopefully starting a true dialogue with other "third world" intellectuals.

4 European culture is of course not a discrete entity unrelated to Arab culture. See, for example, Maria Rosa Menocal (1987).

5 Meaghan Morris's observation on "the modern" as a local reproduction of "something which has already happened elsewhere" is true of the standard of cultural greatness that developed at that time – a greatness which was seen as absent from the contemporaneous time/space, and needed to be captured from a different place, or recaptured from a different time. Morris (1990: 10).

6 For a brief chronological table of events of the West's more obvious interventions in the Arab world, see Badawi, ed. (1992: viii–xi).

7 A varied group of thinkers found that Islam was one way to challenge and offer alternatives to this liberal humanism, though this was not by and large the mode of challenge favored by literary writers.

8 For a richly detailed account of the early modern development of Arabic narrative and its relationship to rising nationalism see Hafez (1993).

9 Yahya Haqqi was another important member of this group. See the analysis of his novella, *The Saint's Lamp*, in Layoun (1990: 56–104).

10 One of the meatiest and most readable depictions of the events of the 1919 revolution, and the brutality of the British in stamping it out, can be found in Nobel laureate Naguib Mahfouz's *Bayn al-Qasrayn* (1956), translated as *Palace Walk* (1990).

11 Hafez also has a detailed analysis of the story, which he thinks "in one sense is a cry against the regression into vulgarity" (1993: 258).

12 For an excellent analysis of the ambivalent attitudes towards women as a result of the encounter with Europe, and how one patriarchy (Islamic) came to be replaced by another (Victorian), as well as how women from different classes were impacted by modernization efforts from Muhammad Ali's time onwards, see Ahmed (1992).

13 Samah Selim (1997) has traced some of these developments through focusing on the Egyptian village narrative. She shows how different is the depiction of the village in the works of the pioneers, such as Haykal's *Zaynab* (1913), from al-Sharqawi's *Al-Ard* (The Land) (1953), where we actually hear the peasants speak in their own simple yet aware and immensely subversive language, making fun of the languages of the educated, and taking matters into their own hands to fight back against the corrupt landowning classes. The peasants are neither reduced to mute imbeciles nor are they romanticized (the impotent language of Romanticism is in fact subjected to hilarious debunking by the earthy village beauty, Wasifa, in her interactions with the educated adolescent school-boy who fancies himself in love with her). The character of the sheik, as well as his relationship with the villagers, is generally negative but still more complex than in "Village Small Talk," for example.

14 For a more detailed analysis of Diyab's and Qasim's novels, see Al-Nowaihi (forthcoming).

15 Exile and imprisonment are a part of the lives of most of the writers I am discussing in this essay.

16 The Egyptian Yahya al-Tahir 'Abdallah, who died in a tragic car accident in 1981, provides an interesting comparison to Munif. His narratives, also written in an innovatively traditional style – folk-like and deceptively simple, take place in the remote

villages of upper (southern) Egypt and cover the same time period. 'Abdallah is not impressed with the modern world, which makes occasional appearances in the form of central government policies that draft the young village men to fight wars in places and for causes they have never even heard of, for example. But he does not depict a benign traditional way of life in these villages either, and masterfully delineates the descending chain of cruelty that accompanies poverty and extreme deprivation, without ostensibly ascribing blame to specific individuals or entities. The central government in Egypt has largely ignored the south in its economic and social plans, and only recently, after the belated realization of the connection between the extreme poverty and hopeless conditions of the region and the outbreaks of violence by religious groups, has the government decided to pour some money into the area and start various "development" projects there. See 'Abdullah (1983a) and the translation of a collection of his short stories (1983b).

17   Palestinians are the major but not the only national group that has suffered from second-rate citizenship and forced dispersal. Another such group is the Kurds, whose suffering has found eloquent expression in the works of the brilliant Salim Barakat.

18   For more discussion of this issue see Maxime Rodinson's classic *Israel: A Colonial-Settler State?* (New York: Monad Press, 1973), and Joseph Massad, 'The 'Post-Colonial' Colony: Time, Space and Bodies in Palestine/Israel," in *The Pre-Occupation of Post-Colonial Studies*, ed. Fawzia Afzal-Khan and Kalpana Seshadri-Crooks (Durham: Duke University Press, forthcoming).

19   For a detailed analysis of this novel, see Layoun (1990: 177–208).

20   For a detailed analysis of some of these issues see Coffin (1998).

21   For the work of her predecessor Assia Djebar, written in French, see note 21, below.

22   She also reveals some of her ambivalence towards the Egyptian communist party as a woman. For a detailed analysis of this autobiography, as well as the autobiographies of the Palestinian Fadwa Tuqan and the Algerian Assia Djebar, see my "Resisting Silence in Arab Women's Autobiographies" (forthcoming), in which I trace the evolving relationships between the political, the sexual, and the textual in the life struggles of these women, as they try to reconcile gendered resistance with the need for national solidarity against hostile external forces.

23   For an excellent depiction of the failures of the revolution due to internal forces, see Mahfouz.

24   This dream has never entirely died. In August 1998, over sixty artists from all the different Arab countries got together and produced a song entitled "Operette al-Hulm al-'Arabi" (The Arab Dream), as a protest against Arab regimes that have been unable to sustain this dream of a united Arab nation. The song began playing on some television stations in October of 1998, and the stations have been inundated with requests to play the song over and over again. The 23 singers made an appearance in Beirut, and the concert was attended by half a million to a million persons, or a quarter to half the population of the city. It must be remembered that if modernity came to the Middle East stained with colonialism, nationalism was stained with the blood of resistance to imperialism.

25   The theme of Arab male/Western female has been an important one in Arabic literature almost from its inception, and is often employed in explorations of the difficulties of cross-cultural and colonial relationships. Perhaps the most well-known

novel dealing with this issue is the Sudanese Al-Tayyib Salih's *Mawsim al-Hijra ila al-Shamal* (Cairo: Dar al-Hilal, 1969), translated by Denys Johnson-Davies as *Season of Migration to The North* (London: Heinemman, 1969). See also Sulayman Fayyad's *Aswat* (Cairo: Kutub 'Arabiyya, 1977), translated by Hosam Aboul-Ela as *Voices* (New York: Marion Boyars Publishers, 1992). For how the situation gets played out when an Arab woman becomes involved with a European man, see, for example, the Palestinian Hamida Na'na's *Al-Watan fi al-'Aynayn* (Beirut: Dar al-Adab, 1979), translated by Martin Asser as *The Homeland* (Reading, England: Garnet Publishing, 1995), and the Egyptian Ahdaf Soueif's *In the Eye of the Sun* (New York: Vintage International, 1992).

26 For a detailed analysis of this wonderful novel, whose humor is unfortunately mostly lost in the translation, see my "Disorienting Spaces: Salwa Bakr's *The Golden Chariot*" (forthcoming).

27 The publishing house was concerned enough about being sued (an extremely rare occurrence in Egypt) that it included the following disclaimer: "The events appearing in some chapters of this novel are taken from Egyptian government-sponsored and opposition newspapers, and reprinting them is not intended to corroborate their accuracy or defame those mentioned. Rather, the author meant to reflect the general media atmosphere that surrounded his characters and influenced them." For a detailed analysis of this novel see Mehrez (1994).

References

'Abdullah, Yahya al-Tahir. (1983a). *Al-Kitabat al-Kamilah*. Cairo: Dar al-Mustaqbal al-'Arabi.

——. (1983b). *The Mountain of Green Tea and Other Stories*, trans. Denys Johnson-Davies. Cairo: American University in Cairo Press.

Ahmad, Aijaz. (1996). "The Politics of Literary Postcoloniality," in *Contemporary Postcolonial Theory: A Reader*, ed. Padmini Mongia. New York: St. Martin's Press.

Ahmed, Leila. (1992). *Women and Gender in Islam: Historical Roots of a Modern Debate*. New Haven: Yale University Press.

Al-Nowaihi, Magda M. (forthcoming). "Constructions of Masculinity in Two Modern Egyptian Novels," in *Intimate Selving: Self, Gender and Identity in Arab Families*, ed. Suad Joseph. Syracuse: Syracuse University Press.

——. (forthcoming). "Disorienting Spaces: Salwa Bakr's *The Golden Chariot*," in *Intersections: Essays on Modern Arab Women Writers*, eds. Lisa Suhair Majaj, Therese Saliba, and Paula Sunderman. Albany: State University of New York Press.

——. (forthcoming). "Resisting Silence in Arab Women's Autobiographies," in *The Postcolonial Word*, eds. Hamid Dabashi and Theodore Riccardi. New York: New York University Press.

al-Shaykh, Hanan. (1986). *Hikayat Zahra*. Beirut: Dar al-Adab. Trans. by Peter Ford as *The Story of Zahra*. London: Quartet Books, 1986.

al-Zayyat, Latifa. (1960). *Al-Bab al-Maftuh* [Open Door]. Cairo: Maktabat al-Anglo.

——. (1992). *Hamlat Taftish: Awraq Shaksiyya*. Cairo: Dar al-Hilal. Trans. by Sophie Bennett as *The Search: Personal Papers*. London: Quartet Books, 1996.

——. (1994). *Sahib Al-Bayt*. Cairo: Dar al-Hilal. Trans. by Sophie Bennett as *The Owner of the House*. London: Quartet Books, 1997.

——. (1994a). "On Political Commitment and Feminist Writing," in *The View from Within: Writers and Critics on Contemporary Arabic Literature*, eds. Ferial J. Ghazoul and Barbra Harlow. Cairo: American University in Cairo Press.

Badawi, M. M., ed. (1992). *Modern Arabic Literature*, in *The Cambridge History of Arabic Literature*. Cambridge: Cambridge University Press.

Bakr, Salwa. (1991). *Al-'Araba al Dhahabiyya La Tas'ad Ila al-Sama'*. Cairo: Sina Lil-Nashr. Trans. by Dinah Manisty as *The Golden Chariot*. Reading, England: Garnet Publishing, 1995.

Barakat, Hoda. (1990). *Hajar al-Dahik*. London: Riad El-Rayyis. Trans. by Sophie Bennett as *The Stone of Laughter*. New York: Interlink Books, 1995.

Chakrabarty, Dipesh. (1996). "Postcoloniality and the Artifice of History: Who Speaks for 'Indian' Pasts?" in *Contemporary Postcolonial Theory: A Reader*, ed. Padmini Mongia. New York: St. Martin's Press.

Chow, Rey. (1995). "In the Name of Comparative Literature," in *Comparative Literature in the Age of Multiculturalism*, ed. Charles Bernheimer. Baltimore: Johns Hopkins University Press.

Coffin, Nancy. (1998). *Representations of Reality in Palestinian Resistance Narratives 1967–1980*. Doctoral dissertation, Columbia University.

Diyab, Mahumud. (1971). *Ahzan Madina: Tifl Fi al-Hayy al-'Arabi*. Cairo: Al-Hay's al-Misriyya al-'Amma Li-l-Kitab.

Gorgy, Nabil Naoum. (1993). "Hulm al-'Abd," in *Al-Zamr fi Iktimal*. Cairo: Dar Sharquiyyat. Trans. by Denys Johnson-Davies as *The Slave's Dream and Other Stories*. London: Quartet Book, 1991.

Habibi, Imil. (1974). *Al-Waqa'i' al-Gharibah Fi Ikhtifa' Sa'id Abit al-Nahs al-Mutasha'il*. Haifa: Al-Ittihad. Trans. by Salma Khadra Jayyusi and Trevor Le Gassick as *The Secret Life of Saeed the Ill-Fated Pessoptimist: A Palestinian Who Became a Citizen of Israel*. London: Zed Books, 1985.

Hafez, Sabry. (1993). *The Genesis of Arabic Narrative Discourse: A Study in the Sociology of Modern Arabic Literature*. London: Saqi Books.

Ibrahim, Son'allah. (1992). *Dhat*. Cairo: Dar al-Mustaqbal al-'Arabi.

——. (1997). *Sharaf*. Cairo: Dar al-Hilal.

Kanafani, Ghassan. (1963). *Rijal fi al-Shams*. Beirut: Dar al-Tali'ah. Trans. by Hilary Kilpatrick as *Men in the Sun and Other Palestinian Stories*. Washington, DC: Three Continents Press, 1978.

Khalifah, Sahar. (1976). *Al-Subbar*. Jerusalem: Manshurat Galileo. Trans. by Trevor Le Gassick and Elizabeth Fernea as *Wild Thorns*. New York: Olive Branch Press, 1989.

——. (1990). *Bab al-Saha* [Saha Gate]. Beirut: Dar al-Adab.

Lashin, Mahmud Tahir. (1929). "Hadith al-Qarya," in *Yuhka Anna*. Cairo: Dar al-'Usur. Trans. by Sabry Hafez as "Village Small Talk," in Hafez (1993).

Layoun, Mary. (1990). *Travels of a Genre: The Modern Novel and Ideology*. Princeton: Princeton University Press.

Mahfouz, Naguib. (1956). *Bayn al-Qasrayn*. Cairo: Maktabat Misr. Trans. by William M. Hutchings and Olive E. Kenney as *Palace Walk*. New York: Doubleday, 1990.

———. (1967). *Miramar*. Cairo: Maktabat Misr. Trans by Fatma Moussa Mahmoud as *Miramar*. Cairo: American University in Cairo Press, 1978.

Mehrez, Samia. (1994). *Egyptian Writers Between History and Fiction*. Cairo: American University in Cairo Press.

Menocal, Maria Rosa. (1987). *The Arabic Role in Medieval Literary History: A Forgotten Heritage*. Philadelphia: University of Pennsylvania Press.

Morris, Meaghan. (1990). "Metamorphoses at Sydney Tower," *New Formations*, 11 (summer).

Mosteghanemi, Ahlam. (1993). *Dhakirat al-Jasad* [The Body's Memory]. Beirut: Dar al-Adab.

Munif, 'Abd al-Rahman. (1978). *Al-Nihayat*. Beirut: Dar al-Adab. Trans. by Roger Allen as *Endings*. London: Quartet Books, 1988.

———. (1984–9). *Mudun al-Milh*. Beirut: al-Mu'assasa al-'Arabiyya Li-l-Dirasat wa-l-Nashr. The first two volumes have been translated into English by Peter Theroux as *Cities of Salt* (New York: Vintage International, 1989) and *The Trench* (New York: Vintage International, 1993).

Qasim, 'Abd al-Hakim. (1969). *Ayyam al-Insan al-Sab'a*. Cairo: Dar al-Katib al-'Arabi. Trans. by Joseph Norment Bell as *The Seven Days of Man*. Evanston, Ill.: Hydra Books/Northwestern University Press, 1996.

Selim, Samah. (1997). *The Divided Subject: Narrative Enactment in the Egyptian Village Novel*. Doctoral dissertation, Columbia University, New York.

Taher, Baha. (1995). *Al-Hubb fi al-Manfa* [Love in Exile]. Cairo: Dar al-Hilal.

Chapter 15

King Kong in Hong Kong: Watching the "Handover" from the USA

Rey Chow

In the weeks prior to July 1, 1997, I kept receiving invitations from the media in Hong Kong and the United States to discuss, orally or in writing, the historic event of Hong Kong's handover from Britain to China. Judging by the enthusiasm of journalistic circles, it was obvious that the entire world was fascinated with the occasion. This was another spectacular moment for China-watching like the Tiananmen Massacre of June 4, 1989 – even though the mood was decidedly different, at least for Chinese populations in different parts of the world. But behind the craze to focus on China and Hong Kong, we see once again the persistence of all-too-familiar ideological tendencies in the West. For anyone who wishes to discuss the current situation of China and Hong Kong with a sense of justice and fairness, the task is daunting: one must write, it seems, not only against the biases that are readily apparent in the large number of reports generated within a relatively short period but also against the weight of opinion and tradition that sustains such biases.

Ever since China "turned red" in 1949, the predominant mainstream attitude in the United States has been one of simple anxiety. Communist China has been seen by US politicians as a symbol of the United States' loss of guardianship over the most populous area of Asia. Unlike the fascistic Guomindang regime under the military dictatorship of Chiang Kai-shek from the late 1920s to the late 1940s, the People's Republic of China has never succumbed to the manipulation of Big Brother Uncle Sam. The latter's realization of custodial loss has gone hand in hand with an increasing amount of apprehension as China's rise to world power, especially after the dissolution of the former Soviet Union, has become apparent. The twin feelings of mournfulness and fearfulness continue to characterize the US media's portrayal of China today, most often by way of a set of binary oppositions, which tend to represent China as the other of all the positive values embraced by the United States. This deliberate process of othering continued from the 1950s and 1960s through the resumption of relations with China after Richard Nixon's visit in 1972, reaching a new climax in 1989, when Chinese authorities ordered tanks to crush civilians demonstrating for democracy at Tiananmen Square. More recently, with allegations that the Clinton administration accepted sizable donations from "foreigners" spearheaded by overseas Chinese lobby groups, suspicious, resentful, and often blatantly racist insinuations about Asian and, particularly, Chinese people are evident in reports across the country. In addition, a spate of China-bashing films, such as *Seven Years in Tibet*, *Red Corner*, and *Kundun*, form part of the US media's concerted effort to attack China in the name of human rights – even and especially while the president of the PRC, Jiang Zemin, toured the United States at the US government's invitation in the fall of 1997. Despite the virtual disappearance of the actual political configurations of the Cold War, the Cold War narrative never quite dies – every time a major event occurs in China, this narrative returns with a vengeance.[1]

Typically, by posing as defenders of democracy and liberty, the US media portrays Chinese events as crises that require not only vigilance but also intervention. Typically, such portrayals are dramatized – staged in palpably demonizing terms so that audiences in the West are obliged to identify with an invisible but adamant moralistic perspective in which the United States is seen as superior. In discussing the US media's treatment of the 1989 Tiananmen Massacre, I have compared it with the film *King Kong* and used the term "King Kong syndrome" to refer to this structure of cross-cultural, cross-racial representation aimed at producing "China" as a spectacular primitive monster whose despotism necessitates the salvation of its people by outsiders.[2] It is important to remember that although many countries lack "democracy" and "liberty," it is China that, simply because it is not the United States' ideological ally, regularly bears the brunt of this process of palpable demonization (along with countries such as Iraq and Iran, as well as Islamic political groups in general). For many in the United States, China is, first and foremost, that "other country" where violence erupts.[3]

Most reports on the Hong Kong handover have not departed from this King Kong syndrome. I will cite merely a couple of examples of the kind of militant goading in the name of democracy that has come from public personalities such as Dan Rather and Tom Brokaw. On July 1, 1997, after Hong Kong officially became Chinese territory again, Chinese military forces moved, according to schedule, into Hong Kong proper, paying the necessary toll to drive through Hong Kong's toll tunnels and heading toward barracks that had been vacated by British troops. However, this entirely legal move was sensationally reported by many Western journalists as a disaster: "Truckloads of People's Liberation Army soldiers rumbled into Hong Kong."[4] Hong Kong's outgoing British governor, Christopher Patten, took the lead in condemning the peaceful Chinese troop transfer and was quickly supported in this by US Secretary of State Madeleine Albright.[5] Even though it has been common for troops to enter civilian spaces after a major national victory – one is reminded of how troops paraded through European city streets at the end of the Second World War, for instance – Britain and the United States clearly did not want to recognize the Chinese resumption of sovereignty in Hong Kong in these terms and instead voiced their criticisms as if China were some sort of foreign invader. Then there followed reports about how China was introducing "harsh new laws" designed to put the clamps on Hong Kong's democracy. Among them were laws prohibiting foreign contributions to local political candidates. Such contributions are, of course, also prohibited in the United States.

Westerners' misconceptions about the level of danger in Hong Kong can be demonstrated by numerous other, less well-known examples. Wayne Wang, who was directing the film *Chinese Box* in Hong Kong at the time of the handover, reported the following incident: Jeremy Irons, who played one of the leading characters in Wang's film, was at the same time cast in another film in Paris. The lawyers for this other film suddenly objected to the plan for Irons to return to Hong Kong for an extra two days of shooting; they demanded that Wang insure Irons for $400,000 in case he should be injured in a crackdown by China in Hong Kong on July 1.[6] A film critic, capitalizing on the King Kong syndrome, introduced his discussion of the Hong Kong cinema by announcing, authoritatively, the passing of a golden age: "Now that Hong Kong has officially been reunited with – or recolonized by – mainland China, a great, tumultuous movie era has passed."[7] A journalist wrote in the pages of the *New Republic* that Hong Kong is "doomed" and in worse shape than we think because, as his investigative report urgently reveals, "China bonds with Hong Kong's underworld."[8] This journalist has obviously forgotten or is naively unaware of the fact that such bonding between the government and the underworld is a feature pertaining to all societies in the world – and that it existed under the former British administration in Hong Kong and exists in the United States as much as it exists in Hong Kong under China.

In habitually stereotyping China as a violent monster, deserving of exposure, discipline, and punishment, the US media – the major national television networks, news journals, and newspapers – seldom if ever discusses in detail the most important event in the complex historical background of Hong Kong's handover to China – the First Opium War of 1839–42.[9] To that extent it also fails consistently to capture and comprehend the strong emotions that accompany what Chinese populations call, in a manner contrary to the bureaucratic terminology of "handover," Hong Kong's *huigui* (return). The originating event of the First Opium War may be briefly recapitulated as follows: Noticing the significantly high outflow of silver from Britain created by the import of Chinese goods such as silk and tea, British politicians began, around the late eighteenth century, to correct the imbalance by exporting large quantities of opium (produced at that time in British India and in Iran) to China. When the Chinese government, seeing the massive harm produced by the so-called foreign mud, made the opium traffic illegal, British officials resorted to what historians refer to as "gunboat diplomacy" and sought excuses for war. Sterling Seagrave summarizes these events succinctly:

While Great Britain was approaching the zenith of its power at the mid-point of the nineteenth century, China had sunk to its weakest point since the Manchu took control in 1644. Corruption was epidemic, and Emperor Tao Kuang's reluctance to act ruthlessly was seen as weakness, inviting more abuses. In the south, Western traders at Canton and Macao flouted the law, smuggling in massive quantities of cheap Indian opium, driving a spike into the heartwood. *Opium became a symbol of China's sovereignty and whether foreigners could violate that sovereignty at whim*; the fact that corrupt Chinese and Manchu officials participated in the trade did not make the issue less real. It became a game among Westerners to provoke the Chinese at every turn and, when the Chinese struck back, to demand concessions from local mandarins. If concessions were not forthcoming, gunboats were called in; China found herself at war over issues that were trumped up and incidents that were greatly exaggerated or entirely imaginary. Many Westerners built successful careers out of bullying the Chinese. . . . In the politics of collision, rude surprises were grasped as great opportunities, and armed force was used to guarantee the outcome, while the public at home was led to believe it was all part of a grand design.[10]

Against Britain's role in the First Opium War, Britain's own William Gladstone protested in Parliament: "A war more unjust in its origin, a war more calculated to cover this country with permanent disgrace, I do not know and have not read of. . . . The British flag is hoisted to protect an infamous traffic; . . . we should recoil from its sight with horror."[11] Britain thus successfully bombarded its way into China by forcing the latter to accept the Treaty of Nanking, the first in a series of what the Chinese call *bu pingdeng tiaoyue* (unequal treaties). It was this treaty that, apart from stipulating heavy reparations to be paid by the Chinese, led to the ceding of Hong Kong Island to Britain and the opening of five Chinese coastal cities – henceforth known as "treaty ports" – to British trade. Subsequently, with more military invasions and the signing of more unequal treaties, Britain obtained part of the Kowloon Peninsula in 1860 and a 99-year lease on the New Territories in 1898. These three major areas – Hong Kong Island, the Kowloon Peninsula, and the New Territories – and some outlying islands then made up what became known as the British Crown Colony of Hong Kong.[12]

To Chinese people all over the world, July 1, 1997 signified the vindication of *this* originating series of events. Regardless of differences in political loyalties and regardless of pronounced ambivalence toward the current regime in Beijing, it was the symbolic closure of the historic British aggression against China which accounted for the unprecedentedly overwhelming expression of jubilation throughout the Chinese-speaking world at the lowering of the British flag in Hong Kong. The predominantly celebratory mood meant that, despite a century and a half of British hegemony, the Chinese never emotionally consented to British colonialism. For 155 years, they had refused to forget that Hong Kong was a Chinese city.

In spite of this well-documented history, in spite of the United States' own history of colonization by Britain, and even more ironically, in spite of the current national campaigns in the United States against the use of drugs, the US media habitually ignores the Opium Wars. Instead of following the lead of the descendants of those who were invaded, the US media chooses to follow the lead of someone such as Patten, who, together with former British Prime Minister Margaret Thatcher, presents Hong Kong's social stability and economic prosperity as the laudable results of British administration. In the preface to the 1997 *Annual Report on Hong Kong*, Patten implicitly called the Chinese government to task for having turned history into an ideological tool in an attempt to revise historical facts that had already taken place.[13] In thus distorting and effacing the facts of history, he proved himself to be, despite his carefully crafted democratic facade,[14] merely another loyal flack of the queen's vanishing empire.

While Patten's loyalty to his rulers does not require elaboration (since, in the British tradition, loyalty may take the form of loyal opposition), what remains at issue is the double standard continually adopted by Britain and the United States when dealing with a country such as the PRC. For instance, the very "social stability" and "economic prosperity" that are emphasized by Patten and Thatcher as being the accomplishments of British rule in Hong Kong are, we hear repeatedly, precisely the objectives emphasized for Hong Kong by the current leaders in Beijing as well. Rather than acknowledging that the PRC and Britain have much in common in their ambitions as the successive rulers of Hong Kong, however, Patten, whenever he was faced with the world's media, typically presented the Chinese authorities as untrustworthy – as the opposite of the benign, indeed benevolent, model set by Britain – and never subjected Britain's own historical objectives in keeping Hong Kong stable and prosperous to any similarly harsh judgment.

What does having a double standard mean in this situation? It does not refer simply to the use of two different sets of criteria for judging the same kind of action – a use that may be attributed to arbitrariness, lack of consistency, or mere arrogance. More pragmatically, it refers to a practice of systematically granting one party more liberties by exempting it from judgments that are, nonetheless, applied with dogged vehemence against another. Historically, such exemptions from what should be a common set of criteria were an essential part of the West's gunboat diplomacy during an era when military and territorial aggression against China was accompanied by demands for what was known as extraterritoriality. This was the legal fiction that deemed that the premises of a diplomatic mission (and by extension, its people) were not within the territory of the state in which they stood but rather in the territory of the sending state, and that such premises and people were therefore excluded from the jurisdiction of the receiving state. In the nineteenth and early twentieth centuries, through an interlocking network of unequal treaties imposed on China by various foreign powers (including Britain, France, Germany, Russia, Japan, and the United States), extraterritoriality ensured that foreign diplomats, troops, merchants, and missionaries living in China were not subject to the same laws (Chinese laws) to which Chinese people were subject – even if they committed crimes on Chinese soil against Chinese citizens. Extraterritoriality also meant, in effect, that the Chinese government itself was never fully sovereign within Chinese territory.

Serving to legitimize (by force) the double standard that allowed the West to act in China without being subject to Chinese jurisdiction *but not vice versa*, extraterritoriality thus gave Westerners the privilege of having to submit exclusively to their own jurisdiction – that is, the privilege of being (judged) *outside* China even when they were acting in China. This privilege was henceforth internalized in Western attitudes toward China and Chinese people as an unexamined, because naturalized, assumption. And, even when Western actions directly affected, subjugated, or injured Chinese citizens within the territory that was supposedly theirs, the West remained in essence not only the agent but also the sole, patronizing arbiter of such actions. China continues to this day to be put in the position of a lowly, uncivilized other on whom the West can act and pass judgment without having to worry about being acted upon or judged itself. The reverse, of course, is not the case: When China acts, even within the bounds of its own territory, it is always subject to the value-laden arbitration of the West.

The lingering effects of this one-way legal and moral structure of extraterritoriality are, I think, what underlie the Anglo–American representation of the Hong Kong handover. All the criticisms of the PRC are made from the vantage point of an inherited, well-seasoned, condescending perspective that exempts itself from judgment and which, moreover, refuses to acknowledge China's sovereignty even when it has been officially reestablished over Chinese soil. Instead, sovereignty – and with it, proprietorship (over judgment as well as political actions) – continues to be imagined and handled as exclusively Western. Sovereignty and proprietorship here are not only about the ownership of land or rule but also about ideological self-ownership, that is, about the legitimating terms that allow a people to be.

It is within this persistently discriminatory process of extraterritorial value production that the proclamations of democracy by the likes of Patten and Thatcher should be understood. Needless to say, Great Britain and the United States are themselves far from having achieved the progressive, democratic ideals upon which they so freely expound when they judge others. The situation in Northern Ireland and the ongoing struggles of African Americans are but two outstanding examples of the reality of these two major powers' double standards, let alone the historical devastation wrought by both countries' practices of colonialism and neocolonialism. But specifically, what does the frequent, rhetorical invocation of democracy by both countries against the PRC achieve?

For the United States, the answer is simple. The concept of democracy serves the function of uniting Right and Left in such a manner as to facilitate the ongoing myth of a single, undivided American culture. Between practical groups who think of China as a market that must not be passed up even while it is, alas, inconvenienced by communism and idealistic groups who think of the Chinese as victims of totalitarianism (thus needing liberal salvation), China stands as that external something – an enemy and an obstacle – against which the otherwise irreconcilable interests of the Right and the Left can effectively coalesce and collaborate.

For Great Britain, the picture is more complicated because of Britain's long presence in Hong Kong. Here, it is necessary to focus as much on the *image* as on the material realities Britain sought to leave behind. That image, in the hands of Patten, is none other than democracy – a memento of colonialism at its hypocritical climax.

Contrary to what was being presented to the world by Patten and Thatcher, British rule in Hong Kong was, for the most part of its 155 years, not at all democratic. Instead, as scholars have repeatedly pointed out, British rule was characterized by brute military force, the continuous monopolization of trading privileges by British companies, the continuous monopolization of the highest levels of the civil service by British administrators, strict class stratification between British and non-British residents (with the Chinese at the very bottom of most social ladders), significant episodes of corruption by British officials, and the sustained channeling of Hong Kong's considerable revenues toward Britain.[15] And even though Hong Kong was originally on the list prepared by the United Nations Special Committee on Colonialism of colonies that were scheduled to be decolonized – that is, granted independent nationhood – the British government under Edward Heath made no objection in 1972 to Hong Kong's removal from that list. Its excuse was that China, upon being voted into the UN in 1971, had requested the removal of Hong Kong and Macao from the list; the fact remains that this crucial decision, which resulted in Hong Kong's loss of the right to self-determination – a decision about which Hong Kong people were never consulted – was made under British rule by British officials.[16] This decision sealed Hong Kong's fate.

It would only be as a parting gesture that a semblance of democracy was introduced, and only in the last few years of colonial rule did Hong Kong begin to have direct elections, which resulted in a legislature that the PRC dismantled on 1 July and replaced with its own appointed provisional legislature. This appointed legislature was judged by the Hong Kong High Court at the end of July 1997 to be legal. Although the PRC's disrespect for Hong Kong's established legal process certainly deserves to be criticized, the Chinese officials' continuing rhetorical challenge to the British has a real point: If the British were such staunch defenders of democracy in Hong Kong, why did they fabricate this appearance of it only in the last instant, as a Parthian shot? As Mark Roberti writes: "It was not until Britain had formally agreed to return Hong Kong to China that the Hong Kong government began introducing democratic reforms. China had every right to feel tricked. *Democracy, it seemed, was good for Hong Kong only when the British were no longer running it.*"[17] Patten's proposals for political reform, Roberti argues, were "a smoke screen put up so the British could avoid feeling guilty about turning six million people over to a brutal regime" (299).

While Britain's motives will always remain a matter of interpretation, from the perspective of colonialist strategy, the eleventh-hour appearance of democratic procedures in Hong Kong nonetheless served a concrete function. This virtual democracy – hastily planted and left behind in the "decolonized" territory like a land mine, no longer part of Britain's responsibility once the HMS *Britannia* steamed out of Hong Kong's harbor in the early morning of July 1, 1997 – created a political situation that was guaranteed to be a permanent source of irreconcilable conflict among the supposedly decolonized natives.[18] We need hardly mention that histories of the aftermath of British colonialism all over the world have provided ample evidence for the systematic nature of such a decolonizing strategy. Whereas in the Middle East, for instance, the departure of the colonial powers left behind a perpetual crisis in the form of an unequal distribution of resources between populations, in Hong Kong, the most likely area for dispute is clearly Western-style "democracy," especially because the leaders of the mother country have long announced that for historical and cultural reasons, China is not yet ready for it. What better way to leave than by implanting the rudimentary structures of democratic elections that would hereafter provide potent grounds for disaffection and dissent against the regime in power? What better way to ensure that the "decolonized" natives would themselves acquiesce in this fraud and nostalgically give their consent to the virtues of British rule precisely when that rule was supposedly over? What better way to give British values and judgments, once again, *extraterritorial legitimacy*?

From this perspective, the autocratic reactions displayed time and again by the PRC toward the West become understandable even when they are not – as I believe they are not – defensible. For the Chinese authorities, the democracy that the West insists on making China accept is not in essence different from the opium imposed by Britain in the nineteenth century. During the earlier period of manipulation, Britain did not actually desire that the Chinese smoke opium. What it desired was that China give Britain not only its silk and tea but its silver as well. Opium – that magical substance supposedly craved by the Chinese themselves – was only a means to this end, a puff of smoke, a substitute satisfaction. Similarly, during the current period of manipulation, the British and the Americans do not actually desire that the Chinese practice democracy. What they desire is that in China's economy, things be done in Western ways. Democracy – that magical substance supposedly craved by the Chinese themselves – is only a means to this end, a puff of smoke, a substitute satisfaction. Democracy in the late twentieth century can be seen, in other words, as the imposition of a set of values China does not want, with implications that recall, precisely, Westerners' demands for trading rights, missionary privileges, and extraterritoriality, which challenged Chinese sovereignty in the nineteenth century. *In both cases, Westerners want cash, and Chinese people get smoke.* In this light, China's frequent objections to the West's "meddling in Chinese internal affairs" – an excuse the PRC has notoriously used to justify all kinds of repressive political practices – must be seen as logical. This logic is the hysteric's logic of a historical memory, a symptomatic resistance to the West, based, as it were, on an inability to forget.[19]

For these reasons, the ideology of democracy will most probably continue to be contentious, controversial, and indeed treacherous in Hong Kong's future. Fighters for democracy such as Martin Lee, Szeto Wah, Cheung Man-kwong, Lee Cheuk-yan, Emily Lau, and their fellow workers have been put in a precarious position less because of their outspokenness than because of the historical complexities that constitute their political situation. This is a situation in which, their personal intentions notwithstanding, they will be perceived, in effect, as agents for "trouble-making" that have been systematically planted and left behind by British colonialism.

I say this in anguish, as someone who is wholeheartedly supportive of their movement.

So far, three major narratives have been invoked: US imperialism and with it, a persistent Cold War perspective on China; British colonialism and its de-colonizing strategies; and China's knee-jerk official position of resisting everything and anything that seems to be imposed by the West. With the West and Hong Kong insisting on the continuation of the status quo in the former British colony, China's creative solution has been to institute "one country, two systems," an unprecedented idea for political management whose long-term validity and efficacy remain to be seen.[20] However, as the world's China watchers bet on whether Hong Kong will change China or China will change Hong Kong, a new, unpredictable narrative – that of global capital – is rapidly gathering momentum.

What does it mean to ask whether Hong Kong will change China or China will change Hong Kong? Almost without exception, discussions of this question focus on Hong Kong's thriving capitalism and the social forces which have helped sustain it.[21] Conventionally, analysts have always attributed Hong Kong's economic prosperity to British colonialism – to the fact that, because colonialism did not allow political choices to be made, Hong Kong people had to channel their energies into the economic sphere. Hong Kong's economic prosperity, in other words, has always been construed *negatively* in relation to political awareness – as a (morally degenerate) compensation for the lack of political possibilities and as what is at best a delusory (because overly materialistic) accomplishment.[22] As Hong Kong's return to China grabs the world's attention, however, a different line of argument has emerged: Most of those who argue for Hong Kong's democracy now seem to think that, on the contrary, it is actually economic prosperity – hitherto always judged pejoratively to be the result of the lack of political opportunities – that makes it possible for people to want political change or democracy in the first place. Thus, in a manner opposed to the conventional pronouncements about Hong Kong, economic prosperity is linked *positively* to political awareness, which is now said to be an outcome of it. When these two seemingly contradictory arguments about politics and economism are juxtaposed, we find, in fact, a coherent, rationalist argument that progresses as follows: Colonialism leads to economism; economism leads to democracy.

What has remained unarticulated, then, in the rather confusing arguments about democracy (which is invariably invoked together with "totalitarianism" in a binary opposition) is that the democratic Hong Kong of the 1990s is the result not of economic forces alone but rather of the *combined* forces of colonialism and capitalism – of a colonialism, moreover, that, even when it granted no political choice, adopted a laissez-faire economic policy that allowed capitalist forces to flourish with the least amount of government interference.[23] If it is indeed Hong Kong's economic prosperity that has led to its current democracy, this democracy is itself a byproduct of colonialism – of a form of government that was not at all democratic.

Even when coming from the most well-intentioned people, therefore, arguments for maintaining Hong Kong's democracy in the post-British period tend, inevitably, to be trapped in a certain ideological impasse. In spite of strong ethnic sentiments against historical foreign exploitation, Hong Kong people find themselves obligated by their unique circumstances to acquiesce in the "merits" of capitalism (since capitalism is what is believed to have led to democracy in the first place) and thus ironically, by implication, to acquiesce in the merits of colonialism as well (since colonialism was what fostered capitalism in Hong Kong). This ideological impasse underlies the collective wish that Hong Kong "remain the same" after being returned to China. This wish, which China has honored by promising "one country, two systems," is predicated on the assumption that any change from Hong Kong's present system can mean one thing and one thing only – a doomed regression toward being like (not-yet-fully-capitalist) China. As Madeleine Albright proclaimed, "We will be watching to see that the Hong Kong of tomorrow is like the Hong Kong of today."[24]

But what kind of wish, promise, and threat is it to say that we should make sure that the Hong Kong of tomorrow is like the Hong Kong of today? It is a strange notion – a curse even – to want any place to remain the same for fifty years.[25] Since Hong Kong has only the beginnings of a democratic system, does it mean that even though it is officially no longer a colony, it need not advance any further *politically* so that it can remain "the same" as we find it today, in 1997?

Despite its moralistic overtones, the new narrative of global capital – the narrative that, to all appearances, wants to defend Hong Kong's democratic present against the encroachment of an absolutist China – is really interested only in the trajectory of Hong Kong's continual *monetary* growth, itself always said to be the (more or less beneficial) result of British colonialism. With this patent economism comes the important question: If economic prosperity takes precedence over everything else and if democracy (despite the West's promoting it as an indispensable part of social progress) has already been discursively constructed as a byproduct (as what *follows* economic prosperity but not vice versa), doesn't that mean that in fact, democracy *can* be sacrificed when necessary – for instance, if Hong Kong fails to sustain its economic prosperity? Conversely, since Hong Kong already thrived economically under British colonial rule, when there was little democracy to speak of, doesn't that mean that democracy is really not a prerequisite for Hong Kong's continued financial growth?

Ironically, this new narrative of global capital with its revealing ambiguities about democracy is the place where the otherwise ideologically competing – and seemingly incompatible – forces of US imperialism, British colonialism, and Chinese nationalism coincide. Like Britain and the United States, with their considerable trade interests in the Far East, the PRC, too, in spite of its overt ideological "difference," is now a giant investor in Hong Kong businesses. Likewise, within the PRC itself, the economy is being drastically reorganized from one based on state ownership to one based on "shareholding" (a description consciously adopted by PRC officials, who shun the word "privatization"). While the PRC may not openly acknowledge it, the government's tolerance for and enthusiastic embrace of capitalist ventures and practices mean that China has, in fact, gone capitalist.[26] And yet, such capitalist ventures and practices are, traditionally, precisely what provide anchorage for Western imperialism and colonialism. As we learn from even the most elementary reading of Marx, the relationship between capitalism and colonialism/imperialism is that of an infrastructure, with its state apparatuses and legal institutions, and a superstructure, with its function of inculcating civilians with the attitudes and behaviors necessary for perpetuating and reproducing the existing system. As Wang Zhangwei and Luo Jinyi write, "At present, the PRC historical discourse is critical of British colonialism, but the PRC officials are staunch defenders of the problematic capitalist strategies brought by the colonists. They are thus breaking up the twin-like character of imperialism and capitalism. Can this work?"[27] By foregrounding the apparent ideological chaos triggered by the PRC's current economic "openness," Wang and Luo have pinpointed the most intriguing theoretical issue in the Hong Kong handover: In their commitment, undoubtedly proclaimed with sincerity and goodwill, to keeping Hong Kong prosperous and stable, the Chinese leaders must stray, it would seem, further and further from the orthodox teachings of Marx, Lenin, and Mao – teachings they nonetheless continue to affirm even when the credibility of their own reputations as administrators is now linked, as one writer puts it, to Hong Kong's Hang Seng Index.[28]

Clearly, just as there are now "red-chip stocks" (stocks issued by nongovernment-owned PRC companies) exclusively available in the Hong Kong stock market, so, too, China has scrambled Marx's fundamental schema of a mutually supportive capitalism and imperialism/colonialism to the point of unrecognizability. While the long-term implications of this scrambling have yet to be understood, it is possible to make some preliminary observations. In Hong Kong,

China's ideological chaos has so far enabled business tycoons to continue exploiting the working classes for maximum commercial benefit in the name of an anti-colonialist ethnic unity.[29] As such exploitation of the labor force is likely to intensify in the decades to come (precisely as China tries to look good by honoring its commitment to keeping Hong Kong economically prosperous), the gap between the rich and the poor, already huge, will probably widen to an unprecedented degree. Should this happen, Hong Kong's economic prosperity will have to be recognized not as bringing about democracy, with its principle of equality among citizens, but rather as bringing about its lack.

In the ongoing frenzy to generate capital and to privilege money as the paramount goal, is not the PRC itself sponsoring, in effect, a kind of opium (as Marx's analysis of capital suggests) that turns people into addicts, deprived of their freedoms and rights and ultimately of their ability to think? If its objective in Hong Kong is simply to keep Hong Kong economically prosperous without those freedoms and rights, how will the PRC be able to distinguish its own rule from British colonial rule? (Does it matter?) Meanwhile, how will countries such as Great Britain and the United States, the self-appointed guardians of the world's moral values, "help" Hong Kong continue its progress toward democracy when, their avowed promises not to forget Hong Kong notwithstanding,[30] they actually share with the PRC the objective of *keeping Hong Kong as it is*, that is, as (nothing less but nothing more than) the capital of freewheeling capital?

With the emergence of global capital, the older narratives of British colonialism, US imperialism, and Chinese nationalism no longer suffice to account for what is operating as a fluid, transnational, collaborationist structure of financial interests that, despite the ideological divergences of the parties involved, have as their mutually self-serving goal the prosperity and stability of the "Pearl of the Orient." In all likelihood, the struggle for democracy will always remain subordinated to this new, fluid global structure. And it is in that subordinated state, which requires them to plot their tactics forever against a perfidious hegemonic situation created jointly by Hong Kong's current and former colonizers, that Hong Kong's democracy fighters will have to chart their arduous future course.

Notes

A short and preliminary version of this essay, "Yao minzhu haishi yao yapian? Cong Meiguo Kan Xianggang huigui Zhonguo," was published in *Xin bao* [Hong Kong economic journal], 15–16 July 1997. I am indebted to Nancy Armstrong and Leonard Tennenhouse for their enthusiasm and encouragement, and for the valuable insights they offered long distance, during the period of Hong Kong's return to China. Austin Meredith was, as usual, the indispensable interlocutor at home. Without the contributions of these people, this essay would not and could not have been written. John Frow was the one who came up with the essay's main title – to him and to the responsive audiences in Sydney and Brisbane, Australia, where an early version of the essay was presented in public for the first time in August 1997, my heartfelt thanks.

1   The resilience of the Cold War narrative and its accompanying attitudes is reflected in, for example, Richard Bernstein and Ross H. Munro, *The Coming Conflict with China* (New York: Knopf, 1997).

2   See Rey Chow, "Violence in the Other Country: Preliminary Remarks on the China Crisis, June 1989," *Radical America*, 22 (July–August 1988): 23–32 (published in Sept. 1989). A much expanded version of this essay, titled "Violence in the Other Country: China as Crisis, Spectacle, and Woman," can be found in *Third World Women and the Politics of Feminism*, eds. Chandra Talpade Mohanty, Ann Russo, and Lourdes Torres (Bloomington: Indiana University Press, 1991), 81–100.

3   Sterling Seagrave has demonstrated that the Western demonization of China had already begun by the late nineteenth century and had reached a sensational point by the first decade of the twentieth century with the depictions (by some English pornographers) of the Empress Cixi (Tz'u Hsi). See his riveting accounts in *Dragon Lady* (New York: Vintage, 1992).

4   Maynard Parker, "The City on a Hill," *Newsweek*, 14 July 1997, 46.

5   "I do not think this is the best way to start off, and I think we have to watch this very carefully," Albright said in regard to Chinese troops moving into Hong Kong (Steven Erlanger, "Uncle Sam's New Role: Hong Kong's Advocate," *New York Times*, 2 July 1997, A8). Patten reportedly asked Albright to "keep watch" over Hong Kong (Melinda Liu, "Beijing's New Babysitter," *Newsweek*, 14 July 1997, 50).

6   Seth Faison, "Casting Hong Kong as a Drama-Filled City," *New York Times*, 1 July 1997, B1.

7   Howard Hampton, "Once upon a Time in Hong Kong: Tsui Hark and Ching Siu-tung," *Film Comment*, July–Aug. 1997, 16–19, 24–7.

8   Fredric Dannen, "Partners in Crime," *New Republic*, 14–21 July 1997, 18–26.

9   An exception is Paul Theroux, "Letter from Hong Kong: Ghost Stories," *New Yorker*, 12 May 1997, 54–65. Theroux writes: "Understanding imperial British drug dealings, which led to the First Opium War, is essential to understanding Hong Kong" (55).

10 Seagrave, *Dragon Lady*, 42–3; my emphasis. Contrast Seagrave's passage with the following neutral-sounding but in fact pro-British description: "In 1839 China clamped down on the hugely profitable trade in Indian opium, conducted largely in British ships. But the subsequent *opium war* of 1839–42 was about more than opium. China had a deep suspicion of all outside 'barbarians'; it insisted that trade with the outside world be conducted only through Canton (modern-day Guangzhou) and only on its own capricious terms. Britain thought it had a right to trade freely, and a God-given right to pummel with cannon any nation that thought otherwise. A clash between the West's traders, led by Britain, and an inward-looking Qing dynasty was inevitable. When it came, China's forces were humbled" ("1898 and All That – A Brief History of Hong Kong," *Economist*, 28 June 1997, 20; emphasis in the original).

11 Shen Wei-tai, *China's Foreign Policy, 1839–1860* (New York: Columbia University Press, 1932), 87–8; quoted in Seagrave, *Dragon Lady*, 46.

12 This well-recorded fact continues to be misrepresented in publications that seek to

capitalize on the global attention Hong Kong is currently receiving. Carol A. Breckenridge, for instance, writes of "this fragile transitional moment, when *the island city of Hong Kong* will move from being a colony of the British Empire into the orbit of the People's Republic of China" ("Editor's Note," *Public Culture* 9 [spring 1997], v; my emphasis).

13 *Annual Report on Hong Kong* (Hong Kong: Hong Kong Government, 1997), preface. Patten's words were widely cited in the Chinese media.

14 This facade included taking regular walks in Hong Kong's most crowded districts, participating in question-and-answer sessions at Legislative Council meetings, and hosting phone-in programs on the radio.

15 See Ming K. Chan, interviewed in *Xin bao* (*Hong Kong Economic Journal*), US ed., 21 June 1997, 6. Chan warns that distrust of the PRC government should not make Hong Kong people unconditionally accept colonialism or believe that British rule in the past was benign. Chan is the editor of the book series Hong Kong Becoming China: The Transition to 1997, published by M. E. Sharpe, Armonk, NY.

16 See Mark Roberti, *The Fall of Hong Kong: China's Triumph and Britain's Betrayal* (New York: J. Wiley, 1996), 10–11.

17 Ibid., 305; my emphasis.

18 When using the word "decolonized" to describe post-British Hong Kong, I am referring primarily to Britain's departure from its former colony rather than to Hong Kong's gaining independence in the technical sense of decolonization. As mentioned a couple of paragraphs above, because of Britain's 1972 decision not to oppose Hong Kong's being taken off the UN list of colonies slated for decolonization, Hong Kong was technically precluded from ever having a chance to be decolonized/independent. It was, properly speaking, never decolonized but simply transferred from one governing power to another.

19 Younger generations of Chinese intellectuals have been capitalizing on this logic to promote a chauvinistic brand of Chinese nationalism. The most prominent examples are two books, by Song Qiang, Zhang Zangzang, and Qiao Bian, *Zhongguo keyi shuo bu* [China Can Say No] and Song Qiang *et al.*, *Zhongguo haishi neng shuo bu* [China Can Still Say No] (Hong Kong: Ming Pao Publishing, 1996). For a related discussion, see my comments in "Can One Say No to China?" *New Literary History*, 28 (winter 1997): 147–51. Elsewhere, I have also substantially criticized the tradition of cultural essentialism that is implicit in the Chinese government's defensive and dismissive attitude toward foreigners "meddling in Chinese internal affairs"; see, for instance, "We Endure, Therefore We Are: Survival, Governance, and Zhang Yimou's *To Live*," *South Atlantic Quarterly*, 95 (fall 1996): 1039–64.

20 According to the Sino-British Joint Declaration, signed in 1984, "Hong Kong's current capitalist system and lifestyle will remain unchanged for fifty years."

21 See, for example, Parker, "City on a Hill," 49; and Fareed Zakaria, "Who Will Change Whom?" *Newsweek*, 7 July 1997, 46. See also the more nuanced accounts "How Hong Kong Can Change China" and "The Hong Kong Handover: All Eyes on China," *Economist*, 28 June 1997, 13–14, 19–22. The cover picture of the latter journal gives the gist of these typical readings: A PRC tank is face to face with the lone figure of a man, reminding us of the world-famous picture of the brave resister halting a tank during the Tiananmen crackdown in 1989, but this time the "resister" is holding up a bag of money in one hand and a pair of scales

(signifying the rule of law) in the other. The caption reads: "How Hong Kong Can Change China."

22 See my discussion of the masculinist implications of this type of argument in "Things, Common/Places, Passages of the Port City: On Hong Kong and Hong Kong Author Leung Ping-kwan," *differences*, 5 (fall 1993): 179–204.

23 Roberti describes this succinctly: "Like the United States government in the nineteenth century, the colonial administration maintained a strict laissez-faire economic policy. It kept taxes low, bureaucratic red tape to a minimum, and often one eye closed to counterfeiting of foreign products and other unscrupulous practices. It provided only the most basic social services and emphasized job creation. Land was provided and infrastructure built to enable private enterprise to expand. The policy worked because standards of living rose steadily and because the predominantly Chinese population relied on family, rather than government, for support" (*The Fall of Hong Kong*, 12).

24 Erlanger, "Uncle Sam's New Role," A8.

25 " 'Hong Kong people ruling Hong Kong ,' in the end, will actually mean a few very rich people ruling Hong Kong. This system is not at all dissimilar to colonial rule at the time the Joint Declaration was signed. The trouble, though, is that Hong Kong has developed a popular political will since then, and China's 1984 promise that Hong Kong's political system would remain 'unchanged' for half a century now looks more like a curse than a blessing" ("The Hong Kong Handover," 21–2).

26 A joke circulating around Beijing recently sums up the situation: "Presidents Bill Clinton, Boris Yeltsin, and Jiang Zemin are each driving down a road and their three cars approach an intersection. Mr. Clinton turns right without signaling. So does Mr. Yeltsin. But Mr. Jiang hesitates and asks his passenger, Deng Xiaoping, which way to go. 'Signal left and turn right,' Deng replies" (Seth Faison, "A Great Tiptoe Forward: Beijing Talks of More Private Enterprise but Seems Unlikely to Stay Out of Its Way," *New York Times*, 17 Sept. 1997, A1).

27 Wang Zhangwei and Luo Jinyi, "Xunzhao disanzhong jiaodu de Xianggang lishi shuxie" [In Search of a Third Perspective for Writing Hong Kong History], *Ming Pao Monthly*, June 1997, 21; my translation.

28 Thomas L. Friedman, "Hang Seng Salvation," *New York Times*, 3 July 1997, A15.

29 Tung Chee-hwa, Hong Kong's chief executive, appealed to this ethnic unity in his inaugural speech in the following manner: "After 156 years of separation, Hong Kong and China are whole again. This is a solemn, stately and proud moment. We are here today to announce to the world, in our language, that Hong Kong has entered a new era" (Maggie Farley and Rone Tempest, "New Era Rises in Hong Kong," *Los Angeles Times*, 1 July 1997, A12).

30 In his speech before the flag ceremony, Prince Charles of Great Britain concluded with this statement: "We shall not forget you, and we shall watch with the closest interest as you embark on this new era of your remarkable history" (ibid.).

Chapter 16

Japan and East Asia

Sandra Buckley

As a nation intent on defining itself as at once modern and Japanese, Japan was constantly confronted with the relationality of each of these emergent conditions to an apparently hegemonic "west." Japan's strategies of colonization and empire building functioned both as a measure of sameness and of difference. The practices and policies of Japanese colonialism were a primary site of staging for the debate over westernization (becoming equal and the same) versus modernization (becoming equal and different) as the defining dynamic of "becoming Japanese" in the international geopolitical theater of the late nineteenth and early twentieth centuries. In 1887 the Minister of Foreign Affairs stated that "we have to establish a new European-style empire on the edge of Asia" (Tsurumi, 1984: 277). The dilemma of a modernizing Japan is captured in these words: Japan is not European – even if westernization was a reasonable strategy it would always be limited to achieving "the style" of Europe – and Japan's modernization can be understood as much as a process of de-asianization as a process of westernization – "on the edge" of Asia and not of Asia – and yet still intimately bound to Japan's desire to colonize and govern in Asia. A core focus of postcolonial work in Japan has been the interrogation of the complicity between the expansionist mechanisms of the colonial project and the bordering mechanisms of demarcating a modern Japanese identity.

By the 1960s the first substantial postwar histories of Japan's colonial policies and actions were being researched and published (Myers and Peattie, 1984). The historical works produced over the 1960s and 1970s were unquestionably postcolonial in simple chronological terms. Those written by scholars of Japan's excolonies, for example Taiwanese or Korean historians, were also the work of postcolonial scholars. However, this does not mean that these works were necessarily postcolonial as that term will be developed here. The historical projects of this period can largely be described as retrievalist – a historical self-accounting for the present. Another strong dynamic evident over this period might be termed an aberrationist strategy of historical production. In works where Japan's imperialism is presented as an aberration there is often an attempt to identify the juncture (and causes) from which Japan could be said to have taken the wrong path. Implicit in this process is the identification of a missed direction – an historical precedent of a healthy democratic Japanese body politic. In those cases where the aberrationist model is transferred onto the history of the colonies it mutates into a "distortionist" model that tracks the impact of Japan's colonial presence and policies on the indigenous potential for "healthy" development. Within both these models the force of imperial Japan is reproduced as a contagion whose symptoms are to be retroactively diagnosed as a crucial step in eradicating the risk of dormant malignancy or inoculating the contemporary body politic. While the value of this period of intensive historical work cannot be underestimated it should be distinguished from the work of the postcolonial space it preceded, even precipitated.

In *Totality and Infinity* Levinas writes:

> If it [history] claims to integrate myself and the other within an impersonal spirit, this alleged integration is cruelty and injustice . . . Though of myself I am not exterior to history, I do find in the Other a point that is absolute with regard to history – but not by amalgamating with the Other, but in speaking with him. History is worked over by the ruptures of history . . . When man truly approaches the Other he is uprooted from history. (Levinas, 1979)

The integrative dynamics of historiography and the universalizing drive of a modernizing project such as Japan's, even (especially) in its colonial manifestation, operate symbiotically. The alternative proposed by Levinas can function as a clear statement of the postcolonial space – a space of "approach," of "speaking with." This is a space of "working over": of shared risks and potentials for parties in encounter with one another. I will develop this essay around a preference for understanding the postcolonial as such a space of "working over." As this essay cannot be all-inclusive, I will begin with a focus on specific processes of the distinctive Ainu and Okinawan projects of "working over" in the 1980s and 1990s and then trace these as they cascade into other areas of postcolonial space.

There is now a strong case for the recognition of the claims of both Ainu and Okinawans to a postcolonial relationship to contemporary Japan. Traditionally excluded from the colonial histories of Japan, the Ainu and Okinawans have each had to challenge the formative assumptions that delimited the boundaries of the unfolding space of modern Japanese identity – the ideological heartland of the expansive territories of Japan's colonial empire. In 1922 the "father of Okinawan studies," Iha Fuyu, described the unifying project of Japanese identity formation in the colonial period:

> Until half a century ago, the Japanese state was a blood state . . . But with the advent of Meiji, the Ryukyuans [Okinawans], who had moved to the southern islands and become a variant race, entered this group. Not only that, in recent years,

Malayans, Chinese, and Koreans have also entered. Now it is the time for Japanese politicians to be tolerant of these different nations of completely differing origins and attempt to create one great citizenry. This is, in fact, the greatest period since our national history began. But the Japanese who have just achieved this political unification are going one step further and attempting to unify it spiritually. (Siddle, 1998: 126)

The "our" of "our national history" is for Iha already a "Japaneseness" inclusive of the people of Okinawa. His understanding of when this history "began" was necessarily defined by the imperialist state Shinto narrative (itself a creation of the modern period) that would trace this unified identity back to godly origins. Recent research has however identified a much more recent consolidation of language, culture, and ethnicity in the eighteenth century as the beginning of a notion of a unified Japanese identity. This work refuses simple narratives of progression, entangling premodern and modern (Naoki, 1993).

It is not a coincidence that language, culture, and ethnicity became pillars of the strategies of unification alluded to (and performed) by Iha. Standardized language, increased literacy, compulsory education, a centralized curriculum, the incorporation of ethical and cultural development into school and public programs, and the implementation of national agendas for health and sanitation, all made a crucial contribution to the modernizing goal of the elimination of difference (and dissent) during the early decades of nation building. These same strategies were then extended into colonial management as powerful tools in the implementation of assimilation policies. From the outset the Meiji government put in place an efficient colonial administrative and policy structure and its first charges were the governance of Hokkaido and Okinawa.

According to the dominant histories of Japan's modernization both the Ainu and Okinawans were sovereign subjects when the Meiji Constitution was promulgated (1899). Many Ainu and Okinawans reject this version of their island histories. Retold outside the constraints and silences of the dominant history these two distinct experiences of the colonial encounter with Japan discredit the authority of the treaties and annexation processes that justified the unproblematic categorization of Hokkaido and Okinawa as *naichi* (internal colonies) and Japanese sovereign territory. The telling of a history of Ainu and Wajin (Japanese) contact dating from the thirteenth century, together with details of trade and territorial agreements negotiated as early as the sixteenth century, challenge the original Meiji claim to Ezochi (the pre-Meiji name) as *terra nullus* in 1869 (Hanazaki, 1997). Similarly, careful research has consolidated diplomatic and other international archival records that destabilize the legitimacy of Japan's 1879 claim to Okinawa as a prefecture (Tomiyama, 1996).

Located at the geographic extremes of the Japanese archipelago, both island territories were the source of strategic anxiety. However, their incorporation as "internal" to Japan exceeded strategic considerations and flowed over into essential processes of the defining of the "Japaneseness" of this emerging modern nation-state. By the turn of the century there was a marked difference in the historical narratives evolving in the space between these two marginal populations and the metropolitan center (Hashimoto, 1997). The high incidence of illness, prevalence of poverty, and decimation of the sociocultural fabric of Ainu communities were not seen as symptoms of centuries of exploitation, compounded by the damage of contemporary colonial policies, but were instead widely interpreted within a Social Darwinist model as evidence of an inferior and weaker race. It was considered the responsibility of the "modern" Japan to save the "not-yet-modern" Ainu. A romantic and popular urban-based mythology of the Ainu as a disappearing race (*horobiyuku minzoku*) was refigured into policy as the Protection Act of 1899 (Kim, 1997: 110–11). Assimilation was seen as synonymous with a process of civilizing–assisted passage into the modern.

In stark contrast, Iha, together with the influential Japanese scholar of folklore, Yanagita Kunio, argued that the Ryukyuans [Okinawans] were a divergent branch of the Japanese "race" and that "lost" elements of Japanese culture were preserved in Okinawan custom and ritual. If Okinawan culture could be understood as a repository of an earlier mode of "Japaneseness," then the problem for modernization was one of eradicating differences created by a long period of divergence – a process of cultural (not racial) sanitization (Hashimoto, 1997: 81–2). Iha himself conducted a lecture tour of Okinawa, tellingly entitled "Race Hygiene" (Siddle, 1998: 126). If Okinawa was to be (re)incorporated as an organ of the modern Japanese body politic it must pose no threat of contagion. The underlying racial assumptions of the "sanitizing" policies of assimilation implemented in Okinawa and Hokkaido were profoundly different but the consequences were devastating in each case.

Work in the postcolonial space on the Ainu and Okinawan encounters with Japan has focused attention on their essential role in the mapping out of a modern Japanese identity. Iha assumed that a modern Japanese nation would have to move beyond a "blood state" in order to unify the racially and ethnically diverse populations of its colonial territories. However, at the time he made this statement the Ainu had already been reduced to a mere 2 percent of the Hokkaido population as a result of aggressive settlement and continued decimation of the population through illness and poverty. Okinawa had also seen the first waves of migration to southeast Asia, Micronesia, and Central America. Faced with the harsh realities of colonial economic and land reforms and yet denied the right of full political participation (a quarantining of the center against the influence of the margins), many Okinawans voted with their feet. By 1935, 15 percent of Okinawans were living offshore (Taira, 1997: 157).

Although Hokkaido was officially designated as "internal" territory, the inclusivity of this relation only extended to the Japanese settler colonists. The Ainu were excluded under the Protection Act. Their identity was defined in terms of absolute difference. For a modernizing Japan, the Ainu came to represent not a premodern Japan but the nonmodern and non-Japaneseness. For the Ainu, assimilation was not a process of "becoming Japanese" but assuming the condition of "non-Japaneseness." Okinawa was also designated as "internal." But, unlike the Ainu, the relationship of Okinawans to "Japaneseness" was defined by proximity. If the distance differentiating Japanese and Ainu was a space of absolute incommensurability, the proximity of Japanese and Okinawans was presented as a space of potentiality – "becoming Japanese." Yanagita conflated center versus periphery with new and hybrid versus old and pure in his search for an ethnographic heartland of identity in the southern islands. It was the literal distance of Okinawa from the metropolitan centre that was an essential element of the pure or originary "Japaneseness" he located there. The seeking out of a pure space, prior to the modern, was itself an invention of the modern (Hashimoto, 1997: 81–5). Ironically, the end point of the colonial project of "becoming Japanese" for Okinawans was at best always a state of "not-yetness," negotiated through their performance "as" Japanese (Tomiyama, 1996: 148–9).

The assumption of any equivalency between performance "as" Japanese and "Japaneseness" was exploded for Okinawans in the final stages of the war. The contingency of the relation of proximity upon the necessities of the center was made explicit when Okinawa was confronted with its expendability: 73,000 Okinawans died in the Battle of Okinawa, a battle the emperor had been advised was futile. The tragedy of the Okinawans who committed "mass suicide" rather than surrender (acting "as" Japanese) only became widely known decades after the war, along with other horror stories of retreating Japanese troops terrorizing and killing innocent Okinawans (Taira, 1997: 169–70; Siddle, 1998: 131). In the surrender Japan ceded Okinawa to the US for an undesignated period but retained residual sovereignty. Although the majority of Okinawans campaigned for reversion to Japan, this was partly a reflection of the restrictions placed on any autonomy of movement under US control. There was also a perception that the extension of the postwar Japanese constitution to Okinawa would mark a dramatic improvement over the limited rights and freedoms experienced under the US administration. Since reversion in 1972 there has been a gradually expanding movement for greater Okinawan autonomy. The presence in Okinawa of over 75 percent of US troops based in Japan, the continued "occupation" of 20 percent of Okinawan land for US military purposes, the refusal of appropriate retroactive compensation for appropriated lands, high levels of unemployment, and low average household incomes are seen as contemporary reminders that Okinawa remains "not yet" Japanese (Taira, 1997: 172).

The disconnectedness of the chronological periodization of prewar, wartime, and postwar distorts the nontemporal and nonlinear continuities and complicities of the encounter with Japan. Approximately 585,000 of the 1,354,000 resident aliens documented in Japan in 1994–5 were self-identified as both permanent residents and as members of households that had resided in Japan or its colonies prior to Japan's defeat in 1945 (Tezuka, 1997: 134–5). The extent of population movement – voluntary and forced – between Japan and its colonies has been widely unrecognized and contributed to a myth of insularity and homogeneity. By 1937 the population of Saipan in the Japanese Micronesian Protectorate was 96 percent Japanese and Okinawan, while 300,000 Koreans resided in Osaka in 1940, and some 400,000 Japanese had to be repatriated from northeastern China at the end of the war. We still know very little of the interaction in daily life and the community conditions that existed between non-Japanese and Japanese both in Japan and in the colonies. The histories that have been written remain predominantly concerned with the instruments of colonial rule and military expansion. The stories of the mundane remain largely untold, even taboo, for the intimacy of the detail of the everyday easily borders on nostalgia – an uncomfortable emotion for colonizer and colonized.

Significant numbers of immigrants, legal and illegal, have arrived in Japan, and Tokyo in particular, over the last two decades. This is consistent with the contemporary pattern of transnational labor migration into global cities like Tokyo (Sassen, 1993). The majority of the recently arrived and established ethnic communities in and around Tokyo today are directly linked to the colonial history of this global center whose urban fringes they now inhabit: for example, Chinese, Koreans, Malays, Filipinos/as, Thai, Micronesian-Japanese. While marginalized on the urbanscape of contemporary Japan, these communities are central to the economic landscape. Contemporary policies of immigrant labor, naturalization, minority education, and ethnic services are increasingly being analyzed within the postcolonial space in an attempt to undo the bracketing effect of "postwar." This ever present (if sometimes silent) prefix of contemporary "Japan" effectively cuts across the historical landscape isolating the period after 1945 from the official policies and practices, as well as the individual and community experiences of the war and prewar periods. The pre- and post- prefixes also function to focus attention on the war as rupture, a gulf separating the before from the after, an aberration. The work of the postcolonial space entangles the movement of people and the settling and unsettling of communities across the artificial divide of this bracketing.

Of the 700,000 Koreans in Japan today the majority do not qualify for naturalization and continue to self-identify as either North Korean or South Korean affiliated. First and second generation Korean residents in Japan have been described as defining their identity within a doubled process of oppositionality – not North Korean or not South Korean *and* not Japanese (Kim, 1998). The processes of making visible the lives of these generations were closely linked to both the historical project of "working over" dominant narratives of Koreans in Japan, and the telling and recording of personal narratives of hardship and exclusion. The postcolonial space of the 1980s and 1990s has continued to support these projects while also working with a new generation of Koreans in Japan who are struggling to renegotiate the possibility of an identity of in-betweeness (Osawa, 1998; So, 1996). This shift from more familiar strategies of identity politics does not represent a desire to erase difference but a desire to move away from a purely oppositional relationship. This new movement disrupts the strategies of positionality that underlie the claiming of an identity – a process of territorializing that seeks stable, bounded ground. At the same time that it is a move away from a Korean identity staked in historical and cultural ground elsewhere, it is also a proposal of something other than "becoming Japanese" and as such poses an alternative to the condition of "not-yetness". Sometimes described as "not at homeness" it is a move beyond nostalgia or longing for a "homeland" as the primary motivation or site of identity formation (Osawa, 1998: 49–53).

There are many within Japan's minority communities who are fearful that a younger generation may be too hasty in its characterization of an oppositional identity politics as a disempowering adoption of victim status or a condition of indulgent nostalgia. In this context the desire for a more fluid and deterritorialized politics of identity is seen as premature in the continued absence of any willingness on the part of the Japanese to acknowledge responsibility and offer appropriate compensation for acts undertaken during the colonial and imperialist period. In this regard, the demand for recognition, apology, and compensation for *ianfu* (comfort women) is the case that has gained the broadest international attention. The history of *ianfu* has been drawn out of obscurity and woven into common knowledge over the 1980s and 1990s.

The exact number of young girls and women forced into this wartime sex trade is unknown, but estimates based on existing documents and oral histories have sometimes been as high as 130,000. With many of the survivors now elderly and in poor health there is an added urgency to the campaign for appropriate compensation. The documenting of personal histories has played a central role in the process of gaining international support and recognition (Yun Chung-ok *et al.*, 1992). Historians and other academics, most notably Yoshimi Yoshiaki, have played a key role in uncovering a paper trail of official wartime documents (Yoshimi Yoshiaki, 1992). The Military Comfort Women Action Network (*Jugun Ianfu Mondai Kodo Nettowaku*) is one example of the community and activist based organizations that have developed international networks in collaboration with academics to produce conferences and publications as well as working papers and petitions to governments.

The *ianfu* issue has developed in an area of postcolonial space where the theoretical work of gender and sexuality intersects with race and ethnicity. Feminism and queer theory have done much to shape the postcolonial topography in Japan. There has been an ongoing critique of the transformation of the Asian traffic in women under the influence of significant shifts in the flow of economic, political, and cultural currency in the region over the last several decades. This analysis has flowed over into both research and activist support projects focused on the increasing problems associated with the growing population of Asian "mail order" brides in Japanese rural communities (Ito, 1996). Another area of focus has been the challenge to the "inevitability" of sexual violence and prostitution at the edges of the US military machine across Asia (Taira, 1997: 170–1). The official response to the global AIDS epidemic met with a concentrated campaign from gay communities and other groups concerned with the homophobic and racist undertones of government information campaigns and policy. The official lines of "defense" where drawn against an external threat. AIDS was designated an infection originating elsewhere and carried into Japan by foreign bodies. The language of infection and sanitization was disturbingly familiar (Buckley, 1997).

The AIDS campaigns of the early 1990s were coincident with the first stage of the internationalization boom. A flood of pop-academic books, radio and television talkshows, and lead articles in major newspapers and magazines heralded the "multiculturalization" and "diversification" of Japan as the way to a viable and healthy future. The same newspaper or talkshow might have carried another story on the mass deportation of illegal Thai prostitutes or the controversy over a call for compulsory AIDS testing of all foreigners applying for Japanese visas. The immigration crackdown and demonizing of foreign sex workers and gays were pulling popular opinion in one direction while the internationalization boom preached diversity and tolerance. The tension produced by these contradictory currents has become a significant area of postcolonial work over the 1990s (Kang, 1998: 82–5).

The space of postcolonial work in Japan is not simply oppositional to strategies of internationalization. Artificial and tired boundaries between theory and practice have been increasingly "worked over" in the transnational, transdisciplinary, and trans-skilling environments of internationalized forums of postcolonial collaborative projects. Ainu and Okinawans have actively pursued new international trajectories that take identity beyond the limitations of nation and race. Ainu have increasingly located their work in the multiple forums of a rapidly emerging global alliance of indigenous peoples (Hanazaki, 1997: 103–6; Siddle, 1997: 34–43). In Okinawa, an Uchinanchu (an older local term for the people of the islands) movement is pursuing an identity that exceeds the physical space of the islands to draw diasporic Okinawans into a new borderless community (Taira, 1997: 167). In both instances Ainu and Okinawans are undoing the work of identity from the margins of "Japaneseness." One consequence of internationalization in the postcolonial space in Japan is the move towards strategies of identity that exceed nation and race and therefore exceed the designated condition of "not yetness."

If there is an engagement with the processes of internationalization there is also a cautious and continuous "working over" of its shifting conceptualization at each new site of articulation: immigration policy, academic research funding, television news, print media editorials, the massive book market in pop-academic texts, comic books, advertising, and soap dramas (Kang, 1998: 82–5). Some critics have cautioned that the rhetoric of internationalization is haunted by the modernization versus westernization debate earlier this century. Internationalization can be mobilized as a potentially unmarked (not western, not Asian) designation of a space for the renegotiation of Japan's place in a global world order. Much recent postcolonial work suggests that in its popularized usage internationalization has come to stand in for the most recent manifestation of the processes of production of "Japaneseness" (Hashimoto, 1997: 78–9; Iyotani and Sugihara, 1996).

The rapid insertion of the concepts of ethnicity and multiculturalism into the space of the popular (fashion, television, advertising, food, travel) is receiving close scrutiny. There is a growing concern that in the staging of Japan's internationalization, multiculturalism and diversity are functioning as a cultural landscape for the performance of a newly tolerant Japan. However, for the "tolerated" this is only one more manifestation of a relationality of difference measured still in degrees of proximity to "Japaneseness." The core assumption of calls for "the cultural diversification of the Japanese" or the "becoming multicultural of Japan" is not the elimination of difference but the transformation of the relations of difference (Iyotani and Sugihara, 1996). If the 1990s have seen an intense multiculturalization of both elite and popular consumer culture in Japan, the same decade has witnessed a concerted move to contain the ethnic diversification of the immigrant laborforce. By the mid-1990s approximately 1,700,000 non-Japanese were resident in Japan. This figure includes an estimated 300,000 to 400,000 undocumented illegal immigrants. By international standards the level of foreign workers in Japan is low – slightly more than 1 percent compared to 4 percent in the UK, 5 percent in Germany, and 6 percent in France (Tezuka, 1997: 134–6). Even so, by the mid-1980s the Japanese government had become so concerned with what it perceived as high numbers of Middle Eastern and Asian legal and illegal immigrants that it sought an alternative closer "to home" to deal with the ongoing need to fill a domestic labour shortfall in "3K" jobs (*kitsui* – tough, *kiken* – dangerous, *kitanai* – dirty). Japan attempted to self-select for ethnicity by liberalizing access to working visas for overseas Japanese. Descendants of Japanese immigrant communities were encouraged to "return" to Japan to work. The intention was to attract a population of low-income workers of Japanese ethnicity, particularly from the weaker economies of Brazil, Peru, and Micronesia.

The experience of Brazilian-Japanese in Japan exposes the constructedness of the notion of an intrinsic "Japaneseness." It is estimated that up to 10 percent of the male working-age Brazilian-Japanese population was located in Japan by the late-1990s. Proud of their independent heritage, this community considers their identity enriched by the Brazilian elements of their culture and are frustrated by derogatory characterizations of a Brazilian contamination of an original Japaneseness. Popular caricatures of messy, noisy, demonstrative, lovers of loud music and dancing, etc. are the discriminatory expressions of disappointment at the difference that indeed locates this immigrant population in greater proximity to some other ethnic communities than to any inherent Japaneseness (Yamashita-Tei, 1998). The everyday life of Japan's multi-ethnic communities is kept at a safe distance, effectively quarantined, from the staging of a multicultural Japaneseness, but much recent postcolonial work has stepped into this space between the image of the tolerant Japanese and the lived experiences of the tolerated communities of established and recent immigrants (Komai, 1995; Iyotani and Sugihara, 1996). The terms ethnicity, identity, diversity, and community might have first surfaced in ad-copy in Japan, but they are now the familiar vocabulary of much academic writing on contemporary Japanese society. The work of the postcolonial space has extended into the conditions of employment and daily life of Japan's minority ethnic communities in a rapidly expanding project of interdisciplinary ethnographic studies grounded in close community collaboration.

The conflation of nation (*kokka*), nationals (*kokumin*), and race (*minzoku*) in Japan's modernizing processes rendered these terms so overcoded that they were shelved by postwar scholars wishing to avoid any accusation of lingering nationalist sentiment. With the popularization of *nihinjinron* (theories of Japanese uniqueness) over the 1960s and 1970s, the language of cultural uniqueness and homogeneity replaced the tainted prewar language of superiority. Seeking nonpolitico-economic rationalizations for the so-called "Japanese miracle," US and Japanese experts alike resorted to theories of cultural difference, but there have been many critics of the thin line dividing cultural accident from racial determinism. Over the period of rapid economic growth Japanese identity came to function as a cultural equivalent of barriers to entry in trade. However, the popularization of the terms ethnicity, identity, and diversity has seen the first attempts to rearticulate the conditions of possibility of nation and national identity. It may be significant that it is the untranslated forms of these terms (rendered as *esunishitei*, *aidenteitei*, and *daibaashitei*) that now regularly appear coupled with the previously avoided *kokka* (nation) and *kokumin* (nationals). The association with the contemporary and foreign character of these terms appears to have liberated the tainted Japanese words from the burden of history.

A multicultural and tolerant Japan is considered by some as a historically uncontaminated ground for the revalidation of nation and national identity beyond the limits of a relation of proximity – "Japaneseness" versus "not yetness." It is not unusual for works in the postcolonial space to now explore the possibilities of a nationhood not bound to racial homogeneity but to multiplicity (Hamaguchi, 1997; Inoue *et al.*, 1997a). Sceptics, however, point to the continued absence of substantial reforms to a juridico-legal system that still sets consanguinity as the core determining criterion of national identity. Others underline the corporatist and interventionist tone of the language often associated with official multiculturalist projects. The special issue of the journal *Impaction* entitled "Violence as Culture, Culture as Violence" explored this harsher side of the cultural politics of diversification (vol. 99, 1996). Another rapidly proliferating strategy has been the avoidance of nation as the ground of identity formation through a shift to the city. In this approach the density of contemporary urbanscapes is presented as the site of inevitable movement towards diversification driven by global forces rather than internally managed policies or designer-marketed trends. The city emerges as the direct zone of impact of global forces on local communities. The move from nation to city and community seems to encourage an erasure of the influence of state and policy. There are some who caution that this erasure is not symptomatic of a weakening state but of a failure to recognize the flexibility and hybridizing potential of the mechanisms and interests of state (Karatani, 1999; Kang, 1998: 193–233).

There have been a number of anticipated endings to "postwar Japan" – end of the Occupation, the Olympics, Osaka Expo, death of the Showa emperor, declaration of the new Heisei era – but these have each been failed moments. There has been an assumption that the accumulation of historical events over time will eventually distance Japan sufficiently from the "rupture" of the war, and it will eventually become something beyond postwar. More recently, however, there has been a shift away from this linear temporal configuration towards a spatial conceptualization – postwar as a space dominated (colonized) by American interests – and identifying the move out of the postwar as a move out of the sphere of influence of the US. Internationalization has come to designate a movement of becoming unAmerican, and the hidden player in this global drama is Asia (Kang, 1998: 85). It is not a coincidence that the internationalization boom saw the publication of a number of bestsellers with titles such as *When Japan Becomes Asian*. Newspaper and magazine articles in the mid-1990s that carried the buzzwords "multicultural," "diversification," "world-ification," etc. located Japan as the global power *in* Asia (if not *as* Asian).

However, any move towards Asia has proven far from uncomplicated or transparent. Oe Kenzaburo has written that:

> in the war of aggression . . . we lost the right to be a part of Asia and have continued to live without recovering that right. Without that rehabilitation we shall never be able to eradicate the ambivalence in our attitude toward our neighbours, the feeling that our relationships aren't real. (Oe, 1995)

For Oe there is an ethical breach that prevents Japan from inhabiting an Asian or global future and keeps it in a tired orbit around the US. For many Asians the unrealness of these relations has only been exacerbated by over two decades of incremental campaigns for the reform of Japanese school textbooks in what many see as a whitewashing or "sanitizing" of Japan's aggression against Asia during the war. The nomination of the Emperor Showa as "Man of the Century" by Prime Minister Obuchi in 1999 was an extreme example of this disjuncture of "realities." However, the nomination rides on a renewed wave of populist revisionism. Fujioka Nobukatsu's so-called "Liberal Historiography Research Group" represents the intensity of the affective response to the accumulative impact of the processes of "working over." Fujioka and the "liberals" promote a rejuvenation of pride in a Japanese national identity and reject much of the accepted historical record of Japanese aggression against Asia as a negative distortion (Fujioka *et al.*, 1996). Others have stopped short of the "liberal" rejection of any call for war apology, but share the concern that Japan has been trapped in a culture of defeat and "twisted" by a peace constitution imposed by an occupying military force. For example, Kato Norihiro does not deny Japan's war

329

responsibility, but proposes that the freedom for Japan to mourn its own war dead is an essential prerequisite to a "healthy" nation(alism) on which Japan can build an ethical and functional relation with Asia (Kato, 1997). Kato collapses the process of individual mourning into a process of collective national healing, but this collapse is only possible because of the confusion of memory and memorializing. The unifiying mechanism of the memorial and the monument is the public performance/production of shared memory. This is achieved at the price of erasure of the intimate solitude of memory and mourning. The ostensible goal of "making whole" through the memorializing project cannot accommodate the diversity of experiences and memories that have already been "worked over" in contemporary Japan and that refuse to resettle into a singular sovereign past or future. Memorializing is by nature exclusionary and so monuments are the frequent site of vandalism and protest. The grief of others, like the singularity of nation, can only be imagined.

In the postcolonial space of "working over," what is at stake is not the past. The intention is not the territorialization and hierarchization of what has come before but instead a process of proliferation – "adding-on," not detracting, subtracting, or excluding. An expansive strategy of multiplication and diversification offers an alternative to the management of a past–present axis through narrative mechanisms of contraction and constraint. The past exceeds itself as the axis shifts from a chronological progression to a multiplicity of "approaches." The space of postcolonial work is a space of encounter – of "speaking with." It is not a sanitized or quarantined space but a space of exposure and "interfection." The result is a spatiotemporal zone of entangled memories that cannot be reduced to the sum of the parts (Japan), an intimate zone of proliferating pasts and potential futures, a possible trajectory beyond the postwar towards a Japan positively "not at home with itself."

References

Buckley, Sandra. (1997). *Broken Silences: Voices of Japanese Feminism*. Berkeley: University of California Press.

Fujioka Nobukatsu *et al*. (1996). *Kyokasho ga oshienai rekishi* (The History Textbooks Don't Teach), Sankei shinbunsha, Tokyo.

Hamaguchi Eshun. (1997). "Kokusaika no naka no nihonbunka" (Japanese Culture in Internationalization), in Inoue *et al*. (1997a: 39–70).

Hanazaki Kohei. (1997). "Ainumoshiri no kaifuku: nihon no senjuminzoku ainu to nihon kokka no taiainu seisaku" (The Revival of Ainumoshiri: Japan's Indigenous Ainu and the Japanese Nation's Anti-Ainu policies), in Inoue *et al*. (1997b: 93–108).

Hashimoto Mitsuru. (1997). "Chuo to chiho" (Centre and Periphery), in Inoue *et al*. (1997a: 71–88).

Inoue Shun *et al*., eds. (1998). *Minzoku, kokka, esunishitei* (Race, Nation and Ethnicity), Gendai shakaigaku (Modern Sociology Series), vol. 24, Iwanami shoten, Tokyo.

——. (1997a). *Nihon bunka no shakaigaku* (Sociology of Japanese Culture), Gendai shakaigaku (Modern Sociology Series), vol. 23, Iwanami shoten, Tokyo.

——. (1997b). *Sabetsu to kyosei no shakaigaku* (Discrimination and Coexistance), Gendai shakaigaku (Modern Sociology Series), vol. 15, Iwanami shoten, Tokyo.

——. (1997c). *Toshi to toshika no shakaigaku* (Sociology of the City and Urbanization), Gendai shakaigaku (Modern Sociology Series), vol. 18, Iwanami shoten, Tokyo.

Ito Yuri. (1996). "Mohitotsu no kokusai rodo ido" (Another Wave of International Labour), in Iyotani and Sugihara, eds. (1996).

Iyotani Toshio. (1996). "Nihon no kokusaika to gaikokujin rodosha" (Foreign Workers and Japan's Internationalization), in Iyotani and Sugihara, eds. (1996).

Iyotani Toshio and Sugihara Toru, eds. (1996). *Nihon shakai to imin* (Japanese Society and Immigration), Gaikokujin teishu mondai (Series on Foreign Permanent Residents Issue), vol. 1. Tokyo: Meiseki shoten.

Kang Sang-Jung. (1998). *Orientarizumu no kaho e: kindai bunka hihan* (To the Limits of Orientalism: Critique of Modern Culture). Tokyo: Iwanami shoten.

Karatani Kojin. (1999). Untitled presentation to American Association of Asian Studies Meetings, Boston, March.

Kato Norihiro. (1997). *Haisengoron* (Theories of Post-Defeat Japan). Tokyo: Kodansha.

Kim Chongmi. (1997). "Kokumin kokka nihon to nihonjin imin" (Nationalist Japan and Japanese Immigration), in Inoue *et al.* (1997b: 109–32).

Kim Sok-Pom. (1998). "Ima zainichi ni totte kokuseki to wa nanika" (What is the Meaning of Citizenship for Korean Japanese Today), in *Sekai*, 10: 131–42.

Komai Hiroshi. (1995). *Migrant Workers in Japan*, trans. J. Wilkinson. London: Kegan Paul International.

Levinas, E. (1979). *Totality and Infinity*, trans. Alphonso Lingus. The Hague: Mertinus Nijhoff.

Morris-Suzuki, T. (1998). "Unquiet Graves: Kato Norihiro and the Politics of Mourning," *Japanese Studies*, 18, no. 1: 21–30.

Myers, R. H. and M. R. Peattie, eds. (1984). *The Japanese Colonial Empire, 1895–1945* Princeton: Princeton University Press.

Oe Kenzaburo. (1995). Article in *New York Times Magazine*, July 2.

Osawa Masachi. (1998). "Neshon to esunishitei" (Nation and Ethnicity), in Inoue *et al.* (1998: 27–66).

Sakai Naoki. (1991). *Voices of the Past: The Status of Language in 18th Century Japanese Discourse*. Ithaca: Cornell University Press.

Sassen, S. (1993). "Economic Internationalization: The New Migration in Japan and the United States," in *International Migration*, 31, no. 1: 73–99.

Siddle, R. (1997). "Ainu: Japan's Indigenous People," in Warner, ed. (1997).

——. (1998). "Colonialism and Identity in Okinawa before 1945," *Japanese Studies*, 18, no. 2: 117–33.

So Kyong-shik. (1996). "Tabunkashugi hihan" (Critique of Multiculturalism), in *Impaction*, 99: 95–112.

Taira Koji. (1997). "Troubled National Identity: Ryukyuans/Okinawans," in Warner, ed. (1997: 140–77).

Tezuka Kazuaki. (1997). "Nihon ni okeru gaikokujinrodosha no kyosei" (The Coexistance of Foreign Workers in Japan), in Inoue *et al.* (1997b: 133–54).

Tomiyama Ichiro. (1996). "Nashonarizumu, modanizumu, koroniarizumu: Okinawa kara no shiten" (Nationalsim, Modernism, Colonialism: The Perspective from Okinawa), in Iyotani and Sugihara, eds. (1996: 129–65).

Tsurumi, P. E. (1984). "Colonial Education in Korea and Taiwan," in Myers and Peattie (1984: 275–311).

Vasishth, A. (1997). "A Model Minority: The Chinese Community in Japan," in Warner, ed. (1997).

Warner, M., ed. (1997). *Japan's Minorities: The Illusion of Homogeneity*. London and New York: Routledge, 106–39.

Yamashita-Tei, K. (1998). "Brazilian-Japanese *Dekasegi* Communities," informal presentation to Centre for Cultural Studies Seminar series, University of California Santa Cruz, spring.

Yoshimi Yoshiaki. (1992). *Jugun ianfu shiryoshu* (Reference Materials on Military Comfort Women). Tokyo: Otsuki shoten.

Yun Chung-ok, *et al.* (1992). *Chosenjin josei ga mita ianfu mondai*. Tokyo: Sanichi shobo.

Chapter 17

Intellectuals, Theosophy, and Failed Narratives of the Nation in Late Colonial Java

Laurie J. Sears

Edward Said's work *Orientalism* has been immensely influential in developing scholarly thinking about representations of the Middle East and South Asia by Europeans and Americans, most effectively in the modern period. Said suggested that the Orient was not allowed to represent itself; it was always already represented as the Occident's "other" (1978: 2, 78). This representation was not innocent: colonial and postcolonial scholars were implicated in the production of the "Orient" as much as were colonial administrators, travelers, merchants, and artists. Said's identification of orientalist discourses has distinguished, in acknowledged Foucaultian fashion, ways in which the Orient and, more importantly, Islam have been presented to European and American audiences. Said focuses mainly on British, French, and American imperial attitudes, but his arguments can be extended to include Dutch colonial behavior in the Indies and especially Dutch attitudes toward Islam. This essay shows a particular example of orientalist discourse in the tensions of empire that influenced both European and Javanese representations of Javanese literary and historical traditions.[1] In this light, one reaction to Said's ideas is pertinent.

> A notable feature of *Orientalism* is that it examines the history of Western textualities about the non-West quite in isolation from how those textualities might have been received, accepted, modified, challenged, overthrown or reproduced by the intelligentsias of the colonized countries: not as an undifferentiated mass but as situated social agents impelled by our own conflicts, contradictions, distinct social and political locations of class, gender, region, religious affiliation, and so on. (Ahmad, 1992: 172)

Although insufficient as a criticism of Said's work on English literature, this observation cogently captures the intent of my project. I am interested in Dutch discourses about Java and Javanese traditions, but I am equally interested in showing how the actions of local elites and intelligentsias, "as situated social agents," were impelled by their own logics and needs, and how these activities intersected, obstructed, or occasionally meshed with Dutch efforts to represent and control Javanese literary and historical productions.

Dutch attitudes toward and representations of Javanese Mahabharata and Ramayana traditions also illuminate the ways in which Dutch scholars promoted these traditions at the expense of Islam (see Florida, 1995). I do not mean to say that the Dutch in any sense "invented" Javanese Mahabharata traditions conveyed in shadow theater performances (cf. Hobsbawm and Ranger, 1983). In fact, the number of Dutch scholars or administrators who could even understand these traditions was quantitatively insignificant even while the influence of those who could was qualitatively profound. Rather, Javanese patrons, authors, and performers of Javanese Mahabharata and Ramayana stories chose to write or perform their texts in ways that would allow them to accrue cultural capital according to the tastes and styles of the time.

In the 1920s and 1930s, for example, this meant that Javanese authors and patrons sought to show that shadow theater and the stories it conveyed were intrinsically mystical because of the values that were placed on mysticism by groups of Javanese and Dutch intellectuals influenced by Theosophical thought. The key representation of shadow theater in the 1930s was, in fact, written in Dutch by the noted scholar, military officer, businessman, and ruler Mangkunagara VII, head of the minor court in the city of Solo in central Java. The prince, greatly influenced by the ideas of Dutch Theosophists, suggested that every Javanese shadow play was a reenactment of a spiritual search for mystical knowledge ([orig. 1933] 1957). He offered these ideas with mixed intent in a learned lecture to a gathering of Dutch and Indies intellectuals: the prince realized that his audience of Dutch scholars and spiritual seekers placed value on mystical knowledge, and the mystical world was one realm in the era of high colonialism where Javanese could be superior or at least equal to the Dutch. This interpretation suggests that the Javanese prince was impelled by his own conflicts and contradictions, but it also shows that he negotiated knowledges on his own terms to accrue power and prestige in the hybrid Javanese-Dutch intellectual world of the interwar years.

The rise and subsequent disappearance of Javanese national consciousness into a pan-Indies nationalism that would result in the declaration of Indonesian independence in 1945 was interlaced with Mahabharata tales, Theosophical thought, and notions of human subjectivity brought to Java in the wake of the early twentieth-century Dutch Ethical policy. The Ethical Period began at the turn of the century when the Dutch Queen urged the colonial government to recognize its huge fiscal debt to the East Indies for all the wealth the exploitation of the colony had brought to Holland (see Penders, 1977: 157–64). In both colony and metropole, the autonomous human subject constituted by nineteenth-century European liberalism had been under attack since the emergence of the thought of Marx, Nietzsche, and Freud, but the devastation of the First World War – the use of science and technology for human destruction – poignantly questioned the connections between the autonomous human subject and nineteenth-century ideas of progress (Adas, 1989; Soetatmo, 1922). Freudian ideas suggested that individuals were much less in control of an autonomous "I" than had previously been thought. Freud and his colleagues brought the uncharted territory of the unconscious into both scholarly and popular discourses, diffusing notions of autonomy and agency that had been the bedrock of many nineteenth-century European philosophical speculations. This essay shows how Javanese intellectuals negotiated their shifting subjectivities and emerging national identities through the interlacing of Javanese and Dutch *mentalités* within discourses of modernity.

Doubts about progress and autonomous subjectivity were compounded in the early years of the twentieth century when the European colonial rulers began to realize the implications of evolutionary theory for their colonies. Education in European languages, available to limited numbers of local elites throughout the colonial world, made colonial subjects question their colonial status, and both colonial subjectivity and autonomous subjectivity came into question (Chatterjee, 1986). At the very moment the autonomous subject was fragmenting within through the opening of the unconscious, the theoretical structures that had produced the colonial subject were coming under attack from without. If subjects were indeed autonomous and Darwinian evolution inevitable, then Asians and Africans could also achieve autonomous subjectivity, threatening the rationale for colonial rule or, at least, anticipating its demise. If, on the other hand, autonomous subjectivity was little more than a fiction held together by the will of imperious or imperial egos, colonial hierarchies were also doomed to implode, turning conqueror into victim in the fragmentation of colonial desires. In the early part of this century, colonial communities often masked these mounting fears of disintegration by strengthening hierarchies of racial and ethnic distinctions and by an uneasy paternalism, the masters preferring to see their colonial subjects as children, possibly even bright ones, who in time – maybe decades, maybe centuries – could be prepared to receive the responsibilities of rule.

Looked at in another way, the contradictions of colonial subjectivity posed equally perplexing problems for those colonial subjects newly educated in European languages. As the recipients of Dutch, English, or French language educations, these eager students became subjected to the thought-worlds of the languages they studied. They became constituted as subjects within a world of European ideas where a variety of ideological positions were introduced that disrupted the familiar hierarchies of colonizer and colonized. But at the same moment that colonial subjects were being initiated into the intricacies of European languages and ideologies, they were also exposed to its vulnerability. Postwar European disenchantment with ideas of progress and technology coincided with the rise of first Javanese and then Indies nationalism, and other Asian nationalisms as well. As a result, many colonial elites rejected European ideas of subjectivity that did not mesh with their own political ambitions.

Asian intellectuals who studied in Europe were aware of the postwar European assault on subjectivity, and different groups of Dutch Indies intellectuals responded in various ways to the implications of ideas of autonomy for their own views of the world. Was autonomous subjectivity in harmony with Islam? Was autonomous subjectivity in harmony with Javanese ideas of ruler and ruled that had been transmitted over the centuries via oral traditions and reconstituted in Dutch philological editions of ancient Javanese texts? Soetatmo Soeriokoesoemo, one of the most persuasive supporters of Javanese rather than Indies nationalism, argued in 1920 that the European concept of equality might not be in harmony with Javanese worldviews. An intellectual connected to the Paku Alaman minor court in Yogyakarta, Soetatmo was willing to accept fraternity [broederschap] in his definition of nationalism, but equality (gelijkheid) seemed to him a dangerous concept, particularly for the prospects of the hereditary elite or priyayi class in Java. Colonial subjects responded in different ways to notions of autonomous subjectivity, opening up questions of identity and difference that continue to confound postcolonial intellectuals in the late twentieth century.

Javanese nationalists argued in Dutch over the legacies of the Javanese past and the implications of those constructions of the past for the future of the Javanese state. Classical imagery of scabbards fitting onto swords (warangka manjing curiga) – one of many metaphors for the union of ruler and ruled – was used to diffuse the possibility of autonomous subjectivity for the Javanese masses, reserving the possibility of subjectivity only for the educated priyayi who felt they had lost the most under Dutch rule. The ruler represented the will of the people – "he" represented and expressed the desires and needs of the people. If the ruler was just, he would address those needs and desires in ways that would be good for the state, for the people, and for himself.

Javanese elite nationalists like Soetatmo Soeriokoesoemo and Noto Soeroto, also connected to the Jogjanese minor court, blurred the autonomy and agency of individual subjects, claiming the moral high ground over their Dutch masters by suggesting that the needs of the many should outweigh the rights of the individual, unless, of course, the individual was working on a higher spiritual plane that would be incomprehensible to the masses. Dutch-educated Javanese intellectuals were influenced by liberal and radical streams of European thought that came into prominence in the Indies and throughout the world in the first decades of the twentieth century at the same time that liberal and mystically inclined Europeans were flocking toward the religions of the "exotic" East. The blending of European and Javanese knowledges gave rise to new ways of thinking and talking about well-known and well-loved Mahabharata tales in Java. These modernist vocabularies allowed Javanese intellectuals to use the popular shadow (wayang) theater and its repertoire of Mahabharata tales to build a case for Javanese or Indies nationalism in their Dutch scholarly writings, and new ways of talking and thinking about ethnicity and nationality interpellated European scholars and Javanese nationalists as subjects of these new discourses.

1 Theosophy and Javanese Nationalism

There have been a number of scholarly studies on the influence of Theosophical thought in the Indies (Tsuchiya, 1987; Perlman, 1993; Nugroho, 1995). Not only Soewardi Soerjaningrat (Ki Hadjar Dewantara), but also Tjipto Mangoenkoesoemo, H. S. Tjokroaminoto, and Soekarno came into contact with Theosophical ideas in their formative years through their association with the Dutch Theosophist D. van Hinloopen Labberton and his wife. Hinloopen Labberton had taken over as editor of the Dutch Indies Theosophical journal *Theosofisch Maandblad van Nederlandsch-Indië* by 1912 and was president of the Indies Theosophical Society from 1912 to 1923 (Tsuchiya, 1987: 43), and Tjipto Mangoenkoesoemo and other young nationalist leaders were heavily influenced by the Hinloopen Labbertons and by their Theosophical beliefs (Shiraishi, 1990: 122, 126; Dewantara, 1952: 227; Ricklefs, 1981: 157).

As a religious movement, Theosophy began in 1875 in America and quickly spread to Europe and Australia.[2] Women played a major role in the movement: Helena Blavatsky, Annie Besant, and Alice Bailey were among the most prominent. The role of women within the Theosophical hierarchy is a conflicted one. Women like H. Blavatsky and A. Besant were very well-respected, but they based their power on their ability to channel the thoughts and desires of disembodied male beings. Blavatsky was said to have channeled many of the teachings from her mystical contact with the disembodied Great (Male) Masters whose task it was to oversee life on this human earth. Leaders of the movement were appointed through psychic contact across continents, particularly between Australia and India in the early twentieth century. When Besant encountered the young Krishnamurti in Adyar, India in 1909 through her association with C. W. Leadbeater, she was convinced she had found the Spiritual Leader of the new century, and Krishnamurti was adopted by the Theosophists and raised to be the Messiah, a role he rejected as soon as he was knowledgable enough to do so, to the great disappointment of his mentors.

The Theosophical teachings themselves were a mix of several world religions with an emphasis on tolerance towards all religious practices. Hinduism, Christianity, Islam, and Judaism could all blend in harmony in the Theosophical worldview, although pre-Islamic Hindu and Buddhist teachings were favored. The Ramayana and Mahabharata became key texts for the Theosophists, especially the Bhagavad Gita which told the ancient story of Arjuna's enlightenment by the god-incarnate Krishna on the battlefield of Kurukshetra. Theosophy, however, was as much a product of social Darwinism as it was of religion; human life was ordered on an evolutionary plane in which the seven Root Races of humanity worked out their path toward perfection. The lost continent of Atlantis played a significant role in Theosophical thought, representing a past stage of human religious and mystical development and the home of the Fourth Root Race (Hoult, 1910: 17). Racialist thought was built into Theosophy from the beginning, albeit in a paternalistic and tolerant way: certain races were considered "naturally" more evolved than others just as humans were more evolved than monkeys. Aryans, deriving from ancient Indo-Europeans, were believed to belong to the Fifth Root Race while most Mongoloid peoples, i.e. Indies natives, belonged to the Fourth. Thus in India, European Theosophists and well-born Indians could mix on equal terms and Krishnamurti could be groomed as a World Savior as a reflection of the way that English and Sanskrit had both been discovered in the mid-nineteenth century to belong to the Indo-European language family (Stocking, 1987: 59).

In Java, the situation was a bit different. When Dutch Theosophists encountered Javanese Ramayana and Mahabharata stories, they realized that the Javanese were also heirs to mystical teachings revered by members of their eclectic religious persuasion. But Javanese were not actually Aryans, unless one counted the mixing of ancient Indo-Aryans with local Javanese whose fruitful union had supposedly produced the great temples of Borobudur and Prambanan. Dutch scholars attributed the present state of Javanese "indolence" and "fanaticism" to the pollution of these early Aryans by Malay blood until most traces of the "higher" race had disappeared ("Rasvershil onder Inlanders," 1912: 123–5). So most Javanese were seen as members of the Fourth Root Race, a race believed to be capable of great development of the heart *chakra* – centered in the feelings – but more limited in their mental development than the members of the Fifth Root Race, the Aryans. Several members of the mystical group Sumarah with whom I studied in the early 1970s maintained that the Javanese were members of the Fourth Root Race and could only excel in the development of *rasa* or feeling while the Euroamericans studying with the group were members of the Fifth Race and could perfect the intellect or *budi*. In Theosophical thought, all the members of a particular root race did not proceed at the same pace as they matured, and the historical evolution of the root races allowed for the overlapping of members of different root races at different points in time (Blavatsky, 1966: 168ff).

When Mevr. C. van Hinloopen Labberton wrote up her thoughts on the Javanese shadow theater (1912?), she believed she saw there the evidence of ancient Javanese contact with higher knowledge. This contact led back to the days of the great Saivite and Buddhist kingdoms of the pre-Islamic period, when colonies of Indians were believed to have brought their higher civilization to Java. Mevr. Hinloopen Labberton's essay on Javanese shadow theater, which appeared in English in 1912 and in two Dutch Indies journals in 1921, seems to be one of the earliest published contributions to a discourse that began to speak about the shadow theater in a new way. Rather than the quaint and degenerate folk art described by nineteenth-century Dutch scholars and missionaries (see Sears, *Shadows of Empire*, pp. 75–120), the shadow theater became a vehicle of higher knowledge, a point of access to an ancient and fading wisdom. Just as Dutch-educated Javanese were beginning to become aware of the potential for making Javanese traditions – articulated in Dutch – the basis for Javanese nationalism by the formation in 1908 of the Boedi Oetomo [Glorious Endeavor], the first European-style association in the Indies (Nagazumi, 1972; Shiraishi, 1990), young Javanese intellectuals who had watched many a shadow play in their youth were quick to respond to this new appreciation of what had previously been valued as a slightly degenerate remainder and reminder of old-fashioned village traditions. Dutch missionaries and scholars in the late nineteenth century had complained about the decadence of the shadow theater, although they saw its potential for influencing the Javanese masses. Some Dutchmen had distinguished between coarse and uneducated *dhalang* (shadow puppeteers) and those with greater knowledge of Javanese literary lore (Poensen, 1873: 164). It was to this latter group that the Theosophists turned for their inspiration.

This new discourse in which the shadow theater were seen as a vehicle of higher wisdom advanced several contradictory propositions: if the shadow theater were decadent, it could be restored; this restoration could be carried out in "modern" ways through the setting up of schools for the puppeteers; the newly restored tradition could then be used as a vehicle for lifting up the Javanese masses who were blinded by their attachments to village rituals – like the shadow theater – and their fanatic but usually faulty understandings of Islam. For those children of lesser *priyayi* who had been given a Dutch-language education in the early twentieth-century Ethical moment in Dutch colonial policy, Islam had often been presented by their Dutch teachers as an undesirable and troublesome feature of Javanese life. Nobility and lesser officials had been cautioned by the colonial government against identifying too closely with Islam throughout the second half of the nineteenth century. A newly constituted *wayang* tradition might help to draw those Javanese peasants who did not yet fully understand Islam toward an identification with older non-Islamic traditions of the past, and a newly refurbished tradition might guide the peasantry successfully into a "modern" future that could displace the poorly understood Islam (cf. Snouck Hurgronje, in Penders, 1977: 157–64). From his speeches and writings it is clear that the nationalist leader Tjipto Mangoenkoesoemo was familiar with the Hinloopen Labbertons' ideas about shadow theater that were being introduced into Javanese and Dutch scholarly and literary discourses in the first decades of the twentieth century (Balfas, 1957: 166–71). But an essay written in 1913 by Tjipto shows that it was not just Theosophy that changed the way Javanese thought and spoke about the central Javanese shadow theater tradition in the twentieth century.

2   Education and Exile

Islam and shadow theater were intertwined in Java in the early nineteenth century (Sears, 1996: 45–51), and these connections came under assault after certain factions of the Javanese nobility had rallied around the Jogjanese noble Dipanagara, who associated his rebellion against the Dutch with Islam in the Java War of 1825–30. By the late nineteenth century Dutch scholarship had placed "Hindu-Javanese" rather than Islamic literary traditions at the center of what they saw as Javanese culture, and *wayang* theater was seen as the only remaining vehicle of older traditions that Javanese elites and peasants could still – albeit imperfectly – understand. The Dutch scholarship of the latter part of the nineteenth century had devoted considerable attention to translating and annotating as many examples of Hindu-Javanese literature as they could find (Florida, 1995). But it was not until the second decade of the twentieth century that the *wayang* theater, through its elevation in Theosophical thought, also became a useful vehicle for the propagation of both Hindu-Javanese mythologies that could serve as the content of a Javanist religion or *agama jawa*, emptied of Islam, and the uplifting of the Javanese native (*de opheffing van de Javaansche inlander*). Rather than an imposition of Dutch colonial rule or even Dutch scholarship, Javanese nationalists themselves seized the initiative and became the manipulators of shadow plays and shadow tales.

Tjipto Mangoenkoesoemo, mentioned above, is a well-known Javanese intellectual who was active in the first quarter of the twentieth century (see Balfas, 1957; Larson, 1987; Scherer, 1975; Shiraishi, 1981; Tsuchiya, 1987). He was one of the three founders of the Indische Partij in 1912 which argued for an Indies rather than a Javanese nationalism; thus Tjipto and his colleague Soewardi Soerjaningrat allowed Dutch imperial conquests to circumscribe their nationalist visions. Although known for his embodiment of many of the ideals of refined Javanese manhood – humility, dignity, and subtlety – Tjipto held a vision of the Indies that saw all the different ethnic groups uniting and, by adopting the fruits of European knowledges, founding an independent nation (Balfas, 1952). Takashi Shiraishi (1981) has elegantly presented the debates over nationalism and culture that Tjipto had with Soetatmo Soeriokoesoemo of the Paku Alaman minor court in Yogya, and Kenji Tsuchiya (1987) has discussed these early nationalists in the first decades of the twentieth century in his excellent book on Soewardi Soerjaningrat and the rise of the Taman Siswa, Garden of Learning, Javanist schools. Both Tsuchiya and Shiraishi have set their studies against a background in which the *wayang purwa* theater assumes a foundational position. The *wayang* in the work of these scholars becomes synonymous with Javanese culture, illustrates basic ideas about Javanese conceptions of power, marks off the frame, here literally a stage, on which Javanese discourses of modernity are enacted. But this assumes an unchanging, ahistorical vision of the shadow theater and its reception by Javanese audiences. I am proposing that the idea of the *wayang* as the essence of Javanese culture was a product of the interlacing of Javanese and Dutch aesthetic visions and intellectual agendas that engendered and were engendered by discourses of modernity. It is an idea that was also congenial to Dutch scholars and government officials – and often the two groups overlapped – because it displaced attention from the threatening potential of Javanese unification under the banner of Islam that had arisen again in 1912 in the form of the Sarekat Islam, the first mass organization in the Indies. For both Javanese and Indies nationalists, positing the *wayang* as the essence of Java and associating the *wayang* with spiritual development and higher wisdom was quickly adopted because it allowed the nationalists to use the *wayang* to talk about politics right under the noses of the Dutch.

An example of this blending of Javanese and Dutch knowledges and purposes appears in an article written by Tjipto Mangoenkoesoemo at the end of 1913 in Holland and published in 1914 in the *De Indische Gids*, the useful guide to the Indies, published in Amsterdam, that brought together summaries of economic data, book reviews, literary fragments, and opinions written mainly by Dutch scholars, travelers, businesspeople, and administrators. Tjipto's essay on shadow theater had a special poignancy, as before or during its writing he was exiled to Holland because of what the colonial government felt were the subversive activities of the Indische Partij and, in particular, the activities of Soewardi Soerjaningrat, Douwes Dekker, and Tjipto. Less than two months after his arrival in Holland, on October 2, 1913, Tjipto collected both old and new thoughts for the Dutch publication.

In his essay "De Wajang" (*De Indische Gids* 36/I (1914): 530–9), Tjipto positioned himself both inside and outside the worldview of the *wayang* world and began to speak about the shadow theater in a new way. It is certainly true, as Shiraishi (1981) has argued, that Tjipto saw himself as a Javanese *satriya* (noble warrior). But his trip to Holland also allowed him to see the *wayang* from a new vantage point. Speaking about the *wayang* from Holland, Tjipto became the puppeteer, began the journey that the Indonesian author, activist, and former political prisoner Pramoedya Ananta Toer (1990: 78) has called "free[ing] himself from the grip of that *wayang* world," and used the techniques of the *wayang* for his own nationalist purposes. Tjipto deftly lulled the Dutch readers of his essay as he presented first the ethnographic and then a mystical Theosophical discourse on *wayang* with images of Higher Beings, inner lives, pain, and suffering.

In [the *wayang*] the Javanese has embodied a good part of his philosophical and mystical insights; he has put into words his inner life. No wonder then that even in the villas of the highest aristocrats as in the poorest neighborhood homes, it has become a beloved folkplay. Old and young spend their hours with pleasure listening to the words of the *dalang*, following him in his stories about gods and kings, about princes and ksatriya's [warriors], how they suffer and conquer, falling captive to their passions, becoming slaves to it, and finally, however, coming out of the battle victorious. The *wajang* is a purely Javanese creation and was already being performed at the court of Daha around the year 800, being revised around 1500 by Sunan Kali Djaga, the Islamic missionary. Exactly because it is a Javanese creation, through it one can learn a great deal about the inner life of the Javanese. The Netherlands Indies branch of the Theosophical Society did a good job of putting on [the Indian play] Sakuntala and writing down the results of the research.

From this passage, we see two important things: Tjipto has read the Dutch scholarship on the *wayang*, especially Hazeu's ideas (1897) about the Javanese, rather than Indian, origins of the *wayang* theater; and he praised the Theosophical Society's influence and efforts to endow the *wayang* with new mystical meanings that reinterpret and displace the nineteenth-century Javanese blendings of the *wayang* with Islamic sufi teachings.

> Behind [the *oil-lamp*] the *dalang*, the performer, will take his place. The Javanese sees in him the source of all life, because without him, no matter how artistically designed, the wajang puppets will never come to life. The Javanese proverb: *wajang manut dalang* [the wajang follows the dalang] adequately expresses how he regards them. What this relationship represents precisely is the image that the Javanese has of his relationship to the Unknowable, the Power-source, without which no life is possible here on earth. Our eye can only observe the sun that gives color to our earthly life; that is the visible source of all life here on earth.
>
> But behind that hides one even Mightier, an unknown Beginning, a Divinity, without whom "not even a bird falls from on high." All, everything is dependent upon that unknown Beginning, without whose will "not even a hair shall be touched." Just as the *wajang* follows the *dalang*, so the creature follows that Source of Life; this [Source] shall determine the role that humankind has to fulfill here on earth.

We see here the origins of what will become the scholarly judgments about the Javanese *wayang* in the twentieth century: *wayang* is the essence of Javanese culture and a window through which the outsider can peer to understand the Javanese "soul." Tjipto also reinscribed the metaphor of Hidden Power coming to life through the puppeteer, as the puppets come to life in performance. Earlier Javanese beliefs connected the *wayang* with Sufi mystical teachings. What seems to be taking place here is a displacement of *wayang* mysticism and a rephrasing of it in non-Islamic terms. In the 1920s and 1930s this Hidden Power came to be interpreted in "Hindu-Buddhist" religious-mystical terms because of Theosophical influence. In the 1950s and especially the 1960s, the Hidden Power was interpreted in the partisan political terms of that period.

Tjipto also described the *wayang* as a good ethnographer would, showing how it can be decoded to yield "meaning." He gave his Dutch readers access to "the Javanese way of thinking."

> It is the never-ending battle of light against darkness. In the Javanese way of thinking, people compare that to the battle of good spirits against the evil ones. As the daylight fades away, when the darkness creeps over the land, that is the time for the evil spirits to come out. In the *talu* [musical introduction] people hear that clearly indicated: the mellow and soft opening notes increase in ferocity, just as the fierceness of the passions of the evil spirits increases more and more as the evening progresses.

But then he used the *dhalang*'s talent for creating *lakon pasemon* as allegories to allude to the political situation in the Indies. As he described the scene where the *dhalang* can slip in criticisms of the government, Tjipto slipped in his *own* criticism of the government.

> The three clowns, Semar, Gareng and Petroek make funny faces and give the dalang the opportunity to keep the audience awake with quips and jokes. At the same time the three clowns give the dalang the opportunity to speak out about the happenings of the day. One often hears then his judgments of government measures poured out in comical form. One hears him complain in joking ways about the heavy fate of the Javanese under the Government of the so paternally-minded white Dutchmen.
>
> That all has the value of an intermezzo. It serves at the same time to drive the sleep out of the eyes of the listeners and spectators and to make sure that the wajang party does not become bored as would be possible with a story that is stretched out for a whole night.

Tjipto presented an astonishing *fait accompli* in which every *wayang* performance provided the *dhalang* with the opportunity to criticize the colonial government. He conjured up an image of Java in which thousands of imaginary puppeteers were constantly criticizing the "fate of the Javanese under the Government of the so paternally-minded white Dutchman." But then Tjipto slipped back into his role of neutral ethnographer. All that was only an intermezzo, something understandable to all the readers of his essay. It was just a technique the puppeteers used to keep their audiences awake in the wee hours of the night.

It becomes obvious to the reader of this article that Tjipto saw the Dutch as the *danawa* (ogre), the *raksasa* (demon), and the *wong sabrang* (foreigner) – all *wayang* characters – whom the *satriya* had to fight. These *wong sabrang* came to Java because they dreamt of the beauty of a Javanese princess, a symbol for the beauty of Java which the Dutch came to rape and pillage. Not until the *raksasa* are killed, Tjipto said, not until the land is returned to children of the ancestors, will Java be at peace again.

> The army of the foreign ruler made up of ogres had set up their camp right in that forest [where the noble prince was walking alone]. A meeting with the noble prince [*satriya*] cannot be prevented. The noble prince, requested to turn back, replies that he would rather die than interrupt his trip. A battle erupts, a battle between the lone noble warrior and the entire army of ogres, one against many, against all.
>
> It does look like a fairytale, the story of the dalang. The little prince against the monstrous ogres, great in number. And do we not see this in real life occurring again and again? Do we not see it often happen that the little man, fortified by the spirit that lives in him, dares to take on the task that under shallow consideration one would think far beyond his powers?!

There is a wonderful example of Tjipto's creative use of hybrid language in this passage: "de reusachtige danawa," or the monstrous monster is the enemy of the noble *satriya*; he has combined Dutch and Javanese in such a way that his meaning his clear in either language. There was no mention in the plot (*lakon*) that Tjipto was creating of the Korawa, the main enemies of the Pandawa heroes in most of the stories. Tjipto created a new telling of the Mahabharata stories in which the Korawa and Pandawa heroes could unite to rid Java of the *wong sabrang*, the Dutch. The Pandawa and Korawa were all cousins and all *satriya*; they all shared the same moral code, the same love for the fatherland. Tjipto used his exile in Holland to continue his struggle against the Dutch, and the Dutch allowed him to use the *Indische Gids*, their own Indies Guidebook, as a forum for his nationalist cause. Even with his mastery of Dutch, he continued to use Javanese words, to force the Dutch to use Javanese words to subvert their own rule. He forced the Dutch to think in Javanese. He closed his essay with the poignant words (1914: 539): "I cannot ignore that the *wajang* made a great impression on me, when I got so far that I could understand it." Tjipto is saying here that he had to go as far as Holland in order to truly understand the *wayang*. He cleverly mocked both Theosophical and Dutch scholarly discourses on *wayang* as he realized that his exile to Holland allowed him to get out of and thus, in a sense, further into his own understanding of what it meant to be Javanese. His trip to Holland opened his eyes to colonial visions of the *wayang* through which he could clearly see Javanese traditions as "culture." He began to see the *wayang* as subject, rather than being subject to its powers. Although Tjipto was later to become known for his dismissal of Javanese culture as a mystification of the masses, he first learned how to use the *wayang* for his own purposes. In contrast to his compatriots in the early nationalist movement, Tjipto's increasing politicization meant that he was forced to spend many years of his life in exile – far away from central Java – as the 1920s and 1930s brought more repressive colonial governments to power. Those nationalists who turned their efforts to the enrichment of education and the reconstitution of Javanese "culture" were able to realize some of their visions through setting up schools that translated Javanese traditions into languages of modernity.

3 Theosophy and Shadow Theater

In 1919 the Java Institute was established in Batavia with the aim of developing the indigenous cultures of Java, Bali, and Madura through congresses, exhibitions, recitals, courses, competitions, and writings. By 1921, after several years of discussion by members of the Java Institute, Dutch-educated intellectuals connected to the courts of central Java decided to teach the village puppeteers how to upgrade their performance styles, and the first school for puppeteers was opened in Solo in 1923 (Clara van Groenendael, 1986). This decision marked how Dutch-educated Javanese elites had adopted the Dutch scholarly evaluation of their shadow theater traditions. But I noted at the beginning of this essay how Theosophical ideas had offered the possibility of elevating the *mayang* by seeing in it the remains of ancient mystical wisdom and the teachings of the Indian Bhagavad Gita. Mevr. Hinloopen Labberton and Tjipto Mangoenkoesoemo were the first to articulate this new way of speaking about the shadow theater through the essays they published in 1912 and 1914 respectively. We can now turn to look at the ways in which Mevr. Hinloopen Labberton presented her ideas and then trace these ideas in the thought of the radical Javanese nationalist Soetatmo and their final perfection in the famous 1930s text of Mangkunagara VII, the elegant Javanese prince so admired by Dutch intellectuals.

> We are taught that there are seven keys which unlock the secret gate of knowledge. Can it be possible that one of those keys unlocks the true meaning of the *Bharata Yuddha* (Great War) and the *Kurukshetra* in the *Lakon Purvo* (Epic of Purvo)?

This opening by Hinloopen Labberton shows immediately that she is on much surer ground in her knowledge of Theosophical thought than in her knowledge of the *mayang*, here awkwardly called "The Epic of Purvo." She tells us that she had lived in India and heard about the existence of a shadow theater there, but had unfortunately never seen it. But even in these few lines, Hinloopen Labberton established the major connections that would designate the scholarly discourses about *mayang* in the twentieth century: she linked the shadow theater of Java, the Bhagavad Gita, and secret knowledges framed in Theosophical jargon. What remained outside her discussion, of course, was Javanese Islam. She went on to note that the *mayang* had become a part of the "racial" life, as well as the moral life, of the Javanese. Expanding on this theme, she concluded: "As the Javanese race is now probably in its decadence, the new forms that have been added to the Wayang are much inferior to the originals."

This discourse of decadence, degeneracy, and the non–originary quality of the *mayang* resonated with the late nineteenth-century Dutch scholarly discourse. But the Dutch scholars who wrote about Javanese shadow theatre in the nineteenth century (see Sears, 1996: 75–120) never felt that the *mayang* could unlock very much except obscene humor and insipid dialogue which were useful mainly for learning about Javanese language, customs, and linguistics. Mevr. van Hinloopen Labberton then focused on several different parts of the tradition, beginning with the light of the *blencong*.

> This light is the symbol of consciousness, and this consciousness is eternal for all periods of growth; without that light there would be no shadows . . . However, here and there an individual in the masses begins to be conscious, and he only is able to begin to understand the laws of evolution.
>
> Without this light the people of the races could not evolve. Without the Dalang there would be no play; the shadows would drag out an inactive life till the oil was exhausted and the light extinguished . . .
>
> The link that connects the parts in the Wajang Play is Shri Krishna's work.

Her focus on the light, the oil-lamp or *blencong*, was echoed in Tjipto's essay in the *Indische Gids* mentioned earlier. Tjipto (1914: 532) spoke too of the light-giving lamp, representative of the sun, "without which the whole earth would be stagnant, just as on the screen no representation is possible without the life-giving and light-giving blentjong." This discourse is produced, of course, by the combination of Theosophical and Javanese knowledges. Hinloopen Labberton could not have spoken about the *wayang* if she had not received her information from Javanese sources. She then took that knowledge and filtered it through her Theosophical worldview. But Tjipto eliminated the racialist thought that permeated Hinloopen Labberton's work. He took and used only that knowledge that would be useful for his nationalist purposes.

Although Tjipto (1914: 535) erased the racialist thought, he accepted the mystical discourse of coming to awareness that the performance of a good *dhalang* could bring. "How exact is his insight, how philosophical his thought that the use of the sense-organs brings a certain pain, and only through this can people become conscious of living in a World of Oppositions." For Tjipto these oppositions often moved out of the world of *wayang* into the contradictions of the colonial experience. But the Theosophical emphasis on the god Kresna and the Bhagavad Gita also surfaced in Tjipto's later thought. He stated in his 1918 speech (see Balfas, 1957: 66–71), on whether there should be Javanese or Indies nationalism, that what formed the distinguishing feature of the popular folk-play, the *wayang*, was the Bhagavad Gita even though, according to Tjipto, the Javanese *wayang* did not have a "*pakem*" or stable tradition connected to that text. Then Tjipto said, relying on the opinion of D. van Hinloopen Labberton, the Dutchman who headed the Indies Theosophical Society from 1912 to 1923, the essence of the Bhagavad Gita is alive in a qualitative way among a large proportion of the Javanese people. Authorizing his remarks with the opinions of Hinloopen Labberton, Tjipto could proceed to give a sketch of the spiritual life of the Javanese.

Tjipto described the subject matter of the Bhagavad Gita: Arjuna is on the battlefield of Kurukshetra with his charioteer Sri Kresna, incarnation of the god Wisnu. Arjuna loses all his will to fight when he sees his relatives arrayed against him on the battlefield. Tjipto then made a surprising detour. Rather than continuing with the teachings of the Gita – nonattachment to the fruits of one's actions – Tjipto used the story to illustrate to his audience the nobility of the character of the Javanese people. Rather than the misguided polytheistic lazy natives that the Javanese were in Dutch eyes, Tjipto asks how a people could not be thought virtuous who valued this story of Arjuna, a man so noble that he would rather die than kill even one of his beloved relatives, a man with such compassion for his enemies. Once again, Tjipto took an element of Indian Theosophical thought and reinterpreted it, using it for his own purposes.

Tjipto's speech went on to compare Arjuna's reluctance to fight with the nineteenth-century rebel Dipanagara's reluctance to kill anyone in the Java War

(1825–30). But what is most striking about the speech, and reappears continually in the writings of Dutch-educated Javanese, is the effort to refute Dutch ideas that see the Javanese as polytheistic immoral humans who will not be able to properly evolve until they become monotheistic. Tjipto showed his understanding of European evolutionary thought when he compared the Javanese notion of a *Goden hierarchie*, a hierarchy of gods, to what existed everywhere on earth:

> A certain gradation of progress achieved in levels that rise gradually from the Hottentot to the races of Heroes, in ancient and recent history, Heroes in spiritual as well as intellectual fields, and on the field of battle.

But then, Tjipto argued, the Javanese believe in one Supreme Being who rules over this evolutionary span from the lowliest to the highest. The Dutch do not have to think that the Javanese worship every stone that looks a little strange or any tree that appears slightly eerie, a reference to village practices that include giving offerings to trees where village guardian spirits were believed to reside.

Tjipto concluded by citing examples from the Old Javanese *Niti Sastra*, again to show that the Javanese were not degenerate and had long had high ethical standards. In this text the king is supposed to know the trials and tribulations of his subjects, help them in times of need, reward them in the face of battle. Tjipto then compared this model behavior of the ancient king with the contemporary *dhalang*. In this way Tjipto both accepted and recontextualized the Theosophical interpretation of the *dhalang* as "the leader of the race" into a leader of the people who helps to bear the suffering of the people and stands out in times of crisis and humbly retreats when happiness and success overflow. Once again we see here a blending of Javanese and Theosophical knowledges to produce new ways of seeing Javanese practices and Javanese beliefs.

Let us turn now to Tjipto's colleague and intellectual opponent Soetatmo Soeriokoesoemo (1923: 30–39) to see how Soetatmo blended Theosophical discourses about the shadow theater in *Wederopbouw*, the Dutch-language Javanese periodical that he launched in 1918, for his very different goal of renewing Javanese culture and making it the essence of Javanese nationalist ideals.

> Whoever has a good understanding of the wajangplay, of its meaning and knowledge, is surprised and moved by the striking likeness there with the outside world, a world of appearance and illusion in which the fragments of Truth play their assigned role with admirable devotion . . . [*sic*] according to the plan of the Teacher, the Dhalang.
>
> Beautiful is the wajangplay without argument!
>
> And in order that the new generation, whose gaze is clouded more or less by a western schooled intellect, could also profit from the beauty of this sacred, national

347

play, I will attempt here with the help of their imagination, to illuminate that wajang as clearly as possible for them, with the (lively) [*sic*] light of the "blentjong" [oil-lamp].

Once again the elements of the discourse on the shadow theater appear that have become familiar from the writings of Tjipto and Mevr. Hinloopen Labberton: the stress on the *dhalang* as a wise teacher, the importance of the oil-lamp or *blencong*, and the high and sacred value of the tradition. Soetatmo too did not just accept the received wisdom; he inserted his own agendas into the discussion. As noted above, Soetatmo was troubled by the tendency of Javanese youth to turn away from their "traditional culture" and replace it with the fruits of modernity provided by their Dutch-language education. But Soetatmo goes even further here and calls the *wayang* a "sacred, national play" ["gewijde, nationalespel"]. But the *wayang* can only be a national play in a nation whose boundaries coincide with the island of Java.

Soetatmo was calling out to the Javanese youth to come back to their shadow play. He hoped to reconstitute them as subjects of the play within the new discourses of the 1910s and 1920s that had elevated the village tradition of the past into the sacred essence of the Javanese nation's future. In Tjipto's essay that he wrote in Holland and published in *De Indische Gids*, Tjipto was attempting to constitute his Dutch audience as subjects of the *wayang* to bring the inequities of the colonial relationship to their attention. Soetatmo's task seems more daunting, more ambitious, and more poignant; he was arguing for the very existence of the Javanese nation.

> The gamelan on such a wajang-evening, announcing the beginning of the performance through the power of its reverberations, invites You with charming notes, Your own being, your highest Self to seek in this dusky realm of shadows. Thou would find thyself inscribed there. Your will be done, your plan fulfilled. And more can you draw from it. The gamelan whispers to you that you yourself are the "gending" [musical piece].
>
> Sa gendingipoen [the melody] . . . Thou shalt not seek in vain.

In this passage I have tried to capture the flavor of Soetatmo's ornate religious style, deliberate use of upper-case letters for emphasis, and high drama. He was speaking very clearly to the educated youth of Java and said earlier in the essay that if they failed to understand his words, it was their fault as much as his. He could only do his best in this foreign language that was not his own, but they too had to strive to understand his meaning.

> The receptivity of your heart is brought about by Yourself; no one can offer You a helping hand. The opening of the gate lies in your power, because the key is in your hand, the golden key, that will allow you to enter the hidden worlds of the East.

348

After their long journey through the discipline of European "science," which Soetatmo often juxtaposed against Javanese "tradition," young Javanese need to be, as it were, reinitiated into their own culture. Because of their Javanese ancestry, they have the power to relearn their own culture that they have supposedly lost through their European training. But, like any other traveler to Java, they must find the key that will open up the mysterious world of the East that they have lost. In Soetatmo's larger argument, he made a sweeping reversal: he made the educated children of elite Javanese aware of a lack. No longer at the center of their "culture," they have become marginal to it. At the center of Java, of Javanese nationalism, was a mysterious essence that can only be unlocked with a secret key – a key forged by European Theosophists – and this essence was contained in the shadow theater.

We must turn to some of Soetatmo's other writings to fill in his argument, because the argument connects shadow theater, Theosophical teaching, nationalism, and the fate of the children of mixed Javanese-Dutch ancestry. In a 1920 essay on Theosophy and Javanese nationalism, Soetatmo had tried to reconcile the teachings of Theosophy with his vision of a Javanese nation state. It is here that he first posited the Javanese folk at the center of his vision and the Dutch-educated Javanese on the margins.

> Javanese nationalism is based on Javanese individuality, on Javanese personality, and acquires a whole other meaning than the nationalism of the West, which comes from the love of the fatherland. Javanese nationalism is the inevitable color of Javanese culture and thus cannot possibly be in contradiction with Theosophy, which here must signify the "divine". The highest nationalism can only be perceived in the nature of things, understood and felt through those [things] that have penetrated to the heart of Javanese culture.

> This can be illustrated by an example. Firstly, the dear Javanese from the neighborhood feels by intuition in his heart that he is Javanese. He understands nothing of the powerful operation of Javanese culture; still he lives this culture without understanding it. Compare that with a cultivated Javanese who since childhood has enjoyed his upbringing in Europe; he then can perhaps truly say that he is Javanese with the knowledge that he was born from Javanese parents, but that feeling of the neighborhood Javanese is strange to him.

Soetatmo linked the concepts that he needed to express his ideas of what the basis for Javanese nationalism must be: Javanese culture, the Javanese village people, and a Theosophical appreciation of racially and spiritually constructed hierarchies. This marks the rise of a discourse which celebrates rather than laments the construction of Javanese subjectivity as different from European subjectivity – the rise of a discourse that is racially constructed but on Javanese rather than Dutch terms. Theosophical hierarchies become useful here, for on the spiritual planes posited within Theosophical thought Europeans and Javanese can meet and be in harmony. But on this human earth, Javanese blood becomes the *raison d'être* of the Javanese nation state. There is one last essay that ties up this argument about the importance of the shadow theater within Soetatmo's thought.

In the very first issue of *Wederopbouw* (I/1 1918: 4–7), Soetatmo had published an essay called "De Javaansche Vraagstuk," or the Javanese Question. In this essay Soetatmo introduced many of the ideas that he would continue to support in his pursuit of Javanese nationalism. The position in the Indies of the people of "mixed-blood" was obviously something Soetatmo had thought deeply about. The conclusions he came to illustrate the conflicted nature of Soetatmo's thought where he could appear as radically conservative or progressively liberal at the same time.

> People will object that it is also egoistic of me not to think about the lot of the small group of Indiers of mixed blood.
>
> I ask myself then: Why can they not dissolve themselves into us? Why must they unconditionally bear the nationality of the father, of the man? Is that of the woman so much less, so insignificant that it is impossible for them to think of it and they prefer to create a new nationality, namely the Indian, even in the case when they no longer wish to bear the nationality of the father? The question would have been solved if our half-brothers themselves were not ashamed of the nationality of the woman and valued it, a shame finally that is out of place and without any basis.

Soetatmo attempted to uplift the native mothers along with his rehabilitation or reconstruction of Javanese culture. Although the rights of women were not foremost in his mind, he is asking why the children of mixed-blood always put their Dutch fathers over their Javanese mothers. In this case, Soetatmo is willing to accept all those who would call themselves Javanese; even a little Javanese blood will suffice.

In his efforts to lift up the Javanese, to make Javanese proud of their heritage, Soetatmo needed role models to show the nobility of the Javanese people. For a brief moment, there is an overlap between Soetatmo's thought and that of Tjipto as they both sought to reclaim the ethical basis of the Javanese in the face of Dutch beliefs about the immorality of the Indies natives. And again for both of them, role models from the *wayang* proved useful. Rather than choosing the Theosophical Arjuna of the Bhagavad Gita as Tjipto did, Soetatmo chose the Arjuna that Javanese knew from the shadow theater – the delicate mystical hero who fights with greedy and uncontroled ogres in every play. Arjuna not only served as the model for the Javanese nobility but also as a suitable role model for the Javanese youth Soetatmo wanted to construct as the subjects of his discourse.

> Ardjoeno, the adventurous hero of the youth, with his ever inspiring inclinations to asceticism, the mystical hero of the searching philosopher, recalls for You the image of the perfect Ksatriya [prince] with his rhythm of voice and action. He is

courteous in every respect, fine and noble in word and deed. He is courageous like no other. I only have to remind you of the meeting of ogre Tjakil with Ardjoeno, the inimitable liveliness and activity in voice and gesture of the first and, as a worthy opponent, the beautiful and still figure of Ardjoeno, who later with one movement of the hand calmly invites the boeto to quiet down and then taunts him directly with the words: "Ogre, what cave [of corpses] are you from . . . . . !

You see there the characterization of the ungovernable, greedy man with his attitude of cunning fickleness, drunk with delusions of power and trusting only on the power of his arms and the sharpness of his teeth, said in a modern style, trusting in the power of violence and the point of the bayonets. Then you find in the immobile Ardjoeno the type of calm and orderly ksatriya with his immovable will and unequalled courage, a courage that he calmly knew to put in his simple question: "Ogre . . . what cave are you from . . . . ! (1923: 31–2)

In Soetatmo's story, however, it is harder to fix with certainty the models for his *wayang* characterizations. The "greedy, ungovernable man" in Soetatmo's story may have referred to Indies natives from the other parts of the Dutch colonial state or even to Javanese who had accepted European values, although most likely the "greedy man" referred to the Dutch themselves. Soetatmo's story was both simpler and more complex. All who were not Javanese had the propensity to act like the ogres of his story, but his mystical thinking would lead him to rehabilitate those who believed in the evolutionary potential of the human soul. Again, the contradictory nature of Soetatmo's thought allows his words to be read and interpreted in various ways. He finally elevated the *wayang* to the point where it encompassed all religious teachings.

> The point of the teachings and moral lessons from the Bible and the Koran are found again there in the stories of Rama and the Maha-Barata. You can think of no philosophical work of any meaning that the wajang does not also know.

The convoluted and contradictory arguments of Soetatmo finally culminated in an elevated vision of the *wayang*, drawing inspiration from Theosophical, evolutionary, and even the racialist thought of his day. Soetatmo's vision of a Javanese nation with Mahabharata tales as its national narratives failed, but the sophisticated scholar-soldier-ruler Mangkunagara VII would again pick and choose from this thickening discourse those elements that were useful for his vision of a more inclusive – and more hybrid – Indonesian national future.

4 Mangkunagara VII and Colonial Discourses

Before he was elevated in 1916 to the position of Mangkunagara VII, the head of the minor ruling house in Solo, Soerjosoeparto was one of only two Javanese to have served in the Dutch army in the First World War. He had interrupted his literary studies at Leiden to join the army but was recalled to Java in 1915 when it became known that Mangkunagara VI wished to abdicate and Soerjosoeparto was one of two eligible contenders to replace him. He also served as the national chairman of the Boedi Oetomo from August 1915 until he accepted the position of Mangkunagara VII in February 1916 by signing away much of the authority of his realm to the colonial government (see Larson, 1987).

It is clear that he had to give up his nationalist activities when he acceded to the throne. In comparison to the then-reigning Paku Buwana X (who reigned 1893–1939), the mysterious anti-Dutch figure of the major Solonese palace, whether Mangkunagara VII is seen as the model modernizing ruler or as a Dutch collaborator, he has had an enduring impact on the interpretation of the Javanese shadow theater by Dutch and other foreign observers since the publication of his essay on shadow theater in 1933. I intend to place that essay within the changing discourses of Javanese shadow theater that I have been tracing from the nineteenth into the late twentieth century. A close reading of his text can show what was new in Mangkunagara VII's text and what he took from his Dutch and Javanese predecessors.

> In the following essay, which except for certain additions remains the same as my reading of last December 1, have I dared to lift a small tip of the veil, to explicate how the wayang encompasses and keeps hidden the secret Javanese knowledge of the deepest meanings of life. (1933: 1)

The Mangkunagara originally gave his talk on December 1, 1932 to the Solonese Cultural-Philosophical Study Circle, a group of Dutch, Eurasians, and Javanese who, as Claire Holt (Mangkunagara, 1957) tells us, were "philosophically oriented intellectuals and professionals" and met monthly for discussions. Like Soetatmo, the Mangkunagara has adopted a Dutch orientalist approach to Java as exotic and mysterious, even though Soetatmo's audience was not the Dutch scholars but the youth of Java. Mangkunagara also said in his short foreword that it was the "great national duty" for those who love the Javanese folk to accommodate the perhaps not yet consciously felt but nonetheless existing need of prominent Javanese minds for deepening the inner life. So the Mangkunagara also saw among "prominent Javanese minds" a lack – a lack in their inner life. It is to fill this lack that he dared to lift the veil. But here is the contradiction: if he were really lifting the veil for his countrymen (*landgenooten*), would they not be able to lift the veil for themselves? Was he not, in fact, lifting the veil for his Dutch listeners and readers, those who really were the ones who lacked what Java has to offer and whose need he would fill through his explication of the shadow play? Yet he said he dared to lift the veil so that the bond with the core of "our entire folklife," of which the *wayang* is a highly important and distinguished expression, will not be broken. Leaving this contradiction in mind, I continue this investigation of his text.

Therefore, the wayang stories, though based on the Indian epics, may be regarded in their Javanese form as creations of our poets and thinkers and as manifestations of a very special and a very high culture. (1933: 80)

Mangkunagara jumped right into the very contentious Dutch scholarly argument over the origins of the *wayang* theater. Although Brandes's (1889) and Hazeu's (1897) thesis of indigenous origin for the *wayang* had recently been contested by Krom (1926), Mangkunagara chose to ignore Krom and to focus on Rassers' new work (1931) on the origins of the Javanese drama, even citing Rassers's support of the ideas of Brandes and Hazeu for an indigenous origin. By positing the stories as the creations of Javanese poets and thinkers despite their rootedness in Indian stories, a link that he certainly does not want to break, Mangkunagara authorizes his own ideas with the latest Dutch scholarship. Moving deftly from the scientific to the philosophical, Mangkunagara once again supports his ideas with Dutch scholarship: in addition to the work of Rassers, he cites the work of Dr. K. A. H. Hidding (1931) who also argued, in *Het Tijd-schrift voor Indische Taal-, Land- en Volkenkunde*, a major Dutch scholarly periodical, that the *wayang* must be a type of initiation for its spectators into "the secrets of earthly existence."

Warming to his subject, the Mangkunagara then introduced the ideas of R. M. Ir. Sarsita, who had lectured to the same group in May of 1932. What Sarsita had established was the very important distinction between magic and mysticism: magic was equated with superstition and low evolution while mysticism resonated with the higher discourses of Theosophical thought. Sarsita argued that every *wayang* performance illustrated the victory of the mystical over the magical, and Mangkunagara used Sarsita's argument to show the high status of the *wayang purwa*. For Mangkunagara's last authorization, as he slowly guided his audience from scientific to mystical interpretations of the *wayang*, he offered the poetic insights of R. M. Noto Soeroto, a member of the Paku Alaman nobility, mentioned above, whom he had gotten to know in Holland and who also had served in the Dutch army (see M. Djajadiningrat-Nieuwenhuis, 1993). It is in the poetry of Noto Soeroto that the deep interlacing of Javanese and Dutch knowledges appears. Noto Soeroto achieved some fame in Holland for poetry that he wrote in Dutch – poetry radically different from older Javanese poetic practices that relied on intricate rhyme schemes. The image of the young Javanese noble studying law in Leiden and pouring out his longing for his native traditions in Dutch unrhymed verse is an illustrative one – probably as representative of the hybrid intellectual worlds of the period as Mevr. Hinloopen Labberton's enchantment with the "Epic of Purvo." As Noto Soeroto wrote:

Thus mirror yourself in my play, Oh Man, and know yourself! On the battlefield of your own heart will the grim war rage between friends and relations. Play then the demon as befits a demon, and play the nobleman as proper for a noble.

This bit of poetry from Noto Soeroto's "Wajang-liederen" or Wayang Songs, quoted by Mangkunagara (1933: 82 and 1957: 4–5), is revealing for what it tells about the thought-world of the author. Noto Soeroto in this passage showed his familiarity with the Bhagavad Gita by stressing the teachings of Krishna to Arjuna, where Krishna alleviates Arjuna's doubts about killing his cousins and teachers by explaining that each person is born into a certain caste and must fulfill the duties of that caste. Arjuna has been born into the warrior caste and must fulfill his duties as a warrior; that is his Dharma. Thus Noto Soeroto's admonition to act according to one's station in life, whether demon or noble, may have suited Mangkunagara's efforts to connect the *wayang* with the noble Indian text, as well as Dutch poetry and, finally, even the essence of European "culture." In the next passage Mangkunagara argues that Noto Soeroto's poetry clearly links the wisdom of the *wayang* to the philosophical views of Plato, who also "regards this world as a reflection of the world of ideas." The wisdom of the *wayang* has now been elevated to Platonic heights.

Having established the firm credentials of the shadow theater through citations from the work of other authors, Mangkunagara felt ready to present his own views. He argued strongly for both an ancient and indigenous past for the *wayang purwa*, offering a synthesis of the Dutch debates by suggesting that dramatic traditions and stories coming from India in the ancient past probably blended with a preexisting Javanese rite of ancestor worship – a view that many might adhere to today (cf. Ras, 1976 and Sears, 1994). More importantly, however, is the Prince's argument that every shadow theater performance is an exercise in *semadi* or meditation, and he illustrated this argument by his explication of two *wayang* plays, the Arjuna Wiwaha (or Ciptoning) and the Dewa Ruci stories.

The Dewa Ruci story was connected in the early nineteenth century with Islamic sufi mysticism, but Mangkunagara made only the briefest reference to his clear knowledge of the Islamic interpretation of this story. He referred his readers to a Javanese book entitled "Soeksma Poesara" by a certain Dr. Bavinck – an Indo or Dutch scholar? – "who introduces *under other names* the well known Arabic conceptions of Aluamah, Amarah, Supiah and Mutmainah" (1933: 87; emphasis added). Here Mangkunagara showed intimate knowledge of the very Islamic interpretation of the Dewa Ruci story through the association of the colors red, yellow, black, and white with human emotions, and the fight between reason and passion (*akal* and *nafsu*) that lies at the heart of much sufi mysticism.

But Mangkunagara preferred to "lift the veil" only partially; he did not dare to tell his audience what most Javanese Muslims knew – that Islamic as well as "Hindu-Javanese" interpretations could be used to explain the *wayang* in mystical terms. Even his description of Arjuna's *semadi* or meditation, supposedly taken from a recitation of a *dhalang* (Mangkunagara, 1933: 90 and 1957: 14), and translated into Dutch, can be read in Islamic terms. But Mangkunagara did not want to draw the attention of his Dutch listeners to Islam, and his Javanese listeners would not need to be reminded. If there were hidden meanings in Mangkunagara VII's text, they pointed to the unspoken presence of Islam, rather than the nationalist messages of Tjipto or Soetatmo. But he drew his text to a close with scholarly charts, modeled somewhat after J. Kats' *wayang wong* programs for Dutch audiences (see Kats, 1923; Mangkunagara, 1957: 21) and his firm conviction: "In any case every lakon should be regarded as a symbol of mystical action – the practice of semadi." Mangkunagara's Dutch text of 1933 remains today a definitive statement on the meaning of central Javanese, especially Solonese, shadow theater.

The Solonese *wayang purwa* performances held at the court of Mangkunagara VII in the 1930s and the *wayang wong* performances staged at the court of Sultan Hamengkubuwana VIII (who reigned 1921–39) of Yogyakarta (see Lindsay, 1985) were produced for hybrid Javanese and Dutch audiences and fashioned to suit the tastes of those audiences. I was told by the late Sanjoto Sutopo Kusumohatmodjo (personal communication, 1983), Head of Palace Affairs at the Mangkunagaran palace, that *wayang* performances held at the court in the 1930s were very private esoteric events with limited audiences. These performances were unique to a particular moment in the colliding trajectories of Javanese and Dutch knowledges. They were neither more nor less "authentic" than other performances styles. Rather, they were created in the context of the colonial encounter, and they disappeared along with that world when colonialism was swept away.

This essay has analyzed the rise of new ways of speaking and thinking about the Javanese shadow theater and has explored the constitution of new Javanese subjectivities through the influences of Theosophy, exile, and imagination. Although the first decades of the twentieth century brought ideas of autonomous subjectivity to Javanese intellectuals, the ambivalence of colonial subjectivity continued to disrupt Javanese identities into the 1920s and 1930s. Although Javanese nationalism had failed by the mid-1920s, the acceptance of a pan-Indies nationalism still showed Javanese intellectuals debating their ideas of identity and autonomy on European terms. As Javanese intelligentsias began their journeys out of the thought-world of Mahabharata stories, theosophy, and shadow puppet traditions, they continued to experience shifting constructions of identity that moved between autonomous and colonial notions of subjectivity. Nostalgia for village life, the encounter with new technologies, and education in European languages all combined to bring Javanese intellectuals into their own particular constructions of modernity.

If Mahabharata shadow theater characters have served to represent Javanese to themselves for centuries, and this process has constantly been in flux, another dramatic shift in thinking and feeling is taking place as today Mahabharata and Ramayana characters are released from the elaborate and restrictive codes set in place by the hybrid intellectual exchanges of the colonial period. As the Mahabharata and Ramayana stories move into comic books, novels, television programs, and romances, the celebration of shadow play stories by European and American scholars as the essence of a Javanese religion that marginalizes Islam becomes both ambiguous and, perhaps, a relic of a colonial past.

Notes

1 This essay was previously published as a section of chapter 3 of my book *Shadows of Empire: Colonial Discourse and Javanese Tales* (Duke, 1996). Please see that chapter for more extensive footnotes and a broader discussion of these issues. I thank Duke University Press for allowing me to publish this revised essay and Henry Schwarz for finding me and encouraging me to contribute to this volume.
2 My discussion of Theosophy draws on Blavatsky, 1966; Lutyens, 1975; Besant, 1912; Hoult, 1910, "Theosofische Vereeniging" (1932); and my own experiences studying and discussing Javanese mysticism in Solo in the early 1970s and early 1980s. "Theosofische Vereeniging" noted that Blavatsky made three trips to Java in 1853, 1858, and 1883.

References and Selected Bibliography

Abdurrachman Surjomihardjo. (1978). "National Education in a Colonial Society," in *Dynamics of Indonesian History*, eds. Haryati Soebadio and Carine A. du Marchie Sarvaas. Amsterdam: North Holland Publishing Company.

Adas, M. (1989). *Machines as the Measure of Men: Scientific and Technological Superiority and Ideologies of Western Dominance*. Ithaca: Cornell University Press.

Ahmad, Aijaz. (1992). *In Theory: Classes, Literatures, Nations*. London: Verso.

Althusser, Louis. (1971). "Ideology and Ideological State Apparatuses," in *Lenin and Philosophy*, trans. Ben Brewster. New York: Monthly Review Press.

Balfas, M. (1957 [orig. 1952]). *Dr. Tjipto Mangoenkoesoemo: Demokrat sedjati*. Jakarta: Penerbit Djambatan.

Benda, H. (1958). *The Crescent and the Rising Sun*. The Hague: W. van Hoeve.

Besant, A. (1912). *The Masters*. Adyar, Madras: Theosophical Publishing House.

Bhabha, Homi, ed. (1991). *Nation and Narration*. New York: Routledge.

Blavatsky, H. (1966). *An Abridgement of the Secret Doctrine*. London: Theosophical Publishing House.

Bosch, F. D. K. (1961). "The Problem of the Hindu Colonisation of Indonesia," in *Selected Studies in Indonesian Archaeology*. The Hague: Martinus Nijhoff, KITLV Translation Series 3.

Brandes, J. L. A. (1889). "Een Jayapattra of Acte van een Rechterlijke Uitspraak can Caka 849," *Tijdschrift voor Indische Taal-, Land- en Volkenkunde*, uitgegeven door het Bataviaasch Genootschap voor Kunsten en Wetenschappen, 32 (1889): 123–4.

Chatterjee, Partha. (1986). *Nationalist Thought and the Colonial World: A Derivative Discourse*. Minneapolis: University of Minnesota Press.

Clara van Groenendael, V. M. (1986). *The Dalang Behind the Wayang*. Dordrecht: Foris Publications.

"Congres voor Javaansche Cultuur-Ontwikkeling." [no author]. (1921). In *Djawa*, 1: 313–17, reprinted from *De Locomotief*.

Dewantara, Ki Hadjar. (1952). *Dari Kebangunan Nasional sampai Proklamasi Kemerdekaan: Kenang-kenangan Ki Hadjar Dewantara*. Djakarta: N. V. Pustaka Penerbit "Endang."

Djajadiningrat-Nieuwenhuis, M. (1993). "Noto Soeroto: His Ideas and the Late Colonial Intellectual Climate," *Indonesia*, 55.

Florida, Nancy. (1995). *Writing the Past, Inscribing the Future: History as Prophecy in Colonial Java*. Durham: Duke University Press.

Hazeu, G. A. J. (1897). *Bijdrage tot de Kennis van het Javaansche Tooneel*. Leiden: E. J. Brill.

Hinloopen Labberton, C. van. (1912?). *The Wajang or Shadow Play as Given in Java*. N.p.

——. (1921). "De Wajang of het Shaduwenspel," in *Wederopbouw*, 4, nos. 8–9.

Hobsbawm, E. and T. Ranger. (1983). *The Invention of Tradition*. Cambridge: Cambridge University Press.

Hoult, P. (1910). *A Dictionary of Theosophical Terms*. London: Theosophical Publishing House.

Iskandar Nugroho. (1995). "The Theosophical Movement in Colonial Indonesia 1912–1917." Unpublished MA thesis, University of New South Wales, Sydney, Australia.

Kats, J. (1923). *Het Javaansche Tooneel I, De Wajang Poerwa*. Weltevreden: Commissie voor de Volkslectuur.

Krom, N. J. (1926). *Hindoe-Javaansche Geschiedenis*. 2nd. ed. 1931. The Hague: Martinus Nijhoff.

Larson, G. D. (1987). *Prelude to Revolution: Palaces and Politics in Surakarta, 1912–1942*. Dordrecht: Foris Publications.

Lindsay, J. (1985). "Klasik Kitsch or Contemporary: A Study of Javanese Performing Arts." Unpublished Ph.D. dissertation, University of Sydney.

Lutyens, M. (1975). *Krishnamurti: The Years of Awakening*. New York: Avon.

Mangkunagara VII, KGPAA. (1933). "Over de wajang-koelit (poerwa) in het algemeen en over de daarin voorkomende symbolische en mystieke elementen," *Djawa*, 13.

——. (1957). *On the Wayang Kulit (Purwa) and its Symbolic and Mystical Elements*, trans. Claire Holt. Data Paper no. 27. Ithaca: Cornell Southeast Asia Publications.

Nagazumi, A. (1972). *The Dawn of Indonesian Nationalism: The Early Years of the Budi Utomo*. Tokyo: Insitute of Developing Economies.

Nugroho, Iskandar P. (1995). "The Theosophical Education Movement in Colonial Indonesia 1912–1917." Unpublished MA thesis, University of New South Wales, Sydney.

Penders, Chr. L. M., ed. and trans. (1977). *Indonesia: Selected Documents on Colonialism and Nationalism, 1830–1942*. St. Lucia, Queensland: University of Queensland Press.

Perlman, M. (1993). "Theosophy in Java and the Re-Indicization of the Wayang Kulit." Unpublished paper.

Poensen, C. (1873). "De Wajang," in *Mededeelingen van wege het Nederlandsche Zendeling-genootschap*, 16–17.

357

Pramoedya Ananta Toer. (1990). *Rumah Kaca* [Glass House]. Kuala Lumpur: Wira Karya.

Ras, J. J. (1976). "The Historical Development of the Javanese Shadow Theater," *Review of Indonesian and Malaysian Studies*, 10.

Rassers, W. H. (1959 [orig. 1931]). *Panji, the Culture Hero*. The Hague: Martinus Nijhoff.

"Rasvershil onder Inlanders." (1912). *De Indische Gids*: 123–5.

Ricklefs, M. C. (1979). "Six Centuries of Islamization in Java," in *Conversion to Islam*, ed. N. Levtzion. New York: Holmes & Meier Publishers, Inc.

——. (1993 [orig. 1981]). *A History of Modern Indonesia since c. 1300*. Rev. ed. Stanford: Stanford University Press.

Said, E. W. (1978). *Orientalism*. New York: Pantheon Books.

Scherer, S. P. (1975). "Harmony and Dissonance: Early Nationalist Thought in Java." Unpublished MA thesis, Cornell University, Ithaca, New York.

Sears, L. J. (1994). "Rethinking Indian Influence in Javanese Shadow Theater Traditions," *Comparative Drama*, 18 (spring).

——. (1996). *Shadows of Empire: Colonial Discourse and Javanese Tales*. Durham: Duke University Press.

Shiraishi, Takashi. (1981). "The Dispute between Tjipto Mangoenkoesoemo and Soetatmo Soeriokoesoemo: *Pandita* vs. *Satria*," *Indonesia*, 32.

——. (1990). *An Age in Motion: Popular Radicalism in Java, 1912–1926*. Ithaca: Cornell University Press.

Soetatmo Soeriokoesoemo. (1918). "De Javaansche Vraagstuk," *Wederopbouw*, 1, no. 1: 4–7.

——. (1919). "Een beschouwing over de vormen der overheersching," *Wederopbouw*, 2.

——. (1920). "Theosofie en Javaansch Nationalisme," *Wederopbouw*, 3, nos. 4–7.

——. (1922). "De Twijfel van Djanaka," *Wederopbouw*, 5, nos, 1–5.

——. (1922). "Geschiedenis van Java: Gelicht uit het prea-advies van R. M. S. Soeriokoesoemo," *Wederopbouw*, 5, nos. 1–5.

——. (1923). "Het Heilige Schrift in beeld. De Wajang," *Wederopbouw*, 6, nos. 1–3: 30–9.

Stocking, G. W., Jr. (1987). *Victorian Anthropology*. New York: The Free Press.

Sutapa. (1921). "De behoefte aan intellectueele dalangs in verband met de ontwikkeling van het wajangspel," *Djawa*, 1: appendix B, 129.

"Theosofische Vereeniging" [no author]. (1932). *Encyclopedie van Nederland Indie*, 391–2.

Tjipto Mangoenkoesoemo. (1914). "De Wajang," in *De Indische Gids*, 36/I: 530–9.

Tsuchiya, Kenji. (1987). *Democracy and Leadership: The Rise of the Taman Siswa Movement in Indonesia*. Honolulu: Univeristy of Hawaii Press.

Woodward, M. R. (1989). *Islam in Java*. Tucson: University of Arizona Press.

Suggestions for Further Reading

Adorno, T. W. and Max Horkheimer. (1972). *The Dialectic of Enlightenment*. New York: Continuum Publishing Company.

Adorno, T., W. Benjamin, E. Bloch, B. Brecht, and G. Lukács. (1980 [1977]). *Aesthetics and Politics*. London: Verso.

Anderson, B. R. O. (1965). *Mythology and the Tolerance of the Javanese*. Ithaca: Modern Indonesia Project – Cornell University.

——. (1990 [1972]). "The Idea of Power in Javanese Culture," in *Language and Power: Exploring Political Cultures in Indonesia*. Ithaca: Cornell University Press.

Becker, A. L. (1979). "Text-Building, Epistemology, and Aesthetics in Javanese Shadow Theater." In *The Imagination of Reality*, eds. A. L. Becker and A. A. Yengoyan. Norwood, NJ: Ablex.

Benjamin, W. (1969). *Illuminations*. New York: Schocken.

Brandon, J. R. (1970). *On Thrones of Gold*. Cambridge: Harvard University Press.

——. (1987). *Wayang Theater in Indonesia: An Annotated Bibliography*. Dordrecht: Foris Publications.

Derrida, J. (1974). *Of Grammatology*. Trans. with an intro. by G. C. Spivak. Baltimore: Johns Hopkins University Press.

——. (1979). "The Supplement of Copula: Philosophy *Before* Linguistics," in *Textual Strategies: Perspectives in Post-Structuralist Criticism*, ed. Josué V. Harari. Ithaca: Cornell University Press.

Foucault, M. (1972). *The Archaeology of Knowledge*. New York: Pantheon.

——. (1979). "What is an Author?" in *Textual Strategies: Perspectives in Post-Structuralist Criticism*, ed. Josué V. Harari. Ithaca: Cornell University Press.

Geertz, C. (1960). *The Religion of Java*. Chicago: University of Chicago Press.

Holt, C. (1967). *Art in Indonesia: Continuities and Change*. Ithaca: Cornell University Press.

Johns, A. H. (1961). "Sufism as a Category in Indonesian Literature and History," *Journal of Southeast Asian History*, 2, no. 2.

Keeler, W. (1987). *Javanese Puppets, Javanese Selves*. Princeton: Princeton University Press.

Lev, D. S. (1985). "Colonial Law and the Genesis of the Indonesian State," *Indonesia*, 40 (Oct.).

McVey, R. (1967). "Taman Siswa and the Indonesian National Awakening," *Indonesia*, 4 (Oct.).

——. (1986). "The Wayang Controversy in Indonesian Communism," in *Context, Meaning, and Power in Southeast Asia*, eds. M. Hobart and R. Taylor. Ithaca: Cornell Southeast Asia Publications.

Moertono, S. ([1968] 1981). *State and Statecraft in Old Java: A Study of the Later Mataram Period, 16th to 19th Century*. Ithaca: Cornell Modern Indonesia Project.

Pemberton, J. (1994). *On the Subject of "Java."* Ithaca: Cornell University Press.

Pigeaud, T. (1938). *Javaanse Volksvertoningen*. The Hague: Martinus Nijhoff.

Stange, P. (1977). "Mystical Symbolism in Javanese Wayang Mythology," *The South East Asian Review*, 1, no. 2.

Sweeney, A. (1987). *A Full Hearing: Orality and Literacy in the Malay World*. Berkeley: University of California Press.

Chapter 18

Settler Colonies

Anna Johnston and Alan Lawson

The adjective "settler" has been applied to a number of widely diverging societies, cultures, colonies, historical situations, narratives, and individuals. It has thus been associated with many different ideological positions, political motivations, and analytical methods. Attempts have been made in several disciplines – notably history, social geography, social theory, literary studies and, more latterly, cultural studies – to describe and characterize different kinds of colonies. It is clear that even within the overseas imperial expansion of a single European nation, many different arrangements were made for the management of colonial relations.

The *Oxford English Dictionary* explains that the word colony is derived from the Latin "to cultivate"; *colon-us* is a farmer, cultivator, or settler. In Roman times, *colonia* was the official term for a settlement of Roman citizens in a newly subdued land. These *colons* retained their Roman citizenship and functioned as a garrison or bulwark that retained the land under Roman occupation. Normally, the colonists were granted land, and many were former soldiers.

At the very broadest level, historians of colonization generally distinguish two kinds of European colonies. These are most commonly called "colonies of occupation" and "colonies of settlement." Others include plantation colonies, occupation colonies, and mixed colonies. Of course, a more detailed analysis would identify a far greater number of different circumstances. Indeed the attempt to theorize settler subjectivity or settler cultural relations is impelled by, and grounded in, a more precise historicization and cultural location. In colonies of occupation, military power (or its representatives) subdued majority indigenous populations, and the political regimes that followed imposed and maintained rule over them. Most of the European colonies in Africa, Asia, and the Pacific were of this kind, even though they varied greatly in the manner in which this power was maintained and in the systems of governance that were established to sustain it. In these cases, decolonization was an often violent or at least revolutionary act of reclaiming majority, democratic rule by the indigenous population, and, in most cases, of restoring indigenous social and cultural practices and institutions.

Within traditional historical discourses, the term "settler colony" has functioned simply as a marker of one of the various types of colonies established by imperial powers. Hugh Egerton (1904: 5), for example, defines colonies as belonging to either of two groups:

> (1) Plantations, and (2) Colonies proper . . . The distinction between a colony which is primarily a settlement of men, of cultivators (from *colere*, to cultivate), and a plantation, which is primarily a settlement of capital, is fundamental.

Other historians note the difference between short-term colonial projects and permanent colonial settlement, and argue that this temporal distinction is what marks the "settler" (see Pollock, 1980). In general, historical definitions of "settler colonies" have relied on the presence of long-term, majority white racial communities, where indigenous peoples have been outnumbered and removed by colonial policies and practices. Thus countries like Australia, Canada, and New Zealand have traditionally been described as "settler colonies," although it is also possible to make more complex arguments about the inclusion of nations such as the US or South Africa, for example. Historians have always delineated the very different issues and problems experienced in settler colonies, but the use of the term "settler colony" in historiography has not traditionally suggested an analytic or political category.

In various places around the world, though, the term "settler" has had real political meaning. In both South Africa and Israel the term has been used to refer to the political agency of specific local communities. In South Africa, Afrikaners descended from seventeenth-century Dutch immigrants define themselves as "settlers," a term which particularly applies to their involvement in agricultural work. Similarly, the so-called "1820 Settlers" were British farmers who occupied, in particular, farming areas in the Eastern Cape. For such immigrant communities, the act of "settling" followed that other great foundational narrative of the Afrikaners, "trekking" into non-European occupied areas of Africa, culminating in "the Great Trek" of the mid-nineteenth century. These narratives of arrival, hardship, and settlement have been integral to their self-definition. Of course, in post-apartheid times, such white claims to land formerly belonging to the indigenous Africans are highly political. In Israel, too, Jewish Israelis who created communities around the contested city of Jerusalem have been called "settlers." For them, the act of "settling" in the very contested land fought over by Israelis and Palestinians was, and still is in places like the Gaza Strip, another highly political act of land occupation. In both these places, the idea of "settlement" as *laying a claim*, both through the literal possession of land and the physical occupation of disputed space, has always been crucial given the contested nature of land and politics in these countries. And as we will argue, the occupation of land formerly owned by others always translates into the cultural politics of representation.

The political nature of "settlement" has not, however, been absent in more obviously "settler" cultures like Australia, Canada, and New Zealand, but in some ways the term "settler colonies" covered up the real politics of these cultures. It seemed to refer mainly to the very obvious majority white populations without taking account of the physical violence and representational erasure done to indigenous communities in order to achieve that "whiteness." In the 1980s, analysts of colonialism and postcolonialism began to reexamine the implications of "settler colonies," often starting by reinstating the more historically accurate term "settler-invader" to emphasize the violence that the single, ostensibly benign, term "settler" concealed. This essay uses the term "settler" for reasons of brevity, but the "invader" rider should always be kept in mind, as it is in the theory. This work has been crucial to settler postcolonial analysis, as it reemphasized the important work of discourse and textuality along with physical and territorial colonization.

In settler colonies, the violence done was often greater – if less enthusiastically acknowledged – as it usually involved the elimination of the majority status of the indigenous population and its replacement by an emigrant, largely European, population. Examples of this type of colony include Argentina, Australia, Brazil, Canada, New Zealand, and the United States. It should be said that the inclusion of the United States in this group is both recent and contentious. These cultures have many significant things in common with other more problematic "settler colonies" such as Algeria, Ireland, Kenya, New Caledonia, Zimbabwe (formerly Southern Rhodesia), Palestine, Mozambique, and South Africa.

The authors of this article are particularly interested in Australia, Canada, New Zealand, and, more complicatedly, South Africa, but this list is by no means exhausts the range of settler colonies. It is fundamentally based on cultures colonized by British settlers roughly during the seventeenth and eighteenth centuries. Other countries whose "settler" status is discussed include the United States, Ireland, (occasionally) Scotland and Wales, parts of East Africa, and Latin America (most notably, Argentina). The "case" for the inclusion of Ireland is a pressing one, and the early trialing of British colonial methods in Ireland has been theorized and documented most notably by David Cairns and Shaun Richards (1988), David Lloyd (1993), and Declan Kiberd (1995). Many of these cultures have been ambiguously positioned in relation to settler postcolonialism, and the place of the United States is especially controversial. Jenny Sharpe notes that "when used as a descriptive term for the United States, *postcolonial* does not name its past as a white settler colony or its emergence as a neocolonial power; rather, it designates the presence of racial minorities and Third World immigrants" (1995: 181).

There are several significant cultural and historical effects that must be noticed here. "Settlers" arrived in the colony under many different circumstances. They may have been: sent forcibly as convicts (to early Australia, for instance); younger sons of downwardly-mobile families; commercial, political, administrative, religious, or military agents who stayed on; "refugees" escaping social rejection, religious persecution, or economic hard times; optimistic opportunists lured by hopes of gold or of cheap land or labor. In each case, they tended to retain a more limited allegiance to the home country than those sent to rule in colonies of occupation. In most cases, and the American colonies are a prime example, they were also subject to greater constraints upon their freedom and their ability to participate in governance than the citizens of the "home" country. They were frequently characterized in domestic cultural and political discourses as ungovernable, uncultured: as "colonials" they were second-class – belated or feral – Englishmen, and often came to be seen as political or economic rivals to the domestic citizens of the "home" country.

These factors produced, in many cases, the feeling of being colonized – of being European subjects but no longer European citizens. Settler postcolonial theory commonly describes this phenomenon in the axiom: the settler is both colonized and colonizing. This colonization was experienced politically, culturally, and socially, and in the most extreme cases led to revolution by the settler-colonists, as in the United States in 1776 and in Southern Rhodesia in 1965. At the same time, of course, the settler was an agent of colonial rule over the proportionally, and usually numerically, shrinking indigenous population.

A key element in settler postcolonial theory is an examination of the processes by which emigrant European settlers "displaced" the indigenous occupants. This displacement took many different forms. It was physical, geographical, spiritual, cultural, and symbolic. Indigenous peoples were characteristically moved from their traditional lands onto less desirable tracts of country: this happened in the history of settlement of the United States, New Zealand, South Africa, Canada, Argentina, and Australia. These movements of native peoples from their lands have often been memorialized and even celebrated in both popular culture (the "Western") and high culture (in historical fictions of the physical arrival of the European into alien physical and cultural space and their hard-earned sense of spiritual belonging). This helps us to remember that the displacement was, almost as importantly, cultural and symbolic as well as physical. It is in the translation from experience to its textual representation that the settler subject can be seen working out a complicated politics of representation, working through the settler's anxieties and obsessions in textual form. Increasingly, the white settlers referred to themselves and their culture as indigenous; they cultivated native attributes and skills (the Mounties, cowboys, range-riders, gauchos, backwoodsmen), and in this way cemented their legitimacy, their own increasingly secure sense of moral, spiritual, and cultural belonging in the place they commonly (and revealingly) described as "new." They also began to tell stories and devise images that emphasized the disappearance of native peoples: the last of his tribe ("the last of the mohicans"), the dying race, even tales of genocide – the Tasmanian aborigines, the San ("Bushmen") of Southern Africa, the Moriori of New Zealand.

There are two distinct impulses here. In the case of the genocide of the Tasmanian Aborigines in Australia in the 1880s, "genocide" accurately describes the intention but not the achievement – some people of Tasmanian-aboriginal descent survived but their existence as indigenous subjects was effectively obliterated by the universally accepted account of genocide. The extraordinary difficulty that they have had in proclaiming their indigenous authenticity testifies to the vigor and persistence of colonialist historical discourse. In New Zealand and Southern Africa, "history" records *pre*-settlement displacements and exterminations. These narratives had the effect of discrediting the "originality" of the current indigenous population by depicting them as violent *arrivistes* who had dispossessed the "true" indigenes. In the long run, the political, legal, and psychological effects were similar: they erased the claim of indigenous peoples to "full" indigeneity and therefore to their rights to land ownership and cultural priority that flowed from that.

The frequent "scientific" observation of the "dying race" in the nineteenth (and indeed the twentieth) century enabled a narrative of ethical indigenization in which the "settler" simply assumed the place of the disappearing indigene without the need for violence (or, of course, the designation "invader"). In South Africa, such narratives circulate around the San people ("Bushmen"). As Goldie rightly and usefully notices, these "last of his tribe" laments are crucial strategies in the replacement of the indigene by forms of white indigeneity such as the pioneer, the Mountie, the bushman: a process he has called "indigenization" (1989: 13). One of the principal functions of the indigenizing narrative is to legitimize the settler; to put the settler in the cultural and discursive place of the indigene whose physical space has already been invaded. The indigenized settler is the figure who is ready to step in when the native "dies out." The native must *make way* for the settler because there was a legal and moral prohibition against "invasion."

The lands the settlers occupied were themselves given special discursive treatment. Wherever possible, the vastness of the land was emphasized and this was often a prelude to or accompanied by an even more strategic emphasis on its "emptiness." The most spectacular example of this was in the case of Australia where the legal term "*Terra Nullius*" (literally "nobody's land" but commonly misunderstood as "empty land") was applied and survived in both popular and legal discourses until successful legal challenges (the Mabo and Wik Cases) in the 1990s. Vast and empty lands, insistently recorded in both texts and visual images, called out, obviously, to the European imagination to be filled, and they were filled by, successively, people, crops, and herds, but also by the stories and histories that, like the economically-productive crops, legitimated the settlement.

For the settler, too, the land had to be empty. Empty land can be settled, but occupied land can only be invaded. So the land must be emptied so that it can be filled with both words and herds. Some evacuations are more obviously in the domain of narrative and metaphor. The "Frontier," the "North," and (in

Australia) the "Center" are still popularly and even academically referred to as empty spaces. These tropes are persistent devices, thoroughly installed in cultural metaphysics and discourses, of clearance and removal, and of effacement. But they are, therefore, also paradoxical reminders of the extent to which the project of "settlement" (which is a project of displacement replacement) has fallen short. The management of the displacement of indigenous peoples moves from the physical domain (where it has been incomplete) to the symbolic domain.

Settler postcolonialism has had to defend itself against the charge of assimilating itself into a single (and thereby self-privileging) postcolonialism. It has also – less stridently – had to distinguish itself from earlier (though still extant) critical practices that were concerned with so-called "national literatures," and with the cultural nationalism of former colonies. Deriving its critical protocols from the evolution of the study of American Literature from the 1920s to the 1960s it concerned itself typically with the development of a national literature as a case study in nation building. Its philosophical roots were in nineteenth-century European notions of romantic nationalism deriving from Herder and Taine, and it was customarily articulated as reading symptomatically for signs of the national character, often figuring it as an evolving – maturing – organic entity reflected in the themes and metaphors of canonical nation-building texts. They were, inevitably if unwittingly, complicit in acts of cultural indigenization.

In the founding and growth of cultural nationalism, then, we can see one vector of difference (the difference between colonizing subject and colonized subject: settler-indigene) being replaced by another (the difference between colonizing subject and imperial center: settler-imperium). We can see this, with the benefit of postcolonial hindsight/analysis, as a strategic disavowal of the colonizing act. In this process, "the national" is what replaces "the indigenous" and in doing so conceals its participation in colonization by nominating a new "colonized" subject – the colonizer or settler-invader. Settlers are colonizers in an ineluctable historical and continuing relationality to indigenes and indigeneity. This necessitates the establishment of legitimizing narratives that will: naturalize their place; resolve the double bind (or what used to be called ambivalence); and explain (or explain away) their relation to indigeneity. But whatever the desire for disavowal, there is no disidentificatory gesture that is available to the settler. The settler seeks to establish a nation, and therefore needs to become native and to write the epic of the nation's origin. The "Origin" is that which has no antecedent, so the presence of Ab-origines is an impediment.

Settler criticism as it has been practiced since the mid-1980s has established itself in a relation of critique to these traditions of critical practice. The keystone of settler analysis is its insistence on the fraught and agonistic relationality that is an inescapable vector of all institutions and subjectivities within the settler culture. It is in concepts of multiple relationality, negotiation, exchange, and ambivalence that settler theory finds its characteristic analytical expression. Postcolonial analyses – as opposed to nativist celebration – of settler subjectivity have been impelled by the inevitable recognition that the term "settler" itself was, and always had been, tendentious and polemical. That is, the word "settler" was itself part of the process of invasion; it was literally a textual imposition on history.

Settler postcolonial studies have always been a part of a more general "postcolonialism," yet the postcolonial "authenticity" of the area is often challenged. In particular, since postcolonial studies began to gain institutional ground in the US academy, settler postcolonialism has often found itself being neglected, or excluded, in favour of more obviously ongoing colonial conflicts and cultures, such as South America or minority cultures within the United States. As Gillian Whitlock states, "Thinking about settlers is deeply unfashionable in postcolonial studies. Settlers have always been unpalatable subjects" (forthcoming, *The Intimate Empire*).

The primary opposition or contestation regarding the inclusion of settler cultures under the rubric "postcolonial" has to do with differing interpretations of the "post-" part of the term. The first comprehensive study of postcolonial literatures, *The Empire Writes Back*, by Bill Ashcroft, Gareth Griffiths, and Helen Tiffin (1989) used the term "postcolonial" "to cover all the culture affected by the imperial process from the moment of colonization to the present day," and argued that

> what each of these [cultures] have in common beyond their special and distinctive regional characteristics is that they emerged in their present form out of the experience of colonization and asserted themselves by foregrounding the tension with the imperial power, and by emphasizing their differences from the assumptions of the imperial center. (1989: 2)

In such a schema settler colonies have an obvious place.

Other critics believe that the inclusion of settler cultures as "postcolonial" is stretching a historical point, that whilst nations like Australia may once have been "colonial" they have now moved into an entirely different political framework. They point out that the tendency of settler cultures to be themselves involved in ongoing neocolonialism in the third world, or with their indigenous minorities, makes the claim to still be "colonized" themselves contentious. Some of these scholars consider that the inclusion of white settler nations is contradictory and possibly offensive to other cultures still in the grip of colonial oppression. Arun P. Mukherjee's problems with *The Empire Writes Back*'s definition of postcolonialism, for example, include the belief that "the theory downplays the different [*sic*] between the settler colonial and those colonized in their home territories, using the term 'colonized' for both of them. I feel that it trivializes the experiences of those who suffered genocide and pauperization under colonial rule, not to mention cultural deprivation" (1996: 15). Other scholars justly argue that the experience of colonialism has been, and continues to be, very different in, say, India and Australia – critics such as Arun Mukherjee, Vijay Mishra, and Bob Hodge object to the coalition of such different (post-)

colonial entities. Vijay Mishra and Boh Hodge want to see "a stronger distinction between the postcolonialism of settler and non-settler countries" (1991: 288), and argue that:

> the postcolonialism [of *The Empire Writes Back*] is a hermeneutic which is vindicated by the conditions in non-settler countries, but is then used unchanged to apply to settler colonies, thus making strategic moves of these settler colonies towards greater political and economic autonomy within a capitalist world economy appear as heroic and revolutionary ruptures . . . From the base of this elision, the construction of meaning in these non-settler colonies takes up a highly postmodern resonance. (1991: 286)

Literary scholars would not find the distinction surprising, but they might well be disturbed by the calls for exclusions that sometimes follow from it. The field of Commonwealth Literatures or Literatures other than English (which preceded and fundamentally informed what we now call "postcolonial" studies) since its inception in about the 1960s had always included settler colonies. Indeed, this discipline was crucially dependent on academics *from* settler colonies for its early energy, as is evident in Helen Tiffin's comprehensive history of post-colonial literary studies in her Introduction to the recent annotated bibliography, *Postcolonial Literatures in English: General, Theoretical, and Comparative, 1970–93* (Lawson *et al.*, 1997). Many of the disagreements about the scope of "the post-colonial" have arisen out of the tension between different disciplinary understandings and applications of the term and its implications.

The authors of this article would argue that the exclusion of settler colonies from postcolonial analyses would in itself constitute an erasure of colonial difference and complexity. As Mishra and Hodge themselves argue, postcolonialism must "acknowledge difference and insist on a strongly theorized oppositional postcolonialism as crucial to the debate, without claiming that this form is or has been everywhere the same wherever a colonizer's feet have trod" (1991: 289). The argument that settler cultures are not admissible as postcolonial states involves a privileging of one kind of colonial experience over others, and in doing so prevents an understanding of the various manifestations of colonial activity. It also smacks of a kind of postcolonial exoticism – a preference for "the more exciting postcolonialism of the non-settler countries" (ibid.).

It is tempting to speculate about the motivation for the sometimes over-determined repudiation of "settler-invader" postcolonialism by some in the US academy. The anxiety it reveals may derive from what outsiders often recognize as a desire in US nation-narration to forget its own colonizing status in favour of a more urgent attention to more recent problems of race: African-American, Chicano, etc. The effacement of Native Americans from discourses of race and colonialism in the US is concomitant with the wish to efface other settler-invader colonies from the domain of the postcolonial. These settler colonies might remind the US of the repressed memory of its own historical circumstance and hence of its painful need to (re)negotiate its own idealized constructions of origin. We would argue that the critical analysis of the literary, historical, political, and economic discourses of the US as a "white settler colony . . . [and] its emergence as a neocolonial power" (Sharpe, 1995: 181) would be intellectually productive, politically effective, and culturally and institutionally urgent.

The arguments against the inclusion of settler postcolonial studies commit by the sin of omission a kind of intellectual colonizing of their own – they attempt to instill a global theory and typology which erases difference. They also tend to rely on purely physical and institutional signs of colonialism, like armies of occupation or overt economic or legislative control by a distant power. In focusing on such overt manifestations of colonial authority, they exclude cultural, intellectual, and symbolic after-effects of Empire. Nicholas Thomas uses the term "colonial projects" to emphasize that:

> colonizing was an array of religious, commercial, administrative and exploratory projects that sometimes proceed in relative harmony but were at other times in tension or outright contradiction . . . Colonialism's culture should not be seen as a singular enduring discourse, but rather as a series of projects that incorporate representation, narratives and practical efforts. (1994: 97, 171)

While different ex-colonies are at different historical stages of temporal "post"-colonization, it is important to bear in mind that the departure of an imperial force (be it a military, administrative, or penal force) does not immediately end the relationship between nations and peoples built under colonial rule.

Not all postcolonial cultures are postcolonial in the same way. The postcolonialism of the metropolitan East-Indian intellectual is indeed not the same as that of the rural Ugandan, nor is the postcolonialism of the Aboriginal Australian the same as that of the white Canadian, nor (even) is the postcolonialism of the Native Canadian the same as that of the Native American, the New Zealand Maori, or the Australian Aborigine. But the "settler" subject cannot be made to disappear in this project of difference. Rather, she/he emerges from the material and textual enactments and enunciations of imperial power as a crucial site for the investigation of colonial power at work. And colonial power is, as Homi Bhabha has shown us, the sum total of the power that is wielded in the colonial situation – not merely the imposition of imperial power from above and center. To read the moment of imperialism in such a unilinear fashion is simply to reconquer the colonial subject.

The theoretical consequences of excluding settler postcolonialism from the broad field of postcolonial analysis are very damaging. It would have the effect of bracketing off from examination the very location where the processes of colonial power as negotiation, as transactions of power, are most visible. It would also risk reproducing an old and simplistic notion of imperialism as a one-way imposition of power from above and thus repeat the moment of imperialism's discursive capture of history. To propose doing so, is to overlook the fact that the important political and theoretical point that the colonial "moment" is a transaction of forces, a relationship – unequal, certainly – but a relationship nonetheless. Colonial power is a product of all of the vectors in the system, and we prevent its interrogation if we exclude any of them from our analysis. As Stephen Slemon observes, this exclusion of settler cultures unreflectingly reinscribes the familiar "binarism of Europe and its Others, of colonizer and colonized, of the West and the Rest, of the vocal and the silent" (1990: 34). Even early critiques of postcolonial theory have noted that locating resistance either in the contradictions of the colonialist text or in an essentialist Third World consciousness serves to conceal the actual operations of resistance (see Parry, 1988).

Settler postcolonial theory has deployed Homi Bhabha's now-familiar observation that "the colonial text occupies that space of double inscription" (1985: 150) in a particular way. It uses that notion as a way of highlighting the endlessly problematic double inscription of authority and authenticity within settler cultures. That "double inscription of authority and authenticity" is then brought together with the understanding that these cultures are both colonizing and colonized. In this way, we can see that there are always two kinds of authority and always two kinds of authenticity that the settler subject is (con)signed to desire and to disavow. The settler subject is signified, then, in a language of authority and in a language of resistance. The settler subject enunciates the authority that is in colonial discourse on behalf of the imperial enterprise, which he (and sometimes she) represents. The settler subject represents, but also mimics, the authentic imperial culture from which he (and more problematically, she) is separated. This is mimicry in Bhabha's special sense – that which is *almost the same but not quite*" (1984: 130) – since the authority is enunciated *on behalf of, but never quite as*, the Imperium.

Out of that mimicry emerges the menace of "the repetitious slippage of difference and desire" (ibid.: 131). In Western art, popular culture, history, fiction, and even in postcolonial theory, mimicry seems always to be found in the pathetic or scandalous performance of the colonized. However, in settler cultures, mimicry is a necessary and unavoidable part of the repertoire of the settler. This comes about because the "settler" subject exercises authority over the indigene and the land at the same time as translating desire for the indigene and the land into a desire for native authenticity. This can be read in numerous narratives of psychic encounter and indigenization. In reacting to that subordinacy, that incompleteness, that sign of something less, the settler mimics, appropriates, and desires, the authority of the indigene.

The typical settler narrative, then, has a doubled goal. It is concerned to act out the suppression or effacement of the indigene; it is also concerned to perform the concomitant indigenization of the settler. In becoming more like the indigene whom he mimics, the settler becomes less like the atavistic inhabitant of the cultural homeland whom he is also reduced to mimicking. The text is thus marked by counterfeitings of both emergence and origination.

The settler postcolonial subject, then, always speaks – wittingly or unwittingly – to both of its antecedent authorities/authenticities. In speaking back against the Imperium, in the interests of its own identity politics, the "settler" site of enunciation will always tend to reappropriate the position of all of those others with and against whom it has mediated that power. We need to identify, for any historicized, gendered, culturally specific site of enunciation, the "prior" sites whose authority either licenses the utterance or provokes the resistance, the contra/diction. The settler, then, is always addressing both the absent (and absentee) cultural authority of the Imperium and the unavailable (and effaced) cultural authority of the indigene.

The crucial theoretical move to be made is to see the "settler" as uneasily occupying a place caught between two First Worlds, two origins of authority and authenticity. One of these is the originating world of Europe, the Imperium – the source of its principal cultural authority. Its "other" First World is that of the First Nations whose authority they not only replaced and effaced but also desired. (Canadian Native peoples have for some decades insisted on being called *First* Nations in response to the Canadian Constitution's reference to the French and English as "founding nations" of Canada.) To each of these First Worlds, the settlers are secondary – indeed, supplementary. That secondariness makes it clear that the settler was also the "go-between" for the European First World with that which it has strategically named the Third. The 'settler" acted as a mediator rather than as a simple transmitter of Imperialism's uncomfortable mirroring of itself. The in-between of the settlers is not unbounded space, but a place of negotiation; colonialism is a relation, an unequal one, but no less a relation for that. The boundaries of cultures are especially porous. Settler cultures are, Joanne Tompkins points out, sites of rehearsal, of (re)negotiation. They are liminal sites at the point of negotiation between the contending authorities of Empire and Native. The settler subject is, in a sense, the very type of the non-unified subject and the very distillation of colonial power, the place where the operations of colonial power as negotiation are made most intensely visible.

The examination of these negotiations of colonial power takes place in interestingly complicated ways in the texts that settler postcolonial critics engage with. The kinds of texts that settler postcolonialism reads are multiple and various, though the issues surrounding theory, writing, and reception that we have discussed throughout this essay remain constant across a range of genres and writing occasions. Settler postcolonialism, as we have earlier suggested, has been central to the reading and analysis of national literatures of individual settler nations as well as enabling a significant number of comparative studies across the national literatures of, for example, Australia and Canada. Within the sphere of the nation, settler postcolonialism has been crucial in examining national structures and images – the work of Graeme Turner, for example, uses ideas about white Australians as postcolonial, settler subjects to explain the "national fictions" of Australia. At the same time, settler postcolonial analysis has examined in some detail a range of historical and popular discourses, like the myth of the dying race mentioned before, or colonial narratives of excessive indigenous sexuality, captivity narratives, miscegenation, and even cannibalism, as projections of settler anxieties about and desire for indigeneity. Textual sources such as the letters and diaries of settlers have provided much inspiration for creative writers and critics. In Canada, writings like Susanna Moodie's *Roughing it In the Bush* provided the source material for Margaret Atwood's rewriting of settler mythologies in her poem cycle, *The Journals of Susanna Moodie*, while diaries like those of Rachel Henning, Lady Barker, Ellen McLeod, and Georgiana McCrae have been recently retrieved by contemporary historical and literary critics and evaluated as instrumental in the construction of the settler psyche. Finally, in a more strictly literary domain, settler postcolonialism has been involved in trying to explicate symbolically laden fictions from the settler nations – writers such as Patrick White and Randolph Stow (Australia), J. M. Coetzee (South Africa), Michael Ondaatje and Margaret Laurence (Canada), and Janet Frame (New Zealand) have all received considerable attention from settler critics.

Gillian Whitlock's work on the writings of the nineteenth-century Canadian author Susanna Moodie is a good example of the practice of settler postcolonial criticism in relation to specific texts and historical and cultural writing "occasions." Susanna Moodie's *Roughing It in the Bush* (1852) and her sister Catherine Parr Traill's *The Backwoods of Canada* (1836) became crucial texts in defining settler femininity in Canada. Whitlock suggests that Traill was "addressing her own kind in England, as both embodiment and instructor of proper conduct for settler women," while Moodie satirizes and caricatures the role of settler gentlewomen, a role very "specific in its relationship to gender, class, and race" (Whitlock, 1992: 20, 21). Whitlock's reading of these two settler women's texts carefully draws out the implications of maternity in the textual construction of the colonial settler woman. She argues that the environment of settler cultures placed particular emphasis on women's fertility and that the welfare of mothers and children was crucial to the colonizing project in these locations. Colonies of occupation saw the role of women as predominantly that of the wife supporting the male in his role within (minority) white colonialist institutions, and women were expected to send their children "Home" for their safety and education. In the settler colonies, Whitlock suggests, white women were expected to give birth to the imperial race that would carry on the work of settler-invasion and, by implication, complete the replacement of indigenous populations. Whitlock's forthcoming book, *The Intimate Empire*, extends the analysis of gender in settler colonies into questions about the place of domesticity in settler colonies, the relationship between settler femininity and masculinity, and the role of evangelical discourses in forming the opinions and representations of devout settler subjects like the Moodies.

It is interesting to note that the focus on autobiographical material has been particularly useful for a range of settler critics, particularly those concerned with

371

examining the place of settler women. Indeed, critics who have combined an analysis of gender and colonialism have done some especially interesting and progressive work in settler postcolonialism. Work in this field includes that of Gillian Whitlock; Margaret Daymond and Dorothy Driver in South Africa; Helen Buss in Canada; and Lucy Frost, Shirley Walker, Susan Sheridan, and Kay Schaeffer in Australia. Driver and Whitlock have been especially prominent in noting the role of the white woman in the reproduction of Empire – biologically, culturally, and politically. The figure of the white woman has also been central to the fundamentalist-imperial notions of racial purity.

Work in settler postcolonialism has incorporated a range of critical approaches from other areas of the humanities and this has extended the scope and application of settler theories. The American historian Louis Hartz observed that colonies function to some extent as persistent fragments of the "parent" culture from which they have derived. That is, it is possible in colonies of settlers or in diasporic communities to observe cultural and linguistic practices and observances long after they have mutated or disappeared in the domestic culture. While this can be noticed in the earlier historical phases of most settler cultures it is a phenomenon more particular to minority populations in colonies of occupation or among significant diasporic populations where the need for a nonlocal cultural allegiance may be more pressing. Settler colonies do exhibit some of the characteristics of diasporas, but since they constitute cultural majorities, the use of diaspora as an analytic term – though superficially attractive – has not so far been found productive.

It is true, however, that much of the writing about settler cultures has appeared to assume that these cultures are ethnically homogeneous populations of Anglo-Celts (as they are often, but inaccurately, called in each of the Anglophone settler colonies) or of Iberians in Lusophone colonies. This has been theoretically convenient but it is not empirically sound. In Canada and South Africa, for instance, this seriously overlooks the fact that they are each constituted from the colonies of two European countries. But like the United States, all of these societies have long been and are increasingly multicultural: it should be noted, however, that this term is not current in New Zealand and its meaning varies widely between countries. There has, then, been an interesting interaction between postcolonial theory and theories of multiculturalism in Canada and Australia in particular in the work of Ien Ang, Sneja Gunew, Linda Hutcheon, Jon Stratton, and Joanne Tompkins. The neocolonialist activities of these settler cultures – most particularly Australia in New Guinea and the Pacific Islands – has been discussed by Robert Dixon and others. More recently, some of the relations between postcolonialism and broad questions of cultural relations and their commodification have been visited in discussions of globalization by Simon During, Arjun Appadurai, James Clifford, and others.

The other major critical issue that has often intersected with discussions of settler cultures has been "race." Most recently, this has been seen in the emergent critical discourses of "whiteness" which recognize that the elision of "white" as a racial category has inhibited investigation of the full panoply of constructions of culture and subjectivity, especially of those which utilize racist binaries in their foundations. The most prominent exponents of this work have been Richard Dyer and Vron Ware.

As the following discussion of various court rulings about land tenure will demonstrate, settler postcolonial approaches have also been useful in thinking about how government policies and cultural institutions have been deeply influenced by the history of colonial settlers and their ideas. Chief Justice Marshall, in delivering the US Supreme Court's ruling in the case of *Cherokee Nation* v. *State of Georgia* (1831) refers to the strong ethical claim that the indigenous people have on the United States. They have, he points out,

> yielded their lands by successive treaties, each of which contains a solemn guarantee of the residue, until they receive no more of their formerly extensive territory than is deemed necessary to their comfortable subsistence.

The counsel for the Cherokee peoples had argued that they had constitutional standing at Court as a "foreign state." Marshall found the argument that the Cherokee constituted a "state" overwhelmingly persuasive but not the argument that they were a "foreign" one. Although the judgment claims that the situation of the United States and the indigenous peoples who live within its formal borders "exists nowhere else," it is actually strikingly similar to that which has obtained in each of the settler colonies. Chief Justice Marshall went on to describe the Cherokee's relationship to the United States as that of "domestic dependent nations . . . in a state of pupilage . . . [whose] relation to the United States resembles that of a ward to his guardian." Although the Court decided to deny the injunction sought by the Cherokee, it drew attention to a clause in the US Constitution which distinguishes three separate constituencies among whom the Congress may regulate commerce: "foreign nations, . . . the several states, . . . the Indian tribes." Regretfully returning to its opening ethical position, Marshall's ruling concludes: "If it be true that wrongs have been inflicted and that still greater are to be apprehended, this is not the tribunal which can redress the past or prevent the future." And as Chief Justice Marshall makes abundantly, if unwittingly, clear, that "double-talk" is inevitably associated with forms of paternalism ("they are in a state of pupilage") and oppression: "domestic dependent nations" is eerily reminiscent of the way in which the South African apartheid state described "its" Bantustans or "homelands."

The relation between what Marshall called the "residue" of indigenous lands and the state whose title over that residue had not yet been exercised was articulated in a decision of the High Court of Australia in June 1992. In a landmark decision in the famous Mabo Case, the High Court concluded two things. First, it concluded that the doctrine of *Terra Nullius*, which had been used for two centuries in British and Australian law to deny native land claims, was itself untenable because the land was certainly not empty at the moment of "settlement." Second, it found that therefore, at least in certain places, a form of native title had not been, as the judgment puts it, "extinguished." *Terra Nullius* had had the discursive effect of "evacuating" the country of its indigenous inhabitants. It is perfectly clear to the present white inhabitants of Australia that it was neither Empty nor Nobody's in 1788 when the first settlers arrived, and the first settlers knew it quite well too. So the doctrine of *Terra Nullius* represents – *inter alia* – a cognitive dissonance, a gap between knowledge and belief; or, to put it another way, a kind of repressed knowledge. It is also bad history.

But three years later, the same High Court revisited the history of the relationship of different forms of land title in a settler colony. The most significant tracts of land were those over which pastoral leases had been granted. These were parcels of land leased for the specific and explicit purpose of grazing sheep. They were granted extensively in the major period of the expansion of frontiers of settlement between the 1840s and the 1890s. At the insistence of the British Colonial Office, these leases quite explicitly "reserved" a form of native title. In the December 1996 Wik case, the High Court ruled that pastoral leases might not fully extinguish Native title since they do not confer absolute title. Reopening the interesting possibility of coexistence became the occasion for mass anxiety about boundaries of various kinds. In effect, then, the Australian High Court in 1996 rediscovered an ethical and legal notion of coexistence by finding that Native title did survive alongside pastoral title (although European title still has precedence over Native title when the two are in direct conflict). Wik, then, requires quite a shift in thinking about the relations of people and of the land they, differently, occupy. It requires not a notion of separateness but a notion of simultaneity, perhaps more accurately, of proximity; it asserts that two laws – or, even more scandalously, two different systems of law – may apply to the one piece of land. In this new conception of colonized space, the space of the colonizer and the colonized are not mutually exclusive. These two sets of spatial relations must then be seen as things that are relatable but not commensurable. What the Wik judgment enables, then, in a settler-postcolonial analysis, is a reading of the sign of the historical relationality from which neither the settler nor the indigene can be separated. The indigene cannot be relegated to something that is merely chronologically prior; the settler cannot merely come at the end of history, "the winning post." This might be a way of giving a "settler" inflection to Homi Bhabha's phrase, "overlapping without equivalence."

That the relation between the settler-state and the indigenous owners of the land which that state now encompasses to itself is heavily fraught and deeply flawed in legal, ethical, and social terms is a common feature of settler societies. In fact, it might be useful to think of it as a defining one. Invariably the relation inspires a kind of double-talk in both legal discourse and also in the public narratives of history. That "double-talk" has been described by some settler society theorists as "ambivalence," as "duplicity," and more recently as a manifestation of what Freud called "the uncanny." It has been described by the Australian writers Ken Gelder and Jane M. Jacobs this way: "in this moment of decolonization, what is 'ours' is also potentially, or even always already, 'theirs'" (1998: 23). They capture the skeptical utopianism of some forms of postcolonial theorizing in the following remarks: "we want to contemplate the possibility of producing a postcolonial narrative which, rather than falling into a binary that either distinguishes 'us' from 'them' or brings us all together as the same, would instead think through the uncanny implications of being in place and 'out of place' at precisely the same time" (1998: 139).

It is appropriate to end this essay with these discussions of textuality and land, as these are perhaps the most enduring obsessions of settler postcolonial theory and practice. More specifically, the contestation between settlers and indigenous peoples for these cultural resources is a crucial site of contemporary cultural critique – for literary scholars such as the authors of this article, it is particularly important to examine the ways in which this is played out in representational practice. Somewhere in the space between these two spheres of identification in settler colonies the complex nature of cultural politics in these environments is played out, in ways which draw on the colonial past and seek to define a postcolonial future.

References and Further Reading

Ashcroft, Bill, Gareth Griffiths, and Helen Tiffin. (1989). *The Empire Writes Back*. London and New York: Routledge.

Bhabha, Homi. (1984). "Of Mimicry and Man: The Ambivalence of Colonial Discourse," *October*, 28: 125–33. Rept. in Bhabha, 1994: 85–92.

——. (1985). "Signs Taken for Wonders: Questions of Ambivalence and Authority under a Tree outside Delhi, May 1817," *Critical Inquiry*, 12, no. 1: 144–65. Rept. in Bhabha, 1994: 92–102.

——. (1994). *The Location of Culture*. New York: Routledge.

Cairns, David and Shaun Richards. (1988). *Writing Ireland: Colonialism, Nationalism, and Culture*. Manchester, New York: Manchester University Press.

Cherokee Nation v. *Georgia*. 5 Peters, 1, 1831.

Denoon, Donald. (1979). "Understanding Settler Societies," *Historical Studies*, 18, no. 73: 511–27.

——. (1983). *Settler Capitalism: The Dynamics of Dependent Development in the Southern Hemisphere*. Oxford: Clarendon Press; New York: Oxford University Press.

Egerton, Hugh. (1904). *The Origin and Growth of the English Colonies and of their System of Government*. Oxford: Clarendon.

Gelder, Ken and Jane M. Jacobs. (1998). *Uncanny Australia: Sacredness and Identity in a Postcolonial Nation*. Carlton, Victoria: Melbourne University Press.

Goldie, Terry. (1989). *Fear and Temptation: The Image of the Indigene in Canadian, Australian, and New Zealand Literatures*. Kingston, Ont.: McGill-Queens's University Press.

Johnston, Anna. (1996). "Australian Autobiography and the Politics of Making Postcolonial Space," *Westerly*, 4: 73–80.

Kiberd, Declan. (1995). *Inventing Ireland*. London: Jonathan Cape.

Lawson, Alan. (1992). "Comparative Studies and Post-colonial 'Settler' Cultures," *Australian-Canadian Studies*, 10, no. 2: 153–9.

——. (1994). "Un/settling Colonies: The Ambivalent Place of Discursive Resistance," in Chris Worth, Pauline Nestor, and Marko Pavlyshyn, eds., *Literature and Opposition*. Clayton, Victoria: Centre for Comparative Literature and Cultural Studies.

——. (1995). "Post-colonial Theory and the 'Settler' Subject," *Essays on Canadian Writing*, 56: 20–36.

——, Leigh Dale, Helen Tiffin, and Shane Rowlands, eds. (1997). *Post-Colonial Literatures in English: General, Theoretical, and Comparative, 1970–93*. New York: G. K. Hall–Simon & Schuster–Macmillan.

Lloyd, David. (1993). *Anomalous States: Irish Writing and the Post-colonial Moment*. Durham: Duke University Press.

Mishra, Vijay and Bob Hodge. (1991). "What is Post(–)colonialism?" Rept. in Patrick Williams and Laura Chrisman, eds., *Colonial Discourse and Post-Colonial Theory: A Reader*. New York: Harvester Wheatsheaf, 1993.

Mukherjee, Arun P. (1996). "Interrogating Postcolonialism: Some Uneasy Conjunctures," in Harish Trivedi and Meenakshi Mukherjee, eds., *Interrogating Postcolonialism: Theory, Text and Context*. Shimla: Indian Institute of Advanced Study.

Parry, Benita. (1988). "Problems in Current Theories of Colonial Discourse," *Oxford Literary Review*, 9, nos. 1–2: 27–58.

Pollock, Norman. (1980). "Colonies, Explorers, Pioneers and Settlers," in Anthony Lemon and Norman Pollock, eds., *Studies in Overseas Settlement and Population*. London and New York: Longman.

Sharpe, Jenny. (1995). "Is the United States Postcolonial?: Multinationalism, Immigration, and Race?" *Diaspora* 1, no. 2: 181–99.

Slemon, Stephen. (1990). "Unsettling the Empire: Resistance Theory for the Second World," *World Literature Written in English*, 30, no. 2: 30–41.

Stasiulis, Daiva and Nira Yuval-Davis, eds. (1995). *Unsettling Settler Societies: Articulations of Gender, Race, Ethnicity and Class*. London: Sage.

Thomas, Nicholas. (1994). *Colonialism's Culture: Anthropology, Travel and Government*. Melbourne: Melbourne University Press.

Tiffin, Chris and Alan Lawson, eds. (1994). *De-Scribing Empire: Post-colonialism and Textuality*. London: Routledge.

Tompkins, Joanne. (1995). "'The Story of Rehearsal Never Ends': Rehearsal, Performance, Identity in Settler Culture Drama," *Canadian Literature*, 144: 142–61.

Whitlock, Gillian. (1992). "Exiles from Tradition: Women's Life Writing," in Gillian Whitlock and Helen Tiffin, eds., *Re-Siting Queen's English: Text and Tradition in Post-Colonial Literatures*. Amsterdam and Atlanta: Rodopi.

——. (forthcoming). *The Intimate Empire*.

Chapter 19

Ireland After History

David Lloyd

The current amazement that the things we are experiencing are "still" possible in the twentieth century is *not* philosophical. This amazement is not the beginning of knowledge – unless it is the knowledge that the view of history which gives rise to it is untenable.

Walter Benjamin

Reflecting on Irish culture and history, I find myself recurring again and again to the insights Walter Benjamin gathered in his essay, "Theses on the Philosophy of History" (1969: 257). As with so much in the theses, this particular reflection is for us absolutely contemporary: it is as relevant to our own shock at the "recurrence of tribalism" or at the persistence of apparently outmoded cultural formations as it was to the disdain of Benjamin's "historicist" prophets of progress for the foregone movements of the past. This essay is concerned with the self-evidence of such amazement and with the forms of historical narrative that make that amazement seem so commonsensical. I offer a critique of current historicism, which continues to adhere to the notion of progress or development and of civility at the expense of the alternative histories and cultures of which the story might be told. Indeed, it is precisely what Benjamin defines as historicism that not only relegates alternatives, past and present, to the condition of irrationality and backwardness, but *produces* them as such. Atavism is to civility as backwardness to modernity, the necessary antithesis that defines by negation the proper forms and formations of civilized society. Historicism reduces the cultural forms and practices of past and subordinated people to mere reaction, folklore or mythology and yet depends on them for its own articulation and for its own myth of a finally triumphant progress. Within its frames, pasts that envisaged different futures are detached from any life to come, are fixed in their extinction, furnishing only debris, remnants, whose excavation proves only the inevitability of their passing, their fundamental incapacity to blend into the onward flow of history. Only, on occasion, they trouble history's stream with interference, eddies, and counterflows.

That is why I attempt not only critique, but a sketch also of possible alternative terms and methods through which to shatter and to displace the common sense of historicism, the sedimented layer of concepts and assumptions on which its self-certainty rests. I refer of course to our own moment, as post-Cold War triumphalists proclaim the end of history and of ideological struggle and seek to reduce the whole globe by force to the mendacious triad of "capitalism, freedom and democracy." Ireland faces its own forms of subjection to a New World Order that has long been in preparation. "Ireland After History" gestures towards other possibilities that have persisted outside the mainstream of developmental history, and suggests that they might be liberated from the regulatory force of an historical ideology that has governed political and economic decisions globally over the last two centuries.

The lines of thought that I follow here emerge in large part from a longstanding concern with colonialism and in particular with its effects on colonized cultures. Such work inevitably demands a comparative approach drawing from the immense body of work, economic, historical, and sociological as well as cultural, that is and continually becomes available. Colonialism is an integrated phenomenon that operates across all the fields that in the West would constitute the public and the private, civil society and the state. No single event that occurs or institutional practice that is implemented is without effects across all the domains of colonized societies, not least because the aim of colonialism is the utter transformation of the colonized culture: the eradication of its structures of feeling, the subjection of the population to the colonizers' notions of legality and citizenship, and the displacement of indigenous forms of religion, labour, patriarchy, and rule by those of colonial modernity. Again, colonialism is also a rationalizing endeavor that leads to the frequent replication of similar institutions and practices across the widely spread and diverse colonies of each imperial power. Not least, colonialism produces powerful and fantasmatic ideologies that are no less fantastic for being woven and sustained through its quasiscientific studies in racial typology, history, and the economics of development. Nowhere more than under colonialism is the deep unreason of reason more compellingy in evidence.

Yet this representation of colonialism is merely a schematization of the norms and ends of a global process. Comparative work on colonialism's processes and effects draws out not only the ubiquity and replication of forms of colonial rule but also the remarkably diverse ways its rationalizing drive is deflected by the particularities of each colonized culture. There are no identical colonial situations; so that in place of comparative, we should in fact employ the term "differential," marking the ways in which quite specific cultural forms emerge in relation to a universalizing process. That relational moment within differential analysis is crucial, for the actual formation of colonial societies takes place precisely within the uneven encounter between a globalizing project founded in and still legitimated by Europe's delusion of universality and the multiple and different social imaginaries at work in colonized cultures. Without such a differential approach, the analysis of colonialism tends towards either bad abstraction or a positivistic catalog of singularities and leads to a conceptual inanity within which the import of the singularity is permanently evanescent. Differential analysis, however, marks the rhythmic insistence of cultural singularities that emerge in relation to colonial structures, so that the study of one given site may be profoundly suggestive for the understanding of another, without the two sites having to display entire congruence.

Evidently, to introduce an essay on Ireland with these reflections on colonialism and modernity is to insist that Ireland has indeed undergone colonialism and in part continues to do so. This assertion about Ireland's cultural and historical status continues to be contested, and not surprisingly, given the political stakes involved. To assert that Ireland is and has been a colony is certainly to deny the legitimacy of British government in Northern Ireland and no less to question the state and governmental structures that have been institutionalized in the postcolonial Free State and Republic of Ireland. It is to demand that each state's claim to the monopoly of violence within their territories be rigorously thought through in light of their own very arbitrary and violent foundations. Such questioning does not, as many will be quick to charge, confer automatic legitimacy on any armed insurrectionary movement, movements all too simplistically and tendentiously termed terrorist. What it does demand, however, is that the phenomenon of violence be understood as constitutive of social relations within the colonial capitalist state, whose practices institutionalize a violence which, though cumulative, daily, and generally unspectacular, is normalized precisely by its long duration and chronic nature. Unlike insurgency, which is usually represented as sporadic and of the nature of a temporary "crisis," the violence of the state operates through its institutions continuously, producing the material effects of poverty, unemployment, sickness, depopulation, and emigration. That these phenomena are generally not seen as state-mediated effects of capitalist and colonial violence forces us to recognize that the violence of the state belongs in its capacity to control representation, both political and cultural, thus regulating to a remarkable extent the "common sense," in Antonio Gramsci's usage, of any given society.

The struggle over representation in every field of social practice accordingly becomes a crucial terrain. The problem of representation and occlusion is a constant preoccupation. The question of the past in Ireland informs the emergence of future possibilities, possibilities that are continually narrowed and occluded by an historical consciousness that seeks to write the complexities of Irish history into a narrative of modernization and the emergence of a well-regulated civil society. That narrative, which has been so amplified in recent years by an uncritical and literally statecensored media, celebrates the passage from Ireland's domination by British colonial capital to its domination by and participation in the neocolonial circuits of global capitalism. Those who have raised fundamental questions about the continuing consequences of Ireland's colonial past have largely been marginalized in public debate, just as those who have raised legitimate questions as to the repression of fundamental issues in the recent Peace Process have not only been marginalized and abused but in some cases, like that of the family of Bernadette Devlin McAliskey, directly subjected to harassment and inhumane treatment by the State. The insistent disavowal of critical questions as to the alternative possibilities has enforced the occlusion not only of a vast historical repertoire of social imaginaries but also of critical analysis of the present. What would it mean not to commit Ireland's future to continuing capitalist colonialism, to the status of construction zone for the electronics industry with its so far concealed but no less disastrous effects on the environment and its labour force? What would it mean, not to disdain but to take seriously the still-persistent recalcitrance of Irish cultural practices to the rhythms and social practices of capitalist modernity? What will it cost to resist not just British occupation and domination, but absorption into the immense injustice of transnational capital and the destructive logic of international military alliances? What does it in practice mean to project what Gerry Adams has called a nonsexist, nonsectarian, and democratic Republic? Hegemonic resistance to addressing these questions is itself a symptom of the unfinished project of decolonization in Ireland and entirely fulfills Fanon's angry prognosis in *The Wretched of the Earth* that the future of the bourgeois postcolony was to become the conduit of neocolonial capital.

The questions raised by Ireland's colonial status are pressing and intellectually profound. It is, therefore, unfortunate that so much of the objection to that claim has been intellectually vacuous, deploying personal vitriol and caricature rather than reasoned argument. The irrationality of such polemic bespeaks its embeddedness in anxiety and disavowal rather than rationally articulable positions, and more often than not it betrays its own astounding ignorance of the postcolonial work it reviles in its cartoons. There are, however, a number of effective arguments in circulation that seek to problematize or refute the claim that Ireland has undergone the historical experience of colonialism and may therefore be considered, at least in part, as a postcolonial nation. These perspectives in general insist that Ireland has never in fact had the status of a colony or that comparison with other countries considered postcolonial reveals only Ireland's vastly more developed social and economic condition. The force of these arguments obliges postcolonial critics to consider more thoroughly the legitimacy of our own claim that Ireland has been and continues to be colonized in distinct and materially significant ways. I want to focus on two essays that have had relatively wide circulation and succinctly address the issues involved, but not in order to attempt a global refutation of these and related arguments, which would only extend a potentially endless round of empirical claims and counterclaims. It seems more valuable to focus and clarify the methodological or theoretical differences that underlie our different interpretations of Irish history. The first of these is Thomas Bartlett's useful historical essay, "'What Ish My Nation?'" (in Bartlett *et al.*, 1988), the second Liam Kennedy's more recent economically based essay, "Modern Ireland: Postcolonial Society or Postcolonial

Pretensions" (1996). I choose these two essays not because they are the only arguments of their kind, but because each, historical and economic respectively, efficiently condenses the principal arguments made everywhere to refute Ireland's colonial history. Though they do overlap at times in their concerns, I will engage each in turn to draw out distinctly a theoretical critique of their disciplinary terms and deployment of concepts, a critique directed foremost at the limitations of empirical method.

The historical arguments against considering Ireland as a colony have yet to be better summarized that by Thomas Bartlett in his essay "'What Ish My Nation?': Themes in Irish History, 1550–1850." Though it must be said from the outset that Bartlett is not solely concerned with the colonial question and that his brief does not include the postfamine era in which the dissemination of nationalism is most extensive, his essay well exemplifies the kind of historical arguments that need to be adduced in order to call colonialist claims into question. Bartlett's arguments are several. In the first place, though he acknowledges that during the late seventeenth and eighteenth centuries "Ireland bears most, if not all, of the hallmarks of a colony" (1988: 46), he notes the fact that "few Irishmen – Protestant or Catholic – accepted that Ireland was a colony with the attendant attributes of inferiority and subordination" (47). The arguments made were generally for its rightful status as a separate kingdom. Secondly, "Unlike other colonies, Ireland was not located in some distant continent, nor did she supply the mother country with otherwise unobtainable raw materials or exotic products" (ibid.). Thirdly, given the massive emigration and transportation of Irish people to other colonies, such as Australia, Canada, Britain [sic] or the USA [sic], "then surely Ireland, so far from being a colony, should be considered a mother country in her own right?" (ibid.).

These arguments are striking and embed a number of assumptions that are worth questioning. Of the third question, it would be enough to say that in some sense, then, South Asian communities in Britain, Singapore, the United States, reconstitute India and Pakistan as "mother" countries for their new states of citizenship. Or Korean immigrants make Korea an American mother country? In other words, it is well known that the effects of foreign military and commercial interventions, from imperial commercial and territorial wars to extensive colonization, displace large segments of indigenous populations who are forced to migrate in order merely to survive. Most often, and especially when coerced, that emigration must be to locations either in the imperial nation or within its territories. More is obscured here, however, than aspects of comparative global history, the ignoring of which leads to an inaccurate "Irish exceptionalism." The comment could not have been made without the apparent *whiteness* of the Irish emigrants, which seems to naturalize their later and complex identification with Ireland as a white European point of origin, and to obscure the massive differences in the meaning of emigration by positing destination rather than point of origin as the significant factor. That some Irish were in their turn to become colonists elsewhere, or to be instruments of colonial rule, like the Senegalese troops or the Ghurkas, for example, says nothing as to the condition of the Ireland they were mostly obliged to leave. There, to a very large degree, they were not in fact considered to be racially identical with "Anglo-Saxons" or other Europeans. On the contrary, their capacity to become colonizers involved, as many have now shown, a considerable labor of redefinition and of racist self-differentiation from the nonwhite populations of their new nations. The apparent whiteness of the Irish is accordingly a frequent casual objection to the idea of Ireland being a "third world" or postcolonial nation. In fact, the doubt usually reveals to a considerable degree the anxiety "white" subjects tend to feel in being identified with peoples of color. What slips in here at the foundation of the argument is both the problematic history of racialization and a prior assumption, masked by the racial issue, as to the incomparability of the Irish experience to non-European ones. We will return to emigration more extensively in the context of Kennedy's essay, pausing here for some more general reflections on the concept of colonialism that Bartlett's work suggests.

For what occurs in his essay is a common enough confusion of the distinct categories of colonization and of the subject positions within which colonialism is apprehended and, over time, conceptualized. There are distinct differences between colonization as exemplified in the colonial Untied States or Australia and colonization as a term used to describe the effects of French or British imperialism and governance in North and West Africa. The "colonial" period in US history refers in the first place not to the colonization of the land and the subordination, displacement, and extermination of its indigenous peoples, but to the relations between a white settler population and England as the dominant and regulative power. "Independence" then refers not to the process of decolonization, as understood by indigenous populations, but to the establishment of an autonomous, but no less European and imperial, state form by the settlers. What for the settlers inaugurates, in anachronistic terms, a postcolonial era, inaugurates for the indigenous and slave populations a period of intensified and increasingly extended colonization. This example embodies two theoretical points: one is that the designations "colonial" and "postcolonial" involve not mere empirical judgment but the consideration of historical human subjects and their social relations as subjects and objects; the other is that the collapsing of the term "colony" into a single set of characteristics ignores the gradual shifts and accumulations of meaning that mark it as a crucially temporal rather than an ideal concept.

Colonialism is, if I may put it so, always a forged concept, one whose significance is subject to iterations and reiterations that are predicated on materially embedded political and cultural struggles. It is accordingly more or less immaterial whether the "Irish lawyers and politicians" of the eighteenth century argued for the status of a separate kingdom for Ireland or conceived of the country as a colony in the American sense. That is an historiographical move which at once privileges the perspective of elite classes and assumes already the historical development of a concept whose full range of meanings emerged gradually through the nineteenth and into the twentieth centuries. I would propose, instead, that we understand the designation colonial to be, in Marx's sense, a "rational abstraction" rather than a transhistorical concept.[1] That is, it is a concept that can only function, like "labor" and "exchange," *a posteriori*, at the point when the phenomena it designates and unifies have emerged in their full material actuality. Thus, just as we can call barter a form of exchange only when the abstraction of "exchange" as a distinct economic process has been made possible, so, for example, we can refer to India as a British colony only at the point where British governmental administration rather than East India Company mercantile practices dominate and the process of administrative rationalization occurs by way of metropolitan decisions and concerns: retrospectively, we can see the work of the East India Company as a phase of colonialism, though the word itself may not have been used. But the mid-nineteenth-century emergence of the British state as governing power is definitive. Indeed, the function of the modern state is virtually everywhere critical to the definition of colonialism.

Like Algeria, Ireland becomes a "colony" rather than a region of the state exactly where the extension of the British state finds its limit in the deep recalcitrance of Irish economic and cultural practices to "modern" institutions and subject formation. Through the nineteenth century, this recalcitrance is increasingly understood as embedded in the Irish "national character" or in racial difference, thus influencing the emergence of state policies that combine deliberate depopulation of the country with projects that entail the radical transformation of Irish subjectivities economically and culturally.[2] In turn, the emergence of nationalism in Ireland is no less shaped by racialized distinctions that come to underlie the cultural and social projects of many nationalists. The intrinsic resistance of Irish ways to modernization thus inflects both the state's incorporative projects and nationalism's alternative conceptions of Ireland's future. An extended interface between modern and nonmodern social formations arises that can best be understood in relation to other colonial sites.

What I imply here about the texture of Irish and, by extension, colonial histories is that within them the characteristically distinct spheres of modernity – economic, political, legal, cultural, etc. – prove impossible to maintain. Furnishing in some cases an opportunity for nationalist mobilization, this lability of social space presents a profound problem for the colonial as for the postcolonial state. It is no less a problem for intellectual disciplines which define their distinct objects in relation to modern institutions and spheres of practice – economics, political science, sociology, art, etc. Disciplines depend on the stable location of a modern subject and develop their assumptions, whether political, economic, social, or aesthetic, entirely within the terms of modernizing rationalities. The final aim of this rationality is the formation of a modern civil society alongside a developed economy; further entailed in it is the generally implicit assumption of an ethical, disinterested subject, disinterested by virtue of a prior formation, and objective or truthful through submission to disciplinary norms.

Hence the all-too-often unbalanced character of attacks on postcolonialism and cultural studies, or on the even more nebulous specter of "postmodernism." In each case, though in quite different ways, these inter- or post-disciplinary intellectual tendencies challenge at once the integrity of the disciplines and the self-evidence of civil society, and in doing so necessarily displace their ethical assumptions. The *moral* criticism of postcolonial work clearly precedes any intellectual engagement with it, since the ethical status of the disciplinary subject is *a priori* at stake. Hence it is possible for an economist like Liam Kennedy to infer "postcolonial *pretensions*" with scarcely a single citation of any scholar or work and without extended engagement with any argument. The positivistic method that substantiates his own position is entirely in keeping with this *a priori* ethical judgment: Kennedy cannot attend to modes of argument that would question the objective validity of facts in abstraction.[3]

For the sake of brevity, I will focus on one exemplary set of statistics that Kennedy offers. The function of such tables is to demonstrate the irrefutability of facts and the validity of empirical comparative method: you cannot disagree with facts. The structuring of the data in a table simultaneously demands, as an unexamined methodological procedure, a remarkable degree of isolation and abstraction. Elements of a given social economy are excised from their differential relationship to historical processes and related formations and placed in comparison with equally isolated elements in a table that seeks to display a set of significant comparisons. What it actually displays is a set of partial relations organized according to an hierarchical axis that embodies unexamined values. Facts become entirely abstracted from the human agencies and acts that have constituted them in relation to a larger matrix of interdeterminant conditions. Kennedy's Table I (1996: 169), reprinted here, is a notable instance of the effects of such abstraction. I cite a few of the statistics from a somewhat longer table, but this is sufficient for the argument I wish to make here, since the point is to examine the effects of a method rather than the accumulation of statistics.

Kennedy's point is quite clear: statistics on the economic structures of "self-evidently" third world countries when compared to Ireland demonstrate that "there is a marked discontinuity between the Irish and these other experiences"

"Kennedy's (1996) Table I: Economic structure: share of the labour force (%) in agriculture and industry around the time of independence"

Country	Agriculture	Industry
India (1950)	72%	10%
Ghana (1960)	68%	10%
Algeria (1954)	88%	5%
Ireland (1911)	43%	25%

(1996: 169). The proper measure for Ireland is rather "the contemporary continental European countries." Ireland cannot therefore be usefully regarded as a postcolonial nation. Comparisons with other European countries were, indeed, frequently made around the time from which these Irish statistics date and throughout the nationalist tradition from Davis through Pearse and Connolly. Primarily, though, the references were made in order to show the discrepancy between Ireland and similarly sized European countries, among which Belgium was most frequently cited. The point was the anomaly of Ireland's underdevelopment in relation to other small European nations and this fact was usually attributed to British rule. Ireland had, indeed, been systemically underdeveloped as a subordinate entity under British imperial capitalism, in much the sense that Andre Gunder Frank and other Latin American theorists have suggested.[4] That underdevelopment took place not so much by laissez-faire or mercantile policies of extraction but by way of deep state-driven policies of social and cultural transformation that had drastic consequences for the population. The formation of modern Ireland occurred through the exercise of constant coercion and violence, that nonetheless never achieved the integration and homogenization of Ireland that would have extinguished nationalist aspirations. The conditions of (under)development themselves produced Ireland's colonial relation to Britain.

The economic underdevelopment of Ireland took place through its role as supplier of agricultural products, processed and unprocessed, to a largely industrialized and militaristic Britain. The cycles of crisis in agriculture and agriculture-based industries are closely linked throughout the nineteenth and early twentieth centuries to the ebb and flow of British industrialization and military ventures throughout the Empire, the post-Napoleonic crisis after 1815 being an early and spectacular instance. Only the northeast escaped this pattern to some extent, being notably the only part of Ireland to undergo vigorous industrialization. *Pace* Kennedy, who thinks it "an irrelevance" (1996: 170) that location is extremely significant to the terms of any colonial analysis: this was the region of Ireland in which the impact of settler colonialism had been most intense and which later maintained, as James Connolly and others frequently observed, its capitalist social relations through the discriminatory and quasi-racialized deployment of settler–native antagonism. The specific development of an industrial proletariat in northeast Ireland was largely predicated on colonial social relations and the systematic exclusion and underdevelopment of the recalcitrant native population on grounds of culture, ethnicity, and religion. In other regions, industry relied principally on agricultural production which was steadily subjected to capitalist rationalization throughout the nineteenth century, with an ever-increasing emphasis on grazing and on cash-crops, such as barley and hops for the brewing and distilling industries. The registration of many of these industries, as, for instance, Guinness, in England is consistent with a long-lasting pattern of net capital outflow from Ireland, where relatively low levels of investment are returned with a correspondingly large proportion of capital extraction.

This pattern has continued up to the present and shows no immediate prospect of amelioration.[5]

The point then is not that Ireland is or is not directly comparable to other "third world countries" on merely empirical/statistical bases. Such positivist assumptions are neither required nor predicted by postcolonial methods. What is at stake is the process by which facts are related and the geographic, economic, and political conditions and the social contradictions out of which they emerged. Structurally the relations between Ghana, India, and Ireland within the British Empire are not entirely different despite the apparent variation in relative labor statistics. Each colony emerged in relation to the extraction of resources and shows marked differentiation between urban and rural locations: the urban and usually coastal centers become *entrepots* for colonial trade and processing industries, while the ruralized hinterlands become locations of raw materials or of artisanal goods whose specific value depends on their differentiation from mass-produced commodities. Each colony in turn becomes the market for finished goods that are imported from Britain. Beyond these general structural correspondences, however, the use of comparison gives way to the detailed and differential analysis that grounds the moment of abstraction once more in the complex and specific relations of geography, demography, history, racialization, culture, etc. One might say that this is precisely what differentiates the study of colonialism from the study of imperialism, which tended to emphasize the macroeconomic flows of trade and industrial and financial capital rather than the specificities and dynamics of particular colonies. In order to grasp the particularity of Ireland's or of any other country's experience within the larger economies of colonialism, economic or other data need to be posed in relation to the specific forms of rule or modes of cultural differentiation and so forth that have determined the actual texture of the society.

One major demographic, cultural, and economic phenomenon that Kennedy's selection of statistics throughout omits to include is emigration, a phenomenon that, where reincorporated into Irish figures, profoundly alters the interpretation of empirical evidence. Large-scale emigration has been a constant of Irish culture since at least the time of the Famine to the extent that the population of Ireland has remained virtually stable for 150 years. Emigration has had a disproportionate effect on the rural laboring classes, their decimation having become a matter of policy in British administrative circles and among the landlords from the Famine on. But it has also held back the growth of an Irish working class and the formation of specifically Irish forms of class political struggle; it has contributed to the official conservatism of Irish culture and religion by permitting the continuing hegemony of large farmers and petty capitalists through to the late 1960s; it acts as a kind of numbed out cultural trauma and emblem of economic hopelessness. At the same time, it has performed great service to the state as a social safety valve and as a means to mask the otherwise potentially devastating consequences of our neocolonial status within the international and transnational moments of the capitalist world system.

We can reexamine Kennedy's statistics in the light shed upon them by the invocation of emigration as a major and anomalous feature of Ireland's colonial experience. Unlike most other colonial and postcolonial locations, emigration has been for us a *programmatic* instrument of colonial rule and policing, and remained the enabling condition of postcolonial economic development for both De Valera's isolationist Free State and the later, modernizing states, north and south of the border. To have achieved proportional effects in India, something like four hundred million people would have had to have emigrated from the subcontinent since, say, the Indian Mutiny of 1857. The internal and global displacement of populations, like periodic genocide, has been a common experience of virtually all colonized peoples, but probably the only proportional analog to the impact of emigration on Ireland would be the effects of the slave trade on West Africa at an earlier moment in capitalist modernity. This is not to assert direct comparison, but to mark emigration as the distinctive form of disciplining that differentiates the Irish colonial experience from most others.

The degree to which, even, if not especially within colonial studies, this factor has been passed over and disconnected from other aspects of Ireland's internal history, is a striking index of how much we take emigration for granted. If, for example, we consider the rates of emigration in the decades preceding 1911, the year from which Kennedy's statistics are drawn, we grasp a quite different set of relations than his analysis would suggest (see Miller, 1985: 569). See table 2.

In the four decades preceding the eve of independence, then, close on two and a quarter million Irish people had emigrated, skewing irrevocably the proportion of agricultural to industrial workers on which Kennedy relies for his sanguine view of the degree of economic development in Ireland at the time. For the most part, they did not leave for mere adventure and the promise of new life; they left in order to survive the economic and cultural devastation that colonialism had inflicted; they left because there was no obvious alternative. Their leaving has left a wake that works continually in Irish culture. It can neither be softened into the contours of a cultural diaspora nor ignored for the sake of exaggerating Ireland's twentieth-century prosperity: both remain predicated on the as yet unceasing patterns of emigration that for some cushions the neocolonial history of our present. The political and cultural meaning of emigration survives its official erasure and economic use-value, returning as the basis for active forms of global solidarity rather than for the empirical disciplining of such "imagined

Table 2

Decade	Number of recorded emigrants
1871–80	542,703
1881–90	734,475
1891–1900	461,282
1901–10	485,461

communities."[6] For the moment, let us simply note that without emigration, the Irish economy in the twentieth century, in terms of large-scale immiseration, disparities of wealth, and social unrest, would probably compare more to the situation of Central American nations or the Philippines in the circuits of US capital and domination than to Spain or Greece on the edges of Europe. In their undialectical abstraction, Kennedy's figures ultimately conceal more than they reveal, not on account of any attempt to deceive, but as an index of the intrinsic inadequacy of empirical method deployed in abstraction from social relations as a whole.

As an alternative, postcolonial method is, nonetheless, not situated to offer a more complex but still empirical proof of Ireland's definitively colonial or postcolonial status. That it cannot do so is neither an index of intellectual or scholarly ineptitude nor evidence of some unethical indifference to reality. It is rather a consequence of the critique of empirical representation and the recovery of alternative conceptions that is at the core of most postcolonial and related work. In fact, arguments based on the acceptance of Ireland's colonial history have indeed shown a greater explanatory power and offered a more inclusive depiction of the dynamics of Irish society than have other approaches. They have not only shown the validity and value of the study of other colonial locations for understanding the general contours of Irish history, but have shown the ways in which administrators and their ideas circulated throughout the colonial network; they have demonstrated similar patterns of cultural and psychic formation across colonial settings; they have shown how methods and approaches developed in other locations prove effective in the analysis of Irish social and cultural phenomena. They will certainly continue to do so. There is, then, no lack of empirical data or methodological acumen here: the reasons for the intensity of the theoretical and interpretive debates lies elsewhere.

Of course, as I have already suggested, part of that intensity stems from the inevitably political implications of the claim that Ireland has been and continues to be a colonized nation. The counterclaims are no less politically interested. Both claims also exceed their immediately apparent object, the status of Northern Ireland and the legitimacy of republican, British, or loyalist military and political agendas. They deeply affect how the future history of Ireland will be determined, in terms of political arrangements, economic self-determination, gender relations, environmental issues, and beyond. In that sense, each set of claims is distinctly performative, in that they at once repeat or reiterate apparently foundational statements and in doing so constitute institutionally effective realities.[7] The performative nature of scholarship cannot, however, be acknowledged within the framework of traditional disciplinary structures: their commitment to objects of knowledge abstracted into distinctive conceptual sets as the *a priori* of empirical method prevents reflection on the constitution of structures of knowing. This is the case not only for the social sciences but across literature and history as disciplines also. The methods of postcolonial projects, on the contrary, trace their genealogies from works that intervened deliberately in the structures of colonialist knowledge and critiqued the relations of domination embedded in apparently empirical utterances: the critique of empirical method has always been at one with the political nature of the intervention, acknowledging that the apparent self-evidence of empiricism is itself an effect of domination.[8]

Along with the necessarily interdisciplinary nature of postcolonial projects, this theoretical self-consciousness as to the production of knowledge has made their arguments often unrecognizable, in both senses of that word, within traditional disciplinary frameworks. Hence the attempt to resolve interpretive differences on empirical bases becomes merely contradictory. Work on colonialism derives its methods in some senses from the dialectics of colonialism itself, grasped as an historical project that is at once global in its aims and effects and absolutely specific in its practice. That specificity is determined by the largely unpredictable repercussions of local conditions and resistances on the reductive procedures of the state. The differential method, which I have already suggested to be the distinctive practice of postcolonial analysis, is in the first place required if one is to elaborate the dynamics of colonialism in its contrary tendencies towards homogenization and differentiation. But, as Stuart Hall has argued concerning the deployment of Gramsci's Marxist concepts on the rather different terrain of racial formation, it is no less the case that the differential method itself is dynamic: concepts and abstractions that we bring to bear from other theoretical work have constantly and self-consciously to undergo modification and sometimes transformation in relation to other sites (Hall, 1986). Ireland proves to be a location in which the relationship between concepts and material history is productively vexed, leading to a high degree of nonreductive conceptual differentiation.

Both abstraction and differentiation operate as effects of capitalist colonialism at every level of the world system. Abstraction, as is well known, is itself a material requirement of capitalist exchange – it is not a merely theoretical algebra. But materially, in order to realize equivalence at the level of the global market, capitalism has always demanded the regulation and production of difference through state intervention. This process can be articulated through many instances and through various state polities. There are, to begin with, intricate variations in the practice of different imperial systems that depend in large part on the historical moment at which given nations gain imperial power and on the extent to which they reiterate or define themselves against the practices of other powers. The Spanish Empire, forged in a virtually pre-capitalist moment, failed to be the engine for primitive accumulation and capitalist development that it was for less powerful rivals like England and Holland. Its colonial social structures were correspondingly less affected by the exigencies of industrial capital and may have collapsed precisely because they proved unable to produce and reproduce a capitalist dynamic. The structures of the British Empire, bound up with the need for materials and markets in the nineteenth century, proved in turn less flexible than the neocolonial structures adopted by the USA after 1898 in the Philippines and Latin America. Each represents, nonetheless, one moment within a larger, evolving system of colonial domination. Within individual imperial systems, differentiations are no less manifest. Although administrative needs led throughout the British Empire to the formation of a native intermediary class, the depth of the penetration of British culture varies widely from Ireland or the Caribbean through India to the virtual apartheid regimes of British Africa. The British system itself differs markedly in intent and institutional practice from the French extension of cultural citizenship through education throughout its empire, or from US attempts to control its colonies through education supplemented by media and commodity fetishism.

The transfer of practices from one imperial site to the other takes place equally at more discrete levels, in the circulation of officials and institutions from one sector to another of the imperial system. Charles Trevelyan is one such instance: after having had a shaping influence on the formation of British education in India in the late 1830s, he transferred the logic of subject transformation from Indian schools to the administration of the Famine in Ireland.[9] Brigadier Frank Kitson is a more contemporary example: as an officer in all of Britain's postwar attempts to contain anticolonial insurgency, in Malaya, Aden, Kenya, and Cyprus, he developed the methods of low intensity warfare and counterinsurgency that have been deployed in turn in Northern Ireland.[10] In doing so he employed policing structures that in many cases had been modeled after the formation of the RIC in colonial Ireland in the early nineteenth century and replicated with local modification throughout the Empire. Each imperial system, within the larger global structures of colonialism, furnishes a complex space of incorporation and differentiation, of generalization and localization, of circulation and localization, all of which require of the analyst an attentive differential practice.

But if the emphasis falls on the differential practices of postcolonial projects, what remains for the function of the moment of comparison? Comparative work across the field of colonial studies operates in several ways: it can identify the transfer of administrative techniques, such as education or policing, from one colony to another; it can observe ways in which the structures of state rule produce similar modes of resistance in quite disparate cultural formations; it can aid in defining the ways in which the characteristics of the colonized are coded and addressed as a conceptual/metaphorical unity across colonial discourses and regions.[11] It can, of course, also be used to shed suspicion on the validity of claiming the specificity to colonialism of certain practices or phenomena, as both Bartlett and Kennedy use it. Another instructive example of this is Kevin Barry's essay, "Critical Notes on Post-colonial Aesthetics," which claims that the organizational structures of Jacobite and agrarian movements in England strongly resemble those of agrarian movements in Ireland in the same period.[12] This is precisely the kind of instance in which the question of similarity has to posed alongside the recognition of differentiation: though similarities certainly exist between movements that resist the extension of capital at the same historical moment, their signification may yet differ in their distinct contexts. The English movements, and their later mutation into the Luddites, certainly shared some tactical and symbolical forms with their Irish counterparts. But such forms of action in England were put down within the purview of longstanding legal interventions, ranging from arrest and trial to the reading of the Riot Act by local militia. No unprecedented legal means were impelled into being and the disturbances remained within the traditional purview of the law. In Ireland, on the contrary, actions were generally aimed at preserving rates of pay for agricultural laborers, controling landlord improvements, and the expansion of grazing: they took place almost entirely in relation to the ongoing rationalizing of agriculture. At the same time, they invoked a range of Celtic personae, often identified with actual persons, which marked the distinction between a native economic and aesthetic mode and a foreign one. Perhaps more significantly still, the British administration's response was to introduce an unprecedented national and armed constabulary to replace the older magistracy – a response which was otherwise and later introduced only in the colonies. For the administration and in hindsight, it was clear that Irish agrarian disturbances signified quite differently than did Jacobism or Luddism and required the methods of coercion that signaled the status of the British as occupiers rather than as mere enforcers of customary law. The distinction between the specific significance of similar social movements in different contexts is clear and crucial to the structure of analysis.

The dialectical relation of comparison and differentiation proposed here is not one that ends in either theoretical or social resolution. The product of comparative work between analyses of the processes of colonialism in various sites is, generally speaking, formal in nature. The study of historians of Indian, Philippine, or Irish social relations leads to the observation of common processes of cultural formation whose ends are non-identical but share a similar "negative dialectic," a staggering movement of swerve and differentiation which I elaborate throughout this book. Dipesh Chakrabarty's and Partha Chatterjee's work on modernization, Kumkum Sangari and Sudesh Vaid's volume on the "reconstitution of patriarchy" in India, or Reynaldo Ileto's work on banditry and religious movements in the Philippines, all resonate interestingly with the implications of work in Irish labor history from James Connolly and William Ryan to Emmet O'Connor, or of T. P. Foley and Thomas Boylan on economics. Each shows how colonial social formations emerge in relation to modernity but always skewed in unpredictable ways that I have already suggested constitute the field of nonmodernity.[13] This perpetual clinamen of the nonmodern issues in the unclosable dialectic between a constantly reiterated form and the particular content that it can neither predict nor incorporate.

This dialectic is in the first instance a problem of incommensurable temporalities: the time of development, which folds all human histories into the same scale as advanced or belated modalities of progress, is always awry to the alternative rhythms of the nonmodern. Modern historiography, across a broad spectrum from conservative to marxist, is embedded in the rationalities of modernity, in the notion of progress or development as emancipation. With differing degrees of self-reflection, historians narrate history as the history of its own end, in the reconciliation and resolution of contradiction, finding closure predominantly in an orderly civil society and reformed state or occasionally in postrevolutionary socialism. In either case, history is written from the perspective of and with the aim of producing a noncontradictory subject. In doing so, history constitutes and differentiates the developed and the undeveloped, the civil and the savage, the rational and the irrational, the orderly and the violent. Resolution is the containment by the state of the crises constantly produced by the power of these differentiations. The outside of the state and the outside of history are the same, determined as irrational: beyond the pale of each lies not only the unknown but what is strictly unknowable to them.

The task, however is not merely the critique of the political and epistemological forms that make alternative modalities invisible, but the immensely difficult work that critique prepares for, which is the attempt to construct an archaeology of the spaces and temporalities that have been occluded.

Such endeavors must be dedicated to the work of retrieving the different rhythms of historically marginalized cultures and to the alternative conceptions of culture and of social relations that account for their virtual occlusion from written history. But it must be no less dedicated to imagining out of that different knowledge the alternative projects that will convert the damage of history into the terms for future survival. For if the forms of social practice that lie athwart modernity's spate are the casualties of its deep unreason, they are no less the ongoing record of its inability to engorge everything. In this subaltern refusal to be incorporated, and this determination to imagine alternative ways of being, a different future finds its means.

Notes

1   On "rational abstraction" see Marx (1970: 205–13).
2   On growing significance of the notion of "national character" in Ireland, see Deane (1997).
3   Kennedy (1996: 167–81). In opening the essay, Kennedy ventures a little sarcasm at the expense of Parnell and Pearse, both of whom compared conditions in Ireland to those of slaves in the United States. He seems then blithely unaware that this comment had previously been made by Gustave de Beaumont, friend of De Tocqueville and well-respected travel writer, and by no less a figure than Frederick Douglass, who might have had reason to know. One could multiply the list of US and other foreign visitors who made similar comparisons irrespective of their relation to nationalism.

4 *Pace* Liam Kennedy, there have been several quite extended analyses of Ireland as a nation that has suffered from, in Gunder Andre Frank's term, "capitalist under-development." The most notable of these is to be found in Raymond Crotty's all too neglected *Ireland in Crisis: A Study in Capitalist Colonial Undevelopment* (1986), chs. 5 and 6. For direct comparison with Latin America, see Regan (1982: 15–20). Coulter (1990) engages in a more political analysis of Ireland's resemblances with Latin America.

5 On the current ratio of investment to profit outflow in Ireland, see O'Hearn (1997). For Ireland's agricultural "undevelopment" in relation to colonial capitalism, see again Crotty (1986), esp. ch. 4.

6 The term "imagined communities" is usually taken from the celebrated book of that title by Benedict Anderson. My usage of that term here is borrowed from Mohanty's redefinition of it in "Cartographies of Struggle: Third World Women and the Politics of Feminism" (1991: 4).

7 The performative is a mode of utterance which inaugurates a new state: "'Let there be light!', and there was light" being the ultimate instance. Where the divine performative is held to be absolutely inaugural, human utterances derive their power to alter states from an assumed anterior institutional authority: the Church, the State, the University, the discipline: "I declare you man and wife," or "I am President" (Austin; Derrida). Yet at the same time, the power of the institution is only realized in such utterances and in their acceptance by those affected by them. In this respect, the performative is a consensual fiction that organizes a community and its relations of authority. It is no less subject to "iteration," the performative always being a citation of a prior encoded utterance. Accordingly, we can say that it is only in its iteration that the authority of any institution is affirmed, each time anew, so that in fact the institution depends on its iteration rather than on any actual founding moment. This opens the space for the parodic destabilization of the performative as *performance*; or for the skewing of official history in its daily reiterations and popular appropriations (Butler; Bhabha). One special instance of the performative and its destabilizing effects is the Declaration of Independence, which constitutes the very people in whose name it claims to speak, while at the same time exposing the arbitrariness of foundation by delegitimating the previously constituted state in power. Though Derrida's *"Déclarations d'independance"* addresses the American document, the Irish version of 1916 is itself an interesting variant of the same problematic, which it performs in the very insistence on the provisionality of its authority.

8 I refer here to Edward Said's *Orientalism* (1979), Frantz Fanon's *Black Skin, White Masks* (1952) and *The Wretched of the Earth* (1961), Chinua Achebe's *Things Fall Apart* (1958), or Chandra T. Mohanty's essay, "Under Western Eyes" (1984). These writings, among some others, have proven to be seminal texts of theoretical work on colonialism. The best anthology of work on colonialism currently is Patrick Williams and Laura Chrisman, eds., *Colonial Discourse and Post-colonial Theory* (New York: Columbia University Press, 1994).

9 On Trevelyan's career as a colonial administrator, see Cooke (1993); and for a recent discussion of Trevelyan's attitudes to the Famine, see Gray (1995).

10 For Brigadier Frank Kitson's writings, see his *Low Intensity Operations: Subversion, Insurgency and Peace-Keeping* (1971) and *Bunch of Five* (1977), an account of his

involvement in several postwar colonial campaigns, including Kenya, Malaya, Muscat and Oman, and Cyprus. On the general logic of counterinsurgency, also written from the perspective of the military and the state, see Scott (1970).

11 See Gauri Viswenathan and Kumkum Sangari on education. David Andrews on policing. Nasser Hussain (Ph.D.: UC Berkeley, 1993) on law.

12 Barry (1996: 6–7). His argument here is directed principally at Gibbons (1996); and at my own essay (1993).

13 See Chakrabarty (1989); Chatterjee (1986); Sangari and Vaid (1989); Ileto (1979); Connolly (1922); Ryan (1919); O'Connor (1988); Foley and Boylan (1992).

References

Barry, Kevin. (1996). "Critical Notes on Post-colonial Aesthetics," *Irish Studies Review*, 14 (spring).

Bartlett, Thomas, *et al.*, eds. (1988). *Irish Studies: A General Introduction*. Dublin: Gill and Macmillan.

Benjamin, Walter. (1969). "Theses on the Philosophy of History," in *Illuminations*, ed. and intro. by Hannah Arendt, trans. Harry Zohn. New York: Schocken.

Chakrabarty, Dipesh. (1989). *Rethinking Working-Class History, Bengal 1890–1940*. Princeton: Princeton University Press.

Chatterjee, Partha. (1986). *Nationalist Thought and the Colonial World: A Derivative Discourse?* London: Zed Books.

Connolly, James. (1922). *Labour in Ireland*. Dublin: Maunsel and Roberts.

Cooke, S. B. (1993). *Imperial Affinities: Nineteenth Century Analogies and Exchanges Between India and Ireland*. New Delhi: Sage.

Coulter, Carol. (1990). *Ireland: Between the First and the Third Worlds*. Dublin: Attic Press LIP Pamphlet.

Crotty, Raymond. (1986). *Ireland in Crisis: A Study in Capitalist Colonial Underdevelopment*. Dingle: Brandon Books.

Deane, Seamus. (1997). *Strange Country: Modernity and Nationhood in Irish Writing since 1790*. Oxford: Oxford University Press.

Foley, Timothy P. and Thomas Boylan. (1992). *Political Economy and Colonial Ireland*. London and New York: Routledge.

Gray, Peter. (1995). "Ideology and the Famine," in *The Great Irish Famine*, ed. Cathal Porteir. Cork: Mercier.

Gibbons, Luke. (1996). "Identity without a Centre," in *Transformations in Irish Culture: Allegory, History and Irish Nationalism*. Cork: Cork University press.

Hall, Stuart. (1986). "Gramsci's Relevance for the Study of Race and Ethnicity," *Journal of Communication Inquiry*, 10 (summer).

Ileto, Reynaldo. (1979). *Pasyon and Revolution: Popular Movements in the Philippines, 1840–1910*. Manila: Ateneo de Manila.

Kennedy, Liam. (1996). "Modern Ireland: Post-Colonial Society or Post-Colonial Pretensions?" in *Colonialism, Religion and Nationalism in Ireland*. Belfast: Queen's University Institute for Irish Studies.

Kitson, Frank (Brigadier). (1971). *Low Intensity Operations: Subversion, Insurgency and Peace-Keeping*. London: Faber.

———. (1977). *Bunch of Five*. London: Faber and Faber.

Lloyd, David. (1993). "Violence and the Constitution of the Novel," in *Anomalous States: Irish Writing and the Postcolonial Moment*. Dublin: Lilliput, and Durham: Duke University Press.

Marx, Karl. (1970). *A Contribution to be Critique of Political Economy*, ed. Maurice Dobb, trans. S. W. Ryazanskaya. Moscow: Progress Publishers.

Miller, Kerby. (1985). *Emigrants and Exiles*. Oxford: Oxford University Press.

Mohanty, Chandra Talpade. (1991). "Cartographies of Struggle: Third World Women and the Politics of Feminism," intro. to *Third World Women and the Politics of Feminism*, eds. Mohanty, Ann Russo, and Lourdes Torres. Bloomington: Indiana University Press.

O'Connor, Emmet. (1988). *Syndicalism in Ireland, 1917–1923*. Cork: Cork University Press.

O'Hearn, Denis. (1997). "The Celtic Tiger: The Role of the Multi-nationals," in *Under the Belly of the Tiger: Class, Race, Identity and Culture in the Global Ireland*, eds. Jim MacLaughlin and Ethel Crowley. Dublin: Irish Reporter Publications.

Regan, Colm. (1982). "Latin American Dependency Theory and its Relevance to Ireland," *The Crane Bag*, 6, no. 2.

Ryan, William. (1919). *The Irish Labour Movement*. Dublin: Talbot Press.

Sangari, Kumkum and Sudesh Vaid. (1989). *Recasting Women: Essays in Indian Colonical History*. Delhi: Kali for Women.

Scott, Andrew M. (1970). *Insurgency*. Chapel Hill: University of North Carolina Press.

Williams, Patrick and Laura Chrisman, eds. (1994). *Colonial Discourse and Post-colonial Theory*. New York: Columbia University Press.

Chapter 20

Global Disjunctures, Diasporic Differences, and the New World (Dis-)Order

Ali Behdad

No theory of cultural contact is conducive to generalization.

Edouard Glissant

Geographical and cultural displacements have radically informed (post)colonial consciousness. Although people have always moved either voluntarily or by force, European colonialism entailed a massive dislocation of people in the form of the slave trade and later indentured labor, as well as generating other movements among European countries and their colonies. More significantly, these displacing practices of colonialism have given rise to a new set of geographical and cultural movements among the ex-colonies and the West since decolonization. And yet, surprisingly, little attention has been devoted to these issues in the field of postcolonial studies. Although many writers and critics have spoken anecdotally about the fact of their displaced identities, ironically, in their scholarly and critical writings, they have not adequately addressed the consequences and implications of these movements. In spite of their insightful readings of colonial history, culture, and subjectivity, these critics have often left the historical question of colonial displacement unexplored, while evading for the most part such crucial contemporary issues as globalization, diaspora, and immigration. The historical rationale for postcolonial readings of colonial relations of power has been to produce the colonized's absent gaze and unwritten text, but these readings have often overlooked the historical juncture where the colonial encounter becomes relevant to our globalized condition and postcolonial consciousness.

My aim in drawing attention to these historical oversights is not to undermine the critical and academic achievements of these readers, but to acknowledge the need for new directions and historiographies in the field of postcolonial studies. I have discussed elsewhere the ways in which the interventionary practices of postcolonial and "minority" critics have led to a more politicized understanding of knowledge and exerted a strong local influence in heralding crucial pedagogic changes in the US academy (Behdad, 1993). But here I wish to make a more critical point about the dominance of colonial historiography to contextualize my discussion of diaspora and globalization and in order to sketch new terrains in postcolonial theory.

The critical focus on European imperialism and the unequal relationship between colonizers and the colonized has often led to at least two problematic tendencies in discussions of postcoloniality: a discourse of marginality derived from the Manichean model of the dominator and the victim, and a misreading of postcolonial relations of power through the rhetoric of colonization. On the one hand, most cultural discourses of identity in the United States academy have continued to position themselves paradoxically within the confining matrix of identification they strive to subvert, a matrix dominated by such colonialist binaries as center/periphery, dominator/dominated, and oppression/opposition. Postcolonial critiques of colonialist literature and culture have often viewed the relationship between the colonizer and the colonized in terms of a "Manichean allegory" that locates one as the source of power and oppression and the other as the victimized other resisting the conqueror's domination (JanMohamed, 1985). Recognizing this problematic bent, Edward Said (1991a) has rightly warned postcolonial readers that

> our point . . . cannot be simply and obdurately to reaffirm the paramount impor-
> tance of formerly suppressed or silenced forms of knowledge and leave it at that,
> nor can it be to surround ourselves with the sanctimonious piety of historical and
> cultural victimhood as a way of making our intellectual presence felt. (26)

On the other hand, the rhetoric and logic of colonization has been problematically employed to study the recent reconfigurations of power relations. Although issues of hybridity, transculturation, and globalism have gained a great deal of currency in contemporary discussions of identity and power, a binary logic continues to be dominant in these debates: new power relations are mostly defined in terms of the inequality between the center and the periphery while identity is often articulated according to the binary logic of oppression/opposition. But as Néstor García Canclini (1992) has cogently argued,

> To study inequalities and differences today is not simply to see mechanisms of
> exclusion and opposition; it is also necessary to identify the processes that
> unequally articulate social positions, cognitive systems, and the tastes of diverse
> sectors. . . . The dense web of cultural and economic decisions leads to asym-
> metries between producers and consumers and between diverse publics. But these
> inequalities are almost never imposed from the top down, as is assumed by those
> who establish Manichean oppositions between dominating and dominated classes,
> or between central and peripheral countries. (34)

It is not that the changes heralded by globalization and new social movements have diminished the importance of identity, nor have they eliminated the unequal access to power and knowledge. Rather, what has been radically altered is "the absolute spatial division between exploiters and exploited," for as

Kenneth Surin (1995) remarks, "the exploiters are [now] everywhere and so are the exploited" (1188). The postcolonial world, in contrast to the polarized colonial context, has indeed become a "confusing world, a world of crisscrossed economies, intersecting systems of meanings, and fragmented identities" (Rouse, 1991: 8).

1   Exiled Writers, Colonial Subjects

The question of cultural and geographical dislocation in the field of postcolonial theory was first posed by Caribbean writers who voluntarily migrated from the West Indies to Europe and North America to pursue their literary careers. Drawing attention to the displacing practices of colonialism – such as slavery and indentured labor – Caribbean intellectuals like George Lamming and C. L. R. James viewed the new set of geographical and cultural movements between the ex-colonies and the West as the inevitable consequences of European imperialism. But these writers reflected also on the productive function of their self-inflicted exile in becoming writers. In *The Pleasures of Exile*, for example, Lamming (1992) appropriates the figure of Caliban to reflect on the paradoxes and pleasures of the Caribbean writer's exile. At once interpolated by and excluded from the master's language and culture, Caliban is reinterpreted as a liminal figure capable of occupying different geographical and cultural spaces. Identifying with him, the West Indian writer, as a colonial subject and an exile, moves to "the tempestuous island of Prospero's and his language" in a journey that would transform him from an alienated subject to an agent of cultural and historical transformation (1992: 13). Such a redemptive journey is important not only as a means of understanding more profoundly the colonizer's culture in its proper context (by way of articulating a more effective politics of opposition), but also because such a self-inflicted movement mediates a dialogic awareness that enables their creativity as writers. For Lamming, exile is at once an alienating and empowering experience:

> In the Caribbean we have a glorious opportunity of making some valid and permanent contribution to man's life in this century. But we must stand up; and we must move. . . . This may be the dilemma of the West Indian writer abroad: that he hungers for nourishment from a soil which he (as an ordinary citizen) could not at present endure. The pleasure and paradox of my own exile is that I belong wherever I am. My role, it seems, has rather to do with time and change than with the geography of circumstances; and yet there is always an acre of ground in the New World which keeps growing echoes in my head. I can only hope that these echoes do not die before my work comes to an end. (50)

Although exile, as an experience of social and psychological disjunction, has led to political disenfranchisement and cultural alienation in the Caribbean, the West

Indian writer hopes to transform this sense of displacement into a cosmopolitan vision that would let him make a significant contribution to humanity. The voluntary move away from home helps the exilic writer to gain a broader perspective about history and culture, thus allowing him to act as the agent of social transformation. The voluntary exile "reverses the colonizing intention of the imperial monologue" (Paquet, 1992: xviii) as the Caribbean writer is able to "relate the West Indian experience from the inside" (38). Exile in this instance is a form of cultural resistance. The "migration of the writer from the Caribbean to the dubious refuge of a metropolitan culture" (Lamming, 1992: 22) invests him with a kind of dialogic imagination at once expressive of his "double consciousness" (Du Bois, 1989) and necessary in developing an alternative narrative of the colonial encounter.

Lamming's elaboration of exile as an enabling form of displacement anticipates the more recent preoccupation of postcolonial theoreticians with various tropes of spatial movement and hybridity. Although recent theoreticians have made some distinctions to specify these notions, the enabling aspect of exile still enjoys a great deal of critical currency in postcolonial theory today, as critics tend to focus on literary and artistic expressions of diaspora rather than the everyday conditions of immigrants around the world. In his "Reflections on Exile," Said (1984) draws attention to the discrepancy between the actual experience of exile as a "crippling" and "unhealable rift forced between a human being and a native place" (159) and the uses of exile as a heroic and triumphant trope in literature. "Exile," he remarks, "is strangely compelling to think about but terrible to experience" (ibid.). Said also makes, in passing, some useful distinctions between exiles, refugees, expatriates, and émigrés, drawing attention to the crucial difference between voluntary departures and forceful displacement. And yet, although Said acknowledges that "the literature about exile objectifies an anguish and a predicament most people rarely experience at first hand," he continues to use the term nonetheless in a salutary manner. On the one hand, Said defines exile as the opposite of nationalism, and as such he considers it a form of resistance against the "triumphant ideology" of nation-state. On the other hand, like Lamming, he emphasizes the transcendental quality of displacement and movement: "Exiles cross borders, [and] break barriers of thought and experience" (1984: 170). Throughout his seminal essay, Said focuses on exilic poets and writers to emphasize how the detachment of these figures from their native lands "makes possible originality of vision" (172).

The tendency to generalize the oppositional, redemptive, and transformative possibilities of displacement is predominant in the field of postcolonialism both in the United States and Europe. Stuart Hall (1990), to cite an example from the British context, uses the notion of diaspora as the opposite of "the old, the imperialising, the hegemonising, form of identity" (235). For him, "Diaspora identities are those which are constantly producing and reproducing themselves anew, through transformation and difference" (ibid.). Here too, diaspora identity is celebrated as a heterogeneous concept that is constantly recreating and refashioning itself, while ethnic identification is devalued as a monolithic and static phenomenon incapable of variation and transformation.

James Clifford (1992) goes a step further as he redefines culture in terms of travel in order to question the normalizing tendencies that are associated with this key concept. Like Said, who offers the notion of exile as "an alternative to the mass institutions that dominate modern life" (1984: 170), he posits the "chronotope" of travel to question the localizing strategies of social sciences and to account for the complex systems of mobility and intercultural exchanges that mediate the relation of the researcher to the researched. As in Said's description of exile, what is emphasized here is the oppositional dimension of nomadic and decentered consciousness. Postcolonial cultures are viewed as sites of contestation traversed by different people and their spatial practices of moving, mapping, migration, immigration, and so on. The point of the chronotope of travel, Clifford points out, however, is not to privilege displacement over localization, but to provide a comparative perspective to "work on the complexities of cultural localizations in post- or neocolonial situations" (1992: 105).

This comparative project recognizes correctly that the movements of postcolonial travelers are overdetermined by a broad range of cultural, economic, and political conditions, conditions that can empower some while oppressing others. The mutable and wavering nature of postcolonial spaces allows for unequal modes of travel and uneven destinies, depending on the traveler's access to power and its discourses – a point I will return to below. But travel's generality and contingency, according to Clifford, make it nonetheless a useful point of comparison to broach the predicaments of postcolonial diasporas and to describe intercultural relations between various communities. What makes the chronotope of travel so attractive to postcolonial intellectuals like him is "precisely because of its historical taintedness, its association with gendered, racial bodies, class privilege, specific means of conveyance, beaten paths, agents, frontiers, documents, and the like" (1992: 110).

Using the chronotope of travel, recent postcolonial theoreticans, like Caribbean writers, have also taken the diaspora condition of the new social space as an invitation to reconceptualize the very nature of intellectual practice itself. Following Edward Said's "Traveling Theories," Clifford (1989) has suggested the return of theory to its etymological root, *theorein*, that is, a "practice of travel and observation, a man sent by the polis to another city to witness a religious ceremony" (177). (Dis)placed in a world of global contacts where communities, economies, and subjectivities constantly crisscross, theory, Clifford argues, "is no longer naturally 'at home' in the West" (179); it has been destabilized by other locations, contested by other trajectories of subjectivity, and displaced by other forms of knowledge. Theory, indeed knowledge, becomes a kind of itinerary conceived through a complex network of diaspora conjunctures, conditions of displacement and transplantation.

The implications of such destabilizing theories are crucial to academic practices of postcolonial critics not only for their connections and references to their self-fashionings, but also for their consequences in the everyday life of institutional space. In "Identity, Authority, and Freedom: The Potentate and the Traveler," Said (1991b) uses the figure of the traveler to critique the notion of national identity, which impinges on academic freedom. By relegating social heterogeneity and cultural differences to the margin, overmastering and monologic notions of identity, such as "arabness," "Americanness," or "Western identity," impair intellectual freedom and suppress creative interaction. "Our model for academic freedom," Said suggests, "should therefore be the migrant or the traveler" (1991b: 17). The figure of the traveler is used here metaphorically to imply mobility and motion in both symbolic and literal senses, that is, "a willingness to go into different worlds, use different idioms, and understand a variety of disguises, masks, and rhetorics" (18). Students and teachers, according to this model, should "discover and travel among other selves, other identities, other varieties of the human adventure" (17). Abandoning fixed positions and ideologies of mastery and detachment, the academic model of the traveler allows the possibility of traversing different intellectual domains and exploring a plurality of subject positions.

2   The Predicaments of Generalizing the Particular

Although notions of travel, exile, and diaspora are useful in delineating an interventionary politics in the academy, they raise more questions than they provide answers. Above all, these tropes tend to generalize precisely at points where generalization proves inadequate. As Edouard Glissant (1989) has cogently remarked, "The permutations of cultural contact change more quickly than any one theory could account for. No theory of cultural contact is [thus] conducive to generalization" (19). Historically, there are fundamental differences, for example, between "the transplanting (by exile or dispersion) of a people who continue to survive elsewhere and the transfer (by the slave trade) of a population to another place where they change into something different, into a new set of possibilities" (Glissant, 1989: 14). In the case of transplantation by exile, the community is able to maintain its sense of collectivity and cultural particularity – as in the Armenian, Indian, and Jewish diasporas – albeit that such notions of identity and culture are always creolized. In contrast, in the case of the slave trade, "a population . . . is transformed elsewhere into another people . . . and enters the constantly shifting and variable process of creolization" (15). Even this process of creolization has taken different shapes in various locations. In the case of Haiti, for instance, the transferred population was able to fashion a sense of national consciousness and gain its independence from France, while in the case of Brazil, the African diaspora became "part of a multiple whole" (Glissant, 1989: 17).

Moreover, the metaphoric uses of spatial tropes have led to a problematic discourse of utopian mobility that conflates the privileged experiences of writers and intellectuals with those of the less fortunate immigrants. Although most critics are attentive to the "historical taintedness" of the metaphor of travel, acknowledging its connection with gendered, racial, and class identities (Clifford, 1992), utopian optimism emerges among many, even sophisticated, readers who sometimes confuse the clearing of a "space for the 'other' question" (Bhabha, 1986) in the academy with the needs, aspirations, and the deteriorating conditions of many neocolonized communities in the Third World as well as in the West. Homi Bhabha's euphoric claim (1990: 7) that "The bastion of Englishness crumbles at the sight of immigrants and factory workers" offers only one example of such a critical confusion.

While many postcolonial artists, writers, and theoreticians celebrate the massive immigration of the twentieth century as a hybridizing phenomenon that eradicates monolithic notions of identity, many underclass immigrants find their displacing movements and liminal conditions anything but salutary. Even a cursory glance at some diaspora communities – such as North Africans in Paris and Lyon, Pakistanis and Indians in Bradford, Afghanis in Teheran – confirms that the everyday conditions of living abroad have actually deteriorated for most recent immigrants due to a whole series of sociopolitical changes – including restrictive immigration acts, the busting of the manufacturing industry and its replacement by high-technology fields, and the transference of production to Third World countries. Gilroy's discussion of nationalism in England (1987), Silverman's study of citizenship in France (1992), and Barbieri's research on Germany's foreign workers (1998) have shown how the equation of nation with an exclusive notion of race has led to restrictive immigration laws that exclude and discriminate against diaspora communities in these and other countries. Immigrants have been the target of xenophobic and nativist attacks both in cases where they have socially and economically succeeded in "host" countries – for example, Southeast Asians in Africa, Asians in California, or Chinese in Malaysia – and where they have held the least desirable and low-income jobs – such as Turks in Germany, North Africans in France, or Latinos in Southern California (Conner, 1986).

Nor is it evident that geographical displacement leads in most cases to originality of vision or the breaking of intellectual and cultural barriers. For even the most superficial acquaintance with the ethnic politics of a city like Los Angeles reveals how stratified and conflictual Third World-origined and minority communities are in this city (Behdad and Pérez, 1995). Not only are there fundamental cultural and economic differences among various diaspora communities, but these differences have also led to the sowing of mutual hostilities across immigrant and minority communities, as the Los Angeles riots painfully demonstrated. In many cases, the sense of loss and disenfranchisement among many diasporic communities have led to "violent articulations of purity and racial exclusivism," as Clifford (1997: 307) also acknowledges. My aim here is not to play a set of empirical observations against the theoretical tropes of mobility;

nor is it to claim a binary relation between the symbolic and the real. Rather, I wish to draw attention to the discrepancy between salutary explorations of diasporic consciousness by academics, writers, and artists *and* the dead-end itineraries of many immigrants caught in the tailspin of a globalization that has taken them away from their hopes for upward mobility into a state of economic and political disenfranchisement.

This discrepancy is symptomatic of the difference between what John Armstrong (1976) calls "mobilized and proletarian diasporas." Acknowledging the vagueness of the term "diaspora" to describe "any ethnic collectivity which lacks a territorial base within a given polity," Armstrong makes a useful distinction between proletarian diaspora as a "disadvantaged product of modernized polities," and mobilized diaspora defined as "an ethnic group which does not have a general status advantage, yet which enjoys many material and cultural advantages compared to other groups in the multiethnic polity" (393). He further discusses a broad range of factors – such as religion, language, labor, cultural myth, networks of family and personal relations – to schematize the critical differences that exist between the two types of diaspora. Although no diaspora community can be neatly situated within these categories, since immigrants occupy a plurality of social and economic positions, his distinction is helpful nonetheless in situating the uneven itineraries of mobile populations. Anderson's typologies and situational discussion of diasporas call into question the free-floating metaphors of travel and hybridity and offer an alternative paradigm to go beyond general, and often homogenizing, theories of movement and displacement. The experience of diaspora, I suggest, is a worldly phenomenon inscribed within material and symbolic fields of power that are always contingent, contradictory, overdetermined, and open-ended.

3   Local Theories, Global Locations

Recognizing the inadequacies of generalizing tropes of mobility to discern the politics of diaspora, some theoreticians have suggested more nuanced and specific ways to grasp the geographical and cultural displacements of our globalized world. Interestingly, much of this work has been done by anthropologists and sociologists who are studying the current cultural contacts between various polities in order to question traditional models of community and culture that consider these to be isomorphic with nation and ethnicity (Appadurai, 1996; Gilroy, 1993; Gupta, 1992; Malkki, 1992). Roger Rouse (1991), for example, has studied the circular movement of labor, capital, goods, and ideas between the small rural community of Aguililla in the state of Michoacán in Mexico and Redwood City in Northern California, to suggest "an alternative cartography of social space" (12). Unable to support themselves in Mexico, and forced to inhabit a transnational space to make a living, Aguilillans, he demonstrates, "have become skilled exponents of a cultural bifocality that defies reduction to a singular order" (15). Like multinational corporations that espouse internationalism to expand their capital, these migrant workers establish transnational circuits to make do economically and culturally. This "transnational migrant circuit" simultaneously problematizes monolithic notions of national identity and community as well as the binary opposition of center/periphery. As various communities accommodate themselves to a heterogeneous and mobile form of capital and participate in diverse and international modes of cultural expression, we encounter a "proliferation of border zones" throughout the world. The boundaries of the first and third worlds are becoming increasingly blurry as capital and production move to the "periphery," while the movement of labor to the metropolitan centers of the West leads to the "peripheralization at the core" (Sassen-Koob, 1987). With the proliferation of transnational circuits that move people, capital, ideas, and information, we are moving to a new kind of social space where "the comforting modern imagery of nation-states and national languages, of coherent communities and consistent subjectivities, of dominant centers and distant margins no longer seems adequate" (Rouse, 1991: 8).

Transnational circuits such as the one between Aguililla and Redwood City are appearing not just in the West but throughout the world. A case in point is the movement of people, goods, and capital between the oil rich countries of the Middle East and the poor communities of Southeast Asia. Since the oil boom of 1973 stimulated the demand for labor in the Gulf states, over 2 million Indians, 1.5 million Pakistanis, and 200,000 Bangladeshis have moved to these countries as contract workers (Knerr, 1990). Working temporarily away from home, these laborers are able to support their families back home through remittances. They can also bring back substantial savings and luxury commodities upon their return, thus improving the quality of their lives and enhancing their economic and consequently social status. According to data provided by the World Bank, the overseas remittances in 1983 accounted for 55 percent of all imports in Pakistan, 42 percent of Bangladesh, and 20 percent of India. What these figures indicate is the crucial role played by the transnational flow of labor and money in transforming the very structure of sociocultural reproduction. Not only does the possibility of earning big money abroad enable these workers to advance their social class, but it also affects their cultural practices and consumer taste in radical ways. The blossoming of the pornographic film industry and cabaret clubs in Kerala and the peddling of American consumer goods in the black markets of Bombay and other Indian cities are only two disjunctive examples of these changes (Appadurai, 1996).

At the same time, the deterritorialization of people and commodities affect also the cultural, economic, and political contexts of "host" societies. In "The Caribbeanization of New York City and the Emergence of a Transnational Socio-Cultural System," Constance Sutton (1987) describes the ways in which Caribbean immigrants have transformed the city. Like Southeast Asian diaspora, Caribbean immigrants maintain close economic, political, and cultural links with the Islands. But unlike the subcontinental workers in the Middle East, they have permanently settled in New York City, while remaining attached to their home-land cultures (Chaney, 1987). As a result, they have tried to articulate a politics of integration that resists the ideology of assimilation. As in the case of Latino and Asian communities in Los Angeles, these immigrants have made capital investment in the city lucrative and attractive by making themselves avail-able as a low-wage and flexible labor force in the garment industry as well as the service sector of the city's economy. They have also been active in New York City's informal economy, from the production of goods and services for their communities to drug trafficking. In addition to these economic contributions, Caribbeans have also brought to the city a wealth of cultural expressions and practices from the islands. "The transposition of this island heritage," Sutton suggests, "has meant that both the street life of local neighborhoods as well as the many public spaces of the city are being infused with Caribbean popular culture . . . [ranging] from reggae and Salsa concerts, Rastas and domino street players, graffiti and politicized street mural arts, to productions of the Caribbean Cultural Center, Joseph Papp's month-long summer Latino/Caribbean perfor-mances, and a growing number of Hispanic and Afro-Caribbean dance and theater groups" (18).

The proliferation of Caribbean cultural forms in New York City, like those of other immigrant communities throughout the world, demonstrates the inade-quacy of the assimilationist model of immigration prevalent in social sciences. Caribbean and other immigrants in the US are not simply assimilated into the dominant culture. Nor do they merely relive their ethnic cultures in their new environment. Rather, they engage actively in and are formed by a complex process of "transnationalism" that borrows from several sources. "Today, immi-grants develop networks, activities, patterns of living, and ideologies that span their home and the host society" (Basch, Glick Schiller, and Szanton Blanc, 1994: 4). The circular movements and interactions of people, capital, ideas, and cul-tural practices, enabled by globalism and advancements in technologies of com-munication and transportation, have allowed "new" immigrants to maintain a heterogeneous notion of identity and forge cultural practices that borrow from multiple sources. In the case of Caribbean immigrants in New York City, the process of hybridization is complicated since it involves not only the socio-cultural interaction between a metropolitan center and a particular island, but also the fusion of various West Indian identities into broader ethnic identities in the United States, such as Latino and African-American. Placed within the city's categories of "Blacks" and/or "Hispanics" – minority communities that have generally experienced downward mobility throughout the United States – Caribbeans, on the one hand, identify with and join these minorities in making demands on the municipal, state, and federal governments. But on the other hand, their upwardly mobile desire to economically empower themselves gives them no incentive to "become Americanized into either of these low-status cat-egories" (Sutton, 1987: 21). As a result, they often "oscillate between particularistic island/ethnic identities and definitions of interests, and more generalized political/racial alliances" with Blacks and Puerto Ricans (ibid.).

The contextual specificities of Caribbeans in New York is significant because they debunk homogenizing theories of African diaspora. That West Indians in New York maintain an ambivalent, if not contradictory, relation with the city's racial minorities demonstrates that crucial differences exist among various African-origin diasporas and that "race" is no guarantee for solidarity. Although as Paul Gilroy (1993) has argued, there are important political and cultural connections between blacks across the Atlantic, each diaspora community is interpolated differently by the particular context in which it is inscribed. For example, while the immigrant experience of Caribbeans in New York is inflicted with the politics of racial minorities in the United States (leading to an ambivalent relationship between this community and African-Americans and Latinos), the colonial context of Caribbean immigration in England has led black Britain to "draw inspiration from [cultural forms] developed by black populations elsewhere" in its struggle against racism, as Gilroy (1987: 154) has shown. It is therefore important to unpack the particular itineraries of immigrant communities and draw specific maps of diaspora in order to account for the complexity and overdetermination of social movements (Sharpe, 1995; Hune, 1989).

4 Toward Situated Models of Diaspora

I have dwelt on the particular cases of Aguilillans in Redwood City, Southeast Asians in the Gulf states, and Caribbeans in New York not merely to offer random examples of transnational circuits of migration, but to draw upon the broader implications of these specific studies of diaspora communities. Above all, the particularities of these diaspora communities provide new insights into the complexities of global culture. The ability of Aguilillans and other immigrants to establish transnational networks of settlements, for example, undermines static and homogeneous notions of community and draws attention to the circular and contingent process of identity formation. As Rouse (1991) points out, "Today, Aguilillans find that their most important kin and friends are as likely to be living hundreds or thousands of miles away as immediately around them" (13). Diasporas develop and maintain crucial networks of material and symbolic exchanges with their homelands as well as with various social groups in receiving countries.

These diasporas' patterns of migration also confirm that disenfranchisement needs not translate into disempowerment. The fact that Aguilillans or Southeast Asians join international circuits of migration to finance their local economies and to realize their hopes for better lives points to a trajectory of empowerment, not a discourse of victimhood. These immigrants do not obey the law of place and geography (de Certeau, 1984) as they defy the socio-arrangements that have disenfranchised them and by inhabiting border zones and cultivating cultural bifocality. In this sense, narratives of diaspora that rely on a politics of victimhood are as inaccurate and inadequate as those which prematurely celebrate diasporas' dismantling of national and ethnic borders.

Moreover, the layered and confusing economies of these diasporic movements draw attention to the disjunctive nature of global culture. "Disjunctures," Arjun Appadurai (1996) has argued, "have become central to the politics of global culture," as "people, machinery, money, images, and ideas now follow increasingly nonisomorphic paths" (37). The fragmented mode of cultural reproduction among Caribbeans and the fractured experiences of Aguilillans confirm Appadurai's proposals that "we begin to think of the configurations of cultural forms in today's world as fundamentally fractal," at the same time that we need to account for their overlaps and resemblances (1996: 46). The particular experiences of these diaspora communities make evident that these disjunctive global flows are fundamentally context-dependent. As a result, only a historical approach that remains attentive to the particular configurations of power in sociocultural relations can account for the complexities of diaspora experiences. Transnational circuits are appearing throughout the world, but their formations are always sociohistorically contingent and culturally specific.

Finally, the examples of diaspora studies I have cited above are useful in providing us with certain methodological criteria to broach the complexities of social movements today. Rouse (1991) concludes his discussion of the particular experience of Aguilillans by suggesting that "we should look not only to art and literature but also to lives of those 'ordinary' people who inscribe their transient texts in the minutiae of daily experience" (19). As I have suggested above, postcolonial discussions of diaspora have problematically privileged literary and artistic expressions of displacement. Thus, they have constructed salutary models of exile that conflate the experience of the cultural elite with the everyday struggles of the ordinary immigrants – models that fail to address the historical specificities of immigrant lives. Recent anthropological and sociological studies of diaspora, however, suggest that there is much to learn from the everyday practices of immigrants as "we try to chart our way through the confusions of the present towards a future we can better understand and thus more readily transform" (Rouse, 1991: 19). My point here is not to prioritize the real over the symbolic, but to suggest a more worldly and contextual approach to the study of diaspora in which the dynamic tension between the cultural products of the elite and the quotidian experiences of ordinary people are addressed. Such an approach will not only circumvent theoretical generalizations that are empirically flawed and socially inadequate, but it will also force a kind of critical rigor that would forestall simplifying complex and uneven cultural relations into singular or binary models of displacement.

References

Appadurai, Arjun. (1996). *Modernity at Large: Cultural Dimensions of Globalization*. Minneapolis: University of Minnesota Press.

Armstrong, John A. (1976). "Mobilized and Proletarian Diasporas," *The American Political Science Review*, 70, no. 2: 393–408.

Barbieri, William A., Jr. (1998). *Ethics of Citizenship: Immigration and Group Rights in Germany*. Durham: Duke University Press.

Basch, Linda, Nina Glick Sciller, and Cristina Szanton Blanc. (1994). *Nations Unbound: Transnational Projects, Postcolonial Predicaments, and Deterritorialized Nation-States*. Langhorne, Pa., and Reading, UK: Gordon and Breach.

Behdad, Ali. (1993). "Traveling to Teach: Third-world Critics in the American Academy," in Cameron McCarthy and Warren Crichlow, eds., *Race, Identity, and Representation in Education* (pp. 40–9). New York: Routledge.

Behdad, Ali and Laura Pérez. (1995). "Reflections and Confessions on the 'Minority' and Immigrant ID Tour," *Paragraph: A Journal of Modern Critical Theory*, 18, no. 1: 64–74.

Bhabha, Homi. (1986). "The Other Question: Difference, Discrimination and the Discourse of Colonialism," in Francis Barker, Peter Hulme, Margaret Iversen, and Diana Loxley, eds., *Literature, Politics and Theory*. London: Methuen.

———. (1990). "Introduction: Narrating the Nation," in Homi Bhabha, ed., *Nation and Narration* (pp. 1–7). London: Routledge.

Canclini, Néstor García. (1992). "Cultural Reconversion." in George Yúdice, Jean Franco, and Juan Flores, eds., *On Edge: The Crisis of Contemporary Latin American Culture* (pp. 29–44). Minneapolis: University of Minnesota Press.

Chaney, Elsa M. (1987). "The Context of Caribbean Migration," in Constance R. Sutton and Elsa M. Chaney, eds., *Caribbean Life in New York City: Sociocultural Dimensions* (pp. 3–15). New York: Center for Migration Studies of New York, Inc.

Clifford, James. (1989). "Notes on Theory and Travel," *Inscriptions*, 5: 177–188.

———. (1992). "Traveling Cultures," in Lawrence Grossberg, Cary Nelson, and Paula Treichler, eds., *Cultural Studies* (pp. 96–112). New York: Routledge.

———. (1997). *Routes: Travel and Translation in the Late Twentieth Century*. Cambridge, Mass.: Harvard University Press.

Conner, Walker. (1986). "The Impact of Homelands upon Diasporas," in Gabriel Sheffer, ed., *Modern Diasporas in International Politics*. Sydney: Croom Helm.

de Certeau, Michel. (1984). *The Practice of Everyday Life*, trans. Steven Rendall. Berkeley: University of California Press.

Du Bois, W. E. B. (1989). *The Souls of Black Folks*. New York: Bantam.

Gilroy, Paul. (1987). *"There Ain't no Black in the Union Jack": The Cultural Politics of Race and Nation*. Chicago: University of Chicago Press.

———. (1993). *The Black Atlantic: Modernity and Double Consciousness*. Cambridge: Harvard University Press.

Glissant, Edouard. (1989). *Caribbean Discourse: Selected Essays*, trans. J. Michael Dash. Charlottesville: University Press of Virginia.

Gupta, Akhil. (1992). "The Song of the Nonaligned World: Transnational Identities and the Reinscription of Space in Late Capitalism." *Cultural Anthropology*, 7, no. 1: 63–79.

Hall, Stuart. (1990). "Cultural Identity and Diaspora," in Jonathan Rutherford, ed., *Identity: Community, Culture, Difference*. London: Lawrence & Wishart.

Hune, Shirley. (1989). "Expanding the International Dimension of Asian American Studies," *Amerasia Journal*, 15, no. 2.

JanMohamed, Abdul. (1985). "The Economy of Manichean Allegory: The Function of Racial Difference in Colonialist Literature," in Henry Louis Gates, ed., *"Race," Writing, and Difference* (pp. 78–106). Chicago: University of Chicago Press.

Knerr, Béatrice. (1990). "South Asian Countries as Competitors on the World Labour Market," in Colin Clarke, Ceri Peach, and Steven Vertovec, eds., *South Asians Overseas: Migration and Ethnicity*. Cambridge: Cambridge University Press.

Lamming, George. (1992). *The Pleasures of Exile*. Ann Arbor: University of Michigan Press.

Malkki, Liisa. (1992). "National Geographic: The Rooting of Peoples and the Territorialization of National Identity among Scholars and Refugees," *Cultural Anthropology*, 7, no. 1: 24–44.

Paquet, Sandra Pouchet. (1992). "Foreward," in George Lamming, *The Pleasures of Exile* (xii–xxvii). Ann Arbor: University of Michigan Press.

Rouse, Roger. (1991). "Mexican Migration and the Social Space of Postmodernism," *Diaspora: A Journal of Transnational Studies*, 1, no. 1: 8–23.

Said, Edward. (1991a). "The Politics of Knowledge," *Raritan*, XI, no. 1: 17–31.

——. (1991b). "Identity, Authority, and Freedom: The Potentate and the Traveler," *Transition*, 54: 4–19.

——. (1984). "Reflections on Exile," *Granta*, 13: 159–172.

Sassen-Koob, Saskia. (1987). "Formal and Informal Associations: Dominicans and Colombians in New York," in Constance R. Sutton and Elsa M. Chaney, eds., *Caribbean Life in New York City: Sociocultural Dimensions* (pp. 278–96). New York: Center for Migration Studies of New York, Inc.

Sharpe, Jenny. (1995). "Is the United States Postcolonial? Transnationalism, Immigration, and Race," *Diaspora: A Journal of Transnational Studies*, 4, no. 2: 181–200.

Silverman, Maxim. (1992). *Deconstructing the Nation: Immigration, Racism and Citizenship in Modern France*. London: Routledge.

Surin, Kenneth. (1995). "On Producing the Concept of a Global Culture," *The South Atlantic Quarterly*, 94, no. 4: 1179–200.

Sutton, Constance R. (1987). "The Caribbeanization of New York City and the Emergence of a Transnational Socio-cultural System," in Constance R. Sutton and Elsa M. Chaney, eds., *Caribbean Life in New York City: Sociocultural Dimensions* (pp. 15–30). New York: Center for Migration Studies of New York, Inc.

Chapter 21

Home, Homo, Hybrid: Translating Gender

Geeta Patel

Hybrid bodies fascinate me.[1] Queer identities, the unruly intersexed bodies of "hermaphrodites," American Indian "berdache" two-spirited, and Indian-Indian hijras hold me in thrall. Scholarship has transmuted these hybrid bodies into gendered ambiguity, variants of masculinity or femininity, genders in their own right, or cyborgs who mediate between machine and organism, social reality and fiction. Hybrid bodies fascinate me not because I view them as marginal beings whose location serves to keep both center and margin stable. They fascinate me not because I view them as marginal, outside, Other, exempt from participating in some fantasy of normalcy. On the contrary, they fascinate me because they already live *inside* the most pedestrian fantasies of what tends to be understood as central, normal, or home.

Hijras, hybrid figures who live in small communities in many North Indian cities, inhabited my Bombay childhood in the 1960s as the protean characters in boogey-person stories. The stories, which seemed to have no specific origin, enacted for me some of the desires and disturbances embedded in my daily routine. In their narrative embodiments, hijras fleshed out my intrigue with a changing body; my fears of homelessness, loss of class, abandonment by my family; and my encounters with being or becoming different.[2]

Before turning to those childhood stories, I want to bring the scholarship on queer as hybrid home, back into the kitchen, ground those stories in the dailiness of who cooks and who eats, who worries and who listens, activities metastasized through race and class, globalization and discursive apparati, where tropes as seemingly innocuous as "mayonnaise" or "hijras" display their complexity under an unexpected lens. I want to put the seamless uniformity of heterosexuality to the test, not merely by pointing to its culturally contingent construction, but by asking what happens when you assume sexuality is neither fixed nor uniform, by asking how it would look if it were hybrid. Queerness then becomes a way to make the center ambivalent, hybridize it, so that hybridity and queerness no longer sit in for "otherness," but, in continuity with Homi Bhabha's injunctions, unsettle the self.[3] So, when one takes sexuality in(to) the kitchen,

410

and not just metaphorically, what happens to the gendered verities built into the hybrid figures (hijras) that have come to stand in for sexual "otherness" in South Asia?

Gender Fudge

At a conference at New York University where I delivered an earlier version of this paper I was confronted by a young upper-middle class Indian lesbian from Bombay. She asked why I was interested in hijras and their imbrication with my sense of self. As I told her about my own history of coming to terms with remembering hijras, she performed a ritual of collective memory. Pulling stories about hijras out of her back-pack, she gave me some from her childhood, and some she had packed away more recently when she came back to the US from her last trip "home." These memories which included hijras her family knew, were laced with the fear that attended the possibility of becoming a hijra. Had she become a hijra, she remembered worrying, she would have been lost to her family and at the same time forced to give up the comforts that had softened her life as a well-to-do Hindu woman in a city recently torn by Hindu–Muslim strife. The home scenes we exchanged in street Hindi spiced with US English glued us together palimpsestically. Their veracity was less interesting than their commonalities. What brought us together was our conjoint awareness that we were remembering together what we once had quickly been trained to kind-of-forget.

When did I realize that I had forgotten about hijras, in the course of laying aside my fears of losing class? Only when I first read Anne Fausto-Sterling's article on hermaphroditism, "The Five Sexes." Not that I had completely dropped hijras from my iconography of childhood-memories. Had I been asked I, like my young interlocutor at NYU, would have pulled some out. But they had been filed away in the category of memories of no real significance, memories of people who had never quite inhabited the spaces I walked as a child. Lost to the same organization of memory were the ways in which servants who worked for my family in Bombay had peopled my early years. I would have recalled those servants, like my nanny and our cook, had a comment specifically called them up. But had I been asked about my family, or thought about my family, the servants would have dropped from immediate view. In memorializing narratives the movements of the complicated play of class and gender in my life became a kind of background music, heard but easily ignored.[4]

Someone had handed me the Fausto-Sterling article about twenty years after I came to the US as a student. The essay piqued my interest not because it taught me something new about people who are intersexed, but because so much of the information in it seemed so familiar. Familiar and yet unremembered. Familiar, yet odd, precisely because most of the other faculty and students who read the article were so thrown by it, when I was not. Reading the piece dredged up memories sedimented in my body. I laid them out in front of me like portraits

411

or yellowed family photographs. This array of the no–longer–forgotten led me to questions about the production of diasporic identities at the nexus of power/knowledge, in the guise of an unremarked reorganization of memory.

When I arrived in the US in the 1970s, the coming out narratives I heard scripted no place for complex notions of a gendered past. American stories about emerging sexuality thrived on a binary opposition between lesbians and gay men, with tomboyish childhood providing the only relief from insistent gender fixations. Like my interlocutor at the conference, my gender plots began to conform to the narratives at hand, leaving the performances of gender played out by hijras nowhere in sight. I was a girl who grew up in Bombay and came into my sexuality in the US. In the process of producing my narratives about gender and sexuality, I forgot the webbed discourses of difference that had inflected my childhood processes of identification.

The stories I created for myself in the US echoed/reflected those written by psychologists and anthropologists. Women appeared in relation to families. Class slipped away, my location blurred. I found myself speaking of myself as a simple "Indian" woman whose difference was marked only by biology, even if the biology was understood as socially constructed. The lessons about biology I had learned as a child that included my questions about hijras (which at one time had also been questions about myself) dropped from sight and memory.

The stories I now told about myself were in translation. In the process, I became translation. I wore all of the accouterments of a fluency as I traversed the distance from a "minor" to a "major" language: Boston, white, upper-middle class. Only in retrospect do I realize that I had translated my gender, without marking the move, into a different set of narratives. The narratives, however feminist, parceled off men from women and separated masculinity and femininity into two oppositional poles. These gendered binaries reproduced themselves in spatial terms, the standard demarcation into public and private with the "outside" streets and political economy given over to men and the domestic "inside" to women. I became a creature of the house, house bound, family bound, woman bound, in my remembrances.

In what follows I intend to undo claims to an easy fluency regarding gender, whether those claims appear in scholarly discussions or diasporic rememberings. In bringing queer home, home and queer become necessarily hybrid, and gender refuses to stay in its allocated places. Disjunction, as both practitioners of translation theory like Carol Maier and queer theory like Jose Muñoz have argued, becomes an intrinsic part of articulating acts of translation that are queer, odd, anomalous, those that don't quite fit into fluent/fluid backs and forths between different diasporic sites. Diasporas themselves begin undoing fluency when texts and people travel as migrants, immigrants, tourists, and refugees.

Maria Lugones, herself a product of the Latina diaspora, has used mayonnaise as a metaphor to talk about power and race. I want to extend that metaphor to discussions of another kind of world-traveling and translation: the stories of gender cooked up and served up for variable consumption.

Bring Out the Hellman's . . .

In "Purity, Impurity and Separation," Lugones begins her discussion of hybridity with a description of her actions as she follows a recipe for making mayonnaise. She waits till further on in the paper to evoke her mother's kitchen, the place where she mixes her ingredients. But with the tangibility and immediacy of her performed cooking activities – "I crack the egg, and now I slide the white onto one half of the shell, and I place the egg white in a bowl" – she implicitly locates those movements and opens her paper with/in the ordinary, domestic space of the kitchen. For Lugones hybridity is precisely that which is situated in and implicated with the heart of her home. Like mayonnaise it is "neither/nor, but kind of both, not quite either, something in the middle of either/or."[5] Hybridity brings with it ambiguity, and with that possibility threatens the orderliness of schematized reality. No wonder it is often labeled anomalous or deviant. The gooey mess sticks to bowls piled in a sink as its constituent ingredients are carefully packed off into the appropriate shelves on refrigerator doors.

How does this discussion of hybridity translate into mayonnaise? Mayonnaise, a condiment that helps certain kinds of edibles go down more easily, looks homogenous. It has the appearance of something made up of identical particles. However, anyone who has mixed it from scratch knows well the slow care with which each ingredient, egg (yolk, white), vinegar (or lemon), and oil, must be separated and whipped to produce the emulsion that is eventually consumed as mayonnaise.[6]

"Home-cooked" mayonnaise supplies a useful metaphor for hybridity because the final product is visually and viscerally different from its constituents. Greated in the mundane space of the kitchen, it is, under ordinary circumstances, used very differently than its components. But its bland uniform yellowy-whiteness, and its slippery light taste and texture elide the tastes, textures, and visual specificities of its component parts. Once you make mayonnaise you cannot revive, isolate, or go back to its "original" ingredients, and its visual homogeneity rests uncomfortably beside egg-shells and mixing bowls.

"Original" does not in the case of mayonnaise map onto simple or pure, both troubled sites in discussions of hybridity at different periods, when complexity (hybrid race, Creole for example) was either juxtaposed against ostensibly unalloyed categories (black/white) or inexorably returned to "naturally" pure, though "degenerate," origins. Any attempt to chart a genealogy of purity would have to enlist the help of experiments in the absurd. Hunched over a chemistry set, one *could* attempt to distill yolk and oil down to "pure" molecules but they would not turn into "ur" origins easily.

To forestall any mythologized "return" of mayonnaise to pure and primitivized origins, I would like to site it as something "cooked," a substance spooned into a bowl that squats on a counter next to a molded glass jar topped in tin,

413

bought in a store. To queer the discursive possibilities of mayonnaise I have to set the process of its agitated mixing in a kitchen alongside its production and circulation, pouring, packaging, and marketing as a commodity. Hybridity under this troping turns nineteenth-century biology, hybrid wheat, miscegenated sperm, and egg, into kitchen/factory phenomena, sperm banks, and turkey basters.[7]

Mayonnaise, like most emulsions, is both stable and unstable. Emulsions of oil and water have a familiar visual history that any child who has tried valiantly to stir one into another should be able to recall with ease: little bobbles floating insistently back to a churned surface. Mayonnaise circumvents the separation of its constituents because of lecithins in egg yolk. Lecithins, the two molecular ends of which are hydrophobic and hydrophilic, coat oil globules and facilitate the links to water that bring water and oil together in uneasy alliance. Mayonnaise can, however, curdle into two. When you make a curdled mess of mayonnaise you are left neither with a smooth, homogenous mixture of oil and yolk, nor with clean oil and clean egg yolk. You are rather left with "yolky oil and oily yolk."[8] No purity here, no effortless resolve into "original" ingredients. Mayonnaise desanitizes hybridity, even as fears of disease, salmonella in the eggs, unclean kitchen utensils, infect the conditions of its making.

Introducing mayonnaise – a word without cognates, and a condiment that violates the strict vegetarian practices of many households – into many South Asian homes on the subcontinent is likely to degenerate into a translator's nightmare. But South Asian families in urban areas could and occasionally did purchase bottles of Hellman's from the all-purpose British grocery stores in English clubs that stocked all the accouterments needed – from Pears soap to white cheese – to make life in the colonies palatable.[9] British-Indian kitchen habits were then absorbed into a classed subcontinental culinary repertoire. My mother's excruciatingly Anglicized, implicitly middle-class, though nationalist, family made mayonnaise at home sometimes, to use in bland English recipes followed assiduously from imported imperial cookbooks. One woman's sandwich blend turned on another's colonial legacy. Mayonnaise, produced in Anglicized (even if temporarily) kitchens, fingered other issues around the directionality of colonial translations, class, and work. Weighing into kitchen decisions were conversations about who qualified as an appropriate cook for English food, whether the servant who usually worked the pots and pans was adequately versed in British tastes, or whether the lady of the house had to perform the operations herself. Who could and did produce mayonnaise? For whom was the condiment in question displayed?

Mayonnaise as the only trope for hybridity turns rancid as it travels; so too does a distilled and bottled queerness. Though queerness, if one mixes up the myriad uses of the term, is closer to an amalgam than an emulsion (in that it falls apart into its components easily), like mayonnaise it looks different than its ingredients – the practices, identities and sexualities that give it texture. In practice queerness has been deployed as an umbrella term for identities and embodied multiplicity (gay, lesbian, bisexual, transgender, butch–femme, cross-dressing, third gender) as well as manipulated to read texts against the grain for sexualities that do not fit "norms."[10] Queerness as *a* (if one can precede the word by the singular article *a*) site produces a space for sexual hybridity alternate to and in excess of simple identity categories. Once identity categories have been dumped under the rubric of "queer," even when people attempt to distill them into something more "elemental," they carry the faint whiff of complexity, the taint of infection.

So although the banality of mayonnaise may seem worlds away from the contrariness of queerness, queerness and mayonnaise call forth similar issues around hybridity. Compounding queerness and mayonnaise allows me to represent queerness as process, as verb (queering, making queer), not as a given; static, and stable. Locating my conversation in the routine of the kitchen and zeroing in on the unstable emulsion that is mayonnaise brings with it an implicit critique of where discussions of sexuality have often situated gendered/erotic difference. In many such discussions, queer positions, readings, identities, activities are relegated to the margins, "with the assumption that queer is anomalous, or is different from hegemonic (heterosexual) ideologies of gender and sexuality."[11] That is, with the presupposition that queerness happens outside, elsewhere, over there, not at the heart of a fantasy called home.

Disquisitions on queerness seem to require acts of untenable translation when they travel through the machinery of race/imperialism/colonialism.[12] Instead of looking for the hybridity in homogeneity, the homogeneity in hybridity, they tend to generate purified sexual subjects. Colored transparencies overlay sameness with difference, an optical illusion of "real lives" cast into high relief. Race codes into color, not white as colorized, or white as contrast produced in necessary relation to racialized othering, but race etched onto the skin of communities whose representatives must be found to speak their own positions.[13]

If one travels, and translates with a "tr" taken not from the Latin "translatus," but from the Hindi/Urdu *tarna*, as in cross over, traverse, be ferried or saved, and *tirna*, as in float or swim, through discussions of hybridity from South Asian postcolonial theory to queer theory, one sinks into a rift common to both. A rift that is so subtly unmarked, yet so obviously, even prosaically *there*, that it seems almost boring to flag it, which is the problem with most constructed silences, in that they are simultaneously violent, violating and remarkably humdrum. This particular one is the hybrid concocted of South Asian and homo, as in sexuality, and its imbrication with gender. Neither Gayatri Spivak nor Homi Bhabha, paradigmatic "postcolonialists," venture near it. Its ghostly outlines mark the outer limits of their theoretical travails; Bhabha because he traverses hybridity through psychoanalysis via Frantz Fanon, and Spivak, because for her the gendered subaltern in circulation is always already hetero. Queer theorists, who have consumed postcolonial theory without much in the way of critical commentary when they have attempted to marry subaltern to queer, have done little to encourage either writer to confront their occlusions.

415

Queer theory, on the occasions when its territorializing impulses depart the US, does tour South Asia, though quickly, settling on the figure of a third, the anthropologized other, "the" hijra.[14] Depicted in the semiotics of purity and primitivism, hijras appear in scholarly literature as authentic urban (though ruralized) savages whose celebrated gender inversion organizes itself around masculinity but slips into some intermediate embodiment. Absent from most of these portrayals is any explicit discussion of class, colonial subjugation, nationalism, or abjection (the allure of a fetishized utopian body newly minted from past anthropological coin having proved too lucrative).[15]

To decolonize such a figure as "the" hijra, to find a place for the hijra stories of my youth and to find a place for myself in the stories so that I am not relegated to a dichotomized fluency, queer must be hybridized not merely into forms that have been permitted by particular technologies of othering, but in terms that interrogate those very technologies and their implication in productions of homo as everywhere and always the same.

Hybridizing Hijras, or Slathering Them with Mayonnaise

Hijras entered my childhood world in Bombay in two different ways. They came to houses, both to my house and those of other relatives, when we celebrated certain family rituals for childbirths and marriages. They were also *in* my house and *in* my body as protagonists of stories that I have since realized affected my sense of embodiment and my relationships with the domestic and social spaces I inhabited.

In Colaba, the region of Bombay where I grew up, my family lived in a capacious, upscale apartment facing the sea, not far from the fisher-huts cobbled together from cardboard, two-by-fours, and tin, that lined the sea wall, always on the verge of being washed away with the monsoon storms. In a city whose real estate prices rivaled New York's, most people who had regular jobs lived in cramped two-room apartments packed tight with bodies or in the shanty towns scattered irregularly throughout Bombay. The hijras who I saw regularly in Colaba lived in either the shanty towns or in groups of tiny rooms perched on rickety wooden buildings enclosed in verandahs, the residue from British attempts to erect structures for laborers who had migrated to the city. I saw them in groups on the narrow street that veered off from my apartment building. I saw them walking past the small shops that ran alongside the road, the place where my mother sent our cook to pick up our rations of wheat and get it ground, the tiny storefront selling miscellaneous things, pencils, erasers, copybooks and multicolored Japanese chewing gum that came in pocket-sized boxes. My differences from these hijras were marked by my knowledge of the class-specific geography that coded the city, which kinds of housing were available to whom.

416

Hijras are usually represented as men who are not quite "normal." Both Indian and western accounts slip and slide on what hijra means, or what the figure of the hijra is supposed to stand for. They have been variously equated in local lore (Indian media, Indian scholarship) with *zenane* ("gay men"), eunuchs, hermaphrodites, transsexuals, and people who are transgendered.[16] Hijras, popular press articles, and anthropologists who have "studied" them seem to agree that hijras sometimes speak of themselves as intersexed "people" or gendered inverts (effeminate men) who may have been castrated or "emasculated." Although many hijras appear to acquiesce to transnamings such as eunuch or hermaphrodite, they distance themselves from *zenane* (gay men), both the category and the name, calling *zenane* inauthentic or incomplete hijras who use the word "hijra" for their own ends.[17] Hijra, sans *zenane*, then, is a bloated umbrella term under which "trans-" bodies and representation collect.

Figures usually taken to complicate masculinity or male sexuality, the hijras I saw in Bombay usually wore clearly classed women's clothing and jewelry – glass bangles dotted unevenly with gold paint and saris, with embroidery that middle-class viewers might consider "gaudy." The castration ceremony that I had heard hijras undergo, penis and/or testicles sliced off by a *dai* (midwife) without benefit of pain-killers, is said by anthropologists like Serena Nanda to include rituals that echo those that women perform during marriage and childbirth. Although the only way that I supposedly knew hijras was through their most visible public function, performance, in interviews some of them say that they do sex-work.[18]

On occasions such as births and weddings hijras dance and sing predominantly Urdu/Hindi songs drawn from genres like mystical (Sufi) *qawwali*, as well as *filmi git* (film songs, often love lyric) and *gali* (bawdy "curse' songs usually sung by women). Paradoxically, hijras dress as women and perform as women (*zenane*) even as they repudiate the application of the term *zenane* (as effeminate men) to them. In their transitivity (neither male nor female) hijras' intersexed bodies embody auspiciousness. Thus the obsessive reiteration of maleness and masculinity – however liminal or contested – in analyses of hijras recapitulates the futility of recovering untainted yolk from home-mixed mayonnaise.

For the luck they bring to a range of households, hijras can demand and are given as much cash as a family can afford. Although many ethnographers have depicted them as figures whose power derives from Hindu mythology and Mata (the Hindu mother goddess hijras worship), their performances are hybrid urban cultural forms that in turn create them as hybrid religious figures. Thus their performances not only complicate sexuality but also challenge purist religious divisions. The purification of hijras into authentic Hindus whose lineage stretches back across vast reaches of mythic Hindu time, is in consonance with their own repudiation of the Arabic term *zenane*. This discursive move colludes with a nationalist politics of religious, racialized abjection that seeks to eject Muslim "infection" to ensure Hindu purity by recording hybrid practices to produce a lineage of authentic pure forms. It also turns them from cyborgs who rely on screened and circulated film for their "authentic" religious performances into authentic real biological types (species) found when story-gatherers venture into the field.

Mayonnaise here slides back from a jar bought for consumption in colonial sites into unadulterated oil and yolk mixed from time immemorial in a local kitchen, from inauthentic to authentic, the two rarely brought into relationship with one another, and neither calling for an interrogation of the politics of continued colonialism. Temporality is delayed, the counterfeit "ur" purity of Hinduism displacing a complex negotiation with racialized, religious subjectivity in ways that belie the violence that accompanies current re-productions of a pure and originary past.[19] Ironically, the circulation of hijras as hermaphrodites in the US is contested by specialists in Indian studies who struggle with the Hindu-ization of hijras, sometimes refusing them a space in discussions of Sanskrit and transsexualism, sometimes including them.[20]

Like most nonwestern accounts of transsexuality and hermaphroditism, Serena Nanda's analysis of hijras is obsessed with masculinity, men, and maleness.[21] As a category, hijras are explored or exploited almost solely in terms of their relationship to men and adolescent boys. By refusing to speak about the places where women and hijras meet, discourses on hermaphroditism treat it as a male error, a male anxiety, a masculine conundrum, and the woman subaltern remains silenced. Why this insistent pull toward masculinity in discussions of a world where space was given over to bodies that did not quite fit into a bisected bi-sexed, bi-gendered, bi-sexualized system?

In contrast to the neocolonialist world-traveling (and text-traveling) that sends people abroad to search for sexual or gender difference, in urban North India hijras bring that difference to your house. Entering supposedly Hindu homes as real Hindu women (though not the same, and not *zenane*), hijras confront women, femininity, and feminization with parody and a theatrics of sexual ambidextrousness. Wearing saris and bangles, dancing "women's" dances, hijras seem to be "conventional" women, even as their over-the-top, ironic renditions of the already campy, bawdy *gali* that some women lob at each other in closed female spaces during marriages belie gendered convention. Yet writers who use hijras to talk about masculinity generally assume that the women who watch those theatrics remain unchanged by hijra performances. Like cartoon characters utterly absorbed in Hindu ritual, the women of the house register no shifts in gender, lives, or sense of self when the performance comes to an end. Instead they become the bland, unremittingly uniform audience in front of whom hijras dance. Even when women are sexualized in these accounts, they seldom get asked questions about hijras and class. How would they feel if their children were born hermaphrodites? What would it mean to imagine one of their children entering a hijra community? To imagine one of their (middle-class) children crossing class lines to enter a hijra community? How might they respond if a person (maybe even a friend or relative) they thought was a woman or girl turns out not to be one? How have they dealt with the possibility that they themselves might have been hijra? Why might they be inclined to push such questions aside?

Gender Bending Inside the Girl's Door

My first memory of actually seeing hijras was at my aunt's wedding, when I was about seven years old. This aunt, my mother's much younger sister, had lived on and off with us after my grandfather died. So my parents held her wedding in our apartment, in lieu of the home that would have ordinarily hosted the marriage. Although my father was Gujarati, the wedding was a typically upper-middle-class Punjabi one, sort of Arya Samaj, since my mother's family was Arya.[22] My cousins and I were running around in a rambunctious herd, pretending to patrol the front door. We kept getting tangled up in the fragrant gold and white garlands of marigolds and champa that the flower man was weaving into designs on our doors. As I tripped over yet another clump of threaded flowers I heard drums. The worn dark teak elevator door in front of me creaked open. A group of vivid women stepped out and formed themselves into two circles. The black and white speckled foyer suddenly felt full.

The inner ring began to dance and bright blue flashed across my face. A harsh, sharp voice following the thin strains of a harmonium and drum rhythms sang a song that echoed those my aunts had exchanged with my uncle-to-be's sisters. Songs about how awful he was, how ugly, dark, and misshapen. I'd sat in a corner the previous night watching the women laugh, not sure if I was expected to do the same. The abrupt clapping beat caught at me, and I looked up at hands arched outward clapping in a way I had never seen before. "Hiru," anxiety creased my mother's voice as she called my father, "get the girls out of there! What are they doing? Get some money!" The dull force of fingers that ringed my arm pulled me backward through a cool corridor into a hot sunny bedroom. My mother's anxiety focused on the girls, her nieces and her daughter, conveying a veiled fear that we, not my brothers or male cousins would be affected by the performance.

Like many other urban children who lived for periods of time with different relatives in a multifaceted family, I grew up surrounded and protected by stories. The aunt who had been married in our house told me macabre tales of medical school, replete with corpses and peculiar diseases. Her husband took us out to borrow American comic books about superheroes from packed store-front lending libraries tucked into the crevices between buildings. He would read Superman, Spiderman, and Wonder Woman aloud to us when we refused to eat dinner. My grandmother and nanny read to me from the *Ramayana* and the Bible, respectively, when I was restless and wandered the house at night. My friends and I, sharing books circulated under wooden desks filed neatly in the Scottish mission classrooms where we attended school, read Dickens, Marie Corelli, war stories about a fighter-pilot called Biggles, and pulp romances like

Mills and Boone. The boogey-person tales, however, were my own, repeated in private clusters among my friends. But I checked the veracity of some of the more puzzling details with the adults in my life, secure in the belief that adults were incapable of fathoming the larger story hinted at by these tidbits.

In other spooky stories, the architecture of my childhood imaginary bolstering the hijra tales, I imagined dark places ensconced deep in the heart of stark daylight; dark places where I was suddenly alone, abandoned inadvertently in thickly black stairwells of apartment buildings, dust crunching under my polished mary-janes.[23] My boogey-person in this instance was a mythic man on the mountain, an ordinary but horrific urban reincarnation of Fagin crossed with a *buniya* Shiva. This man, I'd been told, trafficked in children's bodies. When I asked about him, my mother pointed out his lair, towering high over the largest shanty sprawl in Bombay, as we ambled past in our smoky car en route to the airport. She said, "He kidnaps kids, and chops off their arms and legs, blinds them, pokes holes in their ears, sends them out to beg. Those kids who beg on little carts with wheels, travel in pairs, they're his. They live on the street, and give him the money they earn. I think that they probably make a lot in one day, you know, all of us give them money." Then she read me an exposé of child beggars from the *Times of India*, the local newspaper, to prove her point.

The secret spaces kids crawl into grew monstrous, inhabited by fears of snatching and deformation, displacement and homelessness, encoding abjection around loss of class. But fears that inhabit many children's lives took a different turn when it came to hijra-stories. Hijras, I thought then, in tales I have since seen cataloged by anthropologists, could lay claim to any child born with two sets of sex organs. They would ask for a child, and parents had no choice but to give the child over to live in communities shrouded in mystery. A hijra child could never come back to live with its family, its relationships truncated at or near birth.[24]

My pediatrician aunt explained the bare bones of the embryology of hermaphroditism to me. What I didn't ask her about was the possibility of blastular changes deforming my body as I became aware of the changes in my friends' developing adolescent anatomies. When bodies grew strange accretions, incomprehensible to a child, all accretions, breasts and penises, seemed to belong together. Our bodies, we thought, could go either way, or in both directions simultaneously. So my friends and I talked vaguely about our hijra potential, bodies that might grow breasts and vestigial penises, while we read illicit Mills and Boone novels about westerners and romance. Romance, at a time in our lives when arranged marriage seemed to be the inescapable norm, carried the titillation of running away from home for love, overturning the convention of a familially sanctioned, contained marriage to someone our parents had carefully selected for us. The stories of our potential for physical reformation merged almost without notice into talks about love as a Westernized social transgression.

Hijras haunted me at night. An occasional pre-adolescent insomniac, I would leave my bedroom to wander the house in the dark, feeling my way to the verandah past the sharp corners of scattered furniture. I stood in there cloaked in the tepid peat-smoke color refracted off the sea beyond our house. I would wait and watch in fascination for my body to emerge naked from the night, its shape subtly transformed by growths I still couldn't completely visualize. I expected to be recognized, surprise blocking my parents' mouths, claimed by silent clues I could not name.

In my fantasies hijras would take me away to dance and sing and beg. My days at the time were invaded by my parents' increasingly insistent attempts to gender me appropriately: to change my relationship to my male siblings, transform my walk, alter the way my clothes draped my body, make me sweeter, neater, more docile – but at the same time also encourage my academic turn towards biology. They wanted to shape-shift me into a willing bride spiced with advanced degrees.

The impact of hijra stories on my life raises the specter of the hybrids that I encountered at home, figures who came to our door when ritual events held the promise of familial collectivity, and when narratives articulated social displacement, loss of home. Tales of hijras as women-hermaphrodites lodged in my body, opening up for it possibilities of metamorphosis, possibilities both liberatory and confining, freeing as well as deforming. All the boogey-person stories, including the hijra ones, articulated my fears about loss of class precisely because their teleology narrated a move downwards in Bombay's geography as I implicitly left my home to go to another. They also enacted political economies, like the one embodied in transactions around mayonnaise: who made it in a colonial kitchen, who bought it in bottles in English grocery stores, and who could/would partake. As an upper-middle-class woman, I was part of the group who paid for performance. In this position, I would never be expected to exact payment for my gendered performance from a group of hijras. So moving differently into the dynamics of solicitation, of trafficking in bodies, I would lose the privilege of who paid whom for what.

Like most coming-of-age stories troubled by time, conformities to plot line, and the exigencies of confessional modalities spoken retrospectively in relation to queerness, mine cannot stand in for representations of the real, any more than "real" hijra narratives can. These stories can and do, however, point out contiguities between class and gender and between gender and sexuality in certain urbanized spaces.

In the opening story – my "when I saw my first hijra" story – hijras enacted a theatrics of gender with songs that echoed the bawdy, vibrant, occasionally vitriolic ones (*gali*) exchanged between the women on both sides of a marital equation. Hijras performed in the liminal place of the threshold a set of sexually explicit songs that had otherwise been sung exclusively between and by women inside the home. That connection opened up for me the possibility that gender was sung in multiple sites. It created for me the possibility that I too might

421

perform gender as not-quite-a-woman, markedly at odds with a translation of myself as merely woman.

Weddings were not the only moments when sexuality was addressed in my polymorphous household. My female relatives engaged in explicit discussions of male prowess, impotence, and inability. My memories set up a complicated inter-play between the words of the midwife in my father's village and the medical establishment so well represented by my mother's urban family, the same family that had schooled me so well in menstruation and pregnancies before marriage. But the *gali*, implicitly sung back and forth between the innards of an apartment and its vestibule, split a gendered education open, returning it not to some utopian prelapsarian muddy village site, but to the cool steel table of dissection, enacting hybridity in a modernizing scene. Gender was about learning to tra-verse abjection. Gender played itself out through narratives thoroughly versed in the English curricula of colonial schooling, American comics, and genealogies of displacement where different horrors of urban poverty became palimpsests for each other. Following a Mills and Boone running-away-with-a-man plot to escape one's family, being kidnapped into Dickensian urban child labor, and growing a vestigial penis only to have it chopped off – each scenario no more hybrid, no less gendered than the other.

Revisiting Mayonnaise

Mayonnaise turns rancid as it travels. Jars left unrefrigerated or twisted open past their expiration date smell of sitting on a shelf too long. Hijras, as the alleged embodiments of a third sex/gender, have become heroic gender benders in queer theory. These thirds are manufactured ostensibly to hybridize gender by blend-ing "male" with "female." But ironically, the hijras that anthropologists and queer theorists write up preserve the distinct ingredients, "male" and "female," from which these hijras have been whipped up. Having produced hijras in a cru-cible of gender and sexuality without attention to religion, nationalism, or urban-ized discourses on class, they not surprisingly tend to locate that crucible in a never-never-land far from the mundane tasks of home.

Against utopian gestures that produce pure othered bodies in a hermetically sealed elsewhere, never-at-home, this paper lays out stories to bring that Other back to the center. Hijras in *my* home were not the only feminized subjects in the space. And I, too, was not merely girl. Neither is home a condiment slathered without pause onto doughy white bread. Home is also produced, mixed from dif-ferent discourses, always as acts of translation, sometimes disturbingly fluent, occasionally just disturbing.

Bringing hybridity home and queering the kitchen does not mean that hybrid-ity stops participating in the exigencies of science, technology, or imperialism. The kitchen, too, must be located, classed and raced. One cook's condiment is another's colonial legacy.

422

Hijras as "real" boys, albeit "unruly" boy bodies, are a translator's fantasy, a discursive product of technologies that typologize as they travel. These figures offer the reader hybridity as mayonnaise, whipped up frenetically in some nowhere space, its shiny surface reflecting a beaming declassed, deracinated face. Easily palatable but to whom? What this version of the process of thirding cannot take into account are contiguities with the kitchen scene rolled backwards, a scene that begins with mayonnaise glowing yellow-white in a bowl, and ends with ingredients arrayed splendidly separate on a counter. Like yolky oil and oily yolk, masculinity produced after the fact never looks so clean. Nor does femininity, the unspoken ingredient in the emulsion.

Notes

1   For shared ruminations I would like to thank Lawrence Cohen, Elena Creef, Sabine Golz, Evelynn Hammonds, Fred Moten, Maureen Robertson, Amy Robinson. Without Kath Weston's artful fingerprints, editorial and otherwise, that mark the text substantially, it would not have arrived at the hybrid form it now takes.

2   Typical discussions about gender, desire, and identification in South Asia focus on men and boys. They tend to follow a neo-Freudian familial script, but complicate the oedipal nuclear triad (father, mother, boy) by making the mother a devouring (Kali-like) figure. See *The Inner World: A Psychoanalytic Study of Childhood and Society* by Sudhir Kakar. A new work that explicitly redresses Kakar's presumptions by addressing the identifications of women and girls is *Listen to the Heron's Words: Reimagining Gender and Kinship in North India* by Ann Grodzins Gold and Gloria Goodwin Raheja. Though Gold and Raheja try to address the elision of female sexuality and power in the usual accounts of gender, they succumb to unreconstructed notions of kinship and heterosexuality.

3   Queered selves may very well unsettle even Bhabha's imbrications of other and self.

4   Class was not just economic circumstances, organization of labor, but the directionality of the exchange of labor, the social stratification of city spaces, access to resources like cultural capital, and finally the way in which stories about loss narrated fears about slips away from implied privilege.

5   Lugones, 1994: 459.

6   Geographically diasporic as well as alimentarily hybrid, mayonnaise is an early nineteenth-century term from Mahon, the capital of Minorca.

7   See Part 6: The Politics of Cyborgs, in *The Cyborg Handbook* and *The War of Desire and Technology at the Close of the Mechanical Age*, Allucquere Rosanne Stone, for additional extensive discussions of the interpenetrations of the "natural" and "technological." In his chapter "Colonialism and the Desiring Machine," Robert Young attempts to bring the desiring machine from Gilles Deleuze's and Felix Guattari's work to bear on postcolonial theorizing of desire by mapping global capitalism's flows of desire as waves of reterritorializing postcolonial spaces. Though Deleuze's and Guattari's machine-age cartographies/economies are sometimes troublingly flattening, Young used them to move discussions on hybridity from purist notions

of the "natural" to ones vested with machinery. It is imperative to evoke the apparati engaged in the production of verities, to turn pure figures into cyborgs, so that the mechanisms for biologizing and naturalizing are rendered visible. For this one can always also turn back again to Foucault and "sexuality" produced discursively through "[t]he 'economy' of discourses, their intrinsic technology, the necessities of their operation" (*History of Sexuality*, vol. 1, 68–9). Though this kind of cyborg-gazing move stretches cyborg history back beyond cyberspace, I offer the move to caution against constructing a linear historical trajectory from "that was then natural," to "this is now hybrid/machine."

8   Lugones, 1994: 459.

9   See Anne McClintock for a discussion of race, gender, and commodities in British colonies.

10   See *Radical History Review*, Queer Issue (vol. 62, nos. 1–6, 1995), essays by Martha M. Umphrey and Donna Penn, for a variety of positions on what constitutes "normal," "normalized," "normality," and also for different deployments of queer. Despite the apparent variety, "queer" can perpetrate its own normalizing moves. Note that most of the articles in the issue, with the exception of Kennedy's and Howard's, speak through whiteness as though it were given and transparent.

11   "Making it Perfectly Queer," Lisa Duggan.

12   For a cogent analysis of the racialized ellipses in feminist readings of psychoanalysis, which, though it does not articulate queerness, certainly raises questions on race/desire which echo those Evelynn M. Hammonds asks in "Black (W)holes and the Geometry of Black Female Sexuality," of queerness, see "Re-placing Race in (White) Psychoanalytic Discourse: Founding Narratives of Feminism," by Jean Walton. Walton's article might be fruitfully read alongside Hammonds' expressly at points when Hammonds alludes to psychoanalysis without entering the vexed terrain of the history of deracinating discussions of psychoanalysis.

13   Hammonds raises precisely this issue in "Black (W)holes," where she speaks to Teresa de Lauretis' statement on "constructed silences around the relations of race to identity and subjectivity in the practices of homosexualities and representations of same sex desire." Lauretis "credits" gays and lesbians of color for this lack by charging them with a failure to adequately study their own "experiences."

14   See *The Lesbian and Gay Studies Reader* for a typical version of this kind of touring.

15   *Third Sex, Third Gender: Beyond Sexual Dimorphism in Culture and History*, edited by Gil Herdt, performs such moves first by dividing the book into two sections, "Historical Contributions" and "Anthropological Contributions," and second by consigning "Hijras: Alternative Sex and Gender Role in India" by Serena Nanda to the "Anthropological." This division reinforces the dehistoricity of anthropology as it contributes to the production of hijras as a species, a type, and a fetish.

16   See "The Pleasures of Castration" by Lawrence Cohen for identifications other than *zenane* for effeminate men who "appear" to be hijras but "do not elect castration." *Zenane* is the plural of the Arabic work *zenana* which is literally translated as "woman." As slang, *zenane* has come to mean an effeminate, and therefore gay, man. The two words Cohen uses are *jankha* and *saheli*. *Saheli*, the preferred appellation, exchanged dialogically between anthropologist and supposed interlocutor, is one

with which Cohen chooses to close his article: "But Kamala said to me: 'You really want to be a *saheli*?'" (300). Cohen ends with a call to disrupt the reification of the third into hijra by posing *saheli* as an alternative for thirdness.

17 Cross-dressing *zenane*, who are in sexual relationships with men or who do sex-work, call themselves hijras, sometimes playfully, but occasionally not so playfully. Hijras who object to these "appropriations" of their "name" do so in part because they feel that *zenane* get a cachet from using "hijra" (complete with rights to ritual power) without having to go through ceremonies devoted to Bahu Chara Mata.

18 Cohen also describes in graphic detail a debate between G. M. Carstairs and Morris Opler over the definition of hijra which closes in on a "hermeneutic circle" around "roles" – what they do is what they are – Carstairs opting for sex-work (prostitution) and Opler for ritual specialization. Both writers lapse into clichéd standardized dichotomies that engage femininity – women as hypersexualized, women as asexual – and play into narratives that dubiously gender and hypersexualize Islam (Richard Burton), as well as Hinduism (Abbe Dubois).

19 For analyses of past and authenticity and the ways in which both get called up during Hindu/Muslim riots, see Gyanendra Pandey's moving evocation of his own complicity in representations of violence.

20 Hindu-ization in another form has been called Sanskritization, a process through which groups marked as abject have resignified themselves. Though the term's history of use is problematic, it is useful to recall here, because though it has been used a great deal in Indian Studies, Nanda seems not to have had it in her repertoire.

21 Robert P. Goldman's article speaks to the incredible contortions plots in Sanskrit texts endure when portraying transsexuality in the other direction, female to male, the only example of which is the story of Amba-Shikhandin.

22 Arya Samaj was a "reformist" Hindu movement that started at the beginning of the twentieth century in urban areas of the northern subcontinent.

23 The geography of the building, dark stairs deep in the building that allow one to travel the entire length, maps class, color, cleanness, purity, and fear of falling onto one another.

24 Cohen offers stories of hijras that violate the conventions of the circulating narratives about them (hijra children who stayed home, for example).

References

Balsamo, Anne. *Technologies of the Gendered Body: Reading Cyborg Women*. Durham: Duke University Press, 1996.

Benjamin, Walter. *Illuminations*. Trans. Harry Zohn. New York: Schocken, 1978.

Bhabha, Homi. "Signs Taken for Wonders: Questions of Ambivalence and Authority Under a Tree Outside Delhi, May 1817," *The Location of Culture*. London: Routledge, 1994.

Certeau, Michel de. *The Writing of History*, trans. Tom Conley. New York: Columbia University Press, 1988.

Cohen, Lawrence. "The Pleasures of Castration," *Sexual Nature, Sexual Culture*, eds. Paul R. Abramson and Steven D. Pinkerton. Chicago: The University of Chicago Press, 1995.

Curti, Nicholas and Herve This-Benckhard. "Chemistry and Physics in the Kitchen," *Scientific American*, 270.4 (1994): 66–71.

Davis, Madeline D. and Elizabeth Lapovsky Kennedy. *Boots of Leather, Slippers of Gold: The History of a Lesbian Community*. New York: Routledge, 1993.

Deleuze, Gilles and Félix Guattari. *Anti-Oedipus: Capitalism and Schizophrenia*, trans. Robert Hurley, Mark Seem, Helen Lane. New York: Viking, 1977.

Dhaliwal, Amarpal K, ed. "The Traveling Nation: India and its Diaspora," *Socialist Review*, 24.4 (1994).

Dingwaney, Anuradha and Carol Maier, eds. *Between Languages and Cultures*. Pittsburgh: University of Pittsburgh Press, 1995.

Duggan, Lisa. "Making it Perfectly Queer," *Socialist Review*, 22.1 (1992): 11–32.

——. "The Discipline Problem: Queer Theory Meets Lesbian and Gay History," *GLQ: A Journal of Lesbian and Gay Studies*, 2.3 (1994): 179–92.

Escoffier, Jeffrey, Regina Kunzel, and Molly McGarry, eds. "The Queer Issue: New Visions of America's Lesbian and Gay Past," *Radical History Review*, 62.1–6 (1995).

Fausto-Sterling, Anne. "The Five Sexes," *The Sciences* (1993): 5–21.

Foucault, Michel. *The History of Sexuality*, vol. 1. New York: Vintage, 1990.

Goff, Jacques le. *History and Memory*, trans. Steven Rendall, Elizabeth Claman. New York: Columbia University Press, 1992.

Gold, Ann Grodzins and Gloria Goodwin Raheja. *Listen to the Heron's Words: Reimagining Gender and Kinship in North India*. Berkeley: University of California Press, 1994.

Goldman, Robert P. "Transsexualism, Gender and Anxiety in Traditional India," *Journal of the American Oriental Society*, 113.3 (1993): 374–401.

Gray, Chris Hables, ed. *The Cyborg Handbook*. Cambridge: MIT Press, 1995.

Hammonds, Evelynn M. "Black (W)holes and the Geometry of Black Female Sexuality," *Differences*, 6.2–3 (1994): 126–45.

Haraway, Donna. "A Manifesto for Cyborgs: Science, Technology and Socialist Feminism in the 1980s," *Socialist Review*, 80 (1985): 65–107.

Herdt, Gil, ed. *Third Sex, Third Gender: Beyond Sexual Dimorphism in Culture and History*. New York: Zone, 1994.

Hubbard, Ruth. "Gender and Genitals: Constructs of Sex and Gender," *Social Text*, 14.1–2 (1996): 157–65.

Kakar, Sudhir. *The Inner World: A Psychoanalytic Study of Childhood and Society*. Delhi: Oxford University Press, 1978.

Lachlau, Ernesto and Chantal Mouffe. *Hegemony and Socialist Strategy*. London: Verso, 1992.

Lowenthal, David. *The Past is a Foreign Country*. Cambridge: Cambridge University Press, 1990.

Lugones, Maria. "Purity, Impurity and Separation," *Signs*, 19.2 (1994): 458–79.

McClintock, Anne. *Imperial Leather: Gender, Race and Sexuality in the Colonial Context*. New York: Routledge, 1995.

Muñoz, Jose. "The Autoethnographic Performance: Reading Richard Fung's Queer Hybridity," *Screen*, 36.2 (1995): 83–99.

Nanda, Serena. *Neither Man nor Woman: The Hijras of India*. Belmont: Wadsworth, 1990.

426

Niranjana, Tejaswini. *Siting Translation: History, Post-Structuralism and the Colonial Context*. Berkeley: University of California Press, 1992.

O'Flaherty, Wendy Doniger. *Women, Androgynes and Other Mythical Beasts*. Chicago: University of Chicago Press, 1980.

Pandey, Gyanendra. "In Defense of the Fragment: Writing about Hindu–Muslim Riots in India Today," *Representations*, 37 (1992): 27–55.

Penley, Constance and Andrew Ross. "Cyborgs at Large: An Interview with Donna Haraway," *Technoculture*, eds. Constance Penley and Andrew Ross. Minneapolis: University of Minnesota Press, 1991.

Portelli, Alessandro. *The Death of Luigi Trastuli: Form and Meaning in Oral History*. Albany: State University of New York Press, 1991.

Probyn, Elspeth. *Outside Belongings*. New York: Routledge, 1996.

Shohat, Ella and Robert Stam. *Unthinking Eurocentrism: Multiculturalism and the Media*. London: Routledge, 1994.

Spivak, Gayatri Chakravorty. "The Politics of Translation." *Destablizing Theory: Contemporary Feminist Debates*, eds. Michèle Barrett and Anne Phillips. Stanford: Stanford University Press, 1992.

Stone, Allucquere Rosanne. *The War of Desire and Technology at the Close of the Mechanical Age*. Cambridge: MIT Press, 1995.

Venuti, Lawrence, ed. *Rethinking Translation: Discourse, Subjectivity, Ideology*. London: Routledge, 1992.

Venuti, Lawrence. *The Translator's Invisibility*. London: Routledge, 1995.

Walton, Jean. "Re-placing Race in (White) Psychoanalytic Discourse: Founding Narratives of Feminism," *Critical Inquiry*, 21.4 (summer 1995): 175–204.

Weston, Kath. "Lesbian/Gay Studies in the House of Anthropology," *Annual Review of Anthropology*, 22 (1993): 339–67.

Weston, Kath. "The Virtual Anthropologist," *Anthropology and "The Field": Boundaries, Areas and Grounds in the Constitution of a Discipline*, eds. James Ferguson and Akhil Gupta. Berkeley: University of California Press, (forthcoming).

Young, Robert J. C. "Hybridity and Diaspora," *Colonial Desire: Hybridity in Theory, Culture and Race*. London: Routledge, 1995.

PART III

The Inventiveness of Theory

Chapter 22

Humanism in Question:
Fanon and Said

Anthony C. Alessandrini

One of the claims frequently made about postcolonial theory is that it is, in one way or another, the "child" of postmodernism. The less emphatic version of this claim simply acknowledges the historical overlap between these two intellectual phenomena: "Postmodern discourse and postcolonialism emerged from the same historical moment – the decentering of Europe in the second half of the twentieth century" (Buckland, 1994: 363). The more ambitious step is to go on to link "historical imperialism" with the "intellectual imperialism" which is said to be the condition of modernity: postmodern attempts to under-cut "the Universalism inherent in the Enlightenment project" can then be said to have "major postcolonial implications" (Hutcheon, 1994: 206–7). At its most ambitious, this position seeks to totally conflate postmodern strategies of decentering with the project of decolonization, as in Thomas Docherty's introduction to a series of essays on "Periphery and Postmodernism" in a recent anthology:

> The mode of thinking which would set up "center" against "periphery" in a bipolar structural opposition is unremittingly modernist. It is also just such an opposition which enables the power relations in imperialism and colonialism. . . . In a certain sense, the discourse of postmodernism – although it is a discourse established in a Eurocentered "First" world – is the discourse *of* the periphery, a discourse which imperialism had strenuously silenced but which is now made available. (1993: 445)

There is a sense in which Docherty's comment, which dates from 1993, already seems rather old-fashioned. It would be hard to make the claim today that somehow ridding ourselves of a "bipolar mode of thinking" has done anything to actually change the state of a world-system which must be considered (albeit in an extremely nuanced way, given the complexity of globalization) according to the structure of centers and peripheries. But this linking of the postmodern and the postcolonial – or, more often, the attributing of the existence of the latter

431

as a separate field of study to the theoretical advances of the former – remains with us, in ways worth noting.

For one thing, some rather strange alliances have ensued. Take the example of Arif Dirlik and Robert Young. In his well-known article "The Postcolonial Aura: Third World Criticism in the Age of Global Capitalism," Dirlik explicitly states that postcolonialism is "a child of postmodernism," which in turn allows him to make the argument that, like postmodernism, "postcoloniality is designed to *avoid* making sense of the current crisis" (1994: 348, 353).[1] Young's book *White Mythologies*, on the other hand, makes the extended argument that deconstruction in particular, and postmodernism in general, represent an effort "to decolonize the forms of European thought": according to Young, "Postmodernism can best be defined as European culture's awareness that it is no longer the unquestioned and dominant center of the world" (1990: 19).

While Dirlik complains that a consideration of the links between postcoloniality and global capitalism is absent from the writings of postcolonial theorists, Young consistently criticizes these same theorists (Edward Said, Homi Bhabha, and Gayatri Chakravorty Spivak are at the center of both arguments) for their "residual classical Marxism" (Dirlik, 1994: 352; Young, 1990: 173). And yet the argument that postcolonial theory ultimately descends from postmodernism links the two: if for Young a theorist like Spivak has not sufficiently learned the lesson of poststructuralism, according to Dirlik she and others have learned it all too well. This is not to discount the important insights offered by Dirlik and Young in these texts, but rather to point out that they thus ultimately become two sides of the same coin.

But what if one were to make the counterclaim that postcolonial theory has by and large descended from the Marxist and Marxist-influenced analyses undertaken by figures involved in the post-Second World war movements against imperialism and for national liberation? This would mean that, rather than considering postcolonial studies through the lens of postmodernism, we would need to look more closely at the historical circumstances under which this field has arisen, and especially at the sorts of strategic decisions involved in the adoption or rejection of particular theoretical paradigms. For example, the moment one stops reading the work of Homi Bhabha as simply an elaboration of Derridean and Lacanian protocols of reading and begins to examine it as a particular way of strategizing about British culture, particular Black British culture, in the 1970s and 1980s, and as thus aligned with the more obviously "political" work of writers like Stuart Hall and Paul Gilroy, one finds oneself doing a genealogy of postcolonial theory very different from that undertaken by those who follow either Dirlik's or Young's lead.[2]

Edward Said, whose work I will be considering in detail, has provided us with an elaboration of this sort of analysis. His essay "Travelling Theory" does not deal with postcolonial theory *per se*, but rather with the ways in which the concept of "reification" makes its way through the work of Lukács, Goldmann, and Raymond Williams. But its influence upon postcolonial studies has to do with the assumption and the question with which Said begins. The assumption is that "as a result of specific historical circumstances, a theory or idea pertaining to those circumstances arises"; the question is: "What happens to [the theory or idea] when, in different circumstances and for new reasons, it is used again and, in still more different circumstances, again?" (1983: 230).

In his reading of this essay, Bruce Robbins diagnoses the "central voyage in question" as "the fall of theory from direct, authentic politics . . . into professional routine." Robbins' work has involved a sustained critique of this narrative of the "fall" into professionalism. And in fact, the twist in "Travelling Theory" has to do with its conclusion, in which Williams' academic "distance" becomes the necessary antidote to the theoretical trap laid by Lukács' theory of reification (Robbins, 1992: 64–7).

But since this narrative of the fall into professionalism continues to proliferate in postcolonial studies, there is a moment in Said's essay, one which is de-emphasized by Robbins, that should be reexamined. In his analysis of Goldmann's appropriation of Lukács – a theoretical move which would appear to be the most "degraded" of the three, since, according to Said, Goldmann possesses neither the political commitment of Lukács nor the theoretical distance of Williams – what Said chooses to emphasize is the historical conditions under which Goldmann adapts Lukács' theory of reification. If it is true that this step nevertheless represents a kind of degradation, "it is just that the situation has changed sufficiently for the degradation to have occurred" (Said, 1983: 236).

What this means is not simply criticizing a particular mode of theorizing as reactionary, but rather being sensitive to the conjuncture which produces the conditions for such a reading. It is this insight, one which Said insists upon throughout his work, that provides the framework for the current essay. I apply both the assertion and the question which open "Travelling Theory" to an investigation of humanism in postcolonial theory. Using the work of Frantz Fanon and Said, I examine the way a particular sort of humanism arises in the historical circumstances of anticolonial struggle and ask what happens to this humanism when it is "used again and, in still more different circumstances, again."

1   Towards a Transnational Humanism: Fanon

Fanon's oeuvre is, by all accounts, full of splits, discontinuities, and occasional outright contradictions. This has led to a variety of competing claims to "Fanon's legacy."[3] As the very different work of Homi Bhabha and Lewis R. Gordon has shown – and indeed, I suspect, as some of the essays in this collection might suggest – Fanon can be used both to attack and defend humanism. And this is not merely a matter of moving from the "early" Fanon of *Black Skin, White Masks* to the more "mature" *The Wretched of the Earth*, since these sorts of contradictions proliferate *within* the latter text.

433

Ato Sekyi-Otu has argued (1996: 4–5, 236) convincingly for a reading of Fanon's texts "as though they formed one dramatic dialectical narrative" whose principal subject is "political experience." According to such a reading, these texts feature not "self-enclosed propositions" which contradict each other but rather "positions assumed, stances staged, claims advanced by typical characters in a story of experience." Sekyi-Otu's reading is a great advance over those which would see the splits and discontinuities in Fanon's work as signs of theoretical inconsistencies or simply bad writing. But what might too easily get lost in such a dialectical approach is a sense of these moments in Fanon as symptomatic of his struggle to write about, and bring into existence, an anticolonial liberation movement, combined with a simultaneous struggle against the European humanist tradition which sets itself up as falsely universal. Few have been as good as Fanon at exposing the supposed "essential qualities [that] remain eternal in spite of all the blunders men may make" as "the essential qualities of the West, of course" (Fanon, 1963: 46; further citations will be noted by page no. alone). To understand the complexity of Fanon's struggle to imagine an emergent humanism which can be separated from this false model, we need to pay attention to the splits and discontinuities that mark this struggle.

Fanon's text, I want to argue, is an attempt to stretch certain modernist metanarratives from within; in fact, the inability to stand outside such metanarratives, or to claim to be uncontaminated by them, is central to Fanon's arguments. Fighting a battle against universalism from within, Fanon works to adapt and stretch such tools as Marxism, existentialism, Hegelianism, and psychoanalysis to fit his needs. The tortured *écriture* and melding of genres in *Black Skin, White Masks* and the way in which *The Wretched of the Earth* teems with multiple themes, voices, and methodologies attest to this struggle. This is not the result of theoretical dilettantism. Rather I would argue, as R. Radhakrishnan does in his analysis of Said's *Culture and Imperialism*, that Fanon's work is "profoundly conjunctural in nature" (1994: 15).

This becomes most clear in Fanon's discussion of "national consciousness," particularly in the chapter of *The Wretched of the Earth* translated as "The Pitfalls of National Consciousness." It could be argued that the adventures (and misadventures) of national consciousness is the central narrative of *The Wretched of the Earth* as a whole. In "Concerning Violence," for example, Fanon suggests that the "immobility" of the colonized in the face of colonialism "can only be called into question if the native decides to put an end to the history of colonization – the history of pillage – and to bring into existence the history of the nation – the history of decolonization" (p. 51); in "Spontaneity: Its Strength and Weakness," we are told that the anticolonial war results in "[e]very man and woman bring[ing] the nation to life by his or her action" (pp. 131–2); in "On National Culture," Fanon maintains that "every culture is first and foremost national" and goes on to argue that: "National consciousness, which is not nationalism, is the only thing that will give us an international dimension" (pp. 216, 247); and in "Colonial War and Mental Disorders," Fanon emphasizes the role played by national consciousness in throwing off the neuroses imposed by colonialism: "When the nation stirs as a whole, the new man [*sic*] is not an *a posteriori* product of that nation; rather, he co-exists with it and triumphs with it" (p. 310).

It would be too simple, however, to claim that "national consciousness" is the theme that ties this book together. Insofar as there is a dialectical method at work in this text, we cannot simply read "national consciousness" as the same thing at different moments – both different moments in Fanon's text and different moments in history. As Sekyi-Otu shows, for example, "Concerning Violence" must be read as an argument that the colonial situation leaves the colonized in a world without a public political sphere, with no mediation possible between the rulers and the ruled. It is only under such circumstances that a particular sort of violence is needed to bring about an anticolonial consciousness; as Fanon suggests at one point, for the native, "To work means to work for the death of the settler" (p. 85). This chapter must therefore be read as only the first moment in the development of a fully formed national consciousness (Sekyi-Otu, 1996: 86–7). Similarly, the particular sort of national consciousness found in the quote from the chapter on "Spontaneity" is immediately complicated, since Fanon is concerned about its simplicity as it gets practiced in this historical moment: "Tactics are mistaken for strategy" (p. 132). This is the "weakness" of spontaneity, one which does not always get noticed by those who would simplify Fanon into a prophet of random anticolonial violence.

So "The Pitfalls of National Consciousness" is a crucial moment in the text and in history, located as it is on the border between colonialism and the establishment of the postcolonial (or, more accurately, neocolonial) nation-state. It also becomes a place to investigate Fanon's humanism, since the battle against colonialism, as it is set out in this chapter, begins with an attempt to end "certain definite abuses: forced labor, corporal punishment, inequality of salaries, limitation of political rights." It is from this sort of rights discourse that, according to Fanon, national consciousness begins to emerge: "This fight for democracy against the oppression of mankind will slowly emerge, somewhat laboriously, as a claim to nationhood" (p. 148). But the final goal of this newly-developed consciousness seems to be a return to the very "neo-liberal universalism," expressed in a recognizably humanist vocabulary, it began by attempting to supersede: its final transformation must be "into a consciousness of social and political needs, in other words into *humanism*"; a national government, the chapter concludes, "ought first to give back their *dignity* to all citizens, fill their minds and feast their eyes with *human things*, and create a prospect that is *human* because *conscious and sovereign men* dwell therein" (pp. 204–05, my emphases). In order to argue that the humanism Fanon invokes here is in fact different from the one which he has critiqued in its Eurocentric and neoliberal form earlier, we must investigate the path an "authentic" national consciousness must travel.

The best way to identify this path is by first defining the "pitfalls" (*mésaventures*) Fanon points out in this chapter. He is quite clear – and remarkably prescient – about what will happen after the claim to nationhood: the "national middle class" will ruin everything; through its "unpreparedness," its "laziness," its "cowardice," and the "profoundly cosmopolitan mold its mind is set in," it will turn national consciousness into "an empty shell, a crude and fragile travesty of what it might have been"; it will fail to be "authentic," and "betray the calling fate has marked out for it," proving itself incapable of "fulfil[ing] its historic role of bourgeoisie"; and finally, through its betrayal of national consciousness, it will bar the way to African unity, condemning this as nothing but a "Utopian" vision (pp. 148–50, 153, 164).

It should be apparent that Fanon is here highly invested in a Marxist narrative in which "the bourgeois phase" is a necessary step towards the eventual proletarian revolution. But it is a narrative whose foundational status is far from secure in Fanon's text. After all, Fanon opens the book with his famous comments about the limitations of Marxist analysis in the colonial context:

> The originality of the colonial context is that economic reality, inequality, and the immense difference of ways of life never come to mask the human realities. When you examine at close quarters the colonial context, it is evident that what parcels out the world is to begin with the fact of belonging to or not belonging to a given race, a given species. In the colonies the economic substructure is also a super-structure. The cause is the consequence; you are rich because you are white, you are white because you are rich. This is why Marxist analysis should always be slightly stretched every time we have to do with the colonial context.
>
> Everything up to and including the very nature of pre-capitalist societies, so well explained by Marx, must here be thought out again. (p. 40)

There is a connection which can be drawn between this passage and the well-known moment in *Orientalism* in which Said demurs from Foucault regarding the role of individual authors: "Foucault believes that in general the individual text or author counts for very little; empirically, in the case of Orientalism (and perhaps nowhere else) I find this not to be so" (1994: 23).

I will have more to say about this connection. For the moment, the point is that like Said's position *vis-à-vis* Foucault, Fanon's stance towards Marxism is a complex one which goes beyond questions of mere influence. This is why I would disagree with those who argue, on the one hand, that Fanon's analysis simply represents a "reexamination" or "reinterpretation" of Marxist theory, and is thus similar to Lenin's analysis of imperialism as the highest stage of capitalism; nor would I agree with those who argue, on the contrary, that Fanon rejects Marxist analysis altogether and makes the mistake of interpreting "the violent resistance to colonialism and the ultimate achievement of independence as revolution." (For the first position, see Jinadu, 1986: 98–109; for the second, Clegg, 1979: 236.)

What actually goes on in *The Wretched of the Earth* is more complicated. For example, early in the text Fanon's stated concern is to "stretch" Marxism to fit the Manicheanism of the colonial situation; but this does not mean, as some commentators have suggested, that he believes race to be "the major determinant in the evolution of society" (Nursey-Bray, 1972: 163). Indeed, one would think that the moment at the end of *Black Skin, White Masks* when Fanon takes pains to differentiate between "the quest for disalienation by a doctor of medicine born in Guadeloupe" and that of "the Black laborer building the port facilities in Abidjan" would be enough to testify to this fact (1967: 223). This point becomes crucial to an understanding of "The Pitfalls of National Consciousness," where class analysis (albeit an unorthodox version, as I have pointed out elsewhere – see Alessandrini, 1995) becomes the key to predicting the future of the postcolonial state. Far from being "the [or even a] major determinant," race here becomes the ideological tool of the national middle class:

Africa is divided into Black and White. . . . The national bourgeoisie of each of these two great regions, which has totally assimilated colonialist thought in its most corrupt form, takes over from the Europeans and establishes in the continent a racial philosophy which is extremely harmful for the future of Africa. . . . Thus it is by no means astonishing to hear in a country that calls itself African remarks which are neither more nor less than racist, and to observe the existence of paternalist behavior which gives you the bitter impression that you are in Paris, Brussels, or London. (pp. 161–2)

The point that needs to be made about Fanon's engagement with Marxism is that it did not occur in a theoretical vacuum, but was rather conditioned by specific circumstances which emerged from the Algerian Revolution, circumstances which made a simple relationship to socialism from inside this revolution an impossibility. Fanon's position had to do partly with the complexity of class politics within the FLN. It was also conditioned by conflicts with actually-existing French Communism and socialism. Simone de Beauvoir's *Force of Circumstance* documents the failure of both the PCF and French socialists generally to actively support the struggle for Algerian independence; as she pointed out:

the Communist Party feared it would be cutting itself off from the masses if it appeared to be less nationalistic than the other parties. . . . It made no effort to combat the racism of the French workers, who considered the 400,000 North Africans settled in France as both intruders doing them out of jobs and as a subproletariat worthy only of contempt. (1965: 339)

Fanon made the same sort of criticism of the PCF in his article "French Intellectuals and Democrats and the Algerian Revolution":

The French Communist Party, it says, can support only certain national liberation movements, for what would be the advantage, for us French Communists, of having American imperialism take over Algeria? . . . The Communist Left . . . while proclaiming the necessity for colonial countries to evolve towards independence, requires the maintenance of special links with France. Such positions manifest that even the so-called extremist parties consider that France has rights in Algeria. (1988: 86–7)

As for the Algerian Communist Party, Fanon pointed out elsewhere that it "was for a long time confined within a reformist position . . . and for long months after November 1, 1954, the Algerian Communists denounced *terroristes provoca-teurs* – in other words, the FLN" (1967a: 150). In this sense, Clegg's critique of "Fanonism," which suggests that since Fanon conceived of the Algerian struggle in "racial and cultural terms" the opportunity to form class alliances between the "Muslim and European" [*sic*] communities was lost, betrays a misunderstanding of this particular historical conjuncture (Clegg, 1979: 236–7).

But if we are back to the point raised by Said in "Travelling Theory" that "specific historical circumstances" affect both the emergence and redeployment of a theory, this is not to say that Fanon's example teaches us to be satisfied with "specificity" alone. This is where Fanon's struggle to theorize a new, non-Eurocentric form of humanism becomes crucial. For, as I began to suggest above, Fanon's stretching of class analysis in "The Pitfalls of National Consciousness" seems to end by re-invoking the language of liberal humanism which it hoped to leave behind. But that earlier brand of humanism was involved only with the "ending of certain definite abuses"; in the Hegelian language Fanon so often favors, it is a request to the master for better treatment. The humanism which emerges at the end of the chapter, and (Fanon proposes) at the point at which true national consciousness is achieved, goes beyond the demands of rights discourse, beyond nationalism, and even beyond a united Africa, as a way of empowering "all underdeveloped people" – indeed, as a way of achieving a "human prospect" for all the "wretched of the earth" (p. 204). It looks ahead to the final sentence of the book, which is pointedly addressed not to the colonial masters but to the colonized: "For Europe, and for humanity, comrades, we must grow a new skin, we must work out new concepts, and try to set afoot a new man" (p. 316).[4] This provides an important counterpoint to Fanon's famous exhortation to "[l]eave this Europe where they are never done talking of Man, yet murder men everywhere they find them" (p. 311).

What is significant is the way in which Fanon's analysis moves from a national to a *transnational* consciousness, and towards what might be called an emergent, transnational humanism. This would not be unlike the "transnational rather than national solidarity" which Kwame Anthony Appiah locates in post-colonial African writers like Yambo Ouologuem and V. Y. Mudimbe – and like these writers, Fanon stakes his claim "in the name of humanism" (Appiah, 1992: 155). In his journalistic and other occasional writings on the Algerian Revolution, where we might expect Fanon to engage in the sort of resolute specificity which a critique of Eurocentric humanism might imply, we instead find him insistently placing the anticolonial struggle in the context, not only of national liberation, but of human liberation: "This oxygen which creates and shapes a new humanity – this, too, is the Algerian Revolution"; "The liberation of the Algerian national territory is a defeat for racism and for the exploitation of man; it inaugurates the unconditional reign of Justice"; "The struggle against colonialism, in its specific aspect of exploitation of man by man, thus belongs in the general process of man's liberation."[5]

To say that "the unconditional reign of Justice" did not follow the years of decolonization in the 1960s is to state the obvious. But this is not to say that "the struggle against colonialism" is at an end; history, after all, is not over. Nor is our responsibility to think through the consequences of the new humanism proposed by Fanon in *The Wretched of the Earth*. Neil Lazarus has eloquently described what a version of postcolonial humanism might look like:

> [it] would necessarily be derivative of the narratives of bourgeois humanism and metropolitan nationalism, with their resonant but unfounded claims to universality. But it would not need to concede the terrain of universality to these Eurocentric projections. On the contrary, where postmodernist theory has reacted to the perceived indefensibility of bourgeois humanism and of colonial nationalism by abandoning the very idea of totality, a *genuinely* postcolonial strategy might be to move explicitly, as Fanon already did in concluding *The Wretched of the Earth*, to proclaim a "new" humanism, predicated upon a formal repudiation of the degraded European form. (1993: 92–3)

I sympathize with this line of argument. But I would add two points: first, the act of "proclaiming" is always going to be historically determined, so that the sort of strategic humanism which will arise will be conditioned accordingly. This is the lesson of Fanon's own brand of humanism, which is unrelentingly strategic. The second point deals with Lazarus's suggestion that a new humanism would be "derivative" of bourgeois humanism; while this is undeniably true, it can be overstated in such a way as to accuse the postcolonial theorist of "residual" humanist tendencies. Edward Said has been so accused.

2   Emergent and Residual Humanisms: Said

In his "Afterword" to the new edition of *Orientalism* published in 1994, Said notes that in the fifteen years that had passed since its initial publication, the book, "almost in a Borgesian way, has become several different books"; he attempts to respond to the "strange, often disquieting, and certainly unthought-of polymorphousness" that has resulted from this (1994: 330). Said uses the largest part of this essay to address the book's reception in the Arab world as an exercise in anti-Westernism and "a systematic defense of Islam and the Arabs" (pp. 330–1).[6] In this context, Said insists upon the book's "anti-essentialist, radically skeptical" nature. He also takes several pages to respond to attacks by Bernard Lewis, with the mixture of wit and acidity that his readers have come to expect: "Lewis's verbosity," Said writes, "scarcely conceals both the ideological underpinnings of his position and his extraordinary capacity for getting nearly everything wrong" (p. 342).

What is most worth noting for my current purposes, however, is Said's attempt to address one particular critique of *Orientalism*:

> among American and British academics of a decidedly rigorous and unyielding stripe, *Orientalism*, and indeed all of my other work, has come in for disapproving attacks because of its "residual" humanism, its theoretical inconsistencies, its insufficient, perhaps even sentimental, treatment of agency. (p. 339)

Said does not mince words in his response: "I am glad that it has! *Orientalism* is a partisan book, not a theoretical machine." He goes on to defend the importance of considering "individual effort" as both eccentric and "in Gerard Manley Hopkins's sense, *original*" (his emphasis), as a way to do justice to Orientalism's "combination of consistency *and* inconsistency . . . which can only be rendered by preserving for oneself as writer and critic the right to some emotional force, the right to be moved, angered, surprised, and even delighted" (pp. 339–40). To top it off, Said proceeds to defend Gyan Prakash's "more mobile post-structuralism" against the critiques of Rosalind O'Hanlon and David Washbrook in the debate around subaltern agency, and to praise the work of Bhabha, Spivak, and Ashis Nandy "for *its* contribution to our understanding of the humanistic traps laid by systems such as Orientalism." All this occurs in one paragraph.

What I am trying to bring out is the impatience with which Said responds to his critics here, one which suggests that a discussion carried on with "rigorous and unyielding" academics does not imply the same sort of urgency as that which must be carried on with those readers who want to claim him as an anti-Western nationalist, or that such a discussion would distract his energies from his continuing battle against Lewis and other Orientalists in their attempt to poison public opinion and affect American foreign policy. There is something to be said for this impatience; it is at least partly responsible for making Said such a successful public intellectual.

My purpose here is to expand on Said's quotable but somewhat cryptic response to critics of his "residual humanism." Part of what I want to argue is that it is a mistake to call Said's humanism "residual." If we were to use the terminology of Raymond Williams – who, as Tim Brennan has suggested, was at least as influential as Foucault in the development of the theoretical framework of *Orientalism* – we could instead call it an "emergent" humanism, in a way which is quite similar to Fanon's.[7]

This also means wrestling with the hybridity of Said's theorizing, caused at least in part, I would argue, by its insistence upon being "partisan" rather than machine-like. Said's appreciative reading of *The Wretched of the Earth* begins with the observation that it "is a hybrid work – part essay, part imaginative story, part philosophical analysis, part psychological case history, part nationalist allegory, part visionary transcendence of history" (1993: 269–70). It is fitting that Said finds this disjunctive methodology so appealing, for his own work can be characterized, in much the same way as Fanon's, as split and discontinuous.

A less sympathetic reader might say instead that Said's work is full of contradictions. It would certainly be possible, for example, to point out the inconsistencies in the responses Said makes to his critics in the "Afterword" to *Orientalism*. In defending against the characterization of his book as anti-Western, he must claim that "words such as 'Orient' and 'Occident' correspond to no stable reality that exists as a natural fact," echoing the most Foucauldian argument he makes in *Orientalism*; in attacking Lewis's Orientalism, however, he must use the language of empiricism in order to prove that the Orientalist gets it wrong by "distorting the truth" (pp. 331, 342). We have already explored such moments of seeming contradiction in Fanon's work as symptoms of a struggle with humanism from within; my argument is that Said's work consistently attempts to carry this struggle forward.

In addressing his critics, Said does not directly identify James Clifford's influential review of *Orientalism*.[8] Yet it is hard to imagine that he did not have this piece in mind when he formulated his response, since Clifford refers specifically to, and sharply rebukes, Said's "residual" humanism, which he also calls "humanist cosmopolitanism" (pp. 274–5). Clifford is quite clear about the methodological problems of the text: "Said's humanist perspectives do not harmonize with his use of methods derived from Foucault, who is of course a radical critic of humanism" (p. 264). There is a bit of the Dirlik/Young syndrome at work in the assumption that *Orientalism* is a Foucauldian text: neither Clifford, who criticizes Said's humanism, nor Aijaz Ahmad, who attacks his "reactionary anti-humanism" (1992: 192–3), ever question the influence of Foucault.

A particularly troubling moment for Clifford has to do with Said's attempt to adopt a "hybrid perspective," especially in the passage I cited earlier: "Foucault believes that in general the individual text or author counts for very little; empirically, in the case of Orientalism (and perhaps nowhere else) I find this not to be so." For Clifford, this hybridity has a "mutually weakening" effect, both upon the reading of individual authors and upon the analysis of discursive formations (p. 269). As I have already suggested, this moment in *Orientalism* is comparable to Fanon's attempt to stretch Marxist analysis in the opening of *The Wretched of the Earth*. So perhaps an account of the historical specificity of Said's engagement with Foucault is in order at this point.

Bruce Robbins has pointed out that Said "is manifestly uninterested . . . in reporting at any length on the original French context of Foucault" (1992: 66). At the time Robbins was writing, before the publication of *Culture and Imperialism*, this was indeed the case.[9] Of course, "Travelling Theory" concludes with a warning against "the theoretical trap" which Foucault's theory of power sets up, but this is a critique more of a particular application of this theory rather than of Foucault himself (Said, 1983: 243–7).

Said's critique of Foucault has become more pronounced since then (see Said, 1986, 1988). Especially striking is a moment in *Culture and Imperialism* where Said does in fact show a particular sort of interest in the historical context of Foucault's work. This occurs, fittingly enough, when he compares "the roughly contemporary work" of Foucault and Fanon (1993: 278). In this comparison, Foucault comes in for criticism for "mov[ing] further and further away from serious consideration of social wholes . . . ignoring the imperial context of his own theories . . . [and] represent[ing] an irresistible colonizing movement that paradoxically fortifies the prestige of both the lonely individual scholar and the system that contains him." While Fanon presses the heritage of Western philosophy "into anti-authoritarian service," Said suggests that Foucault "swerves away from politics altogether." Most recently, comparing Foucault's work to that of Ranajit Guha and the Subaltern Studies historians around the issue of sound and silence, Said goes so far as to wonder "how someone as remarkably brilliant as Foucault could have arrived at so impoverished and masochistically informed a vision of sound and silence" (1997: 17).

I am tempted to claim that one can trace a movement from the Foucauldian to the Fanonian in Said's work. This would not, however, be entirely accurate. For one thing, Fanon does not suddenly appear in Said's work after *Orientalism* (although he does not appear *in Orientalism* itself): for example, in a 1976 interview with *diacritics*, Said discusses the influence of Fanon's work upon his own thinking about colonial discourse and the colonial archive.[10] At this point, interestingly enough, Fanon and Foucault are invoked together as providing a way to talk about the relationship between language and colonization.

Similarly, I think that the unproblematized characterization of Said as a Foucauldian at any point in his career could be complicated by a look at the historical circumstances from which his work has emerged – particularly, as I will suggest, by Said's shifting modes of participation in the Palestinian liberation struggle. This is not to deny the tremendous influence exerted by Foucault. *Beginnings* already sets out the major Foucauldian point which was to be developed at length in *Orientalism*: "a society's identity (its self-rarefaction) rest[s] in some measures upon its detachment from what [is] not itself" (1975: 300–1). I would also agree that Said can be considered "a Foucauldian critic" at least partly because, like Foucault, one experiences in Said's work "the shock of his neutrality in unexpected places, a neutrality which distinguishes him at once from the garden-breeds of anti-bureaucratic thought in current circulation" (Robbins, 1992: 61). But note too that what Said has declared to be of value about Foucault's work is its insistence that since "all knowledge is contentious, then criticism, as activity and knowledge, ought to be openly contentious too" (1983: 224). It is in the place of struggle between contentiousness and neutrality – or, in the terms he sets out in "Travelling Theory," between the "political insurgency" of Lukács and "the distance, even the coldness" of Williams's "critical reflections" – that Said's work exists (ibid.). Or, to put it still another way, Said's work could be characterized as critical reflection *as* political insurgency. A look at his position within the Palestinian liberation struggle, and toward the Palestinian Liberation Organization, suggests the historical circumstances which have helped to determine Said's theoretical choices.

In the introduction to *The Politics of Dispossession*, a collection of what he identifies as his "political essays" on the struggle for Palestinian self-determination, Said marks the June 1967 war as the moment that interrupted "the life of a young professor of English and comparative literature"; at that moment, he writes, he "was emotionally reclaimed by the Arab world generally and by Palestine in particular" (1995: xii). One of the things which is so striking about Said's career, of course, is the way in which he does not cease to be a literature professor, with all of the critical rigor that comes along with it, even in his most overtly "activist" moments: for example, in the same essay, he notes that one of the ways in which the Palestinian liberation struggle signaled a break with the past was the way in which it changed the "rhetorical style" of Arabic political writing: "footnotes began to be used systematically in political writing in Palestinian publications" (p. xv).

What goes hand in hand with this point is the fact that even at his most theoretical Said writes from a position of political insurgency, one which affects his work in ways that have not been sufficiently appreciated. To go back to Clifford's critique, one could argue that the alleged "residual humanism," which might appear to be lapses in a Foucauldian analysis, might just as easily be read as symptoms of Said's struggle (which becomes more overt in his political essays) "to abide by universalist principles and yet be concrete and critical at the same time" (p. xix). As I have already suggested, Fanon's writing bears traces of the same struggle.

A return to Said's earliest political essays provides a particular sort of shock. For example, "The Palestinian Experience," written in 1968–9, identifies the emergence of what he calls "Palestinianism" in the aftermath of the 1967 war. This experience is characterized by Said as the movement from a sense of void to one of discontinuity, and is born in a moment of direct political conflict, the military encounter between Israelis and Palestinians at Karameh in March 1968. Said's comments are worth quoting at length:

> At that moment, when an invading Israeli force was *met* by a local one defending what it could no longer afford to give up, the void changed into a direct experience of true political discontinuity: the actual face-to-face enmity between Zionism and Palestinianism. . . . An event like the battle of Karameh was a decisive moment which, for the Palestinians, was suited to be a certain demarcation between what came before it and what came after it . . . the opponents were clearly pitted against each other. . . . Thus Karameh divides the Palestinian experience into a *before* that had refused an encounter . . . and an *after* that finds the Palestinian standing in, becoming, fighting to dramatize the disjunction of his and her history before 1948 with his history at the peripheries since 1948. In this sense, then, a void, felt by

> every Palestinian, has been altered by an event into a discontinuity. And the
> difference between void and discontinuity is crucial: One is inert absence, the other
> is disconnection that requires reconnection. (1995: 9)

The shock is that Said here sounds like Fanon at his most Hegelian – and this
is not to mention the references to Sartre and Erik Erikson that come later in
the piece. Reading such a passage and then returning to Clifford's criticism
that "we–they distinctions of the kind Said condemns are also useful to anti-
imperialism and national liberation movements" (1988: 261), one cannot help but
feel that Said, indeed anyone involved in the Palestinian struggle, hardly needs
such a reminder.

And yet, Clifford is not wrong to find a strong critique of such a we–they
distinction in *Orientalism*. What is striking is how Said works through this theoretical conflict. For example, if we stay with the notion of "discontinuity,"
which is so crucial to this passage, we find that it reappears in Said's appreciative
analysis of Foucault in *Beginnings*. In this context, Said suggests that discontinuity, for Foucault, is what "confirms the triumph of seriality over unity" (1975:
306). This is very far from a discontinuity which marks "a disconnection that
requires reconnection," just as the rhetoric of the emergence of "Palestinianism" from a moment of face-to-face conflict is far from what one would expect
from a Foucauldian critic best known as a practitioner of "colonial discourse
analysis." We may have located another set of boundaries within which, and
against which, Said's theorizing struggles.

But again, allow me to suggest that this is not due to a choice made just at
the level of theory, but rather one affected by a particular set of historical circumstances. I refer to the fortunes of the Palestinian Liberation Organization,
and Said's ambivalent, often agonistic position towards it. Rather than attributing Said's particular position about the role of the critical intellectual to his
Foucauldianism, it makes a certain amount of sense to reverse the terms – the
move to Foucault, that is, allows the space Said needs to maintain both political
insurgency and critical distance, both contentiousness and neutrality of a
particular kind.

Space does not permit an extended analysis of Said's political writing, but two
points in particular need to be made to understand the connections between it and
his more "theoretical" work.[11] The first, as I have begun to suggest in the case of
his engagement with Foucault, is that what may appear to be theoretical choices
are often the result of particular conjunctures in the Palestinian struggle. To give
one example, the force with which Said rebuts those readers who attribute an anti-
Westernism to *Orientalism* can be read as a reinforcement of the most Foucauldian
arguments in the book. On the other hand, one could also link this particular move
to the arguments Said has been making within the Palestinian movement about
the need for a more nuanced understanding of the West.

This sort of argument emerges most clearly in his articles intended for an
Arabic-speaking audience, where Said often criticizes "the problem of believing

that the West is a single, monolithic object, which of course it is not," whether the West is being idealized or vilified (1996: 94). This is, of course, precisely the point which Said has been making about Orientalism as a discourse, with the difference being that Orientalism has enjoyed an institutional power quite different from what might too easily be called "Occidentalism." What emerges from reading Said's political and theoretical writing together is that what might look like theoretical impurities often turn out to be the result of historical pressures. To put it another way, Said objects to fighting Orientalism with Occidentalism not (or not only) because it is theoretically objectionable, but because it is bad political strategy.

The other point, with which I will conclude this section and which will bring us back to the question of humanism, has to do with the way Said has bridged the political and the professional. In a recent interview with Abdullah al-Sinnawi, Said was asked to respond to a number of accusations made against him by Yasser Arafat: that Said's writings on the "peace process" were "absurd," that Said, as an American, was not one of the people who "made the *intifada*," and that "he, in America, does not feel the suffering of his people" (1996: 165; hereafter cited by page no. alone). Having challenged Arafat's presumption in "appointing himself the sole spokesperson for [the *intifada*'s] martyrs and heroes," Said makes his strongest counter-argument on the grounds of professional competence, specifically his own and Arafat's competence as interpreters of texts:

> I leave it to the reader to judge his and my ability to understand texts and interpret them, while wondering simultaneously about how someone who commands the most basic level of these skills could sign tens of documents that erase with the stroke of a pen many of the inalienable rights of the Palestinian people, including their right to independence. (p. 167)

While this may seem surprising ground for a political critique, Said has been consistent in his claim that the disastrous Gaza–Jericho Agreement was a result of fundamental misreadings – for example, that "Arafat's flawed linguistic and political understanding do not permit him to perceive the difference between limited autonomy, which is what he got, and national liberation, which he gave up" (p. 167). "[T]here is a real disagreement," Said concludes, "between my and Arafat's reading of Palestinian history" (p. 168).

Fanon was also concerned with misreadings, especially those performed by what he called "native intellectuals." Whether it involved misreadings of national culture or of the intentions of the colonizers, some of the most memorable moments of *The Wretched of the Earth* are those which detail the possibilities for such misreadings, as well as their consequences:

> The colonized people, who have spontaneously brought their violence to the colossal task of destroying the colonial system, will very soon find themselves with the barren, inert slogan "Release X or Y." Then colonialism will release these men, and hold discussions with them. The time for dancing in the streets has come.

... Those leaders ... suddenly become useless, with their bureaucracy and their reasonable demands; yet we see them, far removed from events, attempting the crowning imposture – that of "speaking in the name of the silenced nation." As a general rule, colonialism welcomes this godsend with open arms, transforms these "blind mouths" into spokesmen, and in two minutes endows them with independence, on condition that they restore order. (pp. 72–3)

Fanon could well be describing the actions taken by Arafat's regime since the "peace process" was initiated, up to and including the agreement with Israel to "restore order" in the face of "terrorism." Like the mainstream nationalist parties which Fanon subjects to his withering critique, the PLO leadership, according to Said, "became far too concerned with its own survival, not enough with learning from the past, capitalizing and building on strength and potential, remaining focused on principles (like freedom and equality for Palestinians) and real goals, and mobilizing its people and their best elements for work in a common cause"; indeed, Said agrees with Al-Sinnawi's suggestion that "Arafat accepted the Oslo terms because he feared that the Occupied Territories were slipping away from his political plans due to the *intifada*" (1995: xviii; 1996: 181).

But like Fanon, Said also finds in this situation the conditions for the emergence of a new sort of humanism. Writing from the darkest part of the struggle, unexpected possibilities arise. These are moments, it should be noted, that must be drawn out through close readings. One final example might suffice. In "Justifications of Power in a Terminal Phase," published in *Al-Hayat* in April 1995, Said makes no bones about the fact that the New World Order has led to American hegemony in the Middle East of an unprecedented sort (1996: 140–6). But he locates in the *language* of US foreign policy an "eternal recurrence of old ideas and phrases that are hopelessly inadequate," and suggests that this betrays "the ultimate limits of US policy." Stripped of pretenses, the US and Israeli leadership "fall back on banal denunciation and unbending brute force"; such responses "reveal power with no place to go, no vision of the future." Said concludes: "the Great White Father . . . has come to the end of his reign. A new era is dawning." As with Fanon's call to his comrades at the end of *The Wretched of the Earth*, this is a statement aimed not at the masters, but at the victims who must also become the victors, the inheritors of a new era that must be brought into existence. This is the language of emergence, not residue; it has always been at the heart of Said's work.

3   Sweetness and Struggle: Working through Humanism

Near the end of *Orientalism*, in his discussion of Erich Auerbach's exile in Turkey and its effect upon the writing of *Mimesis*, Said offers the following quote from Hugo of St. Victor, which is cited in one of Auerbach's final essays: "The man who finds his homeland sweet is still a tender beginner; he to whom every soil is as his native one is already strong; but he is perfect to whom the entire world is as a foreign land" (1994: 259). Readers of Said's work have found in this quote an important clue to understanding his own attempt to, in Benita Parry's words, maintain "a critique of culture and imperialism that situates itself on the borders and boundaries of knowable communities . . . celebrating the unhoused and decentered counter-energies generated by the displaced critical consciousness" (1992: 19). Both Parry, who is sympathetic to this project, and Clifford, who by and large is not, identify it as "cosmopolitanism." In doing so, the implication is once again that this is a moment of residual humanism, in this case of the sort provided by the Auerbachian tradition of comparative philology – an attempt to fall back on the model provided by European humanism.

It is worth noting that Said invokes this quote again at the very end of *Culture and Imperialism*. It appears, however, with a series of variations worth noting. For one thing, it comes, not via Auerbach, but rather directly from Hugo's twelfth-century work *Didascalion*. For another, a longer portion of the passage is quoted than in *Orientalism*:

> It is therefore, a source of great virtue for the practiced mind to learn, bit by bit, first to change about in visible and transitory things, so that afterwards it may be able to leave them behind altogether. The person who finds his homeland sweet is still a tender beginner; he to whom every soil is as his native one is already strong; but he is perfect to whom the entire world is as a foreign place. The tender soul has fixed his love on one spot in the world; the strong person has extended his love to all places; the perfect man has extinguished his. (1993: 335)

As if to call attention to the fact that he is referring back to an earlier moment in his own work, Said follows this quote with a reference to Auerbach's reading of this passage "as a model for anyone – man *and* woman – wishing to transcend the restraints of imperial or national or provincial limits" (p. 335). This is precisely the point he makes about Auerbach in *Orientalism*.

Unlike that earlier moment, however, Said here goes on to complicate this reading: "But note that Hugo twice makes it clear that the 'strong' or 'perfect' person achieves independence and detachment by *working through* attachments, not by rejecting them" (p. 336). It is this "working through" which is crucial, and which I have tried to suggest characterizes Said's emergent, as compared to residual, humanism. It is work which, as always in Said, comes from a particular set of historical circumstances, those of "someone whose homeland is 'sweet,' but whose actual condition makes it impossible to recapture that sweetness, and even less possible to derive satisfaction from substitutes furnished by illusion or dogma" (p. 336).

If our knowledge of the Palestinian struggle forces us to read this passage as autobiographical, and thus to respond to its wrenching beauty, it also obliges us to acknowledge that what is at work here is not merely a theoretical *choice* which

447

provides a privileged place from which to perform a critique, but rather a brave and clear-sighted attempt to find a space for agency in the face of overwhelming historical forces. To borrow a phrase from Spivak, Said plays the hand which history has dealt him. Such a hand can be played more or less skillfully, as Said suggests when he compares his own skills as a reader of history with those of Arafat. This is precisely the point of preserving agency and critical authority: as a way of preventing political quietism, especially in the face of the incompetence and complicity of Arafat's leadership. The goal, as Fanon put it more than thirty-five years ago, is to create a critical consciousness "freed from colonialism and forewarned of all attempts at mystification, inoculated against all national anthems" (1963: 147). If we are to understand the work done by postcolonial theorists – not just the work of Fanon and Said, but also work which has been inspired by their examples – as more than just a particularly successful offshoot of postmodernism (whatever that is), we need to understand precisely what is at stake in their struggles around humanism, especially as it relates to the historical forces which conditioned, and continue to condition, such struggles. This is especially important if we are to acknowledge that while history has not yet ended, neither has the legacy of colonialism.

Notes

My thanks to Debra Curtis, Jillana Enteen, and Bruce Simon for their comments and encouragement on this essay; they should not necessarily be associated with its arguments, and certainly not with its faults.

1   For a trenchant critique of the ultimate "reductionism" and "functionalism" of Dirlik's argument, see Hall (1996: 258–9). Hall goes on to point out more connections between the seemingly "diametrically opposite" positions of Dirlik and Young.
2   I owe this insight to Abena Busia.
3   For a sense of these debates in Fanon studies, see my review essays "Fanon and the Post-Colonial Future" (1997) and "Whose Fanon?" (1998). For a more detailed sense of the field, see the forthcoming collection *Frantz Fanon: New Critical Perspectives* (Routledge, 1999).
4   I have slightly altered Constance Farrington's translation here; for some reason she renders "*il faut faire peau neuve*" as "we must turn over a new leaf," thus losing the way this phrase points back to *Peau Noire, Masques Blancs*.
5   The second quote is from *A Dying Colonialism* 181, the first and third from *Towards the African Revolution* 64, 145.
6   Said suggests that this reception was affected, at least in part, by the particularity of the Arabic translation of *Orientalism* by the Syrian poet and critic Kamal Abu Deeb, which maintained "an almost total avoidance of Arabized Western expressions" (p. 338).
7   Brennan (1992: 77). For Williams' elaboration of dominant, residual, and emergent cultural forms, see *Marxism and Literature* (1977: 121–7).

8 Clifford (1988: 255–76); further citations will be noted in the text. Similarly, Said does not mention Aijaz Ahmad's critique of his work in *In Theory*, except in the most oblique way: "the passages on Marx's own Orientalism in my book were the most singled out by dogmatic critics in the Arab world and India" (p. 338).

9 For Robbins' more recent considerations of Said's work, see his (1994) and (1994a).

10 *diacritics*, 6, no. 3 (1976): 43. As Tim Brennan (1992: 75) suggests, this interview is remarkable in acting "like a compendium of which the rest of his career is a patient and deliberate elaboration."

11 This is a very tenuous distinction, of course; I maintain it for polemical purposes.

References

Ahmad, Aijaz. (1992). *In Theory: Classes, Nations, Literatures*. New York: Verso.

Alessandrini, Anthony C. (1995). "'We Must Find Something Different': Fanon and the Search for a 'Non-Western' Marxism," *Research and Society*, 8.

——. (1997). "Fanon and the Post-Colonial Future," *Jouvert*, 1, no. 2.

——. (1998). "Whose Fanon?" *Minnesota Review*, 48.

Appiah, Kwame Anthony. (1992). *In My Father's House*. New York: Oxford University Press.

Brennan, Tim. (1992). "Places of Mind, Occupied Lands: Edward Said and Philology," in Sprinker, ed., 1992.

Buckland, Warren. (914). Review of Ian Adam and Helen Tiffin, eds., *Past the Last Post: Theorizing Post-Colonialism and Post-Modernism*. *Textual Practice*, 8, no. 2.

Clegg, Ian. (1979). "Workers and Managers in Algeria," in *Peasants and Proletarians*, eds. Robin Cohen *et al.* New York: Monthly Review Press.

Clifford, James. (1988). "On *Orientalism*," in *The Predicament of Culture*. Cambridge: Harvard University Press.

de Beauvoir, Simone. (1965). *Force of Circumstance*, trans. Richard Howard. New York: Putnam.

Dirlik, Arif. (1994). "The Postcolonial Aura: Third World Criticism in the Age of Global Capitalism," *Critical Inquiry*, 20.

Docherty, Thomas, ed. (1993). *Postmodernism: A Reader*. New York: Columbia University Press.

Fanon, Frantz. (1963). *The Wretched of the Earth*, trans. Constance Farrington. New York: Grove Press.

——. (1967). *Black Skin, White Masks*, trans. Charles Lam Markmann. New York: Grove Press.

——. (1967a). *A Dying Colonialism*, trans. Haakon Chevalier. New York: Grove.

——. (1988). *Toward the African Revolution*, trans. Haakon Chevalier. New York: Grove Press.

Hall, Stuart. (1996). "When was the 'Post-Colonial'? Thinking at the limit," in *The Post-Colonial Question*, eds. Iain Chambers and Lidia Curti. New York: Routledge.

Hutcheon, Linda. (1994). "The Post Always Rings Twice: The Postmodern and the Postcolonial," *Textual Practice*, 8, no. 2.

Jinadu, L. Adele. (1986). *Fanon: In Search of the African Revolution*. New York: KPI.

449

Lazarus, Neil. (1993). "Disavowing Decolonization: Fanon, Nationalism, and the Problematic of Representation in Current Theories of Colonial Discourse," *Research in African Literatures*, 24, no. 4.

Nursey-Bray, Paul. (1972). "Marxism and Existentialism in the Thought of Frantz Fanon," *Political Studies*, 20.

Parry, Benita. (1992). "Overlapping Territories and Intertwined Histories: Edward Said's Postcolonial Cosmopolitanism," in Sprinker, ed., 1992.

Radhakrishnan, R. (1994). "Edward Said's *Culture and Imperialism*: A Symposium," *Social Text*, 40.

Robbins, Bruce. (1992). "The East Is a Career: Edward Said and the Logics of Professionalism," in Sprinker, ed., 1992.

——. (1994). Review of *Culture and Imperialism. Nineteenth Century Contexts*, 18.

——. (1994a). "Secularism, Elitism, Progress, and Other Transgressions: On Edward Said's 'Voyage In,'" *Social Text*, 40.

Said, Edward W. (1975). *Beginnings: Intention and Method*. New York: Basic Books.

——. (1976). Interview, *diacritics*, 6, no. 3.

——. (1983). *The World, the Text, and the Critic*. Cambridge: Harvard University Press.

——. (1986). "Foucault and the Imagination of Power," in *Foucault: A Critical Reader*, ed. David Couzens Hoy. Cambridge: Blackwell.

——. (1988). "Michel Foucault, 1926–1984," in *After Foucault: Humanistic Knowledge, Postmodern Challenges*, ed. Jonathan Arac. New Brunswick, NJ: Rutgers University Press.

——. (1993). *Culture and Imperialism*. New York: Vintage.

——. (1994). *Orientalism*. New York: Vintage. First published 1978.

——. (1995). *The Politics of Dispossession*. New York: Vintage.

——. (1996). *Peace and its Discontents*. New York: Vintage.

——. (1997). "From Silence to Sound and Back Again: Music, Literature, and History," *Raritan*, 17, no. 2.

Sekyi-Otu, Ato. (1996). *Fanon's Dialectic of Experience*. Cambridge: Harvard University Press.

Sprinker, Michael, ed. (1992). *Edward Said: A Critical Reader*. Cambridge: Blackwell.

Williams, Raymond. (1997). *Marxism and Literature*. New York: Oxford University Press.

Young, Robert. (1990). *White Mythologies*. New York: Routledge.

Chapter 23

Spivak and Bhabha

Bart Moore-Gilbert

Together with Edward W. Said, Gayatri C. Spivak and Homi K. Bhabha make up what Robert Young describes as "the Holy Trinity" of postcolonial critics who have achieved the greatest eminence in their field (1995: 163). There are certainly good grounds for considering Spivak and Bhabha together, not least because each acknowledges Said's work as their immediate inspiration. Spivak, for example, has described *Orientalism* (1978) as "the source book in our discipline" (1993: 56). Young's irreverent homage to the trio should not, however, be taken to imply unanimity amongst them, whether in terms of their political vision, thematic interests, or methodological procedures. Not only are there important differences in all these respects between Spivak and Bhabha (moreover, they have rarely engaged in any detailed way with each other's work), but both challenge and revise, as well as extend, the work of their mentor in significant ways. This chapter will both explore certain of the more important convergences and divergences between Spivak and Bhabha and outline some distinctive aspects of their respective contributions to postcolonial studies.

One of the most obvious links between Spivak and Bhabha is that each substantially develops the project, initiated by Said, of bringing "radical" western theory to bear on (post)colonial issues and – equally importantly – of bringing the latter to bear on the former. The often formidable challenge of the pair's work perhaps derives more than anything else from their fluency in a diverse range of contemporaray critical theories. The eclecticism of Spivak's theoretical sources led Colin McCabe to describe her, in the foreword to her volume *In Other Worlds* (1987), as "a feminist Marxist deconstructivist." As this formulation might seem to imply, Spivak has no ambition to synthesize these various discourses into a new and unitary form of critique which might be described in any straightforward fashion as "postcolonial theory." Indeed, an important premise of Spivak's criticism is that the critic must not succumb to the temptations of seeking "a totalizable analytic foothold" (1987: 79). Thus the theories on which she draws are brought together in order to demonstrate their mutual incompatibilities as much as their potential complementarity. As "DissemiNa-tion" suggests, Bhabha is just as eclectic and equally suspicious of totalizing cultural explanations of the kind offered in traditional Marxism, or, indeed, in *Orientalism*: "I have attempted no general theory . . . I have taken the measure of Fanon's occult instability and Kristeva's parallel times into the 'incommensu-rable narrative' of Benjamin's modern storyteller to suggest no salvation, but a strange cultural survival of the people" (1994: 170).

Spivak and Bhabha can perhaps be compared and contrasted most economi-cally through an analysis of the way that each responds to the relative lack of attention paid to the colonized subject in *Orientalism*. Following Said's (selec-tive) reading of Michel Foucault, *Orientalism* characteristically implies that the dominant power successfully "maximized" itself at the expense of the subject peoples, who were rendered almost entirely passive and silent by conquest. Unsurprisingly, then, Said's text focuses almost exclusively on the discourse and agency of the colonizer.

Spivak remedies this imbalance by a consistent attention throughout her career to the (less privileged sectors of the) colonized peoples – and to their suc-cessors in the neocolonial era. To describe these social formations, she adapts the term "subaltern" from Gramsci (to whom *Orientalism* is also heavily indebted conceptually), in whose writing it signifies subordinate or marginalized social groups in European (more specifically, Italian) society. In "Can the Subaltern Speak?", her longest and possibly most important essay, insofar as it summarizes so much of her previous thinking on (post)colonial issues and anticipates many of the directions taken in subsequent work, Spivak adapts the term to analysis of the Third World and, more particularly, to India. Here it signifies "subsis-tence farmers, unorganized peasant labour, the tribals and communities of zero workers on the street or in the countryside" (1988: 84). In some later essays it is extended to encompass a range of disadvantaged constituencies within the West, from women as a whole to the class of migrant which Spivak describes as "urban home-workers."

Perhaps Spivak's principal concern is the degree to which the (post)colonial subaltern, in particular, enjoys agency, an issue which she characteristically explores in terms of whether subalterns can speak for themselves, or whether they are condemned only to be known, represented, and spoken for in a distorted fashion by others, particularly by those who exploit them (but also by "con-cerned" outsiders like aid-workers or seemingly "disinterested" scholars, such as anthropologists). The conclusion reached by "Can the Subaltern Speak?" is unequivocal; there is "no space" (1988: 103) from which subalterns can "speak" and thus make their interests and experience known to others on their own terms.

In order to illustrate this argument, Spivak concentrates much of her atten-tion on the mechanics of what she calls the "itinerary of silencing" (1990: 31) which, paradoxically, accompanies the production of the (post)colonial subaltern as a seemingly "freely speaking" subject/agent in the discourses of the domi-nant order. Indeed, "Can the Subaltern Speak?" begins with an analysis of the silencing of the contemporary subaltern by western "radical" intellectuals who ostensibly seek to champion those who are most oppressed by neocolonialism. Spivak's critique is partly methodological, partly political, in nature. First of all, she accuses figures like Deleuze and Foucault of assuming that they are "transparent" *vis-à-vis* the objects of their attention. In other words such "radicals" too easily suppose that they are outside of the general system of exploitation of the "Third World" – in which western modes of cultural analysis and representation (including "high" theory itself) and institutions of knowledge (such as the universities in which such theory is characteristically developed) are in fact deeply implicated. Secondly, while critics like Foucault and Deleuze announce the "death of the (western, liberal, bourgeois, sovereign, male) subject" of traditional humanism in the postmodern episteme, they retain what Spivak sees as a "utopian" conception of the centered subject/agent in respect to marginalized groups, such as prisoners, women, or the Third World subaltern, who purportedly can "speak for themselves" despite all their various disadvantages. However, in ascribing a voice to the subaltern, according to Spivak, such intellectuals are in fact themselves representing (in the sense of speaking on behalf of, or standing in for) the subaltern. (This is not simply a problem in western radicalism. In "Subaltern Studies: Deconstructing Historiography" (1989), Spivak discerns a similarly "utopian" vision of the resistant historical subaltern in the "counter-hegemonic" work of the Subaltern historians of India with whom she – and Said – collaborated in the 1980s.)

In possibly her boldest move, Spivak then links these aspects of contemporary western theory to the colonial history of the construction of subject-positions for the colonized, a topic which she already began to address with great force in essays like "The Rani of Sirmur" (1985a). In making this connection, "Can the Subaltern Speak?" recapitulates some of this earlier work, interposing in its critique of Foucault and Deleuze an account of the debates surrounding the prohibition of *sati* (the immolation of Hindu widows) in early nineteenth-century India. At the heart of this competition to represent the colonized female's "best interests," between "progressive" colonialist males and "traditionalist" indigenous men who defended the custom as a symbol of the integrity of Indian (more specifically, Hindu) cultural identity, was the ascription of "voice" (again representing free will and agency) to the Indian women. In British discourse, this voice supposedly cried out for liberation, thus legitimizing the colonial mission; according to the native male, by contrast, the voice allegedly expressed the subaltern woman's attachment to tradition by assenting voluntarily to *sati*. In both accounts, Spivak argues, the voice of the female subaltern is in fact ventriloquized. Consequently, one can never directly encounter "the testimony of the women's [own] voice-consciousness" (1988: 93).

Spivak offers a further example of this process of subject-constitution on behalf of the colonized woman in the work of Edward Thompson. Despite being an at times fierce critic of colonialism and a committed proponent of Indian women's rights, this influential missionary campaigner in the interwar years also, in Spivak's view, ultimately sees the Hindu woman as "his" to save from the burden of indigenous patriarchal tradition and manipulates the voice of the Indian woman accordingly. Thompson thus provides an historical bridge between classical colonialist "benevolence" of the kind evident at the time of the formal prohibition of *sati* and that of some radical western intellectuals in the contempoary era.

While seeking to correct an obvious lacuna in *Orientalism*, Spivak's work on the subaltern nonetheless in some ways reinforces the substance of her mentor's arguments. According to Spivak, throughout (post)modernity, between the twin poles of (neo-)colonialism and indigenous patriarchy, "the figure of the woman [forever] disappears, not into a pristine nothingness, but into a violent shuttling which is the displaced figuration of the 'third-world woman' caught between tradition and modernization" (1988: 102). Consequently, "Can the Subaltern Speak?", as much as *Orientalism*, conceives of the subordinate as the "silent interlocutor" of the dominant order. To a large degree, Spivak suggests, this is an inevitable consequence of the fact that in colonial discourse the subjectivity of the subaltern is necessarily constructed according to the terms and norms of the dominant culture which produces the archive in which the historical subaltern exists. "Can the Subaltern Speak?" summarizes the dangers of a repetition of this history of subject-constitution by the contemporary nonsubaltern activist/researcher through reference to the production of victimized or traumatized women as speaking subjects in western psychoanalytic discourse:

> As Sarah Korfman [*sic*] has shown, the deep ambiguity of Freud's use of women as scapegoat is a reaction-formation to an initial and continuing desire to give the hysteric a voice, to transform her into the *subject* of hysteria. The masculine-imperialist ideological formation that shaped that desire into the "daughter's seduction" is part of the same formation that constructs the monolithic "third-world woman" . . . Thus when confronted with the questions, Can the subaltern speak? and Can the subaltern (as woman) speak?, our efforts to give the subaltern a voice in history will be doubly open to the dangers run by Freud's discourse. (1988: 92)

On the evidence of this consistent interest in the predicament of the female subaltern more particularly, whom Spivak represents as subject to even greater degrees of economic, cultural, and political marginalization than her already severely disadvantaged male counterpart, Spivak's affiliations to certain forms of feminist politics are clear. Indeed, Spivak's interest in the specificities of women's experience is also evident in her analyses of the colonizing culture. While *Orientalism* acknowledges the masculinist nature of colonial discourse, it fails to pursue the interrelations between empire and issues of gender in any great detail. By contrast, Spivak gives much greater weight to the agency of western women within colonialism in essays like "Three Women's Texts and a Critique of Imperialism' (1985b); and she also sympathetically addresses the symbolic roles which western women are forced to perform in colonial discourse, as pieces like "Imperialism and Sexual Difference" (1986) illustrate.

But if Spivak is the first figure to consistently inflect postocolonial studies with a feminist agenda (and in doing so, she has inspired a range of subsequent critics in the field), one of the most striking themes of her work is a persistent criticism of western feminism for its failure to "dehegemonize," even decolonize, its own guiding presuppositions. Preeminent among these is that "Woman" is implicitly understood as being white, heterosexual, and middle-class, in a manner analogous to the way that in traditional humanism, "Man" was construed in similarly narrow terms. Indeed, the substance of Spivak's critique of "radical" western theorists like Foucault and Deleuze is anticipated in essays such as "French Feminism in an International Frame" (1981) and "Three Women's Texts and a Critique of Imperialism," where certain strands of western feminism are arraigned for an equally self-interested intervention on behalf of the subaltern woman.

In Spivak's eyes, Julia Kristeva's work provides a particularly striking instance of this problem, with *About Chinese Women* (1977) arousing her particular antagonism. Kristeva's interest in the subaltern Chinese woman is, for Spivak, an example *par excellence* of the manner in which "benevolent" First World feminists exploit the Third World woman for the purposes of *self*-constitution, a process which she sees as entirely consistent with the West's long history of appropriations of Oriental cultures. More specifically, Spivak sees Kristeva's text as a symptom of the retreat of western political "radicals," after the disillusioning failure of the May 1968 *évenements* in Paris, to "the individualistic avant-garde rather than anything that might call itself a revolutionary collectivity" (1987: 140). This suggests the irrelevance of Kristeva's work to the project of constructing a genuinely international feminism: "The question of how to speak to the 'faceless' women of China cannot be asked within such a partisan conflict" (ibid.; Spivak's antipathy to Kristeva provides one important contrast between her work and Bhabha's; for the latter, as the quotation from "DissemiNation" in the second paragraph of this chapter suggests, Kristeva is a major source of inspiration – though Bhabha draws on quite different areas of her writing to those deplored by Spivak).

According to "Three Women's Texts and a Critique of Imperialism," another of Spivak's most influential essays, comparable shortcomings are evident in Anglo-American feminism. The piece centers on what it describes as the latter's "basically isolationist admiration for the literature of the female subject" (1985b: 262). For Spivak, the principal problem represented by Anglophone feminism's exorbitant admiration for texts like *Jane Eyre*, which triumphantly record the historical emergence of the western (proto-)feminist subject, is that the role played by the nonwestern woman in this narrative of empowerment tends to get forgotten. In order to remedy this amnesia, Spivak carefully tracks how Jane's development into a heroine of (proto-)feminism is accompanied by, indeed dependent upon, the simultaneous effacement of Rochester's first wife, Bertha Mason, who for Spivak represents "the woman from the colonies." For Spivak, this sets the pattern for western feminism's (non-)engagement with its non-western sisters. Thus a contemporary woman writer who is ostensibly more sensitized to the issues of empire and race, like Jean Rhys, reveals the continuing limitations of modern western feminism in these respects. In *Wide Sargasso Sea* (1966, Rhys's "rewriting" of *Jane Eyre*), the voice of the subaltern woman is silenced once again when the dissenting black servant Christophine is, according to Spivak, "prematurely" expelled from the text "with neither narrative nor characterological explanation or justice" (1985b: 272). For Spivak such shortcomings reveal the need for major reappraisals on the part of western feminism: "The [western] feminist must learn to learn from [Third World women], to speak to them, to suspect that their access to the political and sexual scene is not merely to be *corrected* by our superior theory and enlightened compassion" (1987: 135).

In methodological terms, "Three Women's Texts" demonstrates one of the ways in which Spivak diverges most markedly from Said. In *The World, the Text, and the Critic* (1983), the latter had provided a trenchant critique of Derrida (inspired by Foucault's account of his French colleague in *Madness and Civilization*) for allegedly failing to sufficiently articulate either critical or "primary" cultural texts with "worldly" (by which Said means real, political, historical) issues and engagements. By contrast, Spivak – who translated Derrida's *Of Grammatology* in 1976 – attempts to demonstrate the usefulness of deconstruction to postcolonial studies at precisely this strategic level, in contradiction of the perception that Derrida is "esoteric and textualistic" (1988: 87). Derrida furnishes Spivak with two important tactical maneuvers in this essay. The first is the procedure of reading the text against the grain, or contrary to its ostensible logic. One form this takes is Spivak's technique of "catachresis," exemplified in the way that she turns Bertha into a representative of the colonized woman, despite the fact that Bertha is, objectively, a member of the former slave-owning plantocracy. Secondly, Spivak follows Derrida in taking apparently marginal material (Bertha is a minor character in Brontë's text, the empire is barely referred to in *Frankenstein*, another of the western canonical works discussed in "Three Women's Texts") and using it to forward her strategic project of exposing the racialized nature of the presuppositions informing the "obvious" or usually privileged meanings of the text under discussion. (Compare *Said's* celebrated later reading of Jane Austen's *Mansfield Park* in *Culture and Imperialism*.)

Like Spivak, Homi Bhabha acknowledges the vital influence of Said in initiating his own project. Thus according to Bhabha, too, *Orientalism* "inaugurated the postcolonial field" (1992: 465). Like Spivak, he subjects a range of contemporary western theory to searching analysis from a postcolonial perspective.

For example, in "'Race', Time and the Revision of Modernity" (1991; this is reprinted as the "Conclusion" to *The Location of Culture*), Bhabha takes to task a number of recent accounts of postmodernity (including those offered by Foucault, Benedict Anderson, and Fredric Jameson) for failing to give sufficient weight to the histories and legacies of colonialism. And like Spivak once again, Bhabha seeks to revise and extend aspects of *Orientalism*. In the first instance, this involves a reappraisal of Said's account of the colonizer's agency and identity, which Bhabha perceives as presented in terms which are, respectively, too monolithically powerful and unitary. Bhabha recognizes that Said "hints continually at a polarity or division at the very centre of Orientalism" (1994: 73); but, he concludes, such tensions and contradictions as Said's text notes within the dominant order are in the end (illegitimately) resolved by an insistence on the intentionality and unidirectionality of the colonizing subject's will to knowledge and power.

Like Spivak, Bhabha also seeks to reappraise Said's account of the colonized. However, in marked contrast to Spivak – *The Spivak Reader* (1996), eds. Landry and MacLean, for example, only cites Fanon twice – Bhabha's reconsiderations of (post)colonial agency and identity also involve him in a sustained dialogue with a figure who is now generally recognized as the most innovative thinker in the field of postcolonial studies prior to Said (this is in no small measure a consequence of Bhabha's "readiscovery" of Fanon in the mid-1980s). Nonetheless, while Fanon provides a seemingly fuller and more positive account of the colonized than *Orientalism*, Bhabha finds it in the end to be no less problematic than Said's. Thus whereas *Orientalism* writes out the colonized (and their agency) almost entirely, Bhabha sees texts like *The Wretched of the Earth* (1961) as conceptualizing the agency of the colonized too much in conformity to the model of the heroic sovereign humanist subject which underwrote colonial epistemology. (This is comparable to the objection which "Can the Subaltern Speak?" has *vis-à-vis* Foucault and Deleuze's conception of the agency of "marginal" constituencies.)

Out of Bhabha's dissatisfaction with his mentors in these respects emerged a powerfully revisionist account of (post)colonial agency and identity which is also, however, strikingly different to Spivak's. For Bhabha the relationship between colonizer and colonized is more complex, nuanced, and politically ambiguous than either *Orientalism* or *The Wretched of the Earth* recognize because both identity and agency in the colonial context are deeply inflected by the operations of the "unconscious." For example, a destabilizing "ambivalence" of psychic affect and identification can be detected in the way that the colonizer represents the subject peoples; thus the stereotypes of "the wily Oriental" and "the faithful servant," both common tropes in colonial discourse, express clearly contradictory sentiments towards the colonized. For Bhabha, this kind of affective and discursive conflict suggests that the colonizer is less secure, both psychically and politically, than *Orientalism* implies.

In seeking to reappraise such issues from a psychoanalytic perspective, Bhabha's main debts are to Freud and Lacan (figures who are far less prominent in Spivak's work). Indeed, one reason for Bhabha's deep interest in Fanon is that the application of Lacanian theory, in particular, to the analysis of colonial relations was initiated by the latter's *Black Skin, White Masks* (1952), which for Bhabha offers a much more enabling starting point for his own project than work like *The Wretched of the Earth*. "Remembering Fanon" (1986) praises the earlier text above all for its engagement with the intersubjective sphere (rather than privileging the "public sphere" of military, legal, or economic relations between colonizer and colonized in its critique of colonialism), and for conceiving of engagements in the former domain as dynamic, conflictual, and shifting. *Black Skin, White Masks*, according to Bhabha, offers the crucial insight that the identity of neither party to the colonial relationship is "originary." Rather, each side needs and depends on the other in order to constitute itself (if only by distinguishing itself from what it is not), whether as colonizer or colonized. From this perspective, the "familiar alignment of colonial subjects – Black/White, Self/Other – is disturbed . . . and the traditional grounds of racial identity are dispersed" (1986: ix).

Such arguments have important implications for the questions of agency and resistance. Bhabha's account of these is, in fact, complex – even contradictory. On the one hand, an essay like "Signs Taken for Wonders" (1985) provides what seems to be a fairly conventional account of subaltern agency insofar as the voice of the Indian subaltern is heard questioning the authority of colonialism (in the guise of the missionary enterprise) in a direct and immediately effective manner. Elsewhere, however, Bhabha offers a quite different conception of agency as a consequence of his reconfiguration of "the political" through the prism of psychoanalytical theory. In perhaps his boldest conceptual move, Bhabha extends the site of the political to the zone of psychic relations "in-between" the dominant and subordinate cultures, across which an unstable traffic of continuously (re)negotiated (counter-)identifications is conducted. While Bhabha suggests that such negotiations point to a certain degree of complicity or "partnership" between colonizer and colonized, the affective "borderland" between them also opens up unexpected and hitherto unrecognized ways in which colonial power can be circumvented by the native subject, in a process which might be described as psychological guerrilla warfare.

Bhabha's conception of this kind of agency is illustrated in two particular ways, each of which derives from his reading of Lacan. For Bhabha, the vulnerability of the colonizer's identity (and therefore, also, of the grounds of his authority) is expressed partly in the "narcissistic demand that [the colonizer] should be addressed directly, that the Other should authorize the self, recognize its priority, fulfil its outlines, replete, indeed, repeat, its references and still its fractured gaze" (1994: 98). A refusal to satisfy the colonizer's "narrative demand" for such recognition is, for Bhabha, clear evidence of how the domain of psychic (counter)identification can become the site of oppositional political impulses.

458

Secondly, the colonized subject can resist by returning, in the sense of challenging, the "gaze" of authority. Thus what Bhabha calls "mimickry" is (on one level) "the name for the strategic reversal of the process of domination . . . that turns the gaze of the discriminated back upon the eye of power" (1994: 112).

To this extent Bhabha recuperates the agency of the colonized which is written out in *Orientalism*, without – apparently – reinscribing the unified humanist subject which underwrites the later Fanon's conception of anticolonial resistance. Nonetheless, this account is extremely problematic, not just in itself – because these modes of resistance are themselves somehow "in-between" the conscious and unconscious spheres – but because Bhabha provides no empirical evidence of how effective such kinds of agency actually were in resisting colonialism.

Bhabha complements these models of subaltern agency with a quite different account of the resistance encountered by the colonizer. This derives from what he represents as colonialism's *immanent* liability to challenge in three principal respects. Firstly, following Foucault's *The History of Sexuality* (1976), Bhabha suggests that, like all forms of power, colonial authority systematically, but "unintentionally," incites challenge and refusal. Secondly, following Derrida's *Writing and Difference* (1967), Bhabha suggests that resistance to colonialism can be detected in the vicissitudes to which all language, including the discourse of power, is intrinsically liable, especially through the play of "repetition" and *difference*. Thus according to "Signs Taken for Wonders," English culture (and, indeed, "Englishness" itself), once "repeated" or "translated" (and it is worth remembering that the latter word derives from the Latin for "carried across") into the alien context of the Indian arena, "is no longer a representation of an essence; it is now [only] a partial presence, a (strategic) device in a specific colonial engagement" (1994: 114–15).

Finally, in this context, Bhabha offers a second account of mimickry, also derived from Lacan's *Four Fundamental Concepts of Psychoanalysis* (1973), which produces resistance to colonialism in a quite different way to the first. Paradoxically, this is because mimickry is a strategy of power *as well as* resistance; as such, it works to consolidate hegemony by inducing its subjects to imitate the forms and values of the dominant culture. For Bhabha, however, this strategy can never fully succeed because it also always requires the subordinate to remain sufficiently different from the colonizer in order that the latter can continue to have subjects to control. Moreover, this element of "cultural difference" on which the colonizing power insists necessarily challenges the supposedly "universal" values of western culture on which empire as an assimilative project is based. Consequently, mimickry in this second sense should properly be understood as a dyadic, contradictory structure. It is "the sign of a double articulation; a complex strategy of reform, regulation and discipline, which 'appropriates' the Other"; however, its dependence on the maintainence of elements of cultural difference between colonizer and colonized "poses an *immanent* threat to both 'normalized' knowledges and disciplinary powers" (1994: 86).

In his more recent work, Bhabha has adapted much of his thinking about the issues of agency, identity, and the relationship between dominant and subaltern formations in the colonial context to analysis of postcolonial and, more specifically, contemporary migrant experience. Bhabha is now especially preoccupied by the processes of intercultural negotiations, political resistance, and psychic identification which are entailed by the contiguity of different cultures within the same metropolitan space and which – in contrast to the situation of colonialism – share (ostensibly, at least) relations of equality.

Such interests have involved Bhabha in a complex set of negotiations between the discourses of postcolonialism and postmodernism. On the one hand, his recent work at times suggests that the contemporary world cannot yet be considered to have arrived in a new (postmodern) cultural dispensation, primarily because of the contemporary West's rearticulation *vis-à-vis* the (allegedly) decolonized nonwestern world of the coercive political and economic structures (and forms of cultural or ideological Othering) which developed during the forms of colonialism that constituted one manifestation of Modernity. At other moments, however, Bhabha seems to second some recent accounts of postmodernism insofar as the current era offers at least some possibility of transcending the oppressions experienced by the (formerly) colonized during Modernity.

Bhabha's ambivalence about postmodernity is reflected in his development of the concept of "postcolonial contramodernity," which involves the same destabilizing relationship to the more unthinking celebrations of postmodernity as the facts of colonial history represented for the West's triumphalist historical claims to Modernity. As in his account of agency in the colonial period, the means by which this "postcolonial contramodernity" mounts its challenge to the dominant discourses takes several forms. On the one hand, members of today's migrant cultures express their resistant agency in the same conventional way that was observed in "Signs Take for Wonders." Just as these historical subalterns posed questions which colonial discourse was unable to answer, so the contemporary migrant both interrogates and "hybridizes" the dominant culture's current narratives of self-representation and self-legitimation. This might take the form of confronting dominant metropolitan discourses of "civility" (such as its claims to democracy and equality before the law) with the realities of discrimination against minorities in the contemporary West. At a more specifically "cultural" level, such forms of agency might be illustrated by the way that "migrant" literature so often "rewrites" metropolitan precedents; for instance Rushdie's *Midnight's Children* (1981) and Kureishi's *The Buddha of Suburbia* (1990) both engage in some detail with Kipling's *Kim* (1901), appropriating colonial structures of representation and meaning to illuminate contemporary postcolonial concerns and experience.

By contrast, simply by their insertion into the "host" cultures of the West, migrant cultures also provide an immanent critique of the presumed foundational unity and identity, and everyday norms and values, of those "host" societies. This poses crucial problems of identity and authority for the "host" society.

Traditional understandings of "Englishness," for instance, have been radically, though "unintentionally" unsettled by the very fact of postwar migration from the former British empire (as well as by the more self-conscious kinds of critique alluded to in the previous paragraph). Equally, the same ambivalent processes of (counter-)identification which Bhabha observes in colonial forms of mimickry also structure contemporary intercultural relations. Discourses of "multiculturalism," for example, function conflictually: they are strategies by which the dominant social formation seeks to control minorities but their acknowledgment of cultural difference also opens up spaces of resistance which are negotiated somewhere "in-between" the conscious and unconscious levels.

However, while "postcolonial contramodernity" enables the production of new sites, times, and kinds of resistance for the formerly colonized in the contemporary metropolis, Bhabha strenuously resists seeing it as a process of progression towards a cultural synthesis between "host" and migrant formations of the kind which is implied in the traditional liberal figuration of "the family of Man." The presumption of unity and equality in this projective image (and in the discourses of "multiculturalism" which it underpins) is, of course, implicitly contradicted by the unspoken hierarchy of (western) parents and (migrant) offspring. In Bhabha's eyes, comparable problems attend Marxist thinking, insofar as "the end of history" is to be effected by the triumph of a proletariat which is presumed to be western. "Postcolonial contramodernity" is, then, consistently antiteleological and antidialectical because Bhabha fears the effacement, or sublation, of the particularities of the formerly colonized cultures within the "higher" term of the West. Rather, Bhabha proposes a conception of cultural difference which does not aspire to "equalizing" migrant with "host" cultures by conceiving of their specific social practices (such as "parenting") or institutions (like religion) as interchangably equivalent but which instead respects the heterogenous – even "incommensurable" – histories, identities, and customs of the formerly colonized.

Thus cultural difference as Bhabha understands it is also what *resists* the attempt of a dominant culture to "assimilate" or "translate" a subordinate one on its own terms or in its own image. However, while at pains to deny what he sees as the spuriously "universal" concepts of "the family of Man" and "the dictatorship of the proletariat," together with the "celebration of fragmentation, *bricolage*, pastiche" (1994: 238) which accompanies the "pick-and-mix" conception of intercultural relations in certain strands of postmodernism, Bhabha stresses that – as in the colonial context – the political relationship of subordinate cultures to the dominant one is not simply antagonistic. The ambivalence which each feels towards the other contains some measure of desire and both are in some ways mutually in need of each other. For this reason Bhabha opposes what he sees as foundational doctrines of "cultural diversity" which, like the segregationist regimes of *apartheid* or the old American South, seek to inscribe absolute relations of impermeability between different ethnicities and cultures. Conversely, Bhabha also seeks to "revise those nationalist or "nativist" pedagogies that set up the relation of Third World and First World in a binary structure of opposition" (1994: 173). For Bhabha (as for Spivak), essentialist versions of "cultural nationalism," such as those espoused by some contemporary black separatist movements in the United States, simply reverse, but do not displace, the models of identity and social identification in the discourses of western racism itself. On a more specifically literary level, once again, the *subversive* approach of writers like Rushdie and Kureishi who both engage in dialogue with, but also "return the gaze" of, colonial forerunners like Kipling suggests a more effective kind of cultural politics than one characterized by outright condemnation or rejection of the metropolitan canon.

While both Spivak and Bhabha have made very substantial contributions to postcolonial studies, a number of problems can nonetheless be identified in their accounts of (post)colonial identity and agency. In keeping with the comparative spirit of this chapter it is worth concluding by considering how each critic's work might be used to illuminate some of the problems which the other's poses.

As was suggested earlier, Spivak follows Said in her admiration for Gramsci; this is one symptom of a broader sympathy for the tradition of historical materialism which has led her to describe herself as "an old-fashioned Marxist" (1991: 204). By contrast, Bhabha has at times strongly disavowed both Marxism and the political movements and parties which it has influenced (most notably the "Old" Labour Party in Britain). From an historical-materialist perspective, Bhabha might be accused of minimizing the material realities of (neo-)colonial oppression and, conversely, of discounting the effectiveness of directly oppositional forms of resistance, such as armed movements for decolonization. As critics such as Parry (1987 and 1994), Ahmad (1992), and Dirlik (1994) have argued, one troubling implication of Bhabha's work is that the critic (or artist) who unpicks the symbolic and narrative ordering of the hegemonic order becomes the privileged locus of opposition to the dominant. More specifically, Robinson and Lazarus (both 1993) have questioned the legitimacy of Bhabha's appropriations of Fanon from a Marxist perspective, complaining that he reads Fanon's career backwards, rather than as progressing towards more overt forms of political resistance. As suggested earlier, a related issue is the actual effectiveness of Bhabha's psychoanalytically informed models of resistance – whether in the context of colonialism or in the present moment of the "New World Order." As Spivak comments in another context: "[E]ven if one knows how to undo identities, one does not necessarily escape the historical determinations of sexism [or, one might add, of (neo-)colonialism]" (1987: 144).

Spivak's work offers other useful perspectives on Bhabha's recourse to psychoanalytic theory. As has been seen, "Can the Subaltern Speak?" links Freud quite explicitly to the "masculine-imperialist ideological formation." In contrast to both Spivak (and, indeed, to Fanon's *Black Skin, White Masks*), Bhabha does not really consider whether psychoanalysis should be considered as a specifically western form of knowledge which, as such, may not be unproblematically translatable to analysis of (post)colonial problematics, especially in the context of cultures which might differ radically in their psychic and social organization from turn-of-the-century Vienna or postwar Paris. By not subjecting psychoanalysis to the kind of critique which he performs on figures like Foucault or Jameson, Bhabha tends to imply that the models of psychoanalytic dynamics provided by Freud and Lacan have "universal" application, thus unwittingly reinscribing the figure of "Man" which he is usually so keen to decenter. The political implications of Bhabha's use of psychoanalysis have been taken up from a different perspective by Abdul JanMohamed (1985), who accuses Bhabha of illegitimately conflating the psychic identities of the colonizer and colonized, with the effect of producing a unified model of the colonial subject which discounts the crucial material differences between them. A similar sort of objection is suggested by Spivak's interest in feminism. As Holmlund (1991) and McClintock (1993) point out, Bhabha pays little attention to how gender might complicate his models of psychic identification and interaction. Similarly, it could be objected that Bhabha overlooks the problems posed to his conceptual models by class differences – on both sides of the colonial equation. Would the Indian Rajah and his female palace sweeper respond in the same way to the female missionary, District Collector, and British Other Rank respectively – and *vice versa*?

In terms of Bhabha's more recent work, Spivak's application of Derrida's strategy of "persistent critique" suggests some important instances of what she calls "repetition-in-rupture," in other words the unwitting reinscription of positions or structures which the critic in question is ostensibly seeking to overthrow. For example, while Bhabha claims to be attempting to "provide a form of the writing of cultural difference in the midst of modernity that is inimical to binary boundaries" (1994: 251), his work often reinstates precisely the sort of hierarchies which he is trying to displace. Hybridity, for example, presumes the existence of its opposite for its conceptual force. Thus there is a danger that the hybrid (or postcolonial) will itself become an essentialized and privileged term. Kristeva warns in "Women's Time" (1979; a key point of reference in Bhabha's recent work) that an insistence on understanding gender in irreducibly biological terms may lead to the practice of an inverted sexism. Bhabha risks similar dangers insofar as he represents the "nonhybrid" alternatives to the postcolonial, notably (neo-)colonialism and cultural nationalism, in unitary terms which do not do justice to their manifest internal contradictions and multiplicity of forms.

In turn, Bhabha's work points to some major problems with Spivak's thinking. To start with, his attempt to set up a "third space" mediating between the dominant and the subordinate orders in the contexts of (neo-)colonialism suggests that Spivak's conception of subalternity is sometimes disablingly nonrelational or even essentialized. In Gramsci's writing, of course, subalternity is always engaged with the hegemonic order and is never the "absolute Other" which it sometimes seems to be in Spivak's writings. Moreover, Bhabha's detailed, albeit problematic, attention to the agency of the (formerly) colonized reveals the degree to which Spivak's work contradicts a crucial corollary of the articulation of subalternity with hegemony in Gramsci's thinking (and in Marxism more generally). This is that the oppressed can – through greater consciousness of self and class interest – organize to eventually overthrow the hegemonic order. Thus while Spivak is excellent on "the itinerary of silencing" historically endured by the subaltern, she pays little attention to how the contemporary subaltern might "come to voice" (Jane Eyre, after all, managed to emerge as a (proto-)feminist subject, so why not some contemporary female subalterns at least?). From this perspective, and in the light of abundant historical evidence of the effective resistance of even the subaltern female, Spivak might justifiably be considered to be unnecessarily deterministic and politically pessimistic.

An insistence on the irreducible alterity and muteness of the subaltern, one might argue, paralyzes not just the subaltern, but the would-be ally of the subaltern – who is left in the double-bind of being required to show solidarity with the subaltern without in any way "selfing" that Other or "assimilating" her to the degree that solidarity perhaps inevitably demands. Such an insistence explains some of the key contradictions of Spivak's own work. Perhaps the most striking of these is that insofar as Spivak asserts that the subaltern cannot speak, she is, of course, herself constituting and speaking for, or in place of, the subaltern – the very maneuver for which she criticizes so much western discourse. Indeed, possibly the greatest irony of an essay like "Can the Subaltern Speak?" is that if its account of subaltern alterity and muteness were true, then there would be nothing but the West (and the native elite, perhaps) to write about. Perhaps inevitably, then, Spivak's work implicitly reinscribes the West as the principal "Subject of History"; thus the western intellectual is, in practice, at least as much her object of investigation as the subaltern. Her polemics on the importance of "unlearning one's privilege," for example, are directed primarily at western colleagues, for whom her prescriptions function no less clearly than those of Kristeva's *About Chinese Women*, as "a set of directives for class- and race-privileged literary women" (1987: 136). In recent years, Spivak has acknowledged many of these difficulties and has taken steps to modify her thinking accordingly. For an account of these changes of emphasis and direction, see Moore-Gilbert (1997).

Even when it is vulnerable, however, each critic's thinking characteristically exemplifies the pattern of "success-in-failure" which, according to Spivak, so often accompanies the application of poststructuralist theory to contemporary cultural-political issues. Thus even the occasional tendency to "repetition-in-rupture" in her own and Bhabha's work has produced any number of what Spivak calls "constructive questions, corrective doubts" (1987: 258). Consequently, both critics are likely to remain vital points of reference as postcolonial studies continue to develop.

464

References and Further Reading

Ahmad, Aijaz. (1992). *In Theory: Classes, Nations, Literatures.* London: Verso.

Bhabha, Homi K. (1984). "Representation and the Colonial Text," in Frank Gloversmith, ed., *The Theory of Reading.* Brighton: Harvester, 93–122.

——. (1986). "Remembering Fanon," Foreword to Frantz Fanon, *Black Skin, White Masks* (1952). London: Pluto.

——. (1990). "The Third Space," in Jonathon Rutherford, ed., *Identity: Community, Culture, Difference.* London: Lawrence and Wishart, 207–21.

——. (1992). "Postcolonial Criticism," in Stepehn Greenblatt and Giles Gunn, eds., *Redrawing the Boundaries: The Transformation of English and American Literary Studies.* New York: MLA, 437–65.

——. (1994). *The Location of Culture.* London and New York: Routledge.

——. (1996). "Day by Day . . . with Frantz Fanon," in Alan Read, ed., *The Fact of Blackness: Frantz Fanon and Visual Representation.* London: ICA, 186–205.

——. (1998). "Anish Kapoor: Making Emptiness," in *Anish Kapoor.* London: Hayward Gallery and University of California Press, 11–41.

——, ed., (1990). *Nation and Narration.* London and New York: Routledge.

——, ed., (1997). *Front Lines/Border Posts.* Special issue of *Critical Inquiry*, 23, no. 3.

Devi, Mahasweta. (1994). *Imaginary Maps*, trans. Gayatri C. Spivak. New York and London: Routledge, 1994.

Dirlik, Arif. (1994). "The Post-Colonial Aura: Third World Criticism in the Age of Global Capitalism," *Critical Inquiry*, 20, 329–56.

Easthope, Antony. (1998). "Bhabha: Hybridity and Identity," *Textual Practice*, 12, no. 2: 341–8.

Holmlund, Christine. (1991). "Displacing the Limits of Difference: Gender, Race, and Colonialism in Edward Said and Homi Bhabha's Theoretical Models and Marguerite Duras's Experimental Films," *Quarterly Review of Film and Video*, 13, nos. 1–3: 1–22.

JanMohamed, Abdul. (1985). "The Economy of Manichean Allegory: the Function of Racial Difference in Colonialist Literature," in H. L. Gates, Jr., ed., *"Race", Writing and Difference.* London and Chicago: Chicago University Press, 1986, 78–106.

Landry, Donna and Gerald MacLean, eds., (1996). *The Spivak Reader.* New York and London: Routledge, 1996.

Lazarus, Neil. (1993). "Disavowing Decolonization: Fanon, Nationalism and the Problematic of Representation in Current Theories of Colonial Discourse," *Research in African Literatures*, 24, no. 2: 69–98.

McClintock, Anne. (1993). "The Return of Female Fetishism and the Fiction of the Phallus," *New Formations*, 19: 1–22.

Moore-Gilbert, Bart. (1997). *Postcolonial Theory: Contexts, Practices, Politics.* London: Verso.

Papastergiadis, Nikos. (1996). "Ambivalence in Cultural Theory: Reading Homi Bhabha's DissemiNation," in J. C. Hawly, ed., *Writing the Nation: Self and Country in the Post-colonial Imagination.* Amsterdam: Rodopi, 176–93.

Parry, Benita. (1987). "Problems with Current Theories of Colonial Discourse," *Oxford Literary Review*, 9, nos. 1–2: 27–58.

——. (1994). "Signs of Our Times: Discussion of Homi Bhabha's *Location of Culture*," *Third Text*, 28–9: 1–24.

Perloff, Marjorie. (1998). "Cultural Liminality/Aesthetic Closure?: The "Interstitial Perspective" of Homi Bhabha," http:/wings.buffalo.edu/epc/authors/perloff/bhbha.html, 1–12.

Rai, Amit S. (1998). "'Thus Spake the Subaltern': Postcolonial Criticism and the Scene of Desire," in Christopher Lane, ed., *The Psychoanalysis of Race*. New York: Columbia University Press, 91–19.

Robinson, Cedric. (1993). "The Appropriation of Frantz Fanon," *Race and Class*, 35, no 1: 79–91.

Spivak, Gayatri C. (1985a). "The Rani of Sirmur," in Francis Barker *et al.*, eds., *Europe and Its Others*. Colchester: University of Essex Press, 1985, vol. 1, 128–51.

——. (1985b). "Three Women's Texts and a Critique of Imperialism," in H. L. Gates, Jr., ed., *"Race", Writing and Difference*. London and Chicago: Chicago University Press, 1986, 262–80.

——. (1986). "Imperialism and Sexual Difference," in Robert Con Davis and Robert Schleifer, eds., *Contemporary Literary Criticism*, 2nd edn. Harlow: Longman, 1989, 517–29.

——. (1987). *In Other Worlds: Essays in Cultural Politics*. London and New York: Methuen.

——. (1988). "Can the Subaltern Speak?" repr. in Patrick Williams and Laura Chrisman, eds., *Colonial Discourse and Post-Colonial Theory: A Reader*. Hemel Hempstead: Harvester Wheatsheaf, 1993, 66–111.

——. (1989). "Subaltern Studies: Deconstructing Historiography," in *Selected Subaltern Studies*, eds. R. Guha and G. C. Spivak. New York: Oxford University Press.

——. (1990). *The Post-Colonial Critic: Interviews, Strategies, Dialogues*, ed. Sarah Harasym. New York and London: Routledge.

——. (1991). "Neocolonialism and the Secret Agent of Knowledge," *Oxford Literary Review*, 13, nos. 1–2: 220–51.

——. (1993). *Outside in the Teaching Machine*. New York and London: Routledge.

Young, Robert. (1990). *White Mythologies: Writing History and the West*. London and New York: Routledge.

——. (1995). *Colonial Desire: Hybridity in Theory, Culture and Race*. London and New York: Routledge.

Chapter 24

A Small History of
Subaltern Studies

Dipesh Chakrabarty

Subaltern Studies: Writings on Indian History and Society began in 1982 as a series
of interventions in some debates specific to the writing of modern Indian
history.[1] Ranajit Guha (b. 1923), a historian of India then teaching at the
University of Sussex, UK, was the inspiration behind it. Guha and eight younger
scholars, based in India, the United Kingdom, and Australia, constituted the
editorial collective of *Subaltern Studies* until 1988 when Guha retired from the
team.[2] The series now has a global presence that goes well beyond India or South
Asia as an area of academic specialization. The intellectual reach of *Subaltern
Studies* now also exceeds that of the discipline of history. Postcolonial theorists
of diverse disciplinary backgrounds have taken interest in the series. Much
discussed, for instance, are the ways in which contributors to *Subaltern Studies*
have participated in contemporary critiques of history and nationalism, and of
Orientalism and Eruocentrism in the construction of social–science knowledge.
At the same time, there have also been discussions of *Subaltern Studies* in many
history and social science journals.[3] Selections from the series have come out in
English, Bengali, and Hindi and are in the process of being brought out in Tamil,
Spanish, and Japanese. A Latin American Subaltern Studies Association was
established in North America in 1993.[4] It would not be unfair to say that the
expression "subaltern studies," once the name of a series of publications in
Indian history, now stands as a general designation for a field of studies often
seen as a close cognate of postcolonialism.

How did a project which began as a specific and focused intervention in the
academic discipline of (Indian) history come to be associated with postcolonialism, an area of studies whose principal home has been in literature departments?
I attempt to answer this question by discussing how, and in what sense, *Subaltern Studies* could be seen as a "postcolonial" project of writing history. It should
be clarified, however, that my concentration here on the relationship between
postcolonialism and historiography overlooks the contributions that other disciplines – political science, legal studies, anthropology, literature, cultural studies,
and economics – have made to the field of subaltern studies. This essay is

motivated by a question that has the discipline of history in focus: In what ways can one read the original historiographic agenda of *Subaltern Studies* as not simply yet another version of Marxist/radical history but as possessing a *necessarily* postcolonial outlook? I concentrate on the discipline of history for two reasons: (a) the relationship between the new field of postcolonial writing and historiography has not yet received the attention it deserves, and (b) to answer critics who say that *Subaltern Studies* was once "good" Marxist history in the same way that the English tradition of "history from below" was, but that it lost its way when it came into contact with Said's Orientalism, Spivak's deconstructionism, or Bhabha's analysis of colonial discourse.[5] In a wide-ranging critique of postcolonial thinkers, Arif Dirlik once suggested that the historiographic innovations of *Subaltern Studies*, while welcome, were more applications of methods pioneered by British Marxist historians, albeit modified by "Third World sensibilities." He wrote:

> Most of the generalizations that appear in the discourse of postcolonial intellectuals from India may appear novel in the historiography of India but are not discoveries from broader perspectives. . . . the historical writing of *Subaltern Studies* historians . . . represent the application in Indian historiography of trends in historical writings that were quite widespread by the 1970s under the impact of social historians such as E. P. Thompson, Eric Hobsbawm, and a host of others.[6]

Without wishing either to inflate the claims of *Subaltern Studies* scholars or to deny what they may have indeed learned from the British Marxist historians, I seek to show that this reading of *Subaltern Studies* as an instance of Indian or Third World historians merely catching up with or simply applying the methodological insights of Anglo social history, seriously misjudges what the series has been all about. From its very inception, I argue, *Subaltern Studies* raised questions about history-writing that made the business of a radical departure from English Marxist historiographical traditions, inescapable. I shall develop my argument by concentrating mainly on the work of the historian Ranajit Guha in the period when he acted as the founding editor of *Subaltern Studies*. The particular writings of Guha I discuss are those which could be considered the founding texts of the project.

1   *Subaltern Studies* and Debates in Modern Indian History

I begin by sketching out some of the principal debates in modern Indian history in which early *Subaltern Studies* intervened. The academic subject called "modern Indian history" is a relatively recent development, a result of research and discussion in various universities in India, the United Kingdom, the United States, Australia, and elsewhere *after* the end of British imperial rule in August 1947. In its early phase, this area of scholarship bore all the signs of an ongoing struggle between tendencies which were affiliated to imperialist biases in Indian history and a nationalist desire on the part of historians in India to decolonize the past. Marxism was understandably mobilized in aid of the nationalist project of intellectual decolonization.[7] Bipan Chandra's book *The Rise and Growth of Economic Nationalism in India*, Anil Seal's *The Emergence of Indian Nationalism*, A. R. Desai's *Social Background of Indian Nationalism*, D. A. Low's edited volume *Soundings in Modern South Asian History*, the many seminal articles published by Bernard Cohn (now collected in his *An Anthropologist Among the Historians*), debates around Morris David Morris's assessment of the results of British rule in India, and the work of other scholars in the 1960s, raised new and controversial questions regarding the nature and results of colonial rule in India.[8] Did the imperialist British deserve credit after all for making India a developing, modern, and united country? Were the Hindu–Muslim conflicts that resulted in the formation of the two states of Pakistan and India, consequences of the divide-and-rule policies of the British or were they reflections of divisions internal to South Asian society? Official documents of the British government of India – and traditions of imperial history-writing – always portrayed colonial rule as being beneficial to India and her people. They applauded the British for bringing to the subcontinent political unity, modern educational institutions, modern industries, modern nationalism, a rule of law, and so on and so forth, Indian historians in the 1960s – many of whom had English degrees and most of whom belonged to a generation that grew up in the finals years of British rule – challenged that view. They argued instead that colonialism had had deleterious effects on economic and cultural developments. Modernity and the nationalist desire for political unity, they claimed, were not so much British gifts to India as fruits of struggles undertaken by the Indians themselves.

Nationalism and colonialism thus emerged, unsurprisingly, as the two major areas of research and debate defining the field "modern Indian history" in the 1960s and 1970s. At one extreme of this debate was the Cambridge historian Anil Seal, whose 1968 book *The Emergence of Indian Nationalism* pictured "nationalism" as the work of a tiny elite reared in the educational institutions the British set up in India. This elite, as Seal put it, both "competed and collaborated" with the British in their search for power and privilege.[9] A few years later, this idea was pushed to an extreme by Seal, his colleague John Gallagher, and a posse of their doctoral students in the book *Locality, Province and Nation*.[10] Discounting the role of ideas and idealism in history and taking an extremely narrow view of what constituted "interest." they argued that is was the penetration of the colonial state into the local structures of power in India – a move prompted by the financial self-interest of the Raj rather than by any altruistic motives – that eventually, and by degrees, drew Indian elites into the colonial governmental process. According to this argument, the involvement of Indians in colonial institutions set off a scramble amongst the indigenous elites who combined – opportunistically and around factions formed along "vertical" lines of patronage (in contradistinction to the so-called horizontal affiliations of class, that is)

469

– to jockey for power and privilege within the limited opportunities for self-rule provided by the British. Such, the Cambridge historians claimed, was the real dynamic of that which outside observers or naive historians may have mistaken for an idealistic struggle for freedom. Nationalism and colonialism both came out in this history as straw and foil characters. The history of Indian nationalism, said Seal, "was the rivalry between Indian and Indian, its relationship with imperialism that of the mutual clinging of two unsteady men of straw."[11]

At the other extreme of this debate was the Indian historian Bipan Chandra, a professor in the 1970s at the prestigious Jawaharlal Nehru University in Delhi. Chandra and his colleagues saw Indian history of the colonial period as an epic battle between the forces of nationalism and colonialism. Drawing on both Marx and Latin American theories of dependency and underdevelopment, Chandra argued that colonialism was a regressive force that distorted all developments in India's society or polity. Social, political, and economic ills of postindependence India – including those of mass poverty and religious and caste conflict – could be blamed on the political-economy of colonialism. However, Chandra saw nationalism in a different, contrasting light. He saw it as a regenerative force, as the antithesis of colonialism, something that united and produced an "Indian people" by mobilizing them for struggle against the British. Nationalist leaders such as Gandhi and Nehru were the authors of such an anti-imperial movement for unity of the nation. Chandra claimed that the conflict of interest and ideology between the colonizers and "the Indian people" was the most important conflict of British India. All other conflicts of class or caste were secondary to this principal contradictions and were to be treated as such in histories of nationalism.[12]

Yet, as research progressed in the seventies, there emerged an increasing series of difficulties with both of these narratives. It was clear that the Cambridge version of "nationalist politics without ideas or idealism" would never ring true to scholars in the subcontinent who had themselves experienced the desire for freedom from colonial rule.[13] The nationalist-historian's story, on the other hand, of there having been a "moral war" between colonialism and nationalism wore increasingly thin as research by younger scholars in India and elsewhere brought new material to light. New information on the mobilization of the poor (peasants, tribals, and workers) by elite nationalist leaders in the course of the Gandhian mass movements in the 1920s and 1930s, for example, suggested a strongly reactionary side to the principal nationalist party, the Indian National Congress. Thus Gyanendra Pandey at Oxford and David Hardiman and David Arnold at Sussex (all of them to become later members of the Subaltern Studies collective), Majid Siddiqi and Kapil Kumar in Delhi, Hitesranjan Sanyal in Calcutta, Brian Stoddart in Perth, Max Harcourt in Sussex, and others elsewhere documented the way nationalist leaders would suppress with a heavy hand peasants' or workers' tendency to protest the oppression meted out to them not only by the British but by the indigenous ruling groups as well, and thus to exceed the self-imposed limits of the nationalist political agenda.[14] From the point of view of a younger generation of historians whom Guha, following Rushdie, has called the "midnight's children," neither the Cambridge thesis propounding a skeptical view of Indian nationalism nor the nationalist–Marxist thesis glossing over – or assimilating to a nationalist historiographical agenda – real conflicts of ideas and interests between the elite nationalists and their socially-subordinate followers, was an adequate response to the problems of postcolonial history-writing in India.[15] The persistence of religious and caste-conflict in postindependence India, the war between India and China in 1962 which made official nationalism sound hollow and eventually gave rise to a fascination with Maosim among the urban educated youth in India, the outbreak of a violent Maoist political movement in India (known as the Naxalite movement) which drew many members of the urban youth into the countryside in the late 1960s and early 1970s – all these and many other factors combined to alienate younger historians from the shibboleths of nationalist historiography. All this historiographical discontent, however, was still floundering in the old liberal and positivist paradigms inherited from English traditions of history-writing even as it was searching for a path towards decolonizing the field of Indian history.

2   Subaltern Studies as Paradigm-shift, 1982–7

Subaltern Studies intervened in this situation. Intellectually, it began on the very terrain it was to contest: historiography that had its roots in the scholarly traditions, both of the left and the right, transplanted in India by the colonial education system. It started as a critique of two contending schools of history: the Cambridge School and that of the nationalist historians. Both of these approaches, declared Guha in a statement that inaugurated the series *Subaltern Studies*, were elitist. They wrote up the history of nationalism as the story of an achievement by the elite classes, whether Indian or British. For all their merits, they could not explain "the contributions made by people *on their own*, that is, *independent of the elite* to the making and development of this nationalism."[16] It will be clear from this statement of Guha's that *Subaltern Studies* was part of an attempt to align historical reasoning with larger movements for democracy in India. It looked for an anti-elitist approach to history-writing and in this it had much in common with the "history from below" approaches pioneered in English historiography by Christopher Hill, E. P. Thompson, E. J. Hobsbawm, and others. Both *Subaltern Studies* and the "history from below" school were Marxist in inspiration, both owed a certain intellectual debt to the Italian Communist Antonio Gramsci in trying to move away from deterministic, Stalinist readings of Marx. The word "subaltern" itself – and, of course, the well-known concept of "hegemony" so critical to the theoretical project of Subaltern Studies – go back to the writings of Gramsci.[17] As in the histories written by Thompson, Hobsbawm, Hill, and others, *Subaltern Studies* was also concerned about "rescuing from the condescension of posterity" the pasts of the socially subordinate groups in India. The declared aim of *Subaltern Studies* was to produce historical analyses in which the subaltern groups were viewed as the subjects of their own history. As Guha put it once in the course of introducing a volume of *Subaltern Studies*: "We are indeed opposed to much of the prevailing academic practice in historiography . . . for its failure to acknowledge the subaltern as the maker of his own destiny. This critique lies at the very heart of our project."[18] But Guha's theorization of the project at the same time signaled certain key differences that would increasingly distinguish the project of *Subaltern Studies* from that of English Marxist historiography. With hindsight, it could be said that there were broadly three areas in which *Subaltern Studies* differed from the "history from below" approach of Hobsbawm or Thompson (allowing for differences between these two eminent historians of England and Europe): "subaltern historiography" necessarily entailed (a) a relative separation of the history of power from any universalist histories of capital, (b) a critique of the nation-form, and (c) an interrogation of the relationship between power and knowledge (hence of archive itself and of history as a form of knowledge). In these differences, I would argue, lay the beginnings of a new way of theorizing the intellectual agenda for postcolonial histories.

The critical theoretical break came with the way Guha sought to redefine the category of "the political" with reference to colonial India. He argued that both the Cambridge and the nationalist historians conflated the political domain with the formal side of governmental and institutional processes. As he put it: "In all writings of this kind [i.e. elitist historiography] the parameters of Indian politics are assumed to be or enunciated as those of the institutions introduced by the British for the government of the country . . . [Elitist historians] can do no more than equate politics with the aggregation of activities and ideas of those who were directly involved in operating these institutions, that is, the colonial rulers and their élèves – the dominant groups in native society."[19] Using "people" and "subaltern classes" synonymously and defining them as "demographic difference between the total Indian population" and the dominant indigenous and foreign elite, Guha claimed that there was, in colonial India, an "autonomous" domain of the "politics the people" which was organized differently to the domain of the politics of the elite. Elite politics involved "vertical mobilization," "a greater reliance on Indian adaptations of British parliamentary institutions," and "tended to be relatively more legalistic and constitutional in orientation." In the domain of "subaltern politics," on the other hand, mobilization for political intervention depended on horizontal affiliations such as "the traditional organization of kinship and territoriality or on class consciousness depending on the level of the consciousness of the people involved." They tended to be more violent than elite politics. Central to subaltern mobilizations was "a notion of resistance to elite domination." "The experience of exploitation and labour endowed this politics with many idioms, norms and values which put it in a category apart from elite politics," wrote Guha. Peasant uprisings in colonial India, he argued, reflected this separate and autonomous grammar of mobilization "in its most comprehensive form." Even in the case of resistance and protest by urban workers, the "figure of mobilization" was one that was "derived directly from peasant insurgency."[20]

Guha's separation of elite and subaltern domains of the political, had some radical implications for social theory and historiography. The standard tendency in global Marxist historiography until the seventies was to look on peasant revolts organized along the axes of kinship, religion, caste, etc. as movements exhibiting a "backward" consciousness, the kind that Hobsbawm in his work on social banditry and "primitive rebellion" had called "pre-political."[21] This was seen as a consciousness that had not quite come to terms with the institutional logic of modernity or capitalism. As Hobsbawm put it with reference to his own material: "they are pre-political people who have not yet found, or only begun to find, specific language in which to express their aspirations about the world."[22] By explicitly rejecting the characterization of peasant consciousness as "pre-political" and by avoiding evolutionary models of "consciousness," Guha was prepared to suggest that the nature of collective action against exploitation in colonial India was such that it effectively stretched the imaginary boundaries of the category "political" far beyond the territories assigned to it in European political thought. To ignore the problems that the political sphere could cause for a Eurocentric Marxism would lead, according to Guha, only to elitist histories, for one would then *not* know how to analyze the consciousness of the peasant – the discourses of kinship, caste, religion, and ethnicity through which they expressed themselves in protest – except as a "backward" consciousness trying to grapple with a changing world whose logic it could never fully comprehend.

Guha insisted that instead of being an anachronism in a modernizing colonial world, the peasant was a real contemporary of colonialism and a fundamental part of the modernity that colonial rule gave rise to in India. The peasant's was not a "backward" consciousness – a mentality left over from the past – baffled by modern political and economic institutions and yet resistant to them. Guha's argument implied that the (insurgent) peasant in colonial India did in fact read his contemporary world correctly. Examining, for instance, over a hundred known cases of peasant rebellions in British India between 1783 and 1900, Guha showed that these revolts always involved the deployment by the peasants of codes of dress, speech, behavior which tended to invert the codes through which their social superiors dominated them in everyday life.[23] Inversion of the symbols of authority was almost inevitably the first act of rebellion by insurgent peasants. Elitist histories of peasant uprisings missed the signification of this gesture by seeing it as "pre-political." Anil Seal, for example, dismissed all nineteenth - century peasant revolts in colonial India as having no "specific political content," being "uprisings of the traditional kind, the reaching for sticks and stones as the only way of protesting against distress."[24] Marxists, on the other hand, explained these gestures as either expressing a false consciousness and/or performing a "safety valve" function in the overall social system.[25] What both of these explanatory strategies missed, Guha contended, was the fact that at the beginning of every peasant uprising there inevitably was a struggle on the part of rebels to destroy all symbols of the social prestige and power of the ruling classes. He wrote: "It was this fight for prestige which was at the heart of insurgency. Inversion was its principal modality. It was a *political* struggle in which the rebel appropriated and/or destroyed the insignia of his enemy's power and hoped thus to abolish the marks of his own subalternity."[26]

I have underlined the word "political" in this quote from Guha to emphasize a creative tension between the Marxist lineage of Subaltern Studies and the more challenging questions it raised from the very beginning about the nature of power in non-Western colonial modernities. Guha's point was that the arrangements of power in which the peasant and other subaltern classes found themselves in colonial India contained two very different logics of hierarchy and oppression. One was the logic of the quasi-liberal legal and institutional framework which the British introduced into the country. Imbricated with this was another set of relationships in which hierarchy was based on direct and explicit *domination and subordination* of the less powerful through both ideological-symbolic means and physical force. The semiotics of domination and subordination were what the subaltern classes sought to destroy every time they rose up in rebellion. This semiotics could not be separated in the Indian case from what in English we inaccurately refer to as "religion."

The tension between a familiar narrative of capital and a more radical understanding of it is can be seen in Guha's text itself. There are times when Guha tends to read "domination and subordination" in terms of an opposition between feudal and capitalist modes of production. There is a respectable tendency in Marxist or liberal scholarship to read undemocratic relationships – or personalized systems of authority and practices of deification – as survivals of a precapitalist era, as not quite modern. They are seen as indicative of the problems of transition to capitalism, the assumption being that a full-blown capitalism would or should be logically incompatible with "feudal"-type relationships. Guha's book *Elementary Aspects* sometimes does speak within this tradition of analysis. Direct domination, Guha tells us in some places, is a feature of lingering feudalism:

> Taking the subcontinent as a whole, capitalist development in a agriculture remained merely incipient . . . until 1900. Rents constituted the most substantial part of income yielded by property in land. . . . The element that was constant in this [landlord–peasant] relationship in all its variety was the extraction of the peasant's surplus by means determined rather less by the free play of the forces of a market economy than by the extra-economic force of the landlord's standing in local society and in the colonial polity. In other words, it was a relationship of domination and subordination – a political relationship of the feudal type, or as it has been appropriately described, a semi-feudal relationship which derived its material sustenance from pre-capitalist conditions of production and its legitimacy from a traditional culture still paramount in the superstructure.[27]

This particular Marxist narrative, however, would appear to weaken and under-represent the force of Guha's critique of the category "pre-political." For if one were to accept the Marxism of this quotation, one could indeed come back at Guha and argue that the sphere of the political hardly ever abstracted itself out from other spheres – that of religion, kinship, culture – in feudal relations of domination and subordination, and that in that sense feudal relations of power could not properly be called political. The lingering existence of "feudal-type" relationships in the Indian scene could then be read – as indeed does Guha at the beginning of this quote – as a mark of the incompleteness of the transition to capitalism. By this logic, the so-called semi-feudal relations and the peasant's mentality could indeed be seen as leftovers from an earlier period, still active no doubt but under world-historical notice of extinction. All India needed was to institute more capitalist institutions, and the process of the con-version of the peasant into the citizen – the properly political figure of person-hood – would begin. This indeed was Hobsbawm's logic. That is why his "pre-political" characters – even when they are "broken into" capitalism and even when Hobsbawm acknowledges that the "acquisition of political con-sciousness" by these "primitive rebels" is what makes "our century the most revolutionary in history" – always remain in the position of being classic "outsiders" to the logic of capitalism: "it comes to them from outside, insidi-ously by the operation of economic forces which they do not understand and over which they have no control."[28]

In rejecting the category "pre-political," however, Guha insists on the specific differences in the histories of power in colonial India and in Europe. This gesture is radical in that it fundamentally pluralizes the history of power in global mo-dernity and separates it from any universal history of capital. "Hobsbawm's material," Guha writes, "is of course derived almost entirely from the European experience and his generalizations are perhaps in accord with it. . . . Whatever its validity for other countries the notion of pre-political peasant insurgency helps little in understanding the experience of colonial India."[29] If we see the colonial formation in India as a case of modernity in which the domain of the political, as Guha argues in introducing *Subaltern Studies*, is irreducibly split into two distinct logics which get braided together all the time – the logic of formal-legal and secular frameworks of governance, and that of relationships of direct domination and subordination which derive their legitimation from a different set of institutions and practices inlcuding those of *dharma* (often translated as "religion") – then Guha's writings help to open up a very interesting problem in the global history of modernity.

Ultimately, this is the problem of how to think about the history of power in an age when capital and the governing institutions of modernity increasingly develop a global reach. Foucault's work shows that if we want to understand the key institutions of modernity that originated in the West, the juridical model of sovereignty celebrated in modern European political thought has to be supple-mented by the notions of discipline, biopower, and governmentality. Guha shows that in the colonial modernity of India, this supplementation has to include an extra pair of terms: domination and subordination. And this, not because India is anything like a semimodern or semicapitalist or semifeudal country. Guha goes beyond the argument that reduces questions of democracy and power in the subcontinent to propositions about incomplete transition to capitalism. He does not deny the connections of colonial India to the global forces of capitalism. His point is that the global history of capitalism does not have to reproduce everywhere the same history of power. In the calculus of modernity, power is not a dependent variable with capital playing the role of an independent one. Capital and power could be treated as analytically separable categories. Traditional European-Marxist political thought which fused the two would therefore always be relevant but inadequate for theorizing power in colonial-modern histories. The history of colonial modernity in India created a domain of the political which was heteroglossic in its idioms, irreducibly plural in its structure, interlocking within itself strands of different type of relations which did not make up a logical whole. One such strand critical to the functioning of authority in Indian institutions was that of direct domination and subordination of the subaltern by the elite. As Guha said in his first contribution to *Subaltern Studies*: this strand of domination and subordination ubiquitous in relationships of power in India "was traditional only in so far as its roots could be traced back to pre-colonial times, but it was by no means archaic in the sense of being outmoded."[30]

Domination and subordination of the subaltern by the elite was thus an everyday feature of Indian capitalism itself. This was a capitalism of the colonial type. Reading critically some key texts of Marx, Guha argued that modern colonialism was quintessentially the historical condition in which an expansive and increasingly global capital came to dominate non-Western societies without effecting or requiring any thoroughgoing democratic transformation in social relationships of power and authority. The colonial state – the ultimate expression of the domain of the political in colonial India – was both a result and a condition of possibility of such domination. As Guha put it: "colonialism could continue as a relation of power in the subcontinent only on the condition that the colonizing bourgeoisie should fail to live up to its own universalizing project. The nature of the state it had created by the sword made this historically necessary." The result was a society which no doubt changed under the impact of colonial capitalism but in which "vast areas in the life and consciousness of the people" escaped any kind of "[bourgeois] hegemony."[31]

The cultural history of power in Indian modernity could not, therefore, be produced by a simple application of the analytics of nationalism available to Western Marxism. Contrary to the intellectual tradition that bound the nationalist-Marxist historian Bipan Chandra to the views of left-nationalists such as Jawaharlal Nehru, Guha's argument implied that one could not pit against the story of a regressive colonialism an account of a robust nationalist movement seeking to establish a bourgeois outlook throughout society.[32] For there were no class here comparable to the European bourgeoisie of the Marxist narrative, a class able to fabricate a hegemonic ideology which made its own interests look and feel like the interests of all. The history of the way the elite nationalists in India sought to mobilize the subaltern classes shows a political domain in which the secular languages of law and constitutional frameworks coexisted and interacted with noncommensurable strategies of domination and subordination. The "Indian culture of the colonial era," Guha argued in a later essay, defied understanding "either as a replication of the liberal-bourgeois culture of nineteenth-century Britain or as the mere survival of an antecedent pre-capitalist culture."[33] This was capitalism but without capitalist hierarchies, a capitalist dominance without a hegemonic capitalist culture – or, in Guha's famous terms, "dominance without hegemony."

3   Subaltern Studies and Reorientation of History

Guha's two formulations – that both nationalism and colonialism were involved in instituting in India a rule of capital in which bourgeois ideologies exercised "dominance without hegemony," and that the resulting forms of power in India could not be termed "pre-political" – had several implications for historiography. Some of these were worked out in Guha's own writings and some in what his colleagues wrote. It is important, however, that we clarify these implications, for they are what made Subaltern Studies an experiment in postcolonial historiography.

First of all, Guha's critique of the category "pre-political" challenged historicism by rejecting all stagist theories of history. If the term "pre-political," as we have discussed, took its validity from categorizing certain kinds of power-relationships as "premodern," "feudal," etc., Guha's discussion of power in colonial India resists such a clear distinction between the modern and the premodern. Relations in India that looked "feudal" when seen through a stagist view of history were contemporaneous with all that looked "modern" to the same point of view. From Guha's point of view, the former could not be looked on through geological or evolutionist metaphors of "survival" or "remnant" without such historicism becoming elitist in its interpretation of the past.

Subaltern Studies, then, was in principle opposed to narratives of nationalist histories which portrayed nationalist leaders as ushering India and her people out of some kind of "pre-capitalist" stage into a world-historical phase of "bourgeois modernity," replete with the artifacts of democracy, citizenly rights, market economy, and the rule of law. There is no doubt that the Indian political elite internalized and used this language of political modernity, but this democratic tendency existed alongside and interlarded with undemocratic relations of domination and subordination. This coexistence of two domains of politics, said Guha, "was the index of an important historical truth, that is, the *failure of the bourgeoisie to speak for the nation*."[34] There was, in fact, no unitary "nation" to speak for. Rather the more important question was how and through what practices an official nationalism emerged which claimed to represent such a unitary nation. A critical stance towards official or statist nationalism and its attendant historiography marked *Subaltern Studies* from the beginning. Postcolonial history was thus also a postnationalist form of historiography.[35]

Guha's quest for a history in which the subaltern was "the maker of his own destiny" brought into focus the question of the relationship between texts and power. Historical archives are usually collections of documents, texts of various kinds. Historians of peasants and other subaltern social groups have long emphasized the fact that peasant do not leave their own documents. Historians concerned with recuperating peasant "experience" in history have often turned to the resources of other disciplines for help: anthropology, demography, sociology, archeology, human geography, etc. In his well-known study of nineteenth-century rural France, *Peasants into Frenchmen*, Eugen Weber provides a succinct formulation of this approach: "the illiterate are not in fact inarticulate; they can and do express themselves in several ways. Sociologists, ethnologists, geographers, and most recently demographic historians have shown us new and different means of interpreting evidence."[36] In the sixties and seventies, E. P. Thompson and Keith Thomas and others turned to anthropology in search of ways of getting at the "experiences" of the subaltern classes.[37] Guha's approach is interestingly different from that of these historians. His *Elementary Aspects* starts by recognizing the same problem as do Weber, Thomas, Thompson, and others: that peasants do not speak directly in archival documents which are usually produced by the ruling classes.[38] Like them, Guha also uses a diversity of disciplines in tracking the logic of peasant-consciousness at the moment of rebellion. But he thinks of the category "consciousness" differently. In insisting on the autonomy of the "consciousness" of the insurgent peasant, Guha does not aim to produce generalizations that attempt to sum up what every empirical peasant participating in rebellions in colonial India must have thought, felt, or experienced inside his or her head. For such attempts, however well-intentioned, ended up making peasants into relatively exotic objects of anthropology. Guha's critique of the term "pre-political" legitimately barred this path of thinking. Guha thought of "consciousness" – and therefore of peasant subjecthood – as *something immanent in the very practices of peasant insurgency*. *Elementary Aspects* is a study of the *practices* of insurgent peasants in colonial India, and not of a reified category called "consciousness." The aim of the book was to bring out the collective imagination inherent in the practices of peasant rebellion. Guha makes no claim that the "insurgent consciousness" he discusses is indeed "conscious," that it existed inside the heads of peasants. He does not equate consciousness with "the subject's view of himself." He examines rebel-practices to decipher the particular relationships between elites and subalterns and between subalterns themselves that are acted out in these practices, and then attempts to derive from these relationships the elementary structure, as it were, of the "consciousness" inherent in those relationships.

478

In keeping with the structuralist tradition to which he affiliates his book by the very use of the word "elementary" in its title, Guha describes his hermeneutic strategy through the metaphor of "reading." The available archives on peasant insurgencies are produced by the counter-insurgency measures of the ruling classes and their armies and police forces. Guha, therefore, emphasizes the need for the historian to develop a conscious strategy for "reading" the archives, not simply for the biases of the elite but for the textual properties of these documents in order to get at the various ways in which elite modes of thought represented the refractory figure of the subaltern and their practices. Without such a scanning device, Guha argued, historians tended to reproduce the same logic of representation as that used by the elite classes in dominating the subaltern.[39] The interventionist metaphor of "reading" resonates as the opposite of E. P. Thompson's use – in the course of his polemic with Althusser – of the passive metaphor of "listening" in describing the hermeneutic activity of the historian.[40]

In thus critiquing historicism and Eurocentrism and using that critique to interrogate the idea of the nation, in emphasizing the textual properties of archival documents, in considering representation as an aspect of power-relations between the elite and the subaltern, Guha and his colleagues moved away from the guiding assumptions of the "history from below" approach of English Marxist historiography. With Guha's work, Indian history took, as it were, the proverbial linguistic turn. From its very beginning, *Subaltern Studies* positioned itself on an unorthodox territory of the left. What it inherited from Marxism was already in conversation with other and more recent currents of European thought, particularly those of structuralism. And there was a discernible sympathy with early Foucault in the way that Guha's writings posed the knowledge–power question by asking, "what are the archives and how are they produced?"

4   Subaltern Studies since 1988: Multiple Circuits

Guha retired from the editorial team of *Subaltern Studies* in 1988.[41] In the same year, an anthology entitled *Selected Subaltern Studies* published from New York launched the global career of the project. Edward Said wrote a Foreword to the volume describing Guha's statement regading the aims of *Subaltern Studies* as "intellectually insurrectionary."[42] Gayatri Spivak's essay "Deconstructing Historiography," published earlier in the sixth volume under Guha's editorship in 1986, served as the introduction to this selection.[43] This essay of Spivak's and a review essay by Rosalind O'Hanlon published about the same time made two important criticisms of *Subaltern Studies* which had a serious impact on the later intellectual trajectory of the project.[44] Both Spivak and O'Hanlon pointed to the absence of gender questions in Subaltern Studies. They also made a more fundamental criticism of the theoretical orientation of the project. They pointed out, in effect, that *Subaltern Studies* historiography operated with an idea of the

479

subject – "to make the sublatern the maker of his own destiny" – which had
not wrestled at all with critique of the very idea of the subject itself that had
been mounted by poststructuralist thinkers. Spivak's famous essay "Can the
Subaltern Speak?" – a critical and challenging reading of a conversation between
Foucault and Deleuze – forcefully raised these and related questions by raising
deconstructive and philosophical objections to any straightforward program of
"letting the subaltern speak."[45]

Subaltern Studies scholars have since tried to take these criticisms on board.
The charges about the absence of gender issues and the lack of engagement with
feminist scholarship in *Subaltern Studies* have been met to some degree by some
seminal essays by Ranajit Guha and Partha Chatterjee, and by contributions
made by Susie Tharu on contemporary feminist theory in India.[46] Partha
Chatterjee's 1986 book *Nationalist Thought and the Colonial World* creatively
applied Saidian and postcolonial perspectives to the study of non-Western
nationalisms, using India as an example.[47] This book extended Guha's criticisms
of nationalist historiography into a full-blown, brilliant critique of nationalist
thought itself. With this work of Chatterjee's and with Gyanendra Pandey's
forthcoming book on the history of the partition of India in 1947, postcolonial
critique may be truly said to have become postnationalist critique as well. The
influence of deconstructionist and postmodern thought in *Subaltern Studies* may
be traced in the way Gyanendra Pandey's, Chatterjee's, and Amin's works in the
1990s have come to privilege the idea of the fragment over that of the whole or
totality. Pandey's book, *The Construction of Communalism in Colonial North India*
(1991) and his 1992 essay "In Defense of the Fragment," Chatterjee's 1994 book,
The Nation and Its Fragments, Amin's recent experimental and widely-acclained
book *Events, Memory, Metaphor* – all question, on both archival and epistemological grounds, even the very possibility of constructing a totalizing national
history in narrating the politics of subaltern lives.[48] This move has also understandably given rise to a series of writings from *Subaltern Studies* scholars in
which "history" itself as a European form of knowledge has come under
critical investigation. Gyan Prakash, Ranajit Guha, Partha Chatterjee, Shahid
Amin, Ajay Skaria, Shail Mayaram, and others have made significant contributions on this subject.[49] Gyan Prakash's recently completed study of the discourse
of "science" in Indian nationalist writings shows a deep engagement with the
thoughts of Homi Bhabha.[50]

Where does Subaltern Studies, both the series and the project, stand today?
At the crossing of many different pathways, it seems. The original project – as
understood here as one that effects a relative separation between the history of
capital and that of power – has been developed and furthered in the work of
the group. David Arnold's study of British colonialism in India in terms of
histories of contested bodily practices, *Colonizing the Body*, David Hardiman's
studies of the political and economic culture of subaltern lives caught in emergent forms of capitalism in the Indian state of Gujarat, *The Coming of the Devi*
and *Feeding the Baniya*, Gautam Bhadra's study of a number of texts to do with

peasant society in eighteenth- and nineteenth-century Bengal, *Iman o Nishan* (in Bengali), are examples in which the possibilities of the original theoretic-historiographic project are worked out and illustrated through concrete, historical examples.[51]

At the same time, it has to be acknowledged that *Subaltern Studies* has exceeded the original historiographical agenda that it set for itself in the early 1980s. The series, as I said at the outset, now has both global and even regional locations in the circuits of scholarship that it traverses. This expansion beyond the realms of Indian history has earned for the series both praise and criticism which fall outside the scope of the present discussion. The point of this exercise has been to rebut the charge that *Subaltern Studies* lost its original way by falling into the bad company of postcolonial theory. I have sought to demonstrate – through a discussion of what Guha wrote in the 1980s – some necessary connections between the original aims of the *Subaltern Studies* and current discussion of postcoloniality.

Notes

Thanks are due to Ranajit Guha, Anne Hardgrove, and Sanjay Seth for discussions of an earlier draft. However, I alone remain responsible for what follows.

1   I italicize "subaltern studies" when it refers to the actual volumes in the series by that name or to the series itself. When left unitalicized, I use the expression to refer to an intellectual project, a field of studies or to the editorial collective of the series.

2   As it exists now the collective has the following members: Shahid Amin, David Arnold, Gautam Bhadra, Dipesh Chakrabarty, Partha Chatterjee, David Hardiman, Sudipta Kaviraj, Shail Mayaram, Gyan Pandey, M. S. S. Pandian, Gyan Prakash, Susie Tharu, and Ajay Skaria. Sumit Sarkar and Gayatri Spivak were members of the collective for specific periods in the 1980s and the 1990s respectively.

3   See, for instance, the symposium on *Subaltern Studies* in the December 1994 issue of the *American Historical Review* in which three historians of South Asia (Gyan Prakash), Africa (Frederick Cooper), and Latin America (Florencia Mallon) participated.

4   See their "Founding Statement" in *Boundary 2*, 20, no. 3 (fall, 1993): 110–21.

5   This is the insistent burden of much of what Sumit Sarkar has written in criticism of *Subaltern Studies*. See his *Writing Social History* (Delhi: Oxford University Press, 1997).

6   Arif Dirlik, "The Aura of Postcolonialism: Third World Criticism in the Age of Global Capitalism," in Padmini Mongia, ed., *Contemporary Postcolonial Theory: A Reader* (London and New York: Arnold, 1996), p. 302.

7   See my discussion of the relationship between nationalism and Marxism in Indian historiography in "Marxism and Modern India" in Alan Ryan, ed., *After the End of*

History (London: Collins and Brown, 1992), pp. 79–84. Sanjay Seth's book *Marxism, Theory and Nationalist Politics: The Case of Colonial India* (Delhi: Sage Publications, 1995) provides a good analysis of the historical connections between Marxist thought and nationalist ideologies in British India.

8   Bipan Chandra, *The Rise and Growth of Economic Nationalism in India: Economic Policies of Indian National Leadership. 1880–1905* (Delhi: People's Publishing House, 1969); Anil Seal, *The Emergence of Indian Nationalism: Competition and Collaboration in the Later 19th Century* (Cambridge: Cambridge University Press, 1968); A. R. Desai, *Social Background of Indian Nationalism* (Bombay: Asia Publishing House, 1966; first published 1948); D. A. Low, ed., *Soundings in Modern South Asian History* (Canberra: Australian National University Press, 1968); Bernard S. Cohn, *An Anthropologist among the Historians and Other Essays* (Delhi: Oxford University Press, 1988); Morris David Morris and Dharma Kumar, eds., *Indian Economy in the Nineteenth Century: A Symposium* (Delhi: Indian Economic and Social History Association, 1969).

9   Seal, *The Emergence.*

10 John Gallagher, Gordon Johnson, Anil Seal, eds., *Locality, Province and Nation: Essays on Indian Politics 1870–1940* (Cambridge: Cambridge University Press, 1973).

11 Anil Seal, "Imperialism and Nationalism in India," in ibid., p. 2.

12 Bipan Chandra, *Nationalism and Colonialism in Modern India* (New Delhi: Orient Longman, 1979).

13 As one respected Indian historian wrote, responding to the work of the Cambridge scholars: "once, not so very long ago, to countless Indians nationalism was a fire in the blood." See Tapan Raychaudhuri's review-essay "Indian Nationalism as Animal Politics," *The Historical Journal*, 22, 3 (1979), pp. 747–63.

14 See Gyanendra Pandey, *The Ascendancy of the Congress in Uttar Pradesh, 1926–1934: A Study in Imperfect Mobilization* (Delhi: Oxford University Press, 1978); Majid Siddiqi, *Agrarian Unrest in North India: The United Provinces, 1918–1922* (Delhi: Vikas, 1978); Kapil Kumar, *Peasants in Revolt: Tenants, Landlords, Congress and the Raj in Oudh, 1886–1922* (New Delhi: Manohar, 1984); David Arnold, *The Congress in Tamilnadu: National Politics in South Asia, 1919–1937* (New Delhi: Manohar, 1977); Hitesranjan Sanyal, *Swarajer Pathe* [in Bengali; posthumously published collection of essays] (Calcutta: Papyrus, 1994); Pavid Hardiman, *Peasant Nationalists of Gujarat: Kheda District* (Delhi: Oxford University Press, 1981). See also the essays in D. A. Low, ed., *Congress and the Raj* (London, 1977).

15 See Ranajit Guha's "Introduction" to *A Subaltern Studies Reader* (Minneapolis: The University of Minnesota Press, 1998).

16 Idem, "On Some Aspects of the Historiography of Colonial India," in Guha, ed., *Subaltern Studies I: Writings on South Asian History and Society* (Delhi: Oxford University Press, 1982), p. 3; emphasis in original.

17 See Antonio Gramsci, "Notes on Italian History," in his *Selections from the Prison Notebooks*, trans. and ed. Quintin Hoare and Geoffrey Nowell Smith (New York: International Publishers, 1973).

18 Ranajit Guha, "Preface," to Guha, ed., *Subaltern Studies III: Writings on Indian History and Society* (Delhi: Oxford University Press, 1984), p. vii.

19   Ibid., pp. 3–4.

20   Ibid., pp. 4–5.

21   See E. J. Hobsbawm, *Primitive Rebels: Studies in Archaic Forms of Social Movement in the 19th and 20th Centuries* (Manchester, 1978), p. 2. See the citation in Ranajit Guha, *Elementary Aspects of Peasant Insurgency in Colonial India* (Delhi: Oxford University Press, 1983), pp. 5–6.

22   Hobsbawm, *Primitive Rebels*, p. 2.

23   Guha, *Elementary Aspects*, chs. 1 and 2.

24   Seal, *The Emergence*.

25   Guha's examines and critiques such Marxist positions in his essay "The Prose of Counter-Insurgency," in Guha and Gayatri Chakravorty Spivak, eds., *Selected Subaltern Studies* (New York: Oxford University Press, 1988), pp. 45–86.

26   Guha, *Elementary Aspects*, p. 75.

27   Ibid., p. 6.

28   Hobsbawm, *Primitive Rebels*, p. 3.

29   Ibid.

30   "On Some Aspects," p. 4.

31   Ibid., pp. 5–6; emphasis in original.

32   Both Nehru's writings of the 1930s and Bipan Chandra's of the 1970s assumed without question that the nationalist movement was "essentially a bourgeois movement" (Nehru) and that its function was to establish "bourgeois ideological, political and organizational hegemony . . . over the vast mass of peasants, workers and the lower middle classes" (Chandra). See Jawaharlal Nehru, *India's Freedom* (London, 1962 [1936]), p. 66 and Bipan Chandra, *Nationalism and Colonialism in Modern India*, p. 135.

33   Ranajit Guha, "Colonialism in South Asia: A Dominance without Hegemony and Its Historiography," in *Dominance Without Hegemony: History and Power in Colonial India* (Cambridge, Mass.: Harvard University Press, 1997), pp. 97–8.

34   Guha, "Some Aspects of," pp. 5–6; emphasis in original.

35   This aspect of the project later came to be developed by Partha Chatterjee, Gyanendra Pandey, and Shahid Amin. See below.

36   Eugen Joseph Weber, *Peasants Into Frenchmen: The Modernization of Rural France, 1870–1914* (Stanford: Stanford University Press, 1976), p. xvi.

37   Cf. E. P. Thompson on "experience": "a category which, however imperfect it may be, is indispensable to the historian, since it comprises mental and emotional response, whether of an individual or of a social group, to many inter-related events." E. P. Thompson, "The Poverty of Theory or An Orrery of Errors," in his *The Poverty of Theory and Other Essays* (London: Merlin Press, 1979), p. 199. See also Keith Thomas, "History and Anthropology," *Past and Present*, 24, April 1963, pp. 3–18.

38   Guha, *Elementary Aspects*, chs. 1 and 2.

39   Guha's own reading strategies are spelt out in his essay "The Prose of Counter-Insurgency" and are implicit throughout *Elementary Aspects*.

40   Cf. E. P. Thompson, "The Poverty of Theory," pp. 210, 222. To be fair, Thompson does not only write about "voices clamour[ing] from the past," – "not the historian's voice, please observe; *their own voices*" – he also has much to say

about how historians interrogate their sources in order to listen to the lost voices of history.

41 See Guha's statement in his introduction to *Subaltern Studies VI* (Delhi: Oxford University Press, 1988).

42 Edward Said, "Foreword," to Ranajit Guha and Gayatri Chakravorty Spivak, eds., *Selected Subaltern Studies* (New York: Oxford University Press, 1988), p. v.

43 Gayatri Chakravorty Spivak, "Subaltern Studies: Deconstructing Historiography," in Guha and Spivak, eds., *Selected Subaltern Studies*, pp. 3–32.

44 Spivak, ibid., and Rosalind O'Hanlon, "Recovering the Subject: Subaltern Studies and Histories of Resistance in Colonial South Asia," *Modern Asian Studies*, 22 (1), 1988, pp. 189–224.

45 Gayatri Chakravorty Spivak, "Can the Subaltern Speak?" reprinted in Patrick Williams and Laura Chrisman, eds., *Colonial Discourse and Postcolonial Theory: A Reader* (New York: Columbia University Press, 1994), pp. 66–111.

46 Guha, "Chandra's Death," in *Subaltern Studies V*, reprinted in Guha, ed., *A Subaltern Studies Reader*, pp. 34–62; Partha Chatterjee, "The Nationalist Resolution of the Woman Question," reprinted as "The Nation and Its Women" in his *The Nation and Its Fragments: Colonial and Post-colonial Histories* (Princeton: Princeton University Press, 1994); Susie Tharu and Tejaswini Niranjana, "Problems for a Contemporary Theory of Gender," in Amin and Chakrabarty, eds., *Subaltern Studies*, vol. 9, pp. 232–60.

47 Partha Chatterjee, *Nationalist Thought and the Colonial World* (London: Zed, 1986).

48 Gyanendra Pandey, *The Construction of Communalism in Colonial North India* (Delhi: Oxford University Press, 1991); Gyan Pandey, "In Defense of the Fragment: Writing About Hindu–Muslim Riots in India Today," in *Representations*, winter 1992, reprinted in Guha, ed., *A Subaltern Studies Reader*, pp. 1–33; Partha Chatterjee, *The Nation and Its Fragments*; Shahid Amin, *Event, Memory, Metaphor* (Berkeley: University of California Press, 1995).

49 Gyan Prakash has led the debate on nonfoundational histories with his well-known essays "Writing Post-Orientalist Histories of the Third World: Perspectives from Indian Historiography," *Comparative Studies in Society and History*, 32, April 1990, and "Postcolonial Criticism and Indian Historiography," *Social Text*, 31/32, 1992. Ranajit Guha's essay "An Indian Historiography of India: Hegemonic Implications of a Nineteenth-Century Agenda," in his *Dominance Without Hegemony*, Partha Chatterjee's chapter entitled "The Nation and Its Pasts," in his *The Nation and Its Fragments*, Gyanendra Pandey's essay "Subaltern Studies: From a Critique of Nationalism to a Critique of History' (unpublished), and Shahid Amin's "Alternative Histories: A View From India" (unpublished) are contributions to debates on historiography and the status of historical knowledge that *Subaltern Studies* have given rise to. In this connection, see also Shail Mayaram's treatment of memory and history in her "Speech, Silence and the Making of Partition Violence in Mewat," in Amin and Chakrabarty, eds., *Subaltern Studies*, vol. 9, pp. 126–64 and Ajay Skaria's forthcoming book, *Hybrid Histories* (Delhi: Oxford University Press, 1999).

50 See, for example, Gyan Prakash, "Science Between the Lines," in Shahid Amin and Dipesh Chakrabarty, eds., *Subaltern Studies*, vol. 9 (Delhi: Oxford University Press, 1996), pp. 59–82. Prakash's forthcoming book analyzes the discourses of science and modernity in colonial India.

51 David Arnold, *Colonizing the Body: State Medicine and Epidemic Diseases in Nineteenth-Century India* (Berkeley: University of California Press, 1993); David Hardiman, *The Coming of the Devi: Adivasi Assertion in Western India* (Delhi: Oxford University Press, 1987) and *Feeding the Banya: Peasants and Usurers in Western India* (Delhi: Oxford University Press, 1996); Gautam Bhadra, *Iman o nishan: unish shotoke bangaly krishak chaitanyer ek adhyay, c.1800–1850* [in Bengali] (Calcutta: Subarnarekha for the Centre for Studies in Social Sciences, 1994).

Chapter 25

Feminist Theory in Perspective

Ipshita Chanda

The issue that concerns us here within the rubric of a "Companion" to "post" colonial literatures, is fundamentally a strategy of reading. Reading the "post" colonial needs to be accompanied evidentially, for unless the purely geographical nature of the "post" colonial is fleshed out with adequate philosophical inputs, it seems to remain an airy nothing despite its firm geographical habitation and its many names. Therefore my contribution towards a strategy of reading "post" colonial discourse has a material dimension. I explore the attempts to rewrite gender ideologies, to dismantle the hierarchies or at least rearticulate them, in some societies, through the period of colonial intervention, nationalist struggle and neocolonial "development," relating these attempts to the material reality that structure these hierarchies, the relation between women's work, land or property, and their socioeconomic status. These seem to be the key questions that feminist practice must address, in "post" colonial locations. These locations are characterized by inequalities but this is not unique to them. Rather, it is the attempts by external and internal agencies to negotiate these inequalities and manage them to further their own explicit or implicit agendas that appears to be the "post" colonial world's most contentious problem. In such circumstances, feminist practice must necessarily be political on the ideological, organizational, and personal planes, for feminist practice has, I would hope to show, the potential to become a transformative radical politics. The implications of these intersecting political positions permeate the everyday lives of men and women, affecting the basic material reality with which their livelihood and their consequent social position are produced. Of course, this is not limited to "post" colonial locations alone. As Sangari (1987) has pointed out, "the history of the West and the history of the non-West are by now irrevocably different and irrevocably shared . . . The cultural projects of *both* the West and the non-West are implicated in a larger history." Citing the "stifling monologues of self and other . . . however disordered or decentered" as "orderly discourses of the bourgeois subject," she calls for a "genuinely dialogic and dialectical history that can account for the formation of different selves and the construction of different

486

epistemologies." It appears that this call has been answered by one strand of "post" colonial theory that foregrounds the different ways in which identity is constructed, especially in the case of gender-identity, and the specificities of caste, community, race, and class have been taken into consideration in meticulous detail in these projects (Mohanty, 1984; Minh-ha, 1989). But feminist practice in "post" colonial locations rarely fits so neatly into these categorizations. Shifting parameters for changing allocations of material resources, shifting alignments of gender allegiances maneuvered by shifting party political configurations and varied emphasis at different historical junctures on various elements that go to make up this "identity," lead to a constant process of negotiation, thus threatening all theories based on the assumption of a stable identity whatever complexities this may include. In "post" colonial words, instability and volatility apparently mark the social scenario – results of party-political engineering and big brotherly pressure from the "developed" world. Besides, there is also the vast gap between the still colonized or recolonized upper classes, and the materially deprived, whose attempts at focused organization are constantly combated through divisive violence and formal suppression. Hence, conceptualizing feminist practice often seems a plunge into the gap opened between practical strategy and epistemological tools that will help the bourgeois colonial-language-educated academic to understand and offer ways of reading these strategies to those of her kind on the global circuit.

First I outline what has been called theory about "Third World" coloniality, produced in geographical locations that are in former colonies as well as in western academia. From these feminist analyses I will move to a consideration of gender ideology and more specifically gender discourse[1] in various "post" colonial locations, within colonial, nationalist, and "post" colonial patriarchal formations, attempting to read the rhetoric of "progress," "modernization," and finally "development" which is implicitly gendered, and which regulates and shapes feminist practice.

In a seminal essay, Chandra Talpade Mohanty (1984) has taken issue with the institutionalization of a "reductive and homogenous notion of . . . Third World feminisms that appropriate and 'colonize' the fundamental complexities that characterize the lives of women of different classes, religions, cultures, races and castes." Mohanty signals a challenge to western feminism in the need to "[situate] itself and examin[e] its role in the global economic and political framework" in order to be able to study "the complex interconnections between first and third world countries and the profound effect of this on the lives of women in these countries." In a similar vein, Avtar Brah (1991) focuses more precisely on the process by which "difference" is conceptualized. Firstly, as a "social relation constructed within systems of power underlying structures of class, racism, gender, sexuality," functioning within "the broad parameters set by the social structures of a given society." Secondly, as "experiential diversity . . . the many and different manifestations of ideological and institutional practices in our everyday life." These levels are "mutually inter dependent," the first characterizing "the representation of our collective histories," the second, "personal experience codified in an individual's biography"; but they "cannot be read off from one another."

Both Brah and Mohanty, in these essays, go on to outline commonalities that can forge community across difference in order to combat hegemonic notions of homogenous Difference. Brah's strategy is to forge a "non-essentialist universalism". Rather than a politics of "identity" (Adams, 1989; Parmar, 1989), she advocates a politics of "identification . . . based on understandings of the material and ideological basis of all oppressions in their global manifestations, of the interconnectedness as well as the specificity of each oppression." Mohanty critically analyses the source of homogenization, locating it within the easy theoretical move of identifying and institutionalizing "norm or referent," against which the other, in this case third world women, are constructed as a single category. Western feminists are not free of this "binary analytic," and they construct their self over and against this other.

Mohanty's (1989) identification of "Western feminists [as] the true subjects' of [the] counter-history" where third world women are relegated to "debilitating generality of their 'object' status" has invited criticism from Sara Suleri (1993), who argues that Mohanty's position is not quite free from binarism, and that her analysis is premised on "the irreconciliability of gender as history and gender as culture." She is sceptical that the "ethnic voce of womanhood [can] counteract the cultural articulation" that Mohanty says is the exegesis of Western feminism. Can the "objectification" of third world women be countered by allowing the "authentic" subaltern to speak? Her critique is that "when feminism turns to lived experience as an alternative mode of radical subjectivity, it only rehearses the objectification of its proper subject – 'life' remains the ultimate answer to 'discourse.'" In contrast, she presents "reality" as experienced by the women who live under violent ordinances regulating sexual morality in Pakistan, and attempts to show how patriarchal constructions of culture define gender ideology and influence women's lives, relating this to the reality of US support for the regime that "liberated" Afghanistan from Communism and propagated Islamic law.

One way of negotiating these objections perhaps is by processual understanding of a particular situation with a view to engagement. Spivak (1988) has advocated "the practical politics of the open end" which she sees as two kinds of politics – "the daily-maintenance politics [that] seems to require acting out of line" and the "massive kind of . . . surgical operation-type politics which can go according to morphology." She sees these as bringing each other to "productive crisis" that leads to this "practical politics of the open-end." Innumerable levels of lived reality intervene and the value of theorization is here reduced to a particular case, on one side of which lies impossibility and on the other an idealistic ethical imperative. It is true, perhaps, that this difficult path is an alternative to liberal humanism, to romantic homogenization of the other, but it also may lead to an intensely felt but intensely individualistic private form of practice. Perhaps the "practical politics of the open end" can be seen as a constant negotiation, as a form of daily engagement to mold, shape, and direct feminist practice in dealing with local and global realities, through collective action.

This is the next point that seems to me to characterize feminist practice in postcolonial locations: that it may manifest itself in the acting agent's individual life, but it is processed out of a sense of collective engagement. Our exploration of the construction of collectivity will be aligned along two interrelated axes. First, the symbolic imposition of colonial gender ideology upon the colonized space, its contradictions with material realities of gender roles, and their further complication in "post" colonial locations. Second, the problems posed by the fraught issue of individual and community rights in the context of "post" colonial polities presided over by the moral imperatives of "democracy," "secularism," and "equality" that define the aspirations of various groups with respect to the "post" colonial state. In the first case, the liberal ideology of the Individual and her freedom/choice militates against the formation of collectives so crucial to feminist practice, and adds to material deprivation of women. In the second case, this Individual becomes a citizen, who demands his rights from the democratic state. Here, the masculine nature of this Individual Citizen is glossed over, as are the other markers that locate him in a historical context within which the discourse of rights arose and was universalized (Menon, 1998). Does this necessarily mean that once this Individual Citizen is placed in the context of "post" colonial democracies and made the subject of social movements for equality and justice, once this essentially masculine concept is opened up to include women, the goal of feminist political practice is achieved? In other words, when community rights are the object of struggle, is it possible for women of a particular community to form a collective regardless of internal inequalities of class? What will their relation be to women of other communities who are also thus drawn into a collective within their respective communities? And finally, what is the possibility for forging gender- or class-based collectives across communities? We are regularly told that "caste," "religion," "tribe," are distinguishing marks of "fractured" "post" colonial societies. Are we to accept this description and allow it to regulate feminist practice?

Feminist practice seeks to discern the ways in which capitalist patriarchy and global market forces orient identity politics into individualist or divisive rhetoric, and thus isolate women in the cocoon of individual freedom, and "choice." The construction of the "modern" woman was a project brought to the colony by the metropolis, appropriated and redefined to suit nationalist partiarchy, and then further engineered to accommodate feminist demands as lifestyle choices through the global media. The struggles between "tradition" and "modernity," "progress" and "backwardness," "bondage" and "emancipation" have been variously articulated and have impinged upon hegemonic gender ideology in ways that keep different patriarchal formations in operation. Through all these maneuvers, the accent has been on individuality, on the woman as a person, whether in the nineteenth century or the late twentieth. This has had the effect of "popularizing" feminist agendas as a watered-down version of the cult of self-cultivation, thus creating a larger global market for multinational conspicuous consumption. So, feminist practice in "post" colonial locations has been recuperated by various hegemonic discourses and may well be inoculated to become a prop for patriarchy if its collective nature is not constantly emphasized and kept in view.

There are two reasons why I emphasize the varying effects of colonialist gender ideology and its rearticulation by the "post" colonial state in different "post" colonial locations. Firstly, the specificity of historical geographical and cultural location must be taken into account if the cutting edge of feminist practice is to be preserved. However, and this is the second reason to be considered here, these specificities may well redirect one's thinking to the fundamental anomalies that circumscribe the lives of those who are deprived. If feminist practice is to sustain its role as transformative politics, then these are the anomalies that it must address. Hence, it is important to relate the symbolic construction and ordering of social relations to the material reality of women's lives, especially to discern the ways in which these factors affect women who despite being economically deprived, must carry the ideological burdens of womanhood imposed upon them by the intersecting patriarchal formations that regulate their lives at any given point.

We now turn to the second aspect of the "collective" nature of feminist practice referred to above. It is clear that class is a crucial factor in determining women's status within society, and thus, class itself should influence feminist practice. However, in analysis of "post" colonial societies, the considerations "caste," "community," and "tribe" have been constantly focused upon and made the crux of understanding these societies. Though these factors do mark "post" colonial reality, there is also evidence to suggest that the power attributed to them is in no way "natural."

The divisive strategies of the colonial state with respect to cultural identity were couched in the language of caste in India (Inden, 1990) or tribe in the case of African societies (Colson, 1962; Kopytoff, 1987). This obscures the fact that specificities which now appear as the motive force of struggle for "cultural rights" (Deshpande, 1998) were initially ways of organizing the economic hierarchy, and their perpetuation remains a way of keeping economic inequality in operation. This facilitated the hegemonic group's maintenance of supremacy, and enabled cultural and religious justificaation of this supremacy. What are the implications of this for gender organization, and for feminist practice? As Menon (1998) points out with respect to the debate around the Uniform Civil Code in India, groups who demand autonomy or justice on the basis of culture (in this case specifically, cultural differences predicated on religion) construe their difference from other competing groups on the basis of their "personal law," or their right to protect the private/family sphere which regulates and defines personal relationships, from either homogenization in the interests of uniformity or from interference by some external authority, in this case the state. The "inner" realm that demarcates self from other operates in the domestic/private sphere – so gender is the axis on which this entire process of demarcation turns.

What does this entail for community rights *vis-à-vis* women? Second, if the identity politics that much west-oriented "post" colonial feminist theory advocates is taken on board, would it be possible to construct a collectivity to agitate for women's demands on the national level in "post" colonial locations, given that women would then be divided along tribal/community lines?

As a beginning, we may look at some experiences from the Indian and Nigerian women's movements. The Nigerian women's group WIN (Women in Nigeria) insists on defining itself as a Nigerian group (Imam, 1997). This is its strategic reply to reality in dissension-ridden Nigeria that is torn by "ethnic" strife. Its priority is to foreground the material oppression of women across religious and tribal boundaries. This is one way of dealing with divisive politics. In their detailed study of the rise and directions of the women's movement in India, Shah and Gandhi (1991) describe the repressive political atmosphere of the mid-seventies in which rights and freedoms granted by the constitution were repealed and severe economic hardship marked daily life. Women from a large cross-section of society, charged with the role of provider of basic necessities by traditional gender ideology, were unable to fulfill this role within the economic constraints they were subjected to. Thus began the Anti Price Rise Movement, enabling the formation of a broad-based collective that was not confined within the borders of community. The Shah Bano case and its judgment in 1989 showed clearly the reality for women – however different gender discourse may be in case of different cultural communities, hegemonic gender ideology does not construe women very differently. The "Muslim community" was seen to uphold the official version of the Shariat law that discriminated against the divorced woman demanding maintenance. "Justice" was pronounced on the basis of "community" – this was seen as part of the personal sphere where the law of the community rather than the uniform law of a "secular" state operated. Almost ten years later, the level of consensus in feminist thinking on this is indicative of the different possible directions feminist practice may take. The accent is on reform of personal law, of any religious community, within a comprehensive gender just framework of rights that cover areas covered by personal law, and legislate in areas not covered by either secular or personal laws (Menon, 1998). This effectively means the extension of the area within which wrongs against women are liable to legal redress, such that the discrimination inherent in traditional gender ideology and deemed to be private can be brought onto the public national agenda. Should the concept of personal law itself be retained, when it discriminates against women? If rights are context-specific are all women's demands to be limited to local contexts only? Is national policy outside the agenda of feminist practice?

In referring to material deprivation we are in fact focusing the analysis on class. The different forms in which sociocultural identities are constructed are finally held in operation by the material reality of women's control of resources and the scope women have to negotiate this control in order to fulfill the roles they have been socialized into. If imposed distinctions of tribe, community, or caste are overcome, would class itself be the locus of collective formation?

Class, however, may prove to be a divisive factor too. The derivative class position of women may actually splinter solidarity, as Agarwal (1994a and b) argues, with respect to women's ownership of property. This is a result of assuming a congruence of interests within the household as an economic unit, and the failure to account for the gender-based division and oppression women are subjected to within this so-called unit. It does not mean that a woman has either access to or means of controlling the property that is supposed to belong to her marital or natal family. She may belong to a propertied household, but unless the property is registered in her name it offers her no security or any benefits apart from what the male members of the family may choose to give her.

Property mediates relations between women, and affects collective action. However, the vicarious nature of class privileges among women leads to the distinctions being less pronounced. Also, as actual experience shows, a woman's belonging to a propertied class does not automatically mean she is wealthy herself. The ideology of womanhood may well relegate her to a nominal role – even if the property is registered in her name, its control may lie with the male members of her family. Hence women's poverty is a reality – when and how it becomes a constraining factor and affects her basic existence, depends upon the economic condition of the men from whom her class position is derived, and her conformation to the gender ideology to which they subscribe (Hirschon, 1984). As long as she remains within the bounds of this gender ideology, and does not actively contest it in order to assert her rights, she may be assured of their support. This is only a hypothetical statement; however, as Agarwal (1994a) says, the household is a "complex matrix of relations in which on-going (implicit) negotiations [are] subject to constraints set by gender, age, type of relation . . . [and] undisputed tradition." In this context gender relations may be "seen as historically constructed by a process of contestation" (1994a: 52). Thus, whatever may be women's derivative class position, economic deprivation and other forms of oppression characterize their daily lives. The possibility of collective action may follow the realization that their material circumstances are at odds with the class position they have been socialized into by patriarchy. The consciousness of patriarchal oppression, mediated and intensified by various social and economic formations, is the inception of a feminist view of the world.

The liberal humanist version of feminism posits the "human essence" as the basis of collectivity – but this limits feminist practice in "post" colonial societies. In such societies, the class-based nature of social institutions of control, as well as the material conditions of women within these institutions, are dialectically related. Only if this relation is taken into account can feminist practice move beyond the boundaries of what Sen (1990) calls "woman-specific demands."

492

The status of these demands and their scope of operations differs in different "post" colonial locations. The emphasis on nationalist anticolonial struggle to the detriment of women's issues (Urdang, 1989) and the accusation that feminism is a foreign import are two of the ways in which these "women–specific demands" are both devalued and delinked from the larger issues of decolonization and "post" colonial reconstruction. As Ama Ata Aidoo (1992) forcefully points out, "One must resist any attempts at being persuaded to think that the woman question has to be superseded by the struggle against any local exploitative system, the nationalist struggle or the struggle against imperialism and global monopoly capital." Feminist practice must be, on the one hand, committed to opposing such hierarchization or prioritization on the agenda of transformative politics. On the other hand it must make its own "space" within struggles for social, economic, and political reorganization. As Sen (1990) says, women's "articulation of demands and issues exerts a pressure on their movements to take cognizance of the women in their mass base. At the same time it is important to recognize that the ways in which movements have thus had to define struggles and issues to accommodate the women in their ranks have charted out new dimensions for women's struggles in India."

Among the five "provisional historical political and discursive junctures" for understanding Third World feminist politics that Mohanty (1991) identifies are "decolonization and national liberation movements in the third world, the consolidation of white, liberal, capitalist patriarchies in Euro-America, the operation of multinational capital within a global economy" (p. 39). What we, located in the "post" colonial world and perceiving feminist practice as transformative, are concerned with begins from this understanding, but is not limited to it, because framed by these contexts are our daily lives wherein "personal" choices and assertions have political consequences with respect to gender relations within the family sphere, and with respect to the socioeconomic formations which form the context within which family as an institution operates. The divisive politics of religion and caste, exacerbated by the gulf created by scholarship in the colonizer's language, necessarily comes in the way of collective practice. As with land issues or the debate on dowry in India, or polygamy in African societies, the actual needs of women economically and socially exploited have been at odds sometimes with those who are apparently more privileged but are conscious of domination and deprivation as women. The problem, then, is how to draw these differing positions into the orbit of feminist practice as truly transformative, a practice that will have as its goal an equal society?

In order to enter this area, we require a broad understanding of "development" as its conceptual orientation has changed over the last three decades.[2] This is especially pertinent to those ex-colonies which were yoked to the global market in the colonial era, withdrew to varying extents in the aftermath of "independence," and are now being forced back into the fold in order to "develop," i.e. become economically viable as a part of the global network of capital, and to provide basic necessities to the vast majority of their populations in an imitation of the "developed," "welfare" states that control this capital.

The first phase of development laid emphasis on the economic to the cost of the human indicators in judging development. When the much-vaunted "trickle down effect" failed to actually trickle down, a process of reconceptualization was sought. These shortcomings shifted the focus onto the humane aproach, towards the alleviation of poverty and empowerment of the deprived. The global funding agencies changed the thrust of their programs. A part of this reconceptualization was the "Women in Development" approach, which functioned on the assumption that women had been left out of development plans because the patriarchal nature of the society within which these plans were formulated prevented women from having access to technology. Hence, to add women into the ambit of development would solve the problem. This of course did not account for sophisticated analyses of the varied nature of capital accumulation in different socioeconomic contexts, their varied effects on the production process, and consequently on economic and social organization of gender (Beneria and Sen, 1982, 1987). Apart from this, it assumes that the general model of development posited from a particular hegemonic worldview is universally applicable, and its only problem is that it does not take women into consideration. Once this is done, all will be well. But of course this very concept of development and the assumptions that underpin it are to be seen as socially constructed rather than universally applicable, especially with respect to "Third World" realities (Antrobus, 1987; Sen and Grown, 1988). According to some analysts (Snyder, 1995), the basic change was due to the impact of "second wave" feminism in the west, which forced agencies to look at the effects of the developmental strategies on women in developing societies; in the view of others, the participation of women in the nationalist movements brought them into the public sphere, and enabled them to voice their demands and criticisms of these strategies, and hence create a grass-roots awareness and pressure for a change in orientations. These two levels interacted ideally, it would seem, and the pressures of demand were reflected, further focused, and given specific directions at various international women's conferences, leading up to the one in Nairobi in 1985 to signal the end of the United Nations decade focusing on wommen's issues.

The "feminist" view of development evolved out of ISIS, *Women in Development: A Resource Guide for Organization*, and conceptualizations culminated in the establishment of Development Alternatives Within the New Women (DAWN) at the world conference in Nairobi at the end of the UN decade in 1985. DAWN looked at development from the vantage point of women, taking an ethical vision from women's daily lives rather than a progress or competition oriented approach. The idea of "global feminism" (CCIC, 1987) germinated from these beginnings. As the Canadian Consortuim for International Cooperation document, "Feminist Perspectives on Development," points out, feminism can be seen as a method of transformation, a politics to make the world humane because it "asks the right questions about power, about the links between the personal and the political and because it cuts through race and class. Feminism implies consciousness of all the sources of oppression – race, class, gender, homophobia – and resists them all." This echoes the Dakar document which defined feminism as "international" because it aims at "liberation of women from all types of oppression and provide(s) solidarity among women of all countries" (Dakar, 1982).

Given the history of active intervention in development by feminists, their success in focusing on the implications of development for women is reflected in the new orientation to development, also called "sustainable development," that is the current approach emphasized by international agencies and other donors. Since it is this form of development we are particularly interested in, for reasons that we will enumerate, it is important to trace the growth of this concept itself. The Report of the World Commission on Environment and Development, 1987, also called the Brundtland Commission, shifted the focus from means of remedying environmental degradation to a preventive and human-centered approach to sustainable development (WCED, 1987). This concept is linked with equity and justice on the one hand and with the emphasis on community management and control of resources on which they depend on the other. It promotes "citizens' initiatives, empowering people's organisations and strengthening local democracy" (Wacker, 1994: 9). Though this report does not directly address women's issues, analysts and theoreticians of sustainability have pointed out that women in the "post" colonial (or what they rather neutrally call South) areas, responsible for daily survival tasks dependent upon the environment, are those who traditionally have a fund of knowledge about resource management which does not deplete the natural resources. At the same time, these women, among the poorest groups, are hardest hit when development destroys or uses up scarce resources (Ghai and Vivien, 1990; Dankelman and Davidson, 1988). Some theorists perceive these women as contributing to environmental degradation, but due to the same reason: the male bias in development has led to greater impoverishment of women. Thus, the idea of sustainability encapsulates within itself certain other ideas, like grassroots participation, the use of alternative knowledge systems and the community as focus of development. All these ideas can be linked to the concept of "empowerment" of those who have thus far been silenced or marginalized in the march towards "progress".

The "Second Development Decade" of the United Nations formulated a development strategy in which "sustained improvement in the well-being of the individual" was the focus. Women and development was seen as a holistic concept by organizations like UNIFEM that acted to facilitate women's "legal right and access to existing means for the improvement of oneself and society" within this context. Noeleen Heyzer, Director of UNIFEM since 1994, has defined sustainable livelihoods as "how people survive, produce, consume and reproduce in conditions of social inequality" (Heyzer, 1994: 25). The Bangkok 1979 paper defined "empowerment" as consisting of "internal strength and confidence to

495

face life . . . [and the] right to determine choices towards more just social and economic order." The idea of justice and rights of women in developing societies has been explored by the theorists of capability (Nussbaum and Glover, 1995), who have argued that to qualify as human an individual should "have the necessary resources and conditions for acting in (certain valued) ways" (Nussbaum, 1995: 94–5). In defining the "thresholds of capability" within which an individual may be seen as functioning as a human being, Nussbaum posits two levels. One, beneath which life is so impoverished that it cannot be seen as human life at all; the second, beneath which the characteristic functions are available in such a reduced way that we may judge this life as human, but not as a *good* human life. Nussbaum has designated the second threshold as the sphere of public policy. The state should not consider its responsibility completed in providing the mere minimum requirements for a human life: its moral imperative should be to provide resources needed for a good human life (ibid., 81–2). The problem in developing societies is of a different nature: varities of the "post" colonial state are centralized formations with different emphases. Generally, such states have direct control over most areas. Political unrest as a result of external and internal pressures and of power struggles between various groups, characterize such formations. Thus the state's maneuvering and bargaining for the survival and preservation of sovereignty and integrity, following the ravages of imperial economics, have actually produced and generated underdevelopment. Neo-imperialism further complicates the issue. Therefore, the "threshold" of a "good" human life is not the arena of public policy in the "post" coloniaal state. It is rather the initial threshold which serves as a moral imperative for this state. Feminist practice will urge that development, or "empowerment," will "not be seen as an outside challenge to local culture and tradition but as a local response to changes in local culture and tradition" (Chen, 1995: 55).

At this very basic level, the "post" colonial state had equality on its agenda; in a formal sense, there was to be no discrimination in the eyes of the law on any grounds. Gradually, considerations of political power led to a redefinition of these goals of equality. Some states then explicitly pronounced themselves as adhering to a particular religion instead of espousing the humanist liberal ideal of secularism or implicitly legislating in such a way as to render certain groups perpetually disadvantaged due to lack of legal access or means of redress, or even lack of awareness of laws. If "development" had "empowerment" as its goal, then the explicit discrimination as well as the implicit, built-in structural inequalities are brought within the purview of reorganization. The demand for rights, for equality, in the field of economic opportunity, become threats to the status quo. If this was limited only to a reorganization of the gender hierarchy, only to a battle for meanings and symbolic representation of women's status within the home and in society, there would still be resulting tension. However, the result of gender reorganization is also a form of economic reorganization and vice versa. Hence the very nature of such development will necessarily become radical. This is characteristic of "post" colonial locations because the very notion of "under" development implies a standard, whether in terms of economic progress, or in terms of realization of human capabilities. Neither of these standards are neutral in any way, and their construction as normative is a result of the permeating of "post" colonial areas by the culture that set these norms. In the "post" colonial situation, the "needs" of disadvantaged groups are themselves sites of struggle. The perception of "need" will vary across the class hierarchy, and the lack of consensus on priorities is bound to lead to conflict. Groups with "unequal discursive (and non-discursive) resources compete to establish as hegemonic their respective interpretations of legitimate social needs" (Fraser, 1989). There is little doubt about who wins, and the consequences of changing this structure. Development that involves the poorest and most disadvantaged groups can hardly avoid this outcome. However, this destabilization is a concern, not of donor agencies or international bodies, but "post" colonial communities and individuals who are involved in broad-based struggles for social transformation. The "donor" is an outside agency which has no moral, legal, or political imperative to deal with the outcome of this transformation, despite the utility and good intentions manifested in its project-proposals. Yet, neither development nor empowerment is of continued sustained worth if the resulting pressures exerted upon the beneficiaries by threatened hegemonic sociopolitical institutions and the groups controlling them cannot be combatted. In fact, only if beneficiaries are equipped to combat such pressure will they be "empowered." In the case of Women, especially, this is crucial, for in patriarchal society the violence consequent upon efforts at transformation or radical restructuring has women as the obvious target. The instances of "caste" or "religion-based" violence upon women in "post" colonial locations are the more obvious effects of such economic wars of position.

Apart from this, the economic empowerment of women, leading to a reorganization of gender relations within and between classes, may also lead to further violence against women. Kabeer (1994) makes a detailed analysis of the "needs" and "interests" perceived by women from different classes in groups and individually, and probes the articulation of these perceptions in the process of empowerment. If "development," and especially the gains for deprived groups, including women, are to be sustained, feminist practice must extend beyond the facilitating of donor-funded development, and formulate strategies to deal with the effects this will have on the existing power relations, in order to support and equip women to survive in the throes of change.

It appears that the easy use of "empowerment" as an ideal veers towards a certain liberal idea of the individual. As Tharu and Niranjana (1994: 101–3) point out, with reference to the contraception initiatives introduced in India, the assumption that "choice" will lead to "empowerment" is not always correct. Apart from pointing out the dubious quality of contraceptives that are not used in the west, but made for control of subject or recalcitrant populations, these

497

writers also take issue with the suggestion that contraception is itself "an empowering technical fix that can bypass sexual politics." In conservative- or religion-bound contexts, the possibility of some semblance of control is undoubtedly liberating – but feminist practice must be committed to addressing changes in existing family and social relations which will follow this. Empowerment consisting of elements of self-confidence, inner strength, the ability to control life inside and outside the home, seems to assume a self-contained individual whose social location and context has no effect on her. If this individual is located at the interstice of a gendered and "classed" socioeconomic hierarchy, then these will affect her "empowerment," and the changes wrought within the interacting systems as the result of "empowerment" cannot be separated from the process of "empowerment" itself.

Another anomaly in this concept is its apparent economic neutrality. Agarwal (1994) points out that education and employment seem to have a priority on development agendas, unlike land reforms, in favor of men. The reason, she argues, is because not only land rights but the process of aquiring them requires confrontation of hegemonic gender and class ideology in every sphere. The demand for economic justice is too radical and apparently upsets the distribution of power within society – in that sense, it also calls into question the political equation between donors and recipients, and if pursued far enough would certainly lead to a destabilization of those relations. Agarwal conceives of gender relations as "historically constructed by a process of contestation" in form and content as well as in the different arenas in which these relations are deployed. This approach encapsulates the dynamic process of the construction of gender relations within a socioeconomic context, a dynamism and contextualization absent from an essentialist and implicitly liberal concept of empowerment. As a goal of feminist practice in "post" colonial locations, "empowerment" must be reconceptualized with respect to the relative material realities of target groups. Without this, it remains only partially effective, which may prove detrimental to the interests and material conditions of those very groups it seeks to "empower."

It is this limitation of the concept that is reflected in the division of women's needs into "strategic" and "practical" gender needs in the development literature (Molyneux, 1985; Moser, 1991; Hlupekile-Longwe, 1991). In the former case, these needs arise out of the "analysis of women's subordination to men . . . [those needs] identified to overcome women's subordination will vary depending on the particular cultural and sociopolitical context" (Moser, 1991). The second set derives "from the concrete conditions women experience, in their position within the gendered division of labour, and come out from their practical gender interests for human survival" (ibid.). It is difficult indeed to conceptualize the subordination of women of sociopolitical and cultural contexts without grounding this in the concrete conditions of women's position within division of labor. "Practical gender interests" arise from particular contexts, and the strategies and materials available to women to fulfill these interests are also related to these contexts. The disjunction of one from the other seems to echo the idea of "empowerment" limited to an individual's realization of her "inner resources." As Agarwal (1994) points out, meeting subsistence needs often involves challenging existing production relations and confronting resistance – hence "empowerment" is irrevocably linked to both economic equality and social and political power. Though a distinction has been made between the "welfarist" notion of development and the "empowerment" notion (Snyder, 1995), limiting women's empowerment to the woman's self in isolation from her material reality does not really proceed beyond the rationale underlying the "welfare" notion. If we use Sen's (1992) concept of the "freedom to achieve," i.e., the real opportunity to accomplish what we value, reflected in a person's "capability to function," we are in a position to appreciate the distinction. To expect a woman to acquire "internal strength," "control," "choice," and "ability" without locating her in a social matrix that regulates her "capability to function," as Sen calls it, seems a liberal humanist effort, as if substantive internal qualities await only to be awakened and brought to action. The "real" opportunity that a woman will create or seize, will always be related to a material context, her negotiation with this context in order to identify, produce, or act upon this opportunity as well as her ability to tackle the effects of the change these actions will bring about in her location within a socioeconomic context.

However, the very idea of sustainable development, with its ecofriendly and community-based grassroots approach, has found champions not only among those who deploy development capital, but among feminists in "post" colonial locations as well. Apart from the perception of these projects as means to empower women, they are also seen as remedial for the environmental degradation that has occurred through the technological concept of development, which disempowers women, devalues traditional sources of knowledge, and depletes natural resource (Shiva, 1988). This view has been criticized on several counts (Agarwal, 1996), primarily as an essentialist argument that does not "adequately explore the concrete processes and institutions [by which] ideological constructions of gender and nature have changed." Also, it doesn't recognize the various ideological strands in ethnic and religious diversity, especially in the case of India. The ecofeminist argument singles out the imposition of Western science and developmental concepts on local bases of inequalities but fails to take account of the complex interactions between "colonial and precolonial [formations] that define parameters within which development, resource use and social change have to proceed" (1996: 211). Agarwal proposes instead a "feminist environmentalist" approach, where the relations of men and women with nature are related to the material reality structured by gender and class organizations of production, reproduction, and distribution. The struggle over resources and meanings will lead to material changes in notions of gender and actual division of work and resource allocation between genders, which is the feminist aspect of this approach. On the environmental front, these changes are the results of and will affect the transformed notions about relations between people and nature, as well as actual methods of appropriation of nature's resources by a minority (1996: 212). This concretizes gender and class relations in terms of distribution of property, power, and knowledge, and in the formulation of development policies and programs (241).

It is from this perspective that one can view the practical outcome of "sustainable development" projects in various "post" colonial locations.

Certain writers see the problem realistically, if not from a feminist perspective. For example, Nelson (1981) sees development as a process that must not disturb the social equation – "Women's abilities, productivity and autonomy must be promoted in ways that do not threaten men overtly" (8). The reason is also clear: "Women's lives cannot be transformed in a vaccuum and the men must be brought along with the process of transformation" (ibid.). The conflict between women, whose lives must change, and other groups in society, whether they are men or women of the same or different classes, can be dealt with in two ways. Either, as Nelson sees it, the existing structure of socioeconomic relations should be maintained, and women's "empowerment" through development will mean their full participation in this structure of relations, without causing any disturbance internally. Such projects have been widely documented. The focus is generally on making basic necessities available to women through projects in which they are involved directly, and areas where the roles they are required to take on do not conflict too radically with the social image that they must present (Snyder, 1995: 71–2, 90–1). In some cases, the traditional rights of women over scarce resources, and the replenishment of the environment through traditional resource-management systems are revived in the aftermath of colonial dismantling followed by the effects of development, and then legitimized through the structures of the "post" colonial state (Wacker, 1994).

The other experience is that of Self-Employed Women's Association (SEWA), where unionization and the cooperative principle have been deployed to cover hitherto unorganized women involved in apparently marginal homework, and then the government has been pressurized to legitimize the grassroots initiative. In this case, too, there is an attempt to translate experience into policy – but it is not a process of accommodation to or revival of existing structures. Rather, it is transformative, in that those who were hitherto outside the formal jural scope, and hence to a great extent either invisible or unaccounted for, now become part of the official system of demands and redress (Rose, 1992). In the case of SEWA, the experience and its translation into policy through grassroots pressure meant a consequent broadening and redefinition of the way in which the "mainstream" is conceptualized. As Mohanty (1997) shows, this is crucial in order to clearly perceive the gendered division of labor that keeps multinational capital viable, and to challenge the system that exploits women in "post" colonial as well as ex-colonizer locations. Defining these women as subjects will require reference to class and race, as well as their position in the production process. But the long arm of aid-funded development is likely to reach each of the sites of identity construction, to interact variously with local politics, the traditional gender hierarchy, the class–caste configurations, and produce a different meaning of "empowerment" in each. Kabeer (1994) outlines a method for assessing the "transformatory aspects" of empowerment strategies and emphasizes organizational empowerment. Women struggle within a given set of policy priorities – they must be empowered to challenge and reverse these priorities, to participate beyond micro, i.e. project, level in the broader policymaking agenda.

In the final analysis, what appears to be obvious is that the fruits of sustainable or empowering development may be beneficial to women's material conditions of living – but need not necessarily be "feminist"[3] as Tharu and Niranjana (1994: 107–8) argue with reference to the anti-arrack movement of rural women in Andhra Pradesh. Here familial values were emphasized as the dynamic force of the movement: if men stopped throwing away their earnings on arrack, their families would not have to face economic hardship. This is a question that inevitably comes up on the agenda of feminist practice in "post" colonial locations. In theory, the politics of power within and outside the family, the gender division of labor, and the symbolic representation of women in the public and private sphere are to be questioned. In practice, among the weakest and most deprived sections of women, the issue of a livelihood, or a job, is a survival issue; and in order to secure these, they are ready to question and actively subvert the existing hierarchy of gender and economic power. It seems that practice in these cases is driven by the desire for better material conditions of living – at the most, the ideal of feminine self-fulfillment is something that may be achieved in the process of attaining the material goal. In some cases women appear to have no quarrel with some parts of their traditionally defined role-scripts. But those parts that prevent them from ensuring better material conditions for themselves and their families, especially their children, are those that they challenge.[4] This makes the nature of their engagements different, and this difference will be variously played out in various "post" colonial locations with varied gender organizations and ideologies, a point I have tried to explore in comparisons between different Indian and African societies. Yet, the similarity is in the dynamics of their collective action resulting not only from conscientization about their deprived and oppressed status as women, but also from the struggle to make available material resources with which to combat deprivation and oppression. And this is characteristic of the practice of deprived groups, of those who belong to the economically exploited sections. As Jonasdottir (1985) points out, the "needs" and "interests" perspectives must be taken together in the case of crafting an agenda for feminist practice, if the tension that Molyneux (1985) identifies between "what is" and what "could be" is to be resolved in formulations of policies and programs of development as well as in feminist responses to them. As Kabeer (1994) points out, piecemeal measures for empowerment can threaten women's practical interests in the short term and entail losses that are likely to affect them in the long run as well. "Interests" emerge out of different dimensions of social life, but are rooted in experiences; they are born of routine practices of daily life and discernible through different kinds of practice, which bring about new basis for experience and knowledge (Kabeer, 1994). If the strategy for fulfillment of "needs" furthers women's "interests" in enabling them to discern their *structural* as well as individual status in an exploitative economic and social hierarchy, these needs and strategies may be termed feminist.

It is within this context that "post" colonial feminist practice shapes and is shaped by "post" colonial realities. In the final part of this chapter, I have read the discourse of "development" from the perspective of "post" colonial practice that I have attempted to outline in the first part. This is because the politics and economics of "development" are a rather potent force in shaping material conditions in the lowest rungs of "post" colonial societies as well as in crafting the political response to them. It is through this exploration that I have attempted to pose and come to terms with problem that the western–educated feminist activist/intellectual must face at this historical juncture, when we are critical of globalization but are rather too welcoming to "development." I would argue that we find echoes of our own ambiguous hybridity in "post" colonial theory, and are eager enough to espouse the cause of specificity on the one hand. On the other, as feminists, we also seek links to women's movements in other areas, whether in "post" colonial locations or among the oppressed in ex-colonizer locations. Thus our attempts to articulate the "global" with the "local" – but the final question that then arises is, what is the nature of the "local"? Does it become feminist automatically by addressing women's needs in a general "developmental" way?

In a succinct comment upon the different positions a western-educated woman like me may occupy *vis-à-vis* the feminist movement, Agarwal (1994b) identifies the routes by which we come to feminism. They are intellectual, emotional routes that lead us to sympathy and outrage on behalf of others. Unlike those women who are among the targets of development capital or organized violence, they are not connected with issues of survival. It is in our context that "strategic" and "gender" needs and interests may be separated – but not in the context of those for whom the issue is one of survival. For them, the organization and definition of gender is itself different from our perception of the same categories. It is perhaps time that we organized these categories to reflect this experience from below, rather than fit our version of "local" experiences to a "global" framework. In that sense, perhaps feminist practice can never be a macrolevel concept. More properly, it may well borrow from Sangari's (1987) idea of "the politics of the possible" as "demarcating a domain over which [one] can exercise control," a politics "tied to specific location." Perhaps feminist practice will always be written in lower case and in the plural, as perhaps "feminism" itself should be.

Does that put us back into the isolated divisions deployed by colonialist formulations, and further rearticulated by "post" colonial theory, for different purposes and in different forms? This question can be answered by invoking qualities which I see as characterizing feminism – that it is a transformative politics, with the potential to make change towards a more equitable society. If it may be called an ideology in the established sense of the term, it is an ideology of support for those who are deprived and exploited by the institutionalized structures of control that operate in different forms in different social formations. Feminism's dynamic strength lies in its constant questioning of structure and hierarchy on the one hand and its constant battle against division and isolationism on the other. And because the creation of institutions implies the concentration of power in the hands of some, and poses a consequent barrier to the formation of broad collectives that oppose such concentration, feminism cannot itself become an institutionalized ideology, applicable across space and time, with fixed and unidirectional goals that would identify it with those political ideologies whose end is the seizing of power in the name of various groups. It is from this standpoint that feminism differs. If there are people in power, there will be those who are oppressed. The history of colonization, decolonization, and formation of the "post" colonial state on the one hand, and the history of different forms of exploitation on the other, have made us painfully aware of the dynamics behind apparent change, "progress," "modernization," and "development." Feminist practices in "post" colonial locations are shaped by this realization.

Feminists have long conceptualized the methods of research (Stanley and Wise, 1992) and the theory of knowledge from premises and with goals different to those considered "normal" or "scientific" by patriarchal society. Here I wish to merely emphasize that reciprocity is crucial to the structuring of our realities relative to the different positions we occupy as women in "post" colonial societies, and also to forging a common agenda. This would involve rethinking the liberal/charitable view of structural and functional inequalities that characterize "post" colonial societies, and a naive view of feminist solidarity that attempts to gloss over these inequalities. Confronting the reality of these anomalies and their effect upon our individual and collective lives as women, forms the bases of feminist identity. The commitment to changing these realties towards an equal society forms the bases of a feminist ethics. In "post" colonial locations, we are interpellated by different versions of "feminism." As consumers in a "developing" economy implicated within global structures of capital, women are addressed by a designer version of feminism as a lifestyle choice which hard-sells labor-saving devices to "free" the "modern" woman from bondage to "traditional" female chores. As a bourgeois academic I am addressed by the liberal humanist verson of empowering 'inner-resources' feminism which posits a substantive human essence transcending all forms of socioeconomic power-play. But there is also the ideology and practice that underpins my daily life as a woman inhabiting complex, multilayered realities that must be differentially negotiated in order to best utilize scarce resources to meet basic necessary needs at the collective and individual levels. I share one or more of these positions with women across class, religion, and caste/"tribe" in "post" colonial locations – but the relative force of these often conflicting interpellations are varied and may only be differentially negotiated across class and religious or caste/"tribe" formations. This encapsulates and contextualizes the similarities and differences in our positions in "post" colonial locations: factors that must be understood, and then negotiated through the experience of collective struggle.

This realization is my personal gain from the explorations I have undertaken in the course of writing this essay. It seems appropriate, therefore, to end with an acknowledgment of the "victories that are also warnings" (Spivak 1994) which marks the complex nature of feminist engagements in "post" colonial locations.

An acknowledgment – but perhaps also a question. Positioned as we are, and defined by the constraints of our position, is it not possible to explore the way beyond, the path that breaks through the tangled imposed binaries of Individual and Collective which make our "victories" "warnings"?

An acknowledgment of the warnings – but perhaps also an attempt to keep the dialectic in operation: warnings that are the dynamics behind the victories?

Notes

In gratitude to those who worked as hard as I did to prepare this essay: everyone at the School of Women's Studies office; Sir G. Purakaith, who processed it; and S. Chakravorty Dasgupta and S. Bannerji Chakravorty, who always listen wisely and need I add patiently. Also Henry, without whom . . .

1   I use the concept of "gender discourse" to mean that which allows a woman to make sense of her own experience, as distinct from "gender ideology" that delineates the conceptual space within which the gender roles ascribed to women by hegemonic social and economic formations are deployed and scripted. See J. K. Cowan, "Being a Feminist in Contemporary Greece: Similarity and Difference Reconsidered," in N. Charles and F. Hughes-Freeland, eds., *Practising Feminism: Identity, Difference, Power*. London, New York: Routledge, 1996, pp. 61–85.
2   For a summary of the changing discourse of development and the documents reflecting them, see C. Bunch and R. Carrillo, "Feminist Perspectives on Women in Development," in Tinker, ed. (1990: 72–92). For a critique of "aid" and "development" funded by First World donors from the perspective of global solidarity and feminist internationalism, see Peter Waterman "Hidden From Herstory: Feminism and New Global Solidarity," in *Economic and Political Weekly*, 28 (44) (Oct. 30, 1993): 83.
3   I put "feminist" here within quotes to indicate (and follow) the general line of argument that Tharu and Niranjana also gesture towards here – that feminism is a western import, an extraneous addition that threatens women's natural rights and duties, and that there is a chasm between this ideology-as-false-consciousness and these "natural" rights and duties.

4   The anti-arrack movement in Andhra Pradesh and Haryana were both finally sacrificed to electoral politics, the latter being a casualty of the 1998 elections. The reasons for the failure of prohibition as a "broad-based" rather than a "women's issue-based" political plank were many: the drainage of revenue to other "wet" states where liquor was available, and where men went, crossing the borders, to drink; illicit liquor brewing and liquor smuggling as industries in which women, who had worked to enforce prohibition, participated in order to earn; etc.

References

Adams, M. L. (1989). "There's No Place Like Home: On the Place of Identity in Feminist Politics," *Feminist Review*, 31 (Spring).

Agarwal, B. (1988). *State Community and the Household in Asia*. New Delhi and London, Kali and Zed.

——. (1994a). *A Field of One's Own*. Cambridge South Asia Studies. Cambridge, Cambridge University Press.

——. (1994b). "Positioning the Western Feminist Agenda: A Comment," *Indian Journal of Gender Studies*, 1, no. 2 (July–Dec.).

Antrobus, P. (1991). "Women in Development," in Wallace and March, eds.

Beneria L. and G. Sen. (1979). "Reproduction, Production and the Sexual Division of Labour," *Cambridge Journal of Economics*, 3: 203–25.

——. (1981). "Accumulation, Reproduction and Women's Role in Economic Development: Boserup Revisited," *Signs*, 7: 279–98.

——. (1982). "Class and Gender Inqualities and Women's Role in Eco Development: Theoretical and Practical Duplications," *Feminist Studies*, 8, no. 1: 157–76.

Boserup, E. (1970). *Women's Role in Economic Development*. London, Allen & Unwin.

Brah, A. (1991). "Questions of Difference and International Feminism," in J. Aaron and S. Walby, eds., *Out of the Margins: Women's Studies in the Nineties*. London, Falmer Press, 168–76.

Chen, M. (1983). *A Quiet Revolution: Women in Transition in Rural Bangladesh*. Cambridge, Mass., Schenkman.

——. (1995). "Women's Right to Employment in India and Bangladesh," in Nussbaum and Glover, eds., 37–57.

Colson, E. (1962). "African Society at the Time of the Scramble," in Gann and Duignan, eds., 27–60.

Dankelman I. and J. Davidson, eds. (1988). *Women and Environment in the Third World: Alliance for the Future*. London, Earthscan.

Deshpande, S. (1998). "Impasse in Language of Rights. Questions of Context" *Economic and Political Weekly*, 33, no. 5: 11-13.

Fraser, N. (1989). *Unruly Practices: Power, Discourse and Gender in Contemporary Social Theory*. Minneapolis, University of Minnesota Press.

Gann, H. L. and P. Duignan, eds. (1962). *Colonialism in Africa 1870–1940*, vol. I. Cambridge, Cambridge University Press.

Ghai, D. and J. M. Vivien, eds. (1990). *Grassroots Environmental Action: People's Participation in Sustainable Development*. New York and London, Routledge.

Heyzer, N. (1994). "Market, State and Gender Equity," in Heyzer and Sen, eds.

Heyzer, N. and G. Sen, eds. (1994). *Gender, Economic Growth and Poverty: Market Growth and State Planning in Asia and the Pacific*. New Delhi, Kali International.

Hirschon, R., ed. (1984). *Women and Property: Women as Property*. London & Canberra, Croom Helm; New York, St. Martin's Press, Oxford Women's series.

Hlupekile-Longwe, S. (1991). "Gender Awareness: The Missing Element in the Third World Development Project," in Wallace and March, eds., 149–57.

Inden, R. (1990). *Imagining India*. London, Blackwell.

Jonasdottir, A. G. (1985). "On the Concept of Interests, Women's Interests and the Limitations of Interest Theory," in K. B. Jones and Jonasdottir, eds., *Development Theory and Research with a Feminist Face*. London, Sage.

Kabeer, N. (1994). *Reversed Realities: Gender Hierarchies in Development Thought*. New Delhi, Kali.

Kopytoff, I. T., ed. (1987). *The African Frontier*. Bloomington and Indianapolis, Indiana University Press.

Menon, N. (1998). "State/Gender/Community: Citizenship in Contemporary India," *Economic and Political Weekly*, 33, no. 5: 3–10.

Minh-ha, T. T. (1989). *Woman, Native Other: Writing Postcoloniality and Feminism*. Bloomington, Indiana University Press.

Mohanty, C. T. (1984). "Under Western Eyes: Feminist Scholarship and Colonial Discourse," *boundary 2*, 12 (3), 13 (1) (Spring/Fall): 333–58.

——. (1991). "Cartographies of Struggle," in Mohanty *et al.*, eds., 1–47.

——. (1997). "Women Workers and Capitalist Scripts: Ideologies of Domination, Common Interests and Politics of Solidarity," in Mohanty and Alexander, eds., 3–29.

—— and J. M. Alexander eds. (1997). *Feminist Genealogies Colonial Legacies Democratic Futures*. New York, Routledge.

——, A. Russo, and L. Torres, eds. (1991). *Third World Women and the Politics of Feminism*. Bloomington, Indiana University Press.

Molyneux, M. (1985). "Mobilisation without Emancipation: Women's Interests, State and Revolution in Nicaragua," *Feminist Studies*, 2, no. 2: 227–54.

Moser, C. (1991). "Gender Planning in the Third World: Meeting Practical and Strategic Gender Needs," in Wallace and March, eds., 157–81.

Nelson, N., ed. (1981). *African Women in the Development Process*. London, Frank Cass.

Nussbaum, M. (1995). "Human Capabilities Female Human Beings," in Nussbaum and Glover, eds., 61–96.

—— and J. Glover, eds. (1995). *Women, Culture and Development: A Study of Human Capabilities*. Oxford. Clarendon.

Parmar, P. (1989). "Other Kinds of Dreams," *Feminist Review*, 31, Spring.

Sangari, K. (1987). "Politics of the Possible," *Cultural Critique*, 7: 157–86.

Sen, A. (1992). *Inequality Re-examined*. Oxford, Clarendon.

Sen, G. and C. Grown. (1988). *Development, Crises and Alternate Visions: Third World Women's Perspectives*. London, Earthscan.

Sen, I., ed. (1990). *A Space within the Struggle*. New Delhi, Kali.

Shah, N. and N. Gandhi. (1991). *Issues at Stake: Theory and Practice in the Contemporary Women's Movement*. New Delhi, Kali.

Shiva, V. (1988). *Staying Alive: Women, Ecology and Survival in India*. New Delhi, Kali.

Snyder, M. (1995). *Transforming Development: Women, Poverty and Politics*. London, Intermediate Technology Publications.

Spivak, G. C. (1988). "Can the Subaltern Speak? Speculations on Widow Sacrifice," in C. Nelson and L. Grossberg, eds., *Marxism and the Interpretation of Culture*. London, Macmillan, 271–310.

———. (1990). "Practical Politics of the Open End." Interview with S. Harasym, in S. Harasym, ed., *The Post-Colonial Critic: Interviews, Strategies, Dialogues*. New York, London, Routledge, 95–112.

———. (1994). *Imaginary Maps*. Calcutta, Thema.

Stanley, L. and S. Wise. (1992). *Breaking Out Again*. New York, Routledge.

Suleri, S. (1993). "Woman Skin Deep: Feminism and the Post Colonial Condition," *Critical Inquiry* 18 (4) (Summer): 756–69.

Tharu, S. and T. Niranjana. (1994). "Problems for a Contemporary Theory of Gender," *Social Scientist*, 22, nos. 3/4 (April).

Tinker, I., ed. (1990). *Persistent Inequalities: Women and World Development*. New York: Oxford University Press.

Urdang, S. (1989). *And Still They Dance: Women, War and the Struggle for Change in Mozambique*. London, Earthscan.

Wacker, C. (1994). "Sustainable Development Through Women's Groups: A Cultural Approach to Sustainable Development," in W. Harcourt, ed., *Feminist Perspectives on Sustainable Development*. London and New Jersey, Zed Books.

Wallace, T. and C. March, eds. (1991). *Changing Perceptions: Writings on Gender and Development*. London, Oxfam.

WCED (World Commission on Environment and Development). (1987). *Our Common Future*. Oxford and New York, Oxford University Press.

Chapter 26

Global Gay Formations and Local Homosexualities

Katie King

This is both a breathtaking and daunting historical moment in which to attempt to comment in a postcolonial context on alternatives to "heterosexuality" – experiences and behaviors, identities and politics, institutionalizations, conceptualizations, and scholarship. Contemporary globalization processes are so intertwined with the relevant fields – of study, of action, of power – that whatever one may say will surely prove to be dated momentarily. So rather than be "encompassing" – the wrong move at any moment – I will offer the best "snapshot" of this moment that I can. I will focus less on bibliography, which is breathlessly proliferating right now, and more on broad structural concerns and questions, which are the productive constraints both enabling and limiting our understanding as I write.

1 Globalization Processes and Layers of Locals and Globals

In 1989 I found the phrase "Global Gay Formations and Local Homosexualities" especially useful in thinking about international art activism directed at the worldwide epidemic called AIDS and in response to scholarship on the history of sexuality, understanding each as also a new site for the production of globalizing sexual identities. Under globalization the global and the local pluralize; their relations to material life and to conceptualizations becoming material forces is foregrounded; necessarily relative and relational, their dynamic interactions are fiercely and even brutally productive. Under contemporary regimes of globalized economic processes, repressive or neoliberal, many experience so-called "hyper-oppression": that is, an intensification of exploitation that matches the intensified extension of global capital. Postcolonial analysis has had to take into account not only these forces as contemporary and disjunctive, but also to see them within the long continuous history of capitalist expansion, trade, exploration, underdevelopment, and before, during, and perhaps after, the formation of the nation-state and various colonial, anticolonial, and postcolonial nationalisms.

Sexuality is constituted out of such intensely problematic processes. Global Gay Formations today are multiple examples of these productions, as are any other alternatives to heterosexuality and as are heterosexualities. Local Homosexualities are dynamically interconnected to these globalizations, in refusal, in transformation, in exchange, in contribution, in opposition, in activism. It is its historical, material, and theoretical instability that counterintuitively makes the phrase "Global Gay Formations and Local Homosexualities" a useful descriptor. Problematic and tricky, it is workable only with great difficulty and with questions and elaborate critiques at every point. Immediately the word Gay is an obvious problem: does it include/exclude women, for whom, where and when? What counts as a Global Gay Formation? I began such thinking by considering international AIDS activisms, artistic, educational, medical, but equally salient are others also interconnected and politically problematic, such as Gay tourism in general, or Gay sex tourism in particular. Similarly double-edged are political strategies, such as appropriations of human rights language for political movements and attempts to get such language into new state and governmental documents; for example, ones creating the new European Union. Such extensions of democratic machinery are available only encrusted by late capitalist neoliberalism. Similarly Gay Studies understood as a Global Gay Formation is also problematic. Feminists and Lesbians in EU countries – the Netherlands is one – have complained that men have commandeered resources for Gay Studies and excluded women. Certainly this is a different situation than in the US, where currently women's studies nationally is much more likely to have resources and to house and nurture lesbian studies than gay studies is likely to marshal the same sort of assets. In another register, the word Gay used in this tentatively inclusive way brings up, on the one hand, the possibility of an oppositional alliance of women and men under a common rubric – one salient in earlier gay liberation generations but called into question with the rise of seventies feminism, and sometimes created anew around another term, Queer. On the other hand though, it also bring up only too many realities about male generics more generally, their powers of imperializing inclusions, their production of new marginalities. Of course the phrase rings ironically as well, since Gay as Global provokes oppositional reflection on powerful historical and cultural *specificities*, while simultaneously emphasizing that such very specific formations also travel globally, along lines of activisms, tourisms, and commodities in production, and thus always within fields of power.

Similarly "Local Homosexualities" is also extremely problematic. Emphasizing Homosexualities rather than, say, "Local Sexualities," allows that the medicalized, legalized term, intended to be "universal," is attached to the local – that is, actually historically and culturally specific. Meanwhile the more obviously historically recent activist political term is the one, inverted, that travels so variously. Nonetheless, "homosexuality" is also a traveling set of discourses, used in some places for medicalized forms of oppression, in others for specifying sexual practices that aren't indigenous, in others as a universal term with both its liberations and its dominations. My point is that the phrase "Global Gay Formations and Local Homosexualities" is carefully and deliberately jarring: it is a phrase of great problematic productivity, that emphasizes that there are many "globals," both kinds of and layers of, and many "locals," places, particularisms, and conceptualizations. Thus it is impossible to ignore that globals and locals are plural, are relative and relational, and that each of these overflowing terms are in fact politicized technologies, in layers of globals and locals, for materially producing people (what Donna Haraway calls "an apparatus of bodily production").

Such metaphors and material realities of travel are subject to rich postcolonial and cultural geographical critique as well: without problematically producing such critique comparable theoretical entities can be *too* stable, unable then to point out over and over the fields of power in which they are embedded. Metaphors of cartography, geographical location, and movement, often function as privileged but deeply problematic signs which articulate these "maps" of meanings within fields of power under global capital. The resonances of the term *travel* – from that of tourists, to refugees and immigrants, to political and cultural workers, from USAID to human rights activists – describe both material bodily movement of people in space but also at times the movement of ideas, policies, transgressions, commerce through physical space and now also virtual space. Virtual space, that is, through the internet and the World Wide Web, where activisms, scholarship, NGOs and governmental groups, pornographers, and businesses, and individuals publish, sell to, view, and photograph themselves and others.

Travel connects both locals and globals. We need much more dynamic ways of understanding the anthropology and history of sexuality and of contemporary global social movements that include the point that globalization depends upon a new kind of horizontal integration: that is, "markets" identified as demographic groups beyond rather than within geographical boundaries. For example, sexuality globalized as ethnicity; say, naming and exploiting an international "Gay" market, especially targeting "Gay" people traveling, migrating, and moved around; or say, rhetorical and political naming and consolidating an international "Gay" human rights movement, especially through the production of new NGOs as political activism shifts in relation to the legalities of the nation-state; or say, naming and producing new scientific apparatus and body maps for a "Gay" gene, especially in the context of biotech funding, both by the state and by commerce, for genetic interventions in the apparatus of bodily production. Such globalization creates both commercial and political identities. The generic and the particular are shifted back and forth in layers of locals and globals under globalization, ethnic and sexual and sexual-ethnic mixtures – the morphed – have special salience, necessarily both relative and relational. Valorizations of the local, the particular, or the located have to be distinguished for their political valences. Since "Global" and "Local" are also conceptual terms with political values, it is important to realize that located knowledges are not necessarily local. "Located"

– a term newly revalued and valorized by postcolonial theorists and anthropologists – is not equivalent to "local," even if it is appropriately understood as partial and particular. Nor does "global" always mean universal, singular, ahistorical; it cannot be unilaterally critiqued as simply foundational or humanist, if there are layers of globals also material and conceptualizations with material powers.

Indeed, the density of this moment within multiple histories is palpable in another way as well, since Global Gay Formations can also describe the investments of contemporary gay folk in creating transhistorical continuities, across time and accountable to very local, indeed culturally quite narrow, political meanings and strategies. These too are themselves ephemeral, and soon to be replaced with other objects of knowledge, with other centers producing objects of knowledge, those perhaps also transhistorical or perhaps global by some other conceptual apparatus. The histories of sexuality are fractured by contests to create or refuse such continuities and discontinuities. Local Homosexualities similarly names the varieties of particularisms also created out of other political and pedagogical purposes today. Especially salient are cultural sites in which the constructions that produce heterosexuality and homosexuality as mutually exclusive and diadic, are denied, eroded, refused, or simply not engaged. The term "Same Sex Sex," which has several registers of currency today, is important in this context. Same Sex Sex separates, or refuses to conflate, behaviors and sexual identities. It is a useful term in global HIV education and increasingly in activism around AIDS, and in the anthropology of sexuality. It is less used in, say, the history of sexuality. In this context compare the political and generational currencies of the overlapping, sometimes competing, sometimes oppositional uses of the terms, "Gay" and its ranges of inclusive naming, "Lesbian and Gay," "Lesbian, Gay, and Bisexual," "Lesbian, Gay, Bisexual, and Transgendered" – alongside with "Same Sex Sex," "Homosexual," and "Queer." One might also name a host of terms intended as historically or culturally local or alternative formations, for example, the tribade, or the penetrator.

2   The Productive Instability of the Term Queer

The term "Queer" is conceptually and politically useful precisely because its range of meanings is so unstable today. For example, for historians of sexuality it might allow for a clearly and self-consciously presentist global analytic metacategory that is thus distinct and separable from the historically specific formations focused upon in a politics of disjunction and in a scholarly and pedagogical production of historical alterity. Alternatively, histories of sexuality that celebrate or focus upon the presence of historic homosexualities in a politics of continuity may use Queer as an inclusive term producing such continuities without too much concern for metalanguage. Which terms will function as metaterms or global analytic categories and for what political purposes are some of the contests around the term Queer. Other political appropriations of the term are generational, and postcolonial.

Queer used as a term to mark the differences between generations of political actors can be self-valorizing, or critical, depending on the standpoint of the analysis. For example, Queer as a self-identification can represent a politics that refuses dichotomies between heterosexual and homosexual, or among those heterosexual, homosexual, bisexual, and transgendered, or that allies with sexual and sexual-ethnic minorities otherwise reduced by the term heterosexual. It can valorize "coming-out" earlier in one's life, during socially liminal periods of childhood or adolescence, perhaps made more possible with greater social tolerance, and create generational cohorts with such similar experiences. It can refuse the institutionalized authorities and knowledges associated with Women's Studies or with Gay Studies and the politics of their institutional actors and their pedagogies. It can refuse what it calls "labeling," as an implicit critique of identity politics or as an implicit valorization of individualism. Such generational meanings may be conflated with postcolonial concerns as well, and thus refuse the imperializations of Gay Liberation as a global movement, of human rights discourse as a liberation within neoliberal paradigms, refuse feminisms and women's movements from so-called developed countries and their resources for representation, such as films, books, and other forms of information and propaganda.

Alternatively, critiques of the term Queer may contest for such political evaluations: for example, might refuse as inaccurate and inadequate political assumptions about the powers and resources of Women's Studies, feminism and women's movements, as too various, generationally, geographically, and in institutionalizations, to be made monolithic and unilaterally rejected. Critiques of the term Queer might practice their own generational politics, constructing a self-valorizing history of political movement now misunderstood and not valued by subsequent generations, although indebted to it materially and politically. Queer may be critiqued as a term so saturated by globalized commerce and capitalist appropriations of sexual identities as to be only a creature of late capitalism, without contemporary liberatory value. In this register Queer may be so associated with globalized capital that it is rejected as another agent of cultural, economic, and political imperialism. Queer may be primarily associated with academic cultural analysis and rejected as theoretical and trendy; or Queer may be primarily associated with disruptive avant-garde activisms and performances and rejected as politically self-destructive and/or elitist. In all its forms Queer may be critiqued for overvaluing a discontinuous history of sexual politics rather than one with powerful and material continuities.

I would contend that in no sense does this instability of meanings and politics evacuate the term and render it meaningless. On the contrary, the term Queer is a powerfully productive site from which new alliances, identities, and political strategies are being born – in appropriation, refusal, and critique, in conceptualizations and in activisms. In other words, Queer is a concept coming to have material consequences and powers, just as I've already claimed for the many elements within the phrase "Global Gay Formations and Local Homosexualities." As such a liminal concept, unstable in its formative uses and reformations, Queer has been especially useful in the history of sexuality to mark inchoate pre-institutional processes and formations placed into an epistemological history of social constructions. In terms of political vision, Queer can also stand for new liberatory practices not yet possible but envisionable, or even not yet envisionable, but longed for. Queering – as a verb – can emphasize both history and politics within an epistemological framework that shows how social constructions come-into-being within fields of power. Or Queering can represent new methodologies that emphasize such epistemological historical processes.

Queer may also be used as either an internal or external critique of identity politics. Queer sexualities may be understood as sexualities that don't produce identities, or as sexual politics that don't lead to identity politics, or refuse it. Queer may mark anti-essentialist political intentions, either within identity politics or in a critique that assumes that all identity politics are essentially essentialist. Conversely Queer may be used in a strategic essentialism to produce new collectivities and alliances. In a generational politics of disjunction, Queer may be used in a limiting move, rejecting whole systems of political alliance and academic and political literatures, as a way of processing overwhelming weights of materials, inheritances, generational subjections, and illegitimate uses of generational and geopolitical power.

I am inclined to use the term Gay for some of these purposes, as my use of "Global Gay Formations and Local Homosexualities" suggests, and for largely generational reasons. But I understand Queer and Gay as alternate terms which could each stand as the metacategory to the other, with different political valences. My politics conceptually emphasizes historical epistemologies of social constructions and a longing for ways to enliven the dynamic relations between universal and particular, unmarked and marked uses of Gay, Queer, and Lesbian. I also intend to emphasize the materialities of globalization processes and local powers in an anti-essentialist identity politics that continually comes up with new methods for self-critique and reformulated political visions accountable to changing movements of power, a conceptualization-in-process that I designate under the rubric "layers of globals and locals." I turn to the term "Lesbian" as also alternately universal and historical in terms both relative and relational, and thus implicated in "Global Gay Formations and Local Homosexualities."

Recall that "Man" epitomized the "unmarked" category in liberal humanism, the realized instrumentally active individual with political agency, able to stand in for and represent all humans, but thus also creating other, that is, "marked" categories: on the one hand, humans who can stand only for themselves as a particular kind of human, for example, women; or on the other hand, creating categories of beings only sometimes and contingently human, for example, slaves. Of course, women were sometimes only contingently human as well, and slaves were not accidentally produced as quasi-humans within a racialized economic apparatus of bodily production. Which categories are marked and unmarked shifts depending on the universe of discourse: for example, within feminist politics white women have only too often functioned as if able to represent all women, or heterosexual women held to have more "universal" concerns than lesbians. The words Gay and Queer have self-consciously positioned themselves as unmarked terms, for example, able to stand for many kinds and genders of alternative sexualities, as specific political interventions into several collectivities, and are often useful as such, or have had important political consequences. Yet the word "Lesbian" has not functioned to include men for example, while the term Gay has sometimes claimed to include women. Note how the range of inclusivities in the phrases "Lesbian and Gay," Lesbian, Gay, and Bisexual," and "Lesbian, Gay, Bisexual, and Transgendered" keeps "Lesbian," "Bisexual," and "Transgendered" as marked categories, while the word "Gay" continues to function as both marked and unmarked. I turn at this point in my argument to the term Lesbian, precisely because its ability to function as an unmarked category is limited and still palpably artificial. I want these palpabilities to remain, to sensitize such theorizations and to represent the difficulties and concerns of such politics.

3   Lesbianisms in Multinational Reception

As is the case with the Homosexual, the Lesbian is an object within an epistemological history which can be interrogated within a history of sexuality or within an anthropology of sexuality. Thinking through "Global Gay Formations and Local Homosexualities" emphasizes that diachronic and synchronic investigations are each accountable to and also always metaphors for and about today's sexual politics under the regime of globalized capital. Such investigation requires thinking in layers of locals and globals, emphasizing that they are relative and relational. Thus implicit in a history or an anthropology of sexuality is the question "What counts as a Lesbian?" – where the word Lesbian has multiple uses and meanings, uses and meanings not exhausted by local particularisms, valuable though they are, central though they are to particular projects. What this means is that no localism or particularism is not caught up in the dynamic interactions between globals and locals, be they geographical or across time. This does not however assume that all trajectories are toward the dominations of US/Euro cultural, political, economic formations, or the dominations of presentist conceptualizations of sexuality and the self, rather than the possibilities of multiple "locals" reassertion of the general priority and wide travel of Local forms. Which locals, and their relative powers under the regime of globalization, their material abilities to "travel" and within what fields of power, from immigration to the internet to currency as new archival objects, are the present circumstances that create new gay formations.

Within a global gay human rights activism the question "What counts as a Lesbian?" is made transparently powerful within "sexual orientation" as an element of the humanist individual self that is emancipated through inalienable rights as a human. Anthropological and historical concerns with particularist cultural forms are subordinated to the difficulties of producing international laws, treaties, and conventions that are answerable to democratic machinery that dates from the end of the Second World War and draws upon Enlightenment notions of liberty. Such productions create a new global citizen, whose claims upon human rights are not claims upon single nation-states, but rather upon continually-recreated-as-stable ideas of the "universal." Such "universals" are in fact quiet unstable, produced and reproduced with great difficulty, legally, militarily, economically, scientifically, and through other discourses, representational and materially powerful. Such politics can be understood as "essentialist" but with the caveat that "essentialism" properly marks the moment of stabilization in a contested social construction, a stability that changes momentarily – perhaps continually reproduced as "the same" through the institutionalizations of repressive political powers, or perhaps deconstructed and destabilized by oppositional movements, or perhaps struggled for as a liberatory practice, process, or identity, or most likely, in a complex, always changing mixture of all these contradictions and contestations.

Such politics might make global political interventions with strategic use of such universals. For example, asking of nation-states, as a transparently demographic question, "Where are the missing Gay people?" With the assumption of a range of human variability within "sexual orientation" and with the weight and authority of new genetic research that works to stabilize sexuality as biologically determined, diadic, and mutually exclusive, nation-states might be held accountable for their own insistence that "There are no Lesbians here," the corollary being that such absences mark "disappeared" people, for whom human rights intervention is necessary. That such "human rights" intervention could be put to repressive as well as liberatory purposes is only too obvious, as is also the ever present possibility that a biologically essentialized "Gay" gene is subject to genetic manipulation and attempts at control and genocide.

"There are no Lesbians here" may at other times actually be a local anti-colonial liberation politics that refuses the narrow social institutionalizations of some particular cultural formation, under the term "Lesbian," as inadequate to represent local practices, activisms, sexualities, or identities. The historical and fictive status of colonialism in the production of alternative sexualities, or in the recognition or rejection of indigenous sexualities is various, although the insistence that Homosexuality is an imposition of colonial rule can be repressive. One particular "local" formation, both geopolitically and chronologically local, the US 1970s feminist version of the "Lesbian," may unself-consciously be used as the standard, the unmarked category, by a variety of locals and globals, of the term "Lesbian," especially in the phrase, "There are no Lesbians here." Local, but also materially powerful under processes of globalization, this formation has

515

traveled widely, back through time in various historical and fictional discourses, and today via gay and feminist activisms, tourism, media, commerce, and medical, legal, and psychological discourses. This US 1970s feminist Lesbian's construction can be emblemized by three political claims: "Lesbianism is not a passing phase," "Lesbians don't ape heterosexuals," and "Bisexuals are confused Lesbians." Such claims create disjunctions from other sexual formations, historical or cross-cultural, that at various times have or could have also displayed under the sign "Lesbian."

For example, "Lesbianism is not a passing phase" excludes from naming under the sign "Lesbian," sexual and cultural practices that do not construct as mutually exclusive from marriage (especially) or other institutional forms of heterosexuality, sex, sex play, love, or affection, or varieties of stimulations between females, ones socially sanctioned, socially prohibited, or socially trivial. Especially "Lesbianism is not a passing phase" excludes from naming as this "Lesbian," sexual or cultural practices that are restricted to particular periods or to specific situations in a life cycle which prescribes marriage and motherhood. "Lesbians don't ape heterosexuals" excludes institutionalizations of gender-specialists, such as in some cultural-theatrical communities, or so-called "butch/femme" couplings, the so-called "mannish" lesbian, and sexual play with objects such as dildos, or sexual practices that figure the clitoris as an organ of penetration. Indeed, it is penetration itself that is especially prohibited with this claim. "Bisexuals are confused Lesbians" excludes all practices and identities that are either not accommodated within a mutually exclusive, diadic Homo/Hetero Sexuality, or that insist on identity-priority rather than practice-priority in an epistemology of polymorphous perversity. Bisexuality is figured only as a gateway in the production of Lesbians out of false heterosexuals. What is constructed is a Lesbianism that is life-long, stable after "coming-out," autonomous of heterosexuality, sex-centered, politically feminist, not situational, and exclusive of marriage. That this formation is both powerful and unstable is made clear by the range of contestations in US lesbian feminism over the decades of the 1970s, 1980s, and 1990s, all sorts of debates/struggles from The Lesbian Continuum to Butch/Femme couples to Gays in the Military to Sex Toys and S/M to Lesbian Bed-death and Lesbian Motherhood and Lesbian Domestic Violence and to Gay Marriage. This formation shadows dramatically the question "What counts as a Lesbian?" in any investigation of sexualities historically or cross-culturally. The range of contestations incompletely synthesized here could be taken to demonstrate the material power of this "Local" (both historically and culturally) version of the Lesbian, or conversely could be taken to show how unstable such domination is, how powerful other local formations are in their reassertion of the priority of their own forms. Within an anthropology of sexuality other forms have come to vie for any such power: such forms as The Gender Specialist, The Penetrator, and The Bisexual.

Bisexuality, rather than the identity The Bisexual, may be the formation in greatest global circulation today. As one Global Gay Formation, bisexuality has currency in a globalized economy of niche markets where the most circulated objects are those which can be viewed within the greatest range of divergent local markets as "like-us." This doesn't mean that bisexuality is actually "all things to all people," but rather that a highly commodified version of bisexuality can be exploited as differently important in a local and distinctive reception by a wide range of markets, especially media markets. (One example is the Global Music Industry, with mega-international groups like Queen.) And in any collectivities of activisms that are international, bisexuality must be reprioritized. In such activist locations the term "Bisexuality" is useful in at least three contexts: (1) as a liminal category, such as its use as "gateway" from heterosexuality to homosexuality, in a universe of discourse effectively exhausted by Hetero/Homo Sex; (2) as a third identity, modeled on the "sexual orientations" homosexual and heterosexual, thus bisexual, essentialist or anti-essentialist, within identity politics or in a queer anti-identity politics; (3) as an overflow category, in a universe of discourse not exhausted by Hetero/Homo Sex, and thus representing all other possible local sexual practices without distinguishing among them under the sign "Bisexual." Thus as overflow category, Bisexual can also, like Queer, name and valorize inchoate non-institutionalized processes and formations connected with sexuality, possibly (or fictitiously) not "disciplined." This version of Bisexual may be interchangable with Queer, and participate in a range of its meanings and productive instabilities as well.

The phrase "Lesbianisms in Multinational Reception" suggests that the term Lesbian is plural and various, that in some global locations it is engaged only as an outside term, not there a local term, that there are many kinds of reception of the term, that such receptions are inextricable from its traveling possibilities. Those travels are interconnected with other globalizing processes in an economy of multinationals in late capitalism, an economy also including representations and media, as well as activisms, art, and cyberspace, and inextricably intertwined too with worldwide movements against colonialism. It includes the possibility that Lesbianism is a rejected term, as well as the possibility of using it as an inclusive, unmarked, or continually reconstructed "universal," although plural, not singular. Naming Lesbian in this context, through this phrase, is a method coming-into-being that arises from acts of translation across fields of power. Often one knows such methods when one sees them only in the midst of misunderstandings and struggles, when previously held assumptions are ruptured by micro and macro movements of power. To pay attention to such methodology coming into focus requires a high tolerance for conflict and for beginning again, tasks with emotional, intellectual and political costs. Misunderstandings and mistakes are the paradoxical "common ground" upon which such methodology is made, and misunderstandings and mistakes have their own consequences, sometimes separate from the coming into being of such methodology, and not at all necessarily mended by it. In this vision such conflicts as the ones shaped through political generations and differing geopolitics, and even through (inter)interdisciplinarities in the academy are pivotal in producing "lesbigay" methodology. At this time I consider the most important task to be first the never simple recognition of such methods when we see them. I believe in eclectic methods that emerge in different local politics out of political and institutional struggles, that require always problematic translations, which themselves shape these methods. No generation of political activists can claim mastery or ownership of such methods, nor can any academic disciplines or political theories, nor can any national liberation movements.

Such new methods enable new translations, new visionary reframings of contemporary geopolitical realities. For example, Chela Sandoval translates "hyper-oppression" into another vision, an ironic one which recognizes simultaneously both terror and possibility, calling it "the democratization of oppression," and naming the activities, activisms, and oppressions of a new global citizen brought into being within shifting fields of power under globalization in late capitalism. She speaks of an alignment among decolonial theorists who, surviving "conquest, colonization, and slavery" develop methodologies "crucial to the project of identifying citizen-subjects and collectivities able to negotiate the globalizing operations of the next century," and names Queers as one set of agents in these negotiations. Any new political movements, among them lesbian, gay, and feminist human rights activisms, must be very sophisticated in their understandings of their own commodification within such layered global and local structures, as well as be risk-taking in their appropriations of pleasures, identities, and political strategies.

Bibliographic Note

Rather than attempt bibliography that does justice to the breathtaking range of new work coming out on what I call Global Gay Formations and Local Homosexualities, I would instead direct readers to one institutional site from which such work now emerges, disseminated in conferences, publications, students, and teachers. CLAGS – The Center for Lesbian and Gay Studies of the City University of New York – is this site, which takes advantage of New York City as the Third World in the First World, of international students and teachers, of populations of immigrants, refugees and academic travelers, to engage these new global formations in methodologically diverse ways. I direct your attention to two conferences especially: "Identity/Space/Power: Lesbian, Gay, Bisexual, and Transgender Politics, "February 8–9, 1996; and "Queer Globalization/Local Homosexualities," April 23–5, 1998; each held at the Graduate School and University Center of the City University of New York. Some papers from the 1996 conference are collected in *GLQ – A Journal of Lesbian and Gay Studies* 3/4 (1997), a special issue from the conference. I understand that papers from the second conference will be gathered in a forthcoming book.

By no means is CLAGS the only such site, for others are coming-into-being as we speak, and one way to identify possible such locations is via the World wide Web. I direct readers to look there for a powerfully various and ever-changing range of "nodes" of engagement, activism, discussion, and display. Rather than give URLs, which are only too likely to change, I suggest investing some serious time with various search engines to find sites. Some entries to investigate: Queer Resources Directory, Lambda Institute, International Lesbian and Gay Association (includes paper on "Finding a Place in International Law"), International Lesbian Information Service, Gay and Lesbian International Lobby, International Lesbigay Resources, Lesbian and Gay Immigration Rights Task Force. Links to a wide variety of national sites can be found from these locations.

Readers who want more background on the methodology of which this essay is an example should look at my book, *Theory in Its Feminist Travels*, which also contains an earlier, now perhaps even standard, bibliography on these issues before 1994, and references to the relevant work by Donna Haraway and Chela Sandoval mentioned in the essay.

PART IV

Cultural Studies and the Accommodation of Postcolonialism

Chapter 27

Rethinking English:
Postcolonial English Studies

Gaurav Desai

As someone of (East) Indian origin working in the US academy I frequently find myself having to explain – indeed, often to justify – my presence teaching in an English department. The academy, of course, has now gotten used to having some Indians and other nonwestern scholars among its fold, but this is not always the case beyond it. Outside the ivory tower the thought of an Indian teaching English in America remains an oddity, a manifestation perhaps of yet another sphere in which the new immigrants are taking over. Typically, of course, in such non-academic scenarios after the initial raising of the eyebrows, my interlocutors attempt an explanation. If it almost always includes some awkward remark about "how well" I speak English, it sometimes goes further in suggesting that the British really knew what they were doing when they taught Indians their language.

Although conversations such as these are primarily conducted as smalltalk with say, a fellow passenger on a plane, the issues that they raise are by no means small. What *does* it mean to work in the field of English studies today? And what does it mean for someone to express surprise that a nonwestern foreigner might well be one of the teachers of English in the US academy? What kind of assumptions about the "ownership" of the English language and its native authenticity underwrite the (dubious) notion that Indians speak English well because the *British* (as opposed to Americans) taught them? And finally what does it mean to speak English "well" anyway? These are some of the issues that are at the heart of the rapidly growing scholarly field known as "postcolonial studies" and it is the task of this chapter to highlight aspects of this discourse in relation to the field of English studies as a whole. My interest here is not so much in re-presenting some of the nuanced positions of particular scholars in the field or even of different literary traditions, since this has already been done admirably in previous chapters. Rather my aim is to work *around* these discourses to get a broader sense of the *significance* of postcolonial scholarship to the discipline of English studies. The focus here, as the section heading suggests, is on the disciplinary issues surrounding postcolonialism in the academy with a keen eye towards its institutional "accommodation."

"Accommodation" may well be considered one of the more contentious terms in the study of postcolonialism precisely because it is an essentially ambivalent signifier. "To be accommodating" is to be receptive to difference, to give of oneself, to be willing to negotiate around disagreements and so on. "To accommodate" to something, however, has a distinctly negative valence about it since it connotes co-optation, selling-out, or even defeat. In the realm of colonial relations, who accommodates to whom and by recourse to what – threat or conviction – is a matter that is itself subject to continued debate. Indeed, by the end of this chapter when we touch upon the critique of postcolonial antifoundationalism we will note that one of the important nodes of disagreement between antifoundationalists and their detractors is based in their implicit account of colonial accommodation. And as we will see, it is again the issue of "accommodation" that resurfaces in the debates surrounding the politics of the "postcolonial" intellectual in the Western academy.

If the politics of "accommodation" are central to what we now call "postcolonial critique" then the roots of the anxiety are located in the colonial moment itself. While many postcolonial writers and critics have for long recognized the alienating effect on the colonized subjects of the English language in general and of English literature in particular, new research on the history of English studies has further shed light on such alienation. Through the seminal work of scholars such as Gauri Viswanathan, Rajeswari Sunder Rajan, Susie Tharu, Ania Loomba, and Mahasweta Sengupta, we have learned that the discipline of English literary studies was in fact an invention of colonial India. Thus, for instance, Gauri Viswanathan's study shows that while schoolchildren in England were still being taught the classics and religion, the English in India chose to inculcate in their colonized subjects a love for the English language and its literature. Best characterized by Thomas Macaulay in his famous 1835 "Minute on Indian Education," the idea was "to form a class who may be interpreters between us and the millions whom we govern; a class of persons, Indian in blood and colour, but English in taste, in opinions, in morals and in intellect" (430). If the *technical* knowledge of the English language on the part of this native elite was to serve as a means of communication between the colonial government and the rest of the population, the study of *literary* works was to present to this class a lesson in morality, gentility, and ideal civility as it was exhibited by the best of the English literary tradition. It is in this way, suggests Viswanathan, that the teaching of English literature became a mask that camouflaged the actual terrors of colonialism.

While numerous examples of colonized subjects may be cited to demonstrate the effective creation of such a class of middlemen in the context of colonial India, perhaps the most poignant account of the workings of such a literary education is presented by Mahasweta Sengupta in her recent study of the Bengali writer Rabindranath Tagore. Tagore, a Bengali nationalist who was, in general, skeptical of the English education system, nevertheless developed an interest in the study of English literature. Sengupta writes: "Rabindranath's understanding or misunderstanding of the literary culture of the English led him to believe in the existence of a class among the rulers who were committed to the higher values of truth, justice and equality in the world. The ideal was taken to be the real, and the actual regarded as false, as aberration. Even when he denounced British policy in India, he never doubted the 'cultured' English character as he knew it through his readings of English literary texts, particularly of the Elizabethan, Romantic and Victorian periods" (1998: 228). Towards the end of his life in 1941, suggests Sengupta, Tagore's speeches had a tragic sense to them. "Looking back on his life, Rabindranath was convinced that his loss of faith in the civilizing mission of the English and other European nations derived from his misplaced belief in the professedly liberal attitudes of the colonizer's race as represented in literature" (229).

If by the end of his life Tagore seems to have come to an understanding of the ideological effects of English literature in colonial India, it is arguably the case that such a critique was not forthcoming from many others who shared his predicament. Indeed, Rajeswari Sunder Rajan suggests that English literature "was not indicted on ideological or historical grounds by association with the English ruler. Rather it became the surrogate – and also the split – presence of the Englishman, or a repository of abstract and universal values freely available to the colonized as much as to the colonizer" (1992: 12). Thus, ironically, English literature often became the vehicle through which Indians made anticolonial and nationalist claims. "This is one of the contexts" writes Ania Loomba, "in which the English literary text became, not a site of conflict, but an *accommodative* ideal where the humanistic assumptions of that discipline could include both a Westernized consciousness and a revivalist one" (1992: 15–16, italics mine). And it is this double-edged quality of English literature in the Indian context, we must note, that has made the rethinking of the postcolonial English curriculum in India a complicated enterprise.

The implications of this brief lesson in the history of English as a discipline cannot be overemphasized. If, instead of a naive trickle-down model of literary education from the metropole to the colony we are now provided with a picture of a disciplinary formation in the very midst of a colonial project, then as post-colonial practitioners of the same discipline we carry a heavy burden indeed. In this picture no aspect of English literary studies, whether it be concerned with the Medieval period or the Renaissance or the Romantics can ignore its own colonial conditions of possibility. To say this is not to suggest that one can read the colonial legacy of canonical literatures in any straightforward way. But the highly mediated relationship between English literature and the empire can no longer justifiably escape our scrutiny. Indeed, as I will suggest below one of the most significant contributions of postcolonial studies has been its emphasis on such rereadings of canonical English literature.

To those of us interested in postcolonial literature and to the creative writers writing it, however, the issues raised by this disciplinary history are even more urgent. If English literature was specifically being used by the British in the interests of native alienation, what role, if any, can it play in a *post*-colonial setting? If the English language itself was an instrument in the creation of an elite class, further dividing an indigenous people against itself, would its continued legacy in the postcolonial context not do more harm than good? Would the creation of a national literature written in the ex-colonial language not continue the class divide initiated by the colonizers?

The answers to these questions are many and their variations are the result of the various factors that go into the creation of an intellectual class and of the many specific individuals that constitute it. But it is interesting to note that in general, the debates over language and curriculum have been more urgent in the context of postcolonial Africa than they have been in the Indian subcontinent. While a proper understanding of the reasons for this difference would warrant a more nuanced study, it may be fair to say that the longer tradition of English pedagogy in India with a greater assimilation of Indians into the colonial civil service on the one hand, and a more explicitly racist structure in colonial Africa on the other, meant that in general African subjects were less likely to be enthralled by the virtues of the English literary tradition than were their Indian counterparts. It is in postcolonial Africa then, that we see some of the most intensive debates over the issue of language along with related attempts to Africanize the curriculum and make it more relevant to a postcolonial context (see Ngugi, "On the Abolition").

Obiajunwa Wali's article "The Dead End of African Literature?" published in the Nigerian journal *Transition* is often considered one of the earliest African critiques of European language literary production. He wrote in this piece that "African literature in English and French, is a clear contradiction, just as 'Italian literature in Hausa' would be" (1963: 14) Wali's skepticism was shared by other thinkers, most famously by the Kenyan writer Ngugi wa Thiong'o. At a 1973 teacher's conference in Nairobi, Ngugi pointed out some of the inherent biases in the English language:

> racism is expressed in the very structure of the English language, probably the most racist of all human languages. It was not only the character of black sambo, but also phrases like black market, black sheep, blackmail, blacklist, black everything, would testify to the value assumptions in that linguistic negative definition of blackness. (1981: 14)

To recognize that the language incorporates a racist ideology and to continue to write in it, suggests Ngugi, is to remain complicitous with the colonial order of things. True decolonization involves not only political freedom but also freedom from a colonized mentality (see his 1986). What the example of the negative connotations of "black" in the English language suggests is that "language is not a neutral medium that passes freely and easily into the private property of the speaker's intentions; it is populated – overpopulated – with the intentions of others; expropriating it, forcing it to submit to one's own intentions and accents is a difficult and complicated process" (Bakhtin, 1981: 294).

While Ngugi has over time given up writing in English and turned to Kikuyu and Kiswahili as more relevant languages for his literary expression, other writers in Africa have often taken up the challenge of moulding the English language to carry their own intentions and accents (Desai). Chinua Achebe, for instance, who has consistently defended the use of English by African writers, owes much of his international fame not only to his general ability to tell a captivating story, but also more particularly to his stylistic ability to recast the English language. In his classic essay, "The African Writer and the English Language," Achebe writes about his own use of English:

> Allow me to quote a small example, from *Arrow of God* which may give some idea of how I approach the use of English. The Chief Priest in the story is telling one of his sons why it is necessary to send him to church:

> "I want one of my sons to join these people and be my eyes there. If there is nothing in it you will come back. But if there is something there you will bring home my share. The world is like a Mask, dancing. If you want to see it well you do not stand in one place. My spirit tells me that those who do not befriend the white man today will be saying *had we known* tomorrow." (*Arrow of God*, 55)

> Now suppose I had put it in another way. Like this for instance:

> "I am sending you as my representative among these people – just to be on the safe side if the new religion develops. One has to move with the times, or else one is left behind. I have a hunch that those who fail to come to terms with the white man may well regret their lack of foresight."

> The material is the same. But the form of the one is *in character*. The other is not. (1975: 61–2)

If the first passage from *Arrow of God* is "in character" it is because it inscribes within the English language idiomatic forms and speech patterns that are in fact characteristically Ibo. It is thus a *social* character that is thrust upon the English language by Achebe here and it is the most subtle of the various kinds of adaptations of English that postcolonial writers across the world have conducted. Other strategies of recasting the English language to resonate the cultural specificity of a non-English culture include the incorporation of untranslated indigenous words and the use of pidgins and creoles by individual characters. The self-conscious use of these strategies has allowed writers as varied as Salman Rushdie and Ken Saro-Wiwa (whose novel *Sozaboy* is provocatively subtitled "A Novel in Rotten English") to bring to the world of literature the various hybrid languages that proliferate in postcolonial contexts.

To read such postcolonial literature, then, is to also experience the globalization of the English language and to recognize the myopia involved in any discussion of linguistic purity. For English today is an international language not only of everyday communication but also of literary and cultural production. And this, it goes without saying, is in large part responsible for the rethinking that is taking place in the field of English Studies. As one might imagine, the accommodation of such literatures into the disciplinary framework of English studies has not always been easy conceptually, leave alone politically. Consider, for instance, just one story among many that could be told about the academic emergence of postcolonial literatures in the US academy. If we were to "read" the annual bibliography of the Modern Language Association as an index of the American reception of African literature we would note that until 1964, the MLA bibliographers chose to categorize entries related to African literature depending on the language in which the literature was written. Thus, for instance, literature originating in Africa written in the English language was listed in a special subsection of the larger field of "English Language and Literature." It is with some irony that we may look back today at the heading of this subsection: "Australia, Canada, etc." It was in the "etceteras" that African literature in English first found its discursive space. It is even more interesting to observe that whereas the rest of the English language tradition, too over-whelming to be undifferentiated, was chronologically divided into seven differ-ent eras, the Anglophone African tradition was not placed within any of them. That is, while it was a part of the English literary tradition by virtue of its language, Anglophone African writing in the twentieth century was nevertheless relegated to a space outside of twentieth-century English literary history.

As an increasing amount of material emerged from the continent, and as critical studies of these literatures grew rapidly, the bibliographers chose to provide a new arena for the material. Thus it was that in 1965 and 1966, a new category "Oriental and African literature" was introduced to the "General and Miscellaneous" section of the bibliography. This was the most confused of times. One can, going through the bibliographies of these two years, find entries related to African literatures in the original category of "Australia, Canada, etc.," in the newly designated arena of "Oriental and African literature," in the section entitled "Folklore," and lastly in the various subsections of the literature of the European languages used in colonial Africa. It was in 1967 that African litera-tures (with the exception of a few scattered entries in other categories) began, in the majority, to figure as "national" literatures. Here too, however, the trend was cautious – there was categorization by genres, by larger regions (such as West Africa), in addition to that by nation-states. 1967 also saw the marriage of African literature and African folklore. Though still not discussed under the category of the nation-state, there was, on the part of the bibliographers, an attempt to place African folklore within the rubric of African literatures. A year later, in 1968, African literature finally got a room of its own, no longer sharing the company of the "Oriental."

Little changed for the next few years. And then in 1981 the storm burst. A whole new way of seeing emerged. The MLA completely reorganized its format. Under the category of African literature, were now introduced the subcategories, "African literature: 1600–1699," "African literature: 1700–1899," and so on. Regional subcategories were also historicized, the most telling being the subcategory "North African Literature" divided into "300–399" (making St. Augustine one of the earliest African writers), "400–499," and so on. A sense of history was in some cases conceptualized around the nation-state, the earliest instances found under "Egyptian Literature: 1600 BC." But along with this move towards historicity, the bibliographers chose to exile folklore into its own separate volume away from "African literature."

If this story tells us anything, it is surely not about the capriciousness of the hard-working folks at the MLA. Rather it is a fairly good reflection of the various emphases and debates that were taking place in the inclusion of nonwestern literatures in the Western academy. The trajectory of this history ranges from an initial ethnographic curiosity in such literature to the more recent attention to it as, say, national allegory. It is also, to the disappointment of many, a history of the surely encroaching hegemony of the written over the oral and of the modern/postmodern over the traditional. At the same time it is a demonstration of the complicated negotiations between European language literatures and those written in the languages indigenous to the postcolonial nations. And finally, the appearance of historical categories in the context of African (and other non-western) literatures in the post-1981 bibliographies, is a strong indication of the historicist and culturalist (as opposed to aestheticist and new critical) approaches of such scholarly studies.

What this story doesn't quite tell, however, are the ways in which nonwestern literatures and cultures entered different *disciplinary* spaces in the academy. Sometimes used in anthropology and history classes to provide a "native" voice from the culture under study, at times taught as "Commonwealth" literature in English departments, and at others in the newly emergent Area Studies courses developed in the mid to late sixties, these literatures were for long conspicuously absent in most Comparative Literature programs across the country. These latter programs could well have provided an appropriate home for postcolonial literatures reading them as products and constituents of essentially (and forcibly) hybridized cultures. But in retrospect they seem to have lost out on the opportunity not only of playing a role in dislocating the center–periphery model on which "commonwealth" literary studies was based, but also of refining their own understanding of the nature of the "comparative" in comparative literary studies itself. It is only today that these traditionally Eurocentric (or on occasion "Orientalist" in the Saidian sense) programs have begun to take account of what it means to teach comparative literature in the context of a global culture (see Bernheimer, 1995). And as these programs now inevitably get ready to position themselves to partake of the fruits of postcolonial studies, it would do us well to remember that the credit for the growth of such studies lies not with these programs but with the many individual scholars who began and continued to teach nonwestern literatures despite the prevalent apathy and even the occasional hostility they faced from their peers.

The acknowledgment of world literatures in English as deserving serious study, then, has only come gradually and that too only after the efforts of a good many scholars already working in the field who actively joined hands with fellow colleagues interested in the study and teaching of US minority literatures, women's literatures, and other previously marginalized literary traditions. The political work of these scholars, popularized in the public imagination as the "canon wars" and often maligned by cultural conservatives as catering to the pressures of "special interest groups" has ultimately yielded to the opening up of some space of disciplinary recognition and it is this space that "postcolonial studies" among others occupies. But it is important to note that the emergence of a postcolonial perspective in literary and cultural criticism did not wait until it was sanctioned by the American academy. If Edward Said's *Orientalism* published in 1978 gave a certain newfound legitimacy to a form of critique that gradually began to be labeled "postcolonial," it is clear that the impetus of the critique shared much in common with predecessors such as Frantz Fanon, C. L. R. James, Amilcar Cabral, and Chinua Achebe. In this regard, "postcolonial studies," referring as it often does to the rapid growth in the eighties of scholarly interest in colonial relations and nationalisms, is best understood as a belated project. It is based on a long history of debate and discussion about issues such as the appropriability of the colonial languages, about the role of regional cultures in nationalist traditions, about the marginalization of gender and women's issues in many newly independent nations, and about the role of indigenous traditions in shaping a postcolonial modernity. These debates that took place between and among creative writers and critics, theater workers and teachers, revolutionary thinkers and nationalist leaders at various moments and various sites of the colonial and newly independent world continue to be echoed in contemporary postcolonial scholarship. A history of the continuities of such debates is yet to be written but the "rediscovery" of earlier thinkers (such as Frantz Fanon) writing against colonialism is now rightfully becoming an important dimension of postcolonial scholarship across the globe (see Gates, 1991, "Critical Fanonism"; Gordon *et al.*, 1996).

At the same time however, it would be disingenuous to ignore the fact that postcolonial scholarship in its *contemporary* guise has as one of its enabling conditions of possibility the institutional rise of literary "theory." The (post)structuralist shift from questions of literariness to questions of textuality associated with such thinkers as Roland Barthes and Michel Foucault, the increasing attention paid to issues of subalternity and hegemony by forms of cultural Marxism such as those of Antonio Gramsci and Raymond Williams, the efforts of feminists such as Susan Gubar and Sandra Gilbert to articulate the parameters of the emergence of a women's literary tradition – these are just some of the more visible markers of the kind of theoretically informed and socially conscious cultural criticism that postcolonialists partook of. And likewise, as postcolonial scholarship benefitted from these early efforts, it too has had a critical role to play in the rethinking of these and other related fields: Marxism, Feminism, the

New Historicism as well as that rather amorphous field called "cultural studies," all carry the traces of postcolonial studies today.

To survey the institutional rise of postcolonial literary studies in the US academy, it may help to think of it as participating in two simultaneous projects. *One* aspect of postcolonial scholarship, as I suggested above, has been to reread the canonical texts of English literature and to place them in relation to the larger project of English imperialism and colonialism. Works that immediately come to mind in this context are Chinua Achebe's early essay on Conrad entitled "An Image of Africa: Racism in Conrad's *Heart of Darkness*"; Gayatri Spivak's rereading of the rise of women's individualism and its connections with issues of empire in "Three Women's Texts and a Critique of Imperialism"; Abdul JanMohamed's *Manichean Aesthetics* (1983), which, by juxtaposing English colonial literature with African literary texts already carries over into the project of the *second* mode of postcolonial criticism I describe below; and Patrick Brantlinger's path-breaking study *Rule of Darkness: British Literature and Imperialism, 1830–1914*, (1988), which moved Victorian studies in the direction of a rigorous self-critique. These early works have been followed by a whole coterie of studies in the nineties and include works such as Sara Mill's *Discourses of Difference* (1991), which analyzed the relationship between women's travel writing and colonialism; Sara Suleri's *The Rhetoric of English India* (1992), which like JanMohamed's work (although to radically different ends) also included readings of postcolonial writers; Jenny Sharpe's *Allegories of Reading* (1993), focusing, as its subtitle suggests, on the "Figure of Woman in the Colonial Text"; Firdous Azim's important intervention on Charlotte Brontë in *The Colonial Rise of the Novel* (1993); Edward Said's magisterial survey, *Culture and Imperialism* (1993); the work of critics such as David Lloyd (1993), Enda Duffy (1994), and Vincent Cheng (1995), who have in various ways worked to think of Ireland and canonical Irish writers such as Joyce from within the intellectual context framed by postcolonial theory; and finally the important book by Simon Gikandi entitled *Maps of Englishness: Writing Identity in the Culture of Colonialism* (1996), which invites us to rethink colonial "Englishness" as always–already partaking of the experience and subjectivities of the colonized.

Closely related to this form of postcolonial critique and often overlapping with it is the legacy of what is labeled "colonial discourse studies," an interdisciplinary investigation not only of the literary works but also of letters, memoranda, diaries, political speeches, legal rulings, and so on written by imperial agents and colonial observers. This study of what V. Y. Mudimbe has called the 'colonial library' is interested, much like Said's *Orientalism*, in the intersections of colonial knowledge and power and its "inventions" of colonized spaces and other exotic lands. While many of the books cited above also exhibit these tendencies, of particular note in this context are works such as V. Y. Mudimbe's *The Invention of Africa* (1988) and *The Idea of Africa* (1994), Timothy Mitchell's *Colonizing Egypt* (1988), David Spurr's *The Rhetoric of Empire* (1993), Nicholas Thomas's *Colonialism's Culture* (1994), and the edited collections *Colonialism and*

531

Culture (1992), *Orientalism and the Postcolonial Predicament* (1993), and *After Colonialism* (1995).

If the study of colonialism and its culture is a major preoccupation of the postcolonial project, there is also a *second* aspect of postcolonial scholarship that is no less intriguing. This other project is more concerned with the literary and cultural production of the *colonized* subjects as well as their postcolonial inheritors. At one level, this is the study of what was once called "Commonwealth Literature," but it also takes quite seriously, as Commonwealth literary studies often didn't, the interface between English and the native languages, the negotiations between nationalist and minoritarian representations, the complicated politics of literacy, and masculinist biases and womanist concerns. In the ever-expanding archives of this scholarly terrain one may well encounter such texts as Abiola Irele's masterpiece *The African Experience in Literature and Ideology* (1981); Barbara Harlow's *Resistance Literature* (1987); Timothy Brennan's *Salman Rushdie and the Third World* (1989); *Out of the Kumbla*, a volume of essays on Caribbean women and literature edited by Carole Boyce Davies and Elaine Fido (1990); Neil Lazarus's study of Ayi Kwei Armah, *Resistance in Postcolonial African Fiction* (1990); Rob Nixon's study of Naipaul, *London Calling* (1992); Chikwenye Ogunyemi's *Africa Wo/Man Palava* (1996) on Nigerian women novelists, and innumerable articles in journals such as *Ariel, Callaloo, Research in African Literatures*, and *World Literature Written in English* to mention only a selected few.

Since the literary and cultural production of the colonized subjects is often part of their response to colonialism itself, literary scholars find that their interests overlap significantly with the work of cultural historians and some anthropologists. In this way, given its wide scope, this second mode of postcolonial scholarship too finds recourse in materials not conventionally thought of as "literature" and includes in its analysis performance, film, and even the circulation of food such as *chapatis* (see for instance, Guha, 1983: 239–46; Bhabha, 1994a: "Bread"). Much of what gets labeled postcolonial literary *theory* today is in effect the result of such cross-fertilization between disciplines but it is arguably not disconnected from the emphasis on literature and culture that is the primary interest of the scholars concerned. Despite the differences in their enunciative intent, texts as varied as the polemical *Toward the Decolonization of African Literature* (1980) by Chinweizu, Jemie, and Madubuike, Kwame Anthony Appiah's *In My Father's House* (1992), Rey Chow's *Writing Diaspora* (1993), Paul Gilroy's *The Black Atlantic: Modernity and Double Consciousness* (1993), Gayatri Spivak's *Outside in the Teaching Machine* (1993), and Homi Bhabha's *The Location of Culture* (1994) all share in common a desire to make sense of the discrepant ways in which literatures and cultures – both high and low – get institutionalized and accommodated at various nodes of the public sphere.

Postcolonial English studies, then, comes in several guises. Rereadings of the English canon, investigations of the production of colonial stereotypes and the "inventions" of the other, critical analysis of postcolonial literatures and cultures, "theorizations" of categories such as "subalternity," "ambivalence," "mimicry," and "hybridity" – all these are part of the vast terrain of the "postcolonial" in the academy. And of course, we should note that these are only *some* of the faces of the "postcolonial" since other emphases and other concerns often shape the study of postcoloniality in locations as varied as Kenya, South Africa, Australia, and the Caribbean. If any comprehensive survey of postcolonial literary studies seems impossible, it is due in fact to the plurality afforded by the various local articulations of the "postcolonial" in different global contexts.

This situation, it would seem, would be cause for much elation among those who support such things as the project of decolonization and the access to representation on the part of hitherto unheard voices. But such has not always been the case and of late postcolonial literary studies has seen increasing internal critiques by those who, in the larger scheme of things, might well be considered friends. One aspect of this critique has taken the form of a rejection of recent trends towards an antifoundational postcolonialism. This antifoundationalism, evoked by historians such as Gyan Prakash, and literary critics such as Homi Bhabha and Sara Suleri, has often sought to present colonialism as a messy project of partial alliance rather than one of outright domination (see particularly Bhabha, *Location*; Suleri, *Rhetoric*). This presentation of the colonizer–colonized relationship as based on the oxymoronic notion of the "intimate enemy" (see Nandy) has troubled those who see in it an erasure of colonial force and atrocities. Reading this move as indicative of a general loss of an *anti*-colonial orientation towards a *post*-colonial one, Suvir Kaul, for instance, has questioned the politics behind Suleri's move in *The Rhetoric of English India* to render colonial relations ambivalent. Moving the discourse of colonial relations away from the emphasis on power to an emphasis on complicity, suggests Kaul, "leads to an astonishing flattening of the contours of colonial power sharing, so that we are left with no fundamental distinction between colonizers and the colonized" (1996: 76). The anti-foundationalist response to this accusation is that foundationalist accounts, whether based on a Fanonian Manicheanism, or on an economistic World-Systems theory of global capitalist penetration, or even instead on an idealist focus on the ideologies of imperialism, all ultimately fail insofar as they are unable to account for the historicity of the very categories that underwrite their claims. Thus, for instance, Gyan Prakash suggests that rather than seeing colonialism in India as *reducible* to the development of capitalism in Britain and India, as foundationalist critics would have us do, it makes more sense to "reinscribe the effects of capitalism's foundational status by writing about histories that remained heterogeneous with the logic of capital" (Prakash, 1992: 14–15). Engaging in such antifoundationalism, then, is not to join hands with conservatives but rather to mount more complex accounts of the *discrepancies* of the colonial project. "How is it possible," asks Prakash in this vein, "to write a critical account of capitalism unless we also estrange, disfigure, and deconstruct its colonization of history? Does this not require the displacement of capitalist development as a privileged theme of history and necessitate the defamiliarization of the bourgeois political economy?" (Prakash, 1992a: 369).

Among all the critiques of the politics of postcolonial studies, however, the most acerbic is Aijaz Ahmad's *In Theory: Classes, Nations, Literatures.* Ahmad argues that postcolonial studies, primarily a first-world phenomenon, is blind to the real material conditions of the neocolonial societies it examines. It does this, he claims, inspired by the bad company that it keeps – the company that is, of poststructuralist theory. Emerging only in the aftermath of the civil resistance of the sixties, this alliance of poststructuralism and postcolonialism has served, writes Ahmad, "to domesticate, in institutional ways, the very forms of political dissent which those movements had sought to foreground, to displace an activist culture with a textual culture, to combat the more uncompromising critiques of existing cultures of the literary profession with a new mystique of leftish professionalism, and to reformulate in a postmodernist direction questions which had previously been associated with a Marxist politics" (1992: 1). By way of example, Ahmad presents the fate of nationalist politics in the hands of the postcolonialists. Beginning with an earlier sympathy to the nationalist project in the sixties and seventies, nationalism today, suggests Ahmad, is in disfavour among postcolonial critics not because it has on many occasions been elitist, sexist and exclusionary but rather because it seems to be based on poststructuralist taboos: "the effort to speak of origins, collectivities and determinate historical projects" (38). This seems to Ahmad to be symptomatic of postcolonial criticism's eagerness to fit into western theoretical models and it does so, he claims, at the expense of engaging in any progressive politics. But, continues Ahmad, the lack of a socialist consciousness among postcolonial scholars should come as no surprise. Characteristically members of an upwardly mobile immigrant class, many postcolonial intellectuals in the West found it convenient to ignore issues of class struggle and to embrace instead "narratives of oppression that would get them preferential treatment, reserved jobs, higher salaries in the social position they already occupied: namely, *as* middle-class professionals, mostly male" (196).

Ahmad's attack, rather than being an isolated one, has recently been echoed by others including E. San Juan and Arif Dirlik. Dirlik, for instance, in an essay entitled "The Postcolonial Aura: Third World Criticism in the Age of Global Capitalism," dramatically suggests that the "postcolonial" begins when "Third World intellectuals have arrived in First World academe" (1994: 329). He too, like Ahmad, argues that "postcolonial criticism has been silent about its own status as a possible ideological effect of a new world situation after colonialism" (331) and that it conceals rather than reveals the neocolonial expansiveness of global capitalism.

These critiques of the accommodation of postcolonial studies in the US academy have resulted in angry and often defensive responses by postcolonial scholars. Ahmad's positions in particular have been characterized as journalistic, moralizing, self-righteous, accusatory, "lefter-than-thou," and so on, and while there may be some warrant for such adjectives, when one considers the often contemptuous tone of the responses one gets the distinct sense that Ahmad has raised issues that are perhaps a little too uncomfortable for his detractors (see *Public Culture*, 1993). These issues are particularly troubling not only because they address the political and ethical stakes of specific individuals and their intellectual affiliations but also because they call into question general participation in a disciplinary practice whose politics are, I suggest, necessarily ambivalent. In other words, what makes Ahmad most unpalatable is his crying "sell-out" to left-leaning and left-thinking (postcolonial) intellectuals.

While this is no place to offer it, I would suggest that a rigorous account of the politics of postcoloniality and its relation to poststructuralism might well begin by allowing Ahmad and Dirlik their claim that as intellectuals working at universities, postcolonialists partake of both the economic as well as cultural capital that such a space offers. As Rajeswari Sunder Rajan notes in a critique of Dirlik's pronouncements of intellectual complicity, "The operation of global capitalism as cause is so pervasive that it is only too easy to establish that intellectuals in particular (and of every persuasion) are co-opted within its system. (What would be of considerably more interest is the identification of categories of criticism or critics who could be considered exempt from the embrace of capitalism's reward system – since indeed that appears to be primarily what is at stake here)" (1997: 597). And if such co-optation is not limited to intellectuals with *particular* ideologies, Rajan proceeds to point out that contrary to the implications of Dirlik's (and we may add, Ahmad's) attack on the *immigrant* intellectual, such co-optation does not spare the non-immigrant intellectual either. If we are to take the reach of global capital seriously, as Ahmad and Dirlik would indeed like us to do, then we cannot isolate a pure, uncontaminated space in which such an intellectual might work.

After making this first move of recognizing the class positioning of academic intellectual work, our critique of Ahmad's *In Theory* may move on to the more substantial concerns about the relationship of theoretical work to politics, of the politics of professionalism, and to the accuracies of his accounts of postcolonial work itself. Such an analysis may well emphasize that the politics of a theory are not *intrinsic* to it but are often the result of the specific contingencies of its mobilizations. Poststructuralism, for instance, can and often has been used in ways which may be loosely characterized as conservative, but it has also been used for radical ends. Gayatri Spivak, one of the most important postcolonial critics in the US academy, has always insisted on the possibilities of simultaneously engaging with Feminism, Marxism, and Poststructuralism (see Spivak, 1990). The absence of any engagement with Spivak in Ahmad's text may well speak to the caricatured nature of his polemic. Additionally, one may usefully critique Ahmad's notion of "left professionalism" as being continuous with his general accusation of academic capitalist complicity. Here, one may well follow Bruce Robbins's lead in recognizing that the US cultural left has in fact gained a voice in public political discourse not despite, but rather because of its professionalization and that contrary to the myths of professional redundancy, such

professionalization has often been self-critical and responsive to the needs of the
larger public. Likewise, one may well argue that attention to the ongoing disempowerment of postcolonial subjects has often served, especially in work inspired
by Spivak, as the ethical core of postcolonial scholarship. Our critique of Ahmad
would at this point do well to show that his reading of postcolonial professionalism is based, then, on an untenable equation of professionalism with bad politics. It is this that leads him to ignore not only the work of Spivak, but ironically
also of many other scholars who, while not entirely dismissive of poststructuralism, have nevertheless situated themselves in spaces offered by alternative
theoretical articulations. There is much, then, in the work of critics such as
Abdul JanMohamed, Benita Parry, Biodun Jeyifo, Barbara Harlow, Neil Lazarus,
Rob Nixon, and Anne McClintock to name only a few, which would give the lie
to Ahmad's insistence that issues of history and class struggle have had no place
in metropolitan postcolonial studies.

Having said this, it should be clear that without critiques such as Ahmad's and
Dirlik's, postcolonial studies might well have been less energetic than it currently
is. Debates such as these are the very signs of a healthy critical practice, since
scholarly interventions, even when they seek to discredit the professional standing of their object of critique, often end up ironically being the driving force of
further study. In other words, even as Ahmad chooses to place his own thinking
in a position of virtuous exteriority *vis-à-vis* the discourses of the postcolonial
academy, his critique ends up finding itself an important place within it. If this
is "co-optation" or "accommodation" of a previously unthought or previously
unspeakable position into a receptive academy, then it is that position's triumph
and not defeat. Rather than lose their critical edge (as is often feared by those
who fear institutions and professions) critiques such as Ahmad's often *fulfill* their
interventionist aims precisely by recourse to such accommodation. Becoming a
part of the archive of "postcolonial studies" is a sure sign of the possibilities of
such success.

To say this is to suggest that if we have seen of late a tremendous growth in
postcolonial scholarship, it is still a field very much in the making. One of the
factors which will affect the future of the field, it seems to me, is the increasing
attention paid of late to issues of cosmopolitanism and globalism. Indeed, I want
to suggest that the "global" is fast replacing the "postcolonial" as a category of
analysis, and the future of the field will depend quite heavily on the negotiations
of the interface between these emphases. Just as "gender studies" seemed in its
earlier days a mixed blessing to those working in "Women's studies," so does
"global studies" seem today to some postcolonialists. For while the importance
of issues of globalization and cosmopolitanism cannot be ignored in an increasingly interconnected world, there is, it seems to me, a legitimate fear on the part
of some of the gradual loss of specialized local knowledges. Such a tendency has,
of course, already been in the making – the ever-increasing scope of the "postcolonial" – from Africa to Asia to Australia to Canada to Ireland to the newly
formed nations of Eastern Europe – has at once been both a threat and a promise

of a kind of intellectual wanderlust. While I am convinced that the category of the "postcolonial" is legitimately used in *all* these contexts, it would be a mistake if established practitioners in the field or students interested in entering it ever attempted a "coverage" model of postcolonial scholarship. For it is arguably in the critical tensions afforded by the interface between a historically nuanced, specialist knowledge of a given area and the rather more abstract questions posed by postcolonial theory that the most innovative research often originates. It is these interstices of area studies and postcolonial theory that I believe need to be retained even as we enter – with cautionary optimism – the realm of the global.

References

Achebe, Chinua. (1975). "The African Writer and the English Language," in *Morning Yet on Creation Day* (pp. 55–62). London: Heinemann.

Achebe, Chinua. (1977). "An Image of Africa: Racism in Conrad's *Heart of Darkness*," Rpnt in *Hopes and Impediments* (pp. 1–20). New York: Bantam Doubleday, 1989.

Ahmad, Aijaz. (1992). *In Theory: Classes, Nations, Literatures*. London: Verso.

Appiah, Kwame Anthony. (1992). *In My Father's House: Africa in the Philosophy of Culture*. New York: Oxford University Press.

Azim, Firdous. (1993). *The Colonial Rise of the Novel*. New York: Routledge.

Bakhtin, Mikhail. (1981). *The Dialogic Imagination*, ed. Michae Holquist, trans. Caryl Emerson and Michael Holquist. Austin: University of Texas Press.

Bernheimer, Charles, ed. (1995). *Comparative Literature in the Age of Multiculturalism*. Baltimore: Johns Hopkins University Press.

Bhabha, Homi. (1994). *The Location of Culture*. New York: Routledge.

———. (1994a). "By Bread Alone: Signs of Violence in the Mid-nineteenth Century," in *The Location of Culture*. New York: Routledge.

Brantlinger, Patrick. (1988). *Rule of Darkness: British Literature and Imperialism 1830–1914*. Ithaca: Cornell University Press.

Breckenridge, Carol and Peter van der Veer, eds. (1991). *Orientalism and the Postcolonial Predicament*. Philadelphia: University of Pennsylvania Press.

Brennen, Timothy. (1989). *Salman Rushdie and the Third World*. New York: St. Martin's Press.

Cheng, Vincent. (1995). *Joyce, Race and Empire*. New York: Cambridge University Press.

Chinweizu, Onwuchekwa Jemie and Ihechukwu Madubuike. (1980). *Toward the Decolonization of African Literature*. Enugu: Fourth Dimension Publishing.

Chow, Rey. (1993). *Writing Diaspora*. Bloomington: Indiana University Press.

Davies, Carol Boyce and Elaine Savory Fido, eds. (1990). *Out of the Kumbla: Caribbean Women and Literature*. Trenton, NJ: Africa World Press.

Desai, Gaurav. (1993). "English as an African Language," *English Today*, 9: 4–11.

Dirks, Nicholas, ed. (1992). *Colonialism and Culture*. Ann Arbor: University of Michigan Press.

Dirlik, Arif. (1994). "The Postcolonial Aura: Third World Criticism in the Age of Global Capitalism," *Critical Inquiry*, 20: 328–56.

Duffy, Enda. (1994). *The Subaltern Ulysses*. Minneapolis: University of Minnesota Press.

Gates, Henry Louis, Jr. (1991). "Critical Fanonism," *Critical Inquiry*, 17: 457–70.

Gikandi, Simon. (1996). *Maps of Englishness: Writing Identity in the Culture of Colonialism*. New York: Columbia University Press.

Gilroy, Paul. (1993). *The Black Atlantic: Modernity and Double Consciousness*. Cambridge: Harvard University Press.

Gordon, Lewis R., T. Denean Sharpley-Whiting, and Renee T. White, eds. (1996). *Fanon: A Critical Reader*. Cambridge, Mass.: Blackwell.

Guha, Ranajit. (1983). *Elementary Aspects of Peasant Insurgency*. Delhi: Oxford University Press.

Harlow, Barbara. (1987). *Resistance Literature*. New York: Routledge.

Irele, Abiola. (1981). *The African Experience in Literature and Ideology*. (Rpnt.) Bloomington: Indiana University Press, 1990.

JanMohamed, Abdul. (1983). *Manichean Aesthetics*. Amherst: University of Massachusetts Press.

Kaul, Suvir. (1996). "Colonial Figures and Postcolonial Reading," *Diacritics*, 26: 74–89.

Lazarus, Neil. (1990). *Resistance in Postcolonial African Fiction*. New Haven: Yale University Press.

Lloyd, David. (1993). *Anomalous States: Irish Writing and the Post-Colonial Moment*. Durham: Duke University Press.

Loomba, Ania. (1992). "Imperialism, patriarchy and post-colonial English studies." in *Gender, Race, Renaissance Drama* (pp. 10–37). Delhi: Oxford University Press.

Macaulay, Thomas. (1835). "Minute on Indian Education," in Bill Ashcroft, Gareth Griffiths, Helen Tiffin, eds., *The Post-colonial Studies Reader* (pp. 428–30) New York: Routledge, 1995.

Mills, Sara. (1991). *Discourses of Difference*. New York: Routledge.

Mitchell, Timothy. (1988). *Colonising Egypt*. New York: Cambridge University Press.

Mudimbe, V. Y. (1988). *The Invention of Africa*. Bloomington: Indiana University Press.

——. (1994). *The Idea of Africa*. Bloomington: Indiana University Press.

Nandy, Ashis. (1983). *The Intimate Enemy: Loss and Recovery of Self Under Colonialism*. Delhi: Oxford University Press.

Ngugi wa Thiong'o. (1968). "On the Abolition of the English Department." In *Homecoming: Essays on African and Caribbean Literature, Culture and Politics* (pp. 145–50). Westport: Lawrence Hill and Co., 1972.

——. (1981). *Writers in Politics*. London: Heinemann.

——. (1986). *Decolonising the Mind: The Politics of Language in African Literature*. London: James Currey.

Nixon, Rob. (1992). *London Calling*. New York: Oxford University Press.

Ogunyemi, Chikwenye O. (1996). *Africa Wo/Man Palava: The Nigerian Novel by Women*. Chicago: University of Chicago Press.

Prakash, Gyan. (1992). "Postcolonial Criticism and Indian Historiography," *Social Text*, 31/32: 8–19.

——. (1992a). "Writing Post-orientalist Histories of the Third world: Indian Historiography is Good to Think," in, Nicholas Dirks, ed., *Colonialism and Culture*. Ann Arbor: University of Michigan Press.

——. ed. (1995). *After Colonialism: Imperial Histories and Postcolonial Displacements.* Princeton: Princeton University Press.

Public Culture. (1993). Special Issue on Ahmad's *In Theory*, 6(1), fall.

Robbins, Bruce. (1993). *Secular Vocations: Intellectuals, Professionalism, Culture.* London: Verso.

Said, Edward. (1978). *Orientalism.* New York: Random House.

——. (1993). *Culture and Imperialism.* New York: Alfred Knopf.

San Juan, E. (1998). *Beyond Postcolonial Theory.* New York: St. Martin's Press.

Sengupta, Mahasweta. (1998). "Literature for the Empire: Rabindranath Tagore Reads English," in Susie Tharu, ed., *Subject to Change: Teaching Literature in the Nineties* (pp. 219–37). Hyderabad: Orient Longman.

Sharpe, Jenny. (1993). *Allegories of Empire: The Figure of Woman in the Colonial Text.* Minneapolis: University of Minnesota Press.

Spivak, Gayatri Chakravorty. (1986). "Three Women's Texts and a Critique of Imperialism," in Henry Louis Gates, Jr., ed., *"Race," Writing and Difference* (pp. 262–80). Chicago: University of Chicago Press.

——. (1990). *The Post-colonial Critic.* New York: Routledge.

——. (1993). *Outside in the Teaching Machine.* New York: Routledge.

Spurr, David. (1993). *The Rhetoric of Empire.* Durham: Duke University Press.

Suleri, Sara. (1992). *The Rhetoric of English India.* Chicago: University of Chicago Press.

Sunder Rajan, Rajeswari. (1997). "The Third World Academic in Other Places; or, the Postcolonial Intellectual Revisited," *Critical Inquiry*, 23: 596–616.

——, ed. (1992). *The Lie of the Land: English Literary Studies in India.* Delhi: Oxford University Press.

Tharu, Susie, ed. (1998). *Subject to Change: Teaching Literature in the Nineties.* Hyderabad: Orient Longman.

Thomas, Nicholas. (1994). *Colonialism's Culture: Anthropology, Travel and Government.* Princeton: Princeton University Press.

Viswanathan, Gauri. (1989). *Masks of Conquest: Literary Study and British Rule in India.* New York: Columbia University Press.

Wali, Obiajunwa. (1963). "The Dead End of African Literature?" *Transition*, 10: 13–15.

539

Chapter 28

Postcolonial Legality

Upendra Baxi

1   Introduction

Postcolonialism is a troubled continent of contested conceptions; the challenge and complexity stand aggravated when the unfamiliar guest – the discourse of constitutionalism and human rights – makes appearance at the dining table.

Constitutionalism, most generally understood, provides for structures, forms, and apparatuses of governance and modes of legitimation of power. But constitutionalism is not all about governance; it also provides contested sites for ideas and practices concerning justice, rights, development, and individual| associational autonomy. Constitutionalism provides narratives of both *rule* and *resistance*.

Constitutionalism typically evokes the device of written constitutions; but the texts of the constitution do not always illuminate, much less exhaust, the context of political and social action. Indeed, constitutionalism interrogates the notion of *writtenness* in at least two ways. First, behind every *written* constitution lies an *unwritten* one, which enacts the conventions and usages, the protocols and accouterments of power that resist linguistic codification. Second, the *unwritten* often overrides that which stands elaborately written, such that we have the paradox of "constitutions without constitutionalism" (to adapt a notion of Oketh-Ogando). The defense/war power of the executive furnishes the paradigm case of the first; the second stands illustrated by periods of constitutional dictatorships. In these, the *acquisition of political power* is legitimated through devices prescribed in the written constitution but the modes of *exercise of power* remain relatively autonomous of the corpus of constraints enacted in the text.

The history of evolution of modern constitutionalism is a narrative of growth of asymmetries in domination and resistance. Principles of constitutionalism were perfected in Europe at the very historic moment when colonialism flourished. In retrospect, the narrative of constitutional development in decolonized societies provides a massive indictment of accomplishments of liberal thought.

Colonial/imperial power provides scripts only for governance; by definition, it is a stranger to the idea of fundamental rights of the people. All practices of interrogation of colonial/imperial power constitute acts of subversion and sedition, even treason. Notions of "justice" and "development" in colonial law formations are at best *paternalistic* and at worst *accessories* to imperial domination. Ideas and forms of incipient constitutionalism do occur (at some moments of insurgency against colonial rule) but only as instrumentalities of governance. Thus, for example, colonial governance may entail separation of powers or decentralization of power. But in neither situation is the centralized unity of colonial state power put even to the mildest risk. Separation of powers between executive and judiciary occurs in colonial governance; but more as a design for efficient rule than as mechanism for superior protection of peoples' rights against bad or evil governance. Likewise, "federal" division of powers occurs typically as *decentralization*, and not *devolution*, of power.

All this needs to be stated in order to cure the modern superstition which suggests that constitutional forms and ideals constitute a legacy of colonialism. The reality is otherwise. Colonialism and constitutionalism were always strangers. And the very act of enunciating a constitution marks a historic rupture.

Even so, it would remain true at a broad level to say that colonial legal cultures did affect *forms* of constitutions: the *civil law* and the *common law* traditions render legible the texts structuring the apparatuses of governance. This contrast may, for example, be studied fruitfully through the ways in which concentrations of the supreme executive power, especially through the Imperial Presidency in most parts of "Francophonic" and "Anglophonic" Africa or in the structuration of the adjudicatory powers. Even more fundamentally, the language of the law established, at least initially, the reach of eclectic *mimesis*. Perhaps more decisive to the constitutionalism formation were the contexts of the Cold War, which generated the antithetic discourse between the *liberal bourgeois* and *revolutionary socialist* constitutionalism. The differences proved vital for Third World practices of constitution making:

- the former venerates rights in *private property*, the latter celebrates state ownership of all property.
- political representation in liberal constitutionalism is a function of class domination, whereas in socialist constitutionalism the "state" stood endowed, through the Party, to represent "workers," "peasants," and "masses."
- adjudication is relatively autonomous in liberal constitutions; it is tied to the Party and the State in socialist constitutions, where adjudication has a markedly *pedagogic role in the construction of the new socialist human person*.
- socialist constitutionalism emphasizes *fundamental duties of citizens* whereas liberal constitutionalism foregrounds their *fundamental rights*.
- this last had profound implications on the structuring of *reign of terror*: *gulags* were manifest pathologies of socialist constitutionalism, while the *rule-of-law* societies are able to disperse their own *gulags* as unredressable manifestations

of microfascism of the local state and civil society (e.g. McCarthyism, vicious forms of racism and patriarchy).

- the giantomachy between the two superpowers in the Cold War era contributed, with deep implication for human rights, to the *militarization of the state* in ex-colonial societies.

Both socialist and capitalist forms of imperial hegemony affected the text and context of constitutionalism in decolonized societies.

2   Postcolonial Constitutionalisms

Despite all this, it would be an error to regard the postcolony as one coherent "public place" determined by any single organizing principle. It remains rather a plurality of spheres, arenas, identities (A. Mbembe). And partly these stand shaped by the struggles for decolonization, most of which have entailed militant peoples' movements and colonial state repression. Postcolonial constitutions thus inevitably carry their birthmarks.

Even so, these do stand constituted by a foremost organizing principle of *natural rights*: claims to self-determination not warranted by imperial legality. Mohandas Gandhi inaugurated the historic practice of this right in the early decades of this century, as did Nelson Mandela towards its end. These *performative* practices of natural rights create a new order of institutional facts (*cf.* Searle) confronting the *brute* facts of power and domination.

The practices of the human right to self-determination stood, however, conditioned by the diverse patterns of colonization, as yet been insufficiently theorized. But available accounts suggest a rich diversity. At the one end of the spectrum we have the pattern of complete metropolitan domination as in Mozambique, which was

> completely dominated by Portuguese laws, Portuguese legal officers and Portuguese legal thinking. All legislation was made in Portugal and then applied to the colony.
>
> As one commentator put it, the laws were shipped out to Mozambique like wine or wool. All the judges and prosecutors belonged to Portuguese state service, and all the legal profession consisted almost entirely of Portuguese persons who had gone out to the colony to make their fortunes. No law school existed in Mozambique until the very eve of independence. (Sachs and Welch, 1990: 3)

At the other end of the spectrum were the colonies like the subcontinent of India in which toleration and at times grudging indifference to civilizational and cultural traditions of the colonized, animated by the exigencies of empire-building, entailed recognition of indigenous legal traditions. The Hindu and the Muslim law as practiced for centuries in India required (so tied were these bodies of law to land, forms of property, religion, and culture) sustained recognition in law, policy, and administration. Colonial mediation, of course, resulted in hybrid formations now known as Anglo-Hindu and Anglo-Muslim law (Derrett). And protection of "personal" (religious/customary) law systems thereby became typical stratagems of "divide and rule" practices of communalization of governance and politics.

The diverse interests of the colonizing elite in India (the missionaries, the commercial/industrial, elite and the administrator/law reform networks) produced strikingly different results. As compared with Mozambique, for example, these networks of elites pulled together (without, of course, threatening their collective interests) not to *ship* their laws but to ship *law reform* models! Colonial India became the arena of Benthamite legislative programs: the metropolitan English legal culture, which remained common-law allergic to the very notion of codification, reveled in pioneering the codification of civil and criminal law in India! (Stokes; Dhagamwar). All this generated an increasingly sophisticated Indian legal profession which was to dominate both the nationalist movement (in the figure of Mohandas Gandhi, Rajendra Prasad, Vallabbhai Patel, C. R. Das, K. M. Munshi, Motilal Nehru, M. A. Zinah, B. R. Ambedkar, to mention a few examples) and the making of the Indian Constitution (Austin).

In the middle ranges of the colonial spectrum lies the example of "settler colonialism" in many parts of Africa. For the most part, in what stood named as the "African customary law" the colonial regimes invented various devices of governance, as for example the institution of chieftanship. Of course this invention was a result of complex and contradictory negotiation of interests between colonial administrators and indigenous elites (Mamdani) and has functioned as more than a historic residue in the postcolonial African condition.

When we attend to the difference and diversity of formative colonial contexts and struggles for self-determination, we begin to realize, at least for law and constitutionalism, how reifying the term "postcolonial" is. And this should serve to remind us as well that the term itself often functions as a constituent moment of organization of the politics of memory and of forgetting, devices available for political mobilization within and across nations.

3 Continuities

Postcolonial law registers *breaks* as well as *continuities*.

A salient continuity resides in the simultaneous affirmation and negation of the emancipatory logic of self-determination. The very success of the decolonization project entails a closure: the new nation-state consolidates colonial boundaries, giving rise to the paradox of "nationalism without nation" (Alyousis). The new nation-state appears neocolonial to many groups whose understanding of struggle against colonialism was radically divergent from those who eventually capture state power and apparatus.

Postcolonial legality thus stands sited in the dialectics of repression and insurgency (Daniel). It continues colonial laws' repressive legacies and even innovates these through the regimes of security legislations. These often equate *suspicion* by the authorities with *proof* of guilt. The jurisdiction of suspicion permits dragnet arrests; indefinite incarceration often beyond pale of even bare judicial scrutiny; custodial torture and tyranny; organized *"disappearances"* of the detainees. The colonial Official Secrets Acts continue to convert conscientious citizens into *spies* by declaring a notified public place the *private* space of the security forces; to enter proscribed places is an act of espionage "worthy" of severe repression.

Despite all this, the postcolonial state lives in fear and trembling. Its Constitution must provide means of its own demise through the power to proclaim a state of emergency. These proclamations seldom relate to the objective of preserving the nascent constitutional emergences from external aggression or armed rebellion. More often, emergency powers have been used in aid of the corrupt sovereign who muzzles even the semblance of political dissent, through extrajudicial killings – at times even taking the juridical form of capital punishment. Ken Saro Wiwa emblematizes, at the turn of the century, the extraordinary politics of "constitutionalized" cruelty.

4   Discontinuities

All the same, a major discontinuity inheres in the constitutional project, which installs a new order of representation of the national "selfhood." Constitutions are constructed, as moral autobiographies of "new" nations, promising a new future, vigorously disinvesting the colonial past.

Postcolonial constitutions comprise two contradictory genres of texts: texts of *governance* and texts of *justice*. The social justice texts of constitutions (texts permeated with ideologies of human rights and redistribution) are slender compared with the texts of governance. But postcolonial legality is always characterized by constitutionally anchored contradiction between *governance* and *justice* in ways not characteristic of the original American constitution and many "Western" counterparts. In this sense, the post-Soviet or "transitional" constitutionalism derives as much, if not more, from the Third World traditions than from the post-bicentennial French and American ones.

Postcolonial legality provides a register of creativity within the framework of mimesis. Mimesis consists in the reproduction, with a range of variation, of texts of governance; even here the invention of military constitutionalism, notably in Africa, deploys cruelly the latent antiliberal potential of the Western constitutional genre. Creativity abides in the human rights and social justice constitutional texts illuminating contradictions of transition, not just rites of passage.

The thesis that postcolonial constitutions are exemplars of "catachreis" (a concept-metaphor without any "historically adequate referent": Spivak) negates in the ex-colonial subject any epistemic capability to form languages of rights and justice. It also ignores the historical specificity of anticolonial struggles, which innovate new forms of constitutionalism. It would fly in the face of recorded history to suggest that either the "classical" genre of postcolonial constitutionalism (such as in India) or the radically emergent forms (in South Africa, Namibia, or Eritrea) constitute any form of "catachreis."

Indeed, some of these latter provide inaugural examples in human history of constitution-making not under the auspices of an elective oligarchy but through the means of widespread popular participation, deferring to a logic of government by consent in the very *foundational* endeavor: the making of the constitution itself.

The contribution of constitutionally authored postcolonial legality lies in the mutation of a whole variety of norms and doctrines writ large on the "Western"/ "Northern" constitutional imagination and praxis. We examine below some aspects of forms of discontinuity.

Notions of human rights

Among the most notable transformations is the extension of the "classical" western notions of rights. The Indian Constitution, inaugurally, extends the notion of rights beyond the state to civil society. It outlaws practices based on the ground of "untouchability"; forbids and penalizes practices of forced and bonded labor and markets for trafficking in human beings; and provides a first contemporary example of *empowering* state action in aid of human rights against formations of cruelty in civil society.

Not merely this. The Indian Constitution, in its progressive development, becomes the vehicle of empowerment of the untouchables and indigenous peoples (defined respectively as the "scheduled castes" and "scheduled tribes"). They stand endowed with legislative reservations: under a constitutionally prescribed scheme, a considerable number of seats are reserved in Parliament and state legislatures (see Baxi; Galanter). Quotas in education and state employment for these categories as well as for socially and educationally backward classes and other backward classes stand mandated. The extension of quotas in the federal services in the eighties (through the implementation of the Mandal Commission report) marked a major social and political upheaval, including poignant practices of self-immolation by young people. The Supreme Court has validated this provision, at the same time mandating that such quotas should not exceed a 50 percent limit and should exclude those groups of beneficiaries who have already achieved economic and social well-being.

Affirmative action programs abound, both as devices of *governance* and of *justice*. In Malaysia, the majority of *bhoomiputras* (sons of soil) enjoy benefits denied to the local Chinese and Indian Malaysian citizens. Sri Lanka is in search of acceptable formulas to end a most savage civil war and find a balance of equity between the Sinhalese and Tamils. Similar, and acute, problems bedevil the political economy (of what Horowitz aptly names as) "severely divided societies." Politics of affirmative action enshrined as an aspect of the doctrine of liberal equality, present manifold narratives transcending political labors following the American Supreme Court's heroic endeavors since *Brown* v. *Board of Education*.

State neutrality

The liberal doctrines about state neutrality stand significantly renovated by the development of postcolonial constitutionalism. Constitutions do embody notions of collective moral good that the state is enjoined to promote. In India, for example, the state may justifiably regulate rights to conscience and to religion on the grounds of public health and order and morality. The answer to the questions *which, what* or *whose morality* can regulate even the right to *conscience* has been a contested site named as constitutional *secularism*. Many devout Indian Muslims cannot concede that courts or parliament can reform the *shari'a* in ways beyond what the hermeneutic of Koranic tradition warrants in the name of secular gender equality. Similarly, many a pious Hindu remains perplexed by the constitutional modification allowing untouchables a right to enter and worship in temples. Indian Catholics are no less perturbed by legislative measures which restrict on the ground of morality certain practices of preaching and converting, and by legalization of abortion. All religious communities feel equally distressed by the very notion of a Uniform Civil Code, which remains the constitutional obligation of the Indian State!

When politics stands thus confronted with the might of religious traditions in multireligious society like India, it takes recourse to aspirational *constitutional enunciations*, typically crystallized in the Directive Principles of State Policy and the Charter of Fundamental Duties of Citizens. Not judicially enforceable, these cast a paramount duty on the legislature and the executive. These provide critical social spaces for politics of identity and difference by introducing dissonance in the life of civil society and the state. The fundamental duty to respect and cherish the ideals of the freedom movement; to respect the "composite culture" of India; to develop a scientific temper, spirit of enquiry, and reform; and to renounce practices derogatory of women – all enable discourses of empowerment. These draw legitimation not from some abstract conception of toleration and dignity but from the source of all legality: the Constitution itself. Of course, the discourse on fundamental duties of citizens is not always people-friendly and has been used to trump basic rights in the constitutional experience of socialist societies and in military constitutional dictatorships in the South.

Property relations

From the first generation of Third World Constitutionalism to the third generation,[1] a central problem has been one of redefinition of property relations. Given the diversity of patterns of colonization and national resistance movements, postcolonial legality furnishes divergent narratives.

Often enough, the bourgeoisie who triumphed in nationalist movements embodied fundamental rights against expropriation, necessary to any basic transformation of agrarian relations. Wherever federalism prevails, the power to legislate and implement agrarian reforms lies with the state or province rather than with the national government. The combined impact of the fundamental right to property and the federal principle is to create a juridical maze which mires all prospects of transformation of deeply unequal property relations.

Pitted against this constitutional construction of the *status quo ante* are, of course, the energies of expectations nurtured during anticolonial struggles. Unlike First World constitutionalism, where universal adult suffrage was extended gradually, over long stretches of historical time, most postcolonial societies were born with instant political enfranchisement. This has led to significant agrarian movements, including movements on behalf, if not at the behest, of the rural poor. Unlike First World constitutionalism, postcolonial constitutionalism provides a register of state formative practices centered upon the issue of redistribution and property relations.

Of course, both *rule* and *resistance*, in this arena, depend on the historic *locus*. Socialist (and even postsocialist) Third World constitutions (Mozambique being an exemplar) differ historically from South Africa or Zimbabwe. The latter stands characterized by an entrenched constitutional provision forbidding agrarian reform measures which may disrupt assurances of entitlement to the White settlers (Gato); the former has to confront the necessity of reordering land relations and rights leavened by both colonialism and apartheid. In addition, different systems of property relations colonially constructed on customary law remain obdurate (and not just in Africa). In contrast, for example, the Indian experiment and experience in guarded agrarian reforms successfully abolishes the historic *zamindari* system (of revenue exactions by large landowners) but fares very unevenly (Januuzi; Baxi) in terms of protection of tenancy or agrarian land ceiling.

Despite local variation, the following remain broadly salient in any narrative of comparative postcolonial constitutionalism:

- The militancy of subaltern movements for agrarian reforms reinforces the *raison d'état*. The state is able to justify excessive use of violence, while *condoning structural violence*: the *reign of terror* by state agents and mangers is *justified as the rule of law* (e.g. the state response to the Naxalite movement in India).
- The worst practices of agrestic serfdom continue (e.g. debt bondage; payment of wages in kind, often narcotics, as in Pakistan, to secure a servile workforce; varieties of unfree labor arising from nonpayment of minimum wages and gender-based wage differentiation; unconscionable forms of child labor; trafficking in women).

- By the same token, preservation and promotion of the worst forms of violence against untouchables is practiced by the dominant landowning classes; it knows no restraint, whether in terms of the wise custom or the rule of law governance models (to appreciate the depths of victimage, one has to read the poignant portrayal in Rohintoon Mistry's classic novel *A Fine Balance*, grounded in modern India but of deep relevance elsewhere).
- The regulatory capture becomes versatile: that is, not just the capture by special interests of the making of legislative policies and law reform but also the *systematic* co-optation of the land revenue, local police and adjudication, learned professions including lawyers, and mass media.

The postcolonial quest for equity in property relations continues, though beset by the inheritance of colonial inequities aggravated by malgovernance practices. Constitutional texts and contexts continue to energize both *rule* and *resistance*. The gains of social movements, wherever considerable, as for example in India, stand now threatened by the might of forces of globalization. The spread of foreign direct investment and multinational capital (while posing a different order of challenges to social activism and human rights movements) also presents a relatively bleak future for agrarian reforms. The voracious appetite of multinationals devours prime agricultural lands, forests, and environment (that provide the necessary infrastructure for their profit and power). Postcolonial constitutional texts could not have anticipated the context of globalization; the task of interpretation has to contend with the fact that constitutions become merely the "local" particular that has to adjust somehow to the "universal" in the global.

4   Judicial Activism

Indeed, judicial activism has steadily emerged as a foremost powerful site, making adjudication (as in India) a people's ally contributing to social movement for redemocratization. Judicial activism in India results in two astonishing feats.

First, the Indian Supreme Court enunciated in the seventies an unusual province and function for judicial review by declaring that the power of Parliament to amend the Constitution was subject to judicial review: it may not extend to alteration of the essential features of the basic structure of the Constitution. What these "essential features" were was left for the Justices to enunciate from time to time, but these included the "rule of law," "republican form of government," "federalism," "democracy," "socialism," "secularism," and above all the power of judicial review. The doctrine was not merely enunciated; it was also applied to invalidate several amendments. (In the process, the Court considered the right to property as worthy of deletion.) The result has often been, accurately, described by naming the Indian Supreme Court as a *constituent assembly in permanent session*. And this form of adjudicatory activism has, in turn, traveled to Pakistan, Bangladesh, and Nepal.

Second, the meteoric rise of the social action litigation (SAL, to be distinguished carefully from Public Interest Litigation: PIL) in India represents a process of informalization and democratization of access to appellate courts, including the Supreme Court of India. The inaugural device here is simple: sending letters to justices drawing their attention to violation of the rights of the disadvantaged, dispossessed, and deprived sections of Indian society. The letters are usually based on media horror stories of violations of the rights of the impoverished and vulnerable. Justices usually act upon them, thus inventing an *epistolary jurisdiction*, expanding the standing (the strict rule being that only a person whose rights are affected may approach courts), determining the facts at issue by the device of sociolegal commissions of enquiry and by orders and directions requiring state action.

SAL has thus been deployed to combat: (a) governmental lawlessness and official deviance; (b) compensatory measures of rehabilitation and restitution for cruel, inhumane, and degrading treatment in custodial institutions; (c) environmental degradation; (d) gender inequality and injustice; (e) corruption in high places. In the process, new fundamental rights of the people, not scripted in the Constitution, have been judicially enunciated and enforced (such as: right to work, literacy, education, shelter, environmental integrity, health, education, accountability and transparency in governance (Ahuja; Baxi, 1989, 1998; Sathe, 1996)).

Not all these enunciations bring about immediate impact, so entrenched are some forms of abuse of public power and concentrations of violence in the civil society. But SAL enables, beyond conventional theories about judicial process and power, through continuing social conversation between human rights and social activists, on the one hand, and wielders of adjudicatory power on the other, practices of *redemocratization* of the Indian polity. No doubt, such judicial activism has often been attacked as *usurpation*. And the charge rings somewhat true when the courts actually begin to *administer*, as when they take over the day-to-day investigation in cases of corruption in high places or management of custodial institutions like jails, juvenile homes, and remand homes for women. But this is done only when the institutions of governance fail to heed the directives of the Court. SAL has so far survived attacks based on the Northern prescriptive theories about judicial role (ever anxious about the antimajoritarian character of judicial review). These theories, indeed, provide a good example of Spivak's "catachreis"; the prescriptive theories have no "historically adequate referent" for the phenomenon of such judicial activism!

5 Engendering Constitutionalism

All postcolonial constitutions are characterized by *political gender equality*. Women as citizens have a right to vote and contest at elections, marking a profound transformation in the way the criteria of political legitimation function in actual social life. South Asian constitutionalism has witnessed a steady succession of women heads of state, at a rate unparalleled elsewhere in the world. And this has a major significance for cultural traditions: political Islam, which otherwise enacts patriarchal gender differentiation in all manner of ways, has still enabled women Prime Ministers in Islamabad and Dhaka. Buddhism in Sri Lanka or "Hinduism" in India has not rendered problematic accession to the highest political power by women political leaders. All this symbolizes *political gender equality at work* in South Asian constitutionalism. And, in some ways, this is an achievement in itself when we recall that the two bicentennial constitutions have yet to install a woman as the head of the state.

The issue of engendering politics, of course, goes deeper than women heads of state, unfortunately fated to govern in a robust patriarchal structure of domination. The constitutional agenda for women's movements in the Third World addresses issues of *feminization* of political party structures and processes. In India, controversy rages on a quota system through which at least one-third of seats is "reserved" wholly for women candidates as a fulfillment of representational equality. India has, at long last, made a wholesome beginning by reserving seats for women in local self-governance, both at the levels of *panchayats* (rural self-governance institutions) and in municipal institutions. It is estimated that as many as 300,000 women will thus be empowered to experience the responsibility of grassroots governance. Elsewhere, especially in some Latin American constitutions, attempts have been made to require political parties to provide "blue ribbon" constituencies to women candidates.

All the same, the most agonizing issue confronting postcolonial constitutionalism has been that of achievement of gender equality in civil society, in the family, and the market relations. Forms of constitutionalism have proved woefully inadequate (as in the First World) in coping with sexual aggression in "public" and "private" spaces and in overcoming gender stereotypes. The promise and challenge of postcolonial constitutionalism lies in ways of overcoming the "male in the state."

The Indian example shows that much can be achieved through judicial activism, where a proactive judiciary exposes and nudges a disoriented state executive to constitutional compliance. On the eve of the golden jubilee of Indian Independence, the Indian Supreme Court in *Viasakha* v. *State of Rajasthan* proclaimed, through a judgment, *legislation* outlawing sexual harassment in all (public and private) workplaces. It further declared that unless Parliament enacts a law consistent with the decision, the *law* declared by the Court shall be binding throughout India. This illustrates the fecund scope which judicial power and process holds for combating patriarchy in the state and civil society.

And yet major issues remain on the agenda of the Third World, engendering militant constititutionalism that combats worse violence against women: the dowry-murder (Menski); child sexual abuse; female genital mutilation practiced in some parts of Africa, despite legislation criminalizing these forms of social behavior; sex-based nutritional discrimination; and sex-trafficking signifying nothing less than a new form of *slavery* for women (Human Rights Watch; Baxi, 1999).

Forms of constitutionalism are everywhere notoriously phallocentric. But Third World constitutionalism makes the traditions of patriarchy deeply problematic. Women's human rights movements today question formations of power in state and society in ways which would have literally terrified the founding *fathers* of the formative era of First World constitutionalism.

6 Pathologies of Power

When all is said and done, histories of postcolonial legality provide their distinctive pathologies. The steady emergence of *military constitutionalism* in many parts of Africa and Asia is marked by catastrophic practices of power, particularly against ethic groups. And it is also marked by *quasi-nationalism* which captures the "nation–state and bring(s) authorized violence down ruthlessly against the people who seem to stand in the way of the nation being united and pure as one body," contributing to the rise of a genocidal state (Werbner.)

"Militarization of ethnicity" (Horowitz; Daniel) accentuates militarization of state and at times of civil society. Under such conjunctures, constitutionalism merely marks the cruel cartography of power and resistance to power. The combined impact of the upsurge of collective popular illegalities and state lawlessness cumulatively complicates ideas about authority, rights, justice, pluralism, and law. Under such conditions of postcoloniality the notions about the rule of law acquire synonymity with *the reign of terror*.

Postcolonial legality has proved itself versatile in its toleration of political corruption. Inadequate laws, insufficient investigation, politically debilitated prosecution, labyrinthine adjudication, witness intimidation, anemic law reform – all these combine to produce a legal and political culture rendering public accountability a casualty. Peoples' movements against corruption in public life, when not co-opted with "moral crusades" against rival political parties or factions, are swiftly suppressed. Privileged criminality, of which corruption is an epitome, also bestows postcolonial legality with impermissible pluralism in the administration of criminal justice. Differential justice exists everywhere, but what distinguishes postcolonial law formation is its open espousal of regimes of impunity, perforated by an occasional "truth commission" (Nino). In many a society, the bulk and generality of postcolonial "citizens" are hapless victims of "governance" beyond the pale of accountability. For them, *the law itself assumes the face of fate*.

The aborted fate of postcolonial law needs to be grasped in terms of a global genealogy. Shaped by the imperatives of the Cold War, the contours of postcolonial legality were heavily conditioned by two hegemonic superpowers. Articulatory space for peoples' jural creativity stood confiscated by juristic *dependencia*. Non-Western forms of legal *imaginations* were denied yet again historic time and space for their unfurling, beyond many a worthwhile improvisation (already mentioned earlier). The *material practices of power* (such as global arms traffic; direct military intervention thinly disguised as humanitarian intervention) aborted many a departure from the Western/imperial canons of *law-ness*. Just when the reversal of European history indicated possibilities of transcendence, "globalization" translates the Cold War motto "Making the world safe for democracy" into "Making the world safe for foreign investors"! It seeks to transform all Third World states into the clones of Late Capitalism. If self-determination was the signature of postcolonial legality, the globalization of law calibrates the postcolonial states and law to the carnival of global capital in its myriad forms. International financial capital, lethal multinationals (the Bhopal catastrophe remains an archetype (Baxi and Dhandha)), regimes of suprastatal institutions, international and regional, all combine to escalate networks of power constituting the new global ruling class.

A *paradigm shift* is already under way: a transition from the paradigm of *universal human rights* (to the historic enunciation of which the South contributed a very high order of imagination) to the paradigm of *trade-related, market-friendly human rights*. Aggregations of global capital and technology make problematic the future of languages of human rights. This emergence of global economic constitutionalism has numerous impacts on the theory and practice of post-colonial dialectic between *rule and resistance*.

For example, it makes difficult, and at times impossible

- performance for *redistributive programs and polices* amidst the labyrinthine complexity of conditionalities of structural adjustment governance.
- the achievement of even modicum goals of "sustainable development."
- any historically meaningful pursuit of gender equality towards which global capital is notably hostile (e.g. sweatshops, gender-based wage discrimination, sex tourism).
- respect for fledgling rights of indigenous peoples, which now stand sacrificed at the altar of foreign investment (its "land hunger": that is, dispossession of lands considered necessary for siting profitable projects).
- minimal observance for collective human rights of the labor.
- development of social movements not co-opted by the United Nations patterns of international solidarity, at the behest of global capital though not on its *behalf*, in ways that has potential for registering here-and-now human amelioration.

On all accounts, the globalization of the law is more conducive to legal imperialism than to autonomous development. The most formidable challenge now posed to postcolonial law, in all its complexity and contradiction, is posed by *modest sites* of *resistance to global economic constitutionalism*. It is on this register that the future(s) of postcolonial legality and constitutionalism shall be inscribed.

Notes

1   A notion not commonly used and perhaps also problematic. I wish to indicate by the first generation of Third World constitutionalism law-regions decolonized after the Second World War; by the second generation I designate forms nascent during the various phases of the Cold War; and by the third generation I refer to post-Cold War constitutions.

The first, inaugurally, is the epoch of Indian constitutionalism; the second reaches out to "continental socialist" constitutions in the Third World; the third brings to mind post-Cold War forms such as those in Southern Africa, Ethiopia, Eritrea, Uganda.

The distinctions, historically crucial, await elucidation from the labors of comparative constitutional scholarship.

References and Bibliography

NOTE: In addition to works cited in the text, I include *illustrative* materials cognate to theme of this contribution.

Ahuja, Sangeeta. (1997). *People, Law, and Justice: Casebook on Public Interest Litigation* (Delhi: Sangam).

Alyousis, G. (1997). *Nationalism without a Nation* (Delhi: Oxford University Press).

Austin, Granville. (1964). *The Indian Constitution: Cornerstone of a Nation* (Delhi: Oxford University Press).

Baxi, Upendra. (1980). *The Indian Supreme Court and Politics* (Lucknow: Eastern Book Co.).

——. (1985). *Courage, Craft and Contention: The Suprme Court in Mid-eighties* (Bombay: N. M. Tripathi).

——. (1986). *Towards a Sociology of Indian Law* (New Delhi: Satvahan).

——. (1988). "Taking Suffering Seriously: Social Action Litigation Before the Supreme Court of India," in U. Baxi, ed., *Law and Poverty: Critical Essays 387* (Bombay: N. M. Tripathi).

——. (1989). *Liberty and Corruption: The Antulay Case and Beyond* (Lucknow: Eastern Book Co.).

——. (1997). "Judicial Activism: Usurpation or Redemocratization?" *Social Action*, 47: 341–60.

——. (1999). "From Human Rights to the Right to be a Woman," in A. Dhanda and A. Prashar, eds., *Engendering One Law: Essays in Honor of Professor Lotika Sarkar* (Lucknow: Eastern Book Co.).

——and Amita Dhanda. (1990). *Valiant Victims and Lethal Litigation* (Bombay: N. M. Tripathi).

——and Bhikhu Parkeh. (1993). *Crisis and Change in Contemporary India* (Delhi: Sage).

Chandra, Sudhir. (1998). *Enslaved Daughters: Colonialism, Law and Women's Rights* (Delhi: Oxford University Press).

Daniel, E. Valentine. (1997). *Chapters in an Anthropology of Violence: Sri Lankans, Sinhalas, and Tamils* (Delhi: Oxford University Press).

Derrett, J. D. M. (1968). *Religion, Law and State in India* (London: Faber & Faber).

Dhagamwar, Vasudha. (1994). *Law, Power and Justice* (Delhi: Sage).

Dhavan, Rajeev. (1977). *The Supreme Court of India: A Sociolegal Critique of its Jurisitic Techniques* (Bombay: N. M. Tripathi).

——and Alice Jacob, eds. (1987). *The Indian Constitution: Trends and Issues* (Bombay: N. M. Tripathi).

Fitzpatrick, Peter. (1992). *The Mythology of Modern Law* (London: Routledge).

Galanter, Marc. (1984). *Competing Equality* (Delhi: Oxford University Press).

Gato, Shadruck B. O. (1993). *Human and Peoples' Rights for the Oppressed: Critical Essays on the Theory and Practice from Sociology of Law Perspectives* (Lund: Lund University Press).

Ghai, Yash. (1997). *Hong Kong's New Constitutional Order* (Hong Kong: Hong Kong University Press).

Human Rights Watch/Asia. (1995). *Rape for Profit: Trafficking of Nepali Girls and Women into India's Brothels.*

Horowitz, Donald. (1985). *Ethnic Groups in Conflict* (Berkely: University California Press).

Jannuzi, Tomasson F. (1994). *India's Persistent Dilemma: The Political Economy of Agrarian Reform* (Boulder: Westview Press).

Mamdani, Mahmod. (1996). *Citizen and Subject: Contemporary Africa and the Legacy of Late Colonialism* (Princeton: Princeton University Press).

Mbembe, Achille. (1992). "Provisional Notes on the Postcolony," *Africa*, 62: 3–37.

Mbembe, Achille. (1992). "The Banality of Power and the Aesthetics of Vulgarity in the Postcolony," *Public Culture*, 4: 1–30.

Mendelsohn, Oliver and Marika Vicziany. (1998). *The Untouchables: Subordination, Poverty and the State in Modern India* (Cambridge: Cambridge University Press).

Mendelsohn, Oliver and Upendra Baxi. (1994). *The Rights of the Subordinated Peoples* (New Delhi: Oxford University Press).

Mistry, Rohinton. (1995). *A Fine Balance* (London: Faber).

Nino, Carlos Santiago. (1996). *Radical Evil on Trial* (New Haven: Yale University Press).

Oketh-Oganda, H. W. O. (1991). "Constitutions without Constitutionalism," in I. G. Shivji, ed., *State and Constitutionalism: An African Debate on Human Rights* (Harare: Southern Africa Political Economy Series (SAPES) Trust).

Parekh, Bhiku and Pieterse Jan Nederveen. (1997). *The Decolonization of Imagination* (Delhi: Oxford University Press).

Sachs, Albie and Gita H. Welch. (1990). *Liberating the Law: Creating Popular Justice in Mozambique* (London: Zed Books).

Sangari, Kumkum and Sudesh Vaid. (1989). *Recasting Women: Essays in Colonial History* (Delhi: Kali for Women).

Sathe, S. P. (1996). *Administrative Law in India*, 6th edn. (Bombay: N. M. Tripathi Ltd.).

Searle, John R. (1995). *The Social Construction of Reality* (London: Penguin).

Seervai. (1993). *Constitutional Law of India*, 3 vols. (Bombay: N. M. Tripathi).

Shivji, Issa. "State and Constitutionalism: A New Democratic Perspective," in *State and Constitutionalism: An African Debate on Democracy* (Harare: SAPEST).

Spivak, Gaytri C. (1995). "Constitutions and Culture Studies," in J. D. Leonard, ed., *Legal Studies as Cultural Studies: A Reader in (Post) Modern Critical Theory* (New York: State University of New York Press).

Stokes, Eric. (1959). *The English Utilitarians and India* (Oxford: The Clarendon Press).

——. (1978). *The Peasant and the Raj* (Cambridge: Cambridge University Press).

Tripathi, P. K. (1973). *Some Insights into Fundamental Rights* (Bombay: Bombay University Press).

Werbner, Richard. (1996). "Multiple Identities, Plural Arenas," in *Postcolonial Identities in Africa* (London: Zed Books).

Woodwiss, Anthony. (1998). *Globalization, Human Rights and Labour Law in Pacific Asia* (Cambridge: Cambridge University Press).

Chapter 29

Race, Gender, Class, Postcolonialism: Toward a New Humanistic Paradigm?

Bruce Robbins

"Are race and gender and sexual orientation distractions from basic issues of economic inequality and social class?" In a column for the *Nation*, a widely-read organ of US progressive opinion, Katha Pollitt (1998) says no to this question. Race, gender, and sexual orientation are inextricable from economic inequality, she argues, and proper attention must be paid. Yet Pollitt does not defend "post-structuralism, cultural studies, post-colonial studies" and the rest of "the academic pomo left," which have insistently upheld the same thesis. It would be easier to make the case for race, gender, and so on, Pollitt suggests with some asperity, if only people did not confuse them with "far-out" enterprises like post-colonial studies.[1]

Pollitt is not alone in her exasperation with postcolonial studies. Though the concept has flourished across a wide range of academic disciplines, to date it has won little respect among those working the border between the academy and mainstream culture and trying to speak for a progressive common sense. Common sense, such observers note, is something postcolonial critics seem anxious to avoid. Russell Jacoby's dismissive judgment in *Lingua Franca*, while angrier than most, is probably not unrepresentative: "While post-colonial studies claims to be subversive and profound, the politics tends to be banal; the language jargonized; the radical one-upmanship infantile; the self-obsession tiresome; and the theory bloated" (1995: 37).[2]

This may be mere mud-slinging, but it exposes a painful failure of communication, and the failure is not entirely Jacoby's fault. Peeking out from behind Jacoby's tirade, moreover, there is a positive recommendation that may also give pause to more judicious observers. What has kept the field from linking up with potential allies and thus doing something to realize its political aspirations, Jacoby implies, is its programmatic antihumanism. When postcolonial critics assert "that 'universalism' is the main prop of imperialism" (Jacoby, 1995: 35), they do the non-Western world no favors: "The undeveloped world needs a reaffirmation of universals, not a dismantling of them" (36). Condemning "human rights" as "too Western and imperialist" (36) is not calculated either to assist Third World activists in their present struggles or to drum up support among nonacademic Westerners. In short, if it wants to be treated as a serious political voice, postcolonial studies needs a new humanist paradigm.

This suggestion deserves a more respectful hearing than the mainstream critics seem to believe it will ever get. But respect entails careful deliberation, for example about slippery terms like "universals," "human rights," and for that matter even "new" and "paradigm," as well as about the more evidently ambiguous "humanism." With its long history, humanism is an especially cluttered and devious concept. Its assorted meanings point toward very different options for critics who are inclined to worry over critiques like the one above – and who probably form a sizable majority, it should be said, of those drawn to postcolonial studies in the first place. The fact that such critiques come from inside as well as outside the postcolonial paradigm, which has not always been factored into descriptions of its politics, is another reason for suspecting that humanism in at least one of its established meanings is already part of the paradigm, for better or worse. If so, it would seem paradoxical to ask the same term to redeem the field from its errors, making it new.[2]

Is humanism simply another word for a proper sense of responsibility, antithesis of and antidote to political frivolity? To Jacoby, humanism seems indistinguishable from common sense itself. A minimal and therefore uncontroversial consensus, immediately and universally obvious to the uninstructed reason, it cries out for instant and impassioned implementation. Jacoby's model would seem to be tabloid journalism. This lowest-common-denominator definition does less than full justice to the press, but it is still more prejudicial to the academy. It would put scholars out of business. For their job description involves instruction and reflection (not necessarily in that order), often not intended to be translated immediately into practice, on issues to which common sense is not an adequate guide. The university's (ever-endangered) distance from national and corporate power predisposes it both to speculate about humanity as a whole and to monitor, as if they mirrored its own institutional marginality, the context-dependent limits of humanist universals.

There exist more nuanced and persuasive arguments for the political inevitability of humanism. Consider for example Nancy Fraser's proposal that Michel Foucault is "normatively confused." Although he treats "liberal norms" and their appeals to rights "as simply an instrument of domination," he cannot fully suspend them without depriving his analysis of all critical force. To the extent that he is indeed political, Fraser concludes, Foucault is "presupposing the very liberal norms he criticizes" (1989: 30–1). As Foucault is one of the most influential theorists in the postcolonial field, there are good grounds for subjecting the field to the same hypothesis. Yet this hypothesis also opens up some further questions. Is it possible to be political *without* presupposing such norms? In other words, is all politics humanist by definition? If so, how much room for significant distinctions is there within politics? And if not, then how might one describe a *non*humanist politics? Is it possible, for example, that postcolonial studies has a nonhumanist lesson or two to teach the political allies it is recommended to join up with – lessons appropriate to its own and to their specific institutional locations?[3]

With these questions in mind, it seems less credible to identify humanism with political seriousness as such. Indeed, the humanist emphasis on realizing thought in action can as easily work against politics in any serious, that is to say divisive, sense. Consider humanitarianism, humanism's more practical-minded offspring. To be "humanitarian" ("one of the least contentious of words," Raymond Williams notes in *Keywords* (1976: 123) is to imagine social welfare in so delibe-rately abstract and generalized a fashion, on a scale both so individual and so planetary, that though action is satisfyingly direct, the organized contentiousness of politics is effectively ruled out. If all parties are assumed to be morally equi-valent, what opportunity remains for partisanship? As embodied in institutions like the Red Cross, humanitarianism prides itself on both the immediate and universal self-evidence of the needs it addresses and, logically enough, on being "above" politics.

Like humanitarianism, the humanities as an academic institution have largely tended to favor a "disinterested" sense of humanism. The distinctness of the humanities, first from theology, law, and medicine and then from the social sci-ences, has long seemed to depend on emphasizing the free exchange of ideas rather than the imperative to realize those ideas in policies and projects. But even scholars who accept some version of this imperative, which has become more the rule than the exception in recent decades as the humanities and social sciences have increasingly mingled, ought to recognize that the kind of academic work they perform will always fall short of a satisfying degree of realization. It will always be vulnerable to weighty ethical demands to transmute theory into practice, exhortations to go forth from the ivory tower, ally oneself with like-minded nonacademics, and put one's ideas to the test of action. On the whole this vulnerability is probably a good thing; however uncomfortable, the tension it generates is worth sustaining. By the same token, however, it cannot tell scholars anything very precise or novel about how to renovate their habits or paradigms.

Nothing could be more familiar to academics, after all, than the injunction to re-ground their theory in the interest of acquiring an effective politics. Though it is sometimes launched from afar by hostile journalists, this injunction is also a domestic product churned out daily and in large quantities by academics them-selves. Not just in postcolonial discussions, but across a wide spectrum of fields, the facts of injustice and the urgencies of action and alliance-making are invoked again and again in support of this or that transformation in the reigning intel-lectual paradigm. Yet however topical these facts and urgencies may seem, in one version or another they are always there to be called upon. There is always a need to act, or a need for further action. And the need to act can be called upon against *any* intellectual paradigm, however radical its ostensible politics, so long as its practitioners are located in the academy or indeed are intellectuals at all. Hence the blunt imperative to get real is not very useful as a means of discriminating between better and worse intellectual paradigms. It is useful, no doubt, as a rite of good conscience, gesturing toward a transcendence of the marginality with which the humanities nevertheless remain (thanks in part to the gesture itself) more or less comfortable. But this reassuring role cannot make up for the dangers of what Peter Osborne calls an "anti-explanatory politicism" – dangers like intellectual laziness and evasiveness about hard political questions. Whether in intellectual life or in political life, does anyone benefit from those resounding political pieties that try to make up in earnest decibels for what they lack in fresh insight and analytic rigor? The fantasy of politics as institutional self-transcendence or self-abolition usually ends up leaving everything just as it was, except a little more fatigued and discouraged.

There is clearly much to be said for humanism as normative self-clarification, or coming clean, as Fraser suggests, about the values that underlie one's critique. But this point should not be confused with a disastrously narrow understanding of political seriousness. Nor should it be confused with a blanket endorsement of old-fashioned universalism. Richard Rorty argues, like Jacoby, that "distrust of humanism" on the part of academic leftists, including postcolonial critics, has meant a "retreat from practice to theory" (1998: 37), of which Rorty strongly disapproves. But Rorty also breaks apart Jacoby's equation of humanism with universals, arguing that to reject recent versions of antihumanism does not entail returning to "universalism." This argument corresponds neatly with the ongoing transnational practice of many human rights groups and other Non-Governmental Organizations (NGOs), about which I will say an encouraging word in conclusion.

Noting this slight play or give between humanism and universalism, terms which usually seem almost indistinguishable, allows for an interesting variation on the "return of humanism" theme: the possibility that universalism has already returned, yet disguised in antihumanist form. This possibility is worth elaborating.

The line of argument by which postcolonial studies came to be identified with anti-universalism and antihumanism is laid out with exemplary clarity in Robert Young's *White Mythologies* (1990: 1).[4] Young suggests that poststructuralism, which summed up the internal critique of European humanism, was born at the same moment as decolonization and also expresses the philosophical truth of that historical conjuncture. "If so-called 'poststructuralism' is the product of a single historical moment," Young writes, "then that moment is probably not May 1968 but rather the Algerian War of Independence." This moment is so crucial not just because Third World agents at last found in it independent political and cultural expression, but also because it was marked by a conspicuous absence of support from a largely Marxist, universalist left. The failure of the organized European left to support the Front de Libération Nationale (FLN), a failure which is documented and deplored in Jean-François Lyotard's political writings of the period (1993), helps Young argue that Marxism is "collusively

Eurocentric" (1990: 3). For "gender and race [cannot] be satisfactorily subordi-nated to class" (4). "Rather than the working class being the obvious universal subject-victim, many others are also oppressed: particularly women, black people, and all other so-called ethnic and minority groups" (5). The formerly colonized, along with women and minorities, are assumed to put all the weight of their difference behind an exposure of "the relationship of the enlightenment, its grand projects and universal truth-claims, to the history of European colo-nialism" (9).

This is how you get from "race and gender and sexual orientation" to anti-humanism. There is a genuine historical insight here: who can doubt that the decentering of European thought and the dismantling of European empires have something to do with one another? Yet the logic also raises questions, par-ticularly around Young's use of the word "particularly." What *is* the status of the particular items on (and off) this list? If it is the historical specificity of de-colonization that excludes "sexual orientation" from Young's list of oppressed groups, presumably on the grounds that gays and lesbians were not massively organized as such in movements of national liberation – something of an under-statement, even if one is not thinking about, say, Robert Mugabe's vendetta against Zimbabwean gays – then what about the inclusion of "women"? Did struggles of national liberation indeed foreground issues of gender? Critics like Diana Fuss (1995) and Rey Chow (1995) have suggested that Fanon's treatment of women, for example, consistently subordinated their interests to those of national liberation. On the other hand, gender could serve to represent not rebel-lious Third World plurality, but on the contrary First World universality in its most neocolonial mode. The danger is summed up in Gayatri Chakravorty Spivak's famous, bitter formula: "white men are saving brown women from brown men" (1988: 296).[5] And like gender, class too could easily be perceived as a threat to undermine the national movement, for many of the leaders were members of a relatively privileged, Western-educated elite.

Along with "nation," which is perhaps too morally ambiguous to figure on such lists, the prime category in which colonial oppression was articulated was race. Yet of the various impulses that run through the movements of national liberation and into the newly independent states of sub-Saharan Africa, Mahmood Mamdani argues, the most successful was deracialization. Mamdani writes: "Whether formulated as a program of 'indigenization' by mainstream nationalist regimes – conservative or moderate – from Nigeria to Zaire to Idi Amin's Uganda, or as one of nationalization by radical ones, from Ghana to Guinea to Tanzania, the tendency everywhere was to erode racially accumulated privilege in erstwhile colonies. Whether they sought to Africanize or to nation-alize, the historical legitimacy of postindependence nationalist governments lay mainly in the program of deracialization they followed" (1996: 288). Mamdani's sound bite for the postcolonial situation in sub-Saharan Africa is "deracializa-tion without democratization" (288). In this historically and geographically precise sense of postcoloniality, race drops out. The same would not hold everywhere, of course; it is certainly not true in the metropolis.[6] Yet it remains significant that in much of the world, decolonization stands not for racial difference but for the sudden (if relative) irrelevance of racial difference – the point made, in the postcolonial literary canon, by the comic trope of the "whitening" of native Indians (for example, in Salman Rushdie's *Midnight's Children*) and Africans (for example, in Tsitsi Dangarembga's *Nervous Conditions*) who successfully replace the departing or soon-to-be-departing colonialists in positions of power and prosperity.

It is hard to resist the suspicion, therefore, that in Young's argument "particular" terms like race and gender are standing in somewhat awkwardly for a very general principle, the principle of plurality or anti-universalism. The fact that the list seems to drop and replace at least one item each time it is enumerated ("race, gender, and class" versus "race, gender, and sexual orientation", and so on) suggests that it is not these precise items that are being referred to, but something bigger than they are, yet also not quite nameable: a whole larger than the sum of its seemingly infinite parts, and somewhat independent of those parts.[7] It also suggests that differences and conflicts among these terms are being suppressed in the interest of sustaining that greater, nebulous whole. In other words, the race-and-gender-etc. list serves as an excuse for an anti-universalist return of the universal, the universal that is marked, in Judith Butler's phrase, by the "embarrassed 'etc.' at the end of the list" (1990: 143).[8]

If the moment of decolonization finds expression in poststructuralism's critique of Western humanism, which thus claims to be the universal voice of the anticolonial movements, then universalism returns by the back door. But exactly how much of an embarrassment to postcolonial studies is this return of the universal? The fact that founders like Frantz Fanon and Edward W. Said were not merely critical of humanism, but deeply indebted to it, has of course been long acknowledged (see Anthony Alessandrini's essay in this volume).[9] Young himself writes that "a straightforward anti-humanism was always problematic . . . For humanism itself is already anti-humanist. That is the problem" (1990: 125). This problem is sometimes written out as a history in which poststructuralism, beginning in the 1960s with an unambiguous repudiation of humanism, turns back toward ethics in the middle or late 1980s. "Virtually all the leading voices of the Theoretical Era," Geoffrey Galt Harpham writes, ". . . organized their critiques of humanism as exposès of ethics" (1995: 388). Then came a tidal wave of theorizing on ethics, in Lyotard, Foucault, Derrida, Kristeva, and others, much of which accorded a central place to alterity. "The date of December 1, 1987, does not mark the moment when ethics abruptly returned from its exile in the predeconstructive wilderness, but rather the approximate time when the large fact that all sorts of thinkers had for some time been heavily invested in ethics became inescapable" (392). For Naomi Schor, it is time for French feminists to acknowledge that they have been universalizing all along (1995). And such universalizing may not after all be a bad thing, as she and Ernesto Laclau agree. Indeed, it may be intrinsic both to intellectual work and to politics. Laclau writes: "If social struggles of new social actors show that the concrete practices of our society restrict the universalism of our political ideals to limited sectors of the population, it becomes possible to retain the universal dimension while widening the sphere of its application – which, in turn, will define the concrete contents of such universality. Through this process, universalism as a horizon is expanded at the same time as its necessary attachment to any particular content is broken. The opposite policy – that of rejecting universalism *in toto* as the particular content of the ethnia of the West – can only lead to a political blind alley" (1995: 107).[10]

In an epoch when imperial common sense is quite capable of taking explicitly anti-universalistic form, as it does for example in Samuel P. Huntington's influential "clash of civilizations" thesis (1996), Laclau's critical embrace of universalism, holding onto it as "horizon" even while continually seeking to loosen its attachment to "any particular content," seems better suited to a critical, anti-imperial project than, say, Young's "straightforward anti-humanism" might be. Laclau's version is also arguably a more faithful account of what postcolonial studies has actually been up to. Much energy has been expended in showing that various supposed universals are really only dominant particulars. But such demonstrations have by no means assumed the validity of an anti-universalistic perspective. Aijaz Ahmad's protest against applying the label "national allegory" to all Third World literature was a protest against the universal criterion of "colonialism," which seemed to assign indefensibly distinct roles to First and Third World culture. But it was a protest in the name of a better, more accurate universalism: the universalism founded on struggle not against colonialism, but against capitalism. Thus Ahmad has indignantly denied that he considers the Enlightenment his natural enemy. To presume it is, he argues, is to take sides with the most reactionary forces in his country (1996: 279). Samir Amin's *Eurocentrism* takes a similar stand. Nor is this a position adopted only by defenders of Marxism.[11] Kwame Anthony Appiah (1996) speaks defiantly in the name of an "ethical universal." In recent Indian debates, many voices have been raised against secularism (near-kin to humanism), and many others have suggested, with Rajeev Bhargava, that in some version and with careful local modifications, secularism might yet prove itself a path toward some better resolution of Indian communal realities (See e.g. Bhargava, 1998). Both sides in the discussion argue on the basis of Indian givens and (whatever the language used) in an Indian vocabulary.

In sum, the real issue is not humanism and universalism, neither of which can be identified with a single geographically defined set of interests or simply opposed in the abstract. The issue is what "particular content" (to use Laclau's phrase) has been throwing its weight around under cover of positions either for or against these large abstractions.

The particular content camouflaged by *anti*humanistic arguments, which is perhaps less immediately obvious, probably needs more explication. For example, to believe one is fighting colonialism by deconstructing the Enlightenment is a bit too convenient for European or American scholars. They can study pretty much the same Western tradition they would have studied anyway, for that tradition is assumed to have been proto-imperialist all along, well before actual colonization began – to be, in effect, an imperialist essence. Thus they need not actually find out anything about the rest of the world or listen to people from it. When Eurocentric humanism remains the definitive target, the center around which all critique revolves, the perspective remains imperial. Consider Mike Gane's paraphrase of Baudrillard: "Humanism, the doctrine of universal human rights with its assumption of human equality, like evangelical Christianity, seeks to form the world after its own image and thus reduces radical otherness to domesticated 'differences.' The result is the imperialist process of the homogenization of world culture . . . [which] paradoxically creates a new racism and sexism, phenomena which belong strictly to a culture which cannot tolerate radical alterity" (1998: 586).[12] Is this indeed the voice of the formerly colonized? Have the formerly colonized been asked for their opinion? Is "radical alterity" their self-description, or is it on the contrary a category that preempts their self-descriptions? Are we sure that such a thing exists, or that if it does, European humanism is unique in trying to "domesticate" it? Gane suggests that the West is exceptional in its evil essence – rather than, say, exceptional in that its conquests, unlike earlier ones, were propeled by capitalism, which itself does not express any national or regional essence. This is the symmetrical mistake that readers of Said's *Orientalism* have learned to call "Occidentalism." It involves refusal of any comparison, any sameness, in the name of a "radical alterity" that can register attempts to communicate only as attempts to domesticate or recolonize. Hence difference loses its contingent characteristics, becoming an absolute predicated in advance of any actual contact. According to such postulates it becomes inconceivable that "human rights," say, might be a joint North/South project. It would be an asymmetrical one of course, due to the unevenness of the global division of labor, and therefore exceptionally precarious, but a joint project nonetheless.

Another example of misguided antihumanism is the familiar Heideggerian argument that "the normative idea of humanistic man" always relies on "the aberrant idea of barbaric man" (48). This implies, in Leela Gandhi's words, that "Arnold's humanism . . . asserts the need to maintain the integrity and sovereignty of Europe in the face of its multitudinous and barbaric Others" (1998: 52). Gandhi is no doubt correct about Matthew Arnold. But the theoretical question here is whether humanism is different in this respect from any other normative or positively valued term – for example, respect for cultural difference. If there is no humanism without a concept of the barbaric, is there any normative term about which the same could not be said? And if any normative term, including respect for cultural difference, would similarly produce or presume its own aberration (e.g. European barbarians who do not respect cultural difference), then rather than a genuine argument against normativity, this objection will perhaps seem like mere quibbling, or at best like a good reason for vigilance in the applying of normative judgments – judgments which one has no choice but to make if one wants to exert political pressure against the existing social order.

It is tempting to see such antihumanist arguments, in a reversal of our initial account, as an expression not of the former colonies but rather of the metropolis. One could then say the same about the race-and-gender-etc. list, which seems to correspond not to the exact moment of anticolonial struggle in the colonies but to a later and a largely metropolitan moment.[13] It is in the metropolis rather than at home, for example, that people from the former colonies are likely to experience post-Independence racism most dramatically.

But this is not a simple choice of metropolis or periphery. The decades of delay between decolonization, in the 1950s and 1960s, and the emergence of postcolonial theory, in the late 1970s and 1980s, suggest that the latter was not a simple reflection of anticolonial politics. But they also suggest that postcolonialism represents a reaction to the intervening history in the newly independent states, an intellectual symptom of the general post-Independence failure of democratic reform, sustainable development, and economic justice. The most pertinent analogy is perhaps with Perry Anderson's analysis of how "Western Marxism" emerged after the defeat of the European revolutions in the wake of 1917. This intellectual flowering came about, Anderson suggests, because observers sought reasons for the failure in cultural, psychological, and political factors that the economistic, deterministic Marxism of the earlier period had neglected (1976: ch. 2). In much the same way, postcolonial studies could be thought of as paying attention to factors like gender and class not because these were crucial organizing principles of anticolonial struggle, but precisely because they were not – because, while these social interests proved unassimilable to anticolonial struggle, their non-assimilation appears to have had a huge and calamitous impact on post-Independence history. That is why they guide so much current historical research into what went wrong in the anticolonial movement – the reasons why Independence did not lead to democracy, gender equality, the end of hunger, and so on. The Subaltern Studies initiative is a salient example.

From this perspective the race, class, and gender formula cannot be dismissed as exclusively metropolitan. But if it is *also* a peripheral formula, then this "also" appears to pose a problem in much the same way that the term postcolonial itself does: the problem of universalizing as depoliticizing. In its narrowest and least controversial sense, postcolonial refers to former colonies that became independent states after the Second World War. But its association with poststructuralist antihumanism has made the term promiscuously expansive. As a sort of magical synthesis of First World philosophical self-critique and Third World anticolonial politics, antihumanism of course encourages a blurring of the line between colonizers and colonized. Unmoored from the moment of national liberation struggle, it drifts in both space and time. Thus the line is also effaced between the narrative of European colonialism's postwar defeat and withdrawal, on the one hand, and on the other the very different narrative of successful white settler colonialisms before the twentieth century (the United States, Canada, Latin America, Australia, New Zealand), which are thus seen as staking an illegitimate claim to the genuine victimhood of others. In the same way the term postcolonial also extends to areas of the globe that strictly speaking were not colonized, like Iran and China. By enlarging the guilt of colonialism until it spreads over every item of Western culture since Aeschylus, this mode of backdoor universalizing first overpoliticizes the field and then – by diluting the political strength of specific times and places of struggle – underpoliticizes it. Seeing colonialism everywhere has much the same effect as seeing it nowhere.[14]

One notoriously controversial instance is the supposed virtue of hybridity. This concept emerged from a variety of motives: from poststructuralist anti-essentialism, with its emphasis on the impurity and instability of all identities; from a psychoanalytic resistance to polarizations of us and them, colonizer and colonized, that missed the actual psychological and political complexities of the colonial encounter (Bhabha); from a refusal to play the role of authentic Other assigned to migrant intellectuals by the metropolitan "alterity machine" (Chow, Appiah: see the "hybridity" entry in Ashcroft et al., 1998). All of these motives are compelling. Yet there is no doubt that the hybrid identity asserted against such simplifications (against "the humanist self" as well as against pure, authentic Otherness) looks and smells like a new universal ideal. And like other universal ideals, it privileges some at the expense of others – migrants to the metropolis, for example, at the expense of nonmigrants. To critics, it seems to express the fragmented conditions of diasporic residence, turning them into a global condition and/or a universal solution.[15] In canonizing hybrid works and world views like Rushdie's, Harish Trivedi writes, "the post-colonial project of writing back . . . turns out to be writing back not to the centre but to the former colony one has exiled or displaced oneself from while occupying the centre" (1996: 243). In much the same way, Aihwa Ong and Donald Nonini find it necessary to point out that "there is nothing intrinsically liberating about diasporic cultures" (1997: 325).

Ong and Nonini go on however to propose that via "self-critique," it may be possible to articulate "a cosmopolitan sense of social justice . . . within the diasporic transnational experience" (330). For them, in other words, the problem is not universalism itself. The problem is the wrong universalism, which dangerously elevates diaspora and hybridity into a cosmopolitanism lacking in commitment to "social justice." But what is needed is a better cosmopolitanism, one that can link up all those "persons and groups disempowered by globalization, whatever their ethnic or national affiliations" (330). Arguments like this one constitute evidence that, appearances to the contrary, humanism has never been foreign to the field. More evidence is not hard to come by. "It has appeared to some of my readers recently," Gayatri Spivak writes, "that I seem to be moving towards some notion of universal humanity, and this has surprised them – I am expected to emphasize difference" (1991). Her desire, however, is "to bring humanism and difference together. Contrary to the received assumption, it seems to me that the non-foundationalist thinkers are suggesting that you cannot have any kind of emancipatory project *without* some notion of the ways in which human beings are similar" (227). Spivak argues that "the principles of a universal humanism – the place where indeed all human beings are similar – is . . . lodged in their being different" (228).[16]

This is an argument for changing the subject. The potentially depoliticizing effects of terms like hybridity and diaspora are real. But pointing this out is not an activity worthy of further investment in time and energy. Politics today demands a different debate altogether. Nothing in the recent debates over hybridity or humanism encourages inquiry into actual historical junctures of humanism and difference – say, whether a given set of differences does in fact matter politically, and if so how. Take the example of the nation. Is the nation inherently oppressive to minorities (the antihumanist position), or is it the humanist self writ large, hence a last and necessary bulwark against global capital? Neither position helps solve such genuine mysteries of global injustice as, for instance, how far the forces of global capitalism have and have not pulled free from the interests of particular regions and nation-states.[17] As Buell and Tomlinson suggest (1991), the shift in terminology from imperialism to globalization implies that capital has indeed become autonomous. Masao Miyoshi's (1993) influential essay on transnational corporations (TNCs) elaborates the same suggestion. On the other hand, the much-used term "neocolonialism" suggests that capitalism, far from cutting its ties to national interests, continues to serve them, protecting citizens of some nations to some degree at least and callously sacrificing citizens of other nations. Many observers share the opinion that globalization is a less a global reality than an effective ideological tool of the most prosperous nations. Much is riding on this issue. Yet the postcolonial field has not been addressing it. At the turn of the millennium, the national question seems less likely to involve throwing off a racially-distinct imperial rule in order to bring a nation-state into existence, and more likely to involve secession from an already-established nation-state. What commentary does the field offer on movements for national-independence-via-secession? Here the colonial paradigm is of little assistance, though of course empires can always be blamed (correctly enough, though not very helpfully) both for imposing the nation-state form and for drawing borders so haphazardly. Postcolonial studies has no further analysis, and nothing original to recommend.[18] When outside critics complain of the field's political irrelevance, they have a point.

My own point is a double one. First, this is the sort of argument that postcolonial critics should be having, and perhaps would be having if controversies between humanism and poststructuralism could somehow quietly fade away. Second, arguments like this indicate the genuine political complexity of the postcolonial condition, a condition that both challenges humanism and shows why it cannot simply be abandoned.

As my title suggests, the battery of "race, class, and gender" formulas mark a universalistic and humanistic impulse that has gradually emerged, within cultural studies generally and postcolonial studies in particular, but that was slow to be perceived as such because of the prevailing antihumanism. Planetary in scope, these terms reflect a sense of exile from the apparent (but illusory) political plenitude of the anticolonial moment, a condition in which meanings must be caught on the wing, in situations and among agents whose political identities cannot be presumed in advance or correlated reliably to nation and location. Like poststructuralist antihumanism, which claims them (sometimes minus class) as its natural constituency, these categories cross and undercut the line dividing former colonized from former colonizer. But they are also separable from antihumanism, as Katha Pollitt argued in the passage with which I began.[19]

Aside from the other reasons discussed above, one would *want* to separate them from antihumanism because global analysis and cooperation have become just as indispensable to progressive projects as they are to capitalism, and because action on behalf of ecology, feminism, labor, and human rights depends so directly on emergent transnational norms. A knee-jerk repudiation of normativity and global universals is thus self-destructive, or more likely to reproduce a comfortable (and traditional) sense of academic marginality than to change the world. But an unrepentant reassertion of humanism in its confident imperial mode would of course be no less unproductive. The terminology for a position that avoids these extremes is not easy to come by, but the effort to achieve one seems to be shared, significantly, both by academic theorists like Ong, Nonini, and Spivak and by mainstream commentators like Katha Pollitt.[20] While Pollitt backs off from the humanism that once steamrolled over the resistant, particularizing perspectives of race, gender, and sexual orientation, she seems to move toward a more strenuous, less predictable humanism, one that would have to be built out of these very perspectives. Humanism in this alternative sense would seem to take strength from the existence of international agencies, movements, and NGOs which have been trying to negotiate a provisional working consensus, on issues like women's rights and the environment, out of very real differences of situation and priority. Once "Western" in origin, this discourse is so no longer, as the dramatic impact of Third World feminists on the agenda of the Beijing conference made clear. If the word "universal" applies, it applies not as an already-existing foundation that all reasonable men and women must naturally agree on, but as a risky, uncertain balancing of the different values, vocabularies, and priorities that reasonably emerge from different circumstances.

Any such balancing of course remains partial and imperfect. The influence that the military and economic power of the United States and Europe exerts over United Nations policy, not to speak of the IMF and World Bank, is flagrant.

The disparity between poor grassroots NGOs and rich, metropolitan ones persists. The underpoliticizing that accompanies planetary-scale humanitarianism, with its false impartiality and feel-good irrelevance, is always a risk.[21] Alex de Waal and others have argued that, thanks to the global media, humanitarian NGOs have acquired too much influence over international policy-making to fit their lack of political accountability (de Waal, 1997; see also Minear and Weiss, 1995). Together with the representatives of global capital, they have no doubt had some hand in keeping old-fashioned racism alive in the former colonies. As Mamdani notes, the failure of democratization and economic development in sub-Saharan Africa also limited deracialization, for "an externally managed capital inflow . . . towed alongside a phalanx of expatriates – according to UN estimates, more now than in the colonial period!" (1996: 288). But the imperfection of transnational actions and institutions is not enough of an argument against the new humanist impulse. Or rather, it is an argument that works only for the older humanism, which thinks that if reason cannot transcend differences and inequalities, then it is not really reason at all.

This reasoning about reason also explains why the older humanism is so quick to condemn the university. The university should be a place of ideal universality, protected from the demands of constituencies and the constraints of its particular institutional being. Here too a newer humanism can provide a corrective. It is for reasons that are in part institutionally self-interested that certain areas of the academy, reacting to their own marginality, could put themselves behind the philosophical positions and research projects that Pollitt describes as "far-out." Yet "far-out" here means nurturing certain antinationalist possibilities that have trouble finding sustenance in less marginal sites. It means occasionally evading the burden of national pride and the unconscious us-first, we-are-the-only-ones-who-count special pleading that so often takes up residence, without protest, in common sense – even progressive common sense. If humanism means taking into account the welfare of humanity as a whole rather than one's own little portion of it, then defying (national) common sense should be described as humanist. And the language in which this defiance is staged, which is indeed sometimes awkward to the point of caricature, can lay claim to the same honorable status. The obscurity of much writing in the postcolonial field can perhaps be taken as a sign, in other words, that more than the usual number of constituencies are being implicitly factored in, listened to or at least for; their interests and sensibilities consulted or at least imagined. Such an effort cannot be expected to flaunt the ease of an unselfconscious prose that knows its (national) audience and need not worry about offending readers outside its borders. If a new humanist paradigm is to emerge, this effort will have to be extended. The prevalence of the "race, class, and gender" list, a rhetorical abomination that not even its most fervent adherents can love, is perhaps evidence that this is already happening, that a certain openness to the perspectives of an open-ended list of significant actors is coming to seem like transnational common sense. Let us hope so.

Notes

1 For an interesting debate on economic inequality and sexual orientation, see Butler (1997) Fraser (1997).

2 For one example among many of a pro-universalist position at the heart of the postcolonial field, see Lazarus: "arguably, the specific role of post-colonial intellectualism: to construct a standpoint – nationalitarian, liberationist, internationalist – from which it is possible to assume the burden of speaking for all humanity" (1994: 220).

3 These questions also emerge from within the history of the term. As Raymond Williams points out in *Keywords*, humanism's history is interestingly split between the Renaissance sense of human as opposed to divine or supernatural ("humanism" is often seen as a less objectionable alternative to "atheism") and later, more affirmative senses like courtesy and civility or "human self-development and self-perfection" (1976: 123). The *Oxford Dictionary of Philosophy* (1994) distinguishes analogously between humanism's association with "anti-religious social and political movements," on the one hand, and its optimism about "the powers of the unaided human understanding" and belief in "the possibility of the autonomous, self-conscious, rational, single self," on the other. To put this difference polemically: is humanism a critical or democratic alternative to religious authority, or is it a new form of authority? Can it be the first without also being the second?

4 Compare with Rajeswari Sunder Rajan's observation of "a convergence – not entirely fortuitous – of the itineraries of political (i.e. feminist, postcolonial, black) and theoretical (i.e. poststructuralist, postmodernist) criticisms upon a critique of essentialism" (1993: 10).

5 "Imperialism's image as the establisher of the good society is marked by the espousal of the woman as *object* of protection from her own kind" (1988: 299).

6 Stuart Hall's contribution to the 1977 UNESCO volume *Race and Class in Post-Colonial Society*, which offers one of the earlier uses of the term "post-colonial," explored for example the seemingly anomalous persistence of race beyond Independence in the English-speaking islands of the Caribbean. But this is simply more evidence that the general principle of plurality and difference cannot stand for the actual differences of the post-colonial world.

7 Sound may also matter here. Consider, for example, the difference between the trochees of "gender, race, and class" and the responsible-sounding abandonment of poetry for prose in "race, gender, and sexual orientation."

8 Butler suggests that this sign of incompleteness, "exhaustion," and "excess" is also "a new point of departure for feminist political theorizing."

9 The belief in human universals is also what James Clifford means by "humanism" in his early and influential review of Edward Said's *Orientalism* in *The Predicament of Culture* (1988).

10 See also Butler (1995), who refuses the idea "that there ought to be no reference to the universal or that it has become, for us, an impossibility." She maintains only that "the term gains its meaning for us precisely through the decidedly less-than-universal cultural conditions of its articulation" (129).

11 On the debate about humanism within Marxism, see for example Althusser (1990); E. P. Thompson, *The Poverty of Theory*; Perry Anderson, *Arguments Within Marxism* . . .

12 This is what Arif Dirlik is objecting to, rightly, when he complains that post-colonial studies has taken "the critique of Eurocentrism as its central task" (1996: 298).

13 The fact that three-term references in the "race-class-and-gender" mode usually draw on a religious vocabulary – litany, trinity, or mantra – suggests that these words stand in for the sacred, and that even while it must be repeated, this sacred or normative counteruniversal cannot be openly or unambivalently avowed. That is why such phrases are so rarely to be discovered outside a protective envelope of metropolitan irony.

14 It seems misguided to object, with Ella Shohat, that "post-colonial studies as an emergent discipline" has "potentially depoliticizing implications" (1996: 321). This is true enough, but it would be true of any field. When was the establishment of an academic domain ever the equivalent of taking sides decisively in a political struggle? It is a fine thing to study the social consequences of the Industrial Revolution, but no naming or framing of that field can preclude historians from arguing (rightly or wrongly) the conservative position that in the long term those consequences were beneficial. Giving their object the political label "Third World" rather than "postcolonialism" never hindered scholars from pathologizing its cultural differences from a putative West or espousing brutally partisan models of global development. On the other hand, from a somewhat formalist point of view one might argue that so early in the life of a disciplinary paradigm, it is to be expected that much energy should be devoted to debating the limits of its titular concept. While critics have certainly been right to insist on differences like those I just mentioned, the paradigm itself can be credited with generating these debates, which are valuable and have a better claim to define the reality of the field than any one position inside it does. (Fields, unlike political movements, are constituted by controversies internal to them.) If antihumanism has provided the conceptual rationale for focusing on both the former colonies and the former colonizers at the same time, and "postcolonial studies" has been the institutional site for this blurred distinction, the field has also provided the site and the occasions on which the distinction could re-emerge, embattled, along with others.

15 Opposition to this dominant particular need not insist on its antithetical virtues, like purity or stay-at-home authenticity. It can simply object that the whole problematic of authenticity-versus-hybridity is not equally central to people's lives everywhere. It is arguably a metropolitan problematic occupying space that might be more profitably filled by other, more urgent problematics.

16 Renato Rosaldo performs a similar double gesture. Critical of liberal equality, which favors conformity, homogeneity, and assimilation, he also calls for "an ethical vision" (1994: 240) of solidarity in diversity.

17 The editors of *Dangerous Liaisons* describe the critical move away from seeing the nation "as the embodiment of, in Frantz Fanon's cautionary words, 'the immemorial truth' of the people," and toward seeing it as "a historically produced, unfinished, and contested terrain" (McClintock *et al.*, 1997: 3–4).

18   See Hannum (1998). See also Goldsworthy, *Inventing Ruritania* (1998) as an exception that proves the rule about the awkwardness of the colonial paradigm in contexts – here, the Balkans – where the primary political issue is secession.

19   Indeed, one might conclude from the prominence of class in Pollitt's necessarily sketchy treatment that "race and gender and sexual orientation" are continuous with an older class-based internationalism, correcting it (need one recall that capitalism cannot fully explain gender oppression?) but also sustaining and extending it.

20   "Post-humanist" is one possibility, and perhaps a better one than anti-universal humanism or antihumanist universalism. Another is cosmopolitanism. "Cosmopolitanism has repeatedly emerged at times when the world has suddenly seemed to expand in unassimilable ways," Amanda Anderson writes; " it is at these moments that universalism needs the rhetoric of worldliness that cosmopolitanism provides" (1998: 272). I experiment with cosmopolitanism in the same volume and in *Feeling Global*. On worldliness see Schwarz, *Writing Cultural History in Colonial and Postcolonial India* (1997).

21   Consider the example of the International Committee of the Red Cross (ICRC), which knew about the Nazi extermination camps but made no public protests. According to Jean-Claude Favez (1988), this refusal to use its moral authority led to the Red Cross's loss of credibility.

References

Ahmad, Aijaz. (1996). "The Politics of Literary Postcoloniality," in *Contemporary Postcolonial Theory: A Reader*, ed. P. Mongia. London: Arnold.

Althusser, Louis. (1990). "Marxism and Humanism," in *For Marx*, trans. B. Brewster. London and New York: Verso. First published 1965.

Anderson, Amanda. (1998). "Cosmopolitanism, Universalism, and the Divided Legacy of Modernity," in *Cosmopolitics: Thinking and Feeling Beyond the Nations*, ed. Pheng Cheah and B. Robbins. Minneapolis and London: University of Minnesota Press.

Anderson, Perry. (1976). *Considerations on Western Marxism*. London: New Left Books.

Appiah, Kwame Anthony. (1996). "Is the Post- in Postmodernism the Post- in Postcolonial?", in *Contemporary Postcolonial Theory: A Reader*, ed. P. Mongia. London: Arnold.

Ashcroft, Bill, Gareth Griffiths, and Helen Tiffin, eds. (1998). *Key Concepts in Post-Colonial Studies*. London and New York: Routledge.

Bhargava, Rajeev. (1998). *Secularism and its Critics*. Delhi: Oxford University Press.

Buell, Lawrence and John Tomlinson. (1991). *Cultural Imperialism*. Baltimore: Johns Hopkins University Press.

Butler, Judith. (1990). *Gender Trouble: Feminism and the Subversion of Identity*. New York and London: Routledge.

——. (1995). "For a Careful Reading," in *Feminist Contentions: A Philosophical Exchange*, eds. S. Benhabib, J. Butler, D. Cornell, and N. Fraser. New York and London: Routledge.

——. (1997). "Merely Cultural," *Social Text*, 52/53 (fall/winter): 266–77. (See also Fraser, 1997.)

Chow, Rey. (1995). "The Politics of Admittance: Female Sexual Agency, Miscegenation and the Formation of Community in Frantz Fanon," *The UTS Review*, 1, no. 1 (Aug.): 5–29.

Clifford, James. (1988). *The Predicament of Culture*. Cambridge: Harvard University Press.

de Waal, Alex. (1997). *Famine Crimes: Politics and the Disaster Relief Industry*. London: African Rights and the International African Institute; Bloomington: University of Indiana Press.

Dirlik, Arif. (1996). "The Postcolonial Aura: Third World Criticism in the Age of Global Capitalism," in *Contemporary Postcolonial Theory: A Reader*, ed. P. Mongia. London: Arnold.

Favez, Jean-Claude. (1988). *Une mission impossible: Le CICR, les déportations et les camps de concentration nazis*. Lausanne: Payot.

Fraser, Nancy. (1989). *Unruly Practices: Power, Discourse and Gender in Contemporary Social Theory*. Minneapolis: University of Minnesota Press.

——. (1997). "Heterosexism, Misrecognition, and Capitalism: A Response to Judith Butler," *Social Text*, 52/53 (fall/winter): 279–89. (See also Butler, 1997.)

Fuss, Diana. (1995). "Interior Colonies: Frantz Fanon and the Politics of Identification," in *Identification Papers*. New York and London: Routledge.

Gandhi, Leela. (1998). *Postcolonial Theory: A Critical Introduction*. New York: Columbia University Press.

Gane, Mike. (1998). "Baudrillard," in *A Companion to Continental Philosophy*, eds. S. Critchley and W. A. Schroeder. Oxford: Blackwell.

Goldsworthy, Vesna. (1998). *Inventing Ruritania*. New Haven and London: Yale University Press.

Hall, Stuart. (1977). "Pluralism, Race, and Class in Caribbean Society," in Race and Class in *Post-Colonial Society: A Study of Ethnic Group Relations in the English-speaking Caribbean, Bolivia, Chile, and Mexico*. Paris: UNESCO: 150–82.

Hannum, Hurst. (1998). "The Specter of Secession: Responding to Claims for Ethnic Self-Determination," *Foreign Affairs*, 77, no. 2 (March/April): 13–18.

Harpham, Geoffrey Galt. (1995). "Ethics," in *Critical Terms for Literary Study*, eds. F. Lentricchia and T. McLaughlin, 2nd edn. Chicago and London: University of Chicago Press.

Huntington, Samuel P. (1996). *The Clash of Civilizations and the Remaking of the World Order*. New York: Simon and Schuster.

Jacoby, Russell. (1995). "Marginal Returns: The Trouble with Post-Colonial Theory," *Lingua Franca* (Sept./Oct.): 30–7.

Laclau, Ernesto. (1995). "Universalism, Particularism, and the Question of Identity," in *The Identity in Question*, ed. J. Rajchman. New York and London: Routledge.

Lazarus, Neil. (1994). "National Consciousness and the Specificity of (Post)colonial Intellectualism," in *Colonial Discourse/Postcolonial Theory*, eds. F. Barker, P. Hulme, and M. Iversen. Manchester and New York: Manchester University Press.

Lyotard, J.-F. (1993). *Political Writings*, trans. B. Readings and K. P. Geiman. Minneapolis: University of Minnesota Press.

Mamdani, Mahmood. (1996). *Citizen and Subject: Contemporary Africa and the Legacy of Late Colonialism*. Princeton: Princeton University Press.

McClintock, A., Aamir Mufti, and Ella Shohat, eds. (1997). *Dangerous Liaisons: Gender, Nation, and Postcolonial Perspectives*. Minneapolis and London: University of Minnesota Press.

Minear, Larry and Thomas Weiss. (1995). *Mercy Under Fire: War and the Global Humanitarian Community*. Boulder: Westview.

Miyoshi, Masao. (1993). "A Borderless World? From Colonialism to Transnationalism and the Decline of the Nation-State," *Critical Inquiry*, 19 (summer): 726–51.

Ong, Aihwa and Donald Nonini. (1997). "Toward a Cultural Politics of Diaspora and Transnationalism," in *Ungrounded Empires: The Cultural Politics of Modern Chinese Transnationalism*, eds. Ong and Nonini. New York and London: Routledge.

Oxford Dictionary of Philosophy. (1994). Ed. Simon Blackburn. Oxford and New York: Oxford University Press.

Pollitt, Catha. (1998). "Race and Gender and Class, Oh My!", *The Nation*, 266, no. 21.

Robbins, Bruce. (1999). *Feeling Global: Internationalism in Distress*. New York: New York University Press.

Rorty, Richard. (1998). *Achieving Our Country: Leftist Thought in Twentieth-Century America*. Cambridge: Harvard University Press.

Rosaldo, Renato. (1994). "Social Justice and the Crisis of National Communities," in *Colonial Discourse/Postcolonial Theory*, eds. F. Barker, P. Hulme, and M. Iversen. Manchester and New York: Manchester University Press.

Schor, Naomi. (1995). "French Feminism Is a Universalism," *differences*, 7, no. 1 (spring): 15–47.

Schwarz, Henry. (1997). *Writing Cultural History in Colonial and Postcolonial India*. Philadelphia: University of Pennsylvania Press.

Shohat, Ella. (1996). "Notes on the Post-Colonial," in *Contemporary Postcolonial Theory: A Reader*, ed. P. Mongia. London: Arnold.

Spivak, G. C. (1988). "Can the Subaltern Speak?", in *Marxism and the Interpretation of Culture*, eds. L. Grossberg and C. Nelson. New York: Routledge.

——. (1991). "Remembering the Limits: Difference, Identity and Practice: A Transcript," in *Socialism and the Limits of Liberalism*, ed. P. Osborne. London and New York: Verso.

Sunder Rajan, Rajeswari. (1993). *Real and Imagined Women*. London and New York: Routledge.

Trivedi, Harish. (1996). "India and Post-colonial Discourse," in *Interrogating Postcolonialism: Theory, Text and Context*, eds. Trivedi and M. Mukherjee. Shimla: Indian Institute of Advanced Study.

Williams, Raymond. (1976). *Keywords: A Vocabulary of Culture and Society*. London: Fontana/Croom Helm.

Young, Robert. (1990). *White Mythologies: Writing History and the West*. London and New York: Routledge.

Index

574

589